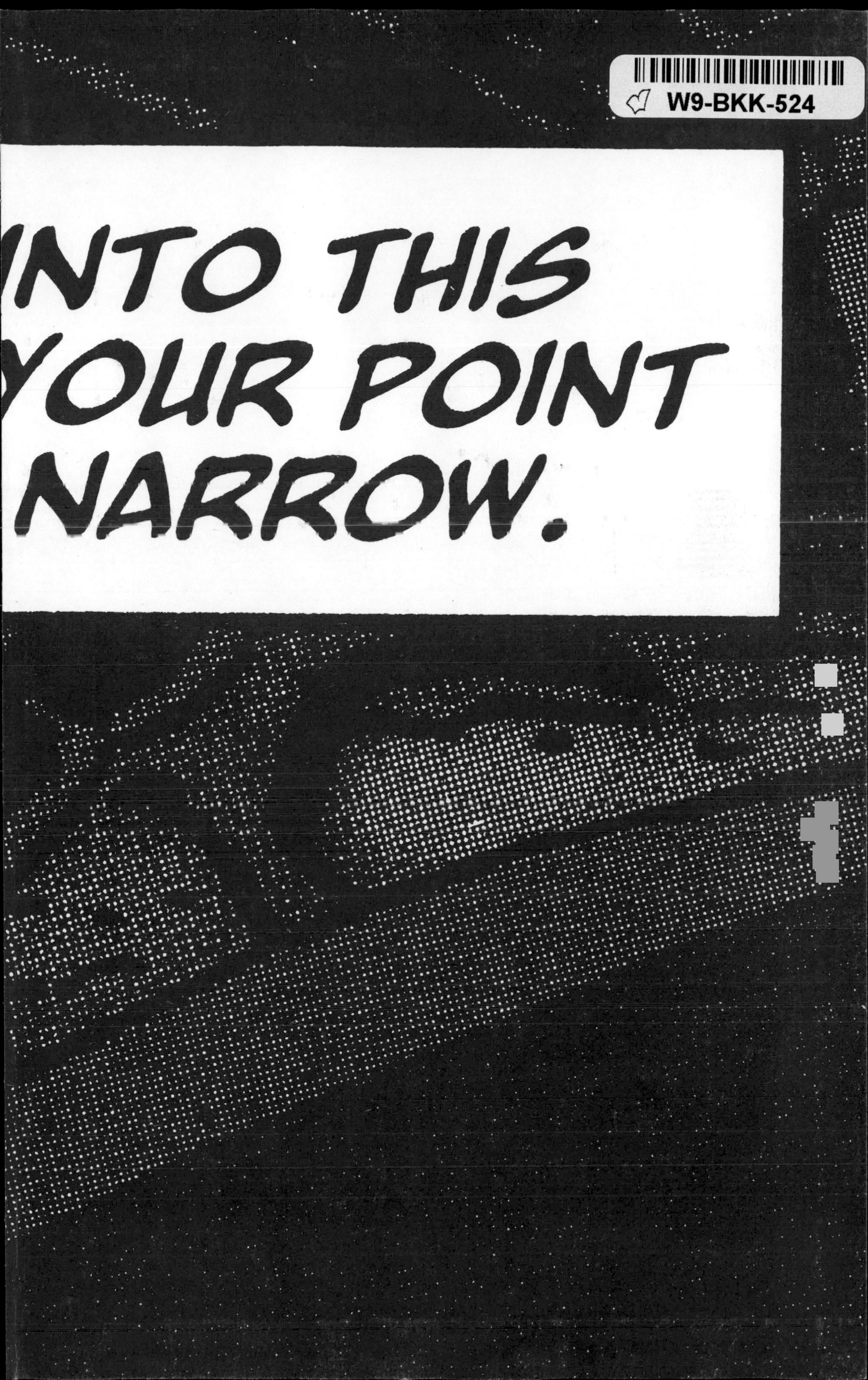
INTO THIS
YOUR POINT
NARROW.

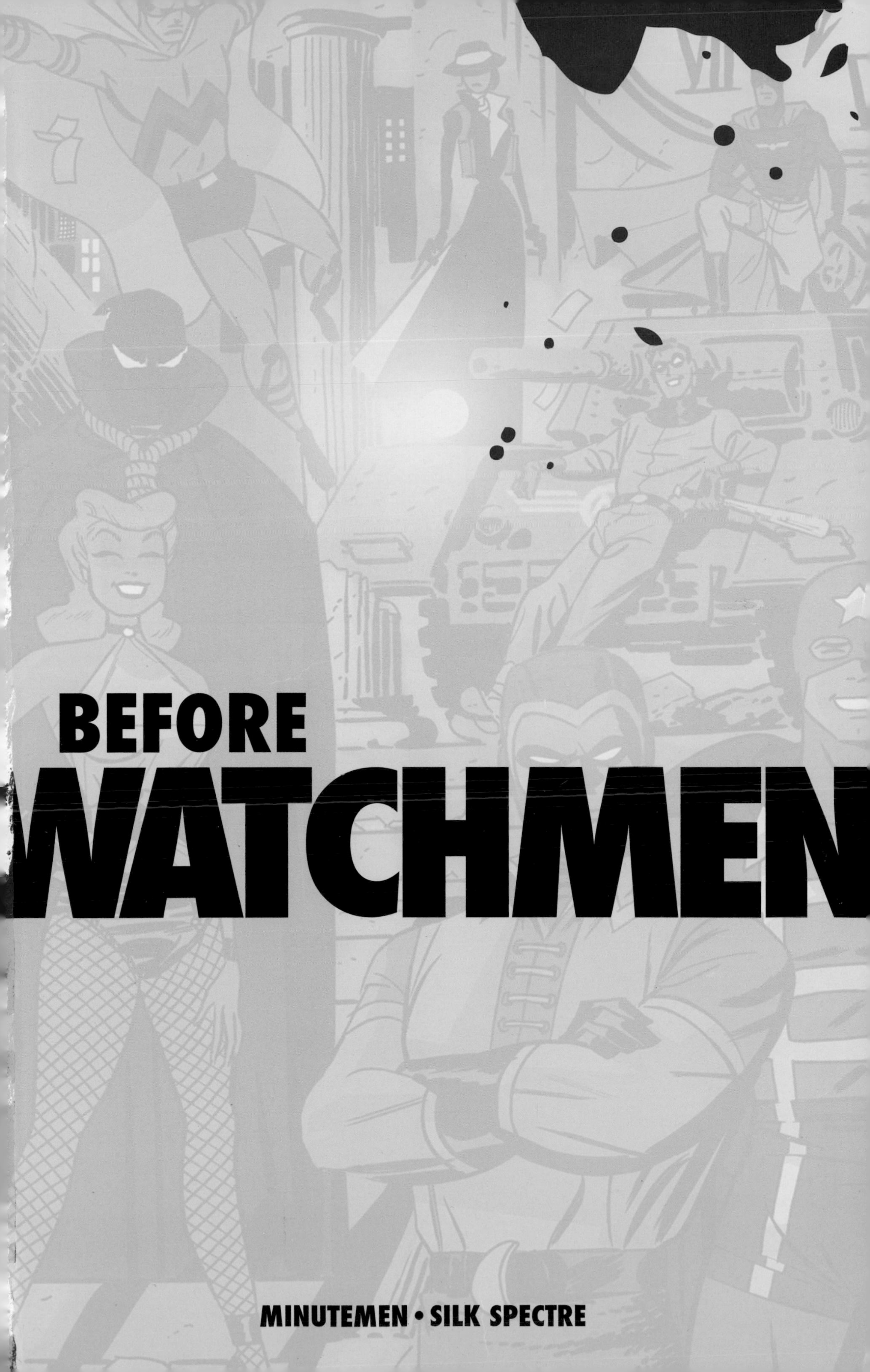

BEFORE WATCHMEN

MINUTEMEN • SILK SPECTRE

BEFORE

WATC

HMEN

MINUTEMEN • SILK SPECTRE

DARWYN COOKE
AMANDA CONNER
writers

DARWYN COOKE
AMANDA CONNER
artists

PHIL NOTO
PAUL MOUNTS
colorists

JARED K. FLETCHER
CARLOS M. MANGUAL
letterers

DARWYN COOKE and **AMANDA CONNER**
with **PAUL MOUNTS** and **PHIL NOTO**
cover artists

Watchmen created by
ALAN MOORE and **DAVE GIBBONS**

MARK CHIARELLO Editor – Original Series

CHRIS CONROY, WIL MOSS Associate Editors – Original Series

CAMILLA ZHANG Assistant Editor – Original Series

PETER HAMBOUSSI Editor

RACHEL PINNELAS Assistant Editor

ROBBIN BROSTERMAN Design Director – Books

ROBBIE BIEDERMAN Publication Design

BOB HARRAS Senior VP – Editor-in-Chief, DC Comics

DIANE NELSON President

DAN DIDIO and JIM LEE Co-Publishers

GEOFF JOHNS Chief Creative Officer

JOHN ROOD Executive VP – Sales, Marketing & Business Development

AMY GENKINS Senior VP – Business & Legal Affairs

NAIRI GARDINER Senior VP – Finance

JEFF BOISON VP – Publishing Planning

MARK CHIARELLO VP – Art Direction & Design

JOHN CUNNINGHAM VP – Marketing

TERRI CUNNINGHAM VP – Editorial Administration

ALISON GILL Senior VP – Manufacturing & Operations

HANK KANALZ Senior VP – Vertigo & Integrated Publishing

JAY KOGAN VP – Business & Legal Affairs, Publishing

JACK MAHAN VP – Business Affairs, Talent

NICK NAPOLITANO VP – Manufacturing Administration

SUE POHJA VP – Book Sales

COURTNEY SIMMONS Senior VP – Publicity

BOB WAYNE Senior VP – Sales

Cover design by CHIP KIDD

BEFORE WATCHMEN: MINUTEMEN/SILK SPECTRE

DC Comics, 1700 Broadway, New York, NY 10019. A Warner Bros. Entertainment Company.
Printed by RR Donnelley, Salem, VA, USA. 5/24/13. First Printing.
ISBN: 978-1-4012-3892-6

SUSTAINABLE FORESTRY INITIATIVE

Certified Chain of Custody
At Least 20% Certified Forest Content
www.sfiprogram.org
SFI-01042
APPLIES TO TEXT STOCK ONLY

Library of Congress Cataloging-in-Publication Data

Cooke, Darwyn.
  Before Watchmen : Minutemen/Silk Spectre / Darwyn Cooke, Amanda Conner.
    pages cm. -- (Before Watchmen)
  "Originally published in single magazine form in Before Watchmen:
Minutemen 1-6, Before Watchmen: Silk Spectre 1-4."
  ISBN 978-1-4012-3892-6
  1. Graphic novels. I. Conner, Amanda. II. Title. III. Title: Minutemen/Silk Spectre.
  PN6728.W386C66 2013
  741.5'973—dc23
                          2013009152

BEFORE WATCHMEN

MINUTEMEN
writer/artist – DARWYN COOKE
colorist – PHIL NOTO
letterer – JARED K. FLETCHER

SILK SPECTRE
writers – DARWYN COOKE & AMANDA CONNER
artist - AMANDA CONNER
colorist – PAUL MOUNTS
letterer – CARLOS M. MANGUAL

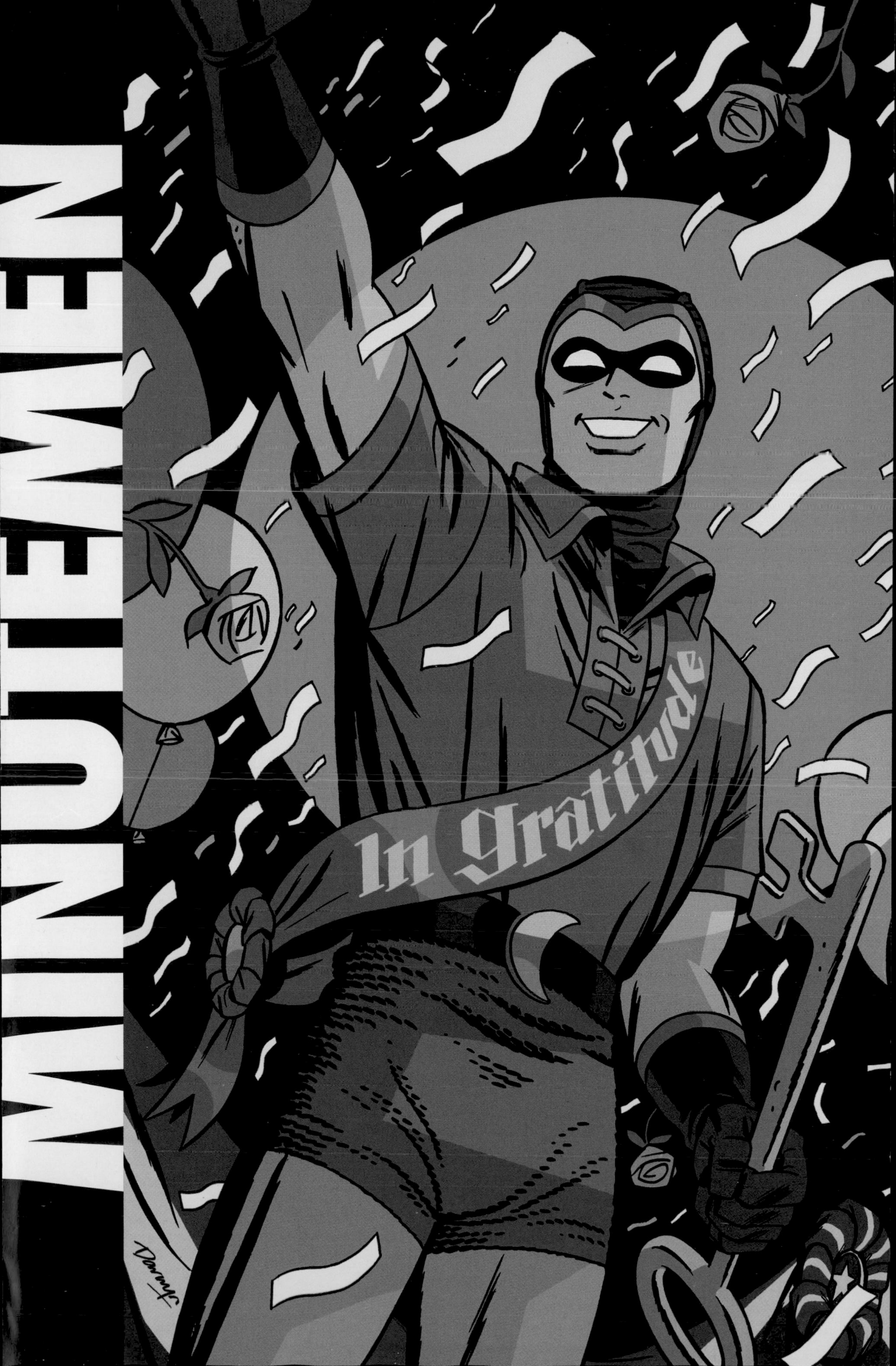
MINUTEMEN
In Gratitude

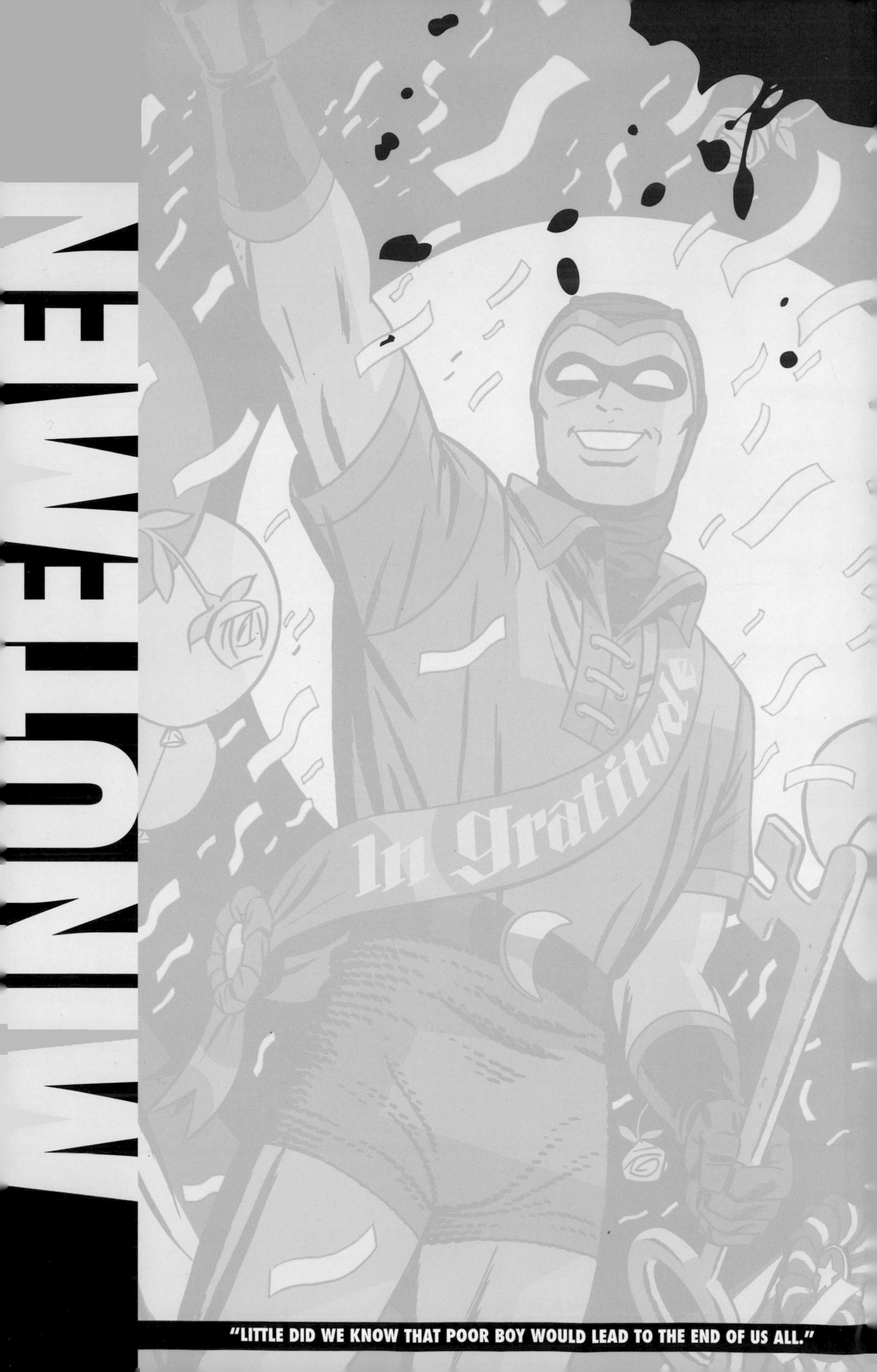
MINUTEMEN
In Gratitude
"LITTLE DID WE KNOW THAT POOR BOY WOULD LEAD TO THE END OF US ALL."

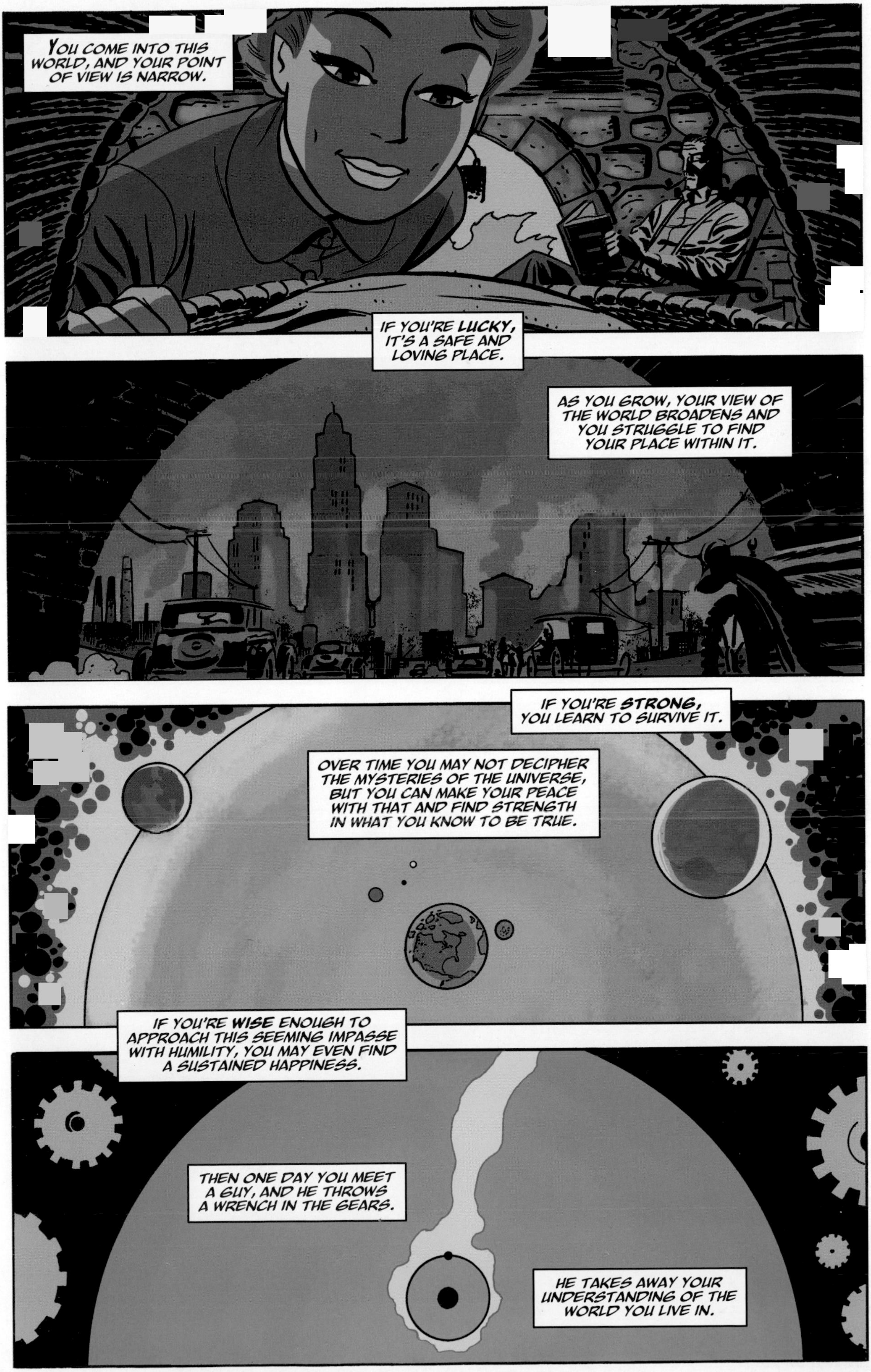
YOU COME INTO THIS WORLD, AND YOUR POINT OF VIEW IS NARROW.
IF YOU'RE LUCKY, IT'S A SAFE AND LOVING PLACE.
AS YOU GROW, YOUR VIEW OF THE WORLD BROADENS AND YOU STRUGGLE TO FIND YOUR PLACE WITHIN IT.
IF YOU'RE STRONG, YOU LEARN TO SURVIVE IT.
OVER TIME YOU MAY NOT DECIPHER THE MYSTERIES OF THE UNIVERSE, BUT YOU CAN MAKE YOUR PEACE WITH THAT AND FIND STRENGTH IN WHAT YOU KNOW TO BE TRUE.
IF YOU'RE WISE ENOUGH TO APPROACH THIS SEEMING IMPASSE WITH HUMILITY, YOU MAY EVEN FIND A SUSTAINED HAPPINESS.
THEN ONE DAY YOU MEET A GUY, AND HE THROWS A WRENCH IN THE GEARS.
HE TAKES AWAY YOUR UNDERSTANDING OF THE WORLD YOU LIVE IN.

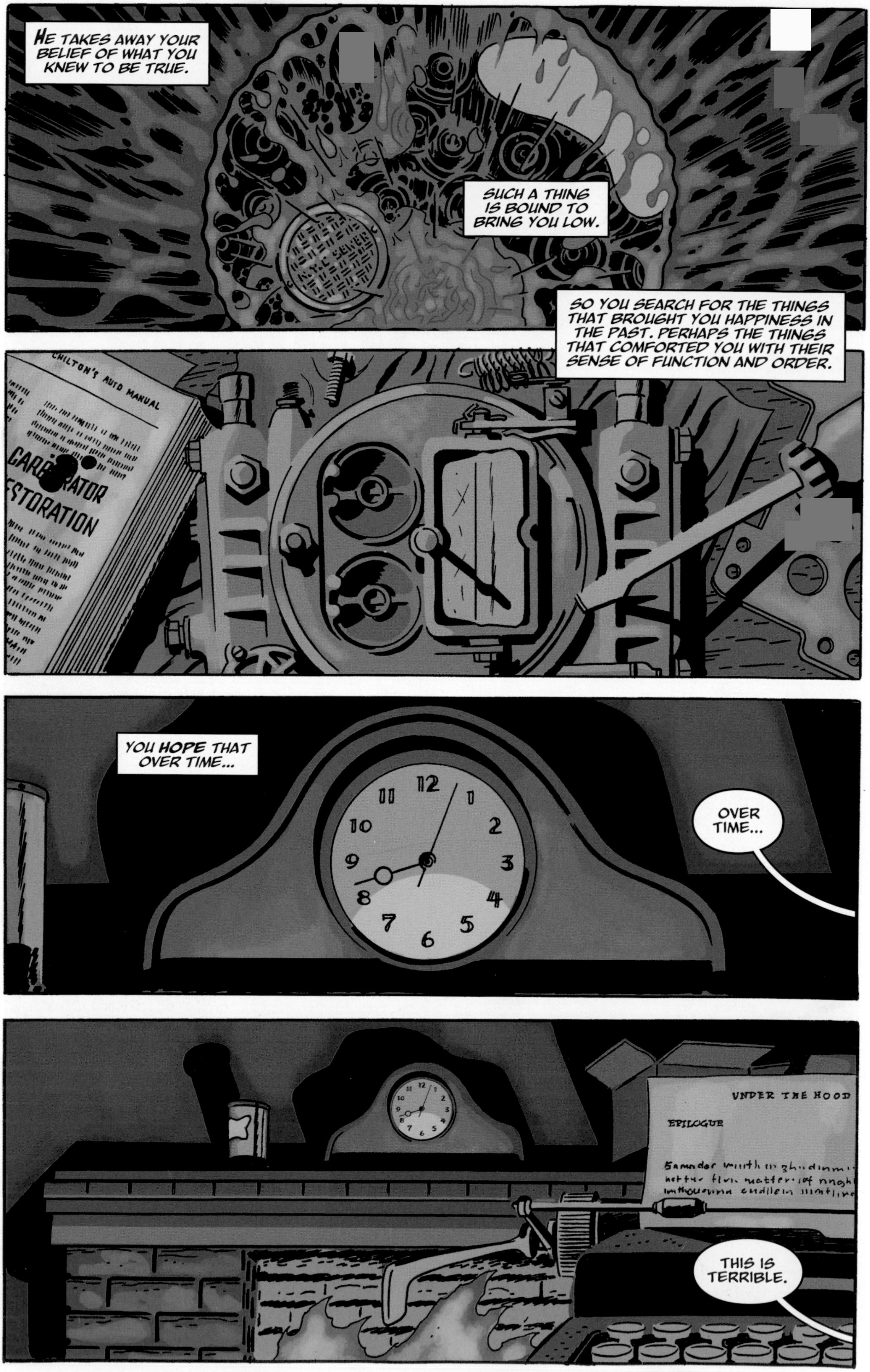
HE TAKES AWAY YOUR BELIEF OF WHAT YOU KNEW TO BE TRUE.
SUCH A THING IS BOUND TO BRING YOU LOW.
SO YOU SEARCH FOR THE THINGS THAT BROUGHT YOU HAPPINESS IN THE PAST. PERHAPS THE THINGS THAT COMFORTED YOU WITH THEIR SENSE OF FUNCTION AND ORDER.
CHILTON'S AUTO MANUAL
YOU HOPE THAT OVER TIME...
OVER TIME...
UNDER THE HOOD
EPILOGUE
THIS IS TERRIBLE.

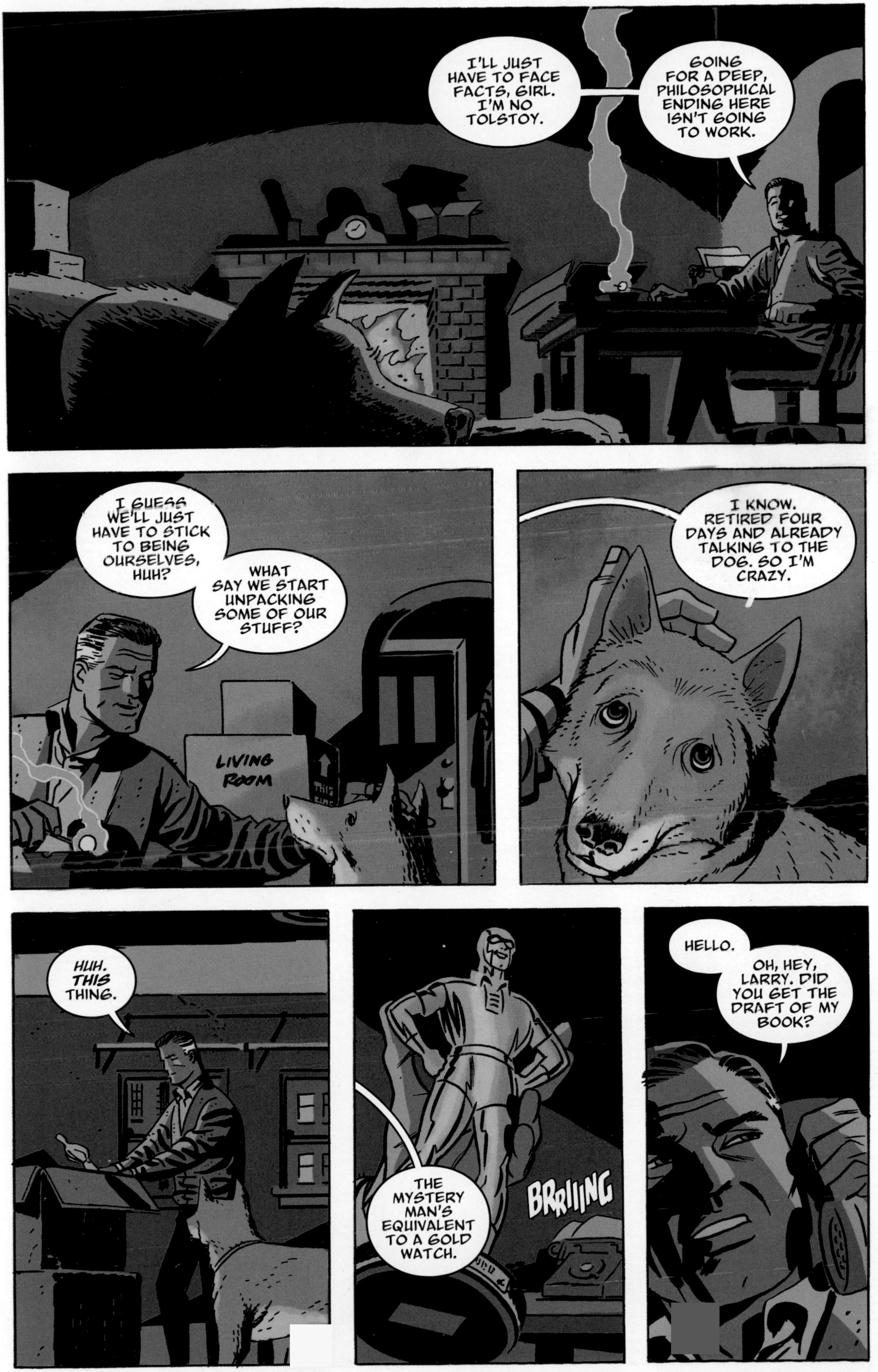
I'LL JUST HAVE TO FACE FACTS, GIRL. I'M NO TOLSTOY.
GOING FOR A DEEP, PHILOSOPHICAL ENDING HERE ISN'T GOING TO WORK.
I GUESS WE'LL JUST HAVE TO STICK TO BEING OURSELVES, HUH?
WHAT SAY WE START UNPACKING SOME OF OUR STUFF?
LIVING ROOM
I KNOW. RETIRED FOUR DAYS AND ALREADY TALKING TO THE DOG. SO I'M CRAZY.
HUH. *THIS* THING.
THE MYSTERY MAN'S EQUIVALENT TO A GOLD WATCH.
BRRIIING
HELLO.
OH, HEY, LARRY. DID YOU GET THE DRAFT OF MY BOOK?

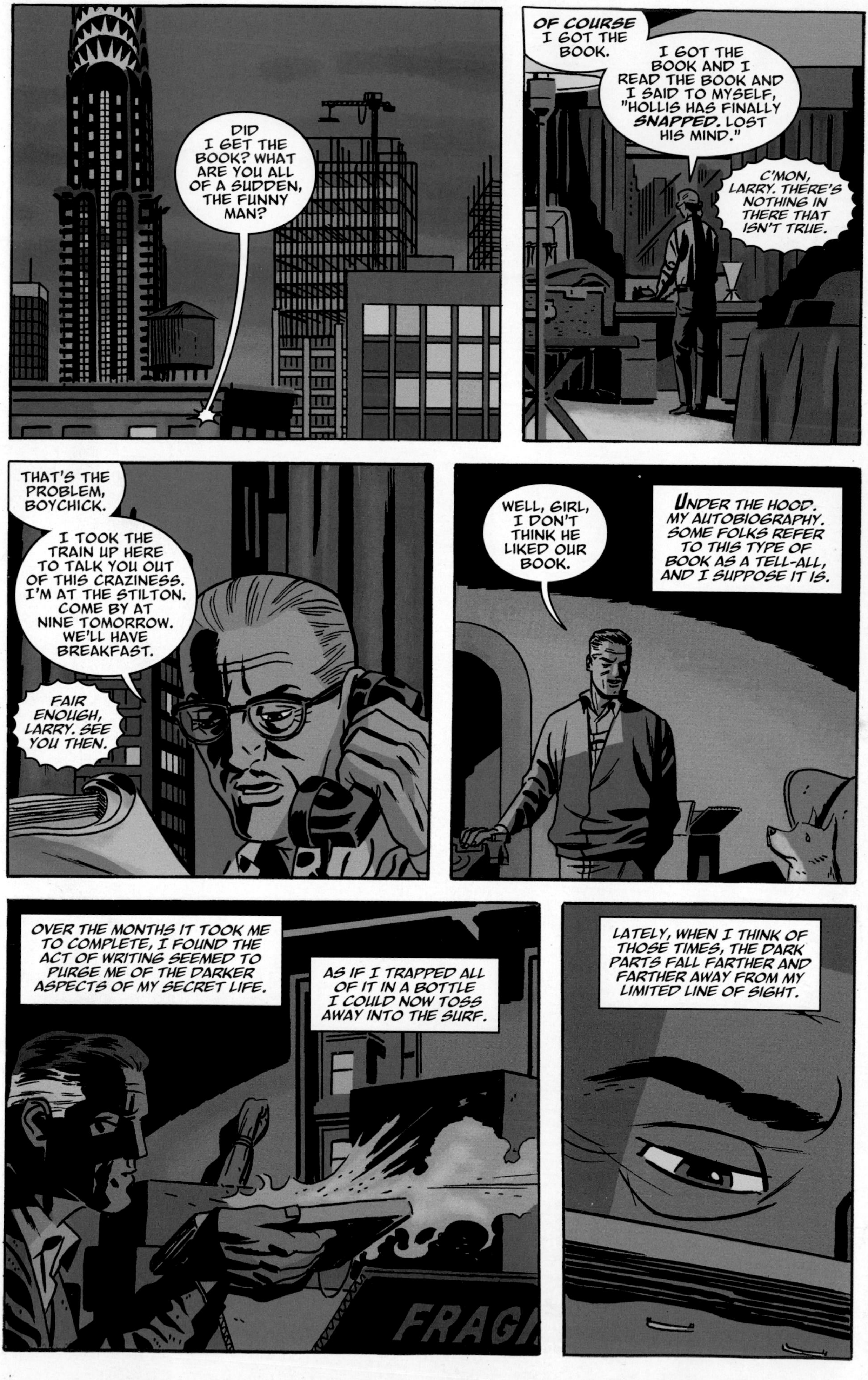
DID I GET THE BOOK? WHAT ARE YOU ALL OF A SUDDEN, THE FUNNY MAN?
OF COURSE I GOT THE BOOK.
I GOT THE BOOK AND I READ THE BOOK AND I SAID TO MYSELF, "HOLLIS HAS FINALLY SNAPPED. LOST HIS MIND."
C'MON, LARRY. THERE'S NOTHING IN THERE THAT ISN'T TRUE.
THAT'S THE PROBLEM, BOYCHICK.
I TOOK THE TRAIN UP HERE TO TALK YOU OUT OF THIS CRAZINESS. I'M AT THE STILTON. COME BY AT NINE TOMORROW. WE'LL HAVE BREAKFAST.
FAIR ENOUGH, LARRY. SEE YOU THEN.
WELL, GIRL, I DON'T THINK HE LIKED OUR BOOK.
UNDER THE HOOD. MY AUTOBIOGRAPHY. SOME FOLKS REFER TO THIS TYPE OF BOOK AS A TELL-ALL, AND I SUPPOSE IT IS.
OVER THE MONTHS IT TOOK ME TO COMPLETE, I FOUND THE ACT OF WRITING SEEMED TO PURGE ME OF THE DARKER ASPECTS OF MY SECRET LIFE.
AS IF I TRAPPED ALL OF IT IN A BOTTLE I COULD NOW TOSS AWAY INTO THE SURF.
FRAGI
LATELY, WHEN I THINK OF THOSE TIMES, THE DARK PARTS FALL FARTHER AND FARTHER AWAY FROM MY LIMITED LINE OF SIGHT.

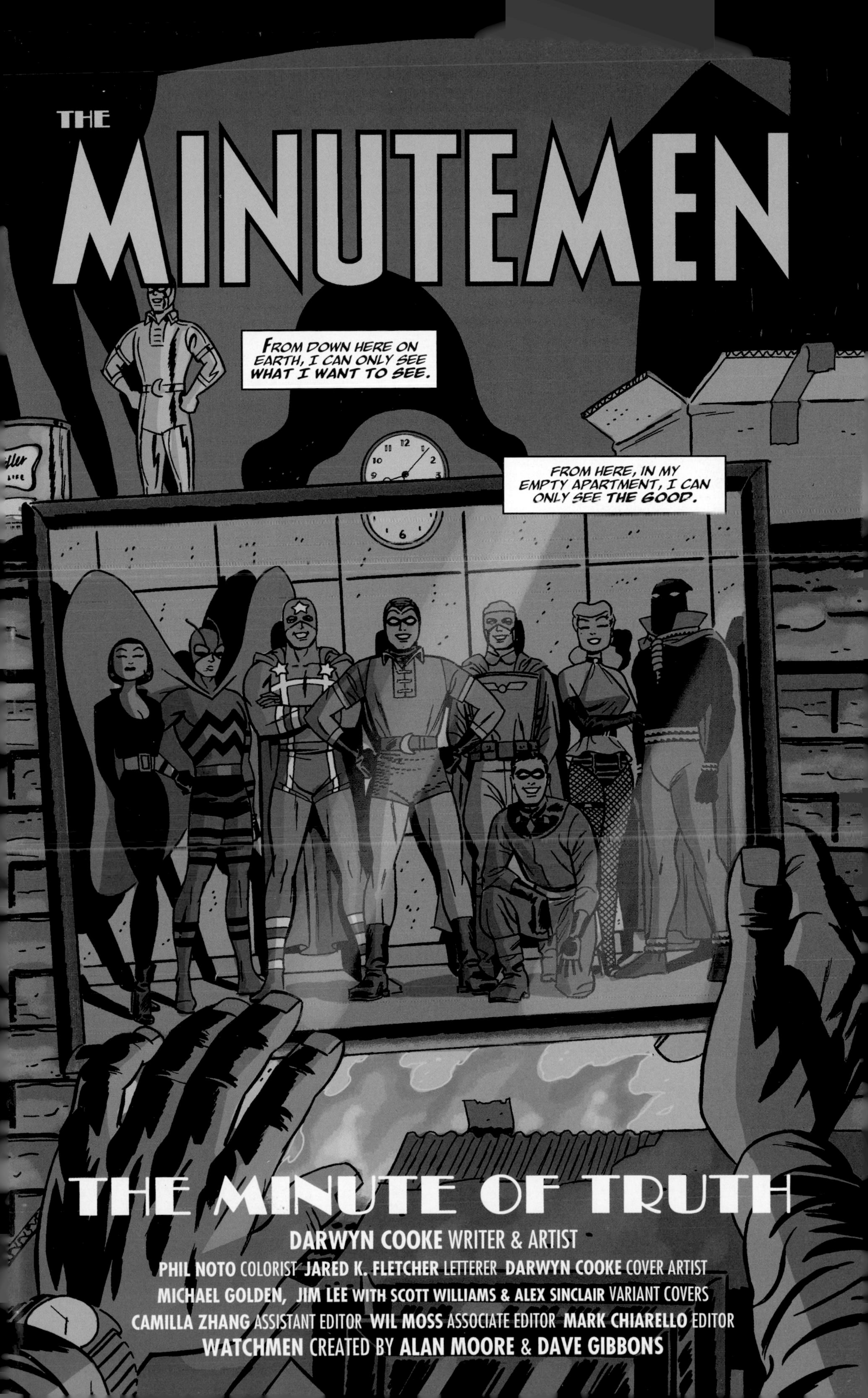
THE
MINUTEMEN
FROM DOWN HERE ON EARTH, I CAN ONLY SEE WHAT I WANT TO SEE.
FROM HERE, IN MY EMPTY APARTMENT, I CAN ONLY SEE THE GOOD.
THE MINUTE OF TRUTH
DARWYN COOKE WRITER & ARTIST
PHIL NOTO COLORIST JARED K. FLETCHER LETTERER DARWYN COOKE COVER ARTIST
MICHAEL GOLDEN, JIM LEE WITH SCOTT WILLIAMS & ALEX SINCLAIR VARIANT COVERS
CAMILLA ZHANG ASSISTANT EDITOR WIL MOSS ASSOCIATE EDITOR MARK CHIARELLO EDITOR
WATCHMEN CREATED BY ALAN MOORE & DAVE GIBBONS

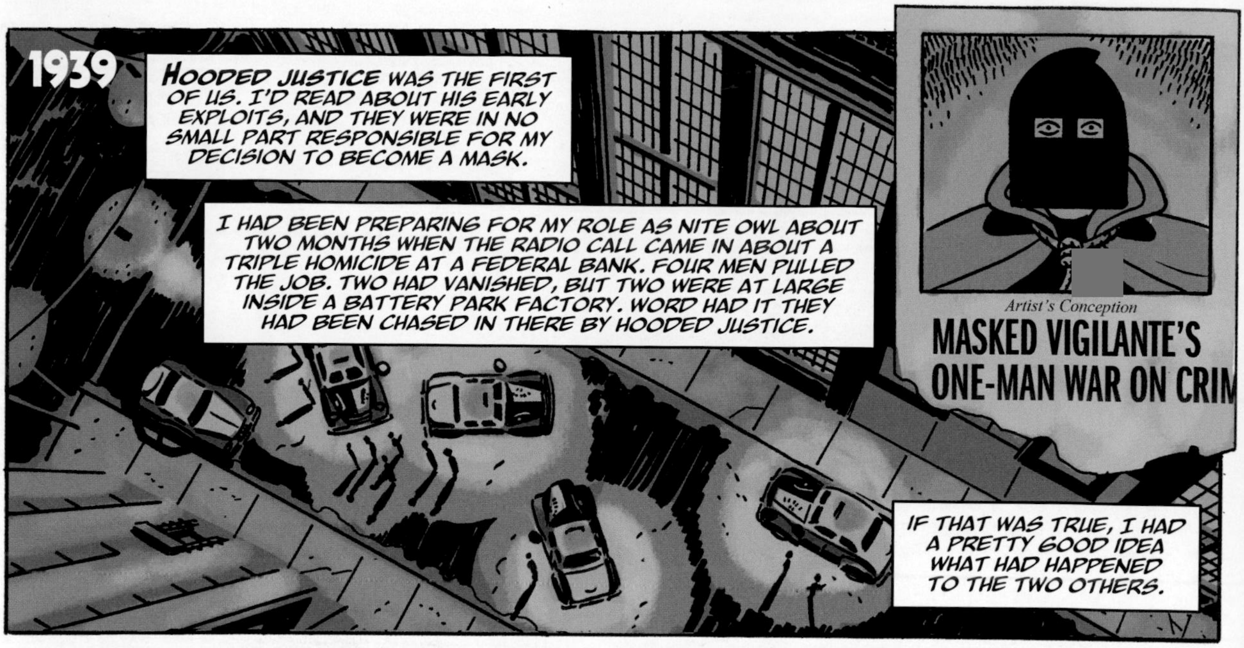
1939
HOODED JUSTICE WAS THE FIRST OF US. I'D READ ABOUT HIS EARLY EXPLOITS, AND THEY WERE IN NO SMALL PART RESPONSIBLE FOR MY DECISION TO BECOME A MASK.
I HAD BEEN PREPARING FOR MY ROLE AS NITE OWL ABOUT TWO MONTHS WHEN THE RADIO CALL CAME IN ABOUT A TRIPLE HOMICIDE AT A FEDERAL BANK. FOUR MEN PULLED THE JOB. TWO HAD VANISHED, BUT TWO WERE AT LARGE INSIDE A BATTERY PARK FACTORY. WORD HAD IT THEY HAD BEEN CHASED IN THERE BY HOODED JUSTICE.
Artist's Conception
MASKED VIGILANTE'S ONE-MAN WAR ON CRIM
IF THAT WAS TRUE, I HAD A PRETTY GOOD IDEA WHAT HAD HAPPENED TO THE TWO OTHERS.

CHAPTER ONE: EIGHT MINUTES

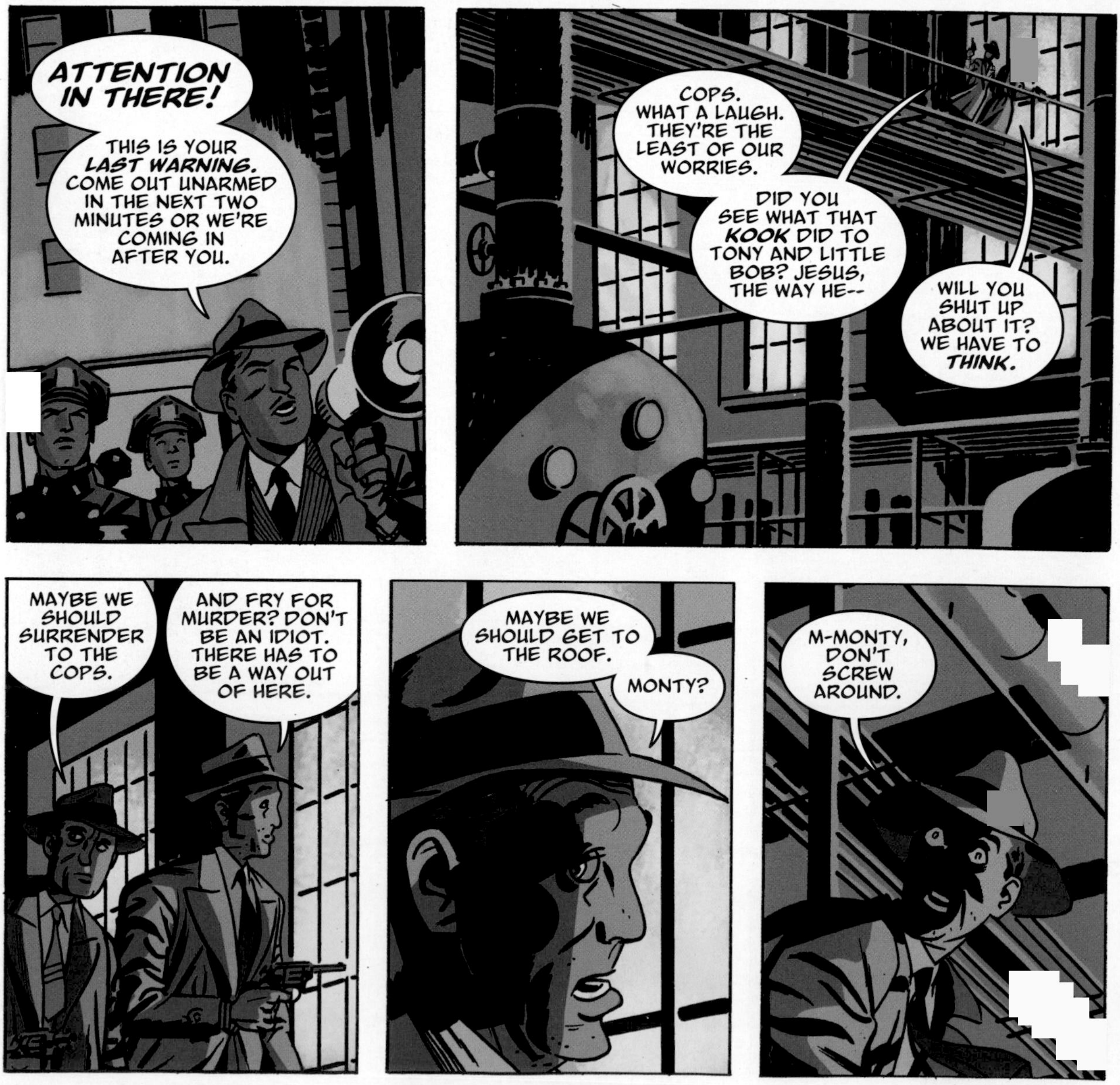
ATTENTION IN THERE!
THIS IS YOUR LAST WARNING. COME OUT UNARMED IN THE NEXT TWO MINUTES OR WE'RE COMING IN AFTER YOU.
COPS. WHAT A LAUGH. THEY'RE THE LEAST OF OUR WORRIES.
DID YOU SEE WHAT THAT KOOK DID TO TONY AND LITTLE BOB? JESUS, THE WAY HE--
WILL YOU SHUT UP ABOUT IT? WE HAVE TO THINK.
MAYBE WE SHOULD SURRENDER TO THE COPS.
AND FRY FOR MURDER? DON'T BE AN IDIOT. THERE HAS TO BE A WAY OUT OF HERE.
MAYBE WE SHOULD GET TO THE ROOF.
MONTY?
M-MONTY, DON'T SCREW AROUND.

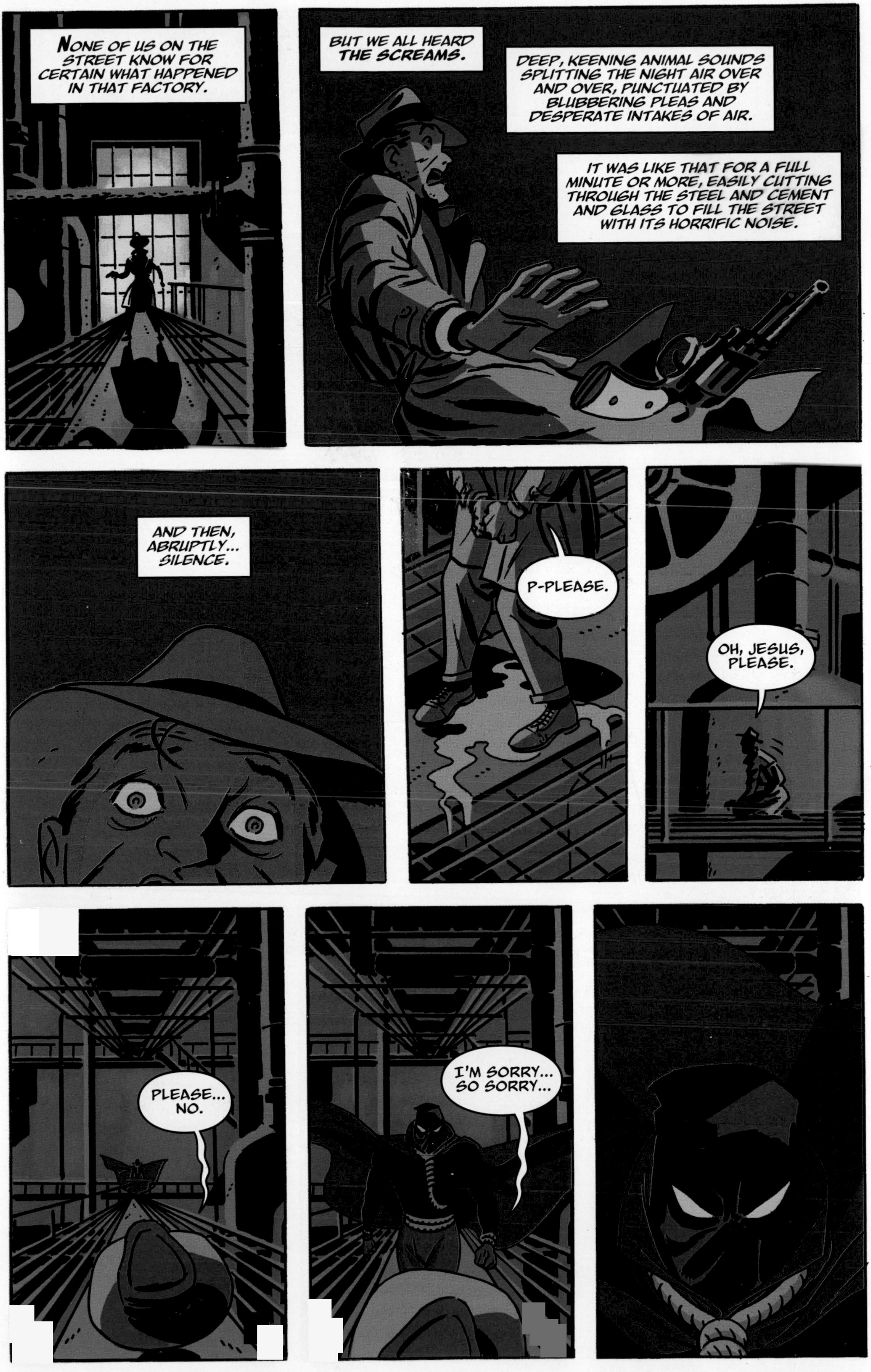
NONE OF US ON THE STREET KNOW FOR CERTAIN WHAT HAPPENED IN THAT FACTORY.
BUT WE ALL HEARD THE SCREAMS.
DEEP, KEENING ANIMAL SOUNDS SPLITTING THE NIGHT AIR OVER AND OVER, PUNCTUATED BY BLUBBERING PLEAS AND DESPERATE INTAKES OF AIR.
IT WAS LIKE THAT FOR A FULL MINUTE OR MORE, EASILY CUTTING THROUGH THE STEEL AND CEMENT AND GLASS TO FILL THE STREET WITH ITS HORRIFIC NOISE.
AND THEN, ABRUPTLY... SILENCE.
P-PLEASE.
OH, JESUS, PLEASE.
PLEASE... NO.
I'M SORRY... SO SORRY...

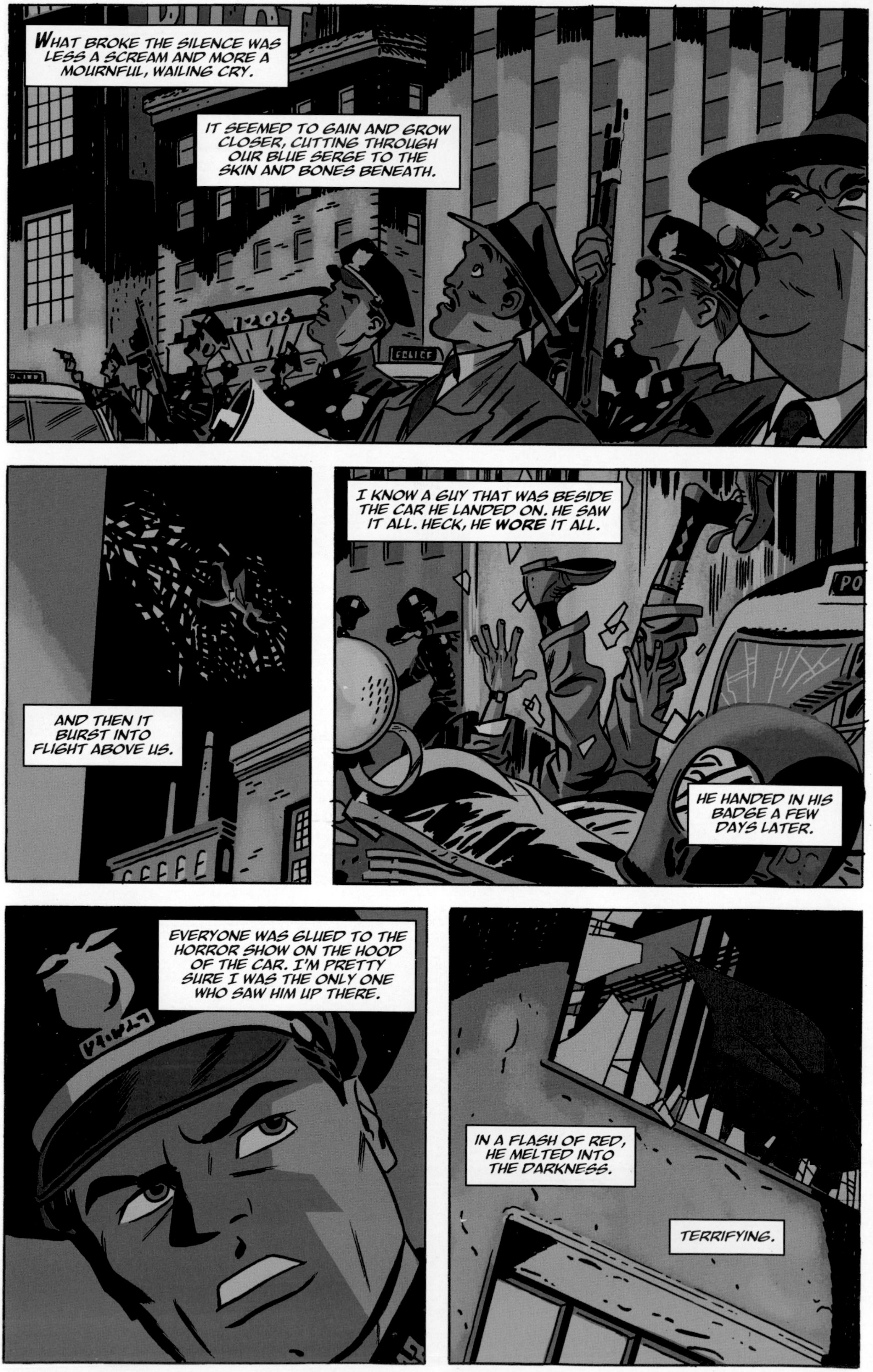
WHAT BROKE THE SILENCE WAS LESS A SCREAM AND MORE A MOURNFUL, WAILING CRY.
IT SEEMED TO GAIN AND GROW CLOSER, CUTTING THROUGH OUR BLUE SERGE TO THE SKIN AND BONES BENEATH.
AND THEN IT BURST INTO FLIGHT ABOVE US.
I KNOW A GUY THAT WAS BESIDE THE CAR HE LANDED ON. HE SAW IT ALL. HECK, HE WORE IT ALL.
HE HANDED IN HIS BADGE A FEW DAYS LATER.
EVERYONE WAS GLUED TO THE HORROR SHOW ON THE HOOD OF THE CAR. I'M PRETTY SURE I WAS THE ONLY ONE WHO SAW HIM UP THERE.
IN A FLASH OF RED, HE MELTED INTO THE DARKNESS.
TERRIFYING.

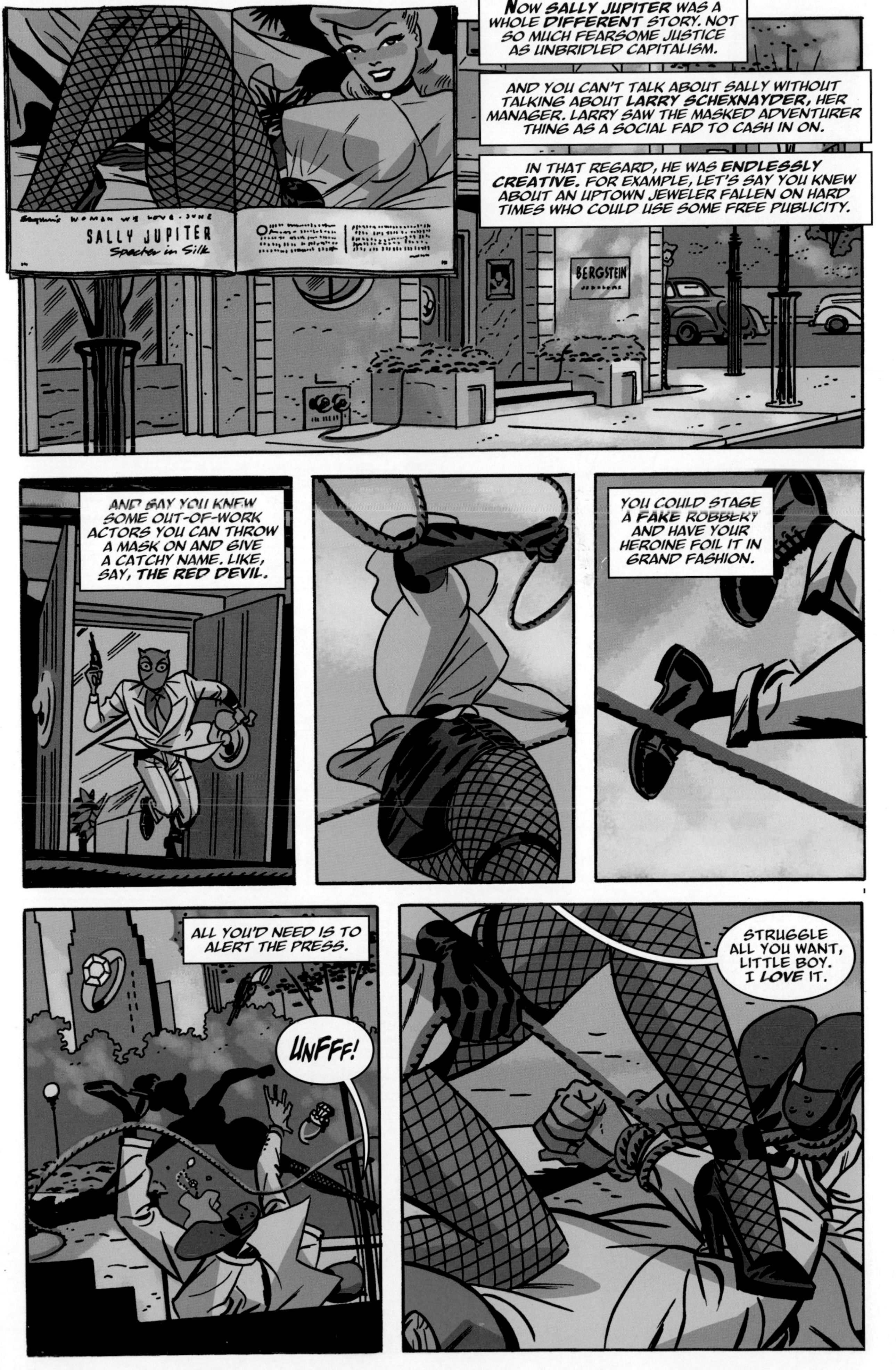
NOW SALLY JUPITER WAS A WHOLE DIFFERENT STORY. NOT SO MUCH FEARSOME JUSTICE AS UNBRIDLED CAPITALISM.
AND YOU CAN'T TALK ABOUT SALLY WITHOUT TALKING ABOUT LARRY SCHEXNAYDER, HER MANAGER. LARRY SAW THE MASKED ADVENTURER THING AS A SOCIAL FAD TO CASH IN ON.
IN THAT REGARD, HE WAS ENDLESSLY CREATIVE. FOR EXAMPLE, LET'S SAY YOU KNEW ABOUT AN UPTOWN JEWELER FALLEN ON HARD TIMES WHO COULD USE SOME FREE PUBLICITY.
SALLY JUPITER
Specter in Silk
BERGSTEIN
AND SAY YOU KNEW SOME OUT-OF-WORK ACTORS YOU CAN THROW A MASK ON AND GIVE A CATCHY NAME. LIKE, SAY, THE RED DEVIL.
YOU COULD STAGE A FAKE ROBBERY AND HAVE YOUR HEROINE FOIL IT IN GRAND FASHION.
ALL YOU'D NEED IS TO ALERT THE PRESS.
UNFFF!
STRUGGLE ALL YOU WANT, LITTLE BOY. I LOVE IT.

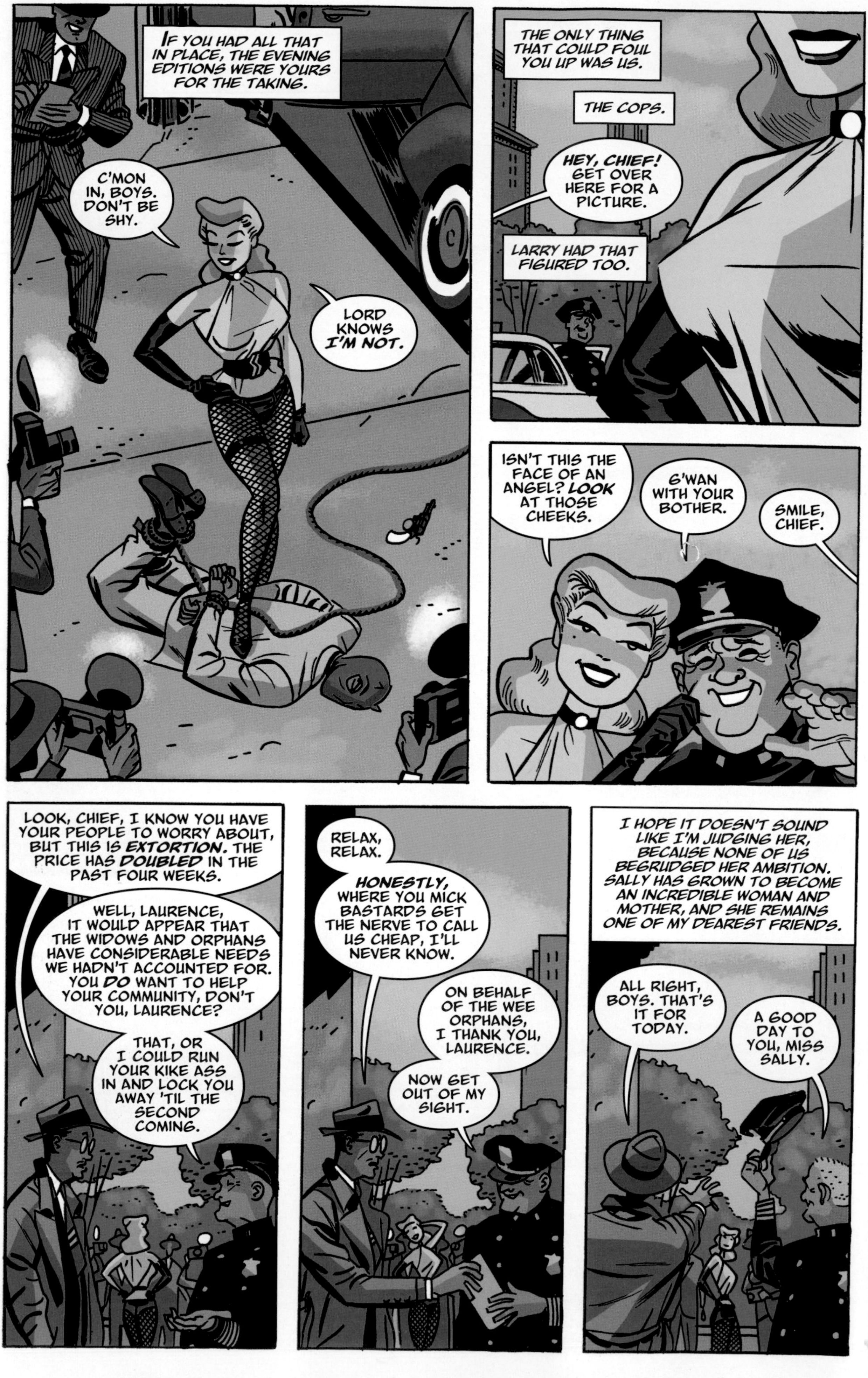
IF YOU HAD ALL THAT IN PLACE, THE EVENING EDITIONS WERE YOURS FOR THE TAKING.
C'MON IN, BOYS. DON'T BE SHY.
LORD KNOWS I'M NOT.
THE ONLY THING THAT COULD FOUL YOU UP WAS US.
THE COPS.
HEY, CHIEF! GET OVER HERE FOR A PICTURE.
LARRY HAD THAT FIGURED TOO.
ISN'T THIS THE FACE OF AN ANGEL? LOOK AT THOSE CHEEKS.
G'WAN WITH YOUR BOTHER.
SMILE, CHIEF.
LOOK, CHIEF, I KNOW YOU HAVE YOUR PEOPLE TO WORRY ABOUT, BUT THIS IS EXTORTION. THE PRICE HAS DOUBLED IN THE PAST FOUR WEEKS.
WELL, LAURENCE, IT WOULD APPEAR THAT THE WIDOWS AND ORPHANS HAVE CONSIDERABLE NEEDS WE HADN'T ACCOUNTED FOR. YOU DO WANT TO HELP YOUR COMMUNITY, DON'T YOU, LAURENCE?
THAT, OR I COULD RUN YOUR KIKE ASS IN AND LOCK YOU AWAY 'TIL THE SECOND COMING.
RELAX, RELAX.
HONESTLY, WHERE YOU MICK BASTARDS GET THE NERVE TO CALL US CHEAP, I'LL NEVER KNOW.
ON BEHALF OF THE WEE ORPHANS, I THANK YOU, LAURENCE.
NOW GET OUT OF MY SIGHT.
I HOPE IT DOESN'T SOUND LIKE I'M JUDGING HER, BECAUSE NONE OF US BEGRUDGED HER AMBITION. SALLY HAS GROWN TO BECOME AN INCREDIBLE WOMAN AND MOTHER, AND SHE REMAINS ONE OF MY DEAREST FRIENDS.
ALL RIGHT, BOYS. THAT'S IT FOR TODAY.
A GOOD DAY TO YOU, MISS SALLY.

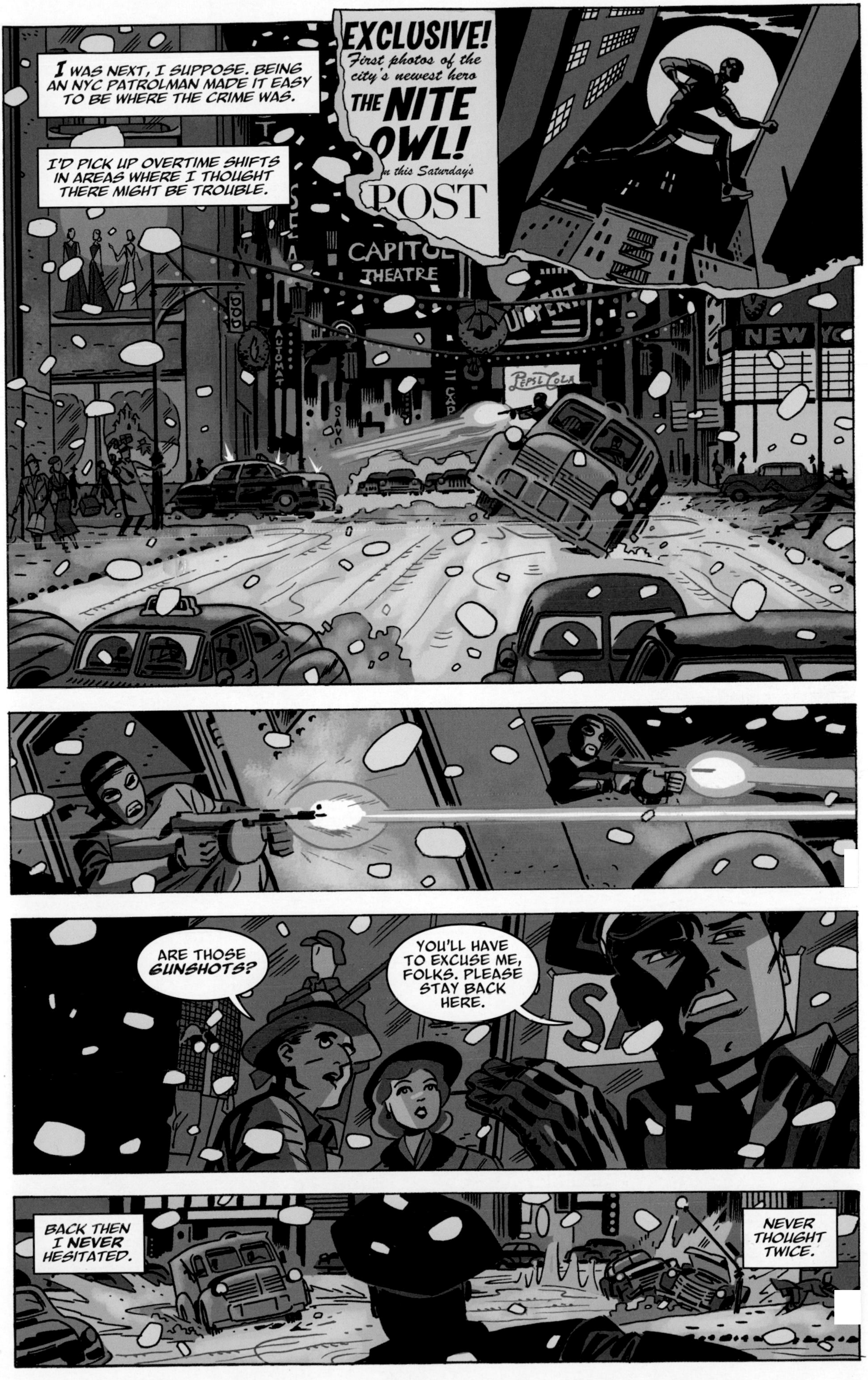
I WAS NEXT, I SUPPOSE. BEING AN NYC PATROLMAN MADE IT EASY TO BE WHERE THE CRIME WAS.
I'D PICK UP OVERTIME SHIFTS IN AREAS WHERE I THOUGHT THERE MIGHT BE TROUBLE.
EXCLUSIVE! First photos of the city's newest hero THE NITE OWL! in this Saturday's POST
CAPITOL THEATRE
AUTOMAT
NEW
PEPSI COLA
ARE THOSE GUNSHOTS?
YOU'LL HAVE TO EXCUSE ME, FOLKS. PLEASE STAY BACK HERE.
BACK THEN I NEVER HESITATED.
NEVER THOUGHT TWICE.

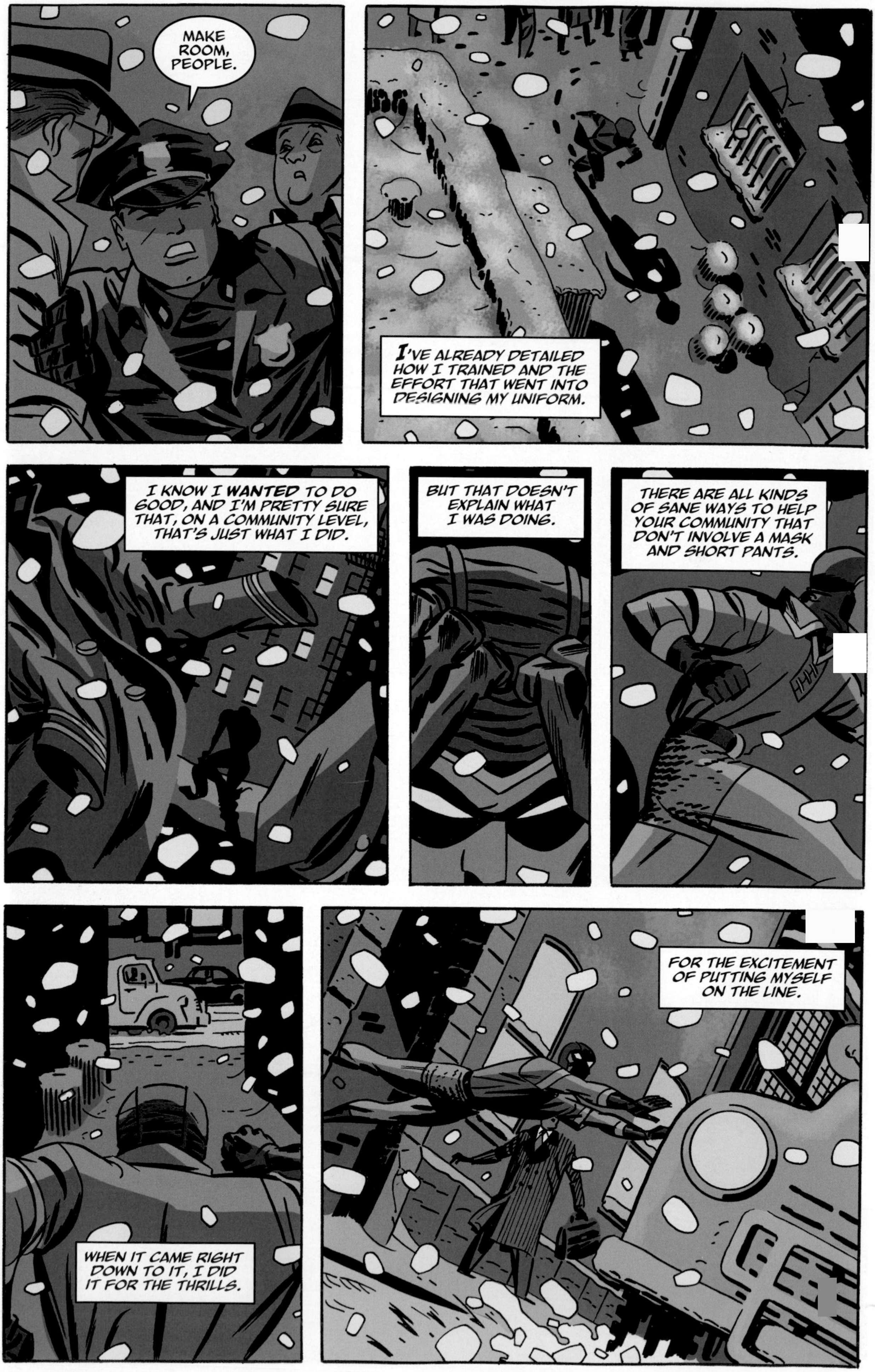
MAKE ROOM, PEOPLE.
I'VE ALREADY DETAILED HOW I TRAINED AND THE EFFORT THAT WENT INTO DESIGNING MY UNIFORM.
I KNOW I WANTED TO DO GOOD, AND I'M PRETTY SURE THAT, ON A COMMUNITY LEVEL, THAT'S JUST WHAT I DID.
BUT THAT DOESN'T EXPLAIN WHAT I WAS DOING.
THERE ARE ALL KINDS OF SANE WAYS TO HELP YOUR COMMUNITY THAT DON'T INVOLVE A MASK AND SHORT PANTS.
WHEN IT CAME RIGHT DOWN TO IT, I DID IT FOR THE THRILLS.
FOR THE EXCITEMENT OF PUTTING MYSELF ON THE LINE.

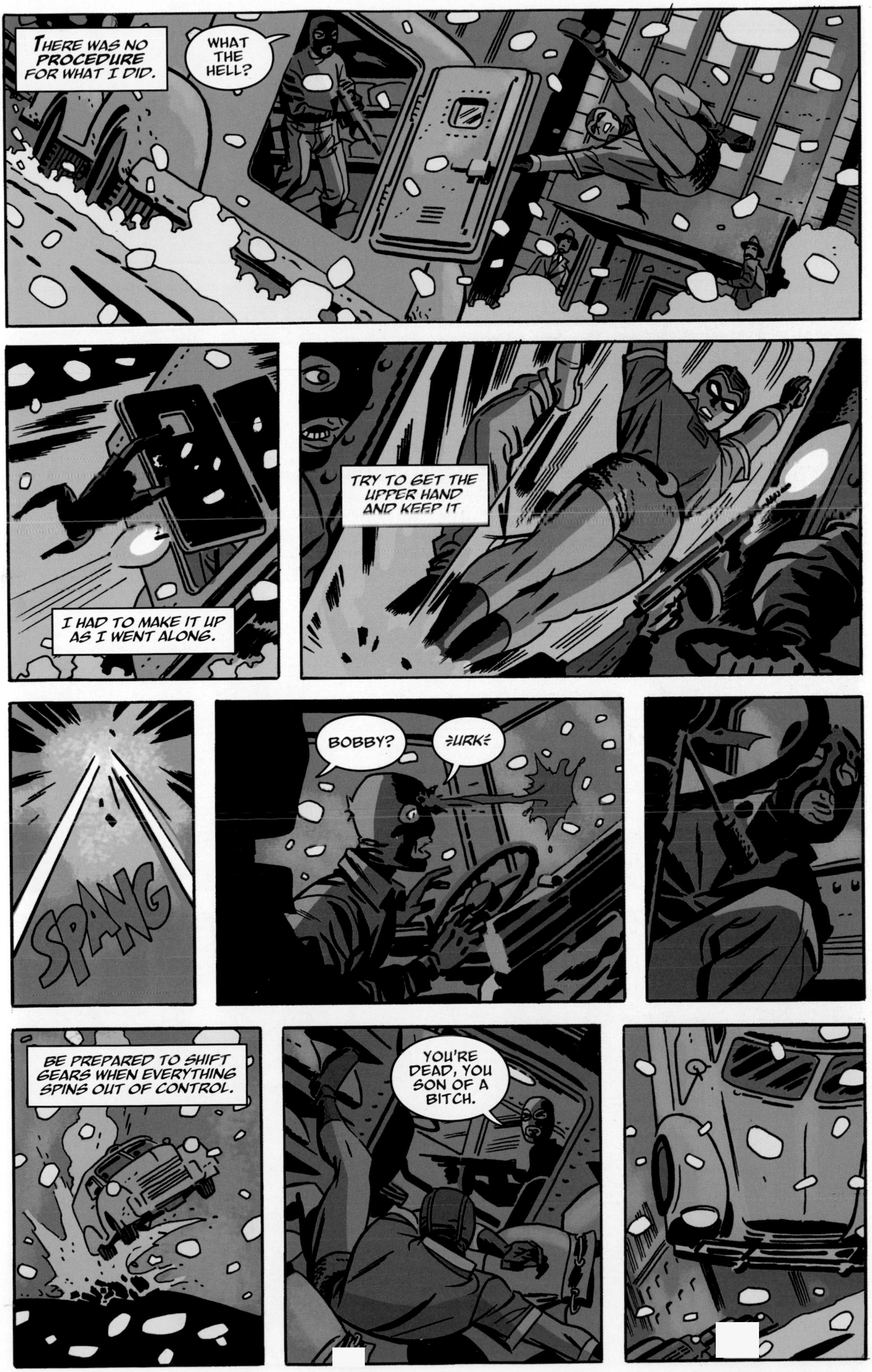
THERE WAS NO PROCEDURE FOR WHAT I DID.
WHAT THE HELL?
I HAD TO MAKE IT UP AS I WENT ALONG.
TRY TO GET THE UPPER HAND AND KEEP IT
SPANG
BOBBY?
URK
BE PREPARED TO SHIFT GEARS WHEN EVERYTHING SPINS OUT OF CONTROL.
YOU'RE DEAD, YOU SON OF A BITCH.

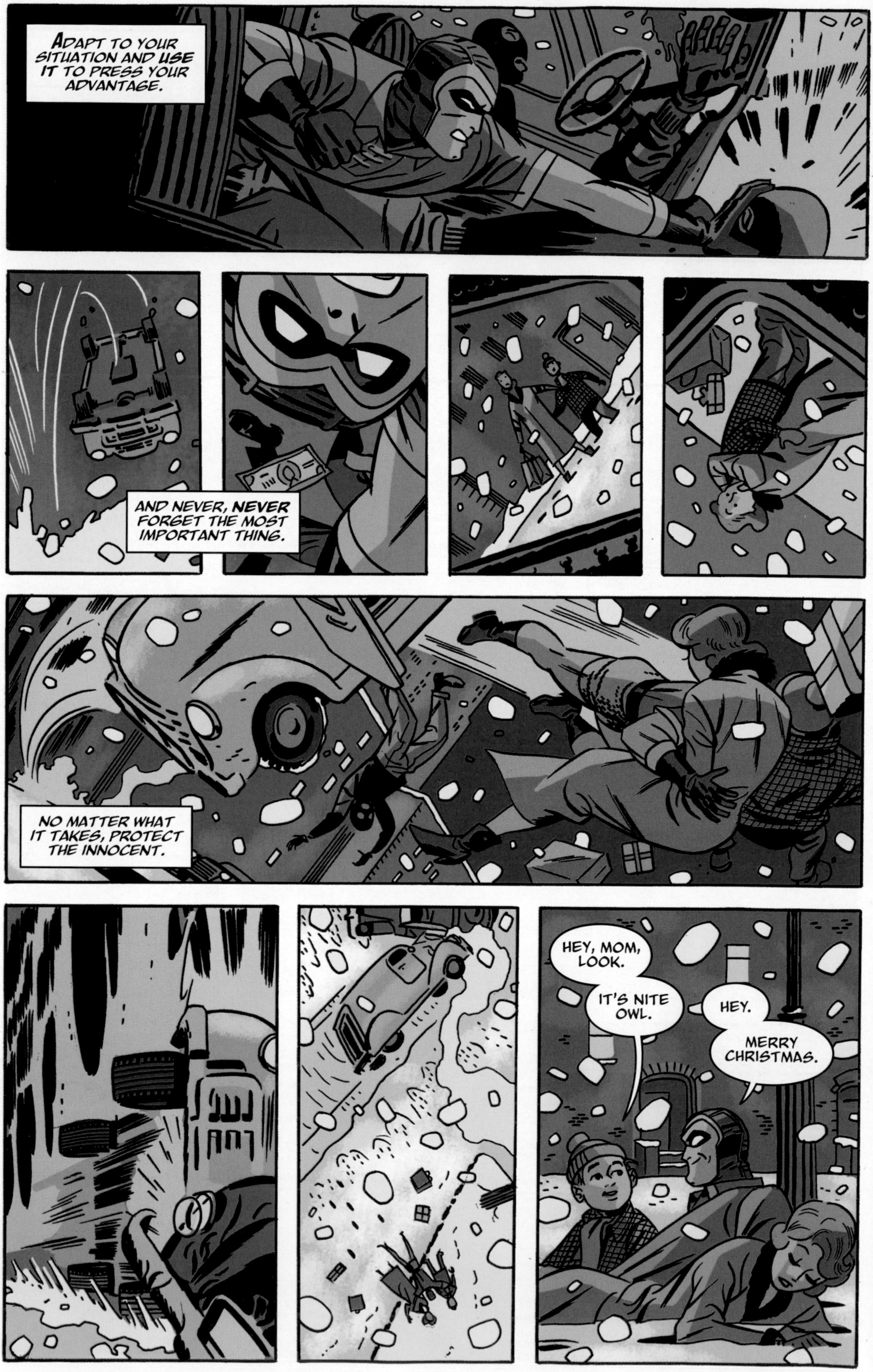
ADAPT TO YOUR SITUATION AND USE IT TO PRESS YOUR ADVANTAGE.
AND NEVER, NEVER FORGET THE MOST IMPORTANT THING.
NO MATTER WHAT IT TAKES, PROTECT THE INNOCENT.
HEY, MOM, LOOK.
IT'S NITE OWL.
HEY.
MERRY CHRISTMAS.

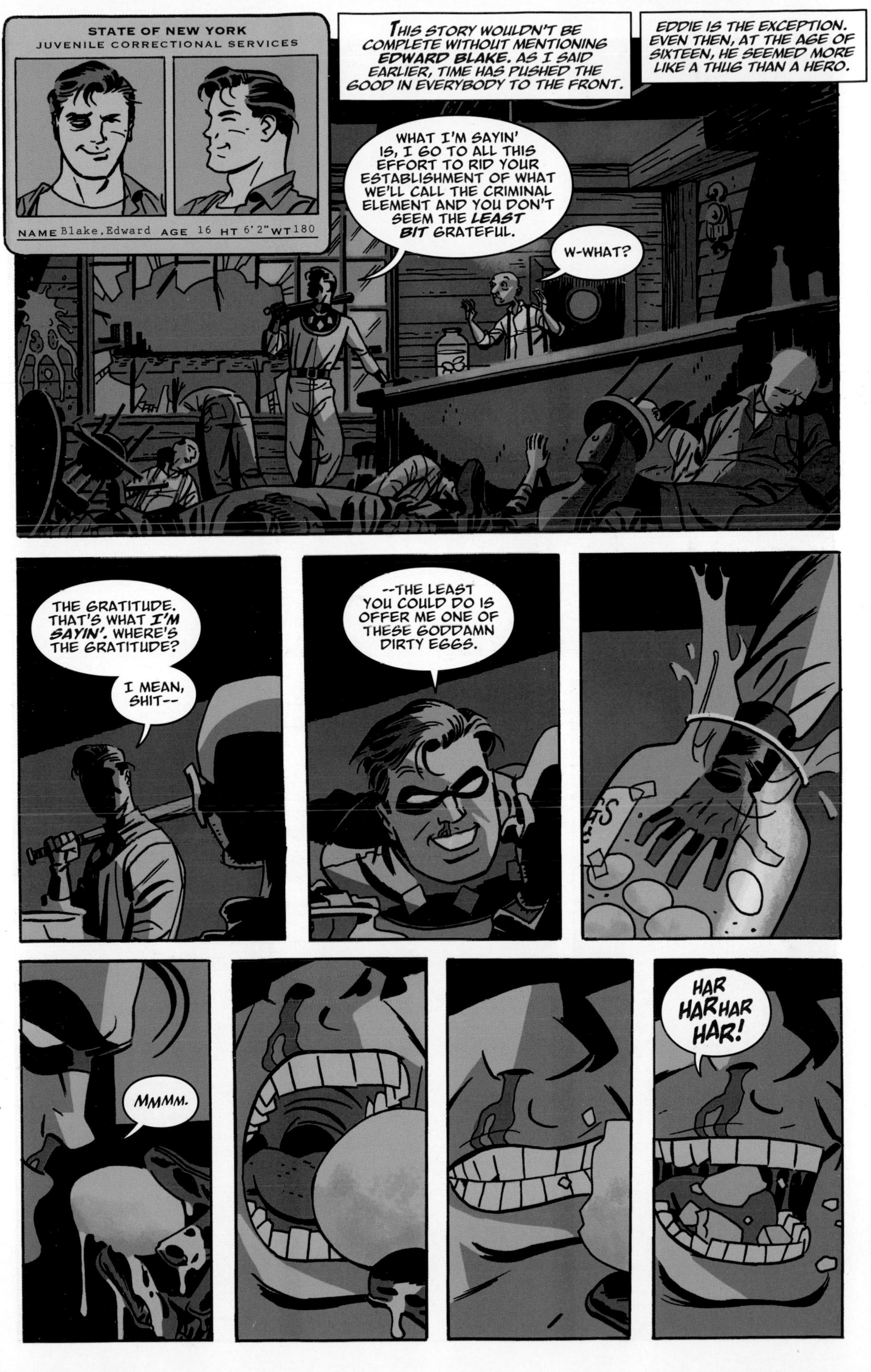
STATE OF NEW YORK
JUVENILE CORRECTIONAL SERVICES
NAME Blake, Edward AGE 16 HT 6'2" WT 180
THIS STORY WOULDN'T BE COMPLETE WITHOUT MENTIONING EDWARD BLAKE. AS I SAID EARLIER, TIME HAS PUSHED THE GOOD IN EVERYBODY TO THE FRONT.
EDDIE IS THE EXCEPTION. EVEN THEN, AT THE AGE OF SIXTEEN, HE SEEMED MORE LIKE A THUG THAN A HERO.
WHAT I'M SAYIN' IS, I GO TO ALL THIS EFFORT TO RID YOUR ESTABLISHMENT OF WHAT WE'LL CALL THE CRIMINAL ELEMENT AND YOU DON'T SEEM THE LEAST BIT GRATEFUL.
W-WHAT?
THE GRATITUDE. THAT'S WHAT I'M SAYIN'. WHERE'S THE GRATITUDE?
I MEAN, SHIT--
--THE LEAST YOU COULD DO IS OFFER ME ONE OF THESE GODDAMN DIRTY EGGS.
MMMM.
HAR HAR HAR HAR!

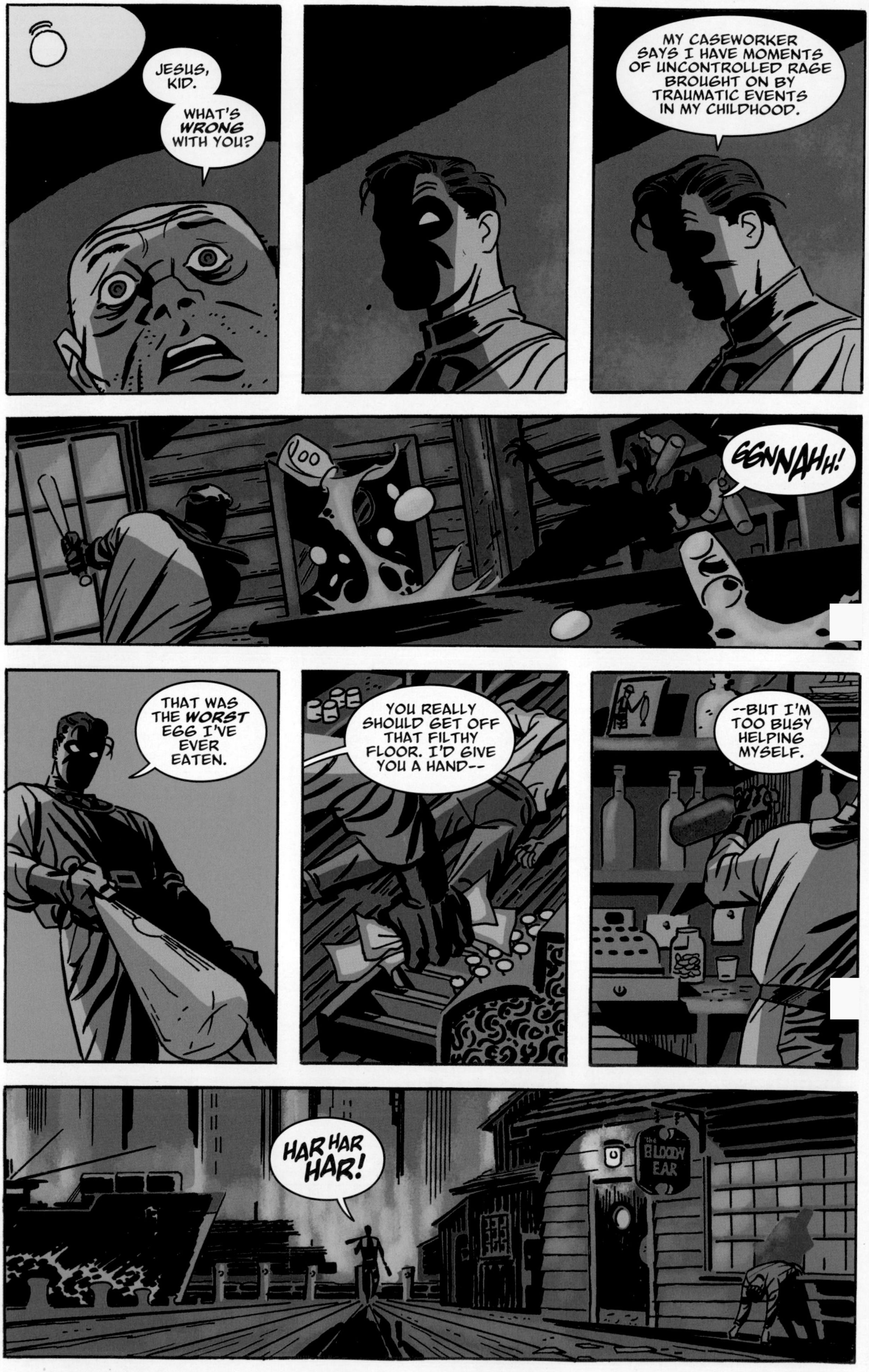
JESUS, KID.
WHAT'S **WRONG** WITH YOU?
MY CASEWORKER SAYS I HAVE MOMENTS OF UNCONTROLLED RAGE BROUGHT ON BY TRAUMATIC EVENTS IN MY CHILDHOOD.
GGNAHH!
THAT WAS THE **WORST** EGG I'VE EVER EATEN.
YOU REALLY SHOULD GET OFF THAT FILTHY FLOOR. I'D GIVE YOU A HAND--
--BUT I'M TOO BUSY HELPING MYSELF.
HAR HAR HAR!
the BLOODY EAR

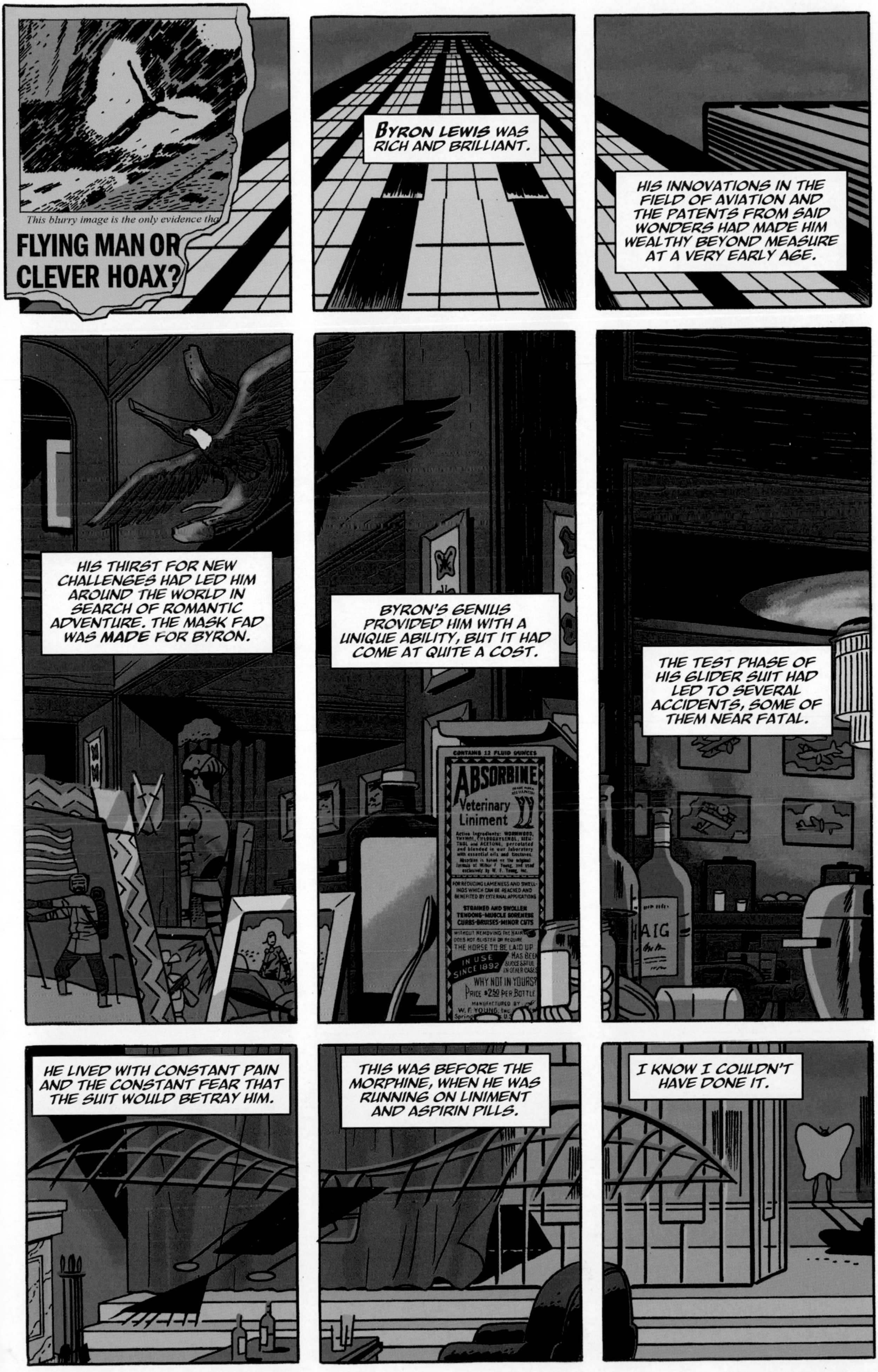
This blurry image is the only evidence tha
FLYING MAN OR CLEVER HOAX?
BYRON LEWIS WAS RICH AND BRILLIANT.
HIS INNOVATIONS IN THE FIELD OF AVIATION AND THE PATENTS FROM SAID WONDERS HAD MADE HIM WEALTHY BEYOND MEASURE AT A VERY EARLY AGE.
HIS THIRST FOR NEW CHALLENGES HAD LED HIM AROUND THE WORLD IN SEARCH OF ROMANTIC ADVENTURE. THE MASK FAD WAS MADE FOR BYRON.
BYRON'S GENIUS PROVIDED HIM WITH A UNIQUE ABILITY, BUT IT HAD COME AT QUITE A COST.
CONTAINS 12 FLUID OUNCES
ABSORBINE
Veterinary Liniment
IN USE SINCE 1892
WHY NOT IN YOURS?
PRICE $2.50 PER BOTTLE
THE TEST PHASE OF HIS GLIDER SUIT HAD LED TO SEVERAL ACCIDENTS, SOME OF THEM NEAR FATAL.
HAIG
HE LIVED WITH CONSTANT PAIN AND THE CONSTANT FEAR THAT THE SUIT WOULD BETRAY HIM.
THIS WAS BEFORE THE MORPHINE, WHEN HE WAS RUNNING ON LINIMENT AND ASPIRIN PILLS.
I KNOW I COULDN'T HAVE DONE IT.

HE HAD TO GAUGE THE WIND AND WEATHER BY THE SECOND.

HIS WEIGHT COULDN'T VARY BY MORE THAN THREE POUNDS.

HE HAD TO STEP OUT OVER SPACE AND *BELIEVE* HE COULD FLY.

IT WAS MUCH LATER HE TOLD ME ALL OF THIS. BEFORE THINGS UNRAVELED COMPLETELY.

YOU SEE, HE WAS *SCARED* OF HIS OWN CREATION.

EVERY TIME HE FLEW, THE FEAR WOULD SWELL INSIDE HIM JUST A LITTLE MORE.

EVENTUALLY HE NEEDED SOMETHING TO HELP HIM BELIEVE.

THE COMMON STORY IS THAT BYRON WAS THE WEAK ONE. THE ONE WHO CRACKED UP.

I SEE IT DIFFERENTLY.

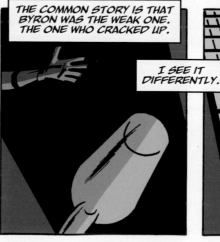

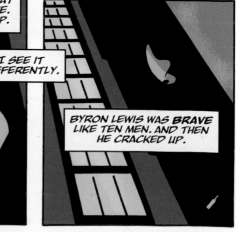

BYRON LEWIS WAS *BRAVE* LIKE TEN MEN. AND THEN HE CRACKED UP.

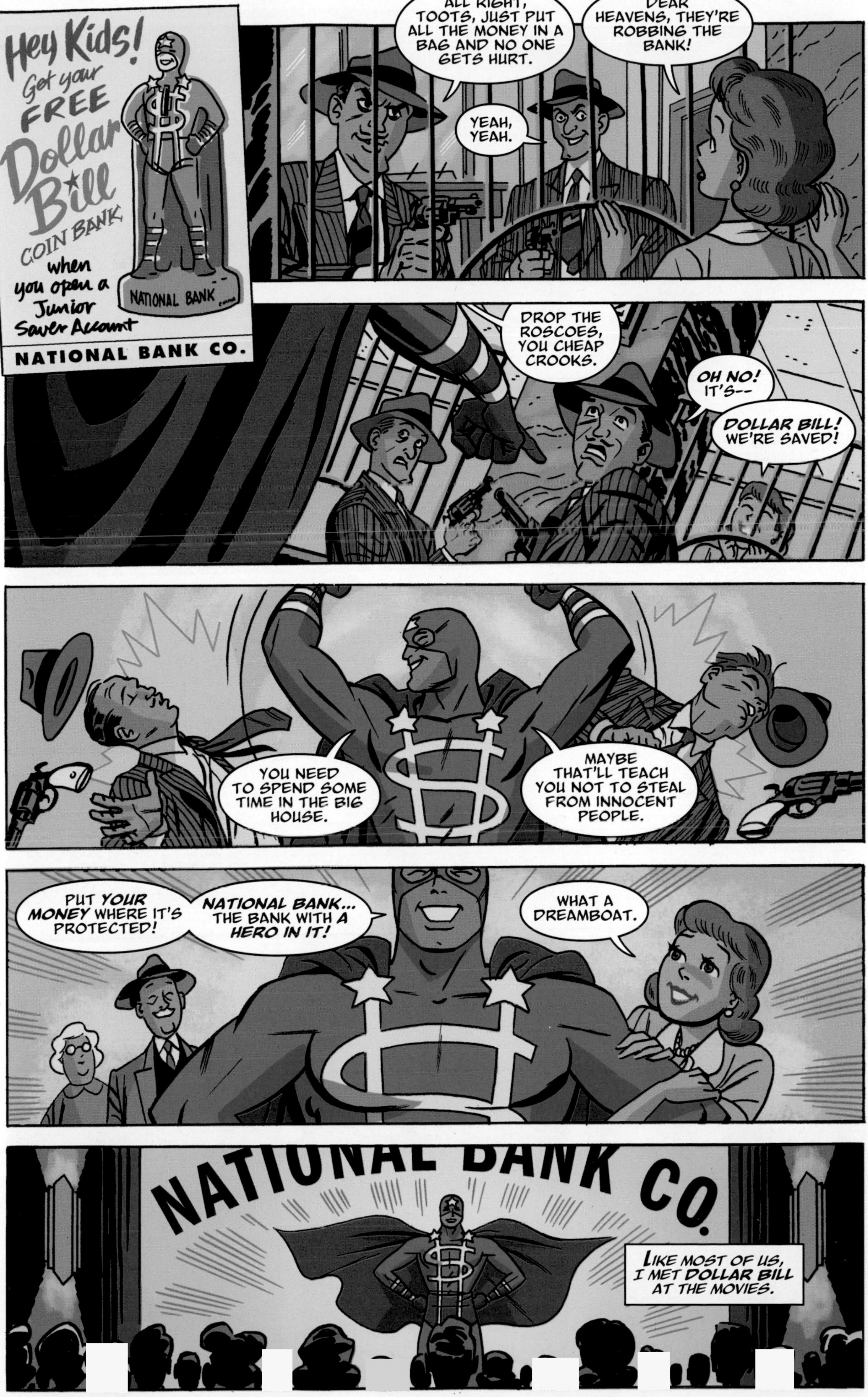
Hey Kids!
Get your FREE Dollar Bill COIN BANK when you open a Junior Saver Account
NATIONAL BANK
NATIONAL BANK CO.
ALL RIGHT, TOOTS, JUST PUT ALL THE MONEY IN A BAG AND NO ONE GETS HURT.
YEAH, YEAH.
DEAR HEAVENS, THEY'RE ROBBING THE BANK!
DROP THE ROSCOES, YOU CHEAP CROOKS.
OH NO! IT'S--
DOLLAR BILL! WE'RE SAVED!
YOU NEED TO SPEND SOME TIME IN THE BIG HOUSE.
MAYBE THAT'LL TEACH YOU NOT TO STEAL FROM INNOCENT PEOPLE.
PUT YOUR MONEY WHERE IT'S PROTECTED!
NATIONAL BANK... THE BANK WITH A HERO IN IT!
WHAT A DREAMBOAT.
NATIONAL BANK CO.
LIKE MOST OF US, I MET DOLLAR BILL AT THE MOVIES.

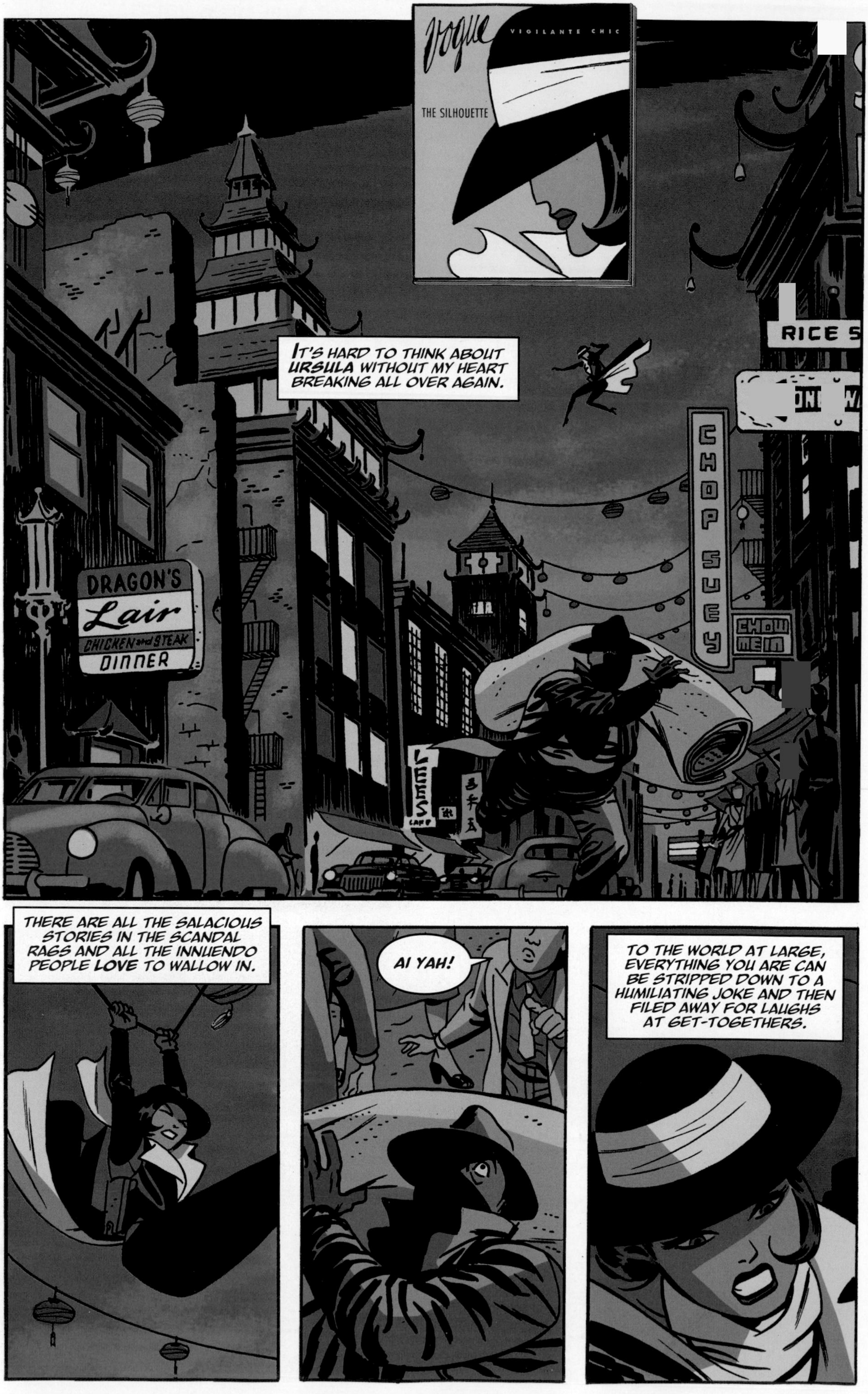
VOGUE
VIGILANTE CHIC
THE SILHOUETTE
IT'S HARD TO THINK ABOUT URSULA WITHOUT MY HEART BREAKING ALL OVER AGAIN.
DRAGON'S Lair CHICKEN and STEAK DINNER
CHOP SUEY
CHOW MEIN
THERE ARE ALL THE SALACIOUS STORIES IN THE SCANDAL RAGS AND ALL THE INNUENDO PEOPLE LOVE TO WALLOW IN.
AI YAH!
TO THE WORLD AT LARGE, EVERYTHING YOU ARE CAN BE STRIPPED DOWN TO A HUMILIATING JOKE AND THEN FILED AWAY FOR LAUGHS AT GET-TOGETHERS.

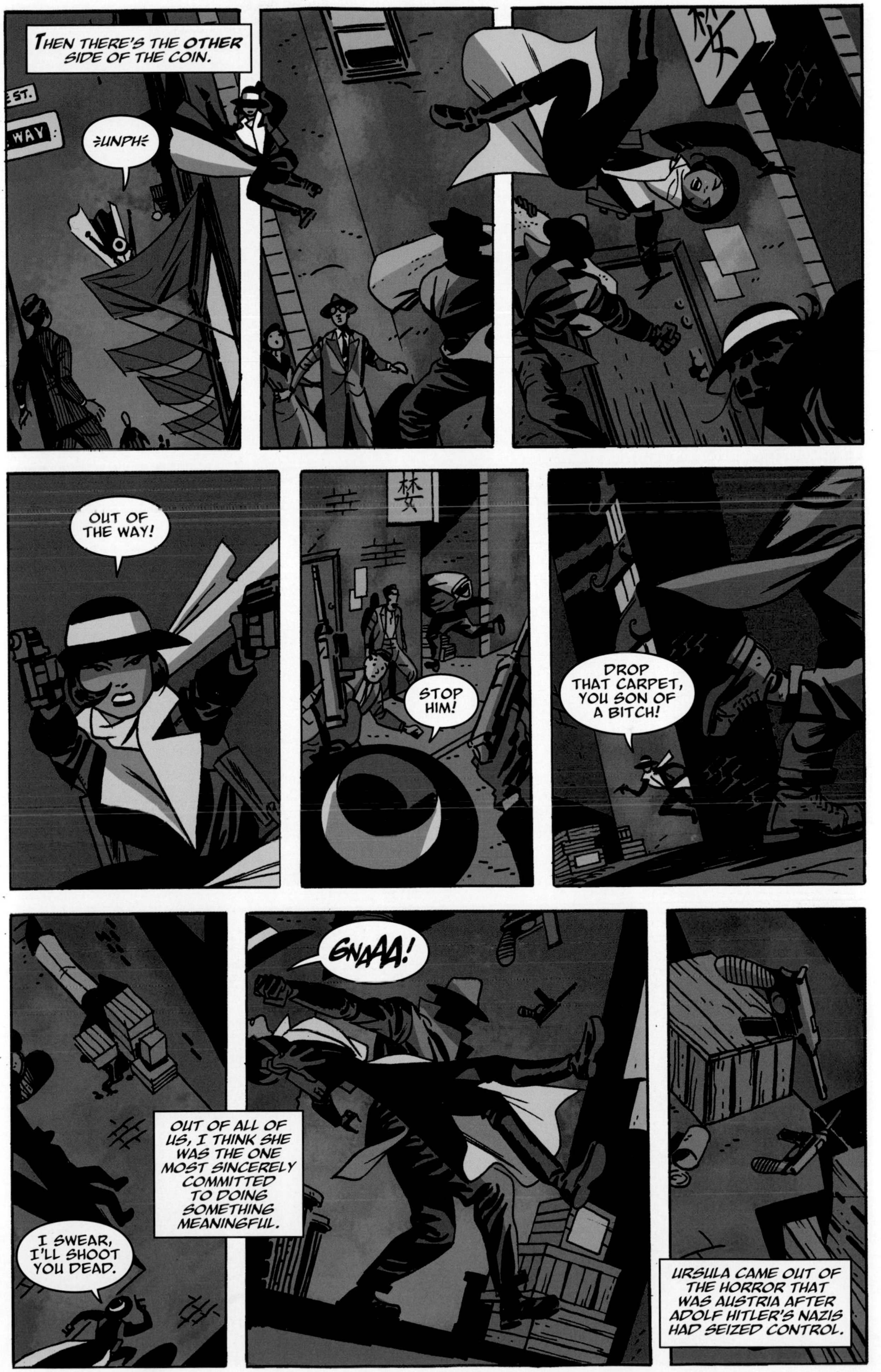
THEN THERE'S THE OTHER SIDE OF THE COIN.
UNPH
OUT OF THE WAY!
STOP HIM!
DROP THAT CARPET, YOU SON OF A BITCH!
I SWEAR, I'LL SHOOT YOU DEAD.
OUT OF ALL OF US, I THINK SHE WAS THE ONE MOST SINCERELY COMMITTED TO DOING SOMETHING MEANINGFUL.
GNAAA!
URSULA CAME OUT OF THE HORROR THAT WAS AUSTRIA AFTER ADOLF HITLER'S NAZIS HAD SEIZED CONTROL.

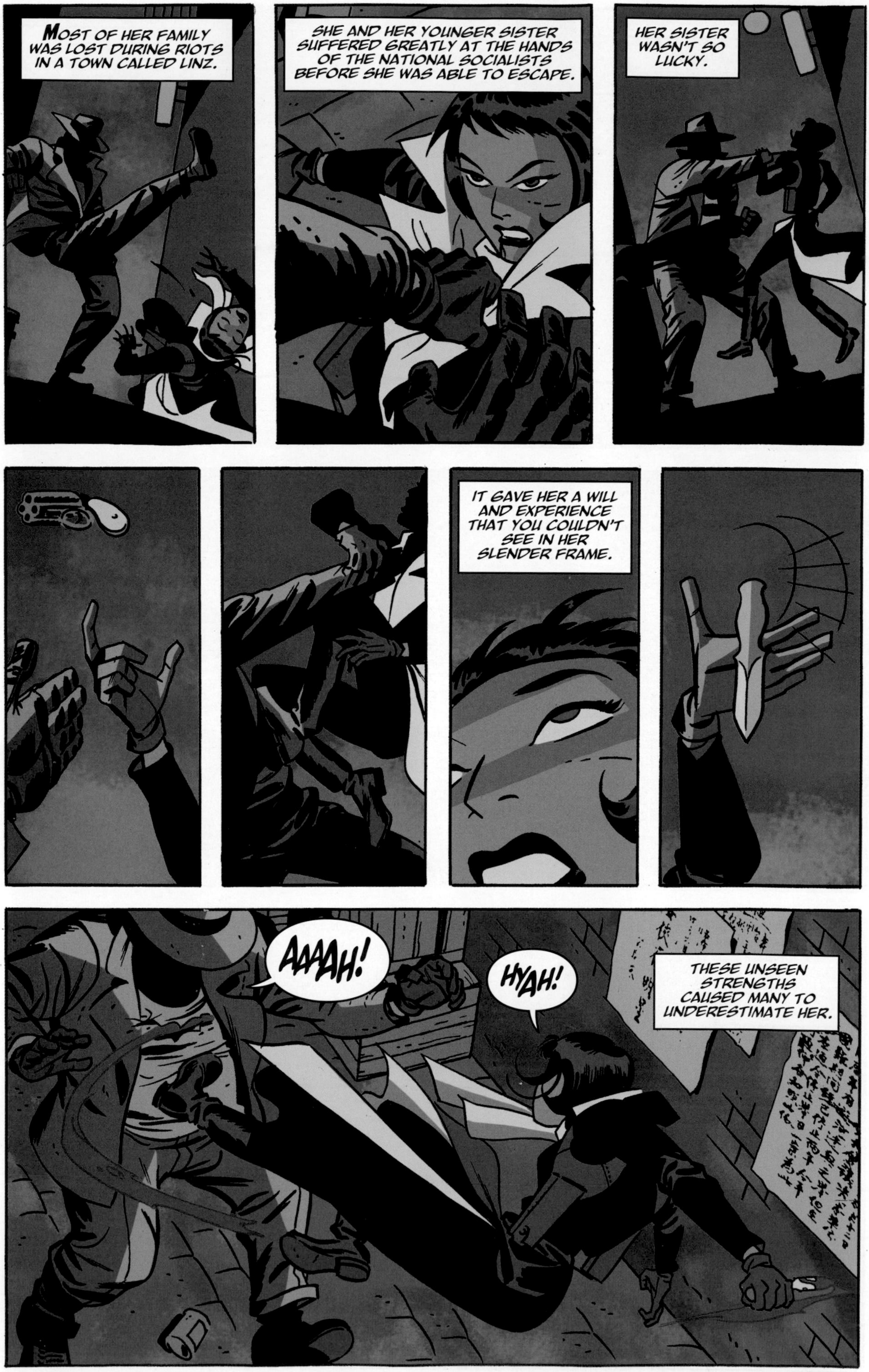
MOST OF HER FAMILY WAS LOST DURING RIOTS IN A TOWN CALLED LINZ.
SHE AND HER YOUNGER SISTER SUFFERED GREATLY AT THE HANDS OF THE NATIONAL SOCIALISTS BEFORE SHE WAS ABLE TO ESCAPE.
HER SISTER WASN'T SO LUCKY.
IT GAVE HER A WILL AND EXPERIENCE THAT YOU COULDN'T SEE IN HER SLENDER FRAME.
AAAAH!
HYAH!
THESE UNSEEN STRENGTHS CAUSED MANY TO UNDERESTIMATE HER.

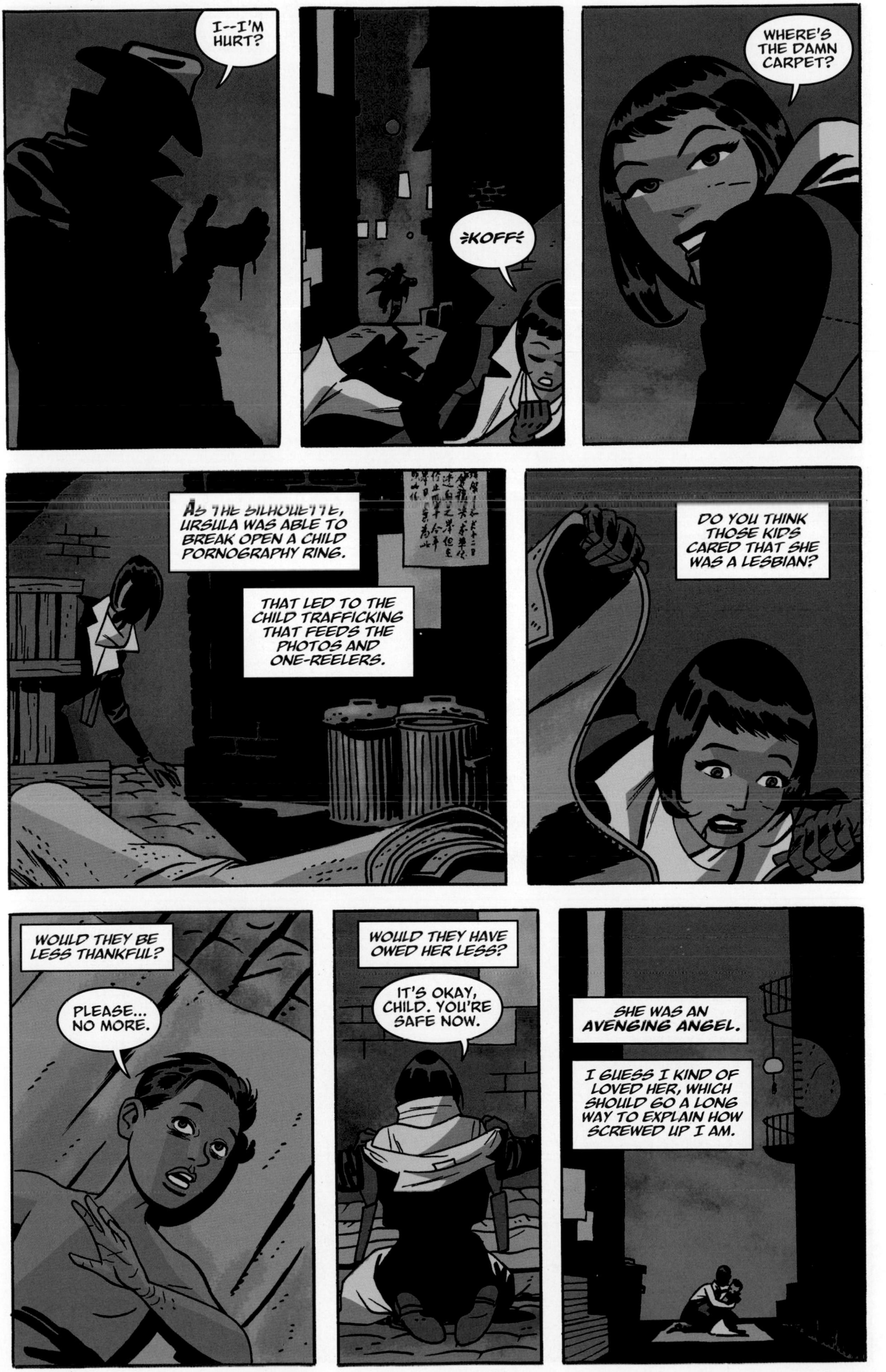
I--I'M HURT?
KOFF
WHERE'S THE DAMN CARPET?
AS THE SILHOUETTE, URSULA WAS ABLE TO BREAK OPEN A CHILD PORNOGRAPHY RING.
THAT LED TO THE CHILD TRAFFICKING THAT FEEDS THE PHOTOS AND ONE-REELERS.
DO YOU THINK THOSE KIDS CARED THAT SHE WAS A LESBIAN?
WOULD THEY BE LESS THANKFUL?
PLEASE... NO MORE.
WOULD THEY HAVE OWED HER LESS?
IT'S OKAY, CHILD. YOU'RE SAFE NOW.
SHE WAS AN AVENGING ANGEL.
I GUESS I KIND OF LOVED HER, WHICH SHOULD GO A LONG WAY TO EXPLAIN HOW SCREWED UP I AM.

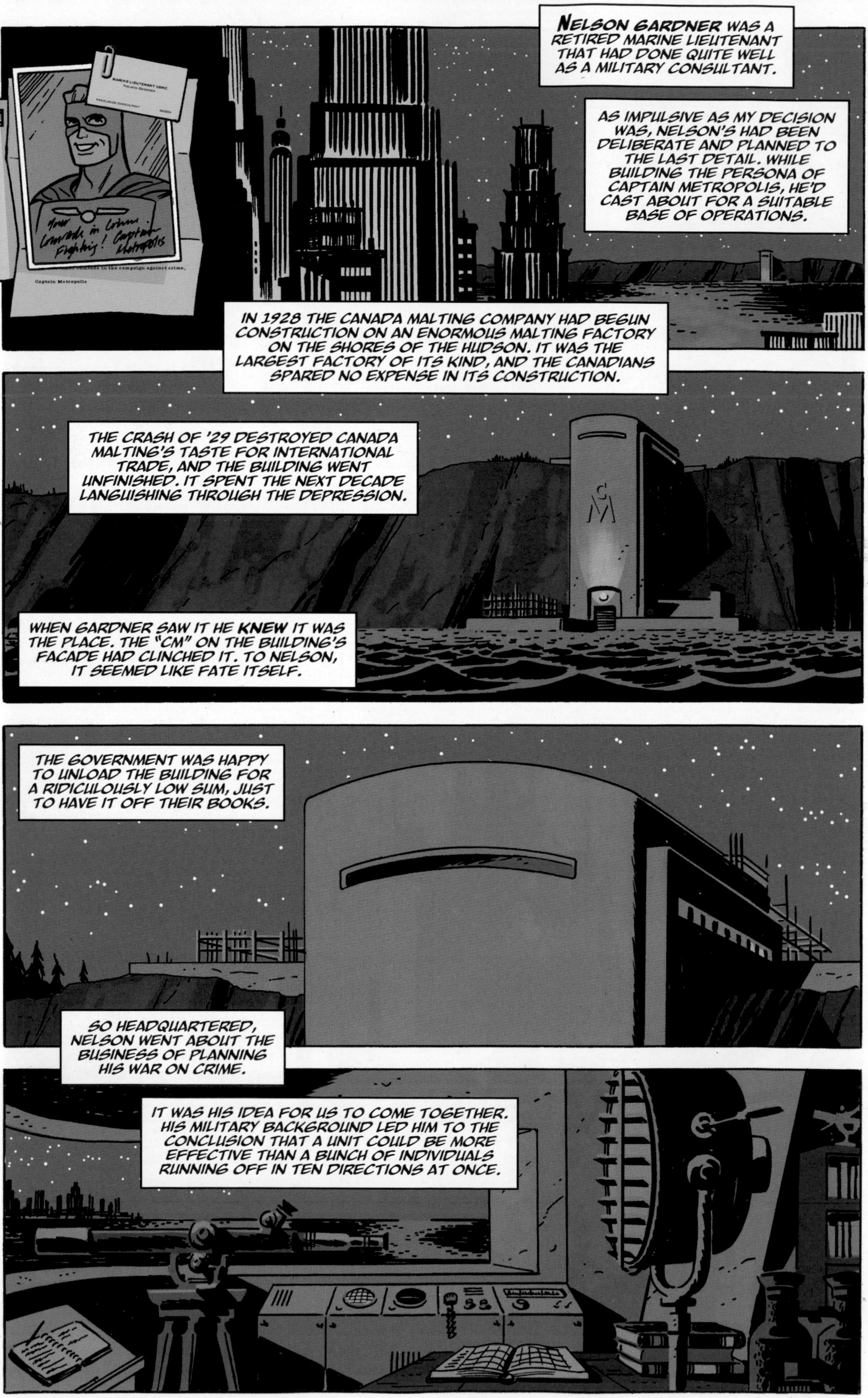
NELSON GARDNER WAS A RETIRED MARINE LIEUTENANT THAT HAD DONE QUITE WELL AS A MILITARY CONSULTANT.
AS IMPULSIVE AS MY DECISION WAS, NELSON'S HAD BEEN DELIBERATE AND PLANNED TO THE LAST DETAIL. WHILE BUILDING THE PERSONA OF CAPTAIN METROPOLIS, HE'D CAST ABOUT FOR A SUITABLE BASE OF OPERATIONS.
IN 1928 THE CANADA MALTING COMPANY HAD BEGUN CONSTRUCTION ON AN ENORMOUS MALTING FACTORY ON THE SHORES OF THE HUDSON. IT WAS THE LARGEST FACTORY OF ITS KIND, AND THE CANADIANS SPARED NO EXPENSE IN ITS CONSTRUCTION.
THE CRASH OF '29 DESTROYED CANADA MALTING'S TASTE FOR INTERNATIONAL TRADE, AND THE BUILDING WENT UNFINISHED. IT SPENT THE NEXT DECADE LANGUISHING THROUGH THE DEPRESSION.
CM
WHEN GARDNER SAW IT HE KNEW IT WAS THE PLACE. THE "CM" ON THE BUILDING'S FACADE HAD CLINCHED IT. TO NELSON, IT SEEMED LIKE FATE ITSELF.
THE GOVERNMENT WAS HAPPY TO UNLOAD THE BUILDING FOR A RIDICULOUSLY LOW SUM, JUST TO HAVE IT OFF THEIR BOOKS.
SO HEADQUARTERED, NELSON WENT ABOUT THE BUSINESS OF PLANNING HIS WAR ON CRIME.
IT WAS HIS IDEA FOR US TO COME TOGETHER. HIS MILITARY BACKGROUND LED HIM TO THE CONCLUSION THAT A UNIT COULD BE MORE EFFECTIVE THAN A BUNCH OF INDIVIDUALS RUNNING OFF IN TEN DIRECTIONS AT ONCE.

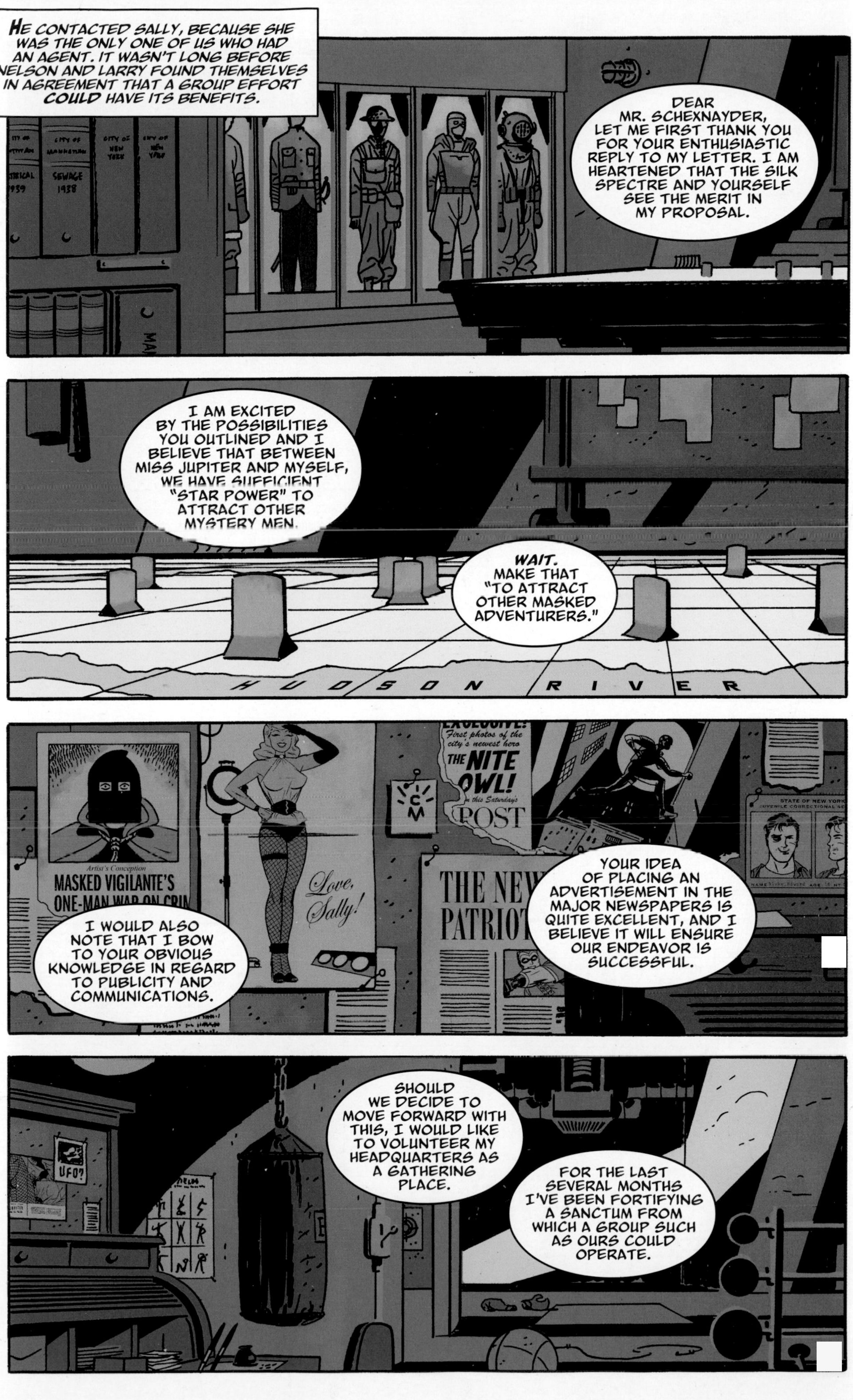
HE CONTACTED SALLY, BECAUSE SHE WAS THE ONLY ONE OF US WHO HAD AN AGENT. IT WASN'T LONG BEFORE NELSON AND LARRY FOUND THEMSELVES IN AGREEMENT THAT A GROUP EFFORT COULD HAVE ITS BENEFITS.
DEAR MR. SCHEXNAYDER, LET ME FIRST THANK YOU FOR YOUR ENTHUSIASTIC REPLY TO MY LETTER. I AM HEARTENED THAT THE SILK SPECTRE AND YOURSELF SEE THE MERIT IN MY PROPOSAL.
I AM EXCITED BY THE POSSIBILITIES YOU OUTLINED AND I BELIEVE THAT BETWEEN MISS JUPITER AND MYSELF, WE HAVE SUFFICIENT "STAR POWER" TO ATTRACT OTHER MYSTERY MEN.
WAIT. MAKE THAT "TO ATTRACT OTHER MASKED ADVENTURERS."
HUDSON RIVER
MASKED VIGILANTE'S ONE-MAN WAR ON CRIM
Love, Sally!
THE NITE OWL!
POST
THE NEW
PATRIOT
I WOULD ALSO NOTE THAT I BOW TO YOUR OBVIOUS KNOWLEDGE IN REGARD TO PUBLICITY AND COMMUNICATIONS.
YOUR IDEA OF PLACING AN ADVERTISEMENT IN THE MAJOR NEWSPAPERS IS QUITE EXCELLENT, AND I BELIEVE IT WILL ENSURE OUR ENDEAVOR IS SUCCESSFUL.
UFO?
SHOULD WE DECIDE TO MOVE FORWARD WITH THIS, I WOULD LIKE TO VOLUNTEER MY HEADQUARTERS AS A GATHERING PLACE.
FOR THE LAST SEVERAL MONTHS I'VE BEEN FORTIFYING A SANCTUM FROM WHICH A GROUP SUCH AS OURS COULD OPERATE.

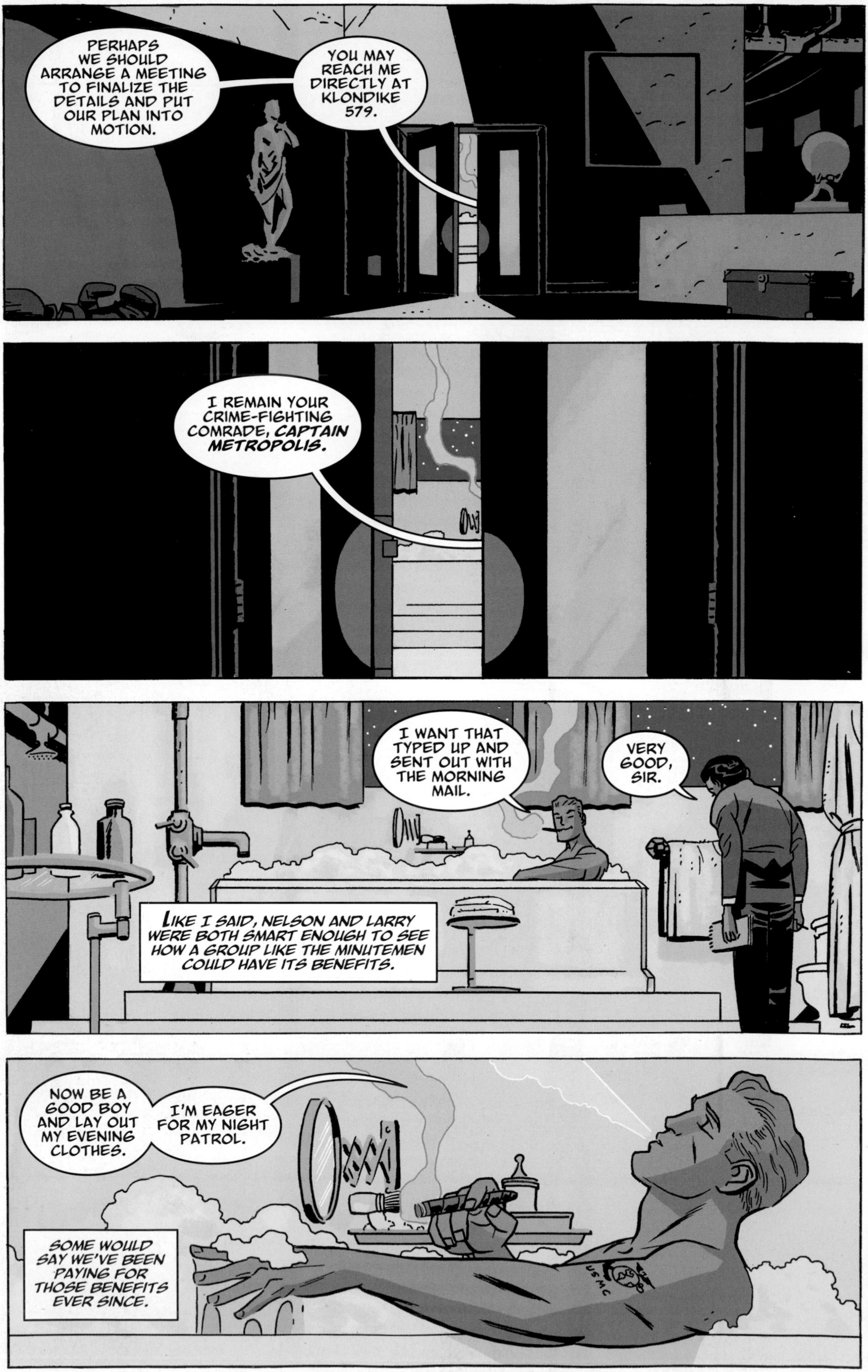
PERHAPS WE SHOULD ARRANGE A MEETING TO FINALIZE THE DETAILS AND PUT OUR PLAN INTO MOTION.
YOU MAY REACH ME DIRECTLY AT KLONDIKE 579.
I REMAIN YOUR CRIME-FIGHTING COMRADE, CAPTAIN METROPOLIS.
I WANT THAT TYPED UP AND SENT OUT WITH THE MORNING MAIL.
VERY GOOD, SIR.
LIKE I SAID, NELSON AND LARRY WERE BOTH SMART ENOUGH TO SEE HOW A GROUP LIKE THE MINUTEMEN COULD HAVE ITS BENEFITS.
NOW BE A GOOD BOY AND LAY OUT MY EVENING CLOTHES.
I'M EAGER FOR MY NIGHT PATROL.
SOME WOULD SAY WE'VE BEEN PAYING FOR THOSE BENEFITS EVER SINCE.
USMC

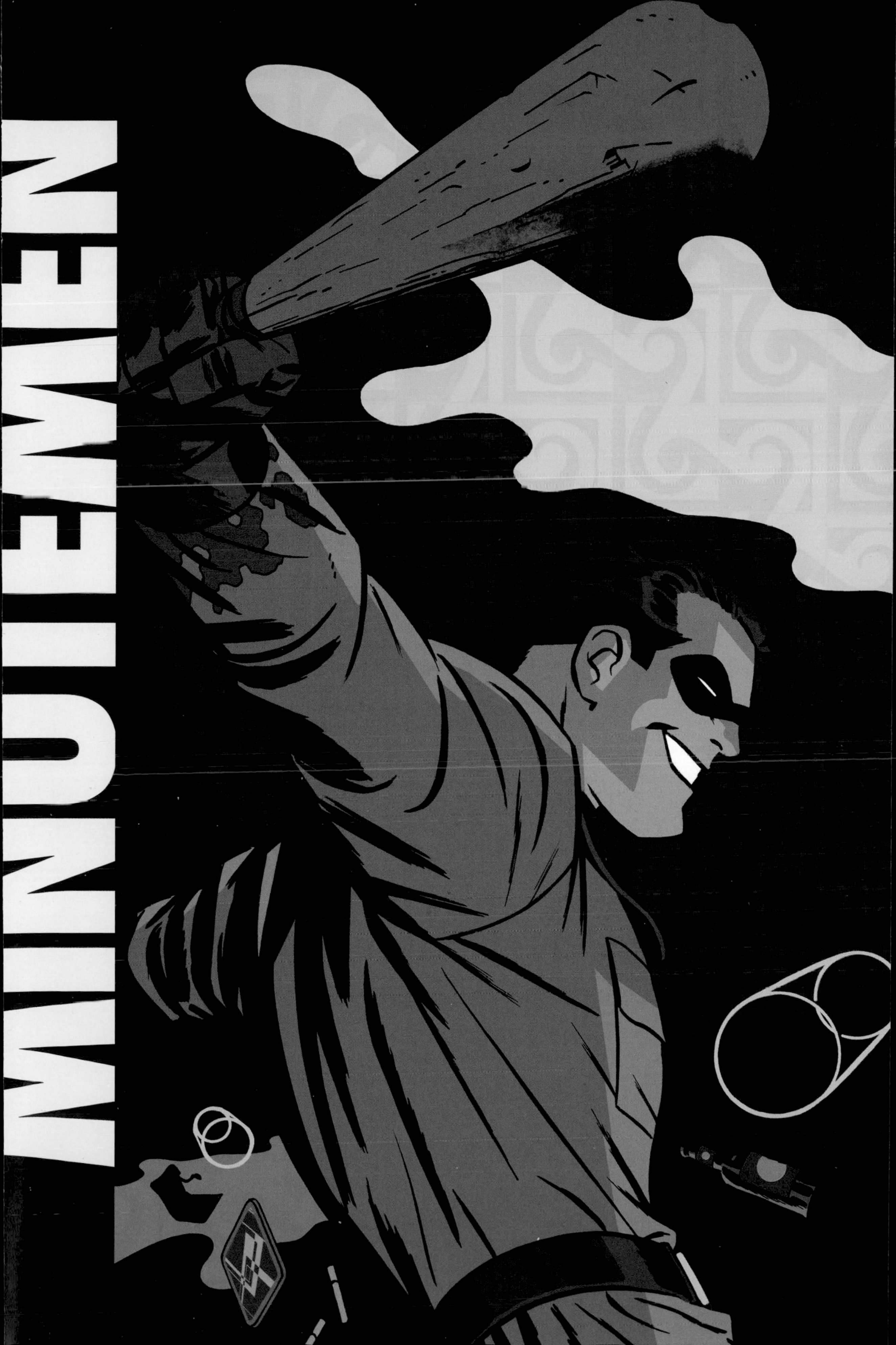
MINUTEMEN

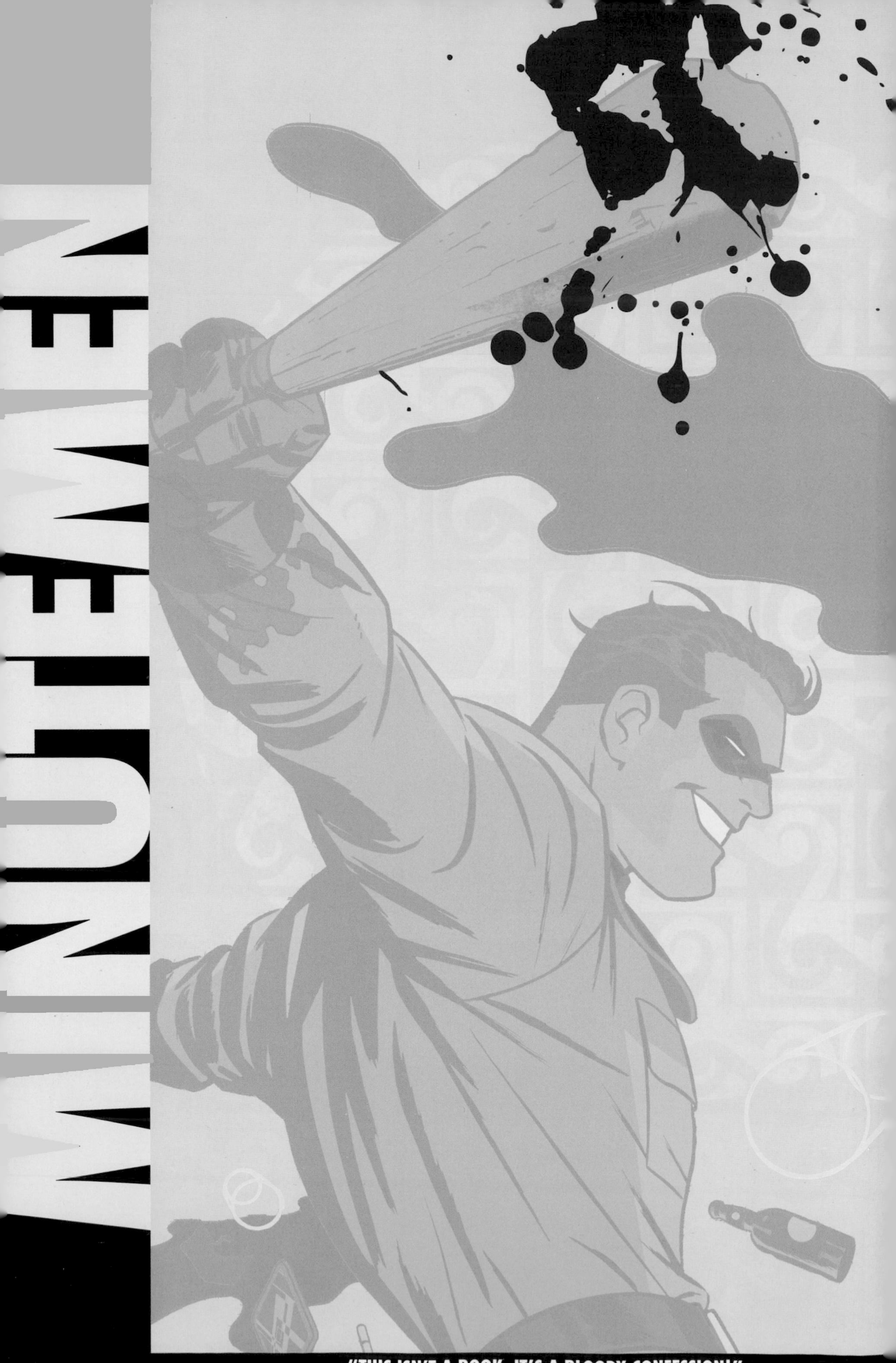
MINUTEMEN

"THIS ISN'T A BOOK. IT'S A BLOODY CONFESSION!"

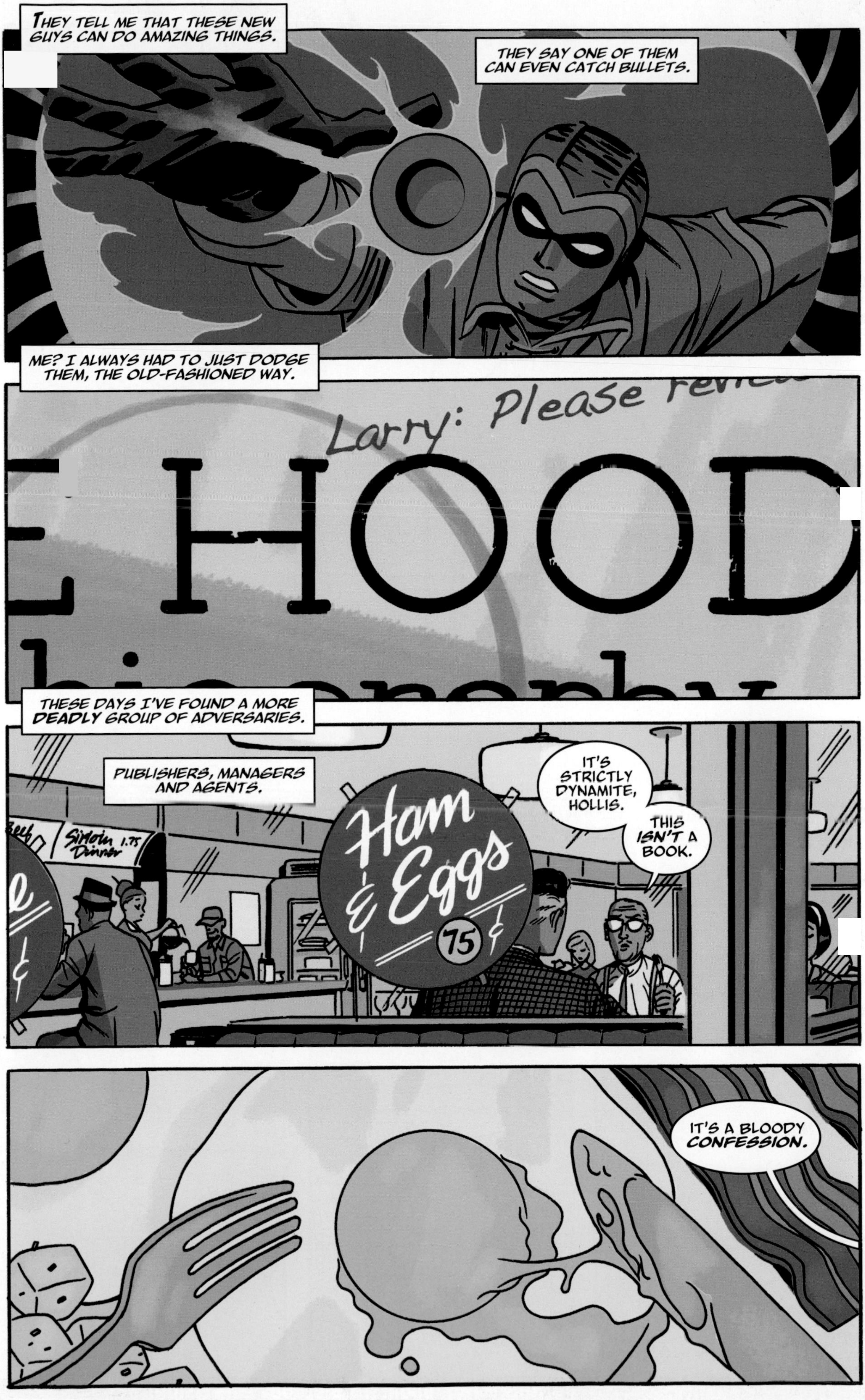
THEY TELL ME THAT THESE NEW GUYS CAN DO AMAZING THINGS.
THEY SAY ONE OF THEM CAN EVEN CATCH BULLETS.
ME? I ALWAYS HAD TO JUST DODGE THEM, THE OLD-FASHIONED WAY.
Larry: Please revie
HOOD
THESE DAYS I'VE FOUND A MORE DEADLY GROUP OF ADVERSARIES.
PUBLISHERS, MANAGERS AND AGENTS.
Ham & Eggs 75¢
Sirloin Dinner 1.75
IT'S STRICTLY DYNAMITE, HOLLIS.
THIS ISN'T A BOOK.
IT'S A BLOODY CONFESSION.

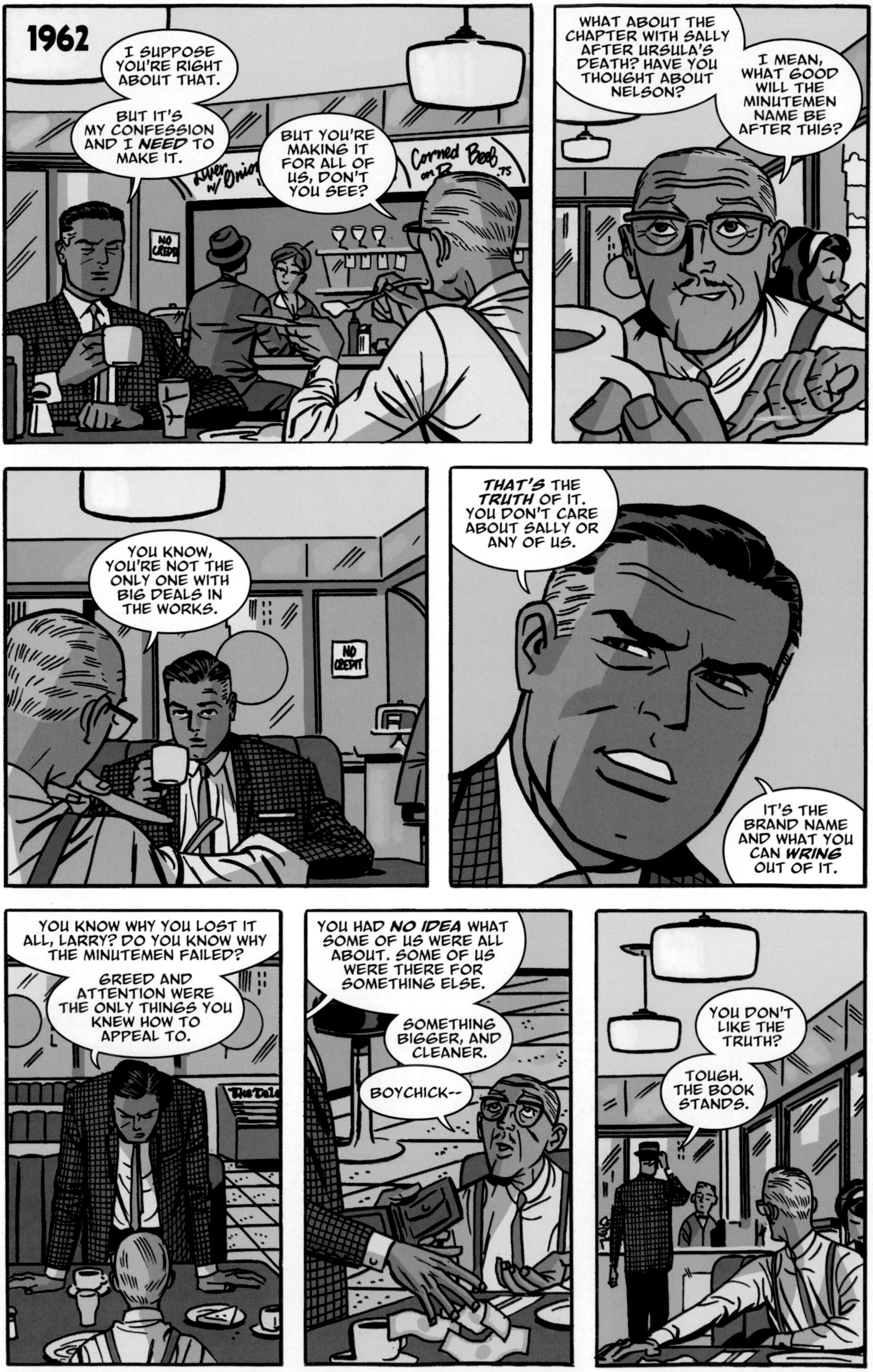
1962
I SUPPOSE YOU'RE RIGHT ABOUT THAT.
BUT IT'S MY CONFESSION AND I *NEED* TO MAKE IT.
BUT YOU'RE MAKING IT FOR ALL OF US, DON'T YOU SEE?
Liver w/ Onion
Corned Beef on
NO CREDIT
WHAT ABOUT THE CHAPTER WITH SALLY AFTER URSULA'S DEATH? HAVE YOU THOUGHT ABOUT NELSON?
I MEAN, WHAT GOOD WILL THE MINUTEMEN NAME BE AFTER THIS?
YOU KNOW, YOU'RE NOT THE ONLY ONE WITH BIG DEALS IN THE WORKS.
NO CREDIT
THAT'S THE *TRUTH* OF IT. YOU DON'T CARE ABOUT SALLY OR ANY OF US.
IT'S THE BRAND NAME AND WHAT YOU CAN *WRING* OUT OF IT.
YOU KNOW WHY YOU LOST IT ALL, LARRY? DO YOU KNOW WHY THE MINUTEMEN FAILED?
GREED AND ATTENTION WERE THE ONLY THINGS YOU KNEW HOW TO APPEAL TO.
YOU HAD *NO IDEA* WHAT SOME OF US WERE ALL ABOUT. SOME OF US WERE THERE FOR SOMETHING ELSE.
SOMETHING BIGGER, AND CLEANER.
BOYCHICK--
YOU DON'T LIKE THE TRUTH?
TOUGH. THE BOOK STANDS.

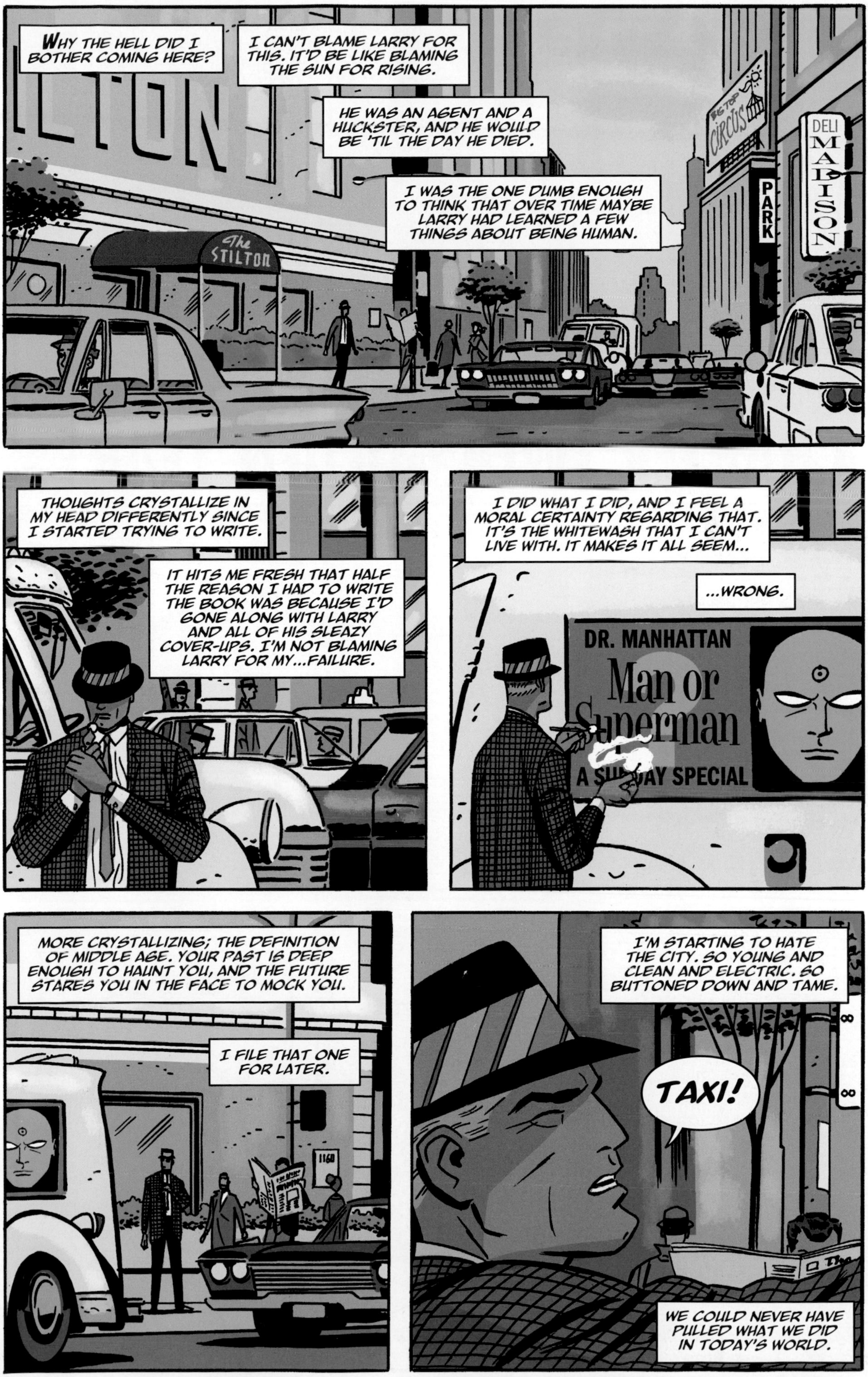
WHY THE HELL DID I BOTHER COMING HERE?
I CAN'T BLAME LARRY FOR THIS. IT'D BE LIKE BLAMING THE SUN FOR RISING.
HE WAS AN AGENT AND A HUCKSTER, AND HE WOULD BE 'TIL THE DAY HE DIED.
I WAS THE ONE DUMB ENOUGH TO THINK THAT OVER TIME MAYBE LARRY HAD LEARNED A FEW THINGS ABOUT BEING HUMAN.
The STILTON
BIG TOP CIRCUS
DELI MADISON
PARK
THOUGHTS CRYSTALLIZE IN MY HEAD DIFFERENTLY SINCE I STARTED TRYING TO WRITE.
IT HITS ME FRESH THAT HALF THE REASON I HAD TO WRITE THE BOOK WAS BECAUSE I'D GONE ALONG WITH LARRY AND ALL OF HIS SLEAZY COVER-UPS. I'M NOT BLAMING LARRY FOR MY...FAILURE.
I DID WHAT I DID, AND I FEEL A MORAL CERTAINTY REGARDING THAT. IT'S THE WHITEWASH THAT I CAN'T LIVE WITH. IT MAKES IT ALL SEEM...
...WRONG.
DR. MANHATTAN
Man or Superman
MORE CRYSTALLIZING; THE DEFINITION OF MIDDLE AGE. YOUR PAST IS DEEP ENOUGH TO HAUNT YOU, AND THE FUTURE STARES YOU IN THE FACE TO MOCK YOU.
I FILE THAT ONE FOR LATER.
I'M STARTING TO HATE THE CITY. SO YOUNG AND CLEAN AND ELECTRIC. SO BUTTONED DOWN AND TAME.
TAXI!
WE COULD NEVER HAVE PULLED WHAT WE DID IN TODAY'S WORLD.

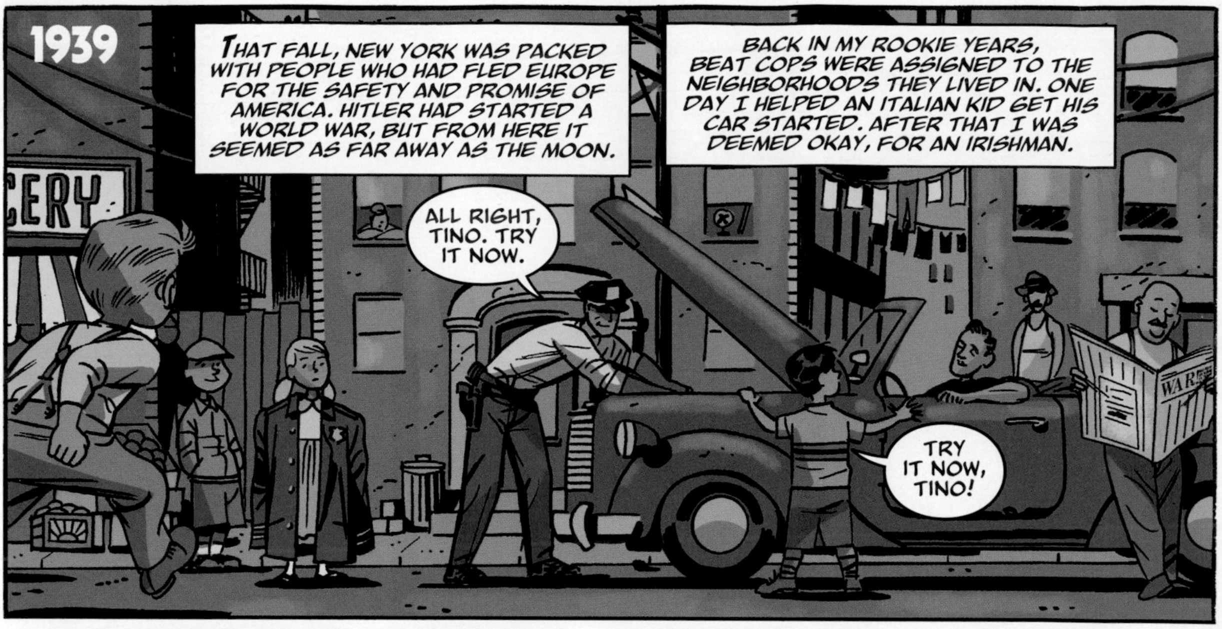
1939
THAT FALL, NEW YORK WAS PACKED WITH PEOPLE WHO HAD FLED EUROPE FOR THE SAFETY AND PROMISE OF AMERICA. HITLER HAD STARTED A WORLD WAR, BUT FROM HERE IT SEEMED AS FAR AWAY AS THE MOON.
BACK IN MY ROOKIE YEARS, BEAT COPS WERE ASSIGNED TO THE NEIGHBORHOODS THEY LIVED IN. ONE DAY I HELPED AN ITALIAN KID GET HIS CAR STARTED. AFTER THAT I WAS DEEMED OKAY, FOR AN IRISHMAN.
ALL RIGHT, TINO. TRY IT NOW.
TRY IT NOW, TINO!
WAR

CHAPTER TWO: GOLDEN YEARS

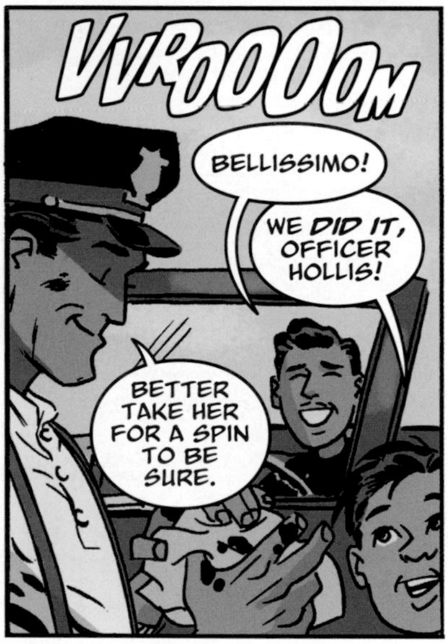
VVROOOOOM
BELLISSIMO!
WE DID IT, OFFICER HOLLIS!
BETTER TAKE HER FOR A SPIN TO BE SURE.

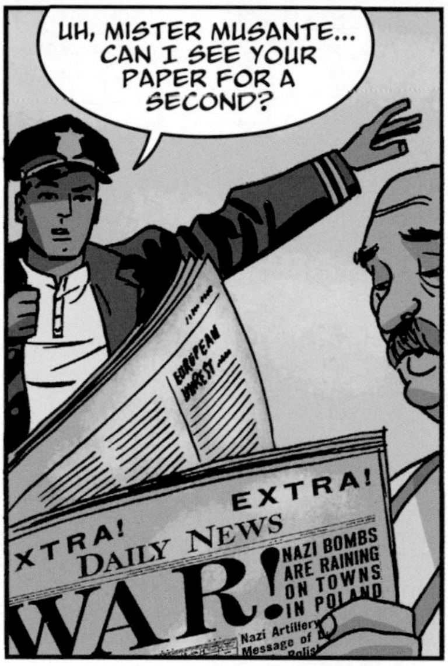
UH, MISTER MUSANTE... CAN I SEE YOUR PAPER FOR A SECOND?
EXTRA!
XTRA! DAILY NEWS
WAR!
NAZI BOMBS ARE RAINING ON TOWNS IN POLAND
Nazi Artillery
Message of

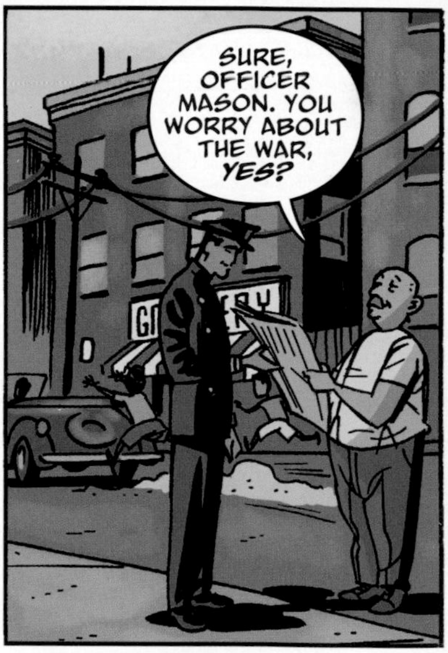
SURE, OFFICER MASON. YOU WORRY ABOUT THE WAR, YES?

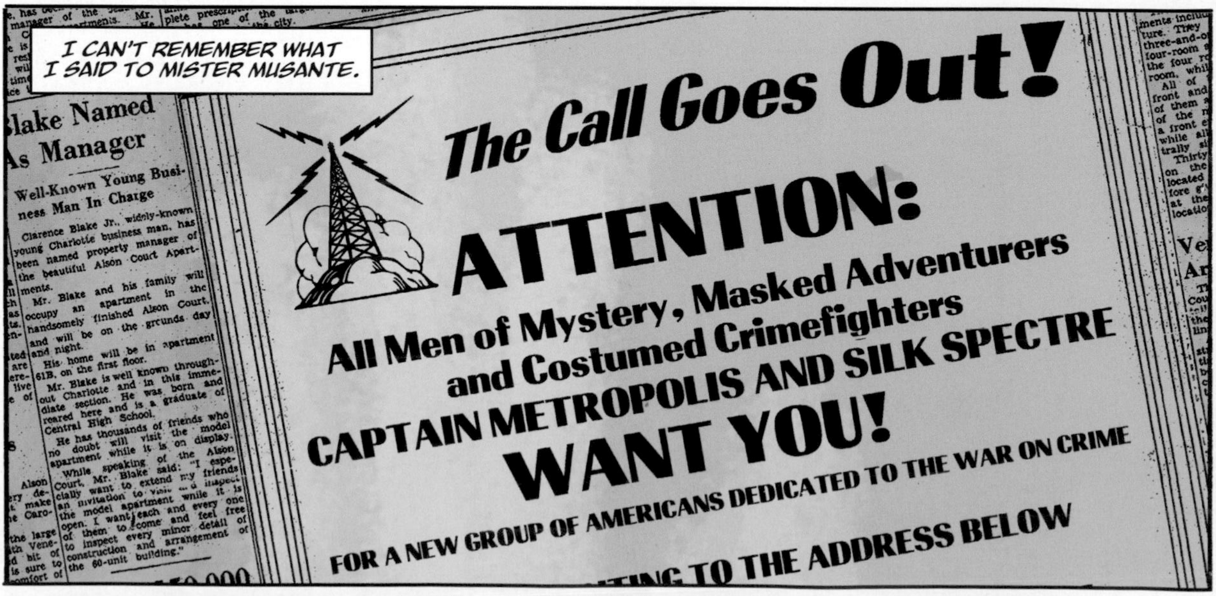
I CAN'T REMEMBER WHAT I SAID TO MISTER MUSANTE.
Blake Named
As Manager
Well-Known Young Business Man In Charge
The Call Goes Out!
ATTENTION:
All Men of Mystery, Masked Adventurers
and Costumed Crimefighters
CAPTAIN METROPOLIS AND SILK SPECTRE
WANT YOU!
FOR A NEW GROUP OF AMERICANS DEDICATED TO THE WAR ON CRIME
TING TO THE ADDRESS BELOW

PHIL NOTO COLORIST **DARWYN COOKE** WRITER & ARTIST **JARED K. FLETCHER** LETTERER
DARWYN COOKE COVER ARTIST **JOSÉ LUIS GARCÍA-LÓPEZ & TRISH MULVIHILL** VARIANT COVER
CAMILLA ZHANG ASSISTANT EDITOR **WIL MOSS** ASSOCIATE EDITOR **MARK CHIARELLO** EDITOR **WATCHMEN** CREATED BY **ALAN MOORE** & **DAVE GIBBONS**

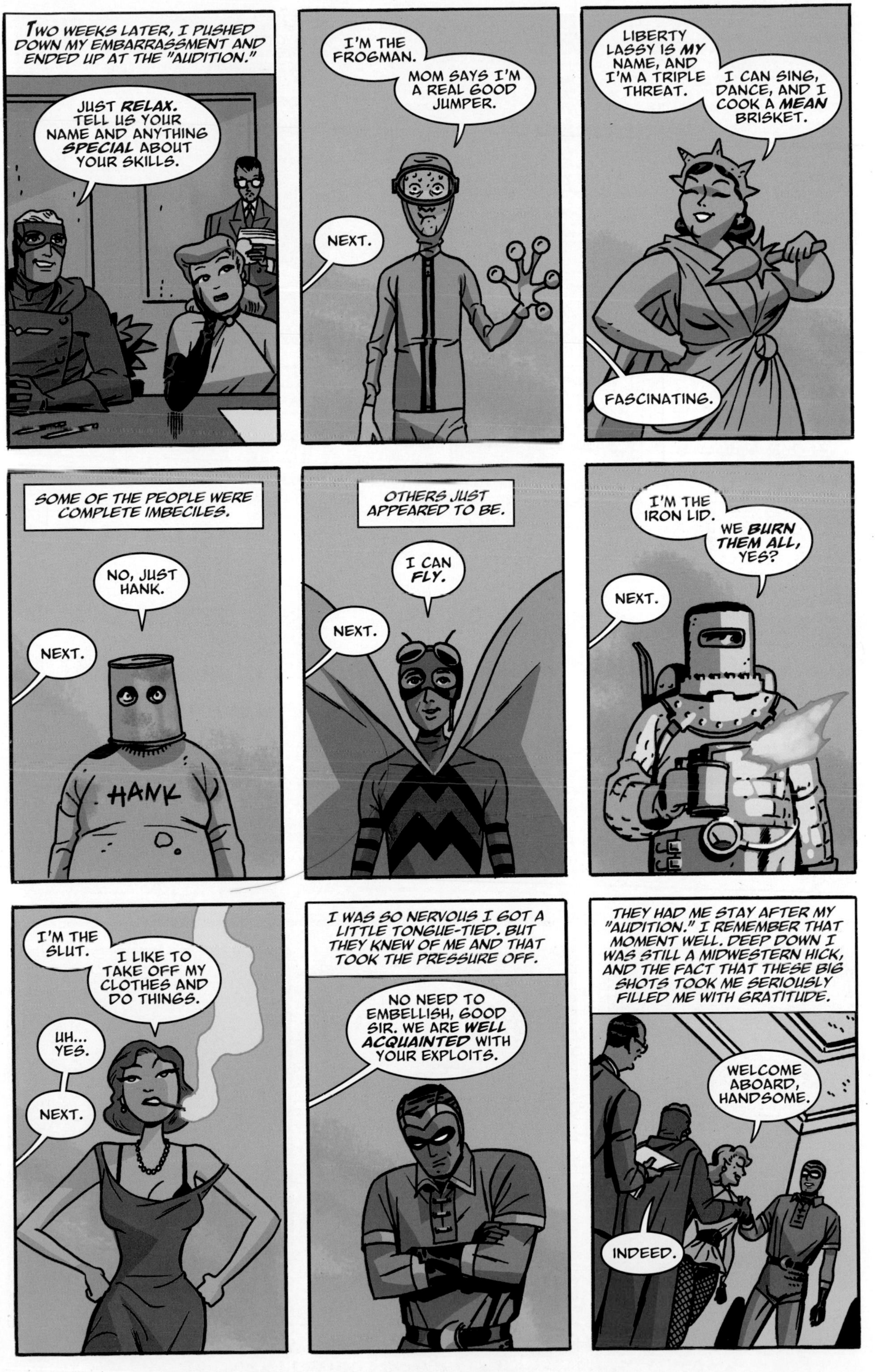
TWO WEEKS LATER, I PUSHED DOWN MY EMBARRASSMENT AND ENDED UP AT THE "AUDITION."
JUST RELAX. TELL US YOUR NAME AND ANYTHING SPECIAL ABOUT YOUR SKILLS.
I'M THE FROGMAN.
MOM SAYS I'M A REAL GOOD JUMPER.
NEXT.
LIBERTY LASSY IS MY NAME, AND I'M A TRIPLE THREAT.
I CAN SING, DANCE, AND I COOK A MEAN BRISKET.
FASCINATING.
SOME OF THE PEOPLE WERE COMPLETE IMBECILES.
NO, JUST HANK.
NEXT.
HANK
OTHERS JUST APPEARED TO BE.
I CAN FLY.
NEXT.
I'M THE IRON LID.
WE BURN THEM ALL, YES?
NEXT.
I'M THE SLUT.
I LIKE TO TAKE OFF MY CLOTHES AND DO THINGS.
UH... YES.
NEXT.
I WAS SO NERVOUS I GOT A LITTLE TONGUE-TIED. BUT THEY KNEW OF ME AND THAT TOOK THE PRESSURE OFF.
NO NEED TO EMBELLISH, GOOD SIR. WE ARE WELL ACQUAINTED WITH YOUR EXPLOITS.
THEY HAD ME STAY AFTER MY "AUDITION." I REMEMBER THAT MOMENT WELL. DEEP DOWN I WAS STILL A MIDWESTERN HICK, AND THE FACT THAT THESE BIG SHOTS TOOK ME SERIOUSLY FILLED ME WITH GRATITUDE.
WELCOME ABOARD, HANDSOME.
INDEED.

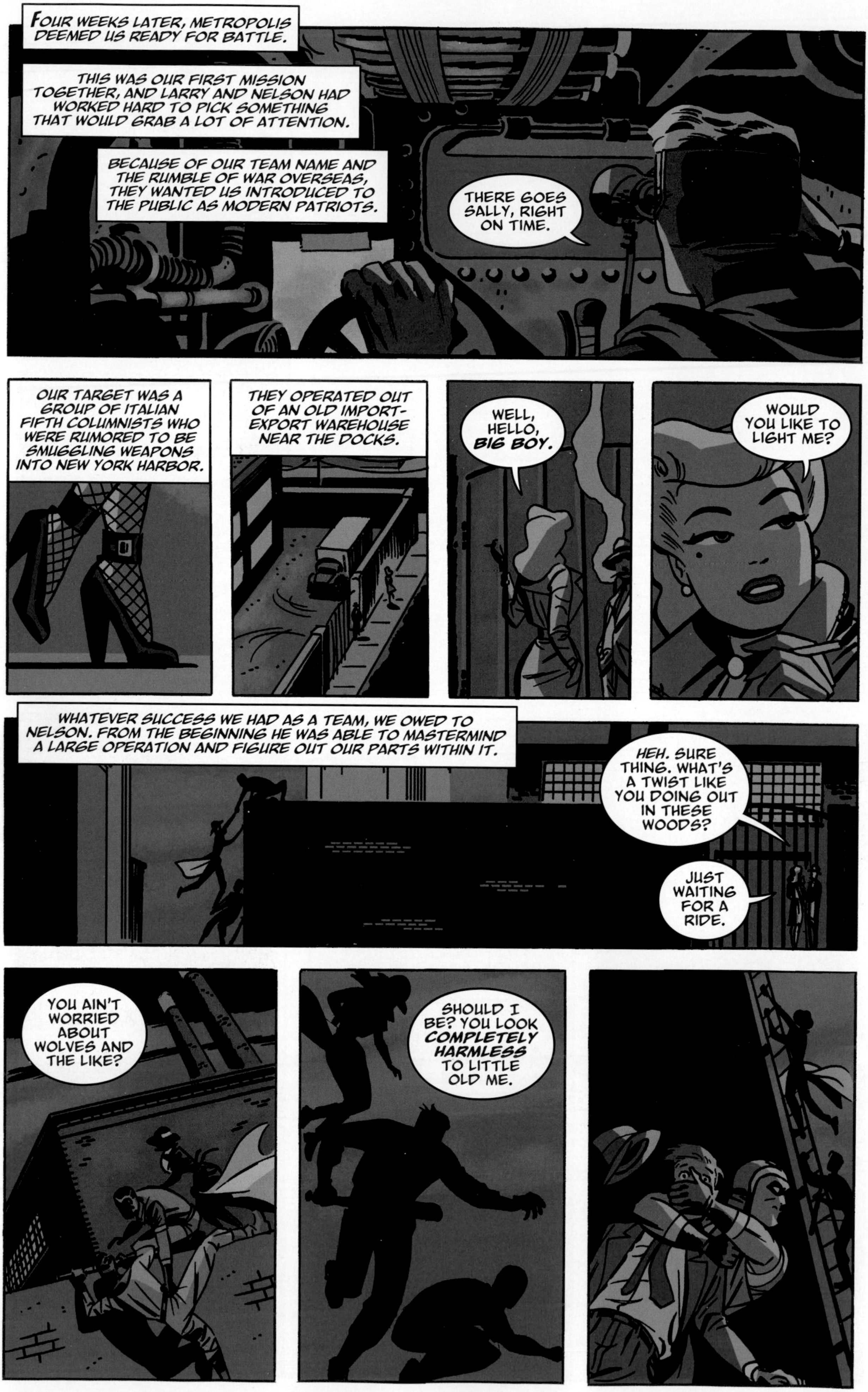
FOUR WEEKS LATER, METROPOLIS DEEMED US READY FOR BATTLE.
THIS WAS OUR FIRST MISSION TOGETHER, AND LARRY AND NELSON HAD WORKED HARD TO PICK SOMETHING THAT WOULD GRAB A LOT OF ATTENTION.
BECAUSE OF OUR TEAM NAME AND THE RUMBLE OF WAR OVERSEAS, THEY WANTED US INTRODUCED TO THE PUBLIC AS MODERN PATRIOTS.
THERE GOES SALLY, RIGHT ON TIME.
OUR TARGET WAS A GROUP OF ITALIAN FIFTH COLUMNISTS WHO WERE RUMORED TO BE SMUGGLING WEAPONS INTO NEW YORK HARBOR.
THEY OPERATED OUT OF AN OLD IMPORT-EXPORT WAREHOUSE NEAR THE DOCKS.
WELL, HELLO, BIG BOY.
WOULD YOU LIKE TO LIGHT ME?
WHATEVER SUCCESS WE HAD AS A TEAM, WE OWED TO NELSON. FROM THE BEGINNING HE WAS ABLE TO MASTERMIND A LARGE OPERATION AND FIGURE OUT OUR PARTS WITHIN IT.
HEH. SURE THING. WHAT'S A TWIST LIKE YOU DOING OUT IN THESE WOODS?
JUST WAITING FOR A RIDE.
YOU AIN'T WORRIED ABOUT WOLVES AND THE LIKE?
SHOULD I BE? YOU LOOK COMPLETELY HARMLESS TO LITTLE OLD ME.

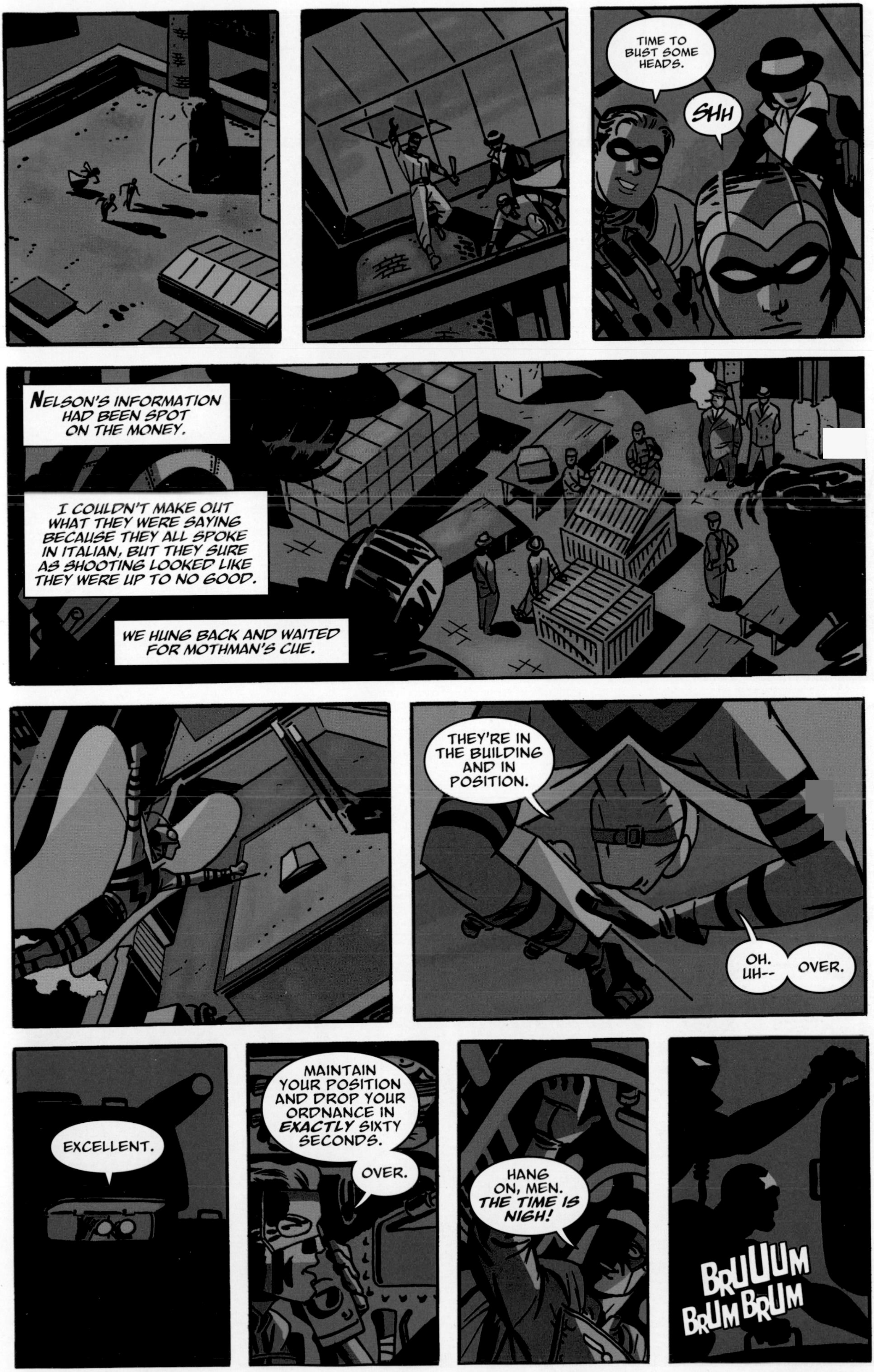
TIME TO BUST SOME HEADS.
SHH
NELSON'S INFORMATION HAD BEEN SPOT ON THE MONEY.
I COULDN'T MAKE OUT WHAT THEY WERE SAYING BECAUSE THEY ALL SPOKE IN ITALIAN, BUT THEY SURE AS SHOOTING LOOKED LIKE THEY WERE UP TO NO GOOD.
WE HUNG BACK AND WAITED FOR MOTHMAN'S CUE.
THEY'RE IN THE BUILDING AND IN POSITION.
OH. UH--
OVER.
EXCELLENT.
MAINTAIN YOUR POSITION AND DROP YOUR ORDNANCE IN EXACTLY SIXTY SECONDS.
OVER.
HANG ON, MEN. THE TIME IS NIGH!
BRUUUM BRUM BRUM

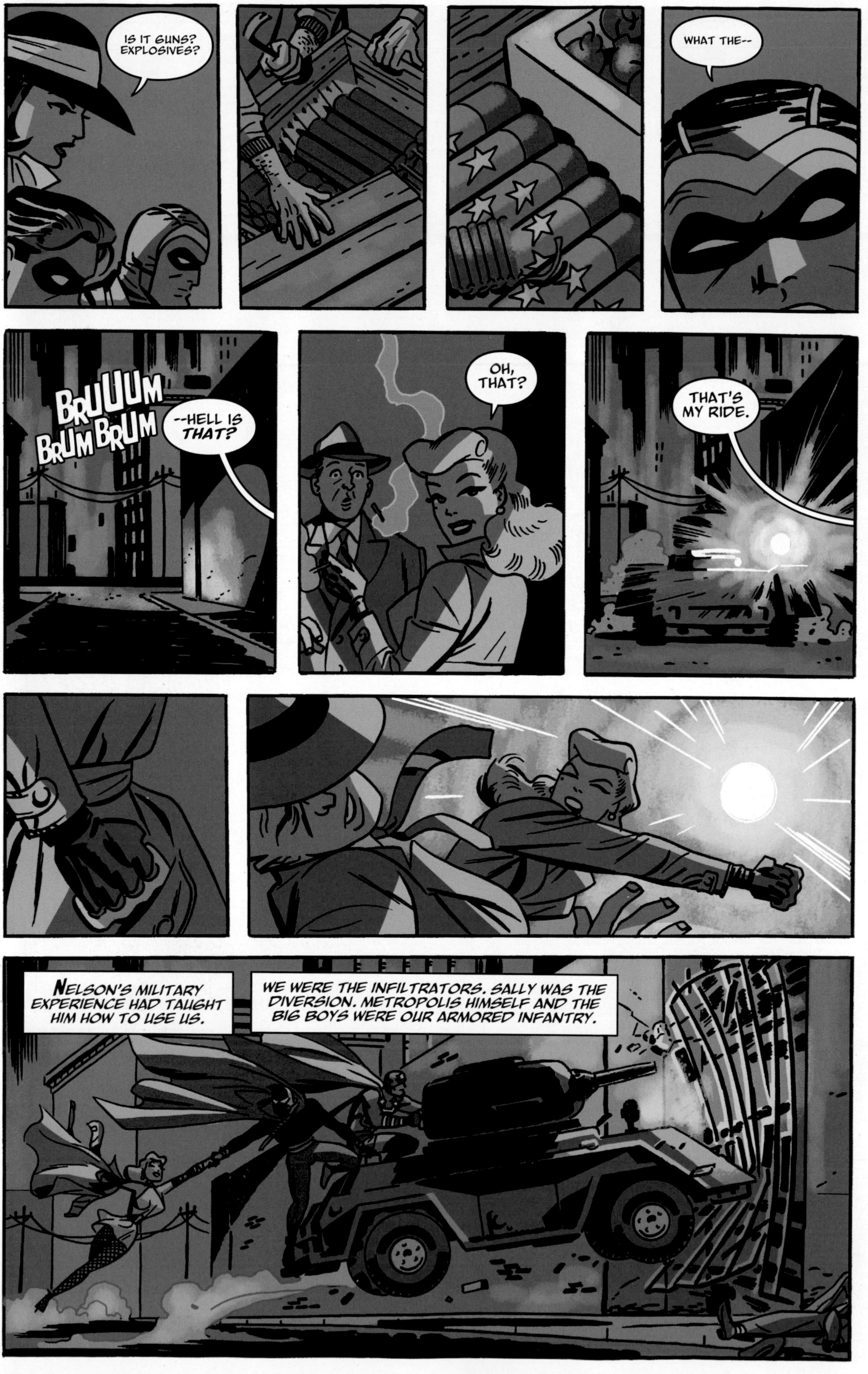

IS IT GUNS? EXPLOSIVES?
WHAT THE--
BRUUUM BRUM BRUM
--HELL IS THAT?
OH, THAT?
THAT'S MY RIDE.
NELSON'S MILITARY EXPERIENCE HAD TAUGHT HIM HOW TO USE US.
WE WERE THE INFILTRATORS. SALLY WAS THE DIVERSION. METROPOLIS HIMSELF AND THE BIG BOYS WERE OUR ARMORED INFANTRY.

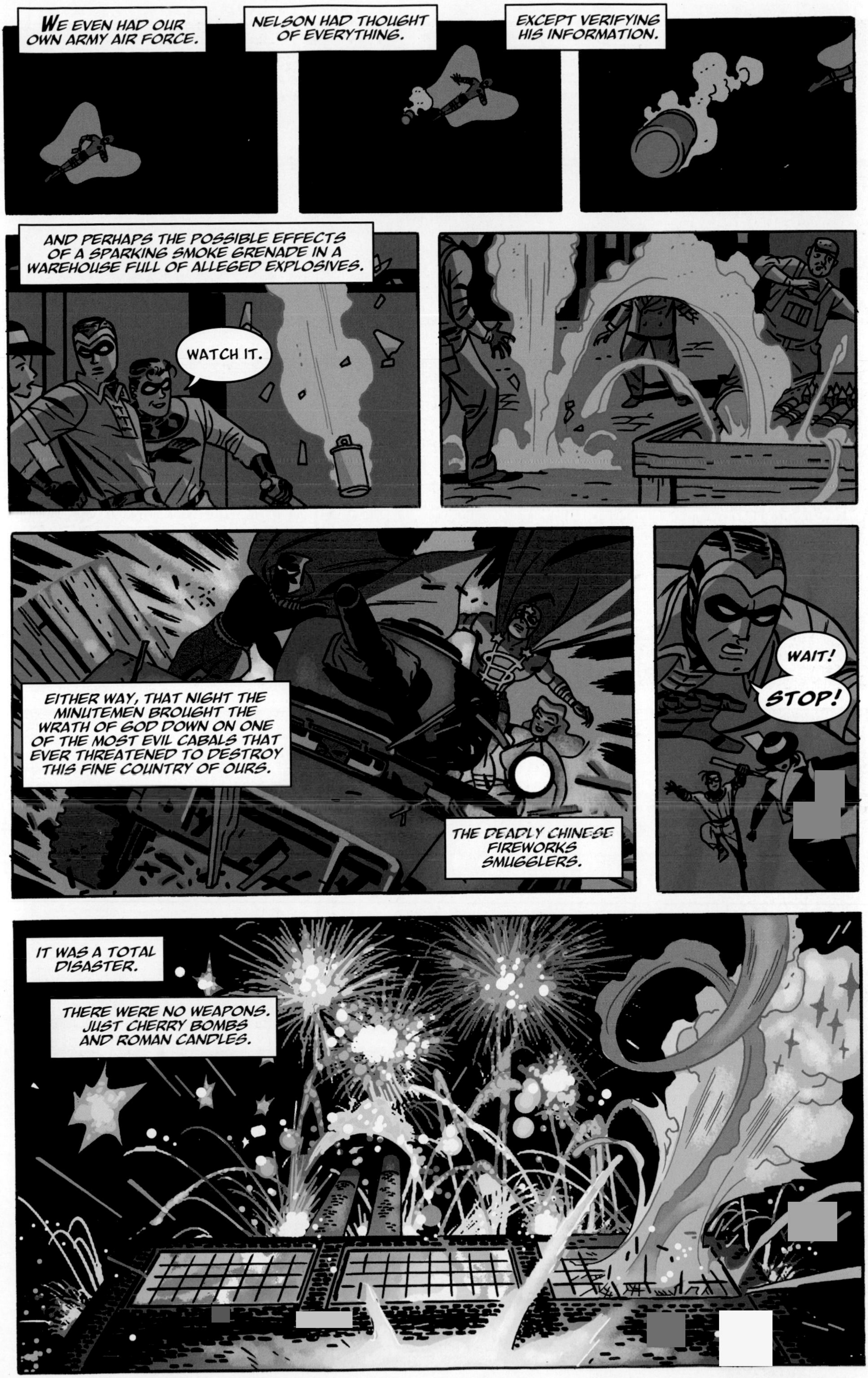

WE EVEN HAD OUR OWN ARMY AIR FORCE.
NELSON HAD THOUGHT OF EVERYTHING.
EXCEPT VERIFYING HIS INFORMATION.
AND PERHAPS THE POSSIBLE EFFECTS OF A SPARKING SMOKE GRENADE IN A WAREHOUSE FULL OF ALLEGED EXPLOSIVES.
WATCH IT.
EITHER WAY, THAT NIGHT THE MINUTEMEN BROUGHT THE WRATH OF GOD DOWN ON ONE OF THE MOST EVIL CABALS THAT EVER THREATENED TO DESTROY THIS FINE COUNTRY OF OURS.
THE DEADLY CHINESE FIREWORKS SMUGGLERS.
WAIT!
STOP!
IT WAS A TOTAL DISASTER.
THERE WERE NO WEAPONS. JUST CHERRY BOMBS AND ROMAN CANDLES.

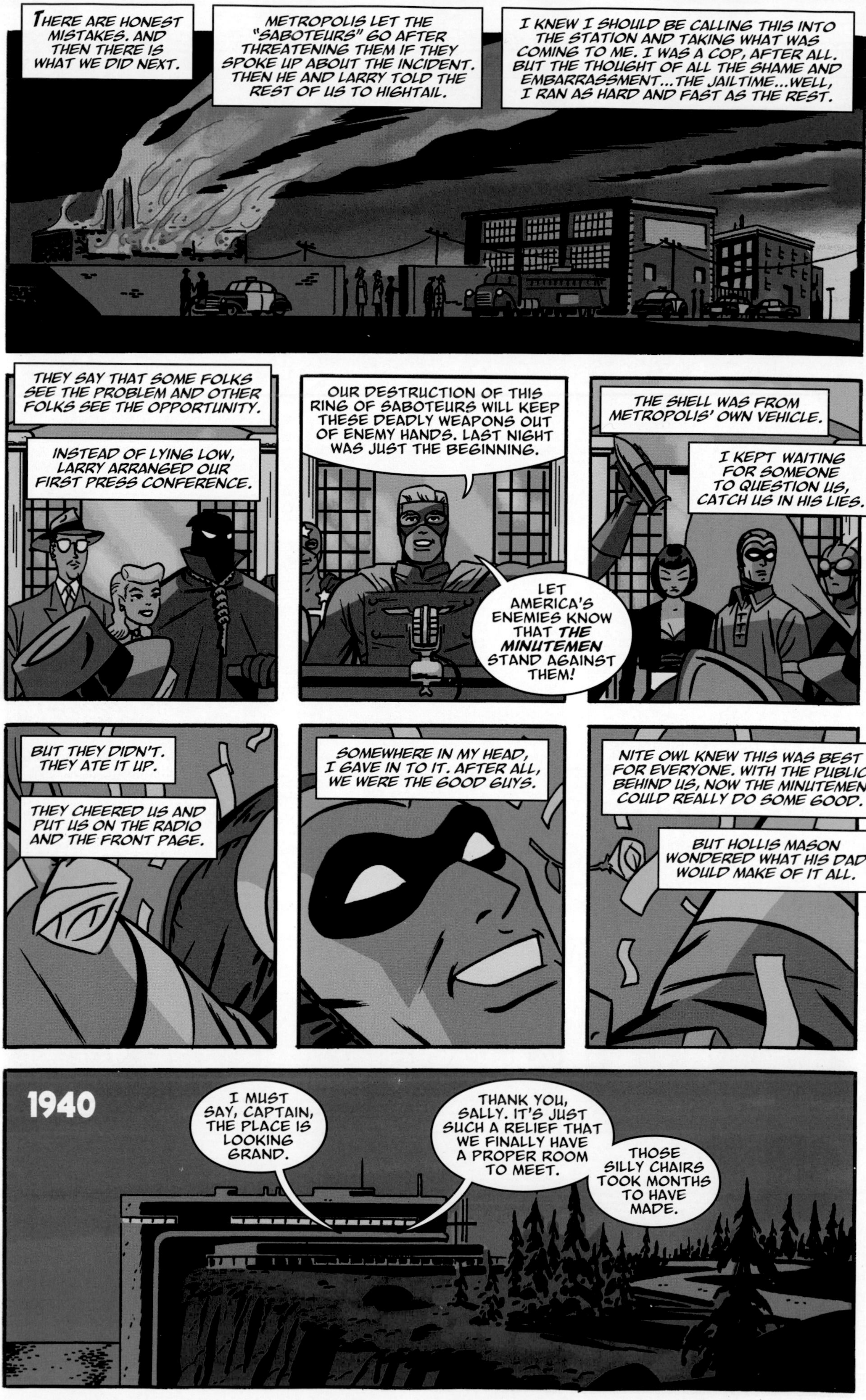
THERE ARE HONEST MISTAKES. AND THEN THERE IS WHAT WE DID NEXT.
METROPOLIS LET THE "SABOTEURS" GO AFTER THREATENING THEM IF THEY SPOKE UP ABOUT THE INCIDENT. THEN HE AND LARRY TOLD THE REST OF US TO HIGHTAIL.
I KNEW I SHOULD BE CALLING THIS INTO THE STATION AND TAKING WHAT WAS COMING TO ME. I WAS A COP, AFTER ALL. BUT THE THOUGHT OF ALL THE SHAME AND EMBARRASSMENT...THE JAILTIME...WELL, I RAN AS HARD AND FAST AS THE REST.
THEY SAY THAT SOME FOLKS SEE THE PROBLEM AND OTHER FOLKS SEE THE OPPORTUNITY.
INSTEAD OF LYING LOW, LARRY ARRANGED OUR FIRST PRESS CONFERENCE.
OUR DESTRUCTION OF THIS RING OF SABOTEURS WILL KEEP THESE DEADLY WEAPONS OUT OF ENEMY HANDS. LAST NIGHT WAS JUST THE BEGINNING.
LET AMERICA'S ENEMIES KNOW THAT THE MINUTEMEN STAND AGAINST THEM!
THE SHELL WAS FROM METROPOLIS' OWN VEHICLE.
I KEPT WAITING FOR SOMEONE TO QUESTION US, CATCH US IN HIS LIES.
BUT THEY DIDN'T. THEY ATE IT UP.
THEY CHEERED US AND PUT US ON THE RADIO AND THE FRONT PAGE.
SOMEWHERE IN MY HEAD, I GAVE IN TO IT. AFTER ALL, WE WERE THE GOOD GUYS.
NITE OWL KNEW THIS WAS BEST FOR EVERYONE. WITH THE PUBLIC BEHIND US, NOW THE MINUTEMEN COULD REALLY DO SOME GOOD.
BUT HOLLIS MASON WONDERED WHAT HIS DAD WOULD MAKE OF IT ALL.
1940
I MUST SAY, CAPTAIN, THE PLACE IS LOOKING GRAND.
THANK YOU, SALLY. IT'S JUST SUCH A RELIEF THAT WE FINALLY HAVE A PROPER ROOM TO MEET.
THOSE SILLY CHAIRS TOOK MONTHS TO HAVE MADE.

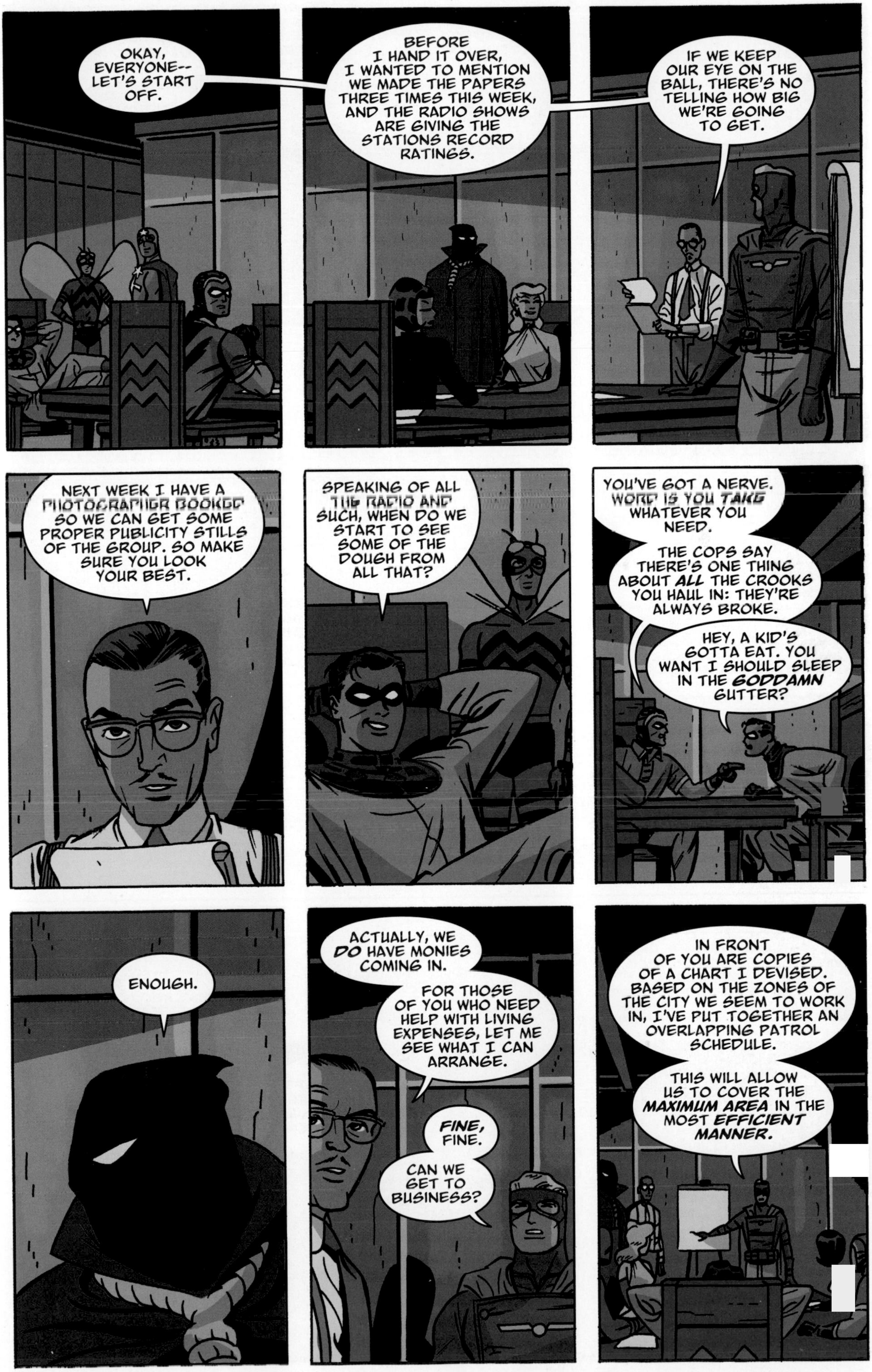
OKAY, EVERYONE-- LET'S START OFF.
BEFORE I HAND IT OVER, I WANTED TO MENTION WE MADE THE PAPERS THREE TIMES THIS WEEK, AND THE RADIO SHOWS ARE GIVING THE STATIONS RECORD RATINGS.
IF WE KEEP OUR EYE ON THE BALL, THERE'S NO TELLING HOW BIG WE'RE GOING TO GET.
NEXT WEEK I HAVE A PHOTOGRAPHER BOOKED SO WE CAN GET SOME PROPER PUBLICITY STILLS OF THE GROUP. SO MAKE SURE YOU LOOK YOUR BEST.
SPEAKING OF ALL THE RADIO AND SUCH, WHEN DO WE START TO SEE SOME OF THE DOUGH FROM ALL THAT?
YOU'VE GOT A NERVE. WORD IS YOU *TAKE* WHATEVER YOU NEED.
THE COPS SAY THERE'S ONE THING ABOUT *ALL* THE CROOKS YOU HAUL IN: THEY'RE ALWAYS BROKE.
HEY, A KID'S GOTTA EAT. YOU WANT I SHOULD SLEEP IN THE *GODDAMN* GUTTER?
ENOUGH.
ACTUALLY, WE *DO* HAVE MONIES COMING IN.
FOR THOSE OF YOU WHO NEED HELP WITH LIVING EXPENSES, LET ME SEE WHAT I CAN ARRANGE.
FINE, FINE.
CAN WE GET TO BUSINESS?
IN FRONT OF YOU ARE COPIES OF A CHART I DEVISED. BASED ON THE ZONES OF THE CITY WE SEEM TO WORK IN, I'VE PUT TOGETHER AN OVERLAPPING PATROL SCHEDULE.
THIS WILL ALLOW US TO COVER THE *MAXIMUM AREA* IN THE MOST *EFFICIENT MANNER.*

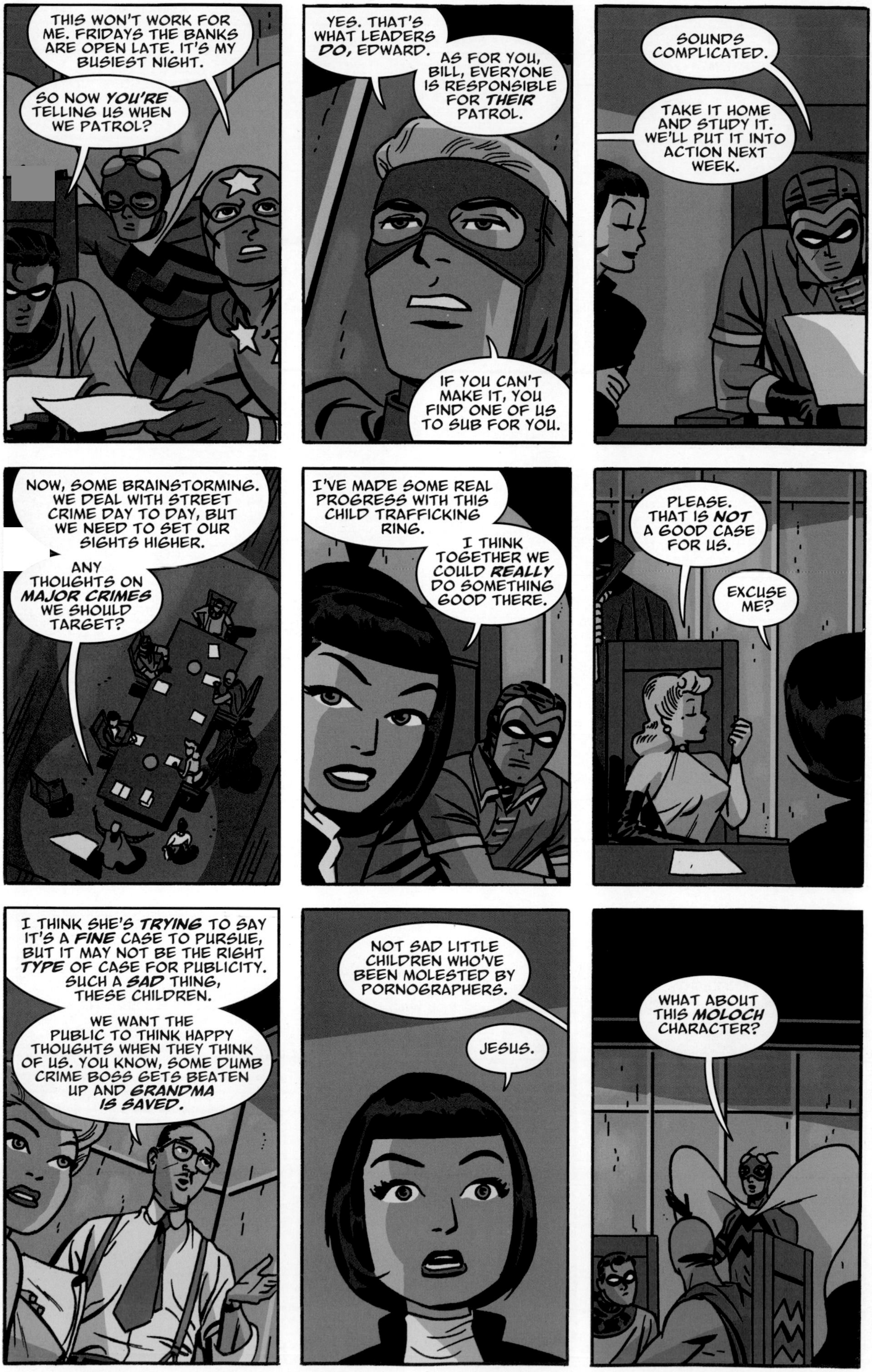

THIS WON'T WORK FOR ME. FRIDAYS THE BANKS ARE OPEN LATE. IT'S MY BUSIEST NIGHT.
SO NOW *YOU'RE* TELLING US WHEN WE PATROL?
YES. THAT'S WHAT LEADERS *DO*, EDWARD.
AS FOR YOU, BILL, EVERYONE IS RESPONSIBLE FOR *THEIR* PATROL.
IF YOU CAN'T MAKE IT, YOU FIND ONE OF US TO SUB FOR YOU.
SOUNDS COMPLICATED.
TAKE IT HOME AND STUDY IT. WE'LL PUT IT INTO ACTION NEXT WEEK.
NOW, SOME BRAINSTORMING. WE DEAL WITH STREET CRIME DAY TO DAY, BUT WE NEED TO SET OUR SIGHTS HIGHER.
ANY THOUGHTS ON *MAJOR CRIMES* WE SHOULD TARGET?
I'VE MADE SOME REAL PROGRESS WITH THIS CHILD TRAFFICKING RING.
I THINK TOGETHER WE COULD *REALLY* DO SOMETHING GOOD THERE.
PLEASE. THAT IS *NOT* A GOOD CASE FOR US.
EXCUSE ME?
I THINK SHE'S *TRYING* TO SAY IT'S A *FINE* CASE TO PURSUE, BUT IT MAY NOT BE THE RIGHT *TYPE* OF CASE FOR PUBLICITY. SUCH A *SAD* THING, THESE CHILDREN.
WE WANT THE PUBLIC TO THINK HAPPY THOUGHTS WHEN THEY THINK OF US. YOU KNOW, SOME DUMB CRIME BOSS GETS BEATEN UP AND *GRANDMA IS SAVED*.
NOT SAD LITTLE CHILDREN WHO'VE BEEN MOLESTED BY PORNOGRAPHERS.
JESUS.
WHAT ABOUT THIS *MOLOCH* CHARACTER?

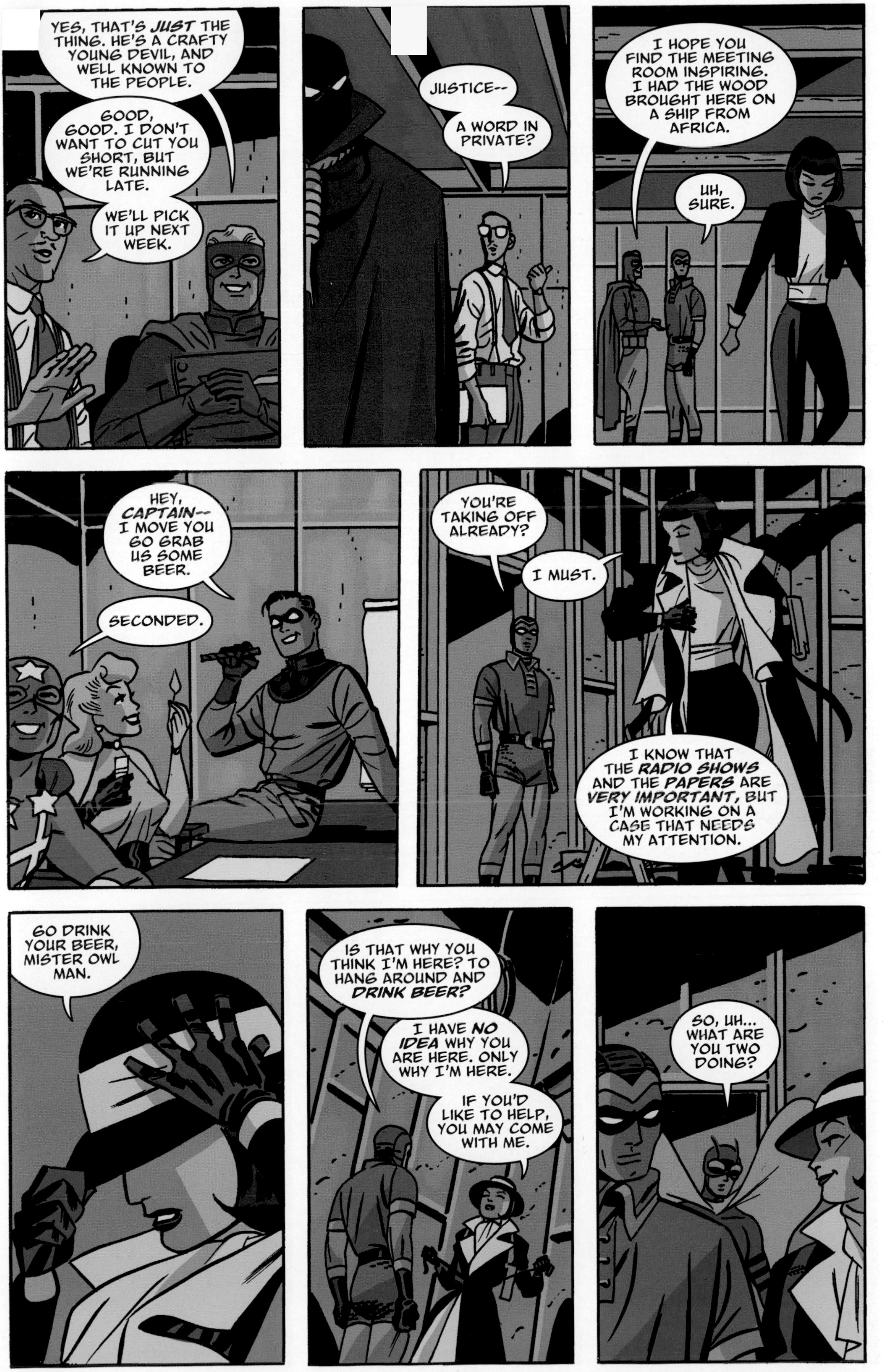
YES, THAT'S JUST THE THING. HE'S A CRAFTY YOUNG DEVIL, AND WELL KNOWN TO THE PEOPLE.
GOOD, GOOD. I DON'T WANT TO CUT YOU SHORT, BUT WE'RE RUNNING LATE.
WE'LL PICK IT UP NEXT WEEK.
JUSTICE--
A WORD IN PRIVATE?
I HOPE YOU FIND THE MEETING ROOM INSPIRING. I HAD THE WOOD BROUGHT HERE ON A SHIP FROM AFRICA.
UH, SURE.
HEY, CAPTAIN-- I MOVE YOU GO GRAB US SOME BEER.
SECONDED.
YOU'RE TAKING OFF ALREADY?
I MUST.
I KNOW THAT THE RADIO SHOWS AND THE PAPERS ARE VERY IMPORTANT, BUT I'M WORKING ON A CASE THAT NEEDS MY ATTENTION.
GO DRINK YOUR BEER, MISTER OWL MAN.
IS THAT WHY YOU THINK I'M HERE? TO HANG AROUND AND DRINK BEER?
I HAVE NO IDEA WHY YOU ARE HERE. ONLY WHY I'M HERE.
IF YOU'D LIKE TO HELP, YOU MAY COME WITH ME.
SO, UH... WHAT ARE YOU TWO DOING?

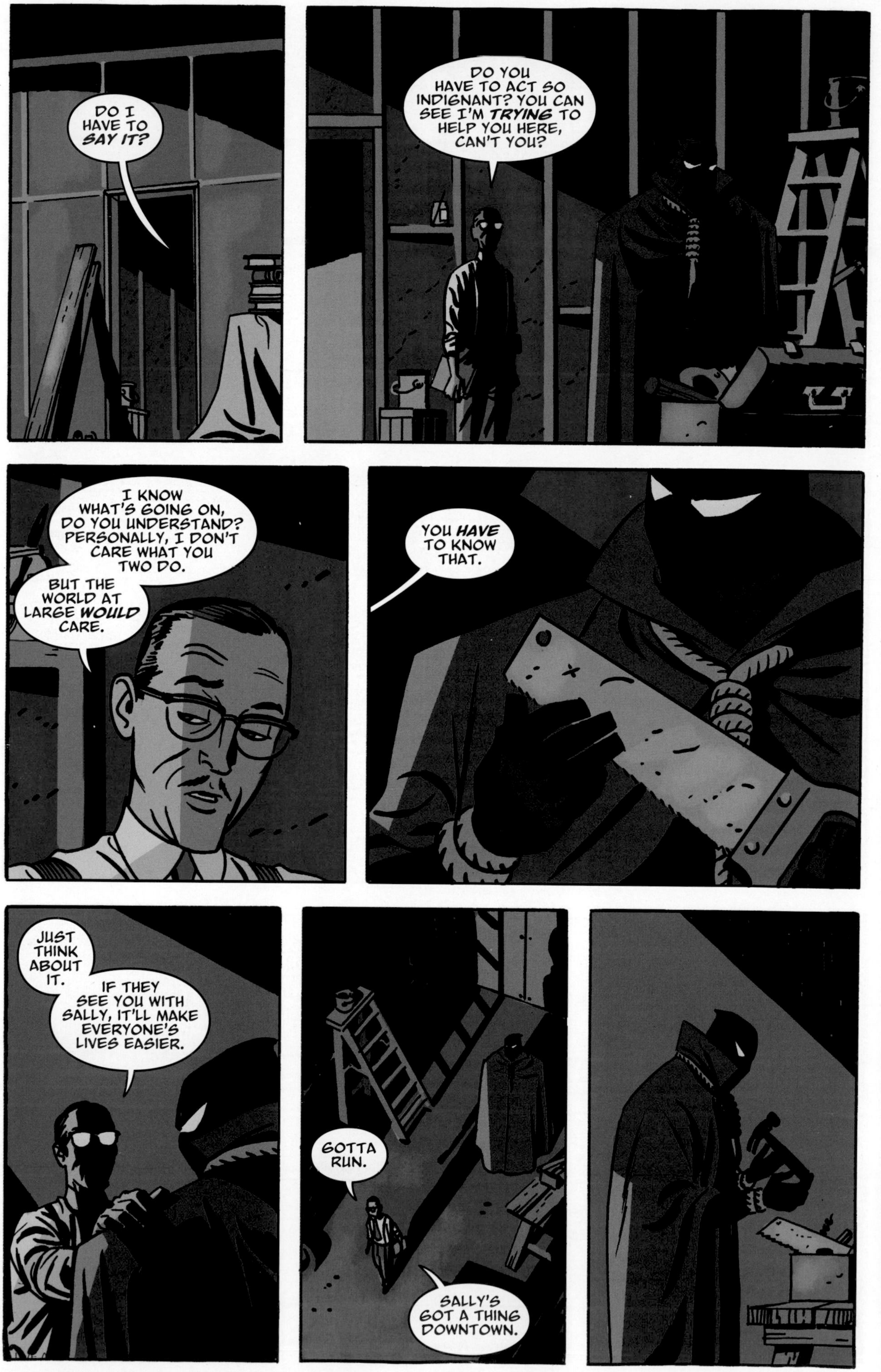
DO I HAVE TO SAY IT?
DO YOU HAVE TO ACT SO INDIGNANT? YOU CAN SEE I'M TRYING TO HELP YOU HERE, CAN'T YOU?
I KNOW WHAT'S GOING ON, DO YOU UNDERSTAND? PERSONALLY, I DON'T CARE WHAT YOU TWO DO.
BUT THE WORLD AT LARGE WOULD CARE.
YOU HAVE TO KNOW THAT.
JUST THINK ABOUT IT.
IF THEY SEE YOU WITH SALLY, IT'LL MAKE EVERYONE'S LIVES EASIER.
GOTTA RUN.
SALLY'S GOT A THING DOWNTOWN.

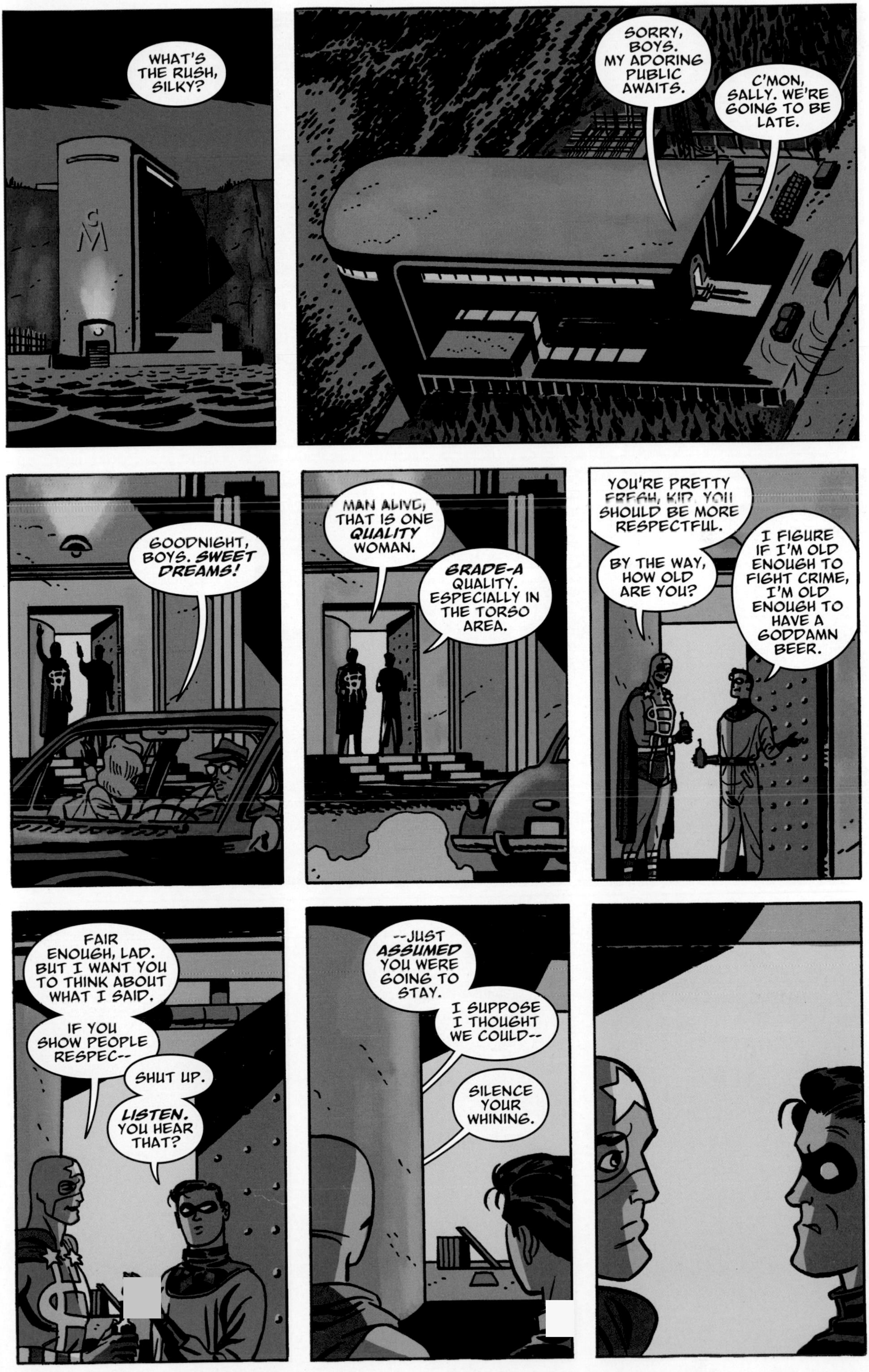
WHAT'S THE RUSH, SILKY?
SORRY, BOYS. MY ADORING PUBLIC AWAITS.
C'MON, SALLY. WE'RE GOING TO BE LATE.
GOODNIGHT, BOYS. SWEET DREAMS!
MAN ALIVE, THAT IS ONE QUALITY WOMAN.
GRADE-A QUALITY. ESPECIALLY IN THE TORSO AREA.
YOU'RE PRETTY FRESH, KID. YOU SHOULD BE MORE RESPECTFUL.
BY THE WAY, HOW OLD ARE YOU?
I FIGURE IF I'M OLD ENOUGH TO FIGHT CRIME, I'M OLD ENOUGH TO HAVE A GODDAMN BEER.
FAIR ENOUGH, LAD. BUT I WANT YOU TO THINK ABOUT WHAT I SAID.
IF YOU SHOW PEOPLE RESPEC--
SHUT UP.
LISTEN. YOU HEAR THAT?
--JUST ASSUMED YOU WERE GOING TO STAY.
I SUPPOSE I THOUGHT WE COULD--
SILENCE YOUR WHINING.

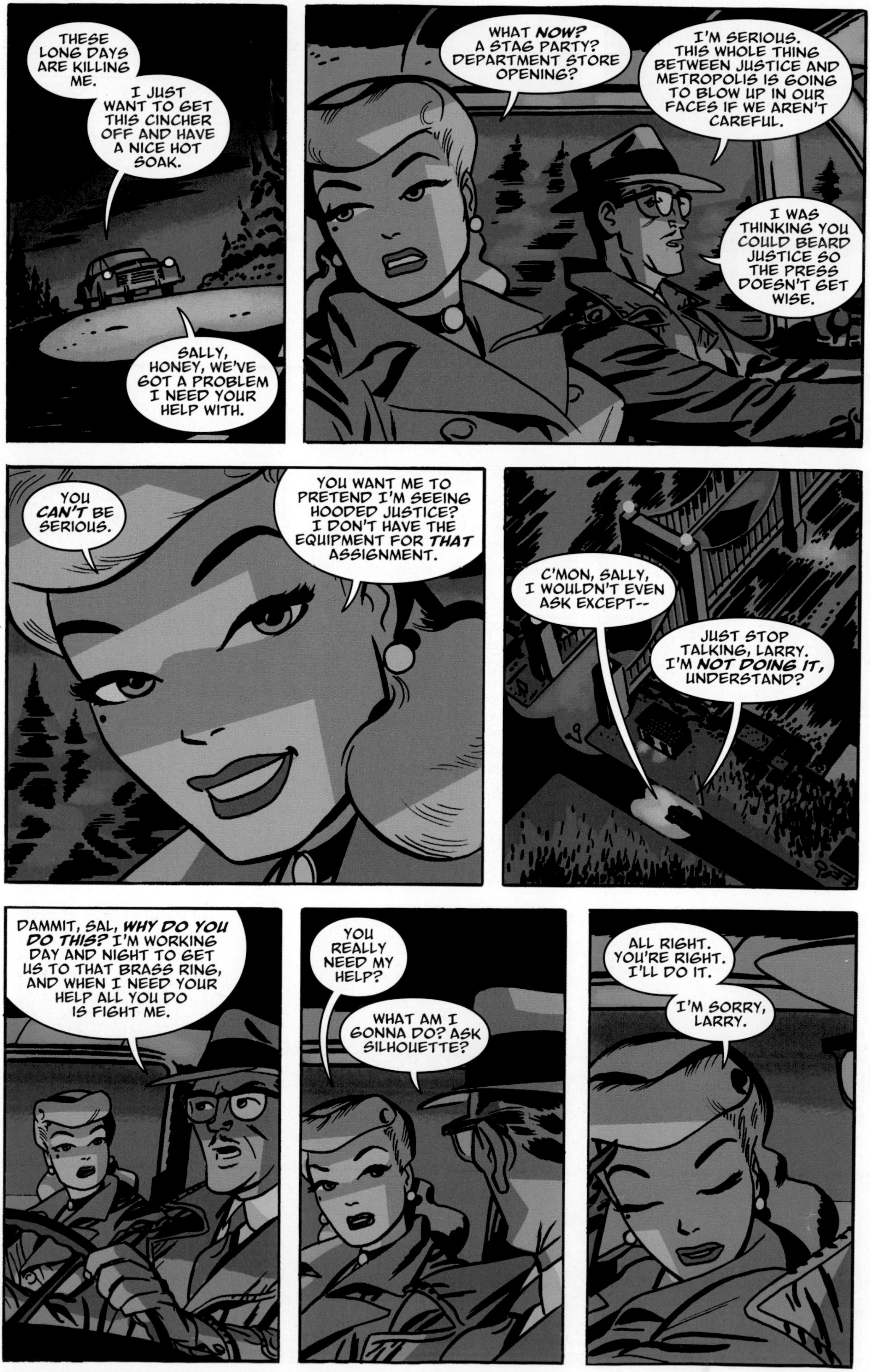
THESE LONG DAYS ARE KILLING ME.
I JUST WANT TO GET THIS CINCHER OFF AND HAVE A NICE HOT SOAK.
SALLY, HONEY, WE'VE GOT A PROBLEM I NEED YOUR HELP WITH.
WHAT NOW? A STAG PARTY? DEPARTMENT STORE OPENING?
I'M SERIOUS. THIS WHOLE THING BETWEEN JUSTICE AND METROPOLIS IS GOING TO BLOW UP IN OUR FACES IF WE AREN'T CAREFUL.
I WAS THINKING YOU COULD BEARD JUSTICE SO THE PRESS DOESN'T GET WISE.
YOU CAN'T BE SERIOUS.
YOU WANT ME TO PRETEND I'M SEEING HOODED JUSTICE? I DON'T HAVE THE EQUIPMENT FOR THAT ASSIGNMENT.
C'MON, SALLY, I WOULDN'T EVEN ASK EXCEPT--
JUST STOP TALKING, LARRY. I'M NOT DOING IT, UNDERSTAND?
DAMMIT, SAL, WHY DO YOU DO THIS? I'M WORKING DAY AND NIGHT TO GET US TO THAT BRASS RING, AND WHEN I NEED YOUR HELP ALL YOU DO IS FIGHT ME.
YOU REALLY NEED MY HELP?
WHAT AM I GONNA DO? ASK SILHOUETTE?
ALL RIGHT. YOU'RE RIGHT. I'LL DO IT.
I'M SORRY, LARRY.

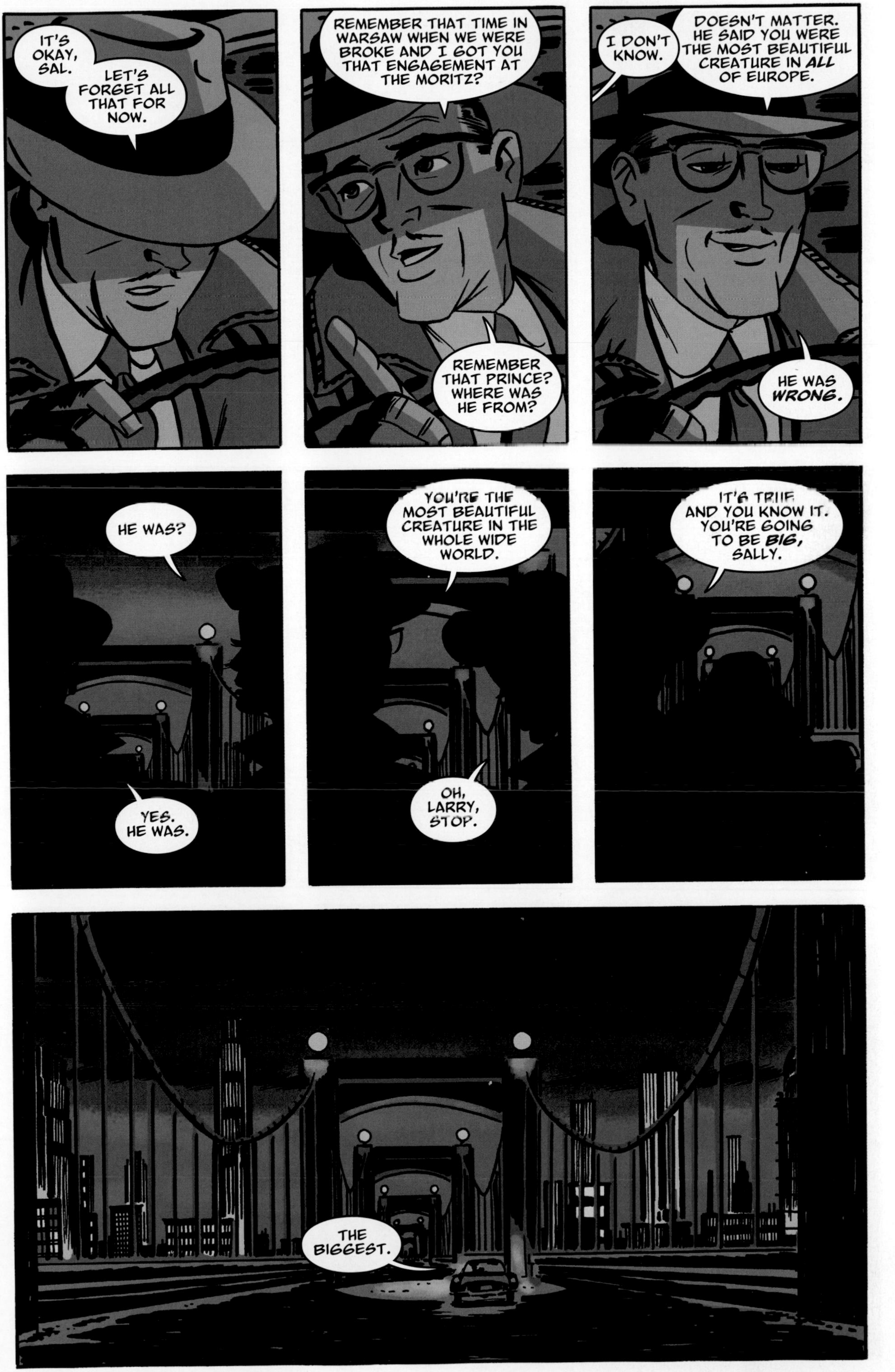
IT'S OKAY, SAL.
LET'S FORGET ALL THAT FOR NOW.
REMEMBER THAT TIME IN WARSAW WHEN WE WERE BROKE AND I GOT YOU THAT ENGAGEMENT AT THE MORITZ?
REMEMBER THAT PRINCE? WHERE WAS HE FROM?
I DON'T KNOW.
DOESN'T MATTER. HE SAID YOU WERE THE MOST BEAUTIFUL CREATURE IN ALL OF EUROPE.
HE WAS WRONG.
HE WAS?
YES. HE WAS.
YOU'RE THE MOST BEAUTIFUL CREATURE IN THE WHOLE WIDE WORLD.
OH, LARRY, STOP.
IT'S TRUE AND YOU KNOW IT. YOU'RE GOING TO BE BIG, SALLY.
THE BIGGEST.

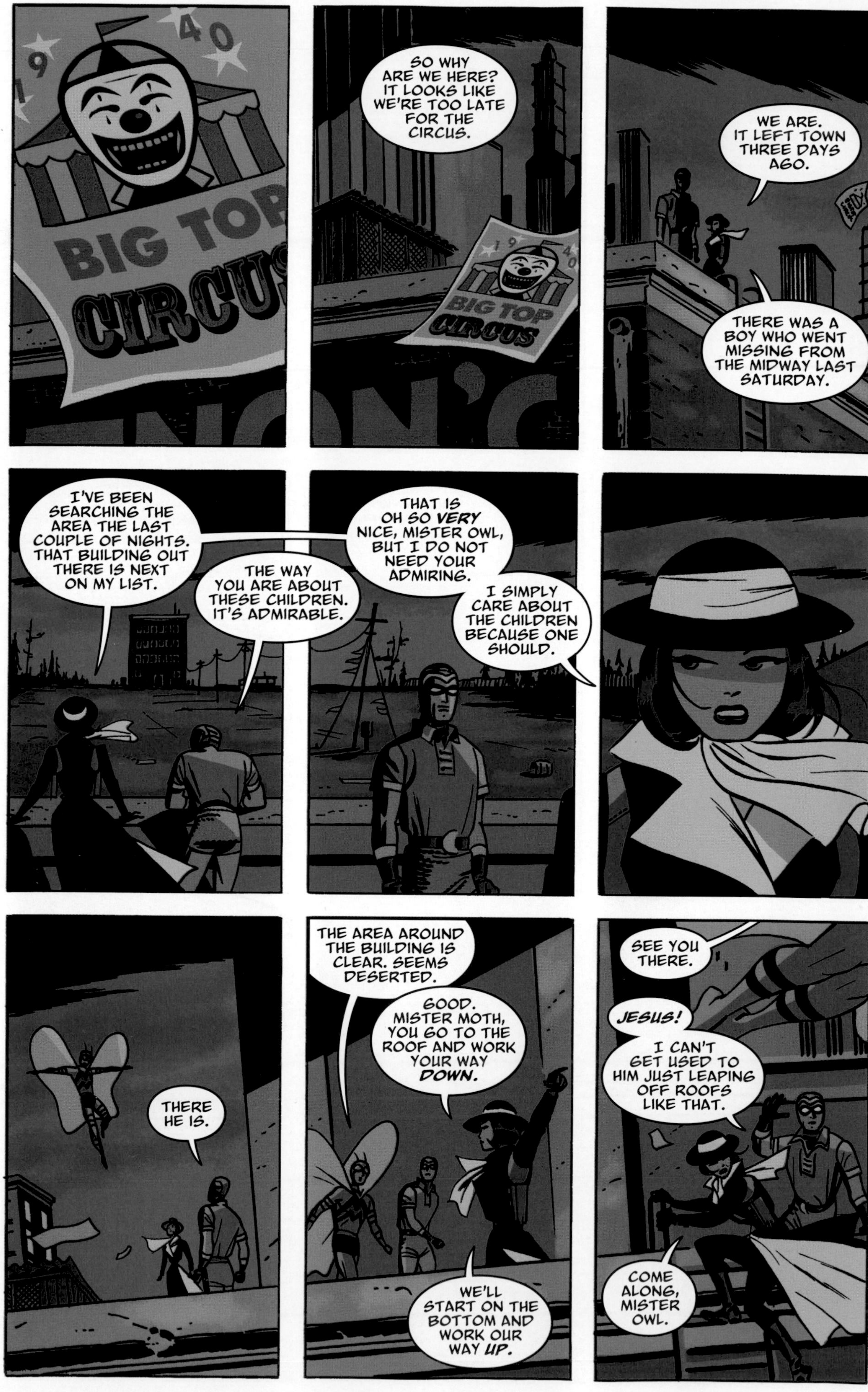
1940
BIG TOP CIRCUS
SO WHY ARE WE HERE? IT LOOKS LIKE WE'RE TOO LATE FOR THE CIRCUS.
BIG TOP CIRCUS
WE ARE. IT LEFT TOWN THREE DAYS AGO.
THERE WAS A BOY WHO WENT MISSING FROM THE MIDWAY LAST SATURDAY.
I'VE BEEN SEARCHING THE AREA THE LAST COUPLE OF NIGHTS. THAT BUILDING OUT THERE IS NEXT ON MY LIST.
THE WAY YOU ARE ABOUT THESE CHILDREN. IT'S ADMIRABLE.
THAT IS OH SO *VERY* NICE, MISTER OWL, BUT I DO NOT NEED YOUR ADMIRING.
I SIMPLY CARE ABOUT THE CHILDREN BECAUSE ONE SHOULD.
THERE HE IS.
THE AREA AROUND THE BUILDING IS CLEAR. SEEMS DESERTED.
GOOD. MISTER MOTH, YOU GO TO THE ROOF AND WORK YOUR WAY ***DOWN.***
WE'LL START ON THE BOTTOM AND WORK OUR WAY ***UP.***
SEE YOU THERE.
JESUS!
I CAN'T GET USED TO HIM JUST LEAPING OFF ROOFS LIKE THAT.
COME ALONG, MISTER OWL.

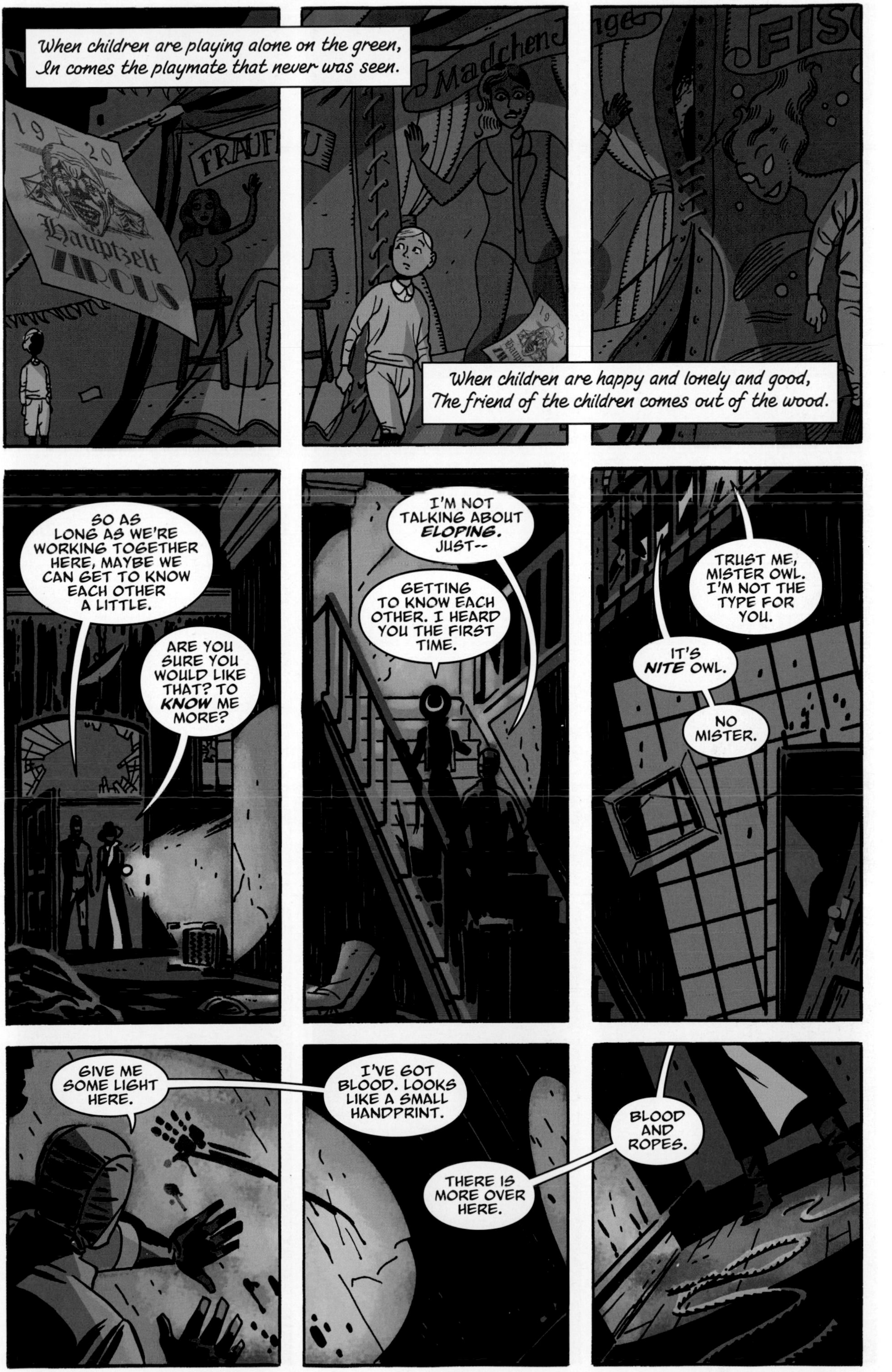
When children are playing alone on the green,
In comes the playmate that never was seen.
1920
Hauptzelt
ZIRCUS
When children are happy and lonely and good,
The friend of the children comes out of the wood.
SO AS LONG AS WE'RE WORKING TOGETHER HERE, MAYBE WE CAN GET TO KNOW EACH OTHER A LITTLE.
ARE YOU SURE YOU WOULD LIKE THAT? TO KNOW ME MORE?
I'M NOT TALKING ABOUT ELOPING. JUST--
GETTING TO KNOW EACH OTHER. I HEARD YOU THE FIRST TIME.
TRUST ME, MISTER OWL. I'M NOT THE TYPE FOR YOU.
IT'S NITE OWL.
NO MISTER.
GIVE ME SOME LIGHT HERE.
I'VE GOT BLOOD. LOOKS LIKE A SMALL HANDPRINT.
THERE IS MORE OVER HERE.
BLOOD AND ROPES.

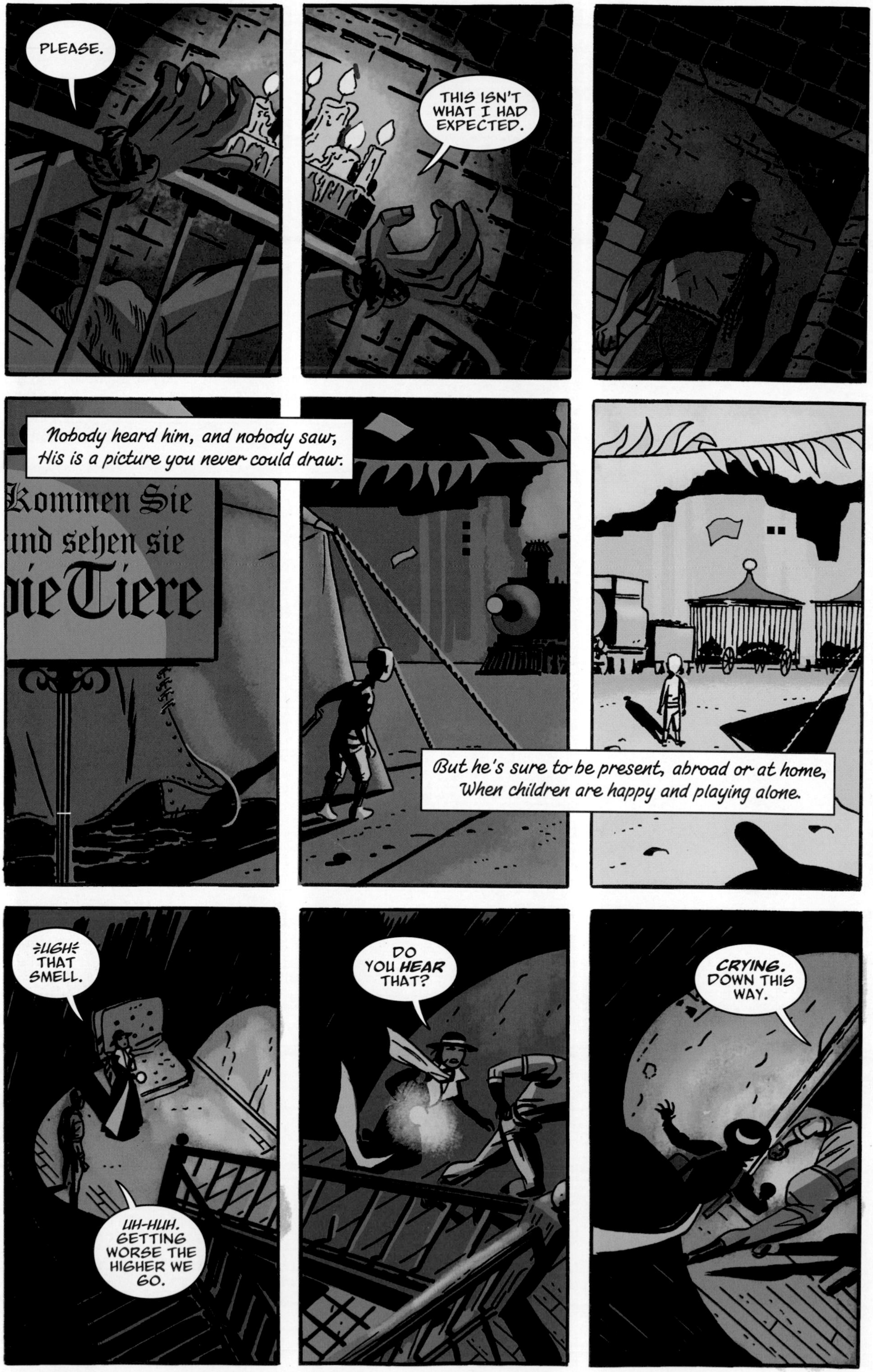
PLEASE.
THIS ISN'T WHAT I HAD EXPECTED.
Nobody heard him, and nobody saw,
His is a picture you never could draw.
Kommen Sie und sehen sie die Tiere
But he's sure to be present, abroad or at home,
When children are happy and playing alone.
UGH THAT SMELL.
UH-HUH. GETTING WORSE THE HIGHER WE GO.
DO YOU HEAR THAT?
CRYING. DOWN THIS WAY.

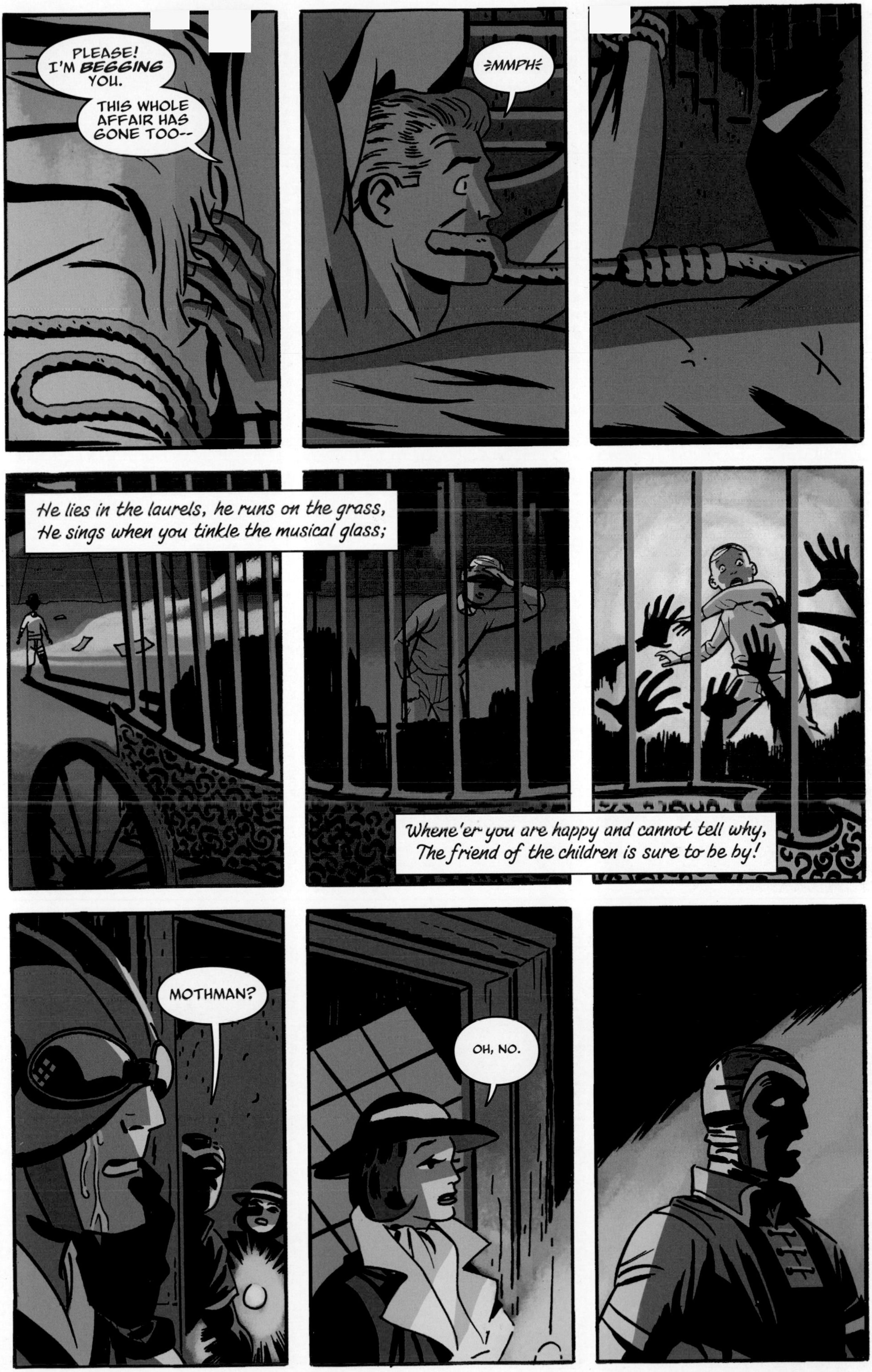
PLEASE! I'M **BEGGING** YOU.
THIS WHOLE AFFAIR HAS GONE TOO--
MMPH
He lies in the laurels, he runs on the grass, He sings when you tinkle the musical glass;
Whene'er you are happy and cannot tell why, The friend of the children is sure to be by!
MOTHMAN?
OH, NO.

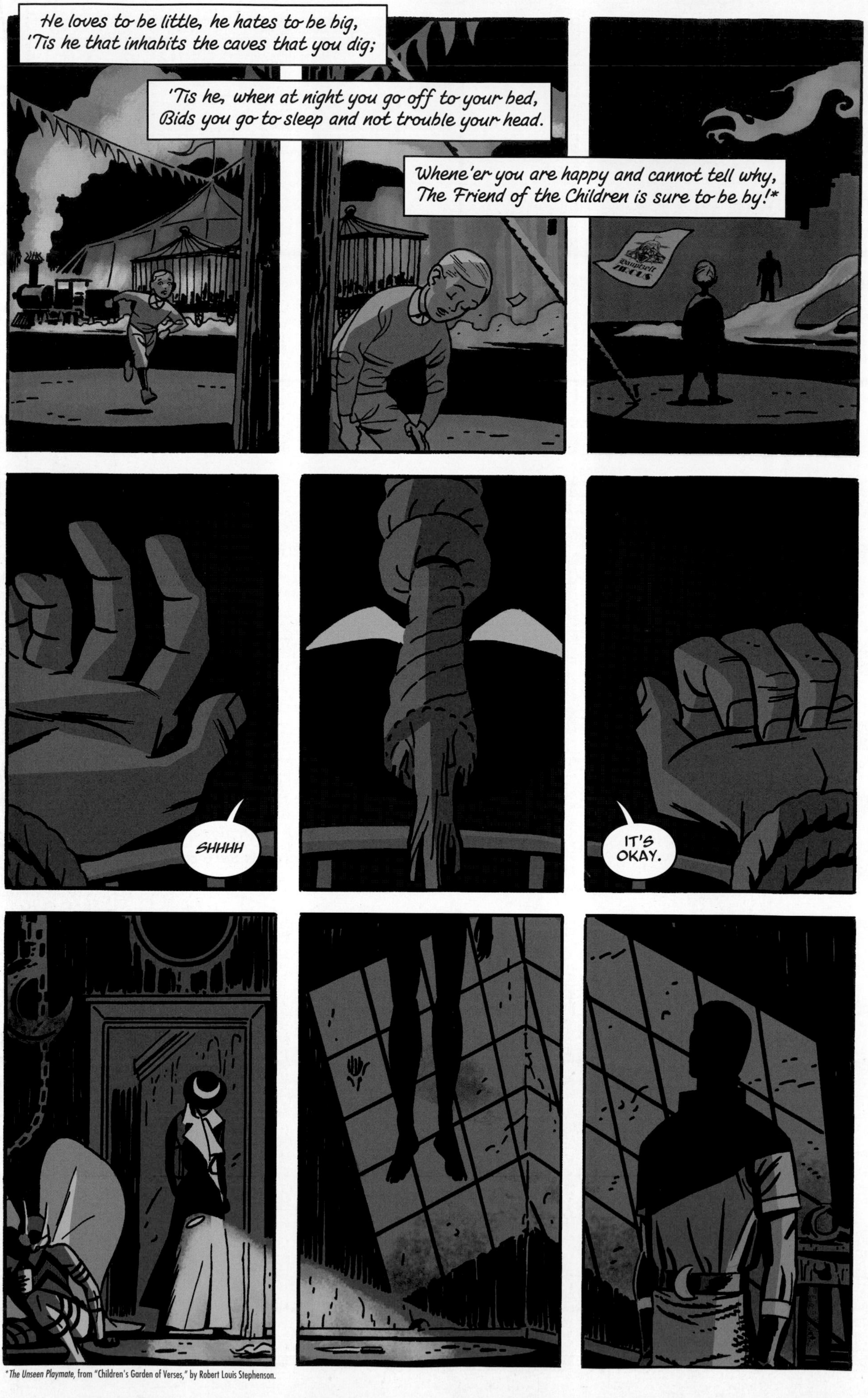
He loves to be little, he hates to be big,
'Tis he that inhabits the caves that you dig;
'Tis he, when at night you go off to your bed,
Bids you go to sleep and not trouble your head.
Whene'er you are happy and cannot tell why,
The Friend of the Children is sure to be by!*
SHHHH
IT'S OKAY.

The Unseen Playmate, from "Children's Garden of Verses," by Robert Louis Stephenson.

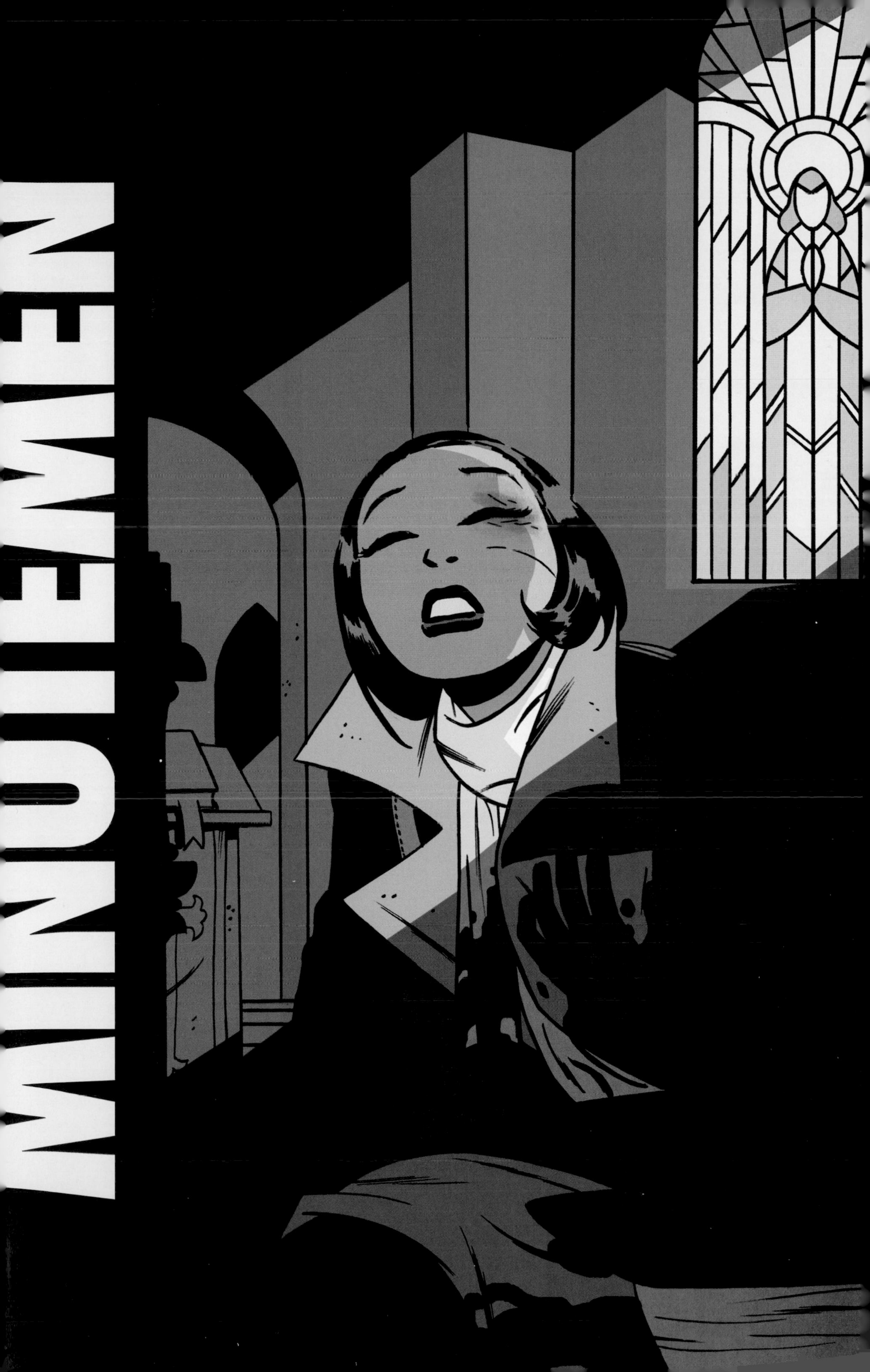
MINUTEMEN

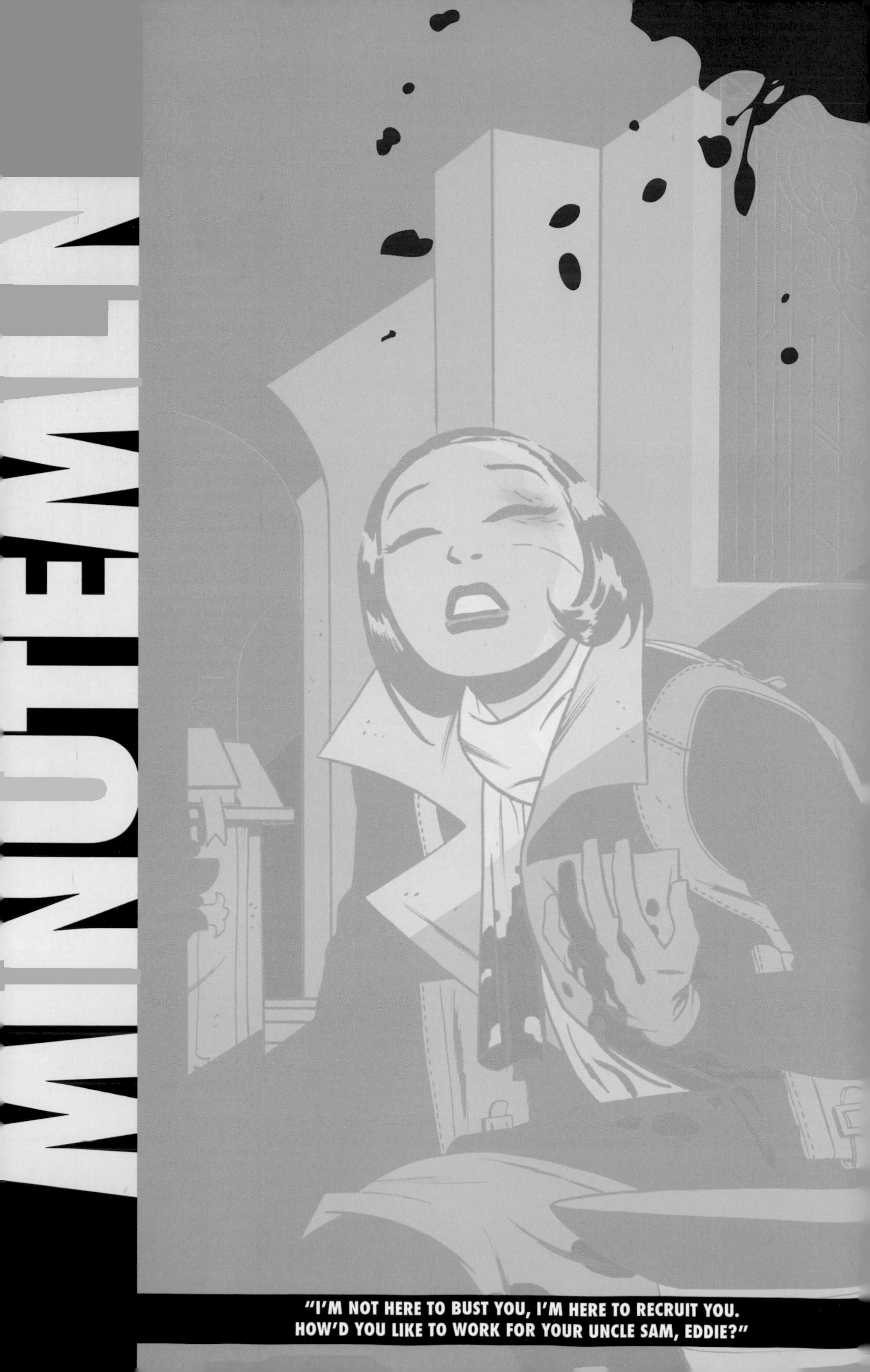
MINUTEMAN
"I'M NOT HERE TO BUST YOU, I'M HERE TO RECRUIT YOU.
HOW'D YOU LIKE TO WORK FOR YOUR UNCLE SAM, EDDIE?"

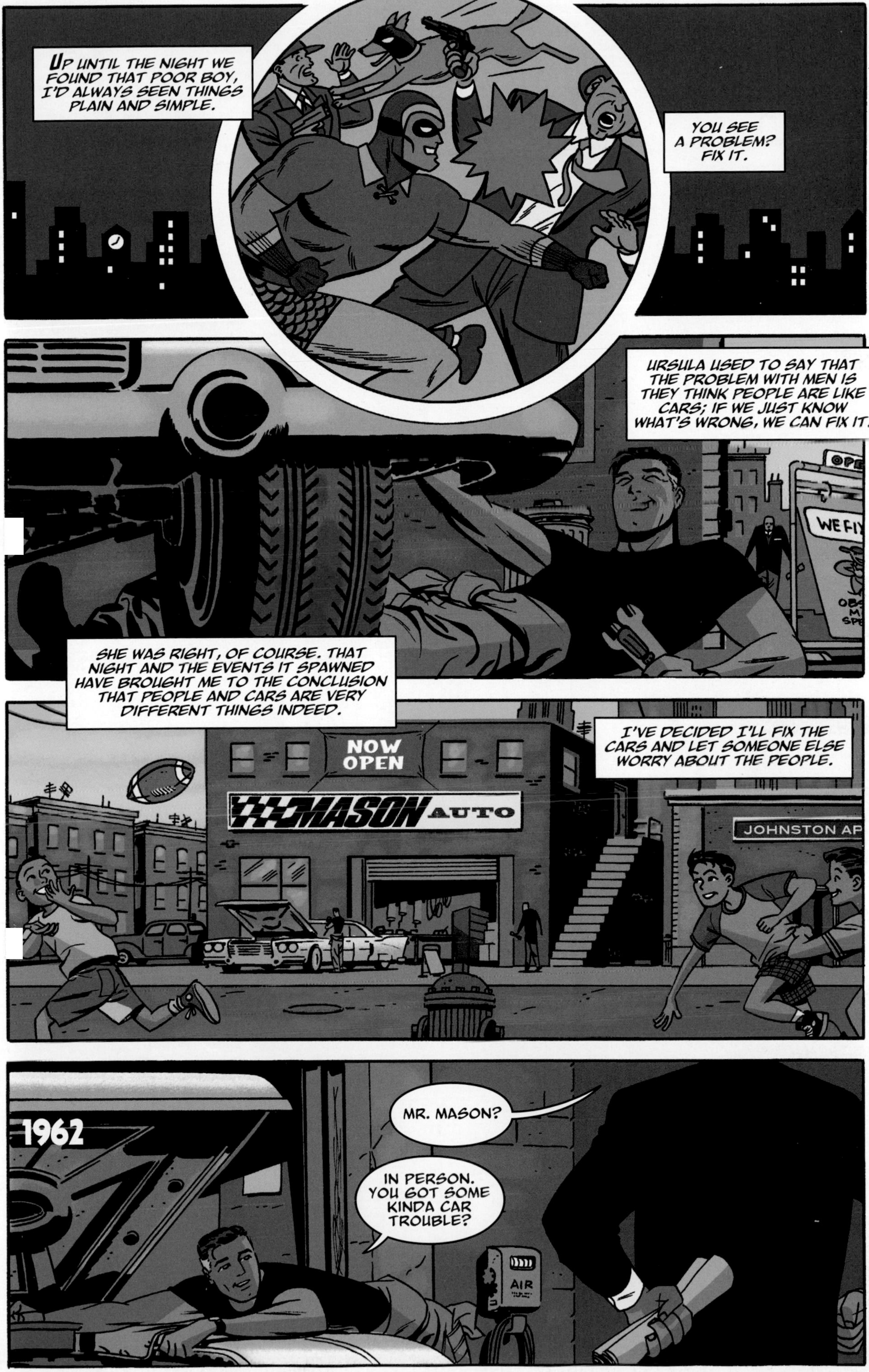

UP UNTIL THE NIGHT WE FOUND THAT POOR BOY, I'D ALWAYS SEEN THINGS PLAIN AND SIMPLE.
YOU SEE A PROBLEM? FIX IT.
URSULA USED TO SAY THAT THE PROBLEM WITH MEN IS THEY THINK PEOPLE ARE LIKE CARS; IF WE JUST KNOW WHAT'S WRONG, WE CAN FIX IT.
SHE WAS RIGHT, OF COURSE. THAT NIGHT AND THE EVENTS IT SPAWNED HAVE BROUGHT ME TO THE CONCLUSION THAT PEOPLE AND CARS ARE VERY DIFFERENT THINGS INDEED.
I'VE DECIDED I'LL FIX THE CARS AND LET SOMEONE ELSE WORRY ABOUT THE PEOPLE.
NOW OPEN
MASON AUTO
JOHNSTON AP
1962
MR. MASON?
IN PERSON. YOU GOT SOME KINDA CAR TROUBLE?
AIR

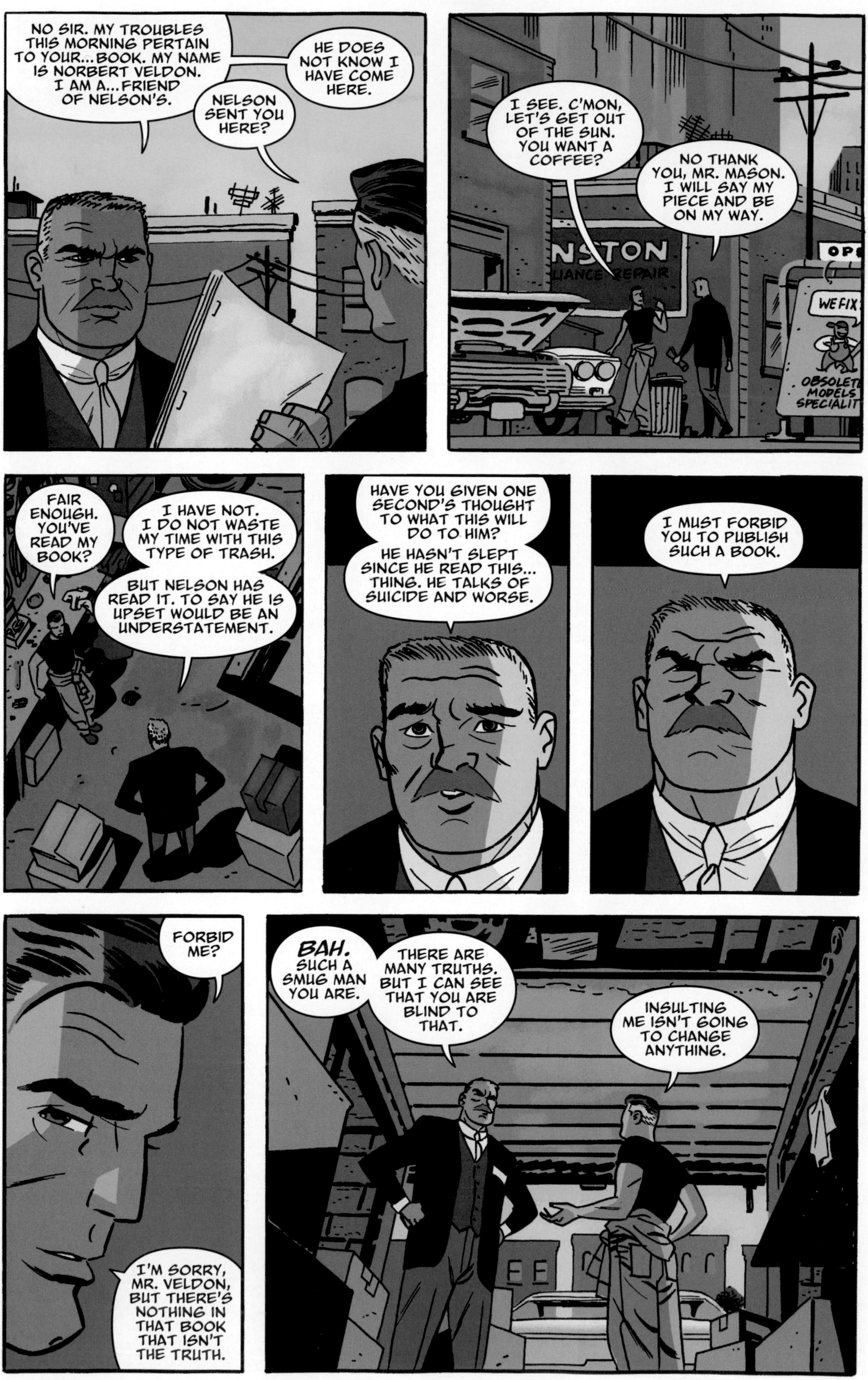
NO SIR. MY TROUBLES THIS MORNING PERTAIN TO YOUR...BOOK. MY NAME IS NORBERT VELDON. I AM A...FRIEND OF NELSON'S.
NELSON SENT YOU HERE?
HE DOES NOT KNOW I HAVE COME HERE.
I SEE. C'MON, LET'S GET OUT OF THE SUN. YOU WANT A COFFEE?
NO THANK YOU, MR. MASON. I WILL SAY MY PIECE AND BE ON MY WAY.
FAIR ENOUGH. YOU'VE READ MY BOOK?
I HAVE NOT. I DO NOT WASTE MY TIME WITH THIS TYPE OF TRASH.
BUT NELSON HAS READ IT. TO SAY HE IS UPSET WOULD BE AN UNDERSTATEMENT.
HAVE YOU GIVEN ONE SECOND'S THOUGHT TO WHAT THIS WILL DO TO HIM?
HE HASN'T SLEPT SINCE HE READ THIS... THING. HE TALKS OF SUICIDE AND WORSE.
I MUST FORBID YOU TO PUBLISH SUCH A BOOK.
FORBID ME?
I'M SORRY, MR. VELDON, BUT THERE'S NOTHING IN THAT BOOK THAT ISN'T THE TRUTH.
BAH. SUCH A SMUG MAN YOU ARE.
THERE ARE MANY TRUTHS. BUT I CAN SEE THAT YOU ARE BLIND TO THAT.
INSULTING ME ISN'T GOING TO CHANGE ANYTHING.

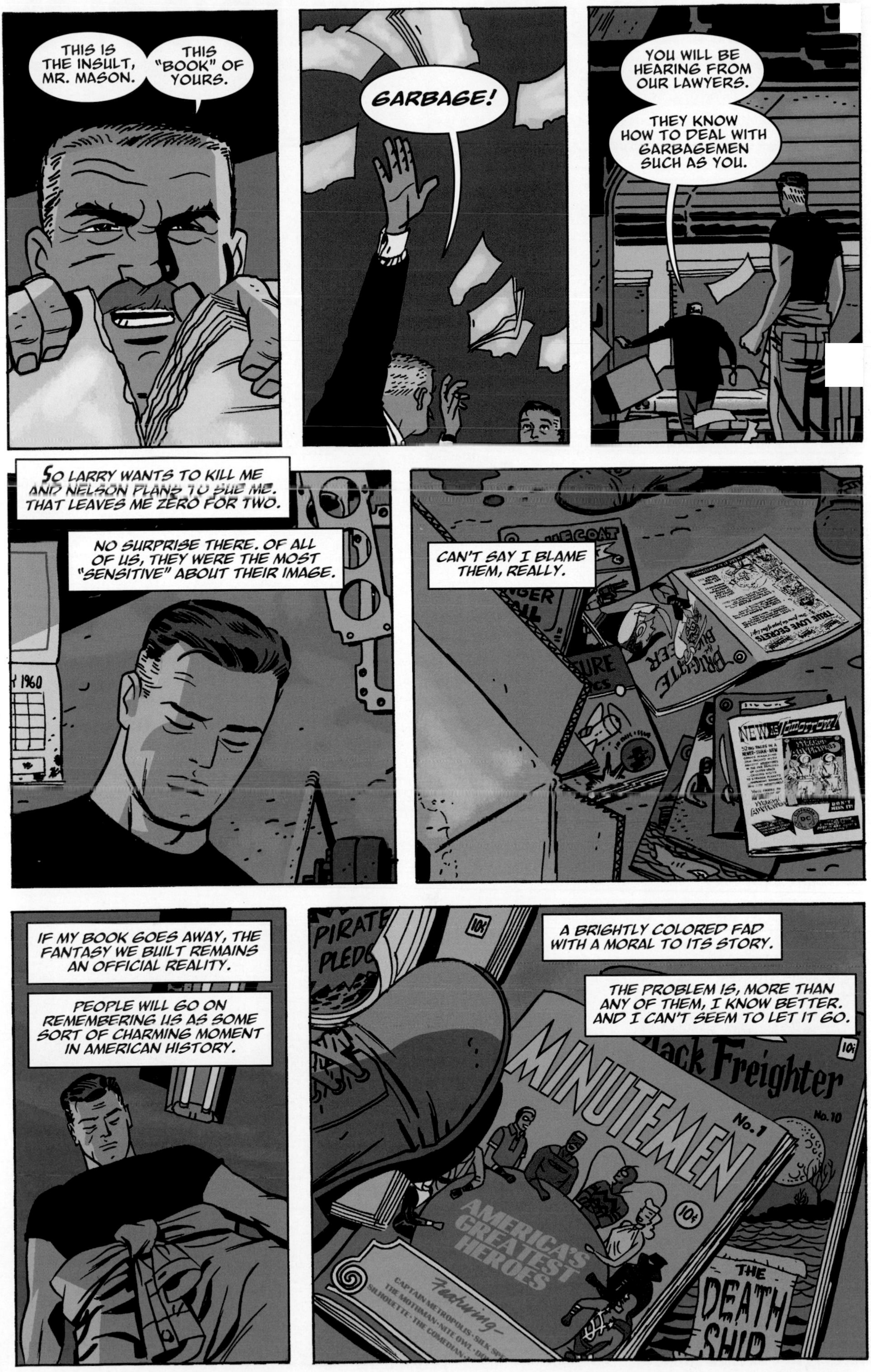
THIS IS THE INSULT, MR. MASON.
THIS "BOOK" OF YOURS.
GARBAGE!
YOU WILL BE HEARING FROM OUR LAWYERS.
THEY KNOW HOW TO DEAL WITH GARBAGEMEN SUCH AS YOU.
SO LARRY WANTS TO KILL ME AND NELSON PLANS TO SUE ME. THAT LEAVES ME ZERO FOR TWO.
NO SURPRISE THERE. OF ALL OF US, THEY WERE THE MOST "SENSITIVE" ABOUT THEIR IMAGE.
CAN'T SAY I BLAME THEM, REALLY.
IF MY BOOK GOES AWAY, THE FANTASY WE BUILT REMAINS AN OFFICIAL REALITY.
PEOPLE WILL GO ON REMEMBERING US AS SOME SORT OF CHARMING MOMENT IN AMERICAN HISTORY.
A BRIGHTLY COLORED FAD WITH A MORAL TO ITS STORY.
THE PROBLEM IS, MORE THAN ANY OF THEM, I KNOW BETTER. AND I CAN'T SEEM TO LET IT GO.
MINUTEMEN No. 1
AMERICA'S GREATEST HEROES
Black Freighter No. 10
THE DEATH SHIP
TRUE LOVE SECRETS
PIRATE PLEDGE

CHAPTER THREE: CHILD'S PLAY

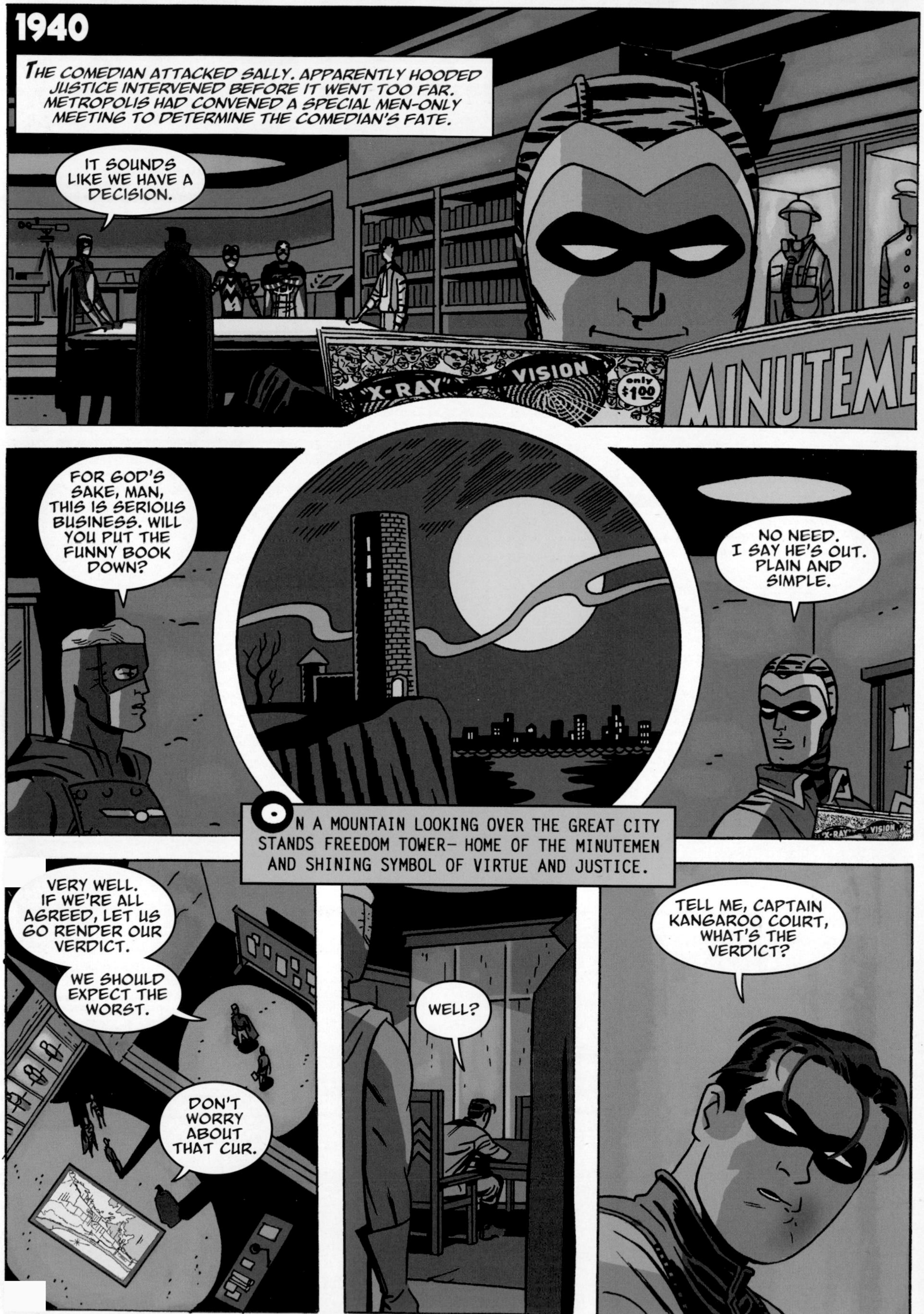

1940
THE COMEDIAN ATTACKED SALLY. APPARENTLY HOODED JUSTICE INTERVENED BEFORE IT WENT TOO FAR. METROPOLIS HAD CONVENED A SPECIAL MEN-ONLY MEETING TO DETERMINE THE COMEDIAN'S FATE.
IT SOUNDS LIKE WE HAVE A DECISION.
"X-RAY" VISION only $1.00
MINUTEME
FOR GOD'S SAKE, MAN, THIS IS SERIOUS BUSINESS. WILL YOU PUT THE FUNNY BOOK DOWN?
NO NEED. I SAY HE'S OUT. PLAIN AND SIMPLE.
ON A MOUNTAIN LOOKING OVER THE GREAT CITY STANDS FREEDOM TOWER— HOME OF THE MINUTEMEN AND SHINING SYMBOL OF VIRTUE AND JUSTICE.
"X-RAY" VISION
VERY WELL. IF WE'RE ALL AGREED, LET US GO RENDER OUR VERDICT.
WE SHOULD EXPECT THE WORST.
DON'T WORRY ABOUT THAT CUR.
WELL?
TELL ME, CAPTAIN KANGAROO COURT, WHAT'S THE VERDICT?

DARWYN COOKE WRITER & ARTIST

PHIL NOTO COLORIST **JARED K. FLETCHER** LETTERER **DARWYN COOKE** COVER ARTIST **CLIFF CHIANG** VARIANT COVER ARTIST

CAMILLA ZHANG ASSISTANT EDITOR **WIL MOSS** ASSOCIATE EDITOR **MARK CHIARELLO** EDITOR

WATCHMEN CREATED BY **ALAN MOORE** & **DAVE GIBBONS**

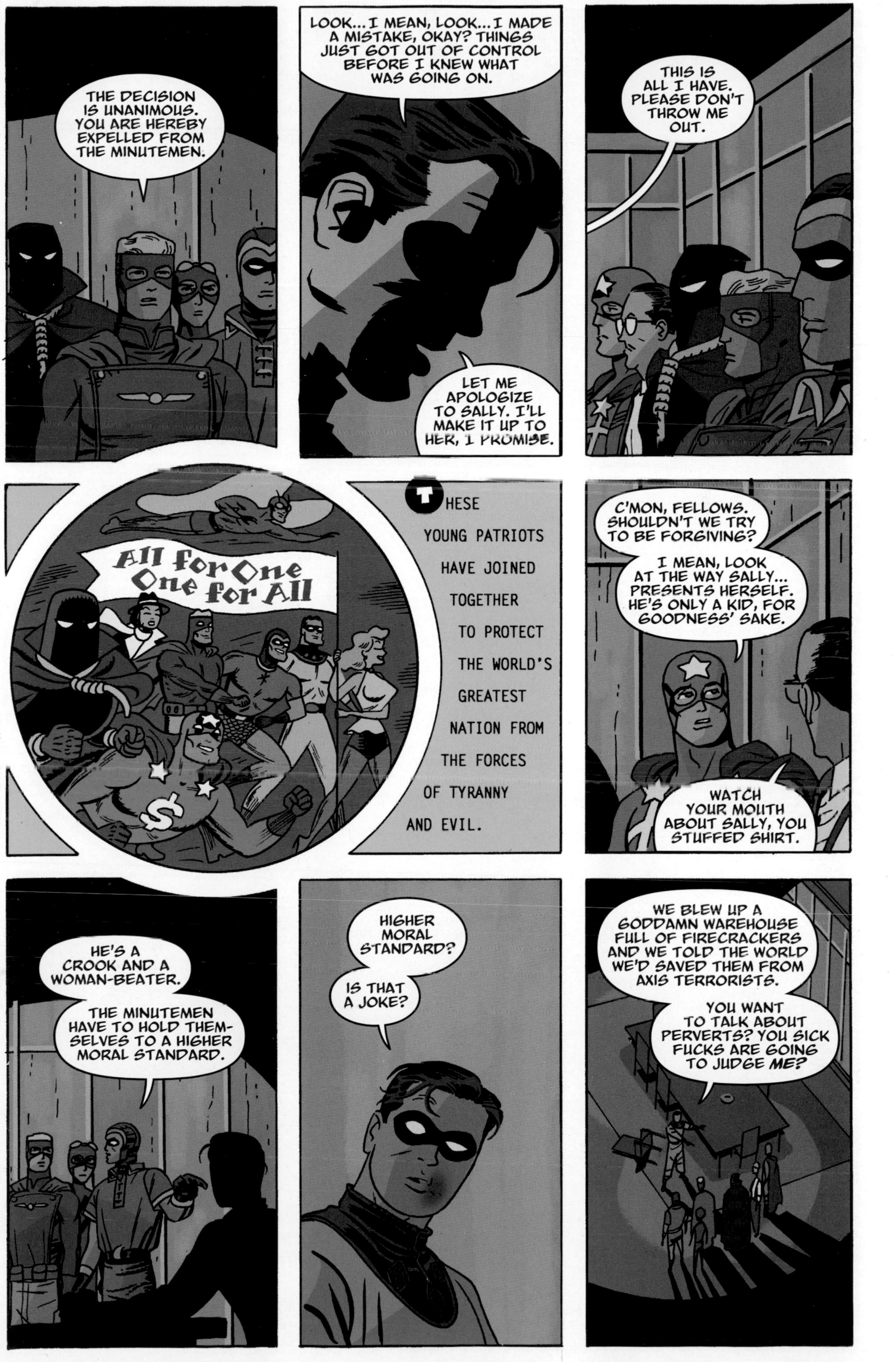
THE DECISION IS UNANIMOUS. YOU ARE HEREBY EXPELLED FROM THE MINUTEMEN.
LOOK... I MEAN, LOOK... I MADE A MISTAKE, OKAY? THINGS JUST GOT OUT OF CONTROL BEFORE I KNEW WHAT WAS GOING ON.
LET ME APOLOGIZE TO SALLY. I'LL MAKE IT UP TO HER, I PROMISE.
THIS IS ALL I HAVE. PLEASE DON'T THROW ME OUT.
All for One One for All
THESE YOUNG PATRIOTS HAVE JOINED TOGETHER TO PROTECT THE WORLD'S GREATEST NATION FROM THE FORCES OF TYRANNY AND EVIL.
C'MON, FELLOWS. SHOULDN'T WE TRY TO BE FORGIVING?
I MEAN, LOOK AT THE WAY SALLY... PRESENTS HERSELF. HE'S ONLY A KID, FOR GOODNESS' SAKE.
WATCH YOUR MOUTH ABOUT SALLY, YOU STUFFED SHIRT.
HE'S A CROOK AND A WOMAN-BEATER.
THE MINUTEMEN HAVE TO HOLD THEMSELVES TO A HIGHER MORAL STANDARD.
HIGHER MORAL STANDARD?
IS THAT A JOKE?
WE BLEW UP A GODDAMN WAREHOUSE FULL OF FIRECRACKERS AND WE TOLD THE WORLD WE'D SAVED THEM FROM AXIS TERRORISTS.
YOU WANT TO TALK ABOUT PERVERTS? YOU SICK FUCKS ARE GOING TO JUDGE *ME*?

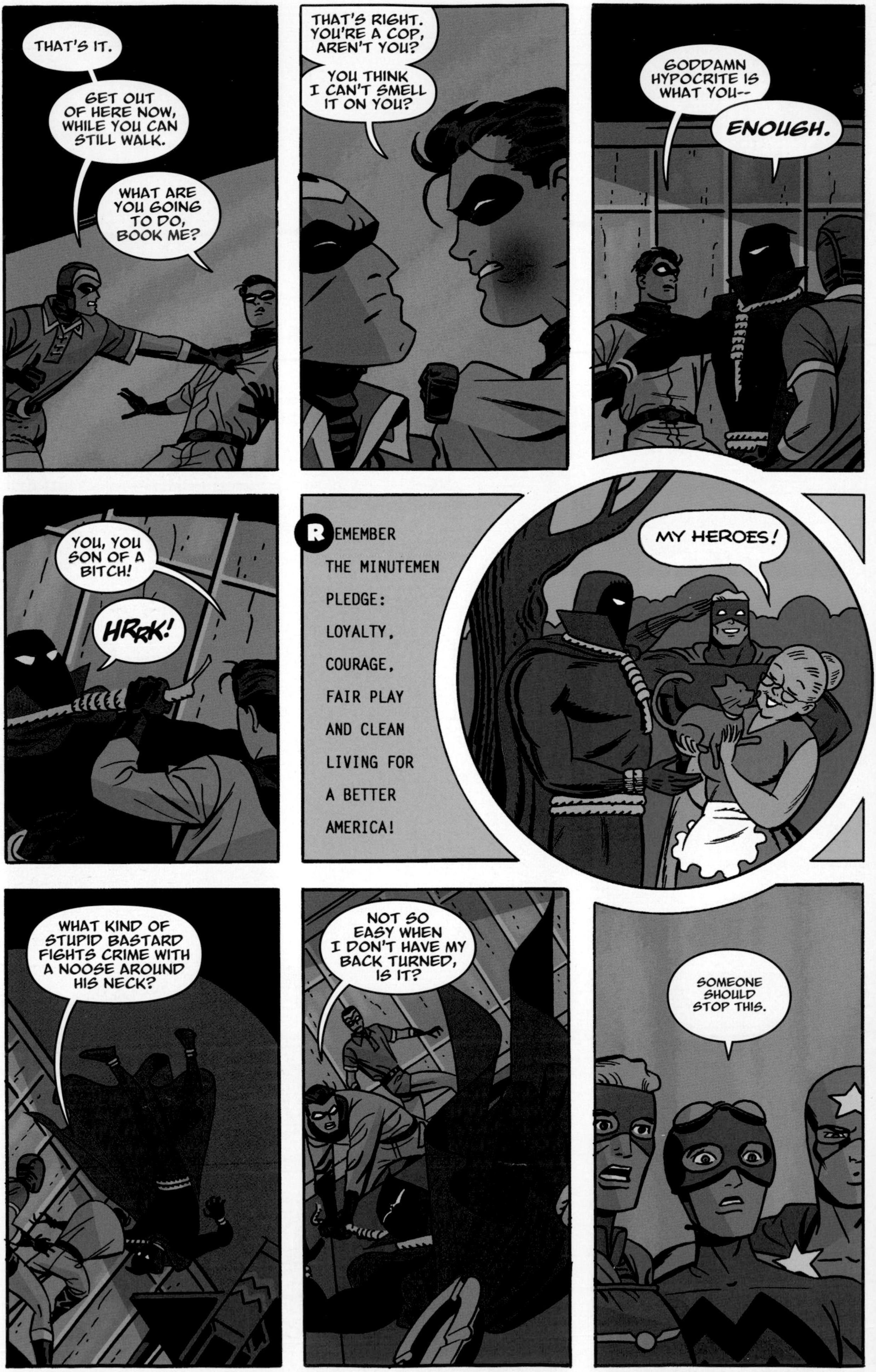
THAT'S IT.
GET OUT OF HERE NOW, WHILE YOU CAN STILL WALK.
WHAT ARE YOU GOING TO DO, BOOK ME?
THAT'S RIGHT. YOU'RE A COP, AREN'T YOU?
YOU THINK I CAN'T SMELL IT ON YOU?
GODDAMN HYPOCRITE IS WHAT YOU--
ENOUGH.
YOU, YOU SON OF A BITCH!
HRRK!
REMEMBER THE MINUTEMEN PLEDGE: LOYALTY, COURAGE, FAIR PLAY AND CLEAN LIVING FOR A BETTER AMERICA!
MY HEROES!
WHAT KIND OF STUPID BASTARD FIGHTS CRIME WITH A NOOSE AROUND HIS NECK?
NOT SO EASY WHEN I DON'T HAVE MY BACK TURNED, IS IT?
SOMEONE SHOULD STOP THIS.

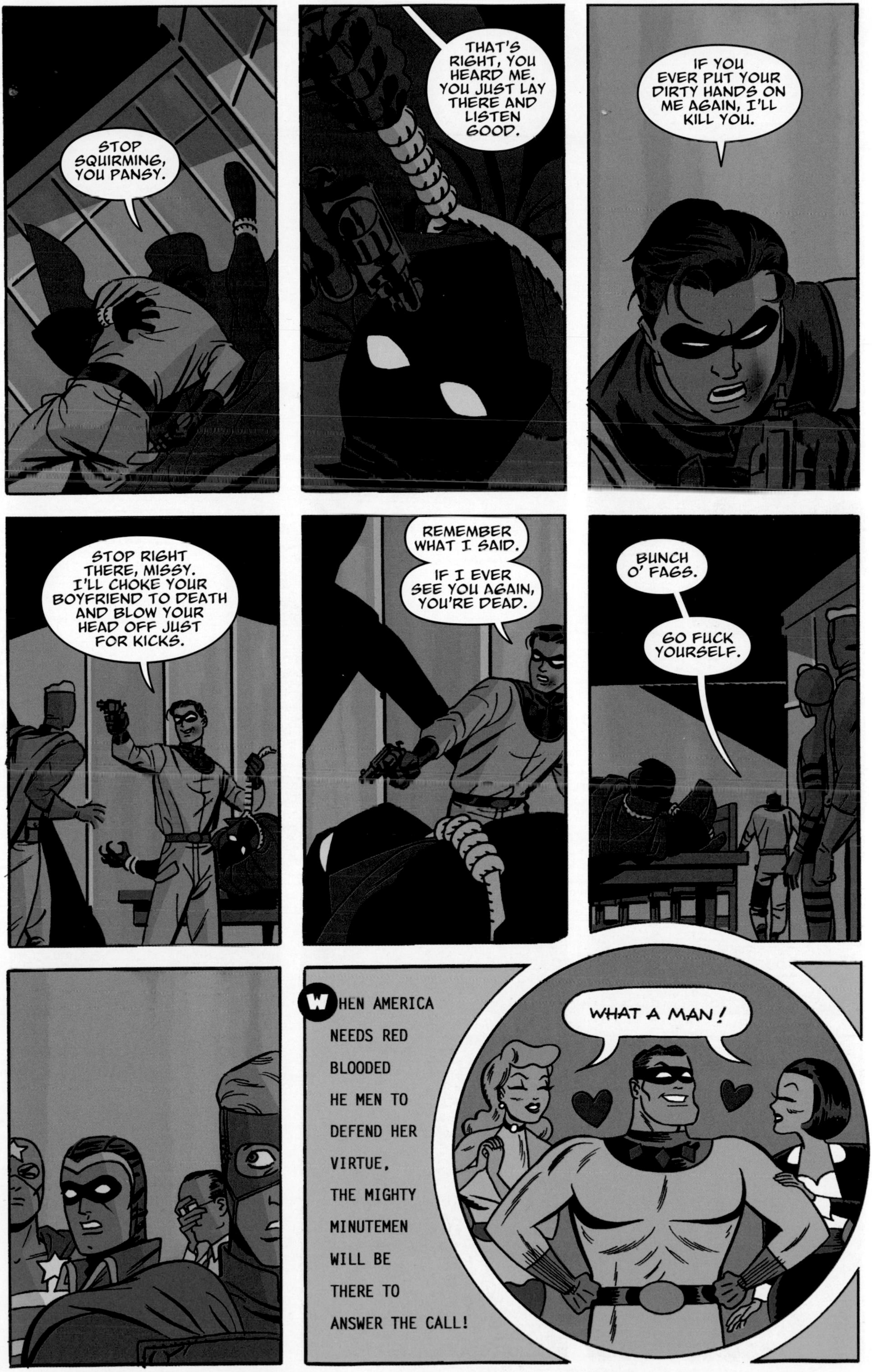
STOP SQUIRMING, YOU PANSY.
THAT'S RIGHT, YOU HEARD ME. YOU JUST LAY THERE AND LISTEN GOOD.
IF YOU EVER PUT YOUR DIRTY HANDS ON ME AGAIN, I'LL KILL YOU.
STOP RIGHT THERE, MISSY. I'LL CHOKE YOUR BOYFRIEND TO DEATH AND BLOW YOUR HEAD OFF JUST FOR KICKS.
REMEMBER WHAT I SAID.
IF I EVER SEE YOU AGAIN, YOU'RE DEAD.
BUNCH O' FAGS.
GO FUCK YOURSELF.
WHEN AMERICA NEEDS RED BLOODED HE MEN TO DEFEND HER VIRTUE, THE MIGHTY MINUTEMEN WILL BE THERE TO ANSWER THE CALL!
WHAT A MAN!

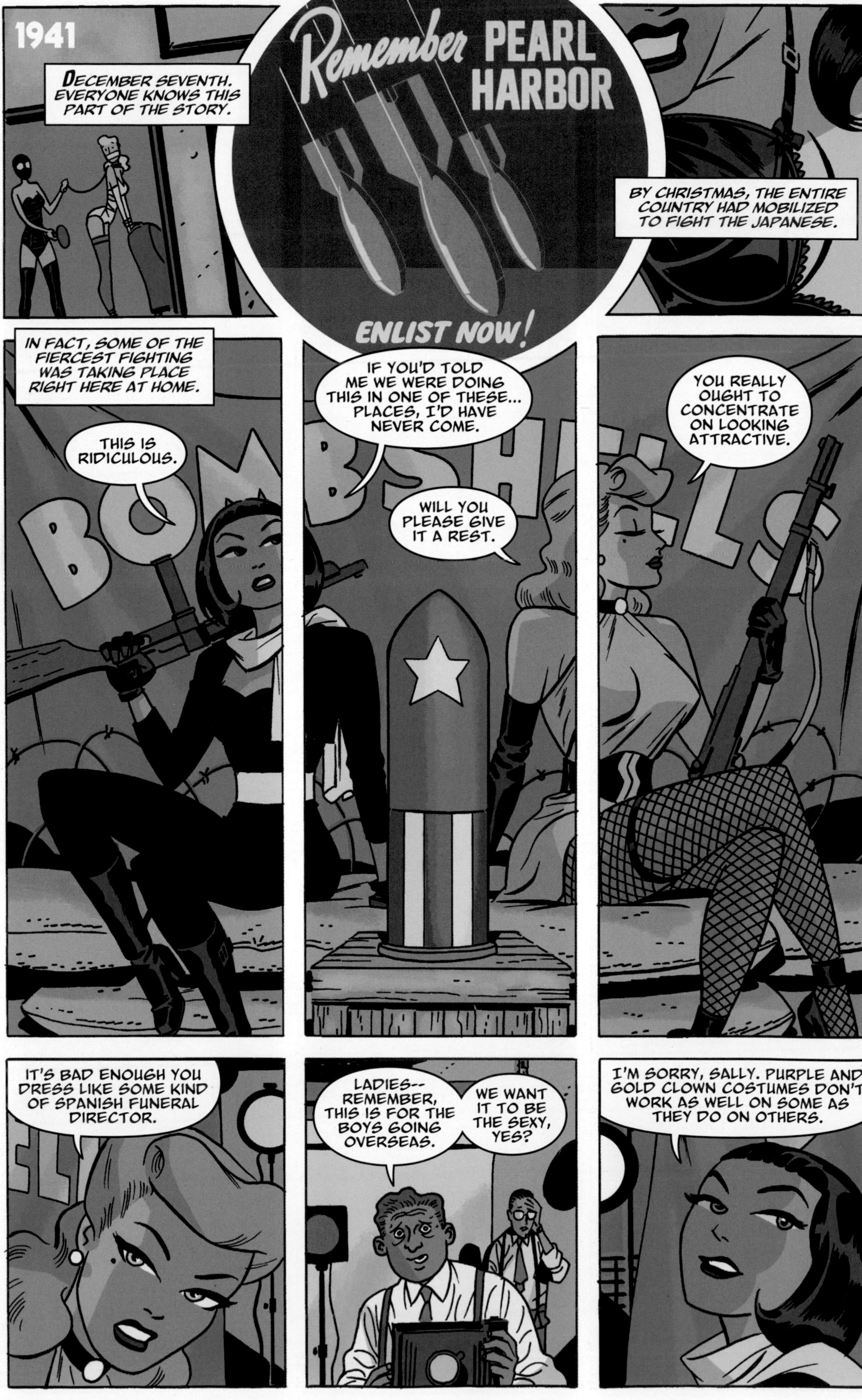
1941
DECEMBER SEVENTH. EVERYONE KNOWS THIS PART OF THE STORY.
Remember PEARL HARBOR
ENLIST NOW!
BY CHRISTMAS, THE ENTIRE COUNTRY HAD MOBILIZED TO FIGHT THE JAPANESE.
IN FACT, SOME OF THE FIERCEST FIGHTING WAS TAKING PLACE RIGHT HERE AT HOME.
THIS IS RIDICULOUS.
IF YOU'D TOLD ME WE WERE DOING THIS IN ONE OF THESE... PLACES, I'D HAVE NEVER COME.
WILL YOU PLEASE GIVE IT A REST.
YOU REALLY OUGHT TO CONCENTRATE ON LOOKING ATTRACTIVE.
IT'S BAD ENOUGH YOU DRESS LIKE SOME KIND OF SPANISH FUNERAL DIRECTOR.
LADIES-- REMEMBER, THIS IS FOR THE BOYS GOING OVERSEAS.
WE WANT IT TO BE THE SEXY, YES?
I'M SORRY, SALLY. PURPLE AND GOLD CLOWN COSTUMES DON'T WORK AS WELL ON SOME AS THEY DO ON OTHERS.

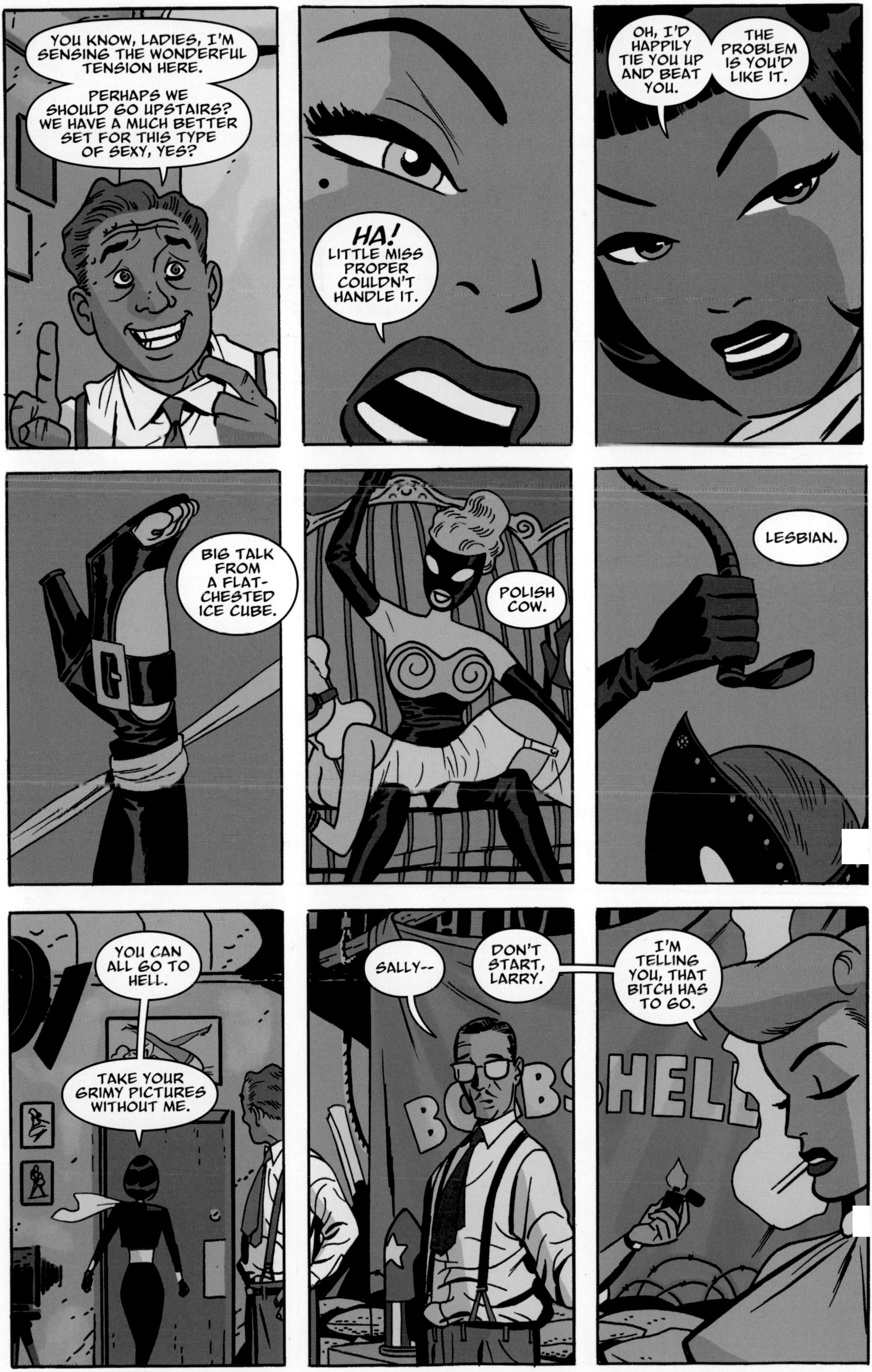
YOU KNOW, LADIES, I'M SENSING THE WONDERFUL TENSION HERE.
PERHAPS WE SHOULD GO UPSTAIRS? WE HAVE A MUCH BETTER SET FOR THIS TYPE OF SEXY, YES?
HA! LITTLE MISS PROPER COULDN'T HANDLE IT.
OH, I'D HAPPILY TIE YOU UP AND BEAT YOU.
THE PROBLEM IS YOU'D LIKE IT.
BIG TALK FROM A FLAT-CHESTED ICE CUBE.
POLISH COW.
LESBIAN.
YOU CAN ALL GO TO HELL.
TAKE YOUR GRIMY PICTURES WITHOUT ME.
SALLY--
DON'T START, LARRY.
I'M TELLING YOU, THAT BITCH HAS TO GO.
BOMBSHELL

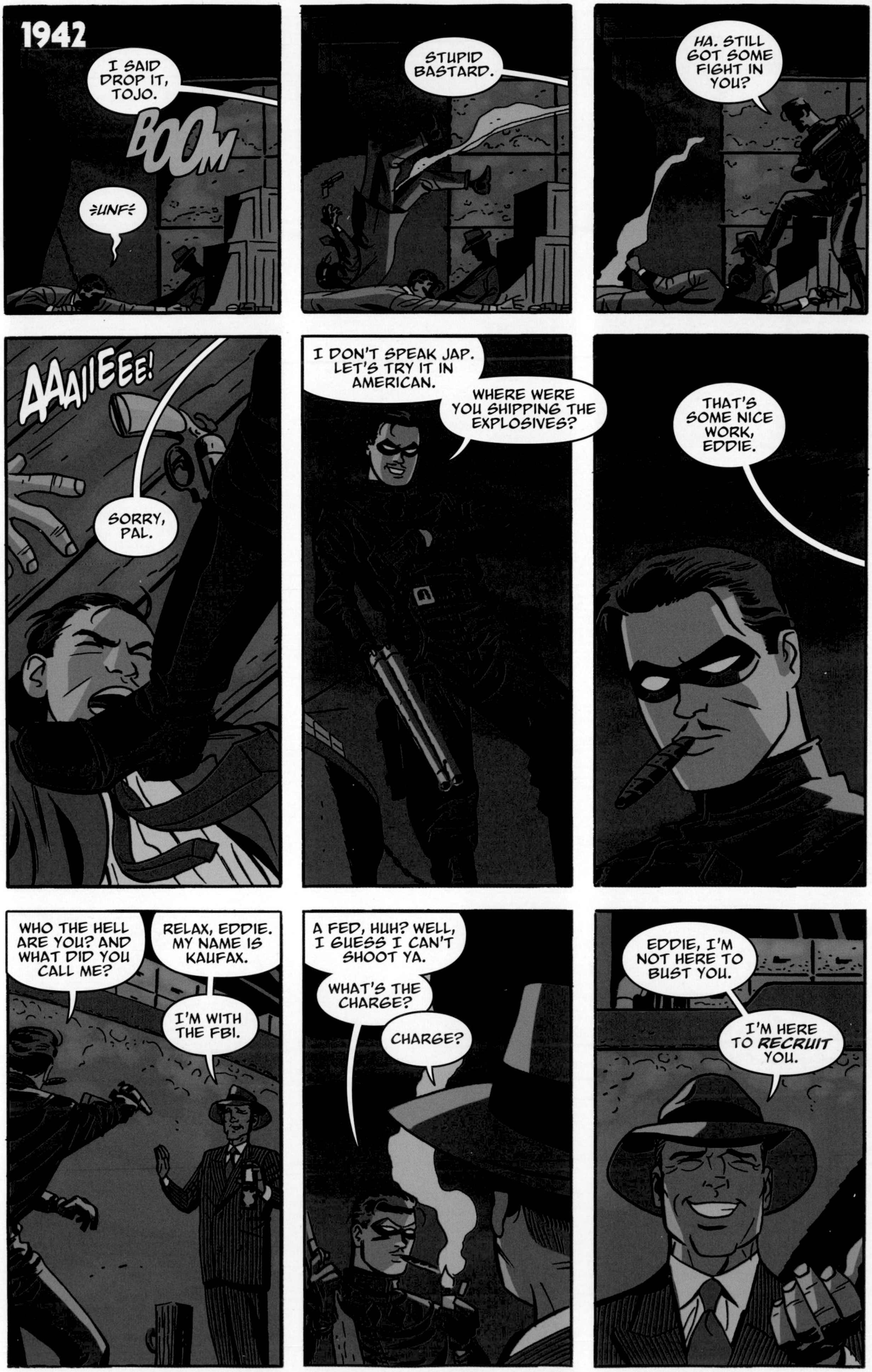
1942
I SAID DROP IT, TOJO.
BOOM
UNF
STUPID BASTARD.
HA. STILL GOT SOME FIGHT IN YOU?
AAAIIEEE!
SORRY, PAL.
I DON'T SPEAK JAP. LET'S TRY IT IN AMERICAN.
WHERE WERE YOU SHIPPING THE EXPLOSIVES?
THAT'S SOME NICE WORK, EDDIE.
WHO THE HELL ARE YOU? AND WHAT DID YOU CALL ME?
RELAX, EDDIE. MY NAME IS KAUFAX.
I'M WITH THE FBI.
A FED, HUH? WELL, I GUESS I CAN'T SHOOT YA.
WHAT'S THE CHARGE?
CHARGE?
EDDIE, I'M NOT HERE TO BUST YOU.
I'M HERE TO *RECRUIT* YOU.

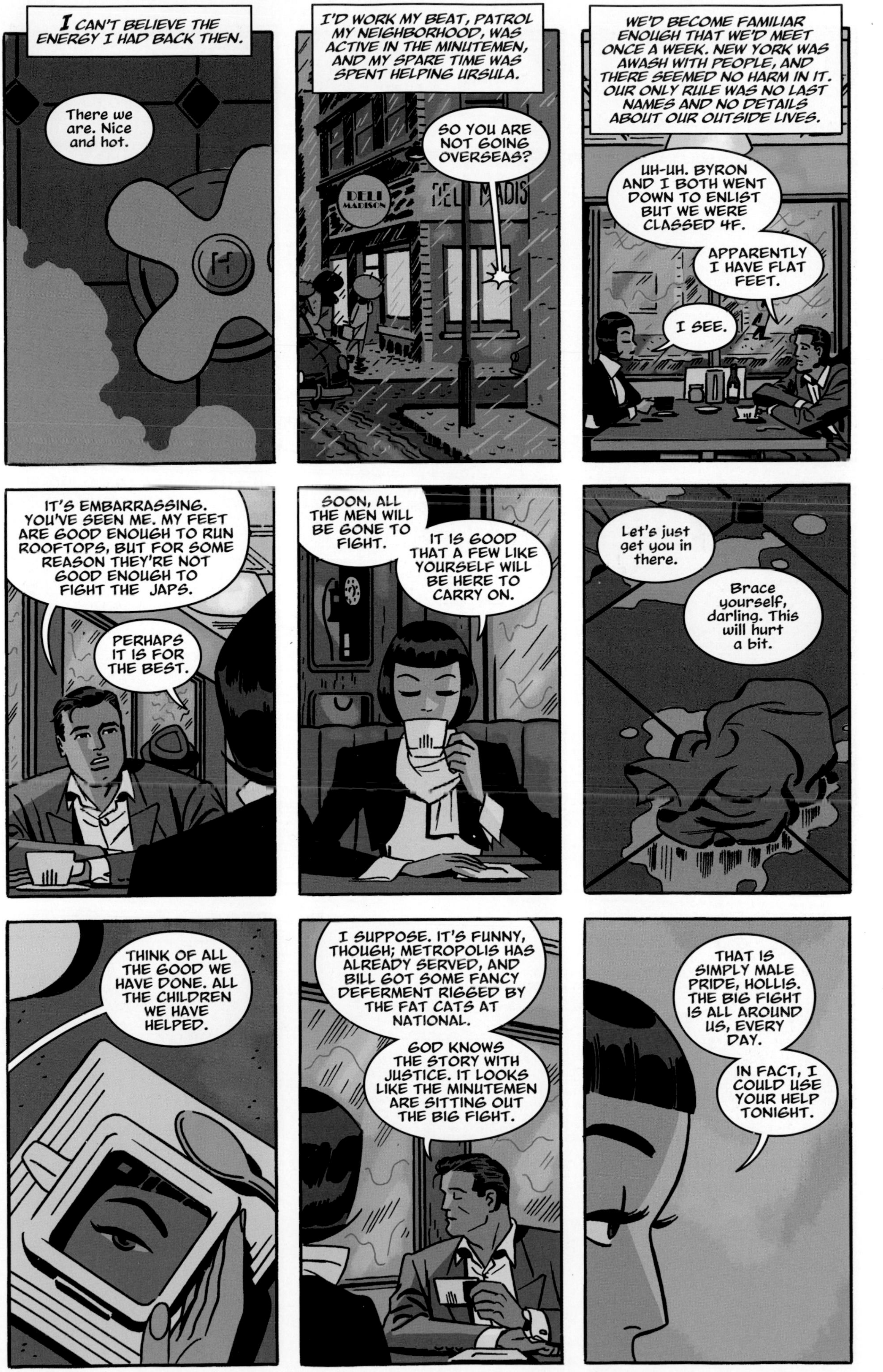
I CAN'T BELIEVE THE ENERGY I HAD BACK THEN.
There we are. Nice and hot.
I'D WORK MY BEAT, PATROL MY NEIGHBORHOOD, WAS ACTIVE IN THE MINUTEMEN, AND MY SPARE TIME WAS SPENT HELPING URSULA.
DELI MADISON
SO YOU ARE NOT GOING OVERSEAS?
WE'D BECOME FAMILIAR ENOUGH THAT WE'D MEET ONCE A WEEK. NEW YORK WAS AWASH WITH PEOPLE, AND THERE SEEMED NO HARM IN IT. OUR ONLY RULE WAS NO LAST NAMES AND NO DETAILS ABOUT OUR OUTSIDE LIVES.
UH-UH. BYRON AND I BOTH WENT DOWN TO ENLIST BUT WE WERE CLASSED 4F.
APPARENTLY I HAVE FLAT FEET.
I SEE.
IT'S EMBARRASSING. YOU'VE SEEN ME. MY FEET ARE GOOD ENOUGH TO RUN ROOFTOPS, BUT FOR SOME REASON THEY'RE NOT GOOD ENOUGH TO FIGHT THE JAPS.
PERHAPS IT IS FOR THE BEST.
SOON, ALL THE MEN WILL BE GONE TO FIGHT.
IT IS GOOD THAT A FEW LIKE YOURSELF WILL BE HERE TO CARRY ON.
Let's just get you in there.
Brace yourself, darling. This will hurt a bit.
THINK OF ALL THE GOOD WE HAVE DONE. ALL THE CHILDREN WE HAVE HELPED.
I SUPPOSE. IT'S FUNNY, THOUGH; METROPOLIS HAS ALREADY SERVED, AND BILL GOT SOME FANCY DEFERMENT RIGGED BY THE FAT CATS AT NATIONAL.
GOD KNOWS THE STORY WITH JUSTICE. IT LOOKS LIKE THE MINUTEMEN ARE SITTING OUT THE BIG FIGHT.
THAT IS SIMPLY MALE PRIDE, HOLLIS. THE BIG FIGHT IS ALL AROUND US, EVERY DAY.
IN FACT, I COULD USE YOUR HELP TONIGHT.

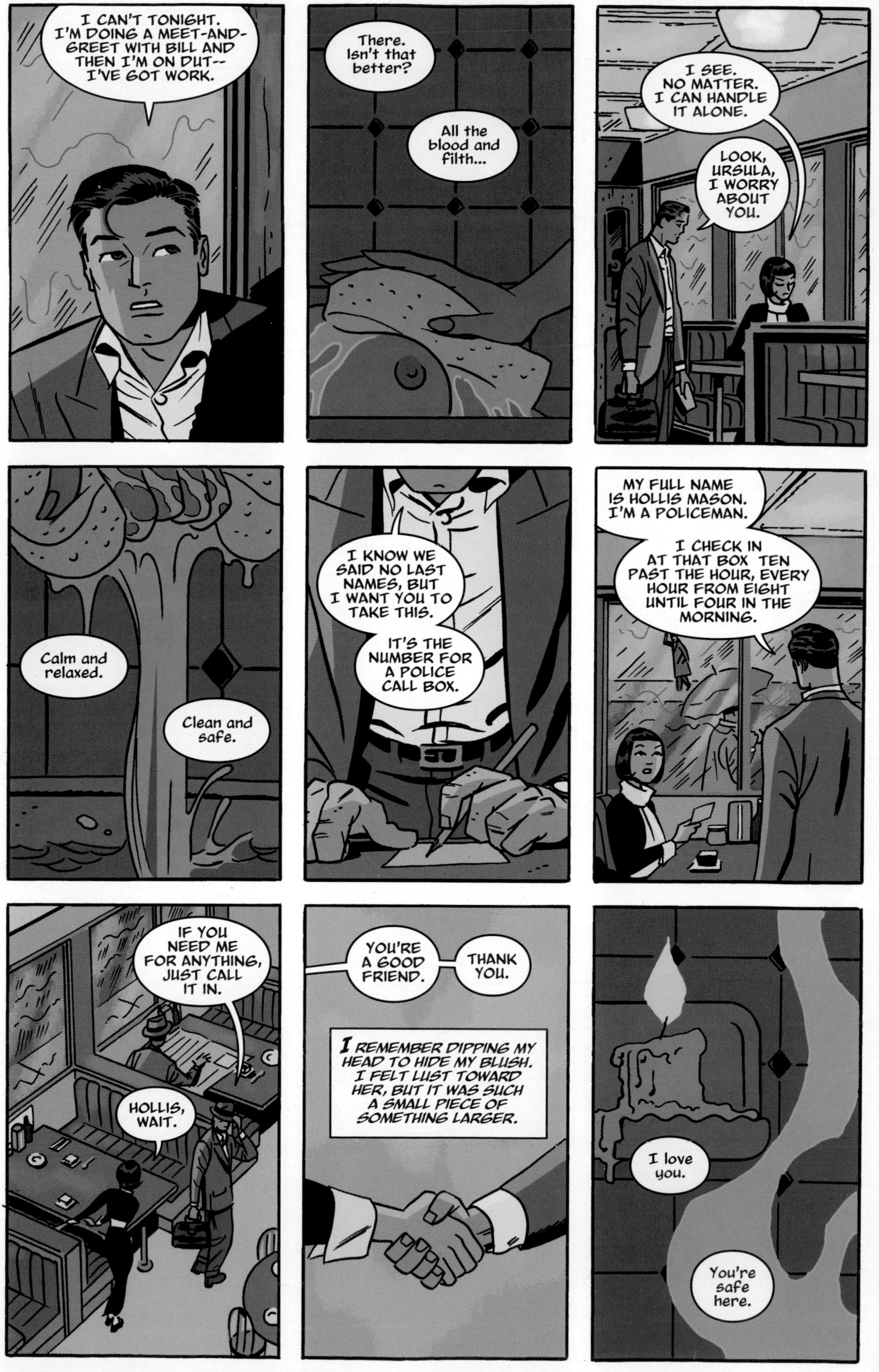

I CAN'T TONIGHT. I'M DOING A MEET-AND-GREET WITH BILL AND THEN I'M ON DUT-- I'VE GOT WORK.
There. Isn't that better?
All the blood and filth...
I SEE. NO MATTER. I CAN HANDLE IT ALONE.
LOOK, URSULA, I WORRY ABOUT YOU.
Calm and relaxed.
Clean and safe.
I KNOW WE SAID NO LAST NAMES, BUT I WANT YOU TO TAKE THIS.
IT'S THE NUMBER FOR A POLICE CALL BOX.
MY FULL NAME IS HOLLIS MASON. I'M A POLICEMAN.
I CHECK IN AT THAT BOX TEN PAST THE HOUR, EVERY HOUR FROM EIGHT UNTIL FOUR IN THE MORNING.
IF YOU NEED ME FOR ANYTHING, JUST CALL IT IN.
HOLLIS, WAIT.
YOU'RE A GOOD FRIEND.
THANK YOU.
I REMEMBER DIPPING MY HEAD TO HIDE MY BLUSH. I FELT LUST TOWARD HER, BUT IT WAS SUCH A SMALL PIECE OF SOMETHING LARGER.
I love you.
You're safe here.

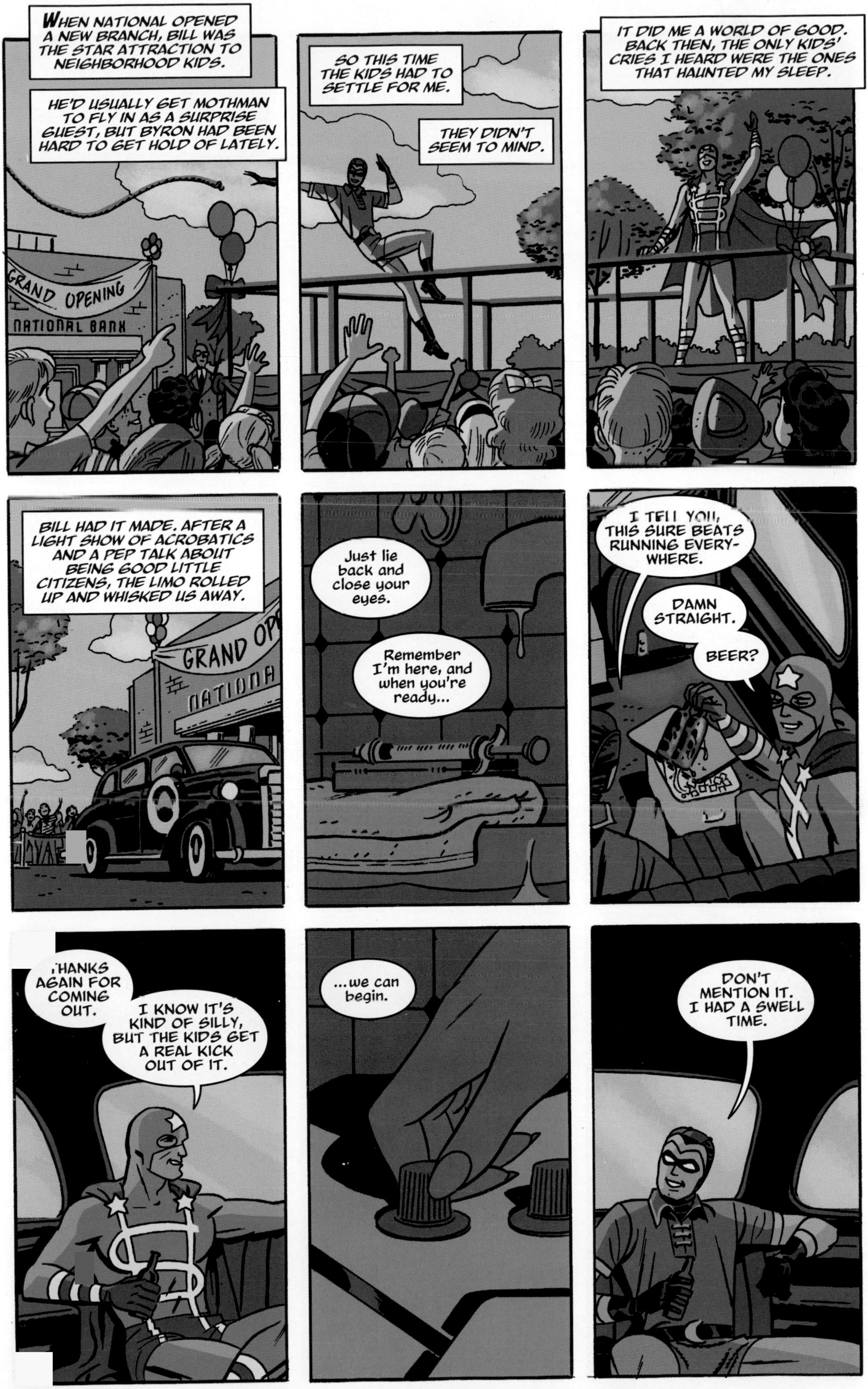
WHEN NATIONAL OPENED A NEW BRANCH, BILL WAS THE STAR ATTRACTION TO NEIGHBORHOOD KIDS.
HE'D USUALLY GET MOTHMAN TO FLY IN AS A SURPRISE GUEST, BUT BYRON HAD BEEN HARD TO GET HOLD OF LATELY.
GRAND OPENING
NATIONAL BANK
SO THIS TIME THE KIDS HAD TO SETTLE FOR ME.
THEY DIDN'T SEEM TO MIND.
IT DID ME A WORLD OF GOOD. BACK THEN, THE ONLY KIDS' CRIES I HEARD WERE THE ONES THAT HAUNTED MY SLEEP.
BILL HAD IT MADE. AFTER A LIGHT SHOW OF ACROBATICS AND A PEP TALK ABOUT BEING GOOD LITTLE CITIZENS, THE LIMO ROLLED UP AND WHISKED US AWAY.
GRAND OP
NATIONA
Just lie back and close your eyes.
Remember I'm here, and when you're ready...
I TELL YOU, THIS SURE BEATS RUNNING EVERY-WHERE.
DAMN STRAIGHT.
BEER?
THANKS AGAIN FOR COMING OUT.
I KNOW IT'S KIND OF SILLY, BUT THE KIDS GET A REAL KICK OUT OF IT.
...we can begin.
DON'T MENTION IT. I HAD A SWELL TIME.

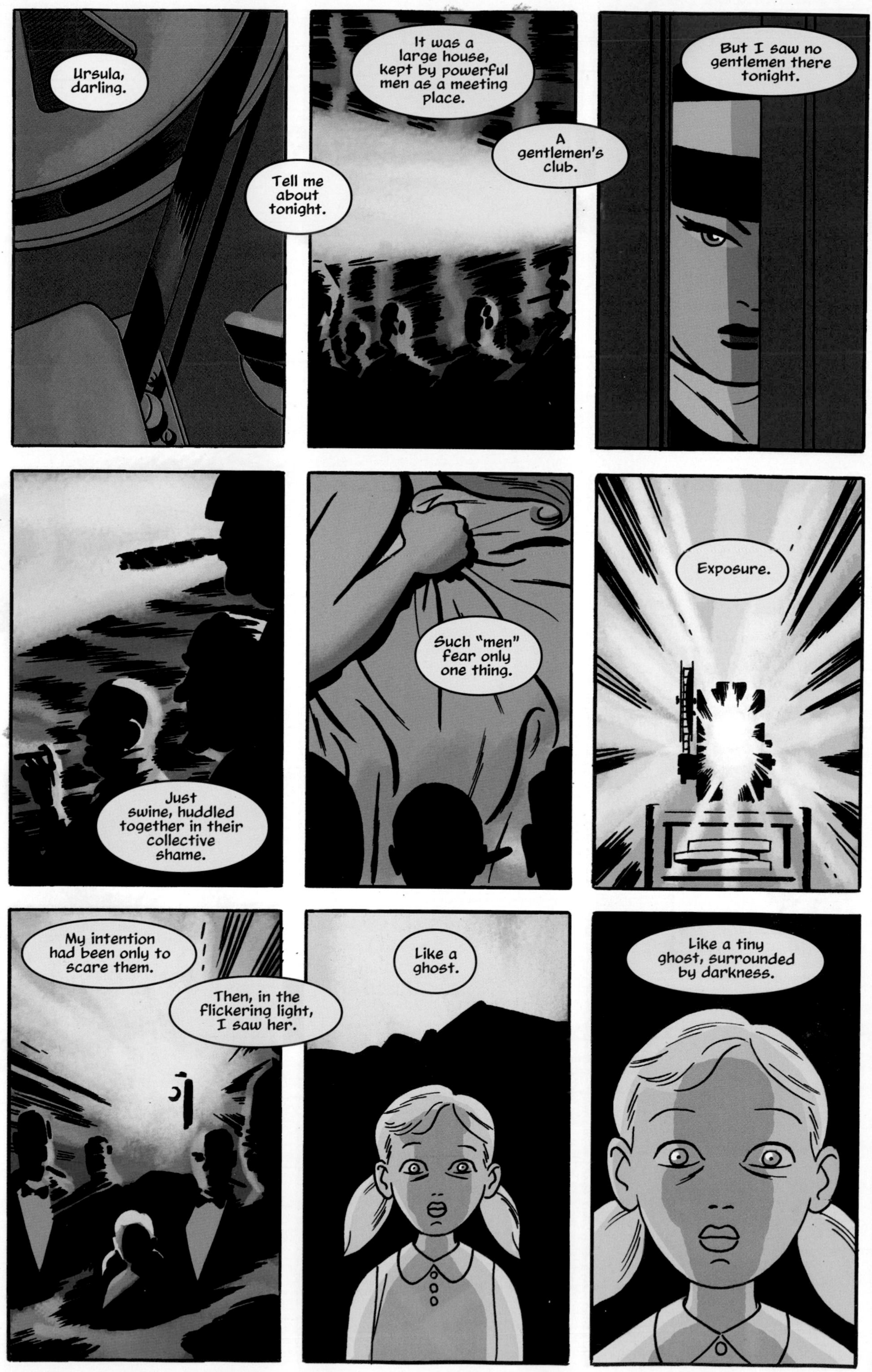
Ursula, darling.
Tell me about tonight.
It was a large house, kept by powerful men as a meeting place.
A gentlemen's club.
But I saw no gentlemen there tonight.
Just swine, huddled together in their collective shame.
Such "men" fear only one thing.
Exposure.
My intention had been only to scare them.
Then, in the flickering light, I saw her.
Like a ghost.
Like a tiny ghost, surrounded by darkness.

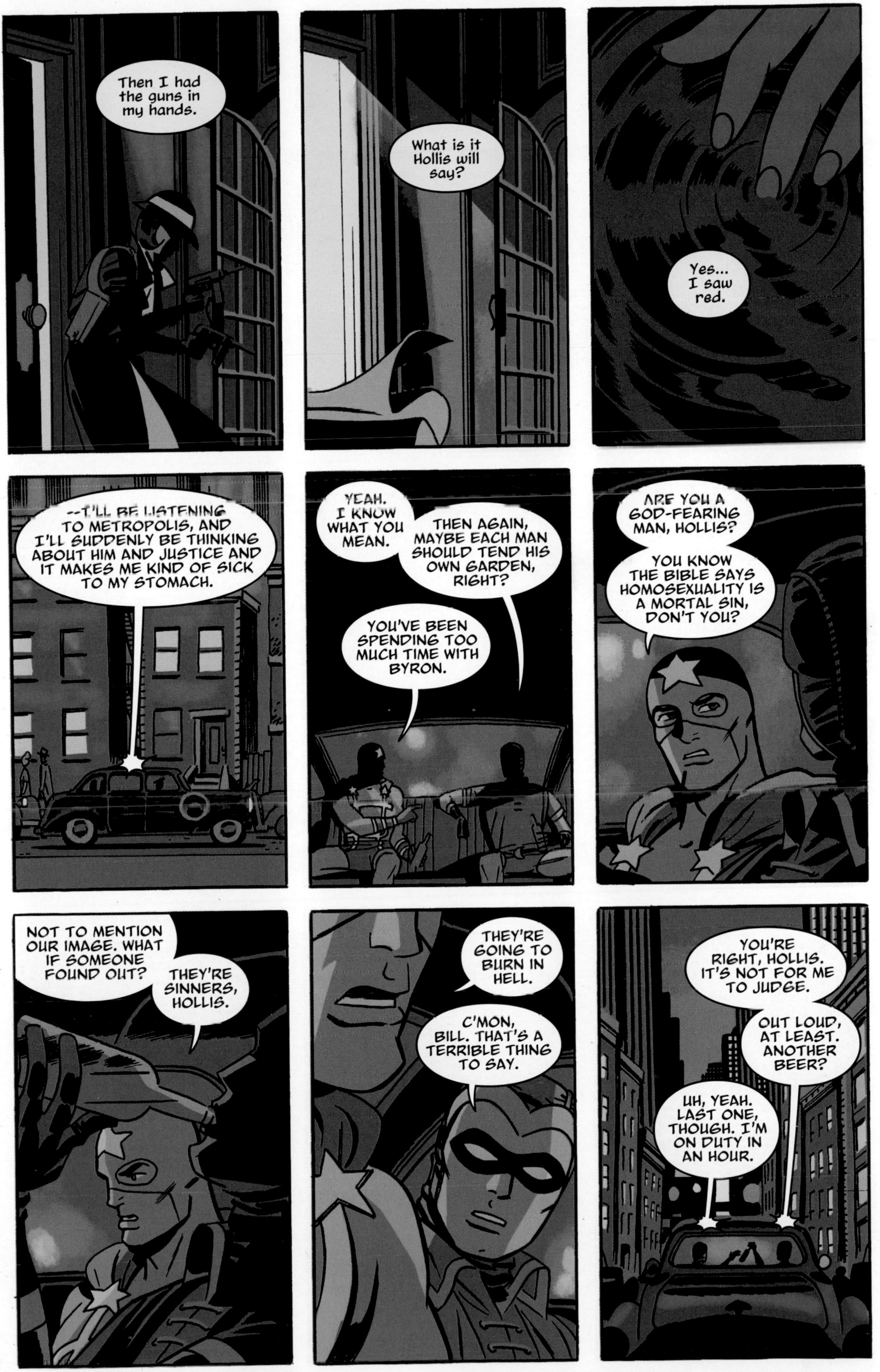
Then I had the guns in my hands.
What is it Hollis will say?
Yes... I saw red.
--I'LL BE LISTENING TO METROPOLIS, AND I'LL SUDDENLY BE THINKING ABOUT HIM AND JUSTICE AND IT MAKES ME KIND OF SICK TO MY STOMACH.
YEAH. I KNOW WHAT YOU MEAN.
THEN AGAIN, MAYBE EACH MAN SHOULD TEND HIS OWN GARDEN, RIGHT?
YOU'VE BEEN SPENDING TOO MUCH TIME WITH BYRON.
ARE YOU A GOD-FEARING MAN, HOLLIS?
YOU KNOW THE BIBLE SAYS HOMOSEXUALITY IS A MORTAL SIN, DON'T YOU?
NOT TO MENTION OUR IMAGE. WHAT IF SOMEONE FOUND OUT?
THEY'RE SINNERS, HOLLIS.
THEY'RE GOING TO BURN IN HELL.
C'MON, BILL. THAT'S A TERRIBLE THING TO SAY.
YOU'RE RIGHT, HOLLIS. IT'S NOT FOR ME TO JUDGE.
OUT LOUD, AT LEAST. ANOTHER BEER?
UH, YEAH. LAST ONE, THOUGH. I'M ON DUTY IN AN HOUR.

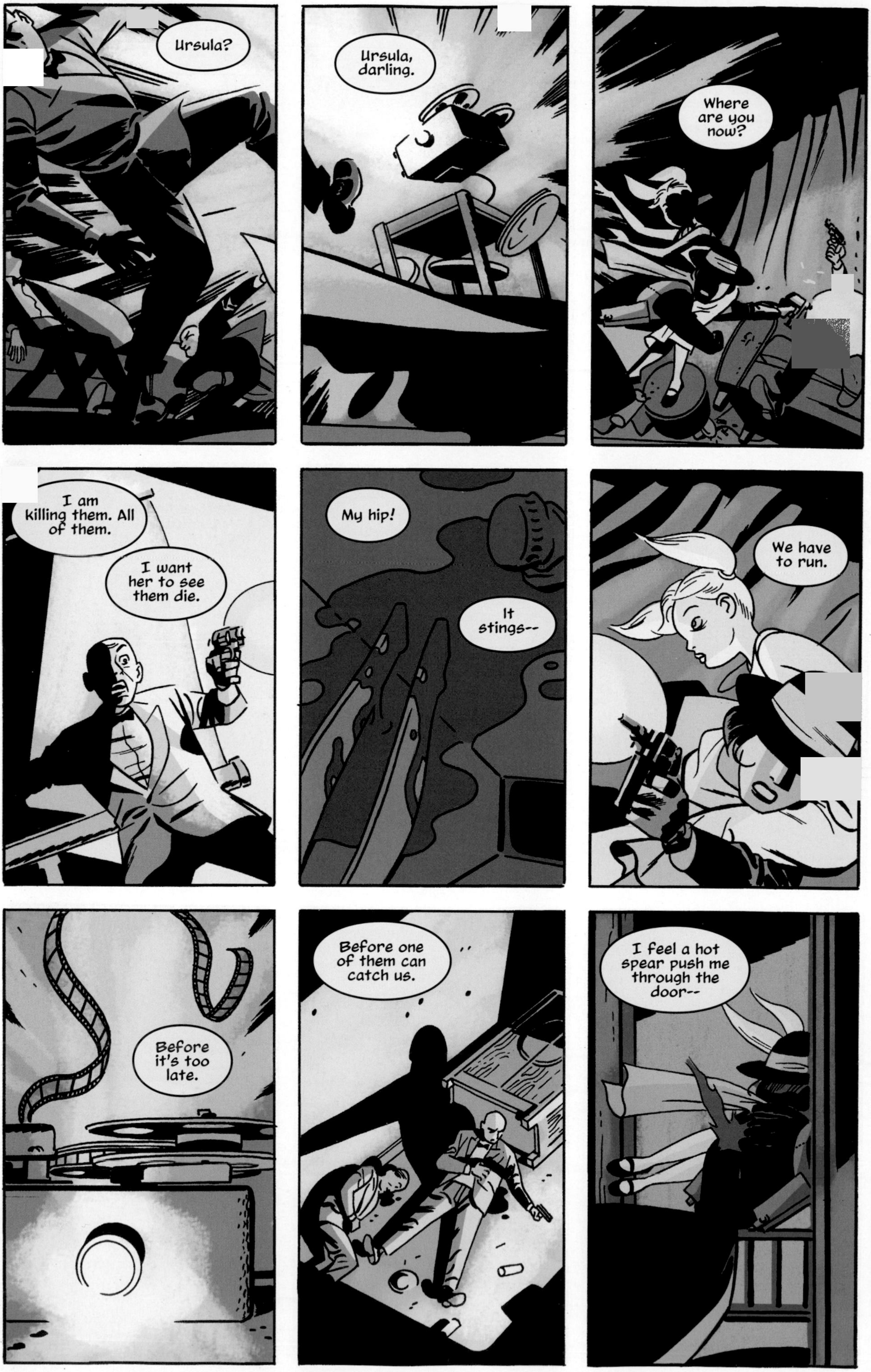
Ursula?
Ursula, darling.
Where are you now?
I am killing them. All of them.
I want her to see them die.
My hip!
It stings--
We have to run.
Before it's too late.
Before one of them can catch us.
I feel a hot spear push me through the door--

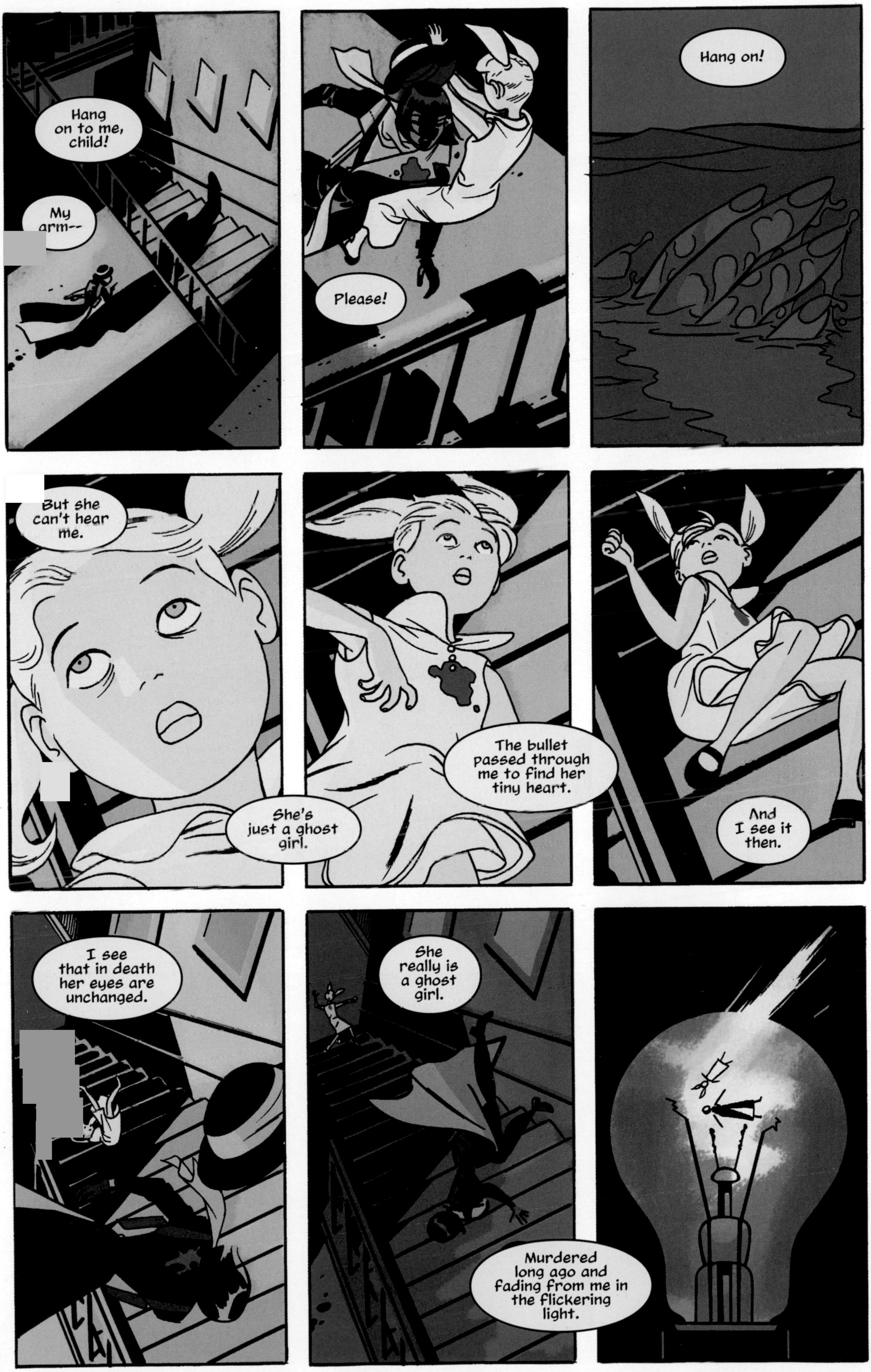
Hang on to me, child!
My arm--
Please!
Hang on!
But she can't hear me.
She's just a ghost girl.
The bullet passed through me to find her tiny heart.
And I see it then.
I see that in death her eyes are unchanged.
She really is a ghost girl.
Murdered long ago and fading from me in the flickering light.

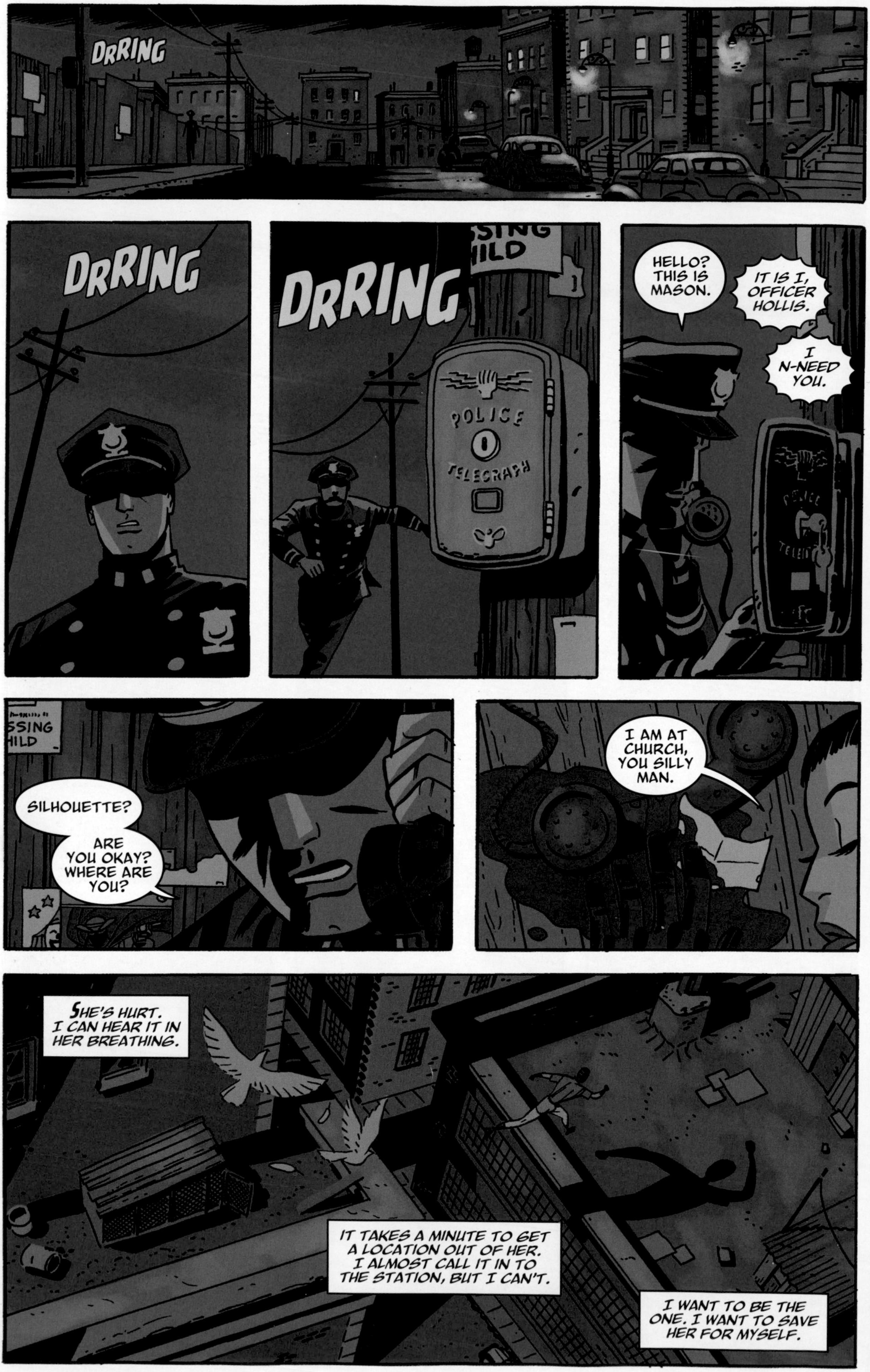
DRRING
DRRING
SSING
HILD
DRRING
POLICE
TELEGRAPH
HELLO? THIS IS MASON.
IT IS I, OFFICER HOLLIS.
I N-NEED YOU.
SSING
HILD
SILHOUETTE?
ARE YOU OKAY? WHERE ARE YOU?
I AM AT CHURCH, YOU SILLY MAN.
SHE'S HURT. I CAN HEAR IT IN HER BREATHING.
IT TAKES A MINUTE TO GET A LOCATION OUT OF HER. I ALMOST CALL IT IN TO THE STATION, BUT I CAN'T.
I WANT TO BE THE ONE. I WANT TO SAVE HER FOR MYSELF.

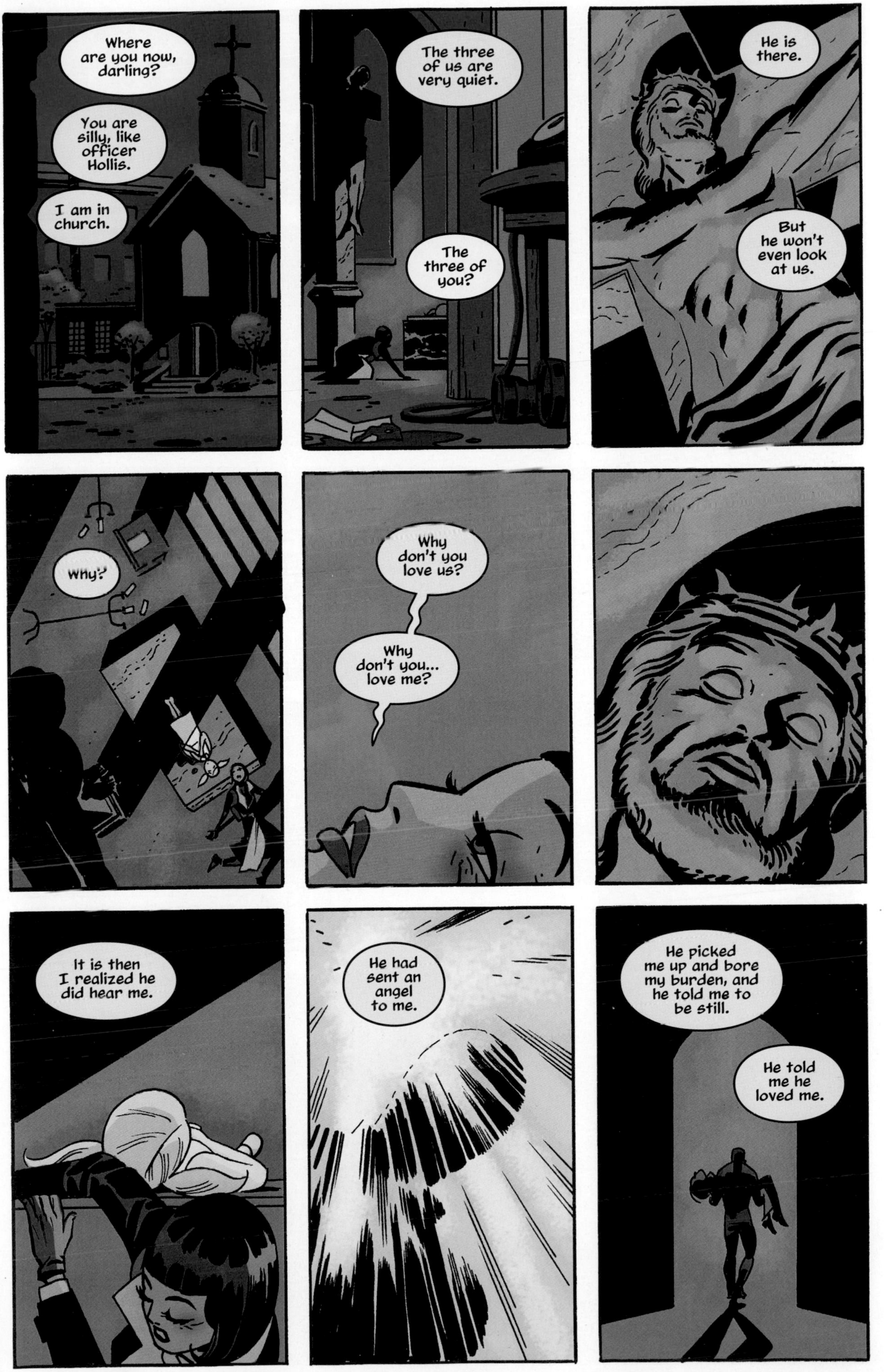
Where are you now, darling?
You are silly, like officer Hollis.
I am in church.
The three of us are very quiet.
The three of you?
He is there.
But he won't even look at us.
Why?
Why don't you love us?
Why don't you... love me?
It is then I realized he did hear me.
He had sent an angel to me.
He picked me up and bore my burden, and he told me to be still.
He told me he loved me.

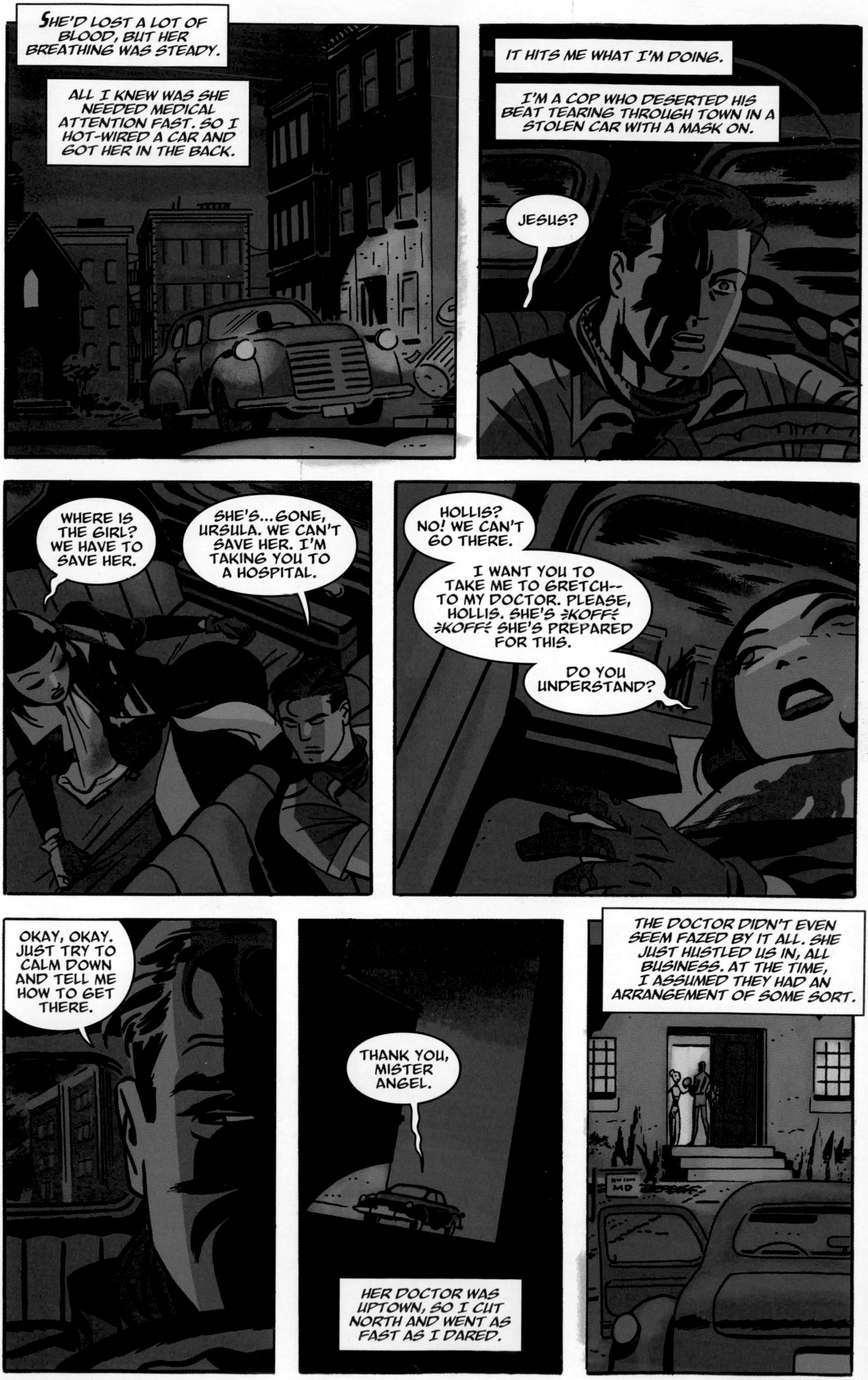
SHE'D LOST A LOT OF BLOOD, BUT HER BREATHING WAS STEADY.
ALL I KNEW WAS SHE NEEDED MEDICAL ATTENTION FAST. SO I HOT-WIRED A CAR AND GOT HER IN THE BACK.
IT HITS ME WHAT I'M DOING.
I'M A COP WHO DESERTED HIS BEAT TEARING THROUGH TOWN IN A STOLEN CAR WITH A MASK ON.
JESUS?
WHERE IS THE GIRL? WE HAVE TO SAVE HER.
SHE'S...GONE, URSULA. WE CAN'T SAVE HER. I'M TAKING YOU TO A HOSPITAL.
HOLLIS? NO! WE CAN'T GO THERE.
I WANT YOU TO TAKE ME TO GRETCH-- TO MY DOCTOR. PLEASE, HOLLIS. SHE'S *KOFF* *KOFF* SHE'S PREPARED FOR THIS.
DO YOU UNDERSTAND?
OKAY, OKAY. JUST TRY TO CALM DOWN AND TELL ME HOW TO GET THERE.
THANK YOU, MISTER ANGEL.
HER DOCTOR WAS UPTOWN, SO I CUT NORTH AND WENT AS FAST AS I DARED.
THE DOCTOR DIDN'T EVEN SEEM FAZED BY IT ALL. SHE JUST HUSTLED US IN, ALL BUSINESS. AT THE TIME, I ASSUMED THEY HAD AN ARRANGEMENT OF SOME SORT.
MD

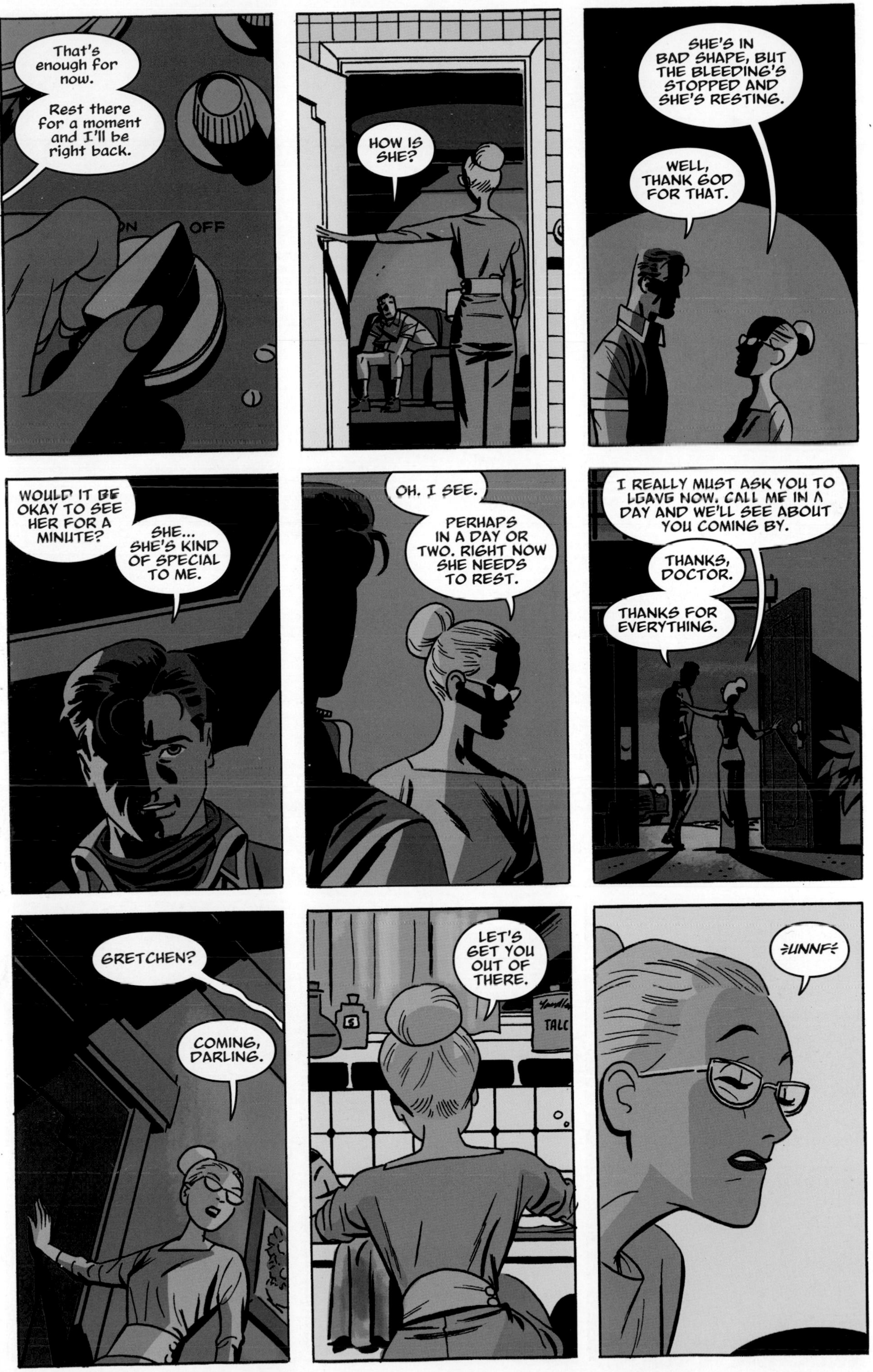
That's enough for now.
Rest there for a moment and I'll be right back.
ON OFF
HOW IS SHE?
SHE'S IN BAD SHAPE, BUT THE BLEEDING'S STOPPED AND SHE'S RESTING.
WELL, THANK GOD FOR THAT.
WOULD IT BE OKAY TO SEE HER FOR A MINUTE?
SHE... SHE'S KIND OF SPECIAL TO ME.
OH. I SEE.
PERHAPS IN A DAY OR TWO. RIGHT NOW SHE NEEDS TO REST.
I REALLY MUST ASK YOU TO LEAVE NOW. CALL ME IN A DAY AND WE'LL SEE ABOUT YOU COMING BY.
THANKS, DOCTOR.
THANKS FOR EVERYTHING.
GRETCHEN?
COMING, DARLING.
LET'S GET YOU OUT OF THERE.
TALC
UNNF

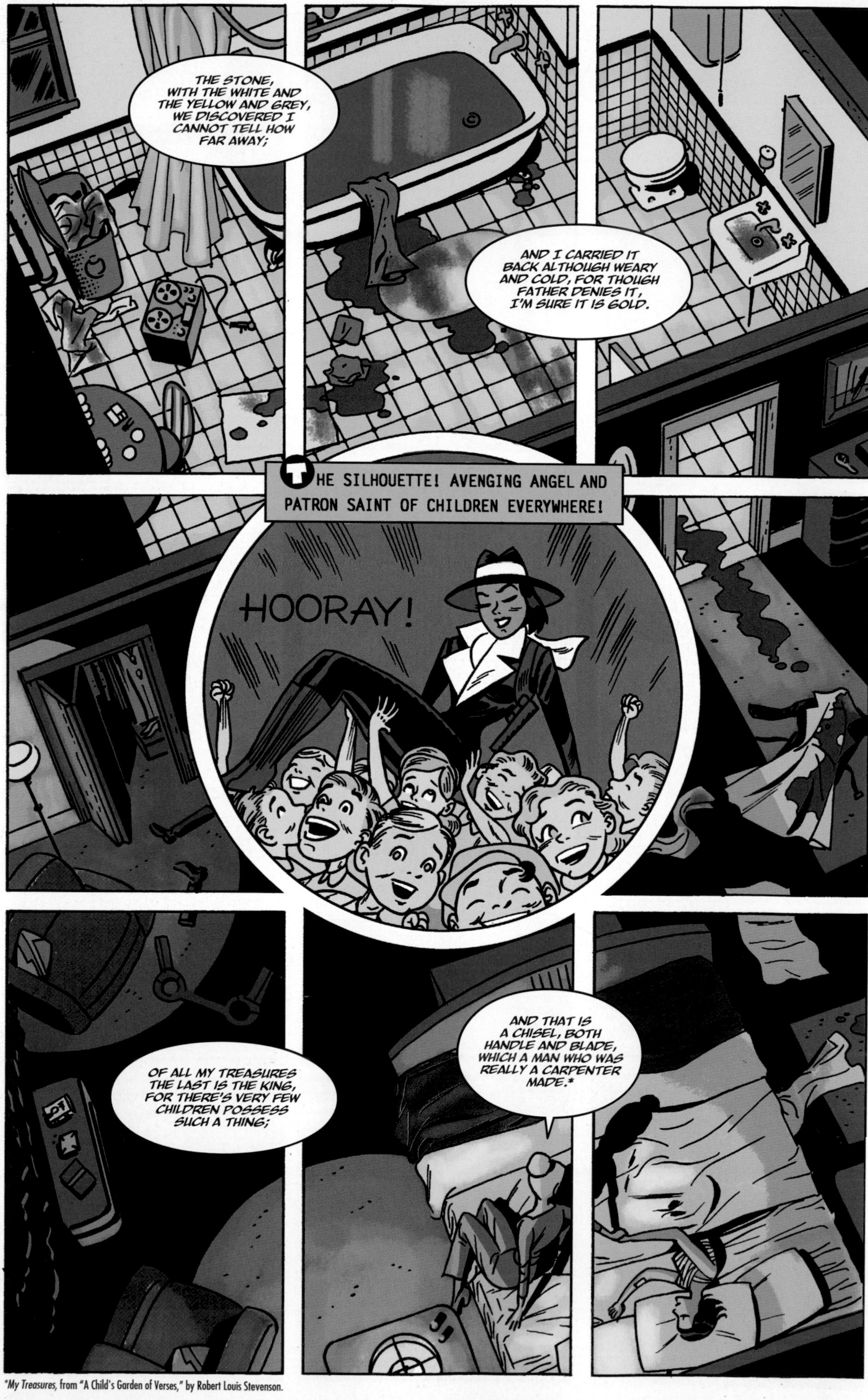
THE STONE, WITH THE WHITE AND THE YELLOW AND GREY, WE DISCOVERED I CANNOT TELL HOW FAR AWAY;
AND I CARRIED IT BACK ALTHOUGH WEARY AND COLD, FOR THOUGH FATHER DENIES IT, I'M SURE IT IS GOLD.
THE SILHOUETTE! AVENGING ANGEL AND PATRON SAINT OF CHILDREN EVERYWHERE!
HOORAY!
OF ALL MY TREASURES THE LAST IS THE KING, FOR THERE'S VERY FEW CHILDREN POSSESS SUCH A THING;
AND THAT IS A CHISEL, BOTH HANDLE AND BLADE, WHICH A MAN WHO WAS REALLY A CARPENTER MADE.*

**My Treasures*, from "A Child's Garden of Verses," by Robert Louis Stevenson.

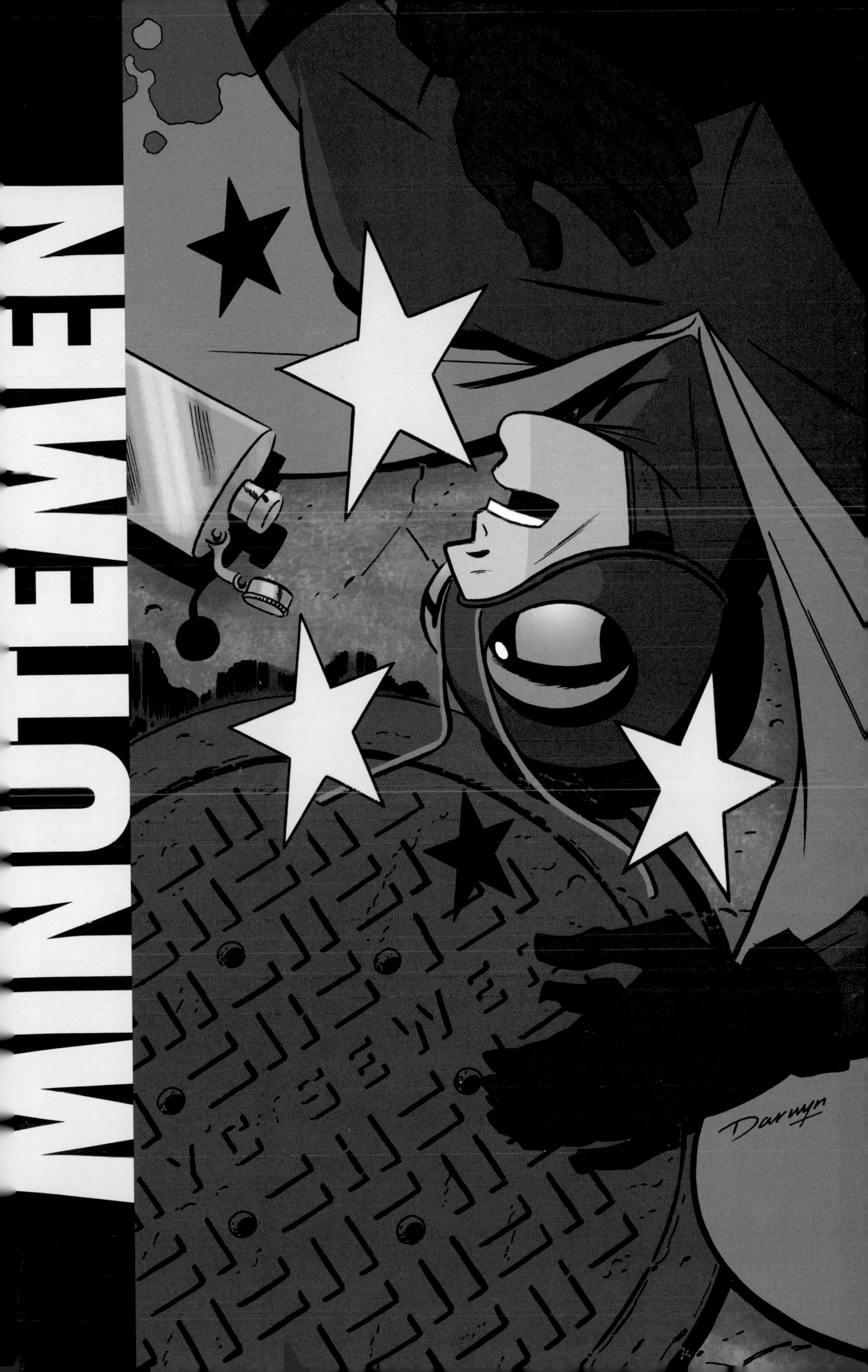
MINUTEMEN
Darwyn

MINUTEMEN

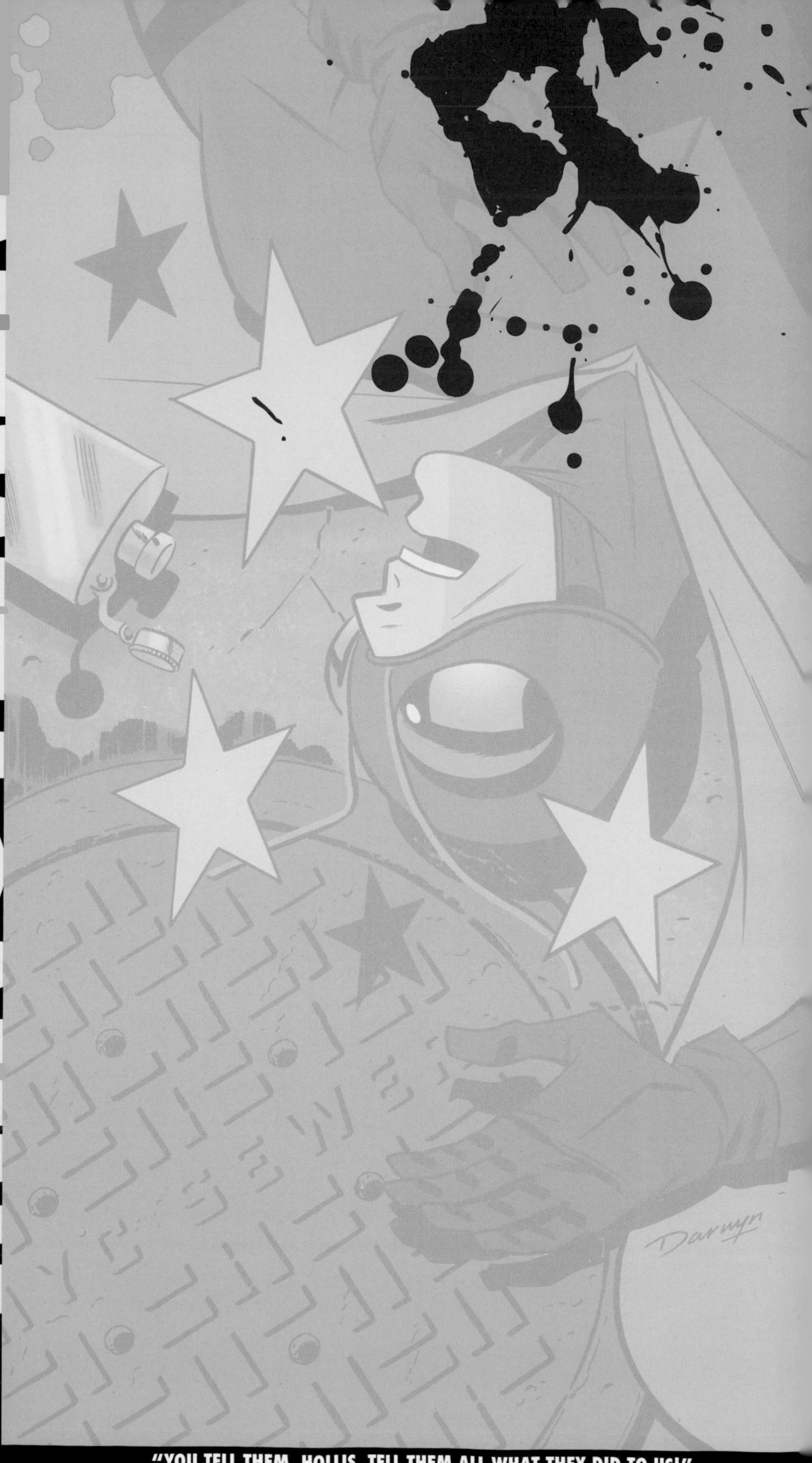

"YOU TELL THEM, HOLLIS. TELL THEM ALL WHAT THEY DID TO US!"

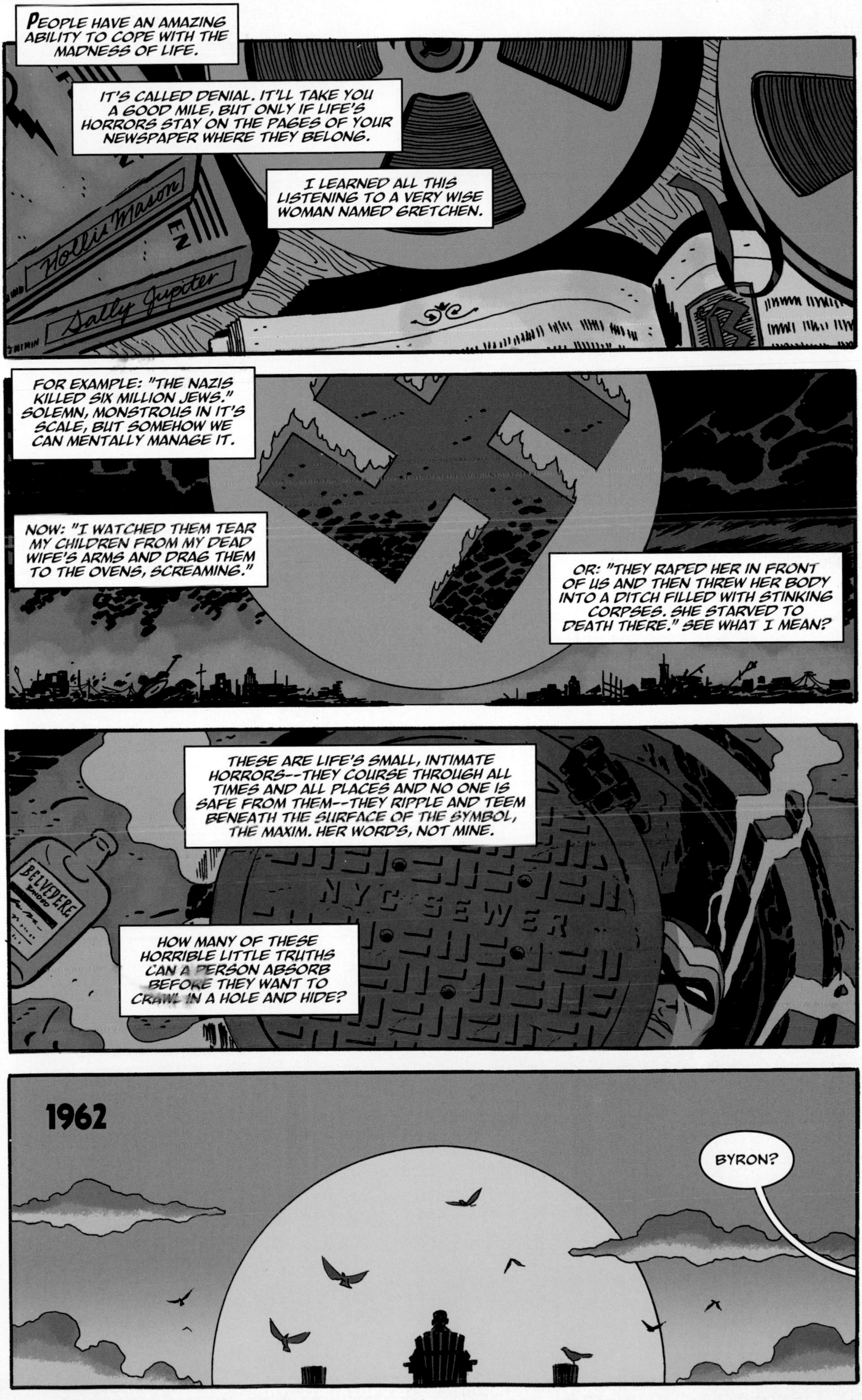
PEOPLE HAVE AN AMAZING ABILITY TO COPE WITH THE MADNESS OF LIFE.
IT'S CALLED DENIAL. IT'LL TAKE YOU A GOOD MILE, BUT ONLY IF LIFE'S HORRORS STAY ON THE PAGES OF YOUR NEWSPAPER WHERE THEY BELONG.
I LEARNED ALL THIS LISTENING TO A VERY WISE WOMAN NAMED GRETCHEN.
Hollis Mason
Sally Jupiter
FOR EXAMPLE: "THE NAZIS KILLED SIX MILLION JEWS." SOLEMN, MONSTROUS IN IT'S SCALE, BUT SOMEHOW WE CAN MENTALLY MANAGE IT.
NOW: "I WATCHED THEM TEAR MY CHILDREN FROM MY DEAD WIFE'S ARMS AND DRAG THEM TO THE OVENS, SCREAMING."
OR: "THEY RAPED HER IN FRONT OF US AND THEN THREW HER BODY INTO A DITCH FILLED WITH STINKING CORPSES. SHE STARVED TO DEATH THERE." SEE WHAT I MEAN?
THESE ARE LIFE'S SMALL, INTIMATE HORRORS--THEY COURSE THROUGH ALL TIMES AND ALL PLACES AND NO ONE IS SAFE FROM THEM--THEY RIPPLE AND TEEM BENEATH THE SURFACE OF THE SYMBOL, THE MAXIM. HER WORDS, NOT MINE.
BELVEDERE
NYC SEWER
HOW MANY OF THESE HORRIBLE LITTLE TRUTHS CAN A PERSON ABSORB BEFORE THEY WANT TO CRAWL IN A HOLE AND HIDE?
1962
BYRON?

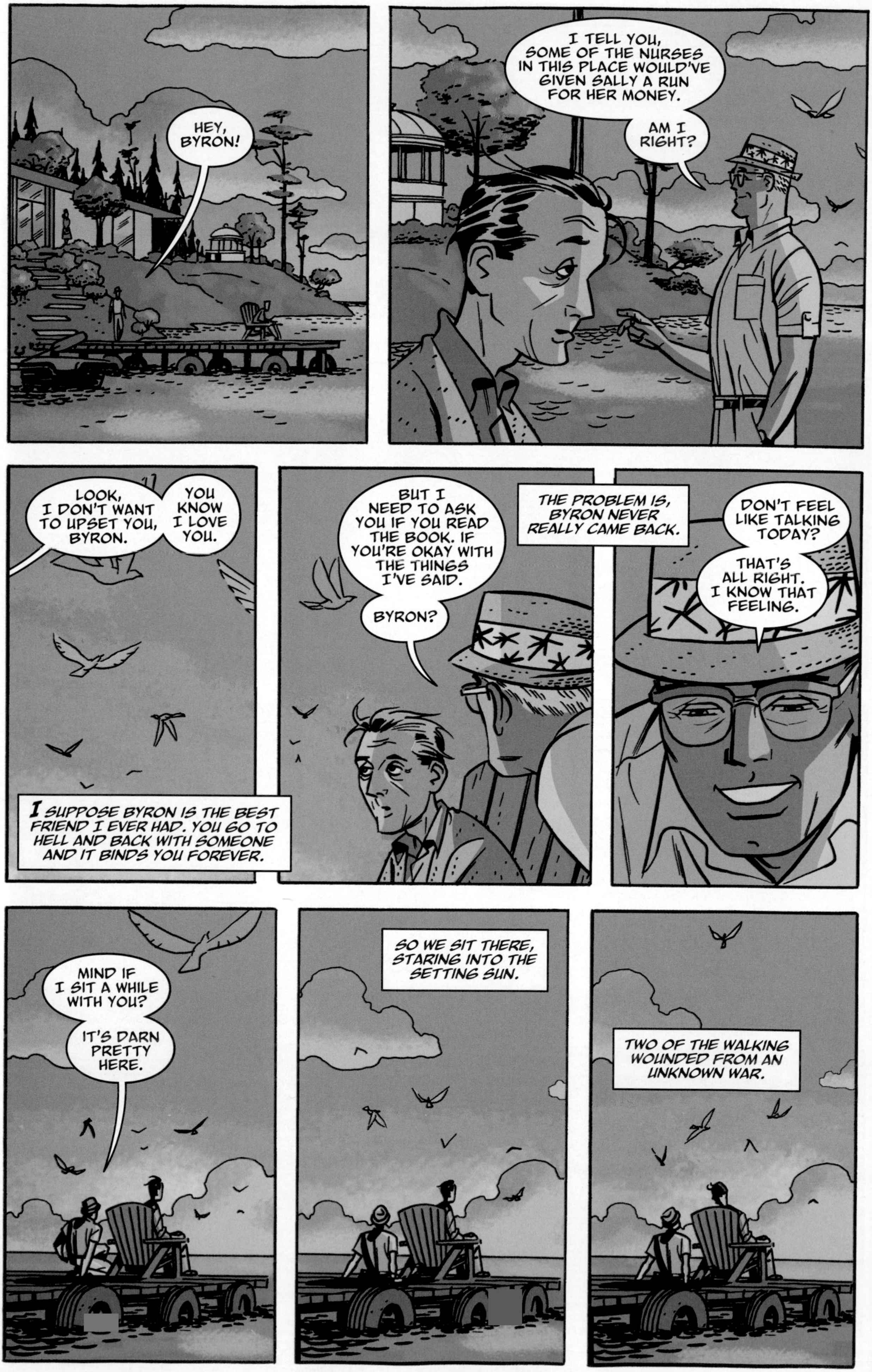
HEY, BYRON!
I TELL YOU, SOME OF THE NURSES IN THIS PLACE WOULD'VE GIVEN SALLY A RUN FOR HER MONEY.
AM I RIGHT?
LOOK, I DON'T WANT TO UPSET YOU, BYRON.
YOU KNOW I LOVE YOU.
I SUPPOSE BYRON IS THE BEST FRIEND I EVER HAD. YOU GO TO HELL AND BACK WITH SOMEONE AND IT BINDS YOU FOREVER.
BUT I NEED TO ASK YOU IF YOU READ THE BOOK. IF YOU'RE OKAY WITH THE THINGS I'VE SAID.
BYRON?
THE PROBLEM IS, BYRON NEVER REALLY CAME BACK.
DON'T FEEL LIKE TALKING TODAY?
THAT'S ALL RIGHT. I KNOW THAT FEELING.
MIND IF I SIT A WHILE WITH YOU?
IT'S DARN PRETTY HERE.
SO WE SIT THERE, STARING INTO THE SETTING SUN.
TWO OF THE WALKING WOUNDED FROM AN UNKNOWN WAR.

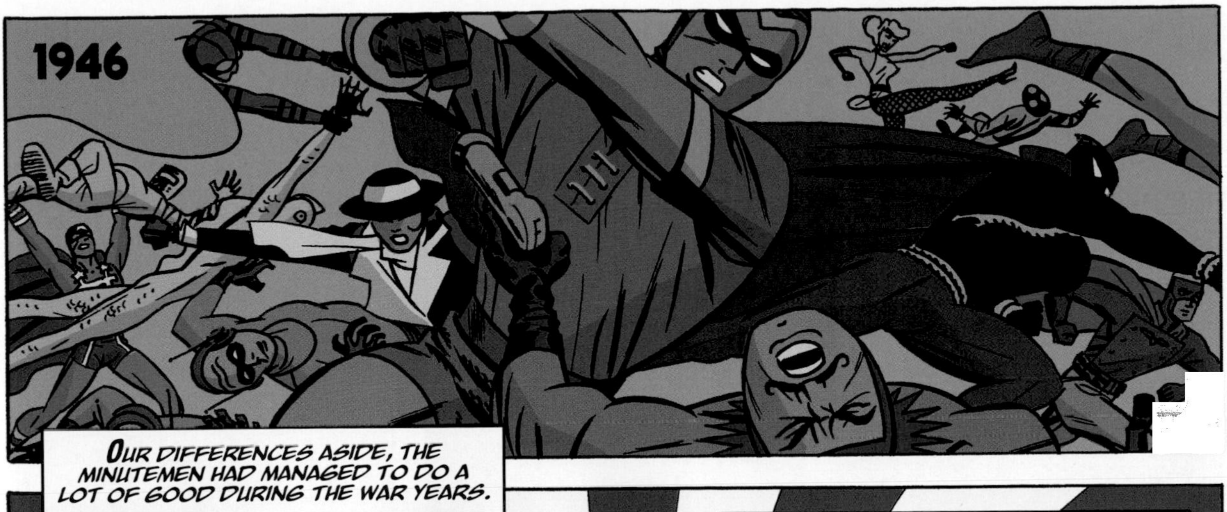
1946
OUR DIFFERENCES ASIDE, THE MINUTEMEN HAD MANAGED TO DO A LOT OF GOOD DURING THE WAR YEARS.

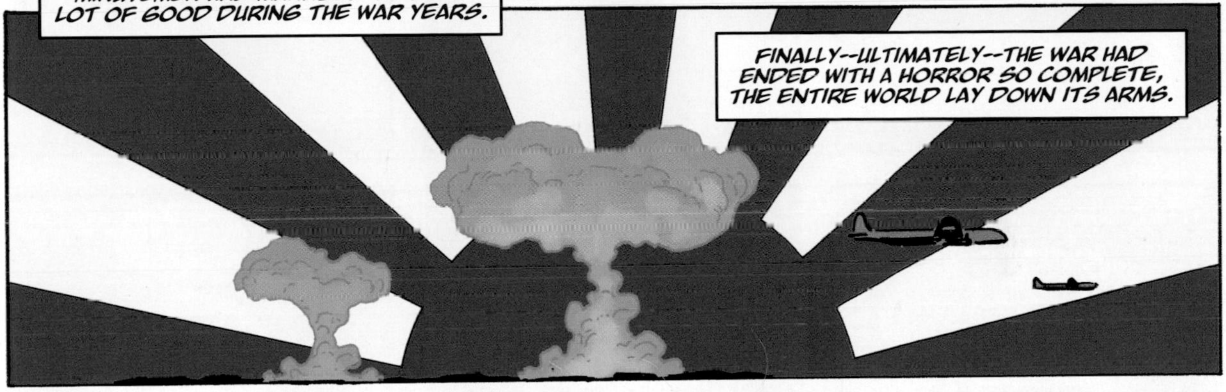
FINALLY--ULTIMATELY--THE WAR HAD ENDED WITH A HORROR SO COMPLETE, THE ENTIRE WORLD LAY DOWN ITS ARMS.

CHAPTER FOUR: WAR STORIES

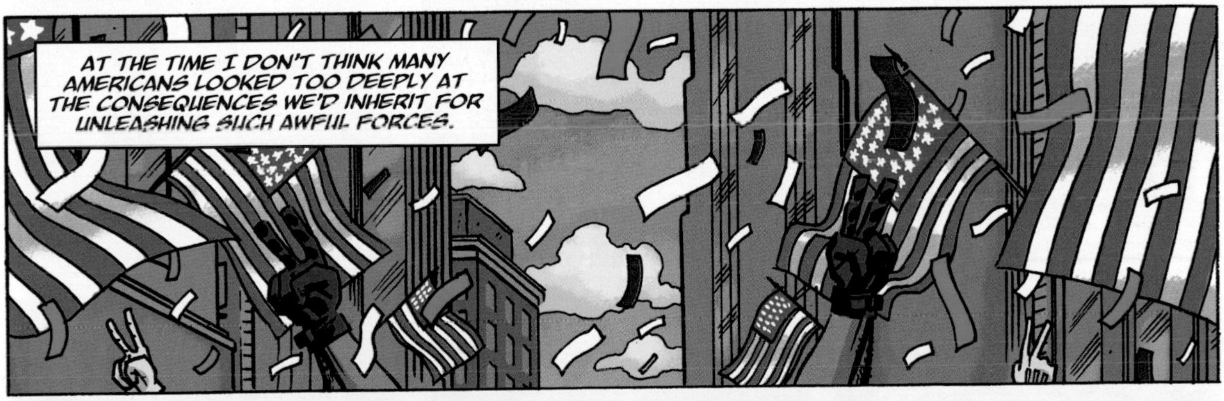
AT THE TIME I DON'T THINK MANY AMERICANS LOOKED TOO DEEPLY AT THE CONSEQUENCES WE'D INHERIT FOR UNLEASHING SUCH AWFUL FORCES.

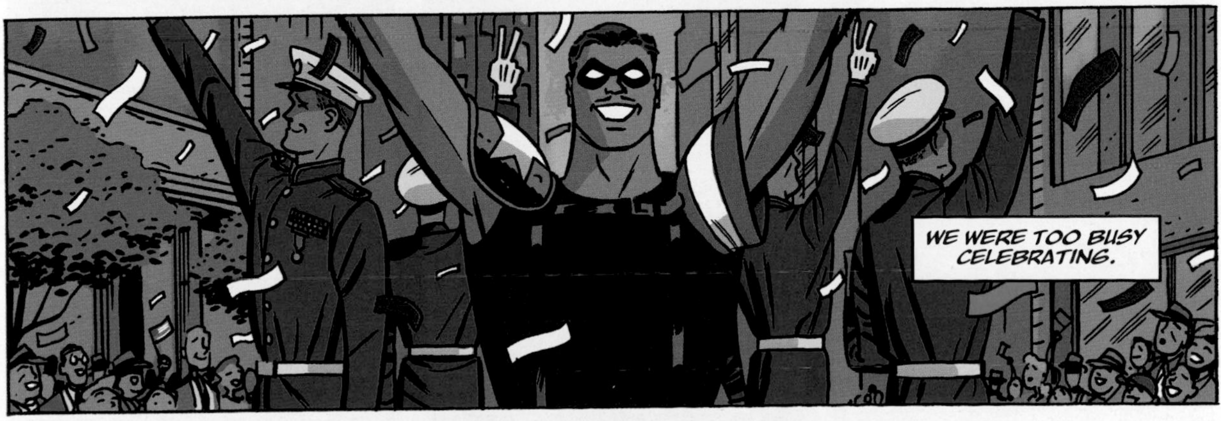
WE WERE TOO BUSY CELEBRATING.

DARWYN COOKE WRITER & ARTIST

PHIL NOTO COLORIST **JARED K. FLETCHER** LETTERER **DARWYN COOKE** COVER ARTIST **STEVE RUDE & GLENN WHITMORE** VARIANT COVER ARTISTS

CAMILLA ZHANG ASSISTANT EDITOR **WIL MOSS** ASSOCIATE EDITOR **MARK CHIARELLO** EDITOR

WATCHMEN CREATED BY **ALAN MOORE** & **DAVE GIBBONS**

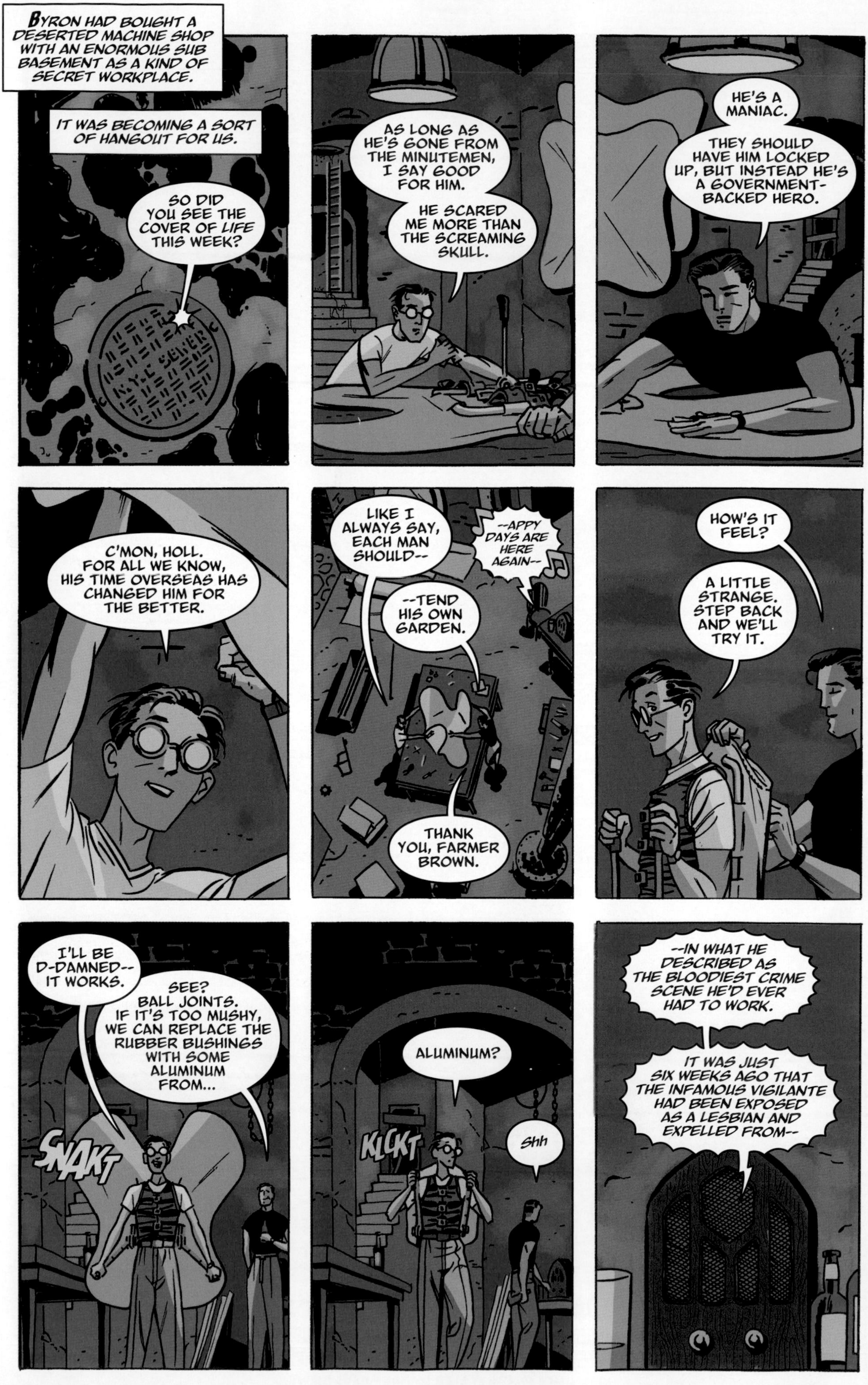
BYRON HAD BOUGHT A DESERTED MACHINE SHOP WITH AN ENORMOUS SUB BASEMENT AS A KIND OF SECRET WORKPLACE.
IT WAS BECOMING A SORT OF HANGOUT FOR US.
SO DID YOU SEE THE COVER OF LIFE THIS WEEK?
AS LONG AS HE'S GONE FROM THE MINUTEMEN, I SAY GOOD FOR HIM.
HE SCARED ME MORE THAN THE SCREAMING SKULL.
HE'S A MANIAC.
THEY SHOULD HAVE HIM LOCKED UP, BUT INSTEAD HE'S A GOVERNMENT-BACKED HERO.
C'MON, HOLL. FOR ALL WE KNOW, HIS TIME OVERSEAS HAS CHANGED HIM FOR THE BETTER.
LIKE I ALWAYS SAY, EACH MAN SHOULD--
--APPY DAYS ARE HERE AGAIN--
--TEND HIS OWN GARDEN.
THANK YOU, FARMER BROWN.
HOW'S IT FEEL?
A LITTLE STRANGE. STEP BACK AND WE'LL TRY IT.
I'LL BE D-DAMNED-- IT WORKS.
SEE? BALL JOINTS. IF IT'S TOO MUSHY, WE CAN REPLACE THE RUBBER BUSHINGS WITH SOME ALUMINUM FROM...
SNAKT
ALUMINUM?
KLCKT
Shh
--IN WHAT HE DESCRIBED AS THE BLOODIEST CRIME SCENE HE'D EVER HAD TO WORK.
IT WAS JUST SIX WEEKS AGO THAT THE INFAMOUS VIGILANTE HAD BEEN EXPOSED AS A LESBIAN AND EXPELLED FROM--

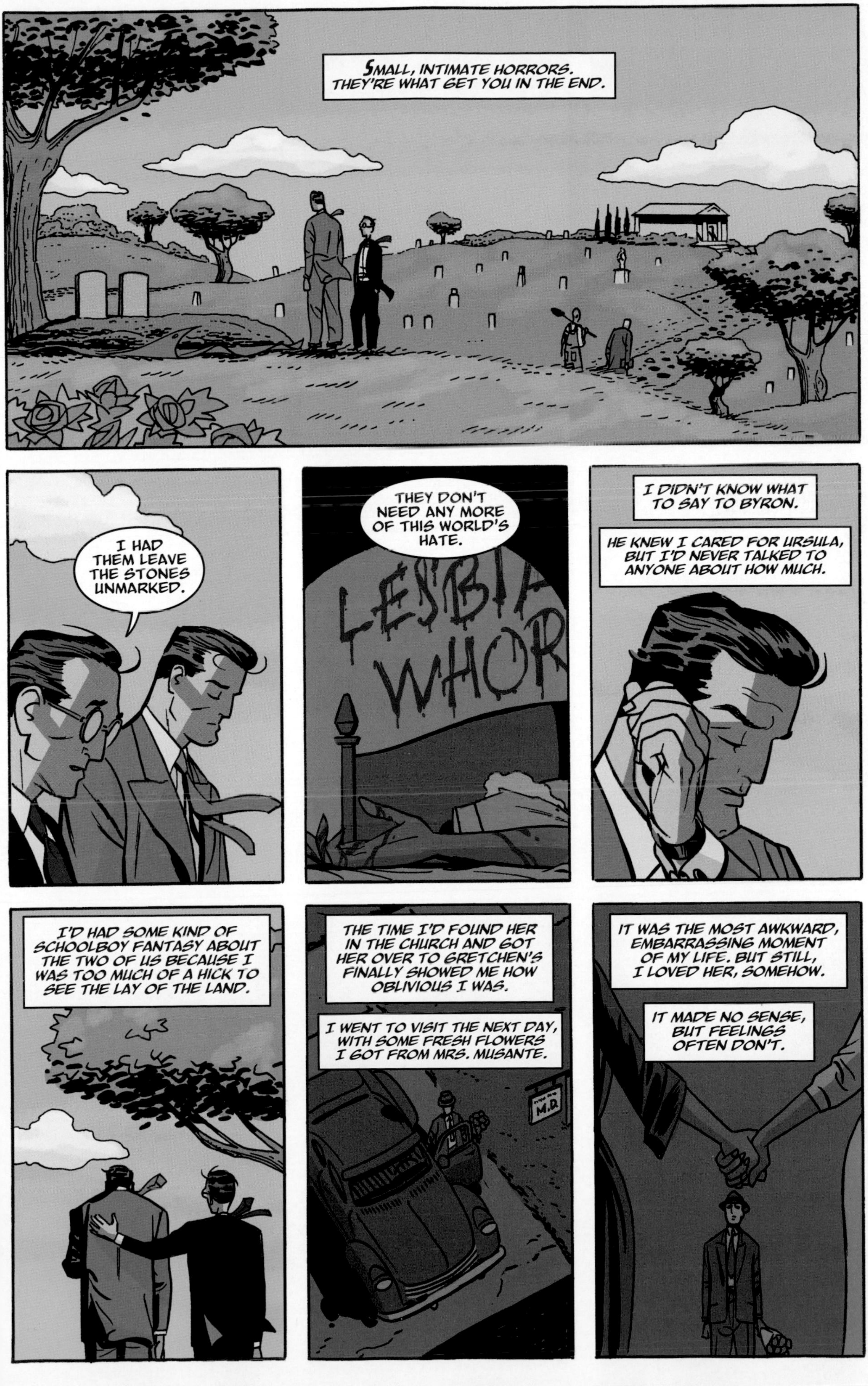
SMALL, INTIMATE HORRORS. THEY'RE WHAT GET YOU IN THE END.
I HAD THEM LEAVE THE STONES UNMARKED.
THEY DON'T NEED ANY MORE OF THIS WORLD'S HATE.
LESBIA
WHOR
I DIDN'T KNOW WHAT TO SAY TO BYRON.
HE KNEW I CARED FOR URSULA, BUT I'D NEVER TALKED TO ANYONE ABOUT HOW MUCH.
I'D HAD SOME KIND OF SCHOOLBOY FANTASY ABOUT THE TWO OF US BECAUSE I WAS TOO MUCH OF A HICK TO SEE THE LAY OF THE LAND.
THE TIME I'D FOUND HER IN THE CHURCH AND GOT HER OVER TO GRETCHEN'S FINALLY SHOWED ME HOW OBLIVIOUS I WAS.
I WENT TO VISIT THE NEXT DAY, WITH SOME FRESH FLOWERS I GOT FROM MRS. MUSANTE.
M.D.
IT WAS THE MOST AWKWARD, EMBARRASSING MOMENT OF MY LIFE. BUT STILL, I LOVED HER, SOMEHOW.
IT MADE NO SENSE, BUT FEELINGS OFTEN DON'T.

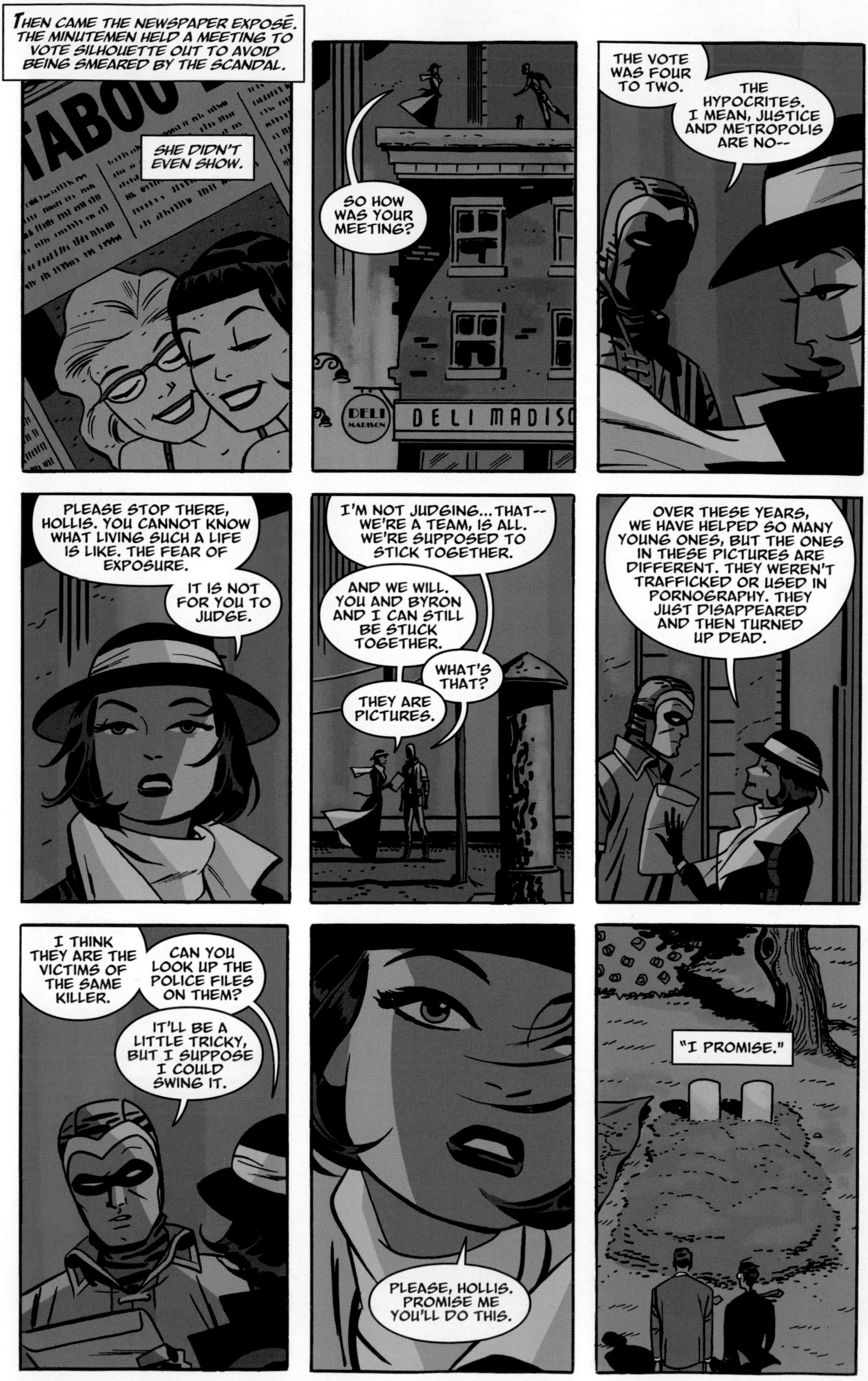
Then came the newspaper exposé. The Minutemen held a meeting to vote Silhouette out to avoid being smeared by the scandal.
TABOO
She didn't even show.
So how was your meeting?
DELI MADISON
DELI MADISO
The vote was four to two.
The hypocrites. I mean, Justice and Metropolis are no--
Please stop there, Hollis. You cannot know what living such a life is like. The fear of exposure.
It is not for you to judge.
I'm not judging... that-- we're a team, is all. We're supposed to stick together.
And we will. You and Byron and I can still be stuck together.
What's that?
They are pictures.
Over these years, we have helped so many young ones, but the ones in these pictures are different. They weren't trafficked or used in pornography. They just disappeared and then turned up dead.
I think they are the victims of the same killer.
Can you look up the police files on them?
It'll be a little tricky, but I suppose I could swing it.
Please, Hollis. Promise me you'll do this.
"I promise."

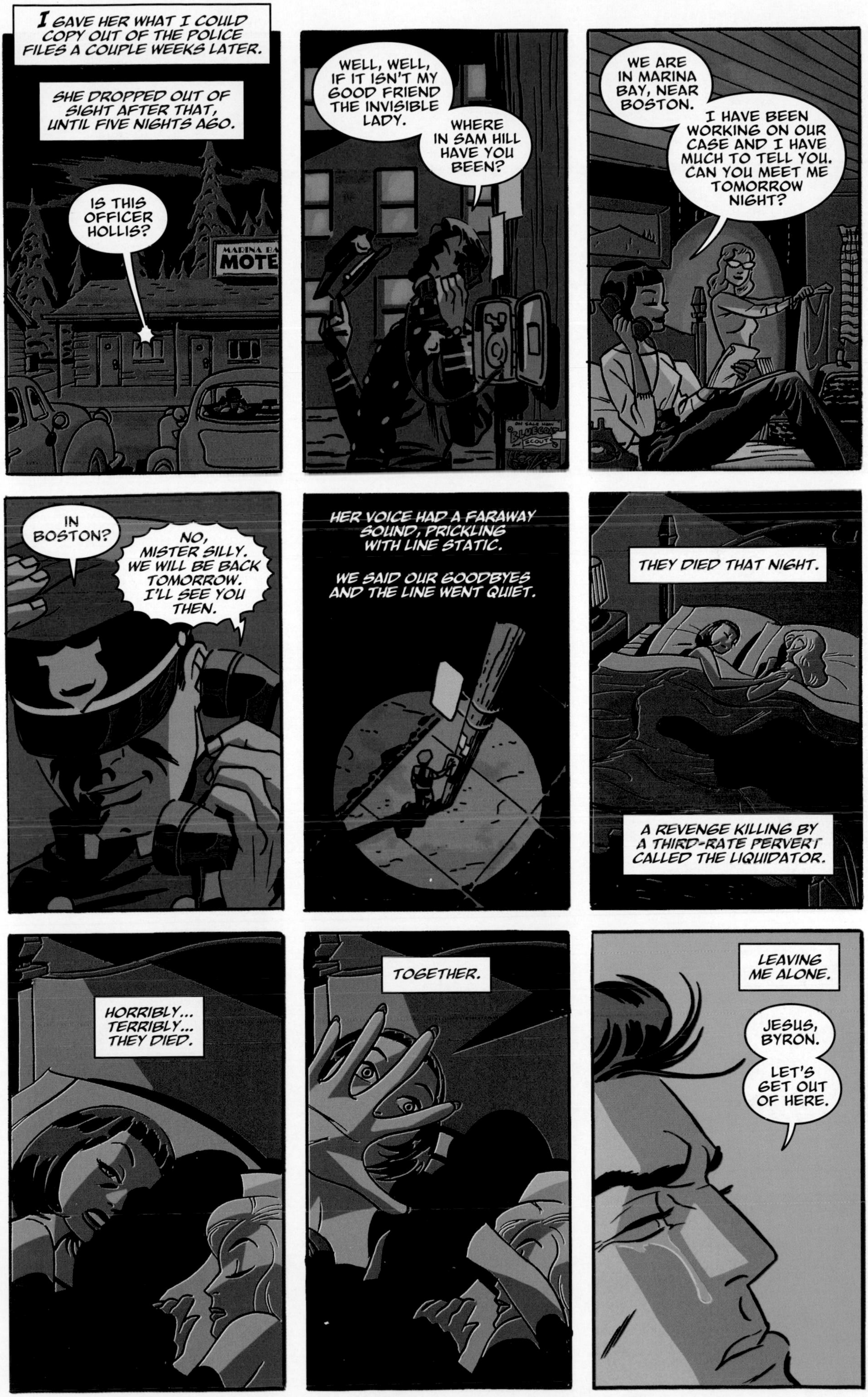
I GAVE HER WHAT I COULD COPY OUT OF THE POLICE FILES A COUPLE WEEKS LATER.
SHE DROPPED OUT OF SIGHT AFTER THAT, UNTIL FIVE NIGHTS AGO.
IS THIS OFFICER HOLLIS?
MARINA BA
MOTE
WELL, WELL, IF IT ISN'T MY GOOD FRIEND THE INVISIBLE LADY.
WHERE IN SAM HILL HAVE YOU BEEN?
WE ARE IN MARINA BAY, NEAR BOSTON.
I HAVE BEEN WORKING ON OUR CASE AND I HAVE MUCH TO TELL YOU. CAN YOU MEET ME TOMORROW NIGHT?
IN BOSTON?
NO, MISTER SILLY. WE WILL BE BACK TOMORROW. I'LL SEE YOU THEN.
HER VOICE HAD A FARAWAY SOUND, PRICKLING WITH LINE STATIC.
WE SAID OUR GOODBYES AND THE LINE WENT QUIET.
THEY DIED THAT NIGHT.
A REVENGE KILLING BY A THIRD-RATE PERVERT CALLED THE LIQUIDATOR.
HORRIBLY... TERRIBLY... THEY DIED.
TOGETHER.
LEAVING ME ALONE.
JESUS, BYRON.
LET'S GET OUT OF HERE.

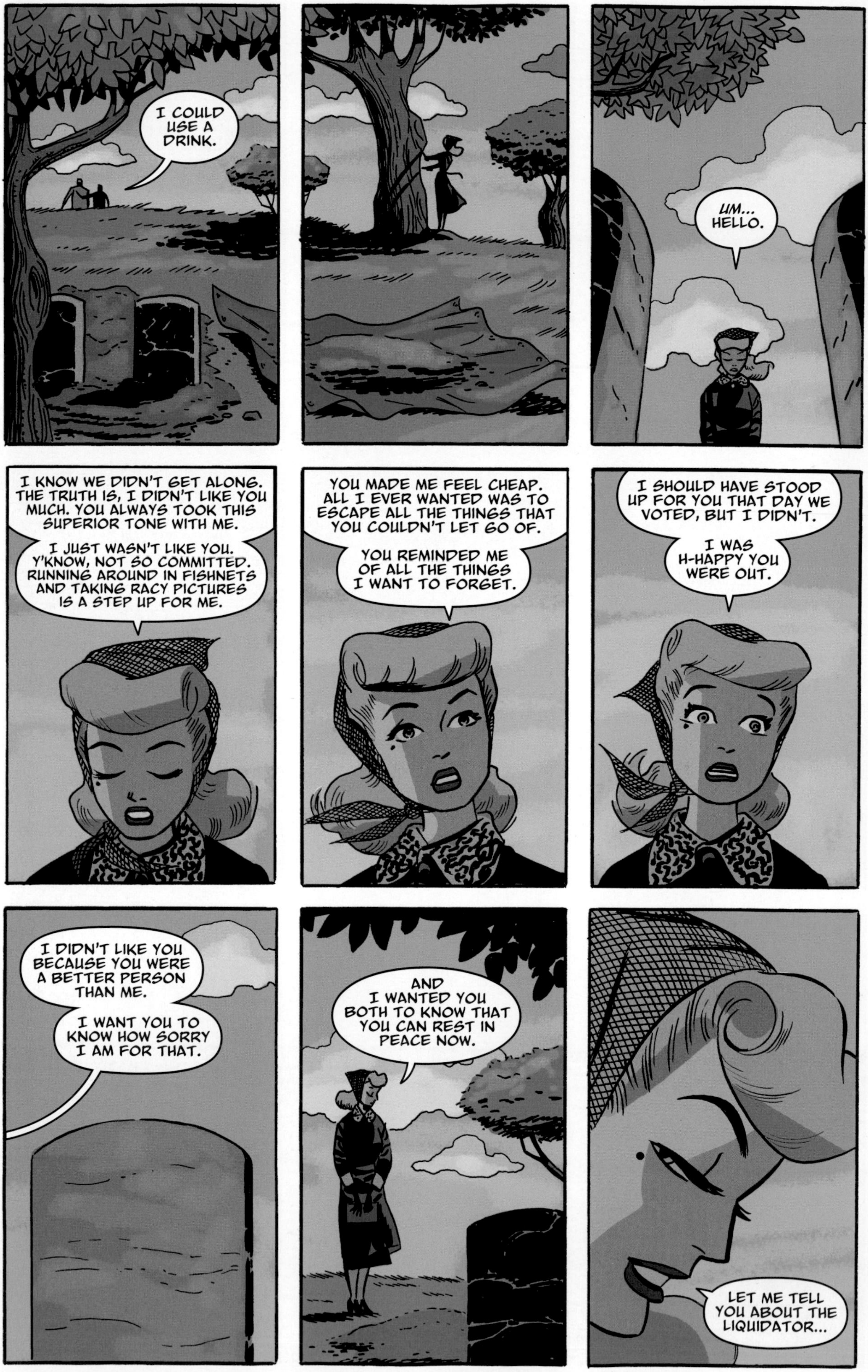
I COULD USE A DRINK.
UM... HELLO.
I KNOW WE DIDN'T GET ALONG. THE TRUTH IS, I DIDN'T LIKE YOU MUCH. YOU ALWAYS TOOK THIS SUPERIOR TONE WITH ME.
I JUST WASN'T LIKE YOU. Y'KNOW, NOT SO COMMITTED. RUNNING AROUND IN FISHNETS AND TAKING RACY PICTURES IS A STEP UP FOR ME.
YOU MADE ME FEEL CHEAP. ALL I EVER WANTED WAS TO ESCAPE ALL THE THINGS THAT YOU COULDN'T LET GO OF.
YOU REMINDED ME OF ALL THE THINGS I WANT TO FORGET.
I SHOULD HAVE STOOD UP FOR YOU THAT DAY WE VOTED, BUT I DIDN'T.
I WAS H-HAPPY YOU WERE OUT.
I DIDN'T LIKE YOU BECAUSE YOU WERE A BETTER PERSON THAN ME.
I WANT YOU TO KNOW HOW SORRY I AM FOR THAT.
AND I WANTED YOU BOTH TO KNOW THAT YOU CAN REST IN PEACE NOW.
LET ME TELL YOU ABOUT THE LIQUIDATOR...

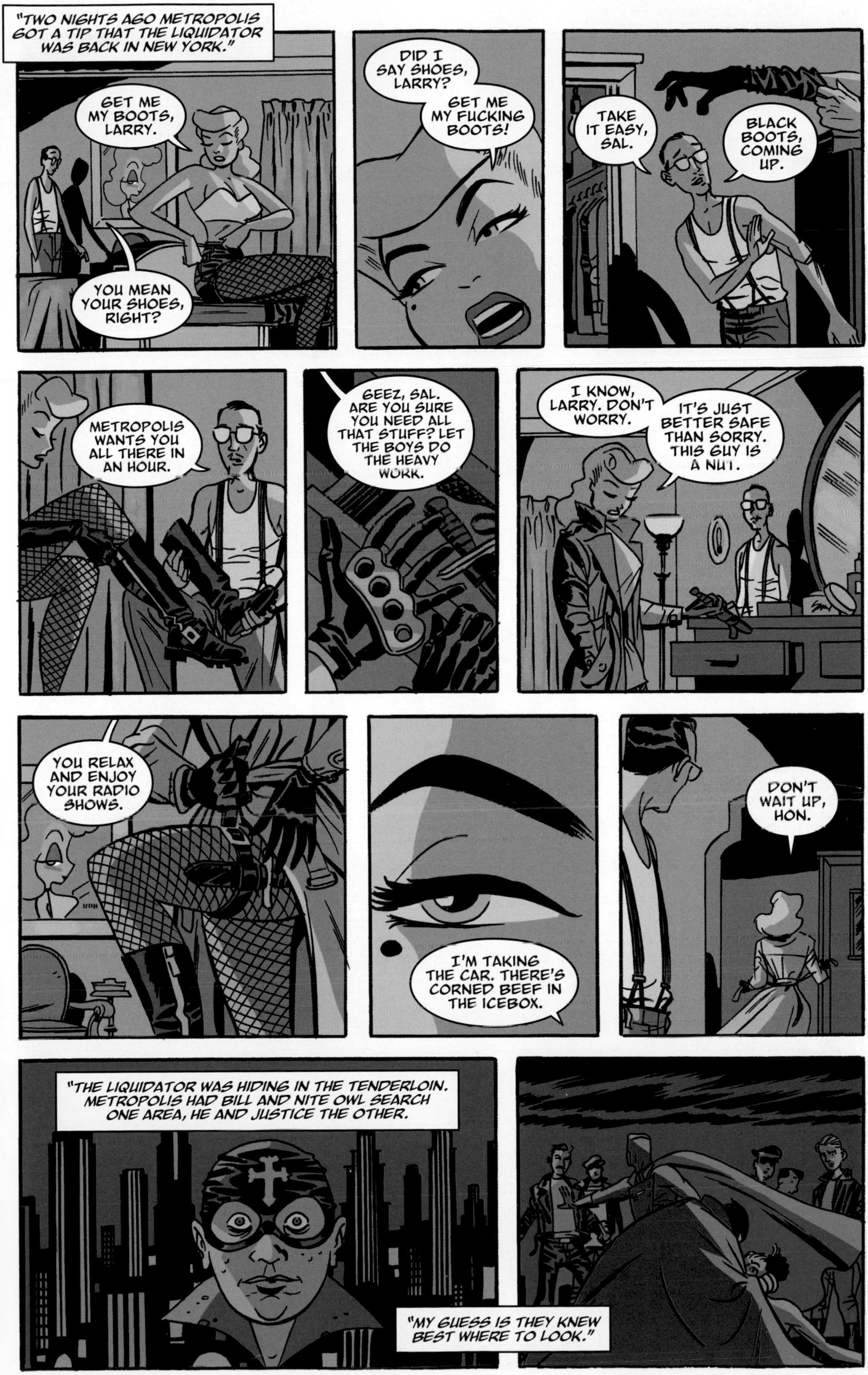
"TWO NIGHTS AGO METROPOLIS GOT A TIP THAT THE LIQUIDATOR WAS BACK IN NEW YORK."
GET ME MY BOOTS, LARRY.
YOU MEAN YOUR SHOES, RIGHT?
DID I SAY SHOES, LARRY?
GET ME MY FUCKING BOOTS!
TAKE IT EASY, SAL.
BLACK BOOTS, COMING UP.
METROPOLIS WANTS YOU ALL THERE IN AN HOUR.
GEEZ, SAL. ARE YOU SURE YOU NEED ALL THAT STUFF? LET THE BOYS DO THE HEAVY WORK.
I KNOW, LARRY. DON'T WORRY.
IT'S JUST BETTER SAFE THAN SORRY. THIS GUY IS A NUT.
YOU RELAX AND ENJOY YOUR RADIO SHOWS.
I'M TAKING THE CAR. THERE'S CORNED BEEF IN THE ICEBOX.
DON'T WAIT UP, HON.
"THE LIQUIDATOR WAS HIDING IN THE TENDERLOIN. METROPOLIS HAD BILL AND NITE OWL SEARCH ONE AREA, HE AND JUSTICE THE OTHER.
"MY GUESS IS THEY KNEW BEST WHERE TO LOOK."

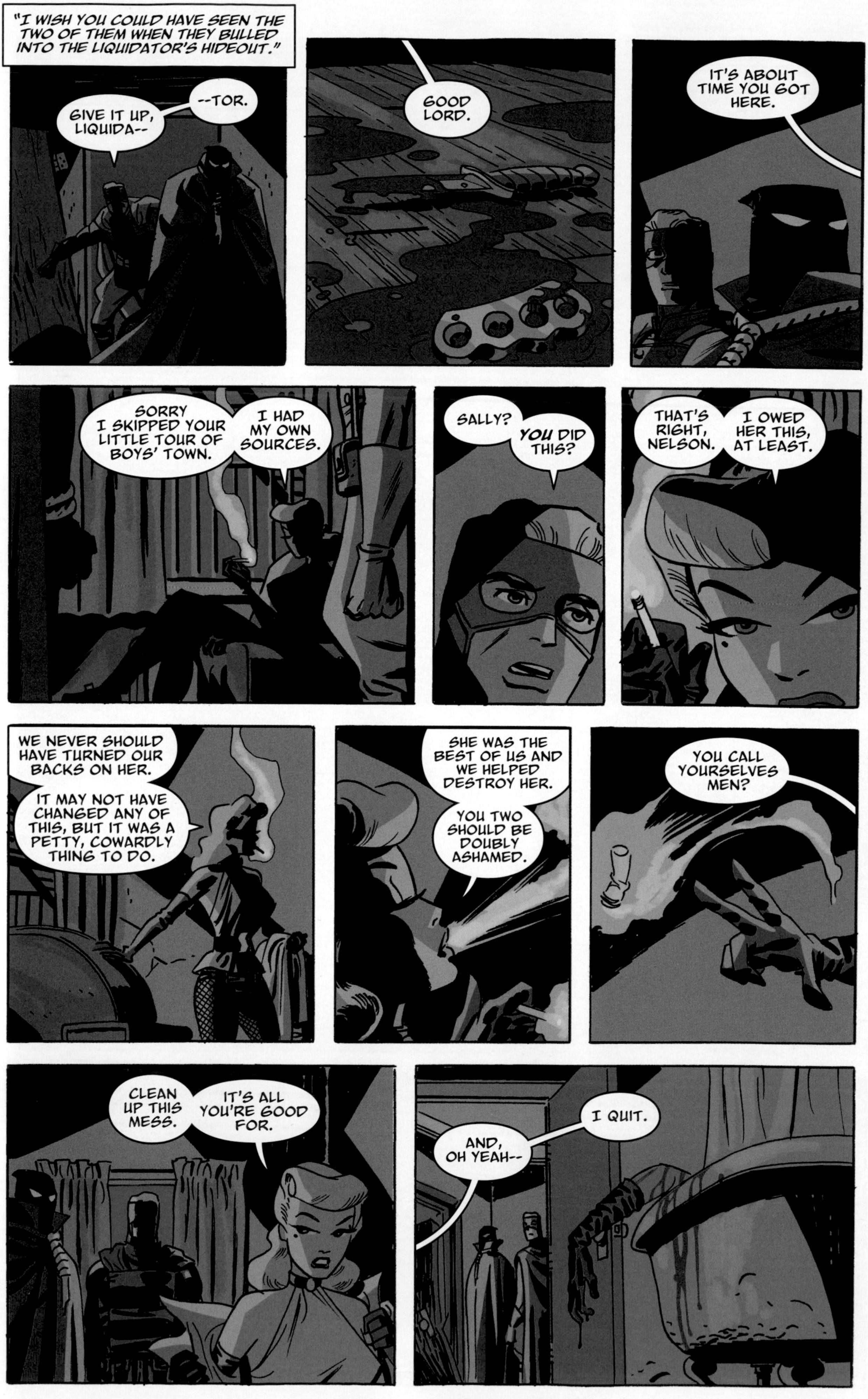
"I WISH YOU COULD HAVE SEEN THE TWO OF THEM WHEN THEY BULLED INTO THE LIQUIDATOR'S HIDEOUT."
GIVE IT UP, LIQUIDA--
--TOR.
GOOD LORD.
IT'S ABOUT TIME YOU GOT HERE.
SORRY I SKIPPED YOUR LITTLE TOUR OF BOYS' TOWN.
I HAD MY OWN SOURCES.
SALLY? YOU DID THIS?
THAT'S RIGHT, NELSON.
I OWED HER THIS, AT LEAST.
WE NEVER SHOULD HAVE TURNED OUR BACKS ON HER.
IT MAY NOT HAVE CHANGED ANY OF THIS, BUT IT WAS A PETTY, COWARDLY THING TO DO.
SHE WAS THE BEST OF US AND WE HELPED DESTROY HER.
YOU TWO SHOULD BE DOUBLY ASHAMED.
YOU CALL YOURSELVES MEN?
CLEAN UP THIS MESS.
IT'S ALL YOU'RE GOOD FOR.
I QUIT.
AND, OH YEAH--

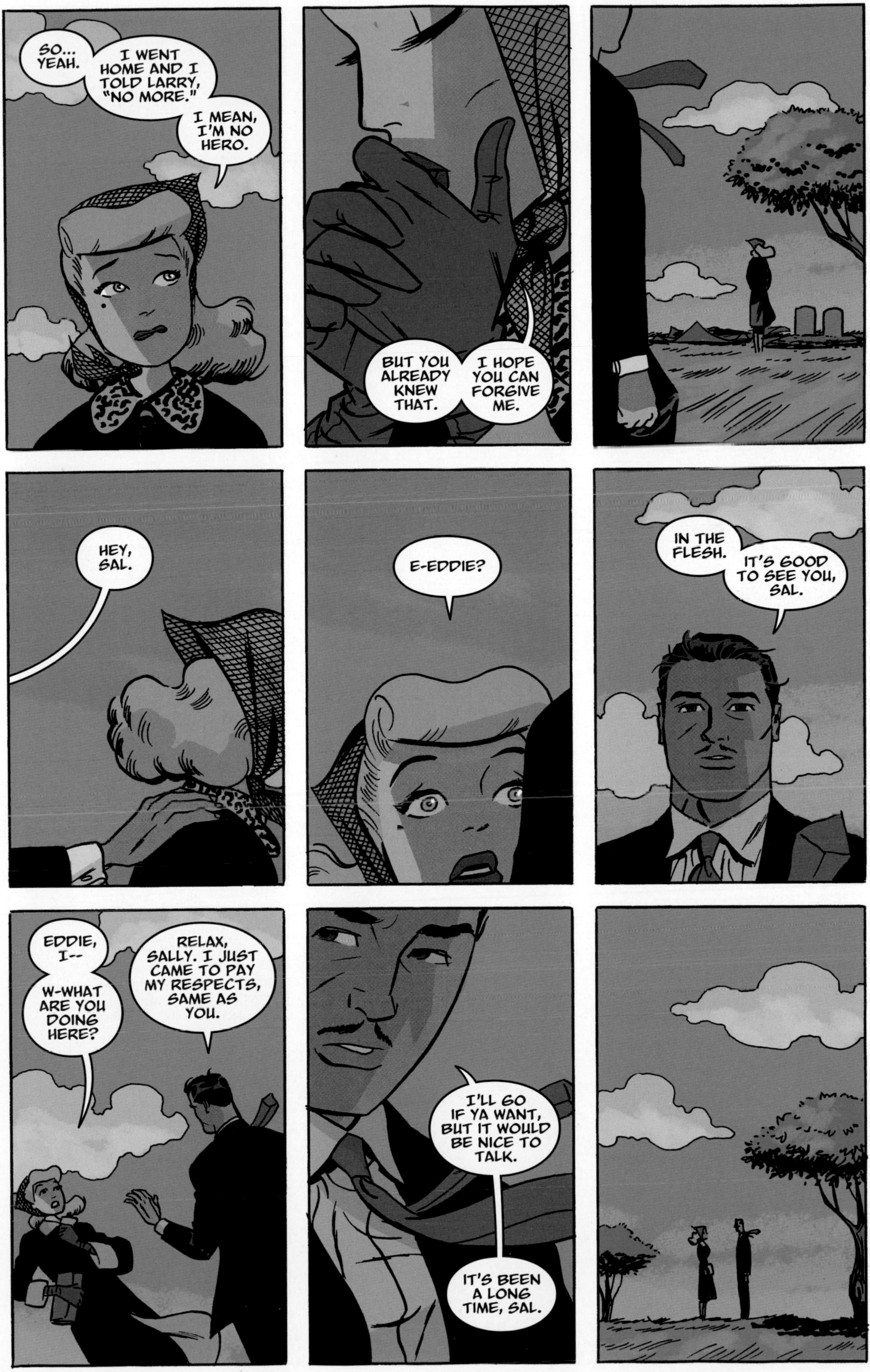
SO... YEAH.
I WENT HOME AND I TOLD LARRY, "NO MORE."
I MEAN, I'M NO HERO.
BUT YOU ALREADY KNEW THAT.
I HOPE YOU CAN FORGIVE ME.
HEY, SAL.
E-EDDIE?
IN THE FLESH.
IT'S GOOD TO SEE YOU, SAL.
EDDIE, I--
W-WHAT ARE YOU DOING HERE?
RELAX, SALLY. I JUST CAME TO PAY MY RESPECTS, SAME AS YOU.
I'LL GO IF YA WANT, BUT IT WOULD BE NICE TO TALK.
IT'S BEEN A LONG TIME, SAL.

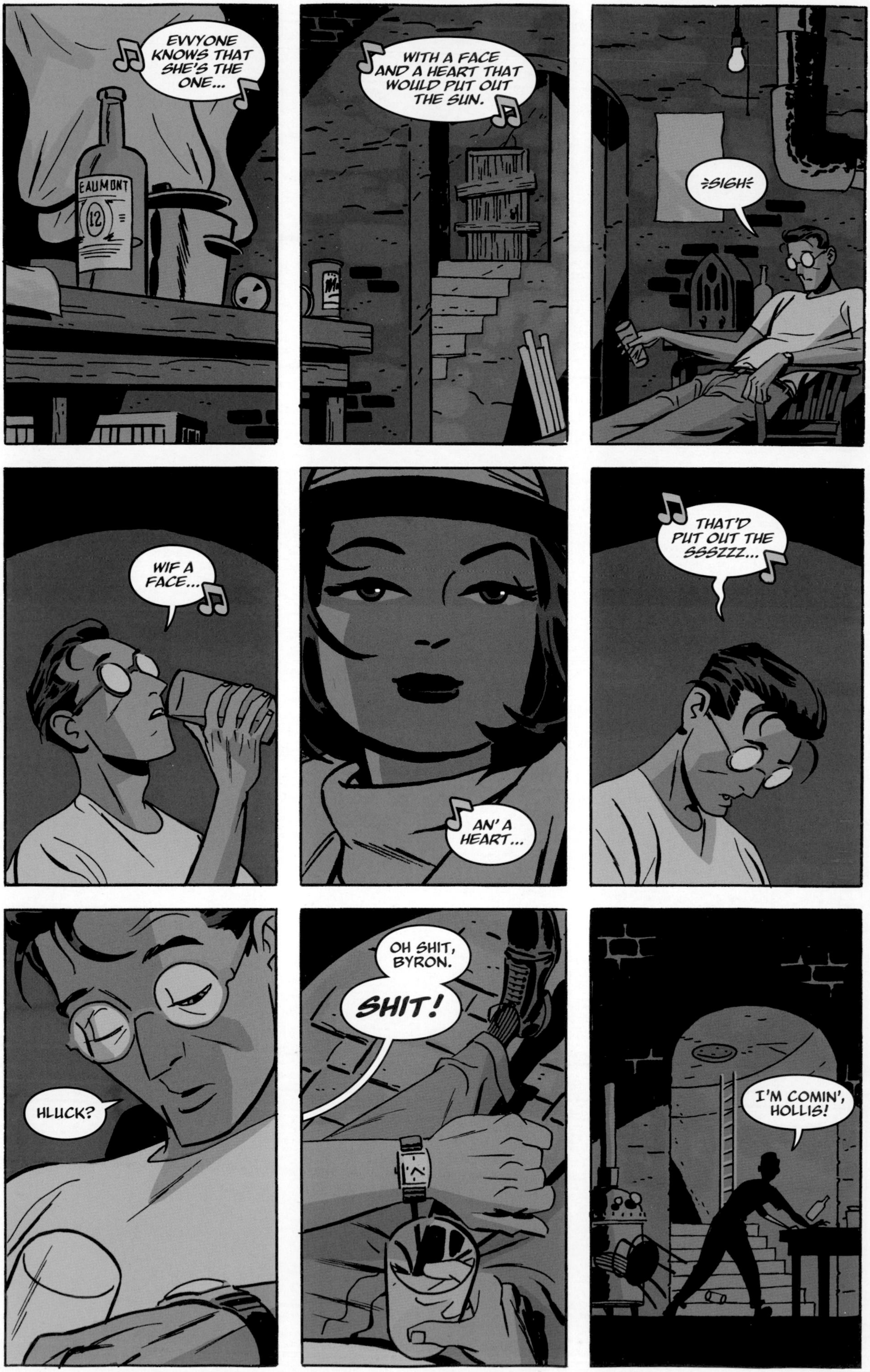
EVVYONE KNOWS THAT SHE'S THE ONE...
WITH A FACE AND A HEART THAT WOULD PUT OUT THE SUN.
≈SIGH≈
WIF A FACE...
AN' A HEART...
THAT'D PUT OUT THE SSSZZZ...
HLUCK?
OH SHIT, BYRON.
SHIT!
I'M COMIN', HOLLIS!

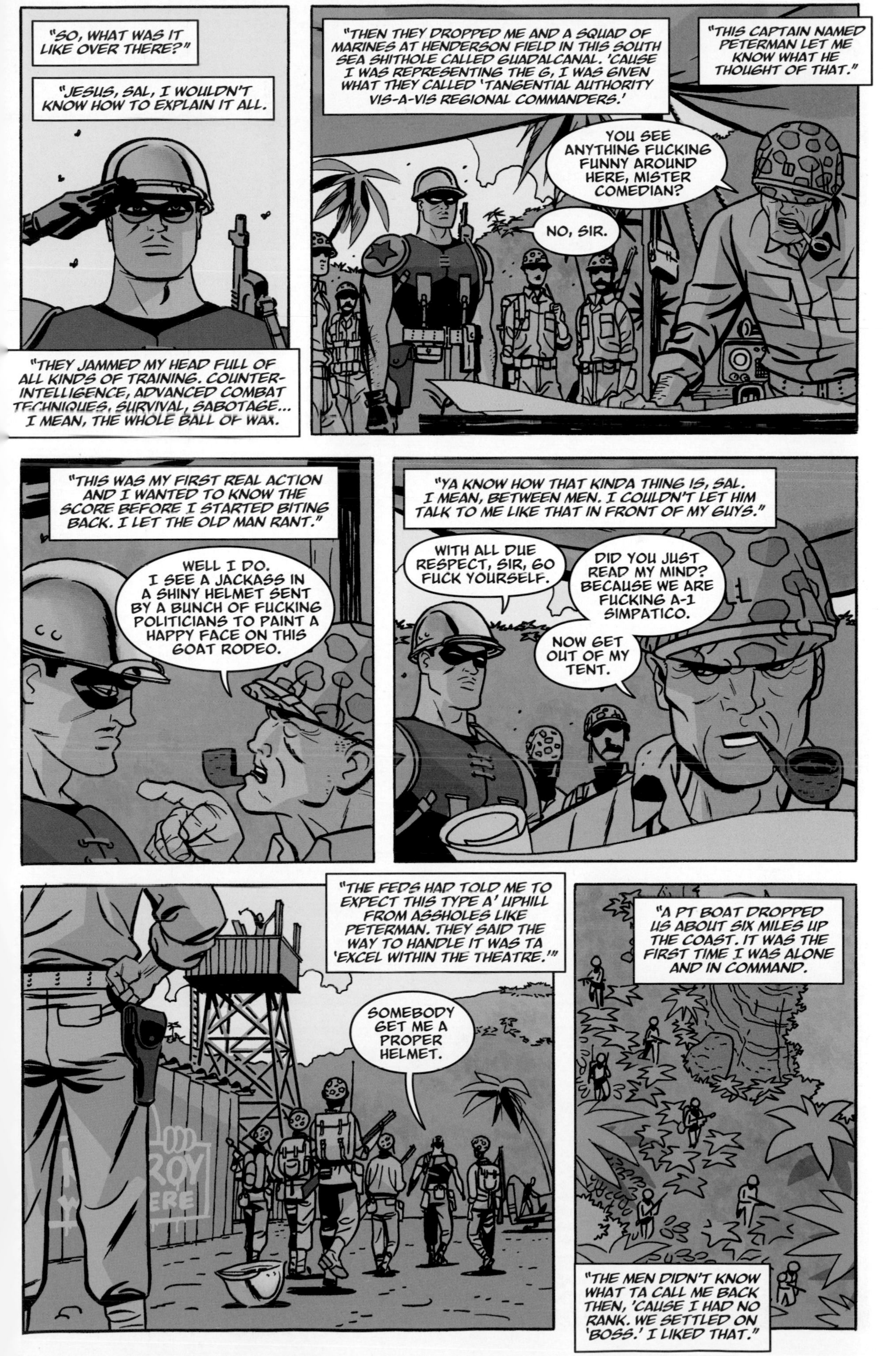
"SO, WHAT WAS IT LIKE OVER THERE?"
"JESUS, SAL, I WOULDN'T KNOW HOW TO EXPLAIN IT ALL.
"THEY JAMMED MY HEAD FULL OF ALL KINDS OF TRAINING. COUNTER-INTELLIGENCE, ADVANCED COMBAT TECHNIQUES, SURVIVAL, SABOTAGE... I MEAN, THE WHOLE BALL OF WAX.
"THEN THEY DROPPED ME AND A SQUAD OF MARINES AT HENDERSON FIELD IN THIS SOUTH SEA SHITHOLE CALLED GUADALCANAL. 'CAUSE I WAS REPRESENTING THE G, I WAS GIVEN WHAT THEY CALLED 'TANGENTIAL AUTHORITY VIS-A-VIS REGIONAL COMMANDERS.'
"THIS CAPTAIN NAMED PETERMAN LET ME KNOW WHAT HE THOUGHT OF THAT."
YOU SEE ANYTHING FUCKING FUNNY AROUND HERE, MISTER COMEDIAN?
NO, SIR.
"THIS WAS MY FIRST REAL ACTION AND I WANTED TO KNOW THE SCORE BEFORE I STARTED BITING BACK. I LET THE OLD MAN RANT."
WELL I DO. I SEE A JACKASS IN A SHINY HELMET SENT BY A BUNCH OF FUCKING POLITICIANS TO PAINT A HAPPY FACE ON THIS GOAT RODEO.
"YA KNOW HOW THAT KINDA THING IS, SAL. I MEAN, BETWEEN MEN. I COULDN'T LET HIM TALK TO ME LIKE THAT IN FRONT OF MY GUYS."
WITH ALL DUE RESPECT, SIR, GO FUCK YOURSELF.
DID YOU JUST READ MY MIND? BECAUSE WE ARE FUCKING A-1 SIMPATICO.
NOW GET OUT OF MY TENT.
"THE FEDS HAD TOLD ME TO EXPECT THIS TYPE A' UPHILL FROM ASSHOLES LIKE PETERMAN. THEY SAID THE WAY TO HANDLE IT WAS TA 'EXCEL WITHIN THE THEATRE.'"
SOMEBODY GET ME A PROPER HELMET.
"A PT BOAT DROPPED US ABOUT SIX MILES UP THE COAST. IT WAS THE FIRST TIME I WAS ALONE AND IN COMMAND.
"THE MEN DIDN'T KNOW WHAT TA CALL ME BACK THEN, 'CAUSE I HAD NO RANK. WE SETTLED ON 'BOSS.' I LIKED THAT."

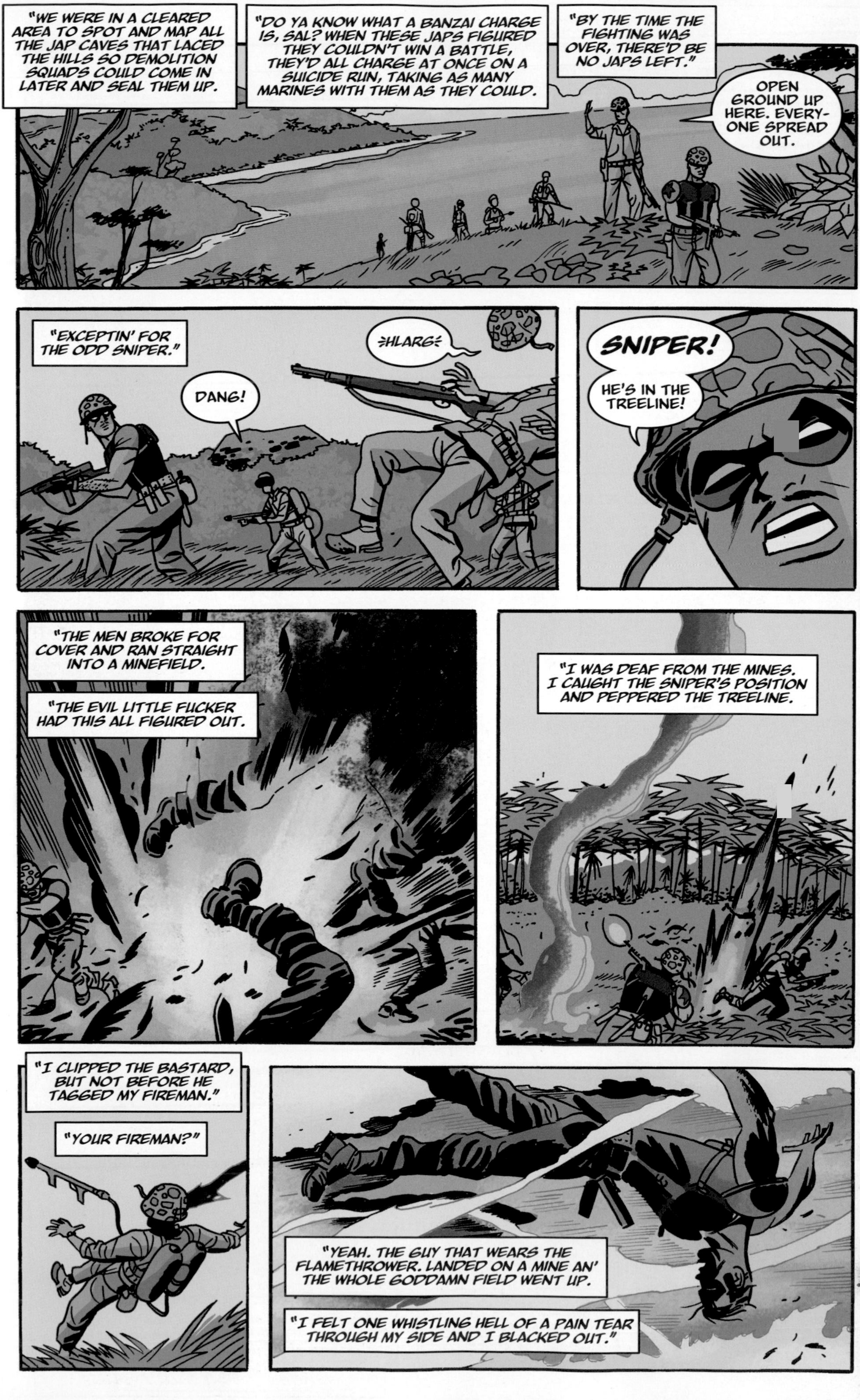
"WE WERE IN A CLEARED AREA TO SPOT AND MAP ALL THE JAP CAVES THAT LACED THE HILLS SO DEMOLITION SQUADS COULD COME IN LATER AND SEAL THEM UP.
"DO YA KNOW WHAT A BANZAI CHARGE IS, SAL? WHEN THESE JAPS FIGURED THEY COULDN'T WIN A BATTLE, THEY'D ALL CHARGE AT ONCE ON A SUICIDE RUN, TAKING AS MANY MARINES WITH THEM AS THEY COULD.
"BY THE TIME THE FIGHTING WAS OVER, THERE'D BE NO JAPS LEFT."
OPEN GROUND UP HERE. EVERY-ONE SPREAD OUT.
"EXCEPTIN' FOR THE ODD SNIPER."
DANG!
HLARG
SNIPER!
HE'S IN THE TREELINE!
"THE MEN BROKE FOR COVER AND RAN STRAIGHT INTO A MINEFIELD.
"THE EVIL LITTLE FUCKER HAD THIS ALL FIGURED OUT.
"I WAS DEAF FROM THE MINES. I CAUGHT THE SNIPER'S POSITION AND PEPPERED THE TREELINE.
"I CLIPPED THE BASTARD, BUT NOT BEFORE HE TAGGED MY FIREMAN."
"YOUR FIREMAN?"
"YEAH. THE GUY THAT WEARS THE FLAMETHROWER. LANDED ON A MINE AN' THE WHOLE GODDAMN FIELD WENT UP.
"I FELT ONE WHISTLING HELL OF A PAIN TEAR THROUGH MY SIDE AND I BLACKED OUT."

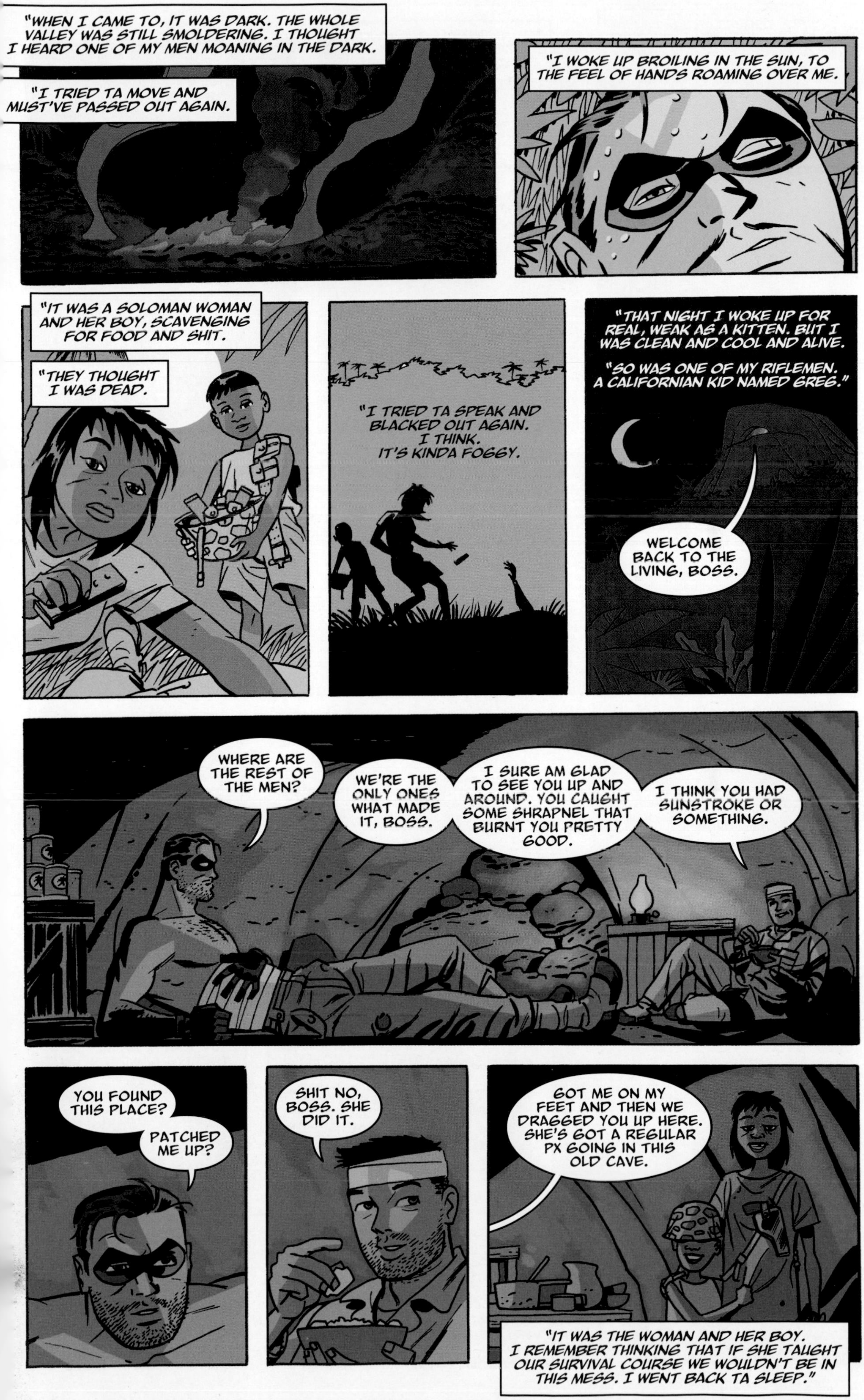
"WHEN I CAME TO, IT WAS DARK. THE WHOLE VALLEY WAS STILL SMOLDERING. I THOUGHT I HEARD ONE OF MY MEN MOANING IN THE DARK.
"I TRIED TA MOVE AND MUST'VE PASSED OUT AGAIN.
"I WOKE UP BROILING IN THE SUN, TO THE FEEL OF HANDS ROAMING OVER ME.
"IT WAS A SOLOMAN WOMAN AND HER BOY, SCAVENGING FOR FOOD AND SHIT.
"THEY THOUGHT I WAS DEAD.
"I TRIED TA SPEAK AND BLACKED OUT AGAIN. I THINK. IT'S KINDA FOGGY.
"THAT NIGHT I WOKE UP FOR REAL, WEAK AS A KITTEN. BUT I WAS CLEAN AND COOL AND ALIVE.
"SO WAS ONE OF MY RIFLEMEN. A CALIFORNIAN KID NAMED GREG."
WELCOME BACK TO THE LIVING, BOSS.
WHERE ARE THE REST OF THE MEN?
WE'RE THE ONLY ONES WHAT MADE IT, BOSS.
I SURE AM GLAD TO SEE YOU UP AND AROUND. YOU CAUGHT SOME SHRAPNEL THAT BURNT YOU PRETTY GOOD.
I THINK YOU HAD SUNSTROKE OR SOMETHING.
YOU FOUND THIS PLACE?
PATCHED ME UP?
SHIT NO, BOSS. SHE DID IT.
GOT ME ON MY FEET AND THEN WE DRAGGED YOU UP HERE. SHE'S GOT A REGULAR PX GOING IN THIS OLD CAVE.
"IT WAS THE WOMAN AND HER BOY. I REMEMBER THINKING THAT IF SHE TAUGHT OUR SURVIVAL COURSE WE WOULDN'T BE IN THIS MESS. I WENT BACK TA SLEEP."

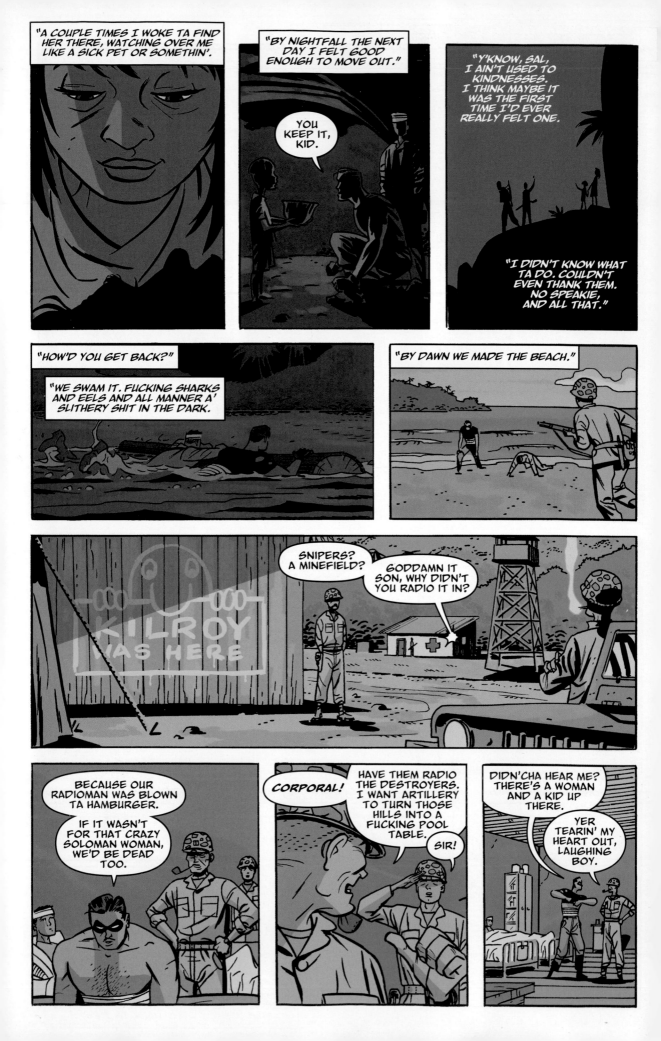

"A COUPLE TIMES I WOKE TA FIND HER THERE, WATCHING OVER ME LIKE A SICK PET OR SOMETHIN'.

"BY NIGHTFALL THE NEXT DAY I FELT GOOD ENOUGH TO MOVE OUT."

YOU KEEP IT, KID.

"Y'KNOW, SAL, I AIN'T USED TO KINDNESSES. I THINK MAYBE IT WAS THE FIRST TIME I'D EVER REALLY FELT ONE.

"I DIDN'T KNOW WHAT TA DO. COULDN'T EVEN THANK THEM. NO SPEAKIE, AND ALL THAT."

"HOW'D YOU GET BACK?"

"WE SWAM IT. FUCKING SHARKS AND EELS AND ALL MANNER A' SLITHERY SHIT IN THE DARK.

"BY DAWN WE MADE THE BEACH."

KILROY WAS HERE

SNIPERS? A MINEFIELD?

GODDAMN IT SON, WHY DIDN'T YOU RADIO IT IN?

BECAUSE OUR RADIOMAN WAS BLOWN TA HAMBURGER.

IF IT WASN'T FOR THAT CRAZY SOLOMAN WOMAN, WE'D BE DEAD TOO.

CORPORAL!

HAVE THEM RADIO THE DESTROYERS. I WANT ARTILLERY TO TURN THOSE HILLS INTO A FUCKING POOL TABLE.

SIR!

DIDN'CHA HEAR ME? THERE'S A WOMAN AND A KID UP THERE.

YER TEARIN' MY HEART OUT, LAUGHING BOY.

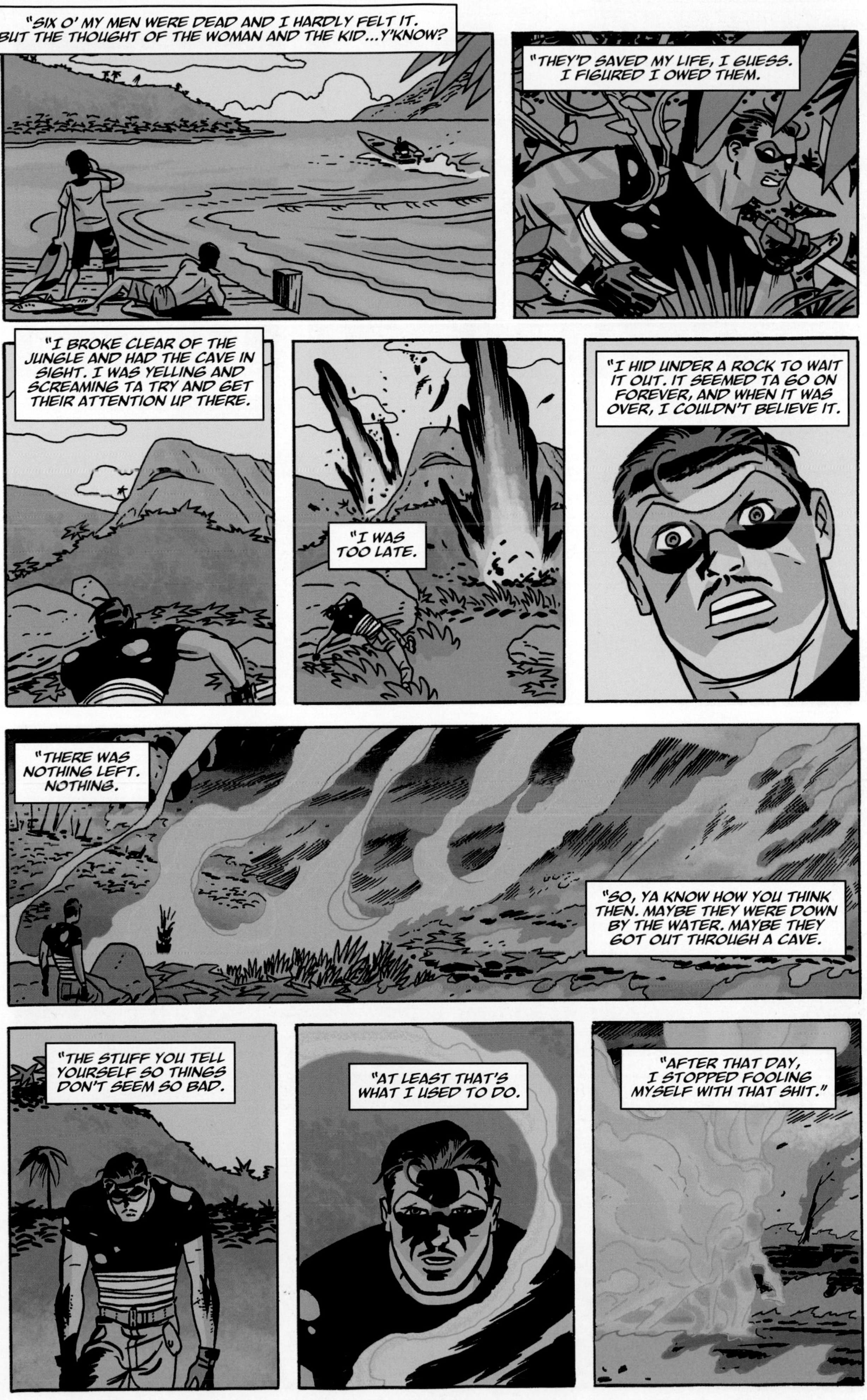
"SIX O' MY MEN WERE DEAD AND I HARDLY FELT IT. BUT THE THOUGHT OF THE WOMAN AND THE KID...Y'KNOW?
"THEY'D SAVED MY LIFE, I GUESS. I FIGURED I OWED THEM.
"I BROKE CLEAR OF THE JUNGLE AND HAD THE CAVE IN SIGHT. I WAS YELLING AND SCREAMING TA TRY AND GET THEIR ATTENTION UP THERE.
"I WAS TOO LATE.
"I HID UNDER A ROCK TO WAIT IT OUT. IT SEEMED TA GO ON FOREVER, AND WHEN IT WAS OVER, I COULDN'T BELIEVE IT.
"THERE WAS NOTHING LEFT. NOTHING.
"SO, YA KNOW HOW YOU THINK THEN. MAYBE THEY WERE DOWN BY THE WATER. MAYBE THEY GOT OUT THROUGH A CAVE.
"THE STUFF YOU TELL YOURSELF SO THINGS DON'T SEEM SO BAD.
"AT LEAST THAT'S WHAT I USED TO DO.
"AFTER THAT DAY, I STOPPED FOOLING MYSELF WITH THAT SHIT."

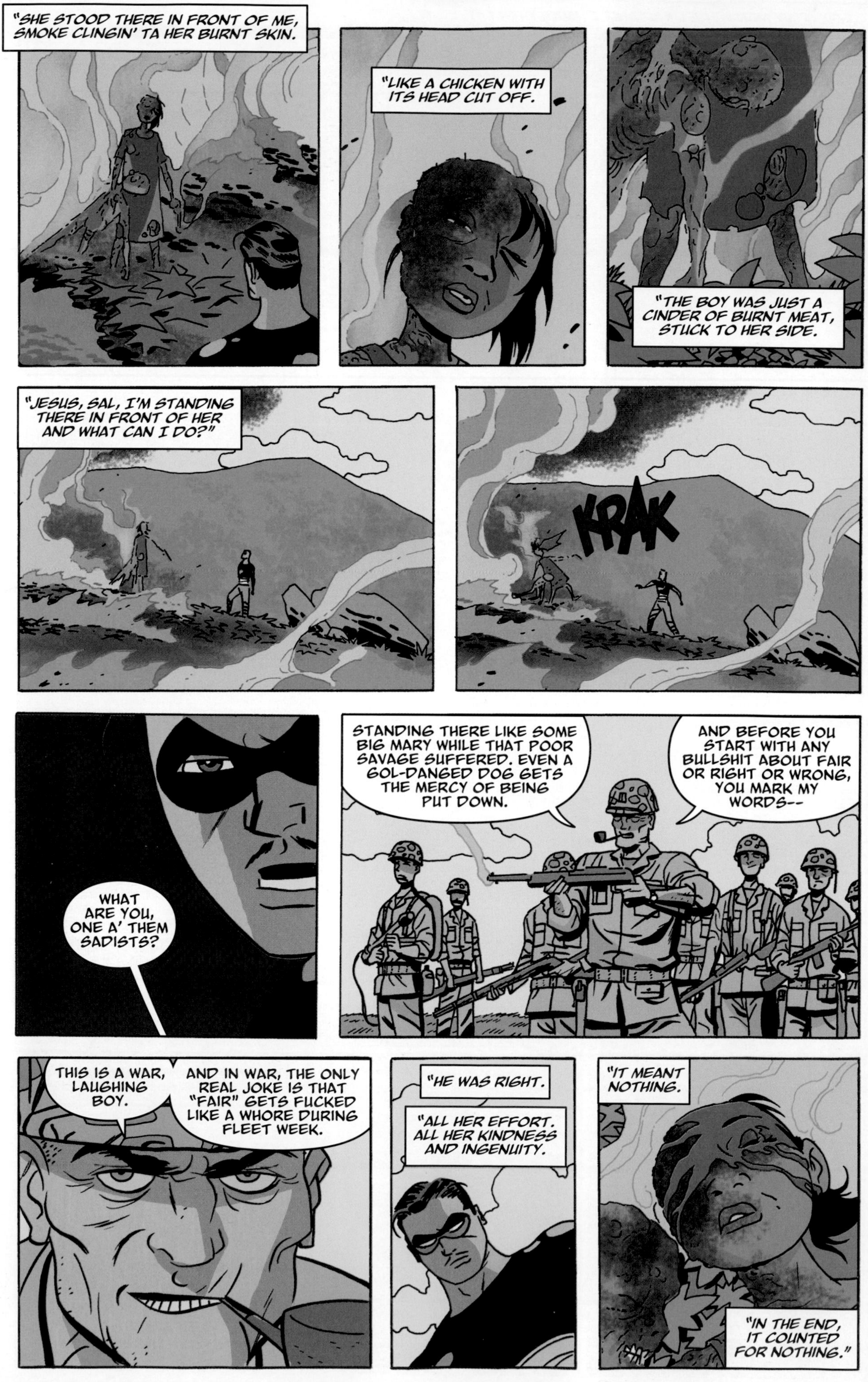
"SHE STOOD THERE IN FRONT OF ME, SMOKE CLINGIN' TA HER BURNT SKIN.
"LIKE A CHICKEN WITH ITS HEAD CUT OFF.
"THE BOY WAS JUST A CINDER OF BURNT MEAT, STUCK TO HER SIDE.
"JESUS, SAL, I'M STANDING THERE IN FRONT OF HER AND WHAT CAN I DO?"
KRAK
WHAT ARE YOU, ONE A' THEM SADISTS?
STANDING THERE LIKE SOME BIG MARY WHILE THAT POOR SAVAGE SUFFERED. EVEN A GOL-DANGED DOG GETS THE MERCY OF BEING PUT DOWN.
AND BEFORE YOU START WITH ANY BULLSHIT ABOUT FAIR OR RIGHT OR WRONG, YOU MARK MY WORDS--
THIS IS A WAR, LAUGHING BOY.
AND IN WAR, THE ONLY REAL JOKE IS THAT "FAIR" GETS FUCKED LIKE A WHORE DURING FLEET WEEK.
"HE WAS RIGHT.
"ALL HER EFFORT. ALL HER KINDNESS AND INGENUITY.
"IT MEANT NOTHING.
"IN THE END, IT COUNTED FOR NOTHING."

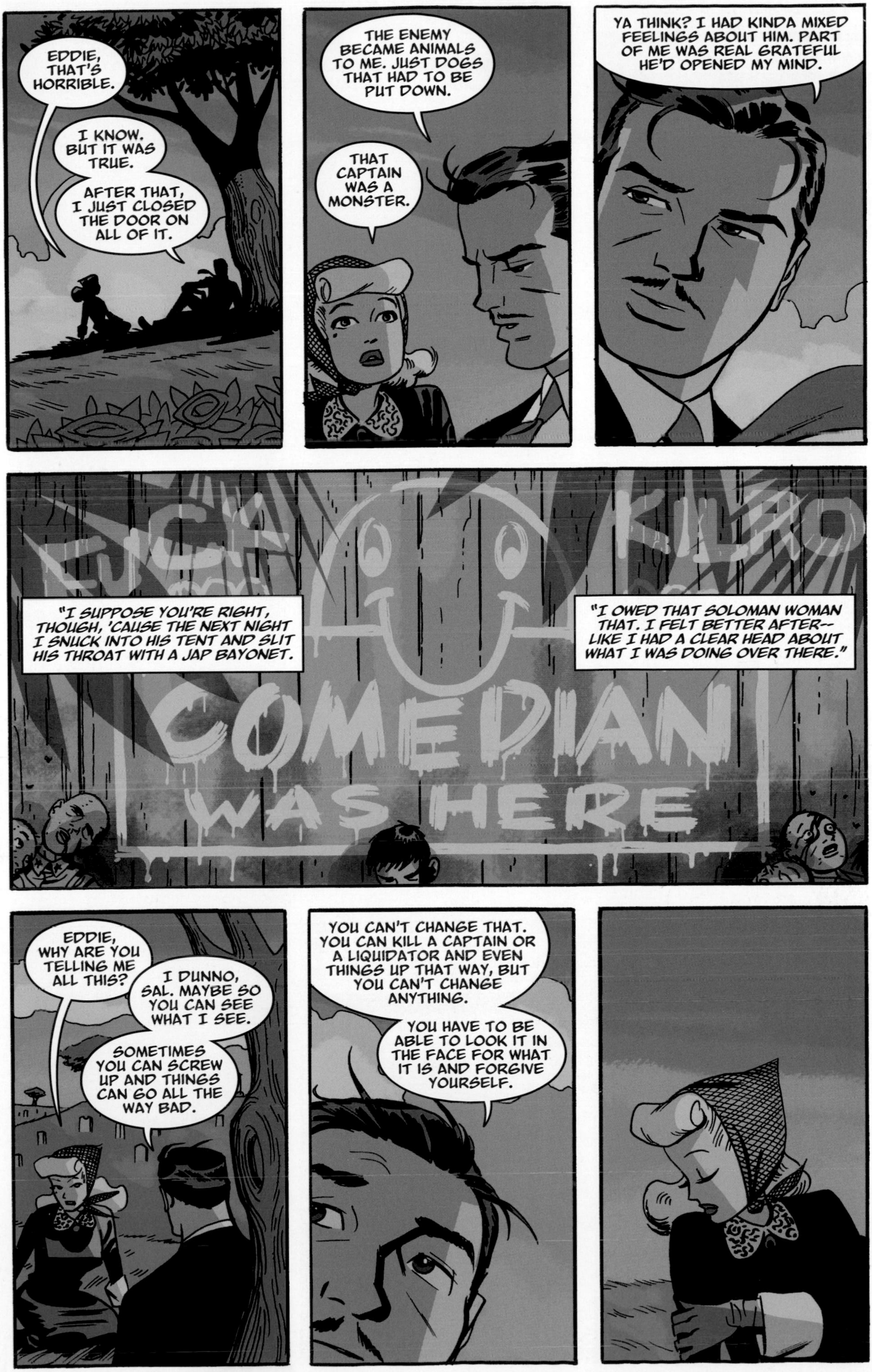
EDDIE, THAT'S HORRIBLE.
I KNOW. BUT IT WAS TRUE.
AFTER THAT, I JUST CLOSED THE DOOR ON ALL OF IT.
THE ENEMY BECAME ANIMALS TO ME. JUST DOGS THAT HAD TO BE PUT DOWN.
THAT CAPTAIN WAS A MONSTER.
YA THINK? I HAD KINDA MIXED FEELINGS ABOUT HIM. PART OF ME WAS REAL GRATEFUL HE'D OPENED MY MIND.
"I SUPPOSE YOU'RE RIGHT, THOUGH, 'CAUSE THE NEXT NIGHT I SNUCK INTO HIS TENT AND SLIT HIS THROAT WITH A JAP BAYONET.
COMEDIAN WAS HERE
"I OWED THAT SOLOMAN WOMAN THAT. I FELT BETTER AFTER-- LIKE I HAD A CLEAR HEAD ABOUT WHAT I WAS DOING OVER THERE."
EDDIE, WHY ARE YOU TELLING ME ALL THIS?
I DUNNO, SAL. MAYBE SO YOU CAN SEE WHAT I SEE.
SOMETIMES YOU CAN SCREW UP AND THINGS CAN GO ALL THE WAY BAD.
YOU CAN'T CHANGE THAT. YOU CAN KILL A CAPTAIN OR A LIQUIDATOR AND EVEN THINGS UP THAT WAY, BUT YOU CAN'T CHANGE ANYTHING.
YOU HAVE TO BE ABLE TO LOOK IT IN THE FACE FOR WHAT IT IS AND FORGIVE YOURSELF.

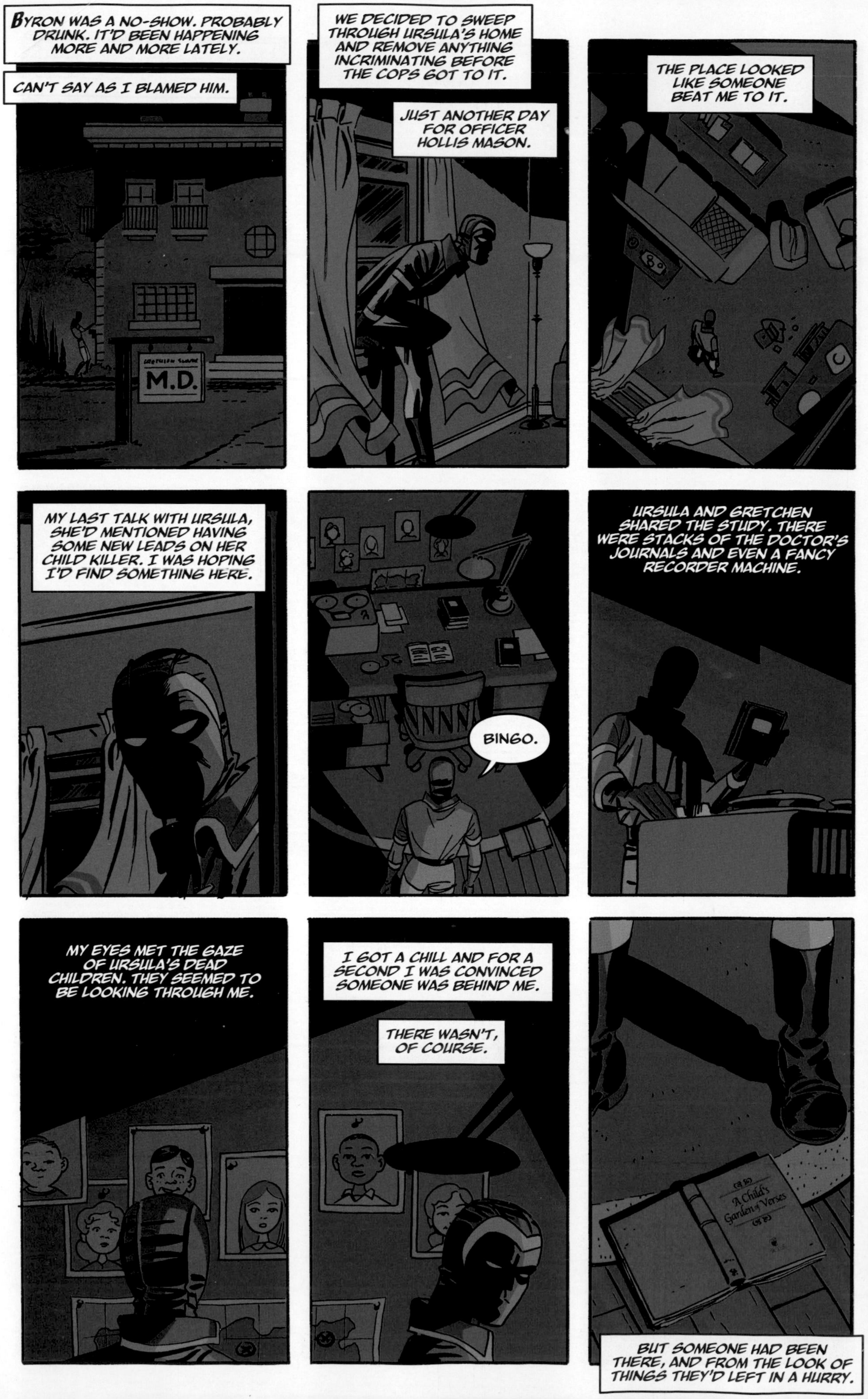

BYRON WAS A NO-SHOW. PROBABLY DRUNK. IT'D BEEN HAPPENING MORE AND MORE LATELY.
CAN'T SAY AS I BLAMED HIM.
M.D.
WE DECIDED TO SWEEP THROUGH URSULA'S HOME AND REMOVE ANYTHING INCRIMINATING BEFORE THE COPS GOT TO IT.
JUST ANOTHER DAY FOR OFFICER HOLLIS MASON.
THE PLACE LOOKED LIKE SOMEONE BEAT ME TO IT.
MY LAST TALK WITH URSULA, SHE'D MENTIONED HAVING SOME NEW LEADS ON HER CHILD KILLER. I WAS HOPING I'D FIND SOMETHING HERE.
BINGO.
URSULA AND GRETCHEN SHARED THE STUDY. THERE WERE STACKS OF THE DOCTOR'S JOURNALS AND EVEN A FANCY RECORDER MACHINE.
MY EYES MET THE GAZE OF URSULA'S DEAD CHILDREN. THEY SEEMED TO BE LOOKING THROUGH ME.
I GOT A CHILL AND FOR A SECOND I WAS CONVINCED SOMEONE WAS BEHIND ME.
THERE WASN'T, OF COURSE.
A Child's Garden of Verses
BUT SOMEONE HAD BEEN THERE, AND FROM THE LOOK OF THINGS THEY'D LEFT IN A HURRY.

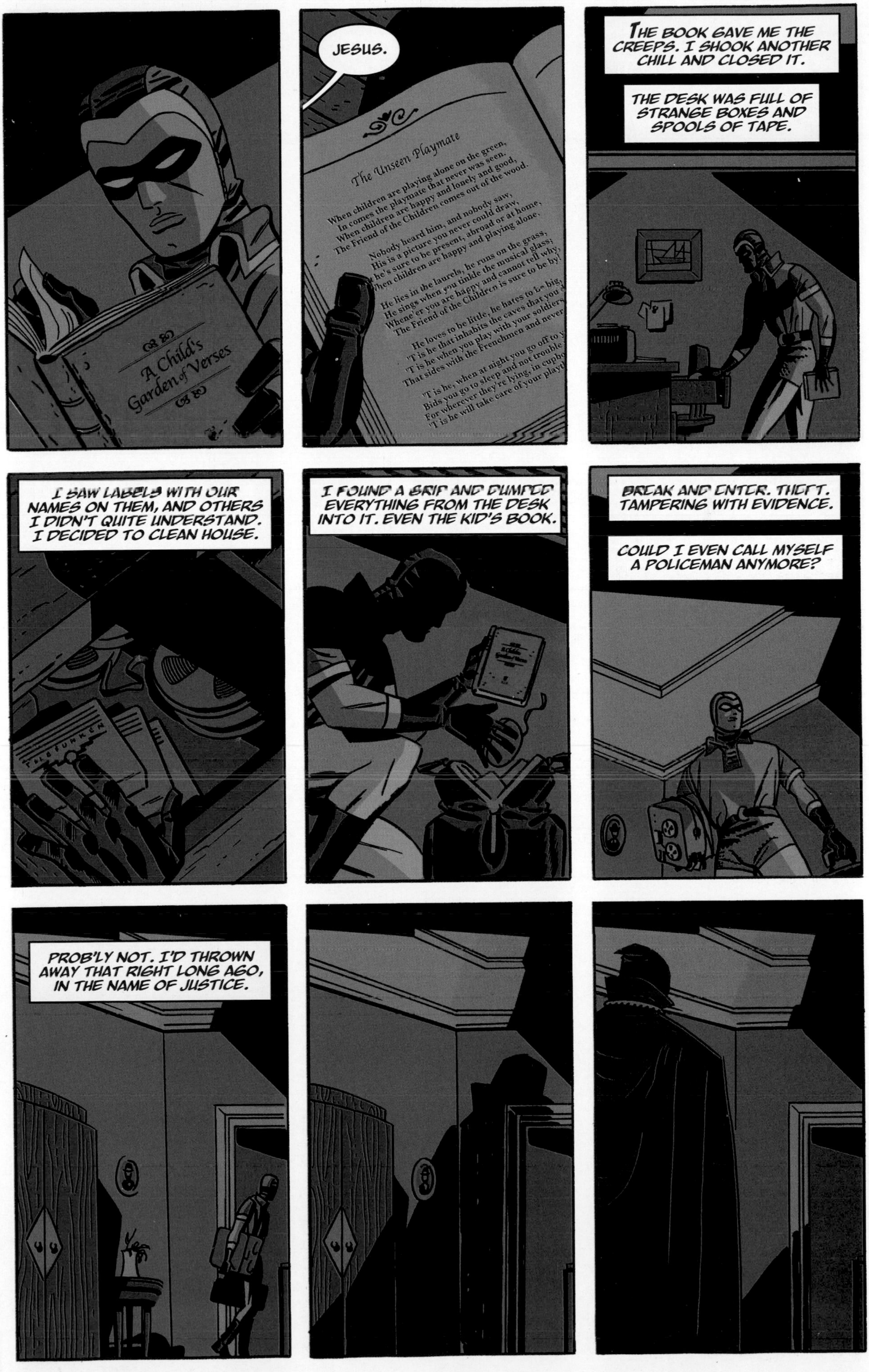
A Child's Garden of Verses
JESUS.
The Unseen Playmate
When children are playing alone on the green,
In comes the playmate that never was seen.
When children are happy and lonely and good,
The Friend of the Children comes out of the wood.
THE BOOK GAVE ME THE CREEPS. I SHOOK ANOTHER CHILL AND CLOSED IT.
THE DESK WAS FULL OF STRANGE BOXES AND SPOOLS OF TAPE.
I SAW LABELS WITH OUR NAMES ON THEM, AND OTHERS I DIDN'T QUITE UNDERSTAND. I DECIDED TO CLEAN HOUSE.
I FOUND A GRIP AND DUMPED EVERYTHING FROM THE DESK INTO IT. EVEN THE KID'S BOOK.
BREAK AND ENTER. THEFT. TAMPERING WITH EVIDENCE.
COULD I EVEN CALL MYSELF A POLICEMAN ANYMORE?
PROB'LY NOT. I'D THROWN AWAY THAT RIGHT LONG AGO, IN THE NAME OF JUSTICE.

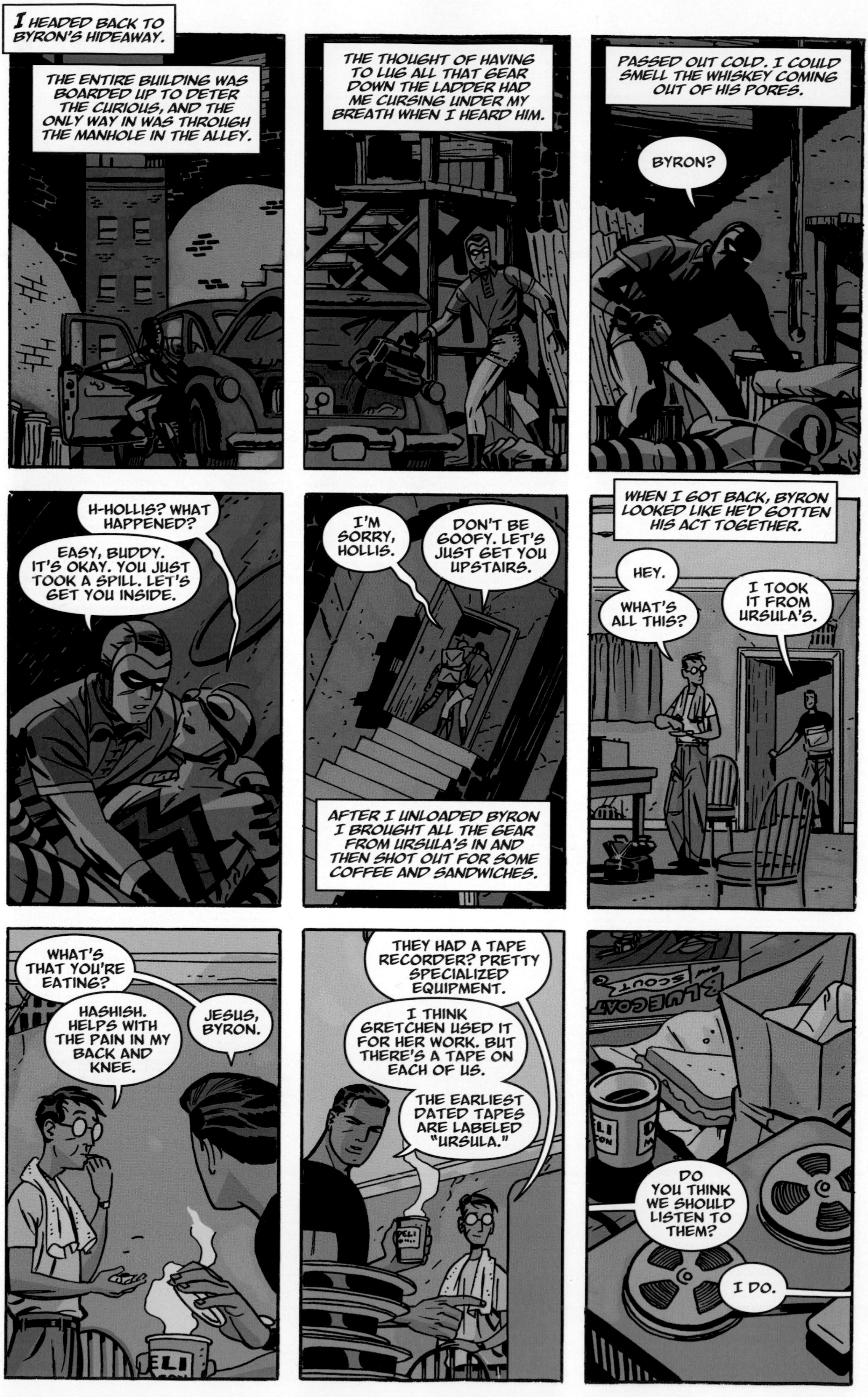
I HEADED BACK TO BYRON'S HIDEAWAY.
THE ENTIRE BUILDING WAS BOARDED UP TO DETER THE CURIOUS, AND THE ONLY WAY IN WAS THROUGH THE MANHOLE IN THE ALLEY.
THE THOUGHT OF HAVING TO LUG ALL THAT GEAR DOWN THE LADDER HAD ME CURSING UNDER MY BREATH WHEN I HEARD HIM.
PASSED OUT COLD. I COULD SMELL THE WHISKEY COMING OUT OF HIS PORES.
BYRON?
H-HOLLIS? WHAT HAPPENED?
EASY, BUDDY. IT'S OKAY. YOU JUST TOOK A SPILL. LET'S GET YOU INSIDE.
I'M SORRY, HOLLIS.
DON'T BE GOOFY. LET'S JUST GET YOU UPSTAIRS.
AFTER I UNLOADED BYRON I BROUGHT ALL THE GEAR FROM URSULA'S IN AND THEN SHOT OUT FOR SOME COFFEE AND SANDWICHES.
WHEN I GOT BACK, BYRON LOOKED LIKE HE'D GOTTEN HIS ACT TOGETHER.
HEY.
WHAT'S ALL THIS?
I TOOK IT FROM URSULA'S.
WHAT'S THAT YOU'RE EATING?
HASHISH. HELPS WITH THE PAIN IN MY BACK AND KNEE.
JESUS, BYRON.
THEY HAD A TAPE RECORDER? PRETTY SPECIALIZED EQUIPMENT.
I THINK GRETCHEN USED IT FOR HER WORK. BUT THERE'S A TAPE ON EACH OF US.
THE EARLIEST DATED TAPES ARE LABELED "URSULA."
DELI
BLUE GOAT SCOUT
DO YOU THINK WE SHOULD LISTEN TO THEM?
I DO.

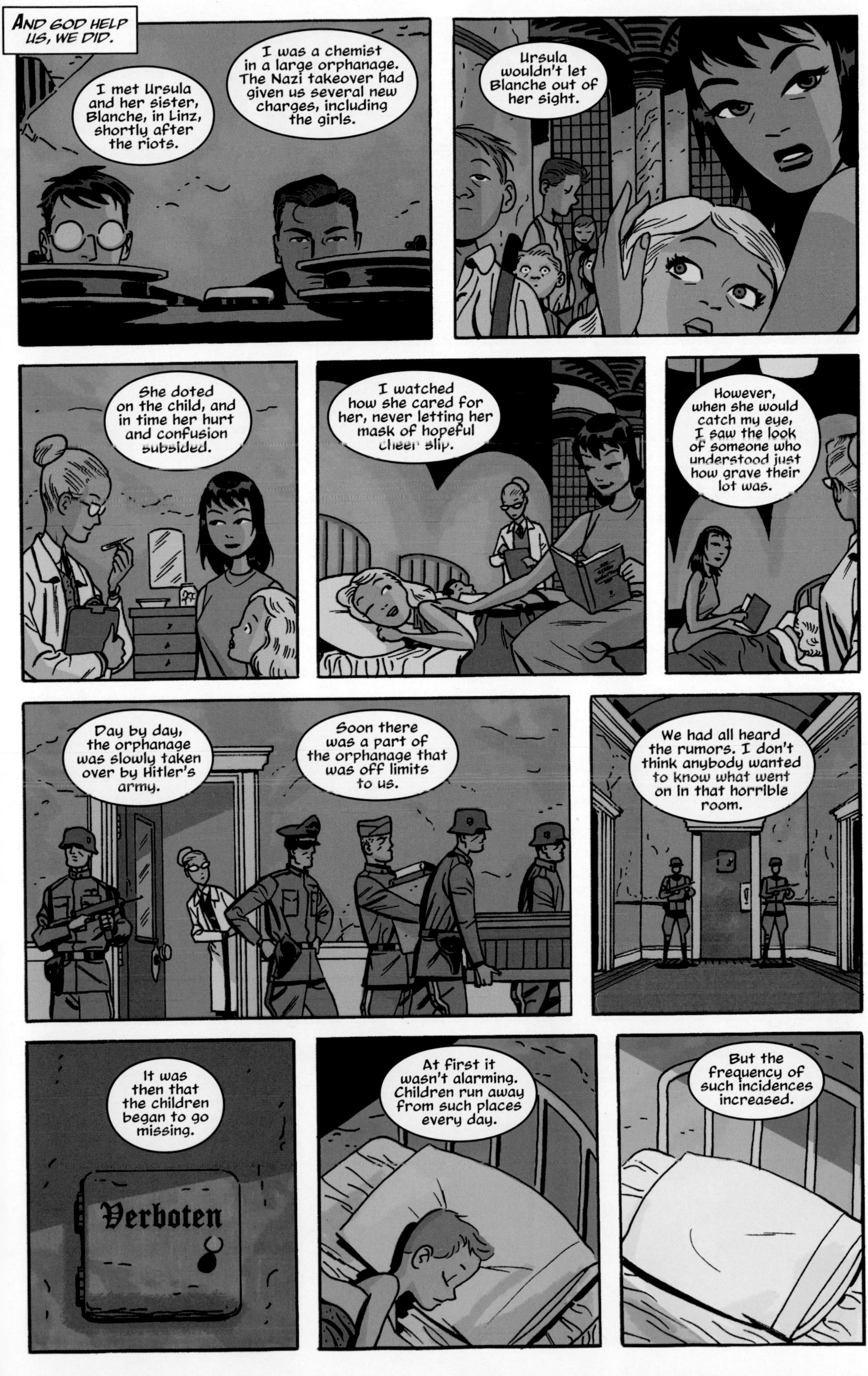
AND GOD HELP US, WE DID.
I met Ursula and her sister, Blanche, in Linz, shortly after the riots.
I was a chemist in a large orphanage. The Nazi takeover had given us several new charges, including the girls.
Ursula wouldn't let Blanche out of her sight.
She doted on the child, and in time her hurt and confusion subsided.
I watched how she cared for her, never letting her mask of hopeful cheer slip.
However, when she would catch my eye, I saw the look of someone who understood just how grave their lot was.
Day by day, the orphanage was slowly taken over by Hitler's army.
Soon there was a part of the orphanage that was off limits to us.
We had all heard the rumors. I don't think anybody wanted to know what went on in that horrible room.
It was then that the children began to go missing.
Verboten
At first it wasn't alarming. Children run away from such places every day.
But the frequency of such incidences increased.

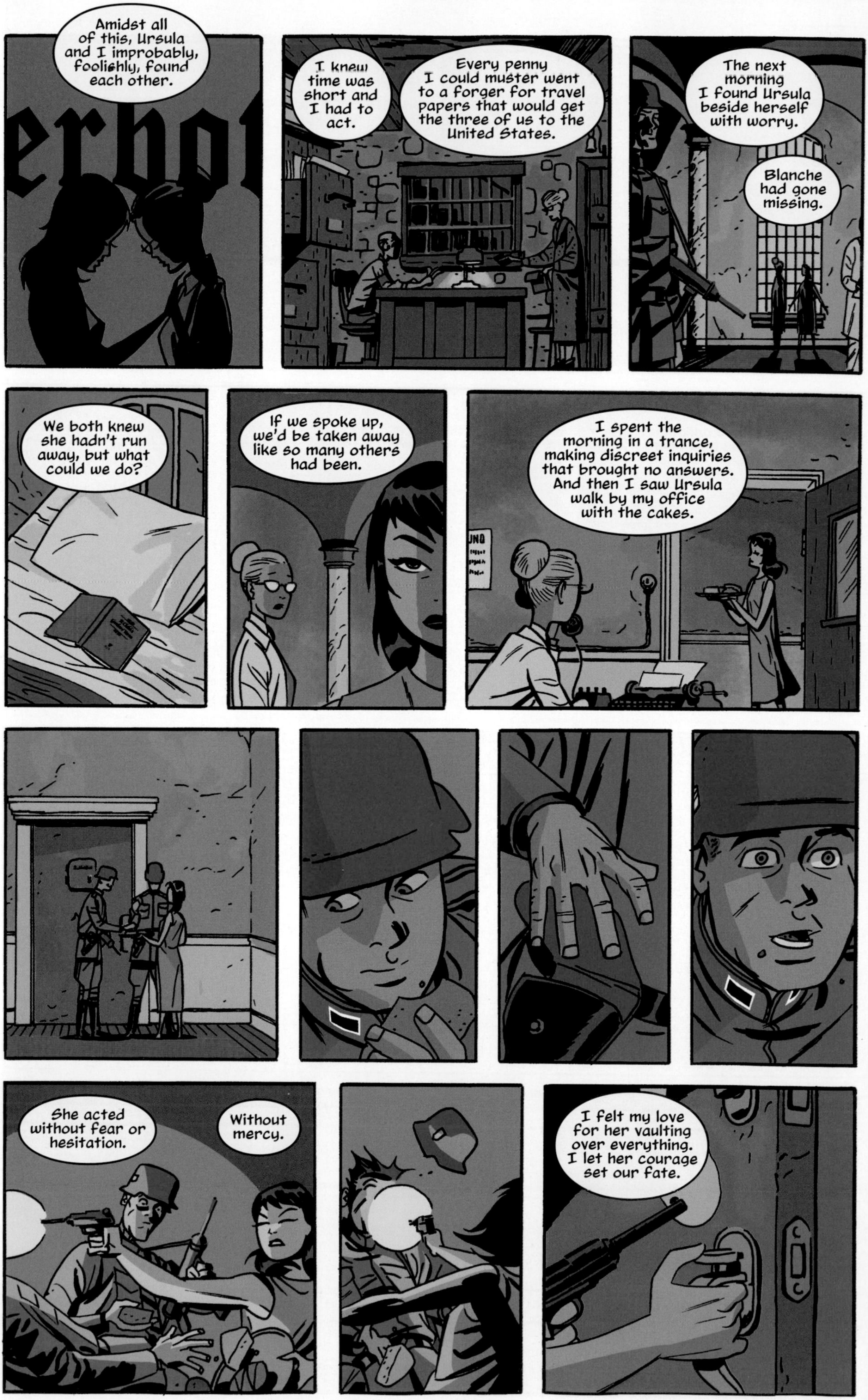
Amidst all of this, Ursula and I improbably, foolishly, found each other.
erbot
I knew time was short and I had to act.
Every penny I could muster went to a forger for travel papers that would get the three of us to the United States.
The next morning I found Ursula beside herself with worry.
Blanche had gone missing.
We both knew she hadn't run away, but what could we do?
If we spoke up, we'd be taken away like so many others had been.
I spent the morning in a trance, making discreet inquiries that brought no answers. And then I saw Ursula walk by my office with the cakes.
She acted without fear or hesitation.
Without mercy.
I felt my love for her vaulting over everything. I let her courage set our fate.

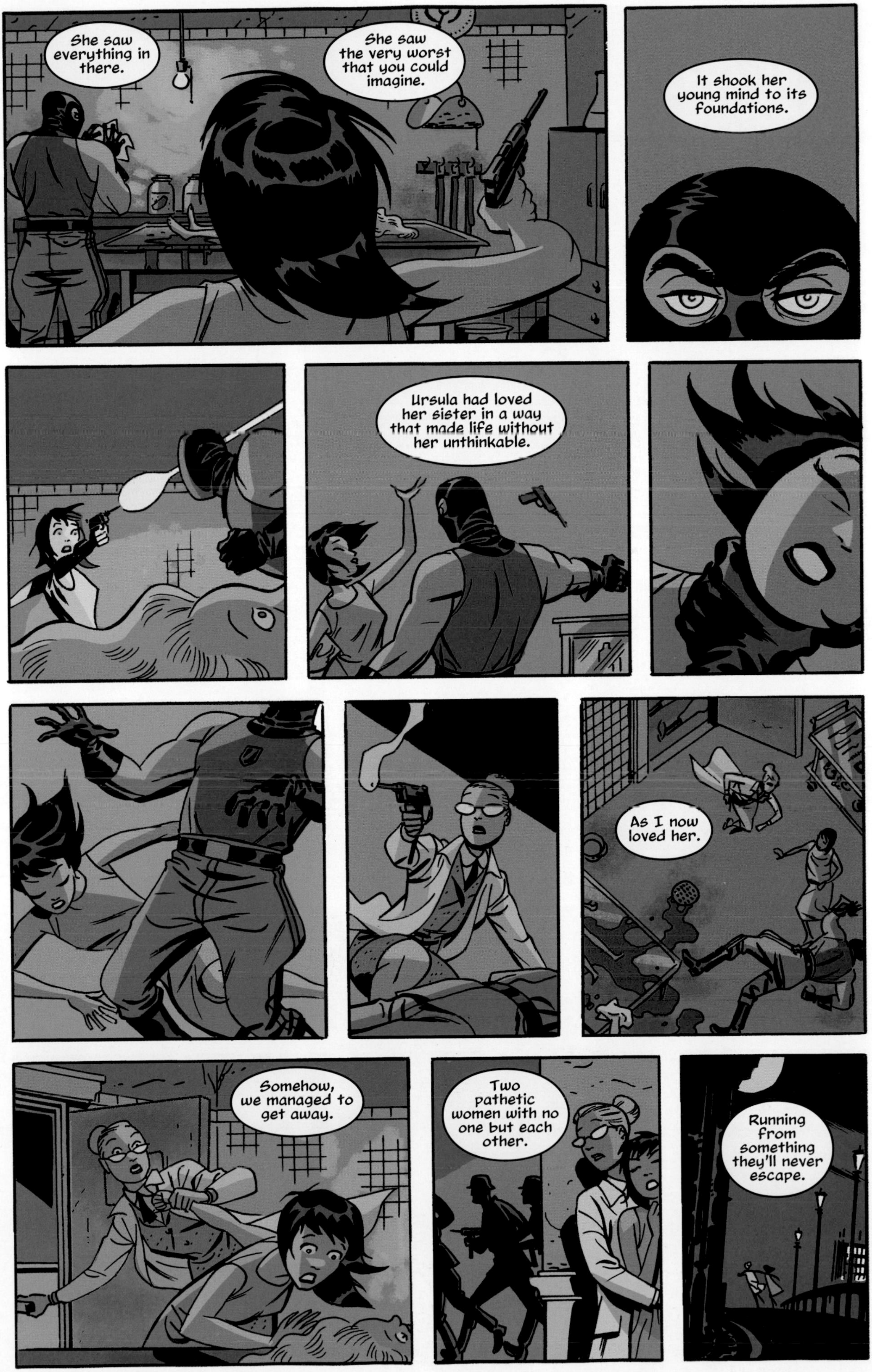
She saw everything in there.
She saw the very worst that you could imagine.
It shook her young mind to its foundations.
Ursula had loved her sister in a way that made life without her unthinkable.
As I now loved her.
Somehow, we managed to get away.
Two pathetic women with no one but each other.
Running from something they'll never escape.

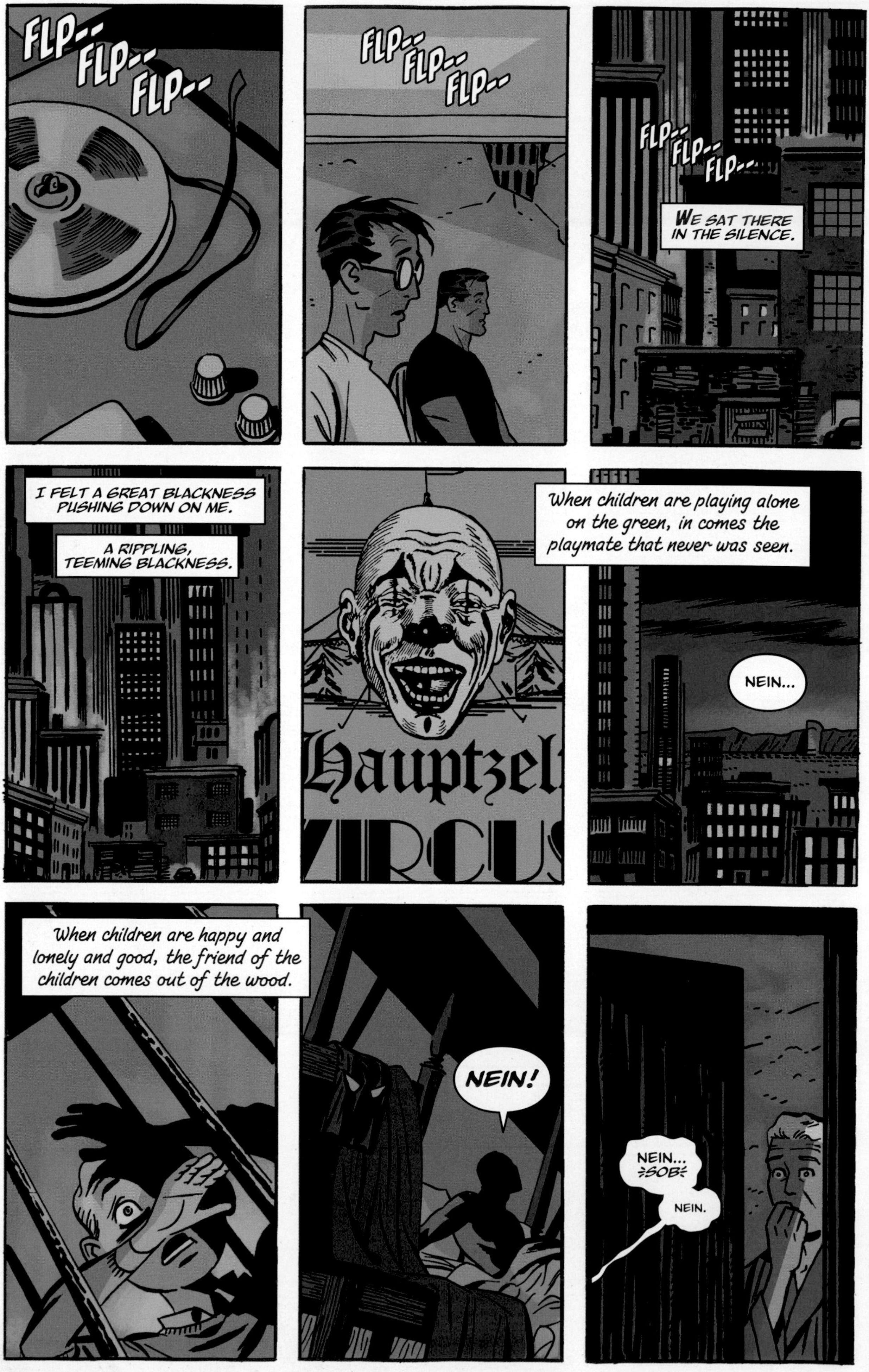
FLP--
FLP--
FLP--
FLP--
FLP--
FLP--
FLP--
FLP--
FLP--
WE SAT THERE IN THE SILENCE.
I FELT A GREAT BLACKNESS PUSHING DOWN ON ME.
A RIPPLING, TEEMING BLACKNESS.
Hauptzel
ZIRCUS
When children are playing alone on the green, in comes the playmate that never was seen.
NEIN...
When children are happy and lonely and good, the friend of the children comes out of the wood.
NEIN!
NEIN... SOB
NEIN.

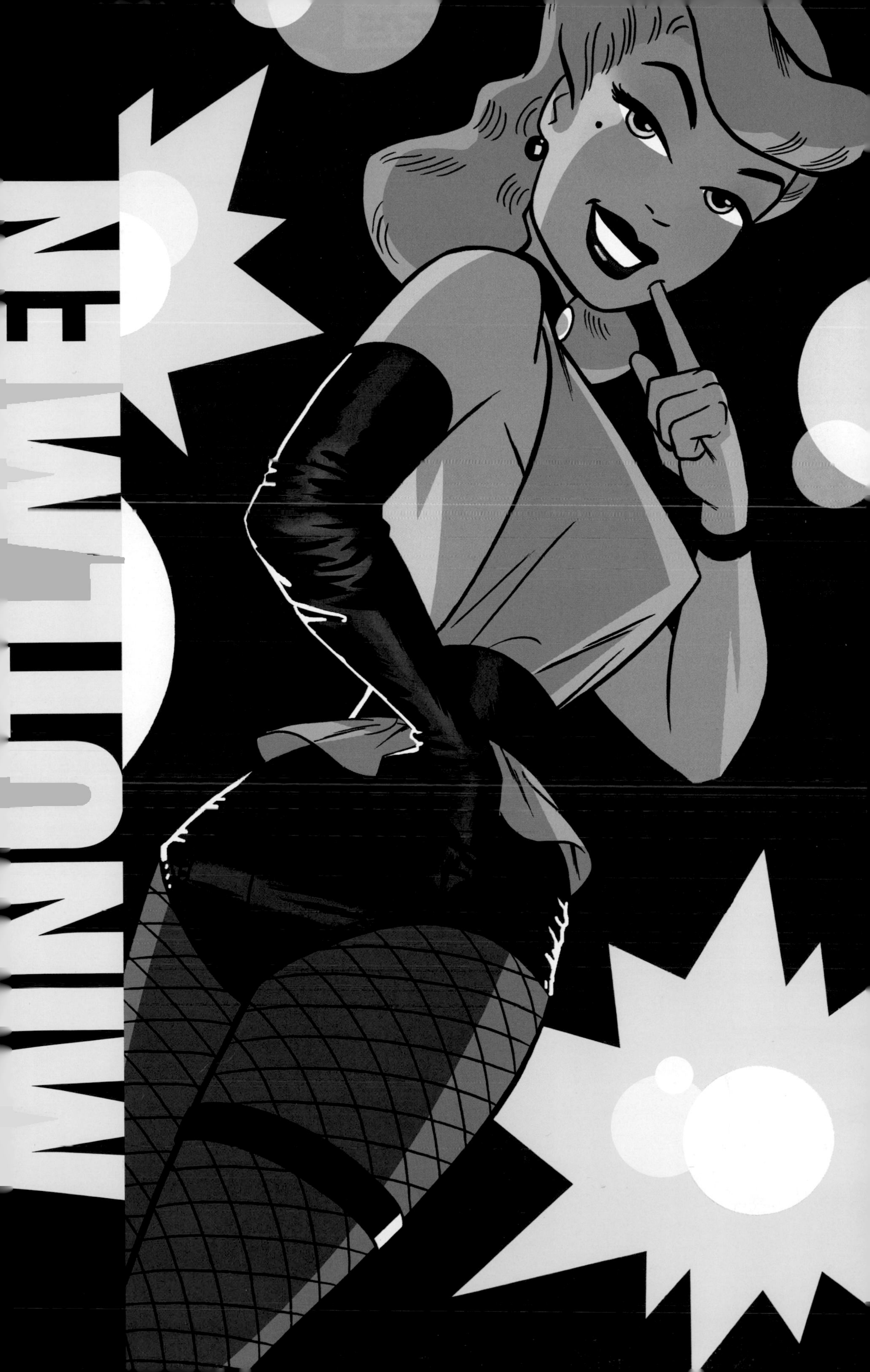

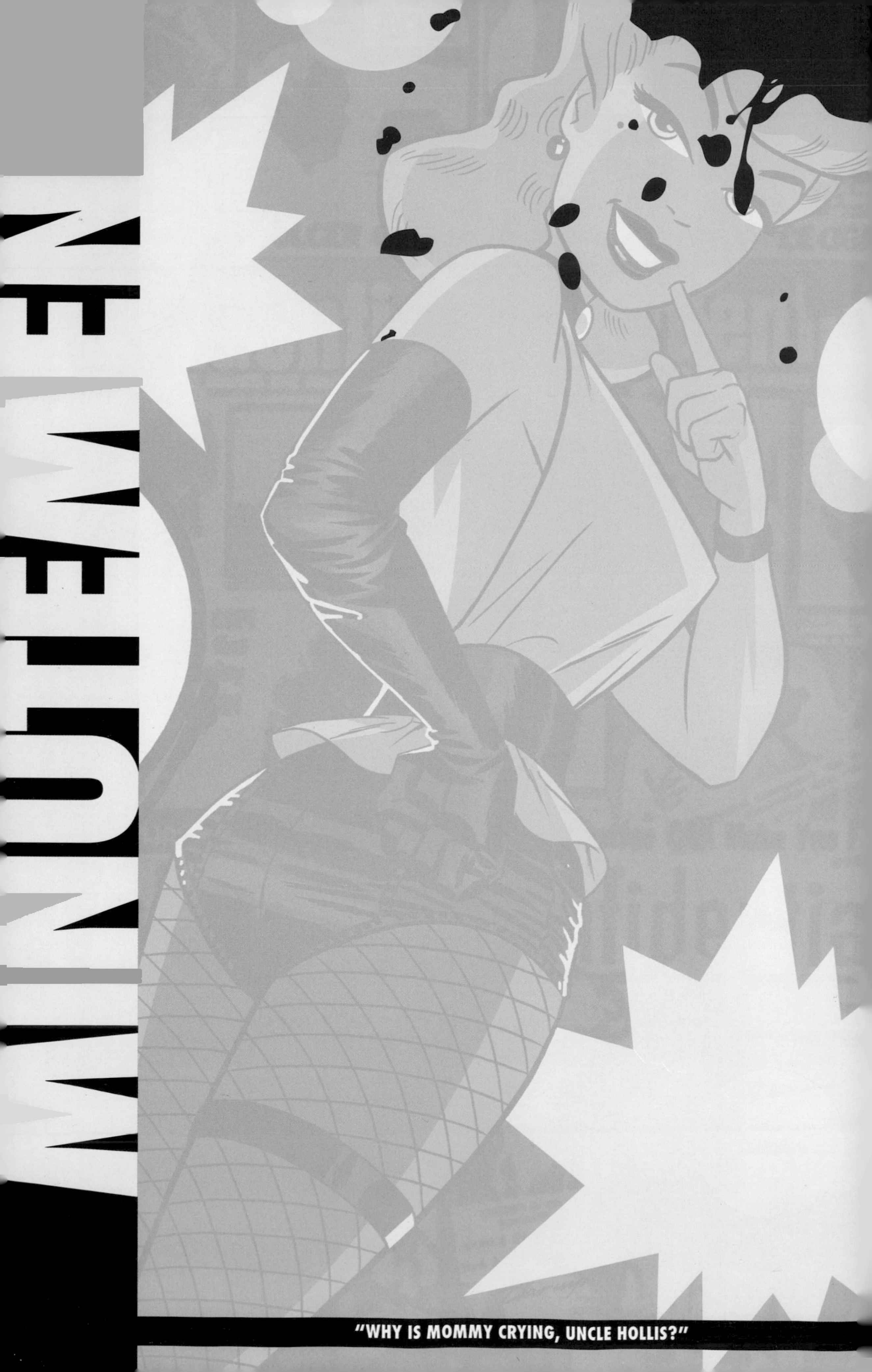
MINUTEMEN
"WHY IS MOMMY CRYING, UNCLE HOLLIS?"

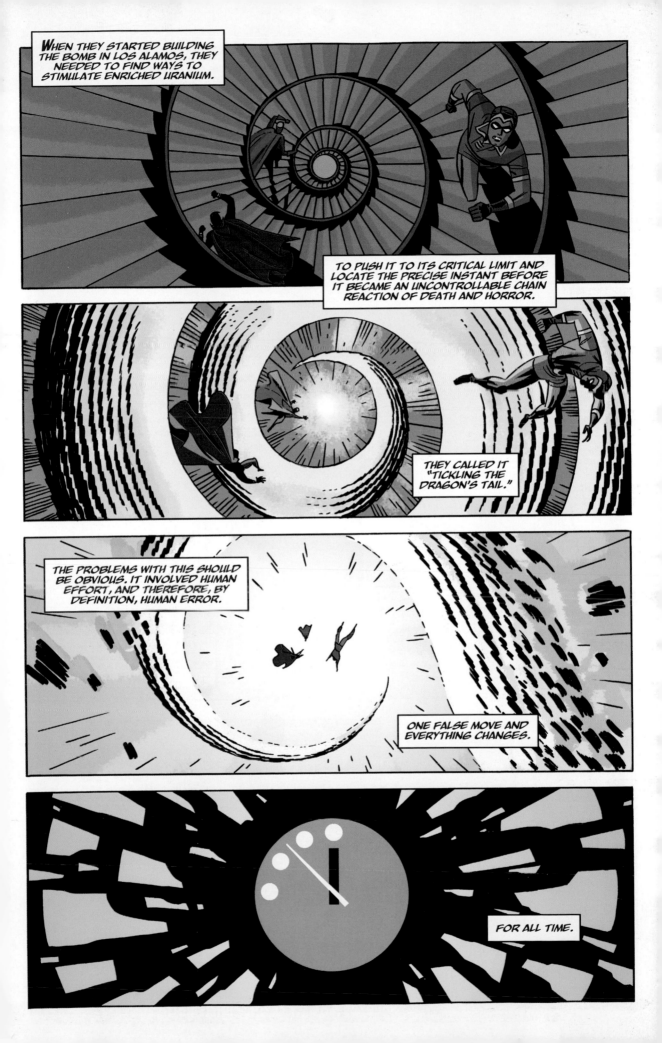

WHEN THEY STARTED BUILDING THE BOMB IN LOS ALAMOS, THEY NEEDED TO FIND WAYS TO STIMULATE ENRICHED URANIUM.

TO PUSH IT TO ITS CRITICAL LIMIT AND LOCATE THE PRECISE INSTANT BEFORE IT BECAME AN UNCONTROLLABLE CHAIN REACTION OF DEATH AND HORROR.

THEY CALLED IT "TICKLING THE DRAGON'S TAIL."

THE PROBLEMS WITH THIS SHOULD BE OBVIOUS. IT INVOLVED HUMAN EFFORT, AND THEREFORE, BY DEFINITION, HUMAN ERROR.

ONE FALSE MOVE AND EVERYTHING CHANGES.

FOR ALL TIME.

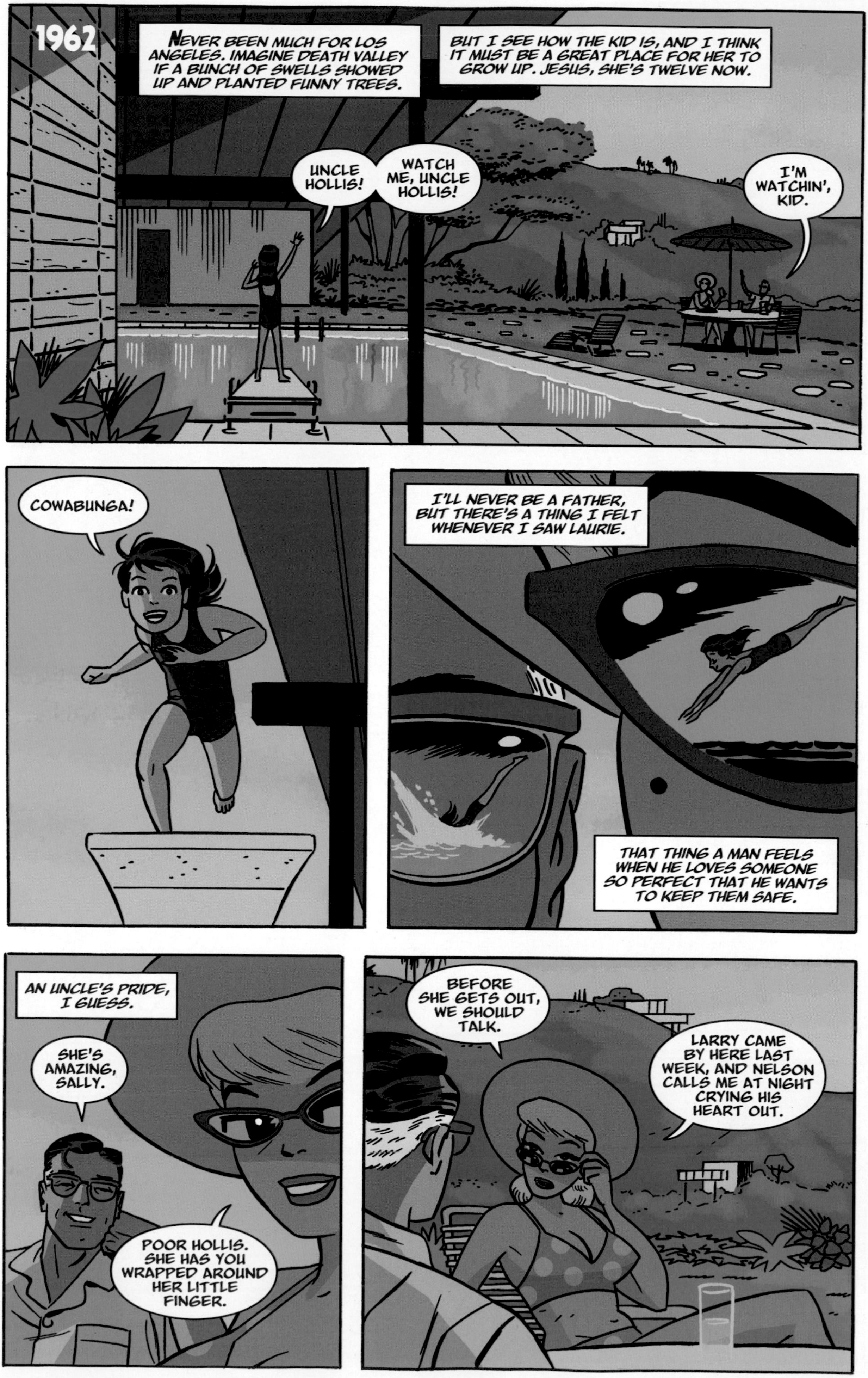
1962
NEVER BEEN MUCH FOR LOS ANGELES. IMAGINE DEATH VALLEY IF A BUNCH OF SWELLS SHOWED UP AND PLANTED FUNNY TREES.
BUT I SEE HOW THE KID IS, AND I THINK IT MUST BE A GREAT PLACE FOR HER TO GROW UP. JESUS, SHE'S TWELVE NOW.
UNCLE HOLLIS!
WATCH ME, UNCLE HOLLIS!
I'M WATCHIN', KID.
COWABUNGA!
I'LL NEVER BE A FATHER, BUT THERE'S A THING I FELT WHENEVER I SAW LAURIE.
THAT THING A MAN FEELS WHEN HE LOVES SOMEONE SO PERFECT THAT HE WANTS TO KEEP THEM SAFE.
AN UNCLE'S PRIDE, I GUESS.
SHE'S AMAZING, SALLY.
POOR HOLLIS. SHE HAS YOU WRAPPED AROUND HER LITTLE FINGER.
BEFORE SHE GETS OUT, WE SHOULD TALK.
LARRY CAME BY HERE LAST WEEK, AND NELSON CALLS ME AT NIGHT CRYING HIS HEART OUT.

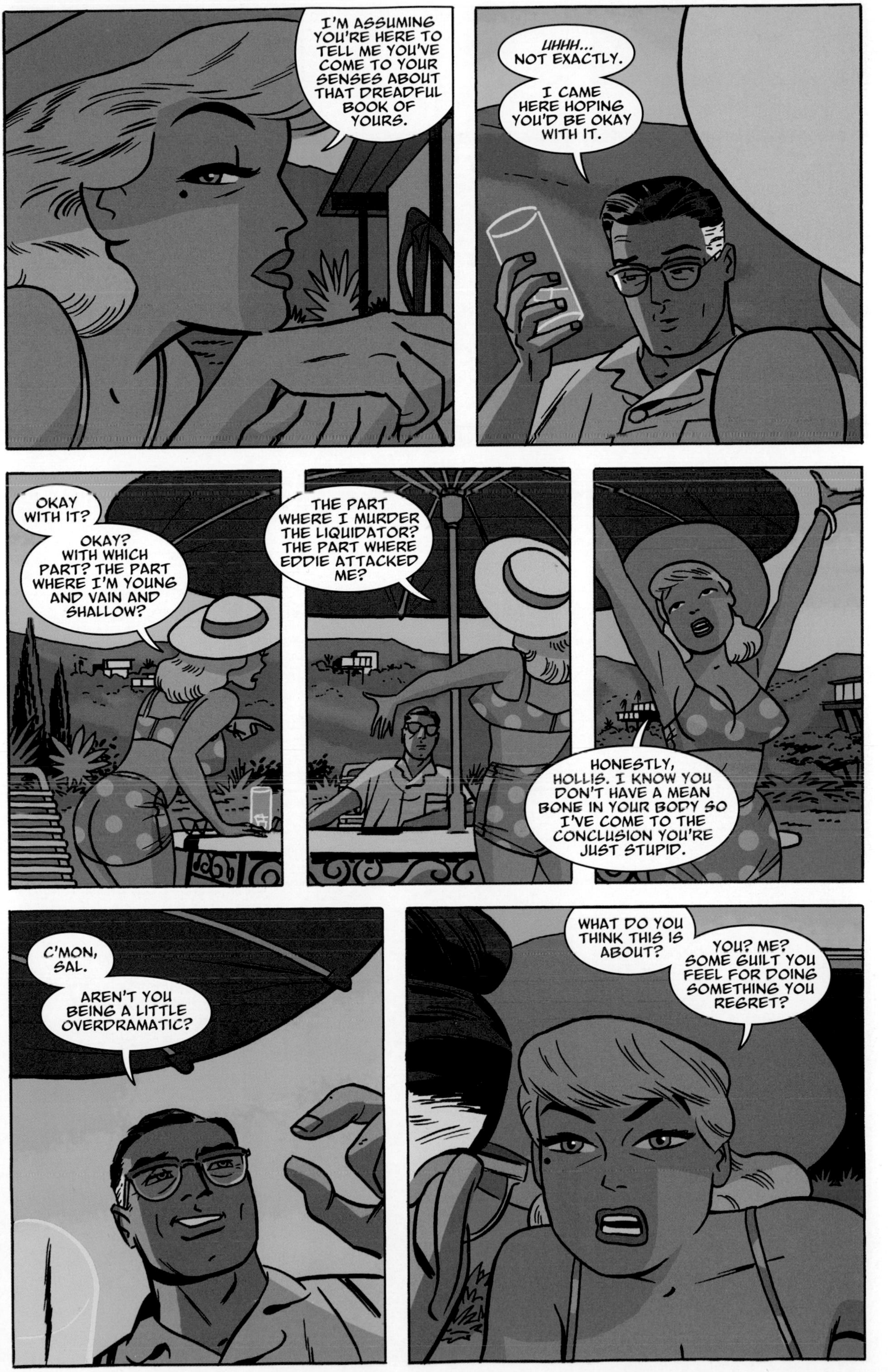
I'M ASSUMING YOU'RE HERE TO TELL ME YOU'VE COME TO YOUR SENSES ABOUT THAT DREADFUL BOOK OF YOURS.
UHHH... NOT EXACTLY.
I CAME HERE HOPING YOU'D BE OKAY WITH IT.
OKAY WITH IT?
OKAY? WITH WHICH PART? THE PART WHERE I'M YOUNG AND VAIN AND SHALLOW?
THE PART WHERE I MURDER THE LIQUIDATOR? THE PART WHERE EDDIE ATTACKED ME?
HONESTLY, HOLLIS. I KNOW YOU DON'T HAVE A MEAN BONE IN YOUR BODY SO I'VE COME TO THE CONCLUSION YOU'RE JUST STUPID.
C'MON, SAL.
AREN'T YOU BEING A LITTLE OVERDRAMATIC?
WHAT DO YOU THINK THIS IS ABOUT?
YOU? ME? SOME GUILT YOU FEEL FOR DOING SOMETHING YOU REGRET?

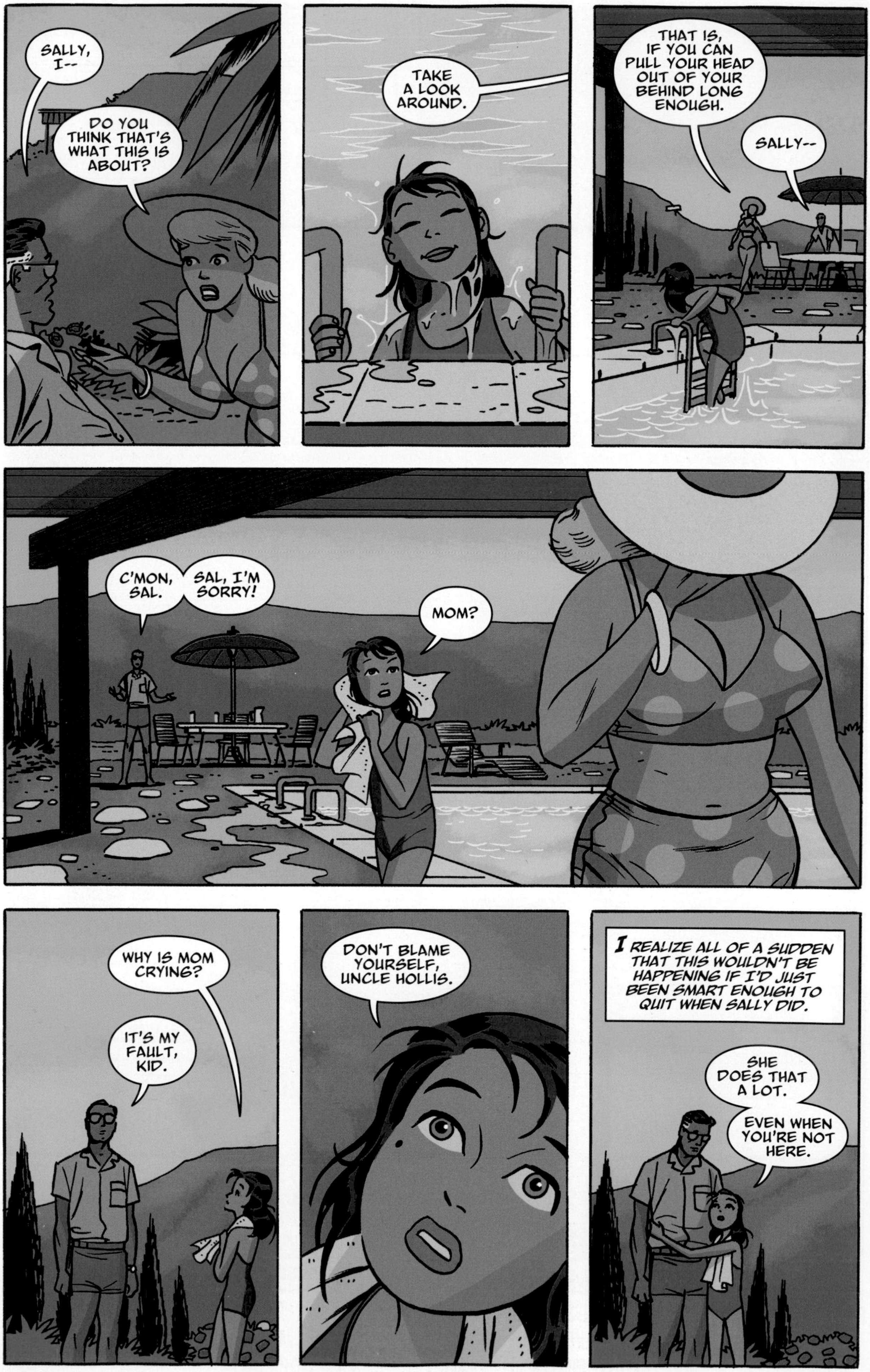
SALLY, I--
DO YOU THINK THAT'S WHAT THIS IS ABOUT?
TAKE A LOOK AROUND.
THAT IS, IF YOU CAN PULL YOUR HEAD OUT OF YOUR BEHIND LONG ENOUGH.
SALLY--
C'MON, SAL.
SAL, I'M SORRY!
MOM?
WHY IS MOM CRYING?
IT'S MY FAULT, KID.
DON'T BLAME YOURSELF, UNCLE HOLLIS.
I REALIZE ALL OF A SUDDEN THAT THIS WOULDN'T BE HAPPENING IF I'D JUST BEEN SMART ENOUGH TO QUIT WHEN SALLY DID.
SHE DOES THAT A LOT.
EVEN WHEN YOU'RE NOT HERE.

CHAPTER FIVE: THE DEMON CORE

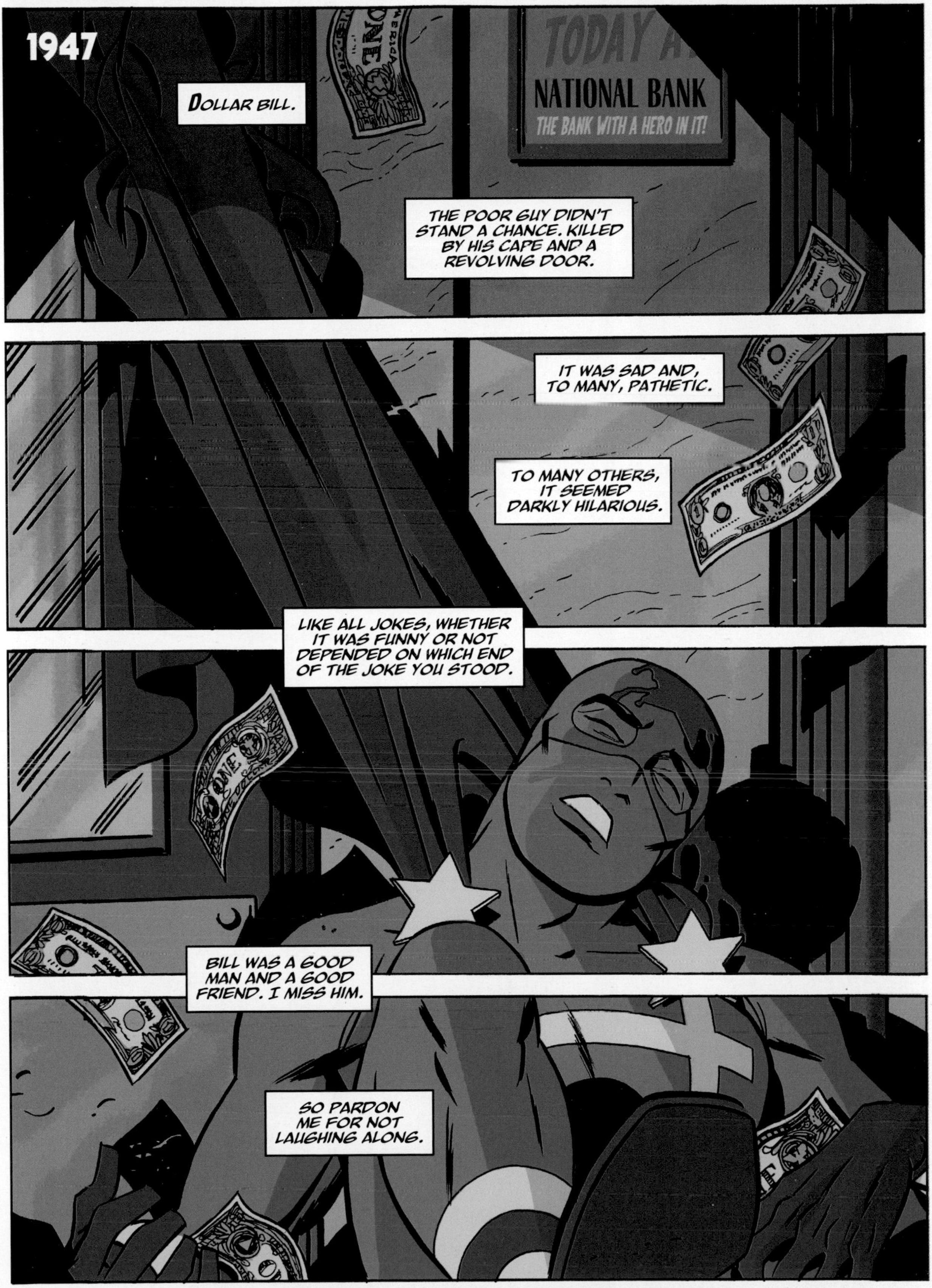
1947
TODAY AT
NATIONAL BANK
THE BANK WITH A HERO IN IT!
DOLLAR BILL.
THE POOR GUY DIDN'T STAND A CHANCE. KILLED BY HIS CAPE AND A REVOLVING DOOR.
IT WAS SAD AND, TO MANY, PATHETIC.
TO MANY OTHERS, IT SEEMED DARKLY HILARIOUS.
LIKE ALL JOKES, WHETHER IT WAS FUNNY OR NOT DEPENDED ON WHICH END OF THE JOKE YOU STOOD.
BILL WAS A GOOD MAN AND A GOOD FRIEND. I MISS HIM.
SO PARDON ME FOR NOT LAUGHING ALONG.

DARWYN COOKE WRITER & ARTIST

PHIL NOTO COLORIST **JARED K. FLETCHER** LETTERER **DARWYN COOKE** COVER ARTIST **MICHAEL CHO** VARIANT COVER ARTIST
CAMILLA ZHANG ASSISTANT EDITOR **WIL MOSS** ASSOCIATE EDITOR **MARK CHIARELLO** EDITOR
WATCHMEN CREATED BY **ALAN MOORE** & **DAVE GIBBONS**

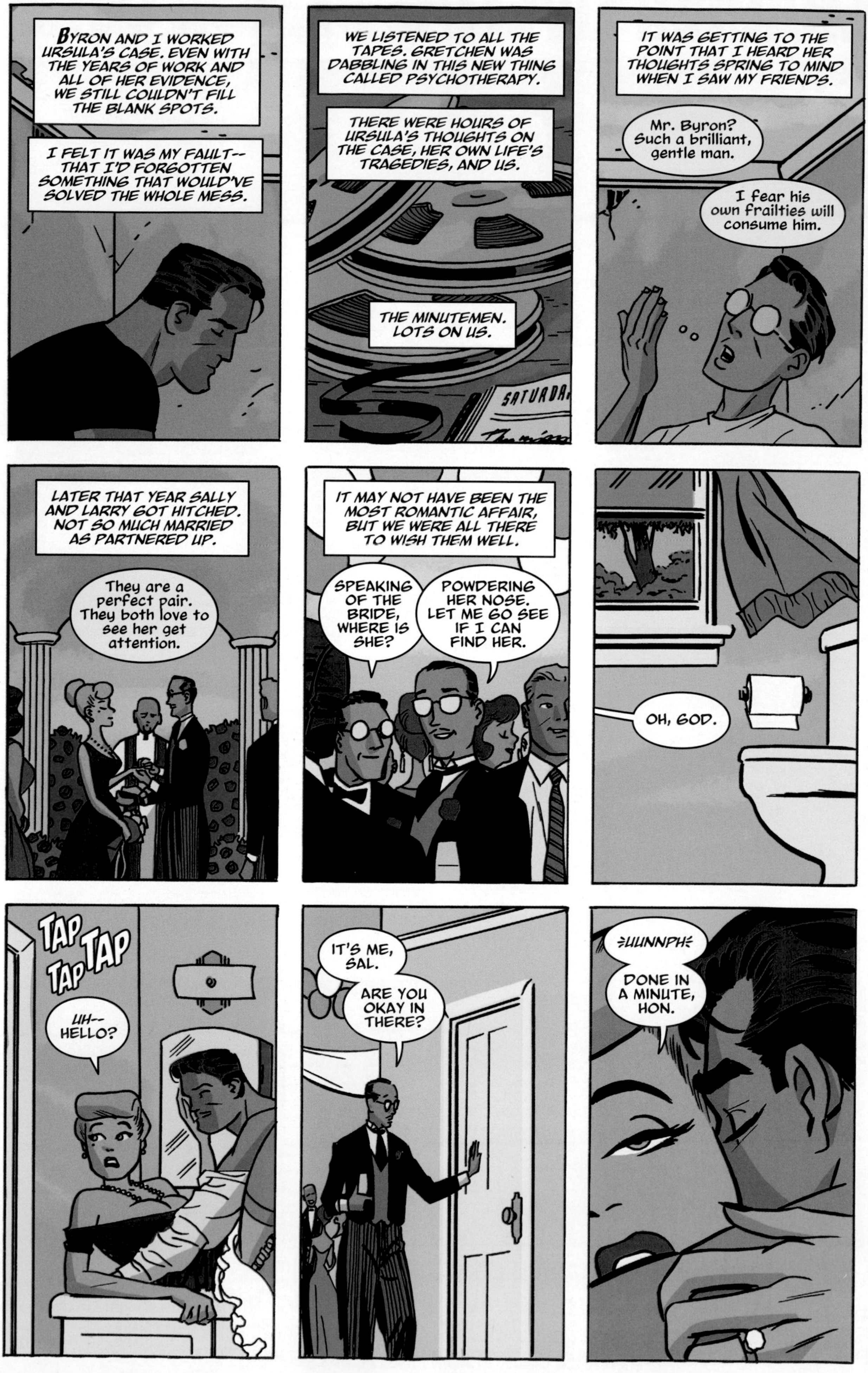
BYRON AND I WORKED URSULA'S CASE. EVEN WITH THE YEARS OF WORK AND ALL OF HER EVIDENCE, WE STILL COULDN'T FILL THE BLANK SPOTS.
I FELT IT WAS MY FAULT-- THAT I'D FORGOTTEN SOMETHING THAT WOULD'VE SOLVED THE WHOLE MESS.
WE LISTENED TO ALL THE TAPES. GRETCHEN WAS DABBLING IN THIS NEW THING CALLED PSYCHOTHERAPY.
THERE WERE HOURS OF URSULA'S THOUGHTS ON THE CASE, HER OWN LIFE'S TRAGEDIES, AND US.
THE MINUTEMEN. LOTS ON US.
IT WAS GETTING TO THE POINT THAT I HEARD HER THOUGHTS SPRING TO MIND WHEN I SAW MY FRIENDS.
Mr. Byron? Such a brilliant, gentle man.
I fear his own frailties will consume him.
LATER THAT YEAR SALLY AND LARRY GOT HITCHED. NOT SO MUCH MARRIED AS PARTNERED UP.
They are a perfect pair. They both love to see her get attention.
IT MAY NOT HAVE BEEN THE MOST ROMANTIC AFFAIR, BUT WE WERE ALL THERE TO WISH THEM WELL.
SPEAKING OF THE BRIDE, WHERE IS SHE?
POWDERING HER NOSE. LET ME GO SEE IF I CAN FIND HER.
OH, GOD.
TAP TAP TAP
UH-- HELLO?
IT'S ME, SAL.
ARE YOU OKAY IN THERE?
UUNNPH
DONE IN A MINUTE, HON.

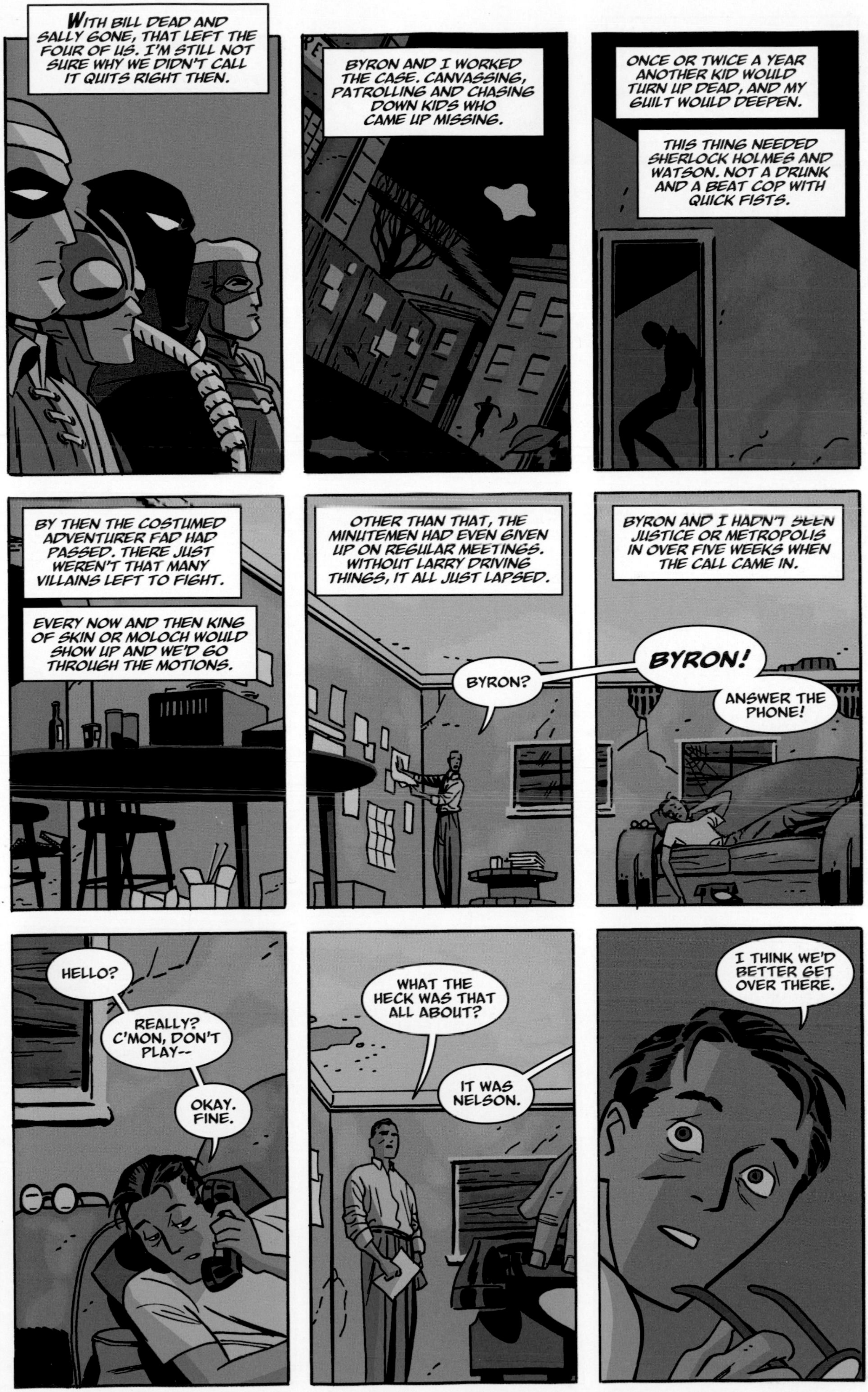
WITH BILL DEAD AND SALLY GONE, THAT LEFT THE FOUR OF US. I'M STILL NOT SURE WHY WE DIDN'T CALL IT QUITS RIGHT THEN.
BYRON AND I WORKED THE CASE. CANVASSING, PATROLLING AND CHASING DOWN KIDS WHO CAME UP MISSING.
ONCE OR TWICE A YEAR ANOTHER KID WOULD TURN UP DEAD, AND MY GUILT WOULD DEEPEN.
THIS THING NEEDED SHERLOCK HOLMES AND WATSON. NOT A DRUNK AND A BEAT COP WITH QUICK FISTS.
BY THEN THE COSTUMED ADVENTURER FAD HAD PASSED. THERE JUST WEREN'T THAT MANY VILLAINS LEFT TO FIGHT.
EVERY NOW AND THEN KING OF SKIN OR MOLOCH WOULD SHOW UP AND WE'D GO THROUGH THE MOTIONS.
OTHER THAN THAT, THE MINUTEMEN HAD EVEN GIVEN UP ON REGULAR MEETINGS. WITHOUT LARRY DRIVING THINGS, IT ALL JUST LAPSED.
BYRON AND I HADN'T SEEN JUSTICE OR METROPOLIS IN OVER FIVE WEEKS WHEN THE CALL CAME IN.
BYRON?
BYRON!
ANSWER THE PHONE!
HELLO?
REALLY? C'MON, DON'T PLAY--
OKAY. FINE.
WHAT THE HECK WAS THAT ALL ABOUT?
IT WAS NELSON.
I THINK WE'D BETTER GET OVER THERE.

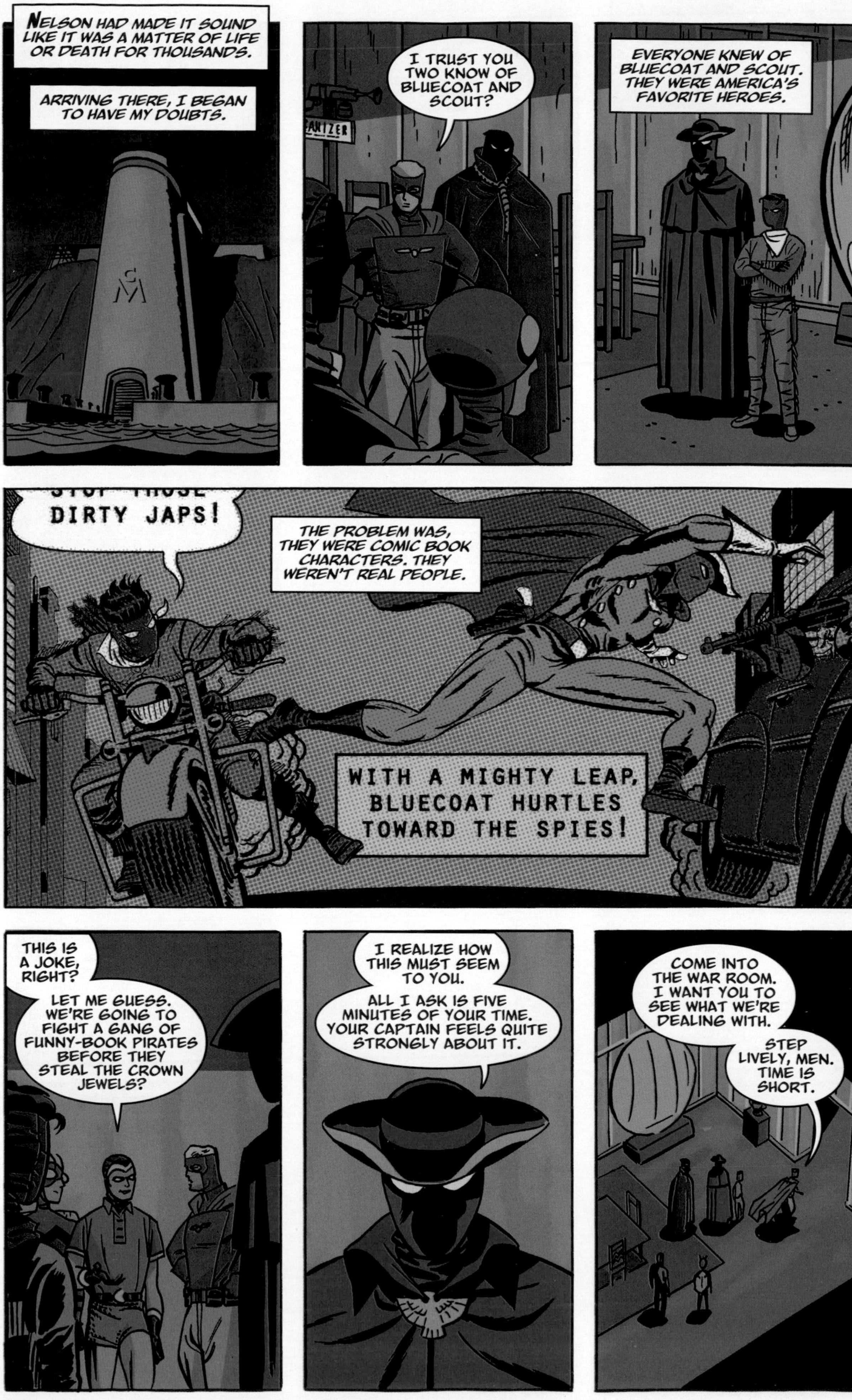
NELSON HAD MADE IT SOUND LIKE IT WAS A MATTER OF LIFE OR DEATH FOR THOUSANDS.
ARRIVING THERE, I BEGAN TO HAVE MY DOUBTS.
I TRUST YOU TWO KNOW OF BLUECOAT AND SCOUT?
EVERYONE KNEW OF BLUECOAT AND SCOUT. THEY WERE AMERICA'S FAVORITE HEROES.
DIRTY JAPS!
THE PROBLEM WAS, THEY WERE COMIC BOOK CHARACTERS. THEY WEREN'T REAL PEOPLE.
WITH A MIGHTY LEAP, BLUECOAT HURTLES TOWARD THE SPIES!
THIS IS A JOKE, RIGHT?
LET ME GUESS. WE'RE GOING TO FIGHT A GANG OF FUNNY-BOOK PIRATES BEFORE THEY STEAL THE CROWN JEWELS?
I REALIZE HOW THIS MUST SEEM TO YOU.
ALL I ASK IS FIVE MINUTES OF YOUR TIME. YOUR CAPTAIN FEELS QUITE STRONGLY ABOUT IT.
COME INTO THE WAR ROOM. I WANT YOU TO SEE WHAT WE'RE DEALING WITH.
STEP LIVELY, MEN. TIME IS SHORT.

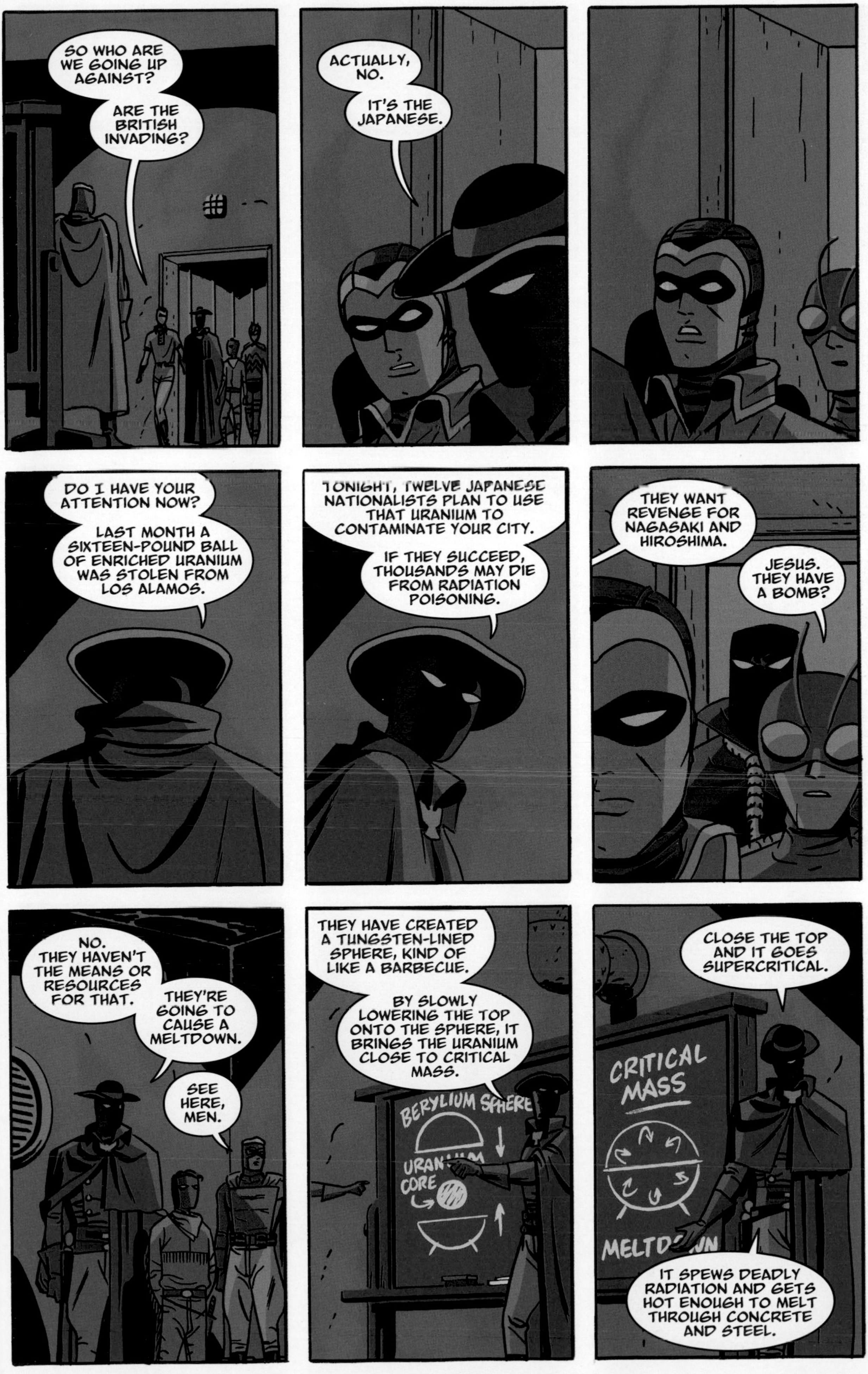
SO WHO ARE WE GOING UP AGAINST?
ARE THE BRITISH INVADING?
ACTUALLY, NO.
IT'S THE JAPANESE.
DO I HAVE YOUR ATTENTION NOW?
LAST MONTH A SIXTEEN-POUND BALL OF ENRICHED URANIUM WAS STOLEN FROM LOS ALAMOS.
TONIGHT, TWELVE JAPANESE NATIONALISTS PLAN TO USE THAT URANIUM TO CONTAMINATE YOUR CITY.
IF THEY SUCCEED, THOUSANDS MAY DIE FROM RADIATION POISONING.
THEY WANT REVENGE FOR NAGASAKI AND HIROSHIMA.
JESUS. THEY HAVE A BOMB?
NO. THEY HAVEN'T THE MEANS OR RESOURCES FOR THAT.
THEY'RE GOING TO CAUSE A MELTDOWN.
SEE HERE, MEN.
THEY HAVE CREATED A TUNGSTEN-LINED SPHERE, KIND OF LIKE A BARBECUE.
BY SLOWLY LOWERING THE TOP ONTO THE SPHERE, IT BRINGS THE URANIUM CLOSE TO CRITICAL MASS.
BERYLIUM SPHERE
CORE
CLOSE THE TOP AND IT GOES SUPERCRITICAL.
CRITICAL MASS
IT SPEWS DEADLY RADIATION AND GETS HOT ENOUGH TO MELT THROUGH CONCRETE AND STEEL.

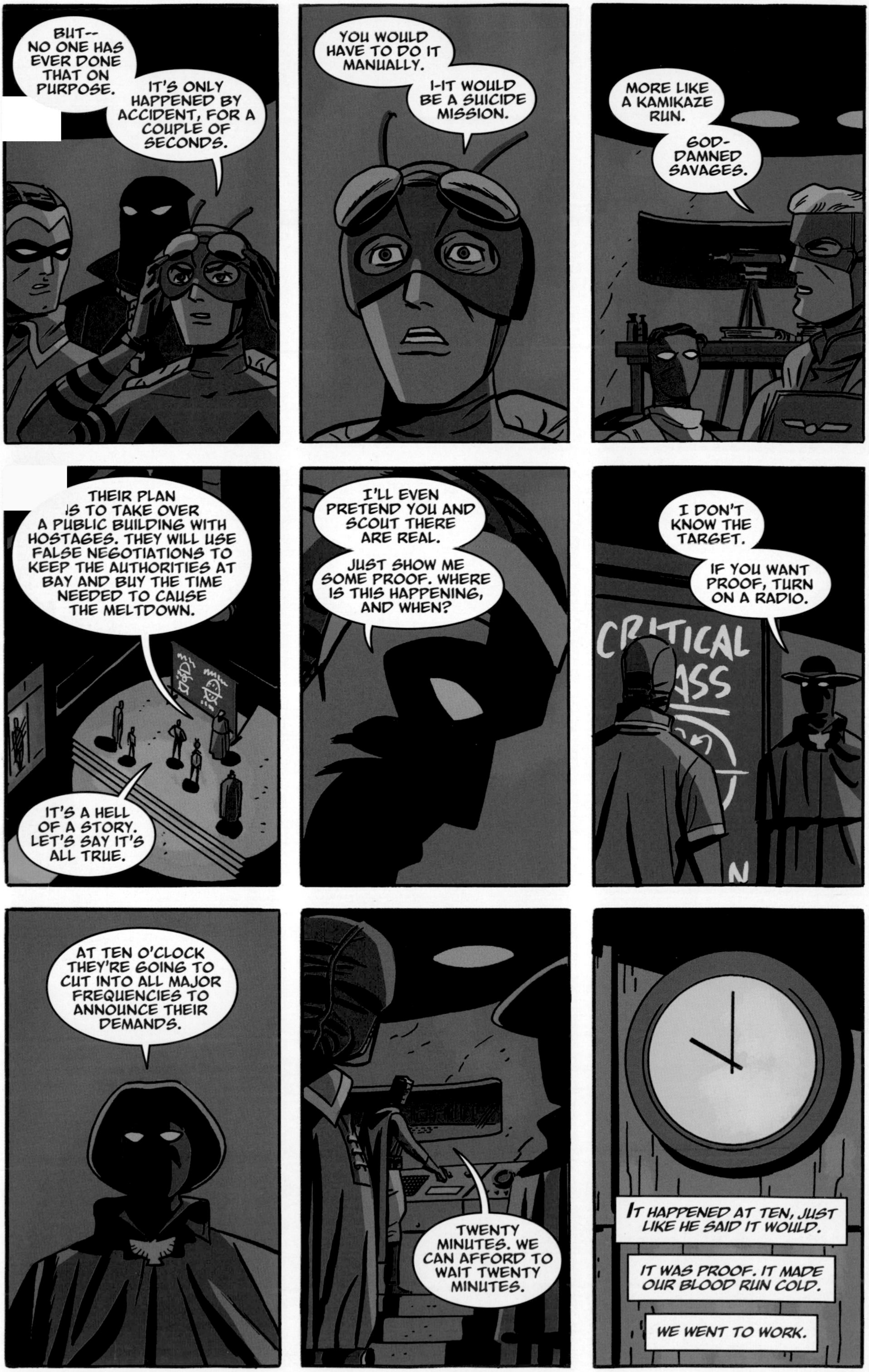
BUT-- NO ONE HAS EVER DONE THAT ON PURPOSE.
IT'S ONLY HAPPENED BY ACCIDENT, FOR A COUPLE OF SECONDS.
YOU WOULD HAVE TO DO IT MANUALLY.
I-IT WOULD BE A SUICIDE MISSION.
MORE LIKE A KAMIKAZE RUN.
GOD-DAMNED SAVAGES.
THEIR PLAN IS TO TAKE OVER A PUBLIC BUILDING WITH HOSTAGES. THEY WILL USE FALSE NEGOTIATIONS TO KEEP THE AUTHORITIES AT BAY AND BUY THE TIME NEEDED TO CAUSE THE MELTDOWN.
IT'S A HELL OF A STORY. LET'S SAY IT'S ALL TRUE.
I'LL EVEN PRETEND YOU AND SCOUT THERE ARE REAL.
JUST SHOW ME SOME PROOF. WHERE IS THIS HAPPENING, AND WHEN?
I DON'T KNOW THE TARGET.
IF YOU WANT PROOF, TURN ON A RADIO.
CRITICAL
ASS
AT TEN O'CLOCK THEY'RE GOING TO CUT INTO ALL MAJOR FREQUENCIES TO ANNOUNCE THEIR DEMANDS.
TWENTY MINUTES. WE CAN AFFORD TO WAIT TWENTY MINUTES.
IT HAPPENED AT TEN, JUST LIKE HE SAID IT WOULD.
IT WAS PROOF. IT MADE OUR BLOOD RUN COLD.
WE WENT TO WORK.

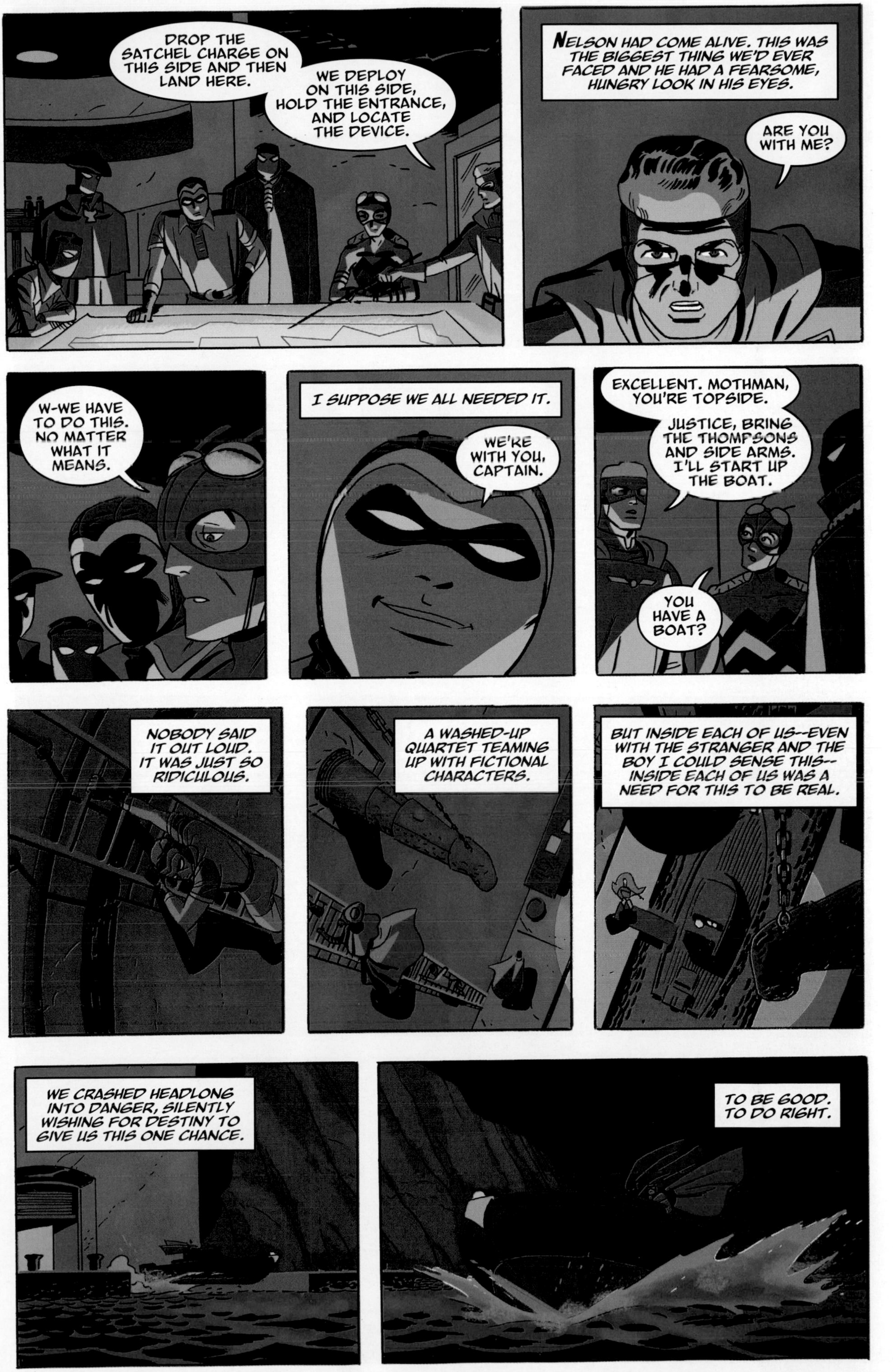
DROP THE SATCHEL CHARGE ON THIS SIDE AND THEN LAND HERE.
WE DEPLOY ON THIS SIDE, HOLD THE ENTRANCE, AND LOCATE THE DEVICE.
NELSON HAD COME ALIVE. THIS WAS THE BIGGEST THING WE'D EVER FACED AND HE HAD A FEARSOME, HUNGRY LOOK IN HIS EYES.
ARE YOU WITH ME?
W-WE HAVE TO DO THIS. NO MATTER WHAT IT MEANS.
I SUPPOSE WE ALL NEEDED IT.
WE'RE WITH YOU, CAPTAIN.
EXCELLENT. MOTHMAN, YOU'RE TOPSIDE.
JUSTICE, BRING THE THOMPSONS AND SIDE ARMS. I'LL START UP THE BOAT.
YOU HAVE A BOAT?
NOBODY SAID IT OUT LOUD. IT WAS JUST SO RIDICULOUS.
A WASHED-UP QUARTET TEAMING UP WITH FICTIONAL CHARACTERS.
BUT INSIDE EACH OF US--EVEN WITH THE STRANGER AND THE BOY I COULD SENSE THIS--INSIDE EACH OF US WAS A NEED FOR THIS TO BE REAL.
WE CRASHED HEADLONG INTO DANGER, SILENTLY WISHING FOR DESTINY TO GIVE US THIS ONE CHANCE.
TO BE GOOD. TO DO RIGHT.

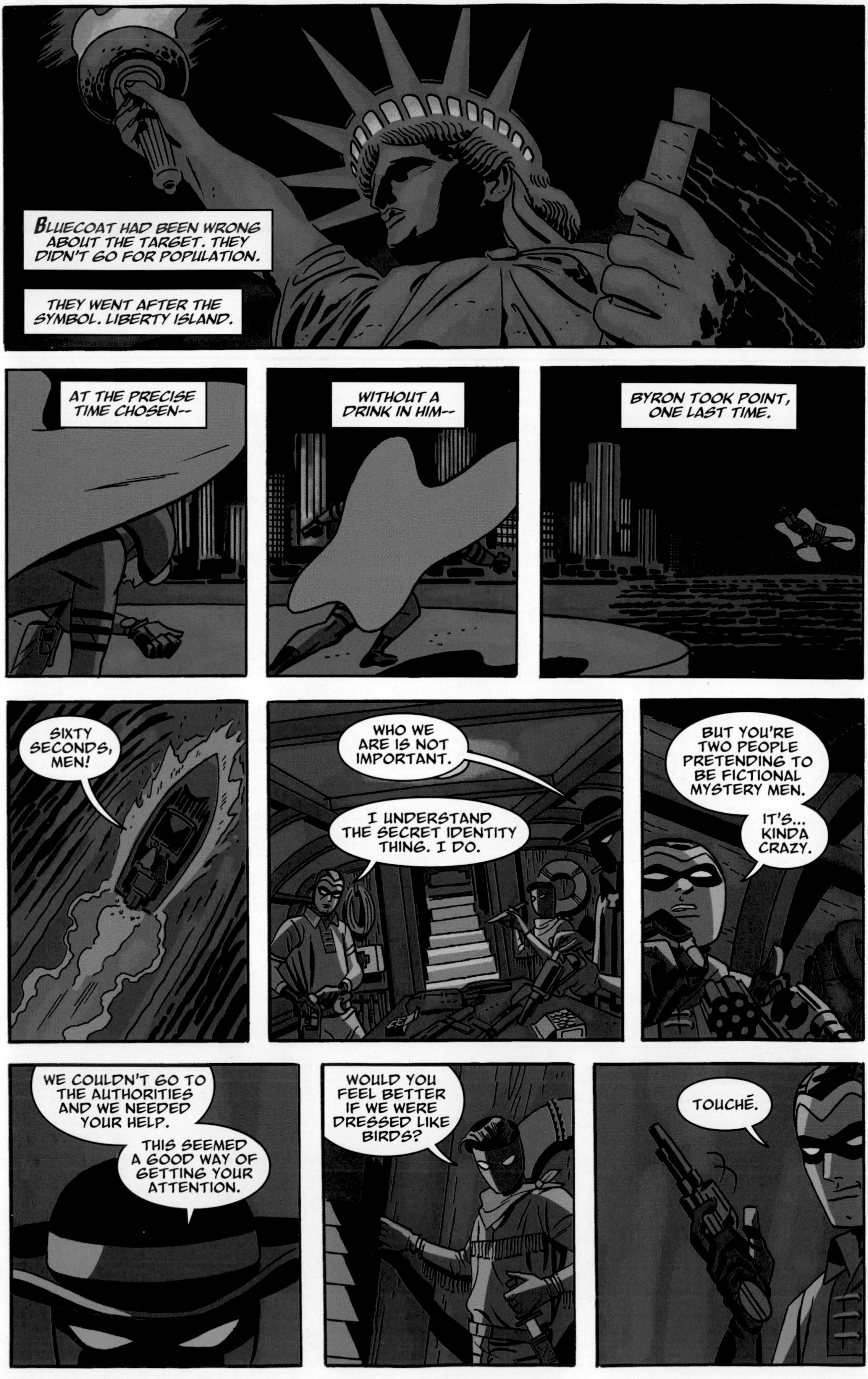
BLUECOAT HAD BEEN WRONG ABOUT THE TARGET. THEY DIDN'T GO FOR POPULATION.
THEY WENT AFTER THE SYMBOL. LIBERTY ISLAND.
AT THE PRECISE TIME CHOSEN--
WITHOUT A DRINK IN HIM--
BYRON TOOK POINT, ONE LAST TIME.
SIXTY SECONDS, MEN!
WHO WE ARE IS NOT IMPORTANT.
I UNDERSTAND THE SECRET IDENTITY THING. I DO.
BUT YOU'RE TWO PEOPLE PRETENDING TO BE FICTIONAL MYSTERY MEN.
IT'S... KINDA CRAZY.
WE COULDN'T GO TO THE AUTHORITIES AND WE NEEDED YOUR HELP.
THIS SEEMED A GOOD WAY OF GETTING YOUR ATTENTION.
WOULD YOU FEEL BETTER IF WE WERE DRESSED LIKE BIRDS?
TOUCHÉ.

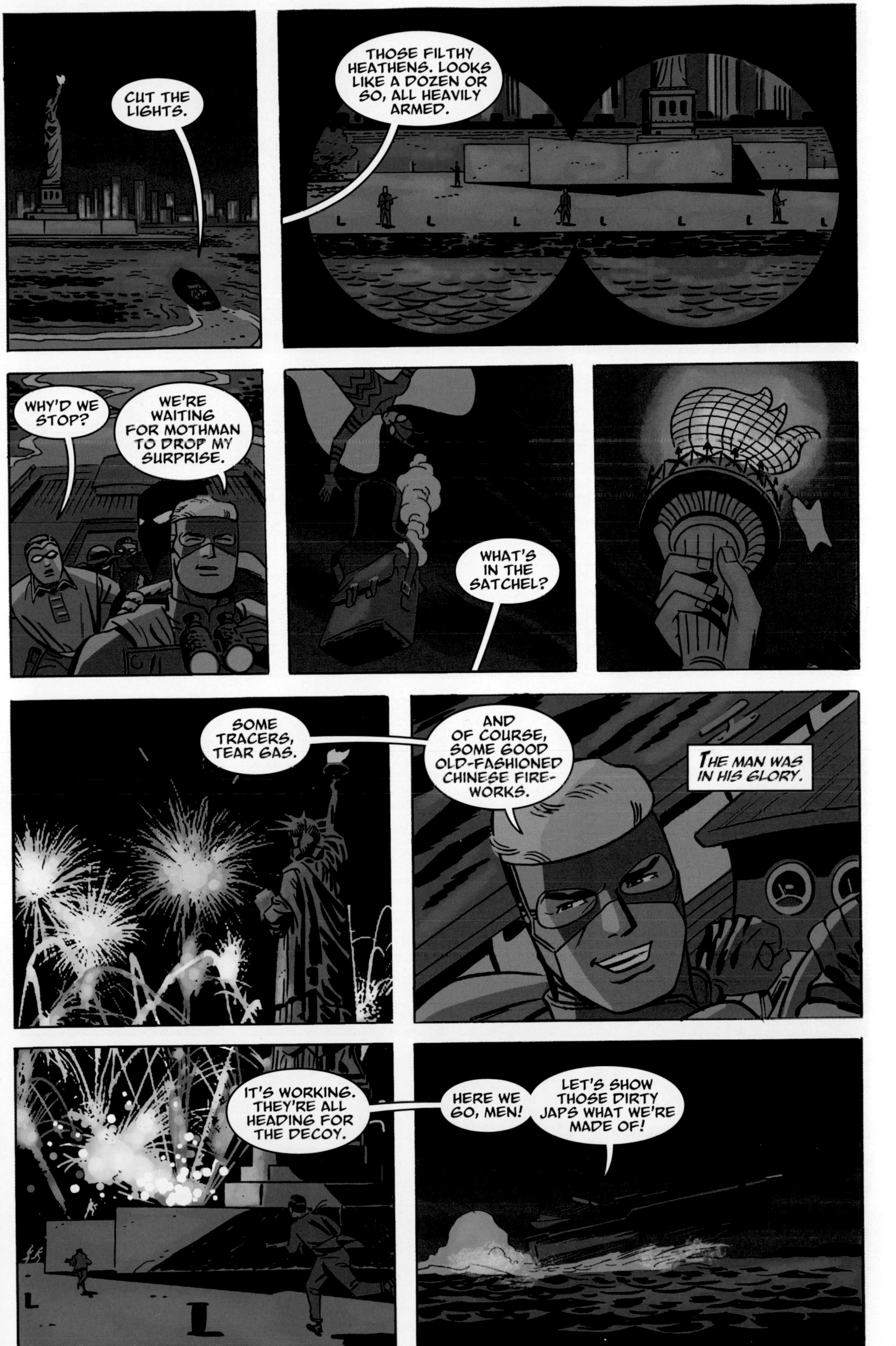
CUT THE LIGHTS.
THOSE FILTHY HEATHENS. LOOKS LIKE A DOZEN OR SO, ALL HEAVILY ARMED.
WHY'D WE STOP?
WE'RE WAITING FOR MOTHMAN TO DROP MY SURPRISE.
WHAT'S IN THE SATCHEL?
SOME TRACERS, TEAR GAS.
AND OF COURSE, SOME GOOD OLD-FASHIONED CHINESE FIRE-WORKS.
THE MAN WAS IN HIS GLORY.
IT'S WORKING. THEY'RE ALL HEADING FOR THE DECOY.
HERE WE GO, MEN!
LET'S SHOW THOSE DIRTY JAPS WHAT WE'RE MADE OF!

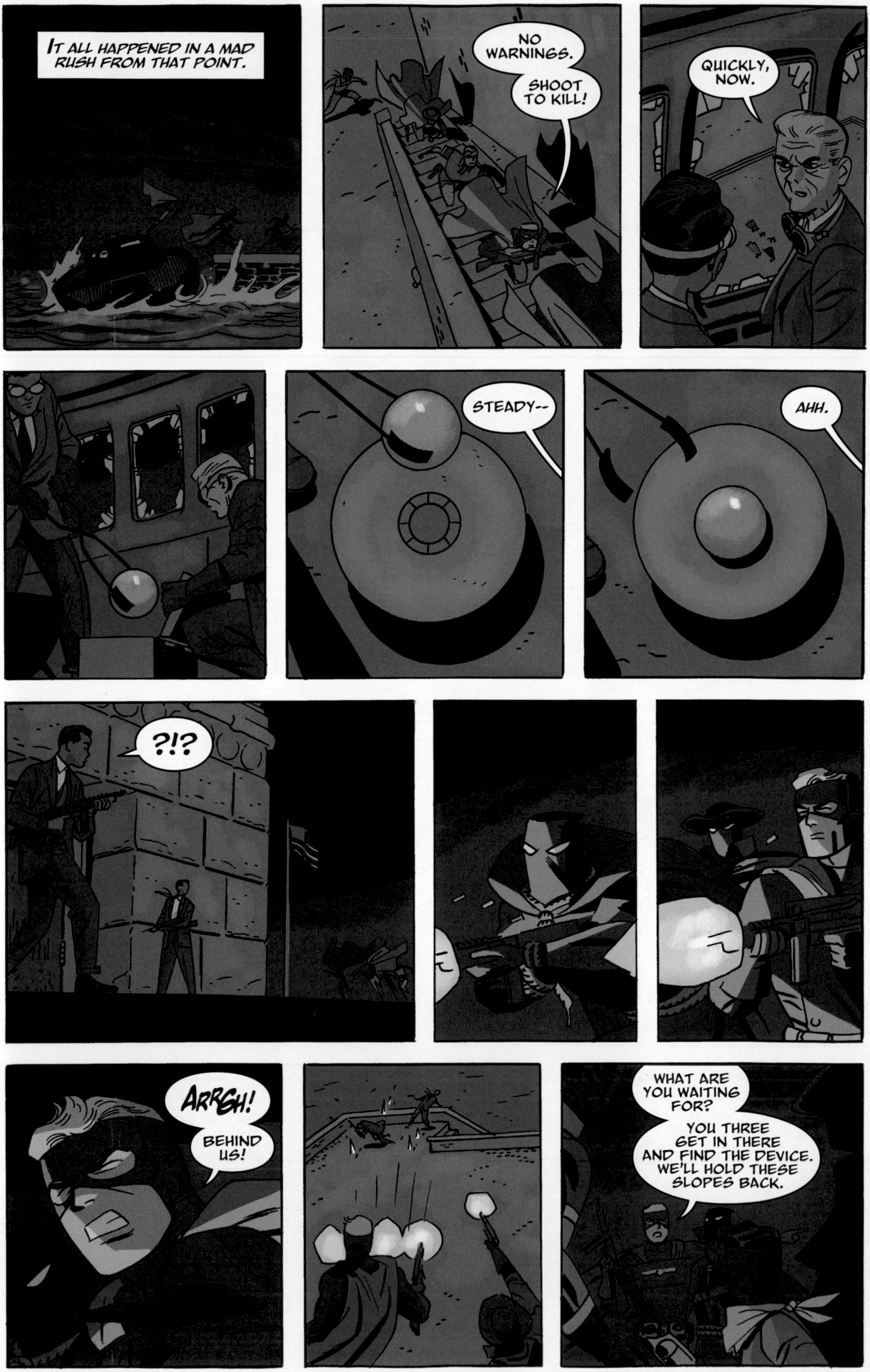
IT ALL HAPPENED IN A MAD RUSH FROM THAT POINT.
NO WARNINGS.
SHOOT TO KILL!
QUICKLY, NOW.
STEADY--
AHH.
?!?
ARRGH!
BEHIND US!
WHAT ARE YOU WAITING FOR?
YOU THREE GET IN THERE AND FIND THE DEVICE. WE'LL HOLD THESE SLOPES BACK.

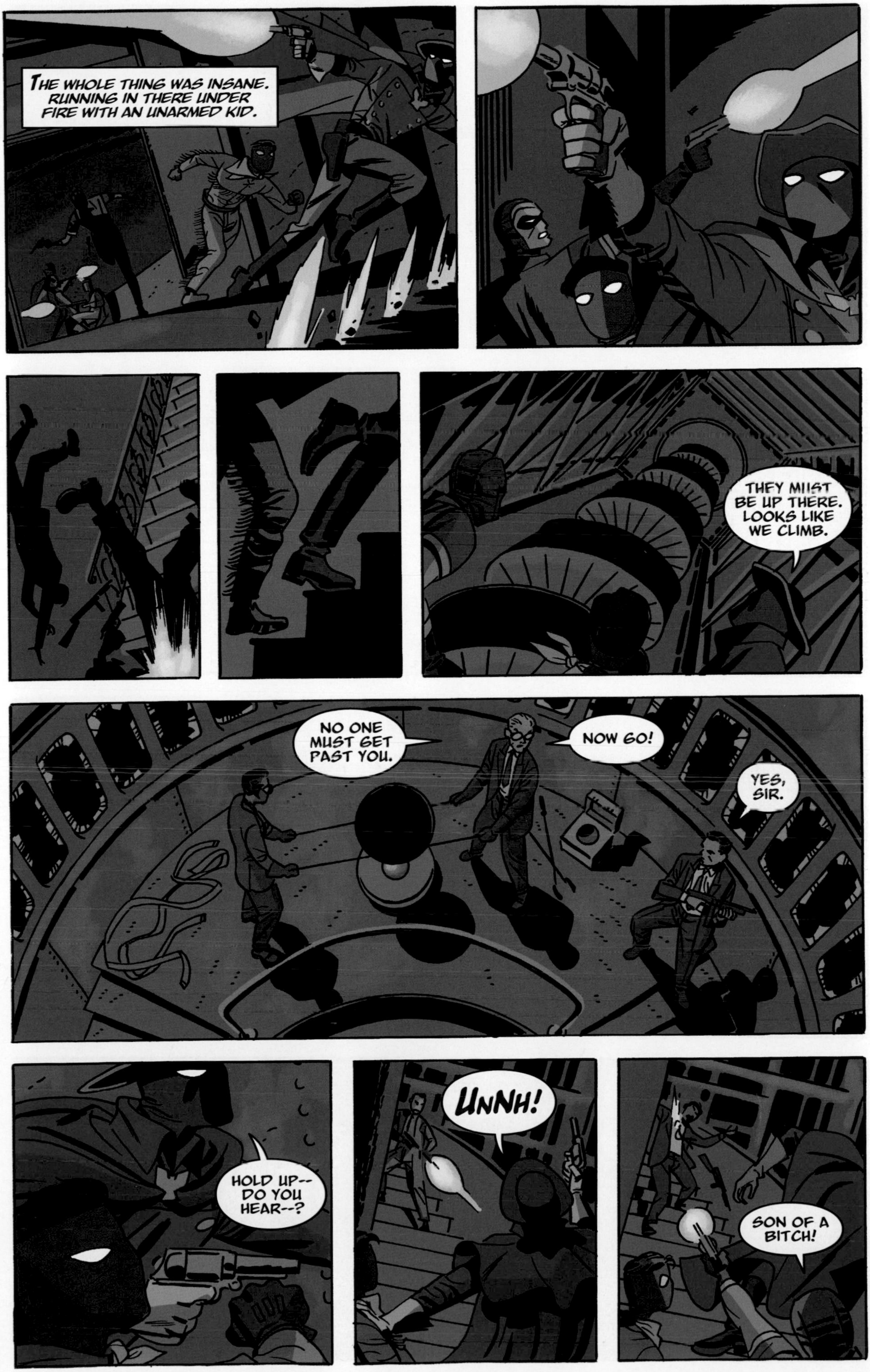
THE WHOLE THING WAS INSANE. RUNNING IN THERE UNDER FIRE WITH AN UNARMED KID.
THEY MUST BE UP THERE. LOOKS LIKE WE CLIMB.
NO ONE MUST GET PAST YOU.
NOW GO!
YES, SIR.
HOLD UP-- DO YOU HEAR--?
UNNH!
SON OF A BITCH!

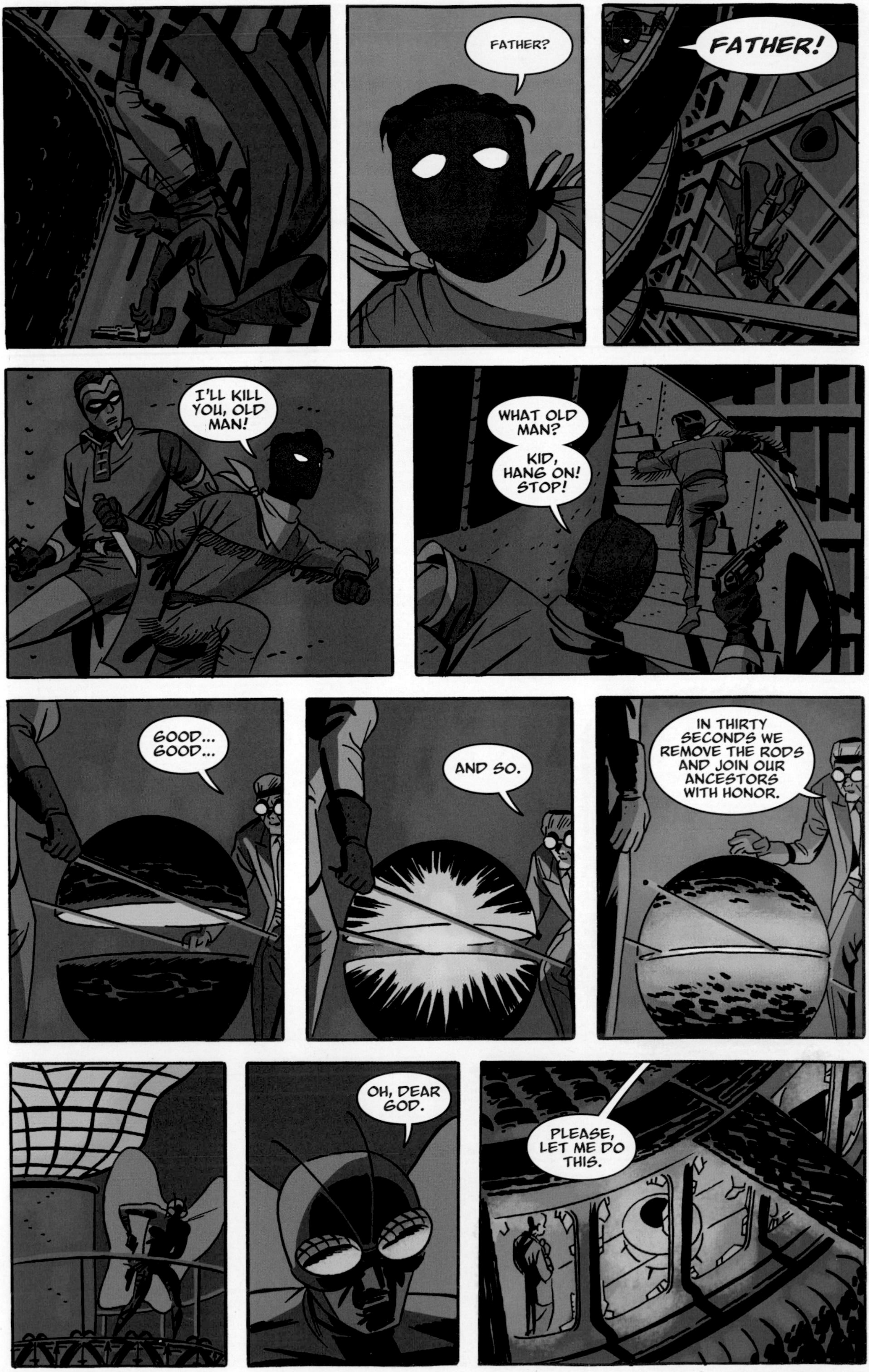
FATHER?
FATHER!
I'LL KILL YOU, OLD MAN!
WHAT OLD MAN?
KID, HANG ON! STOP!
GOOD... GOOD...
AND SO.
IN THIRTY SECONDS WE REMOVE THE RODS AND JOIN OUR ANCESTORS WITH HONOR.
OH, DEAR GOD.
PLEASE, LET ME DO THIS.

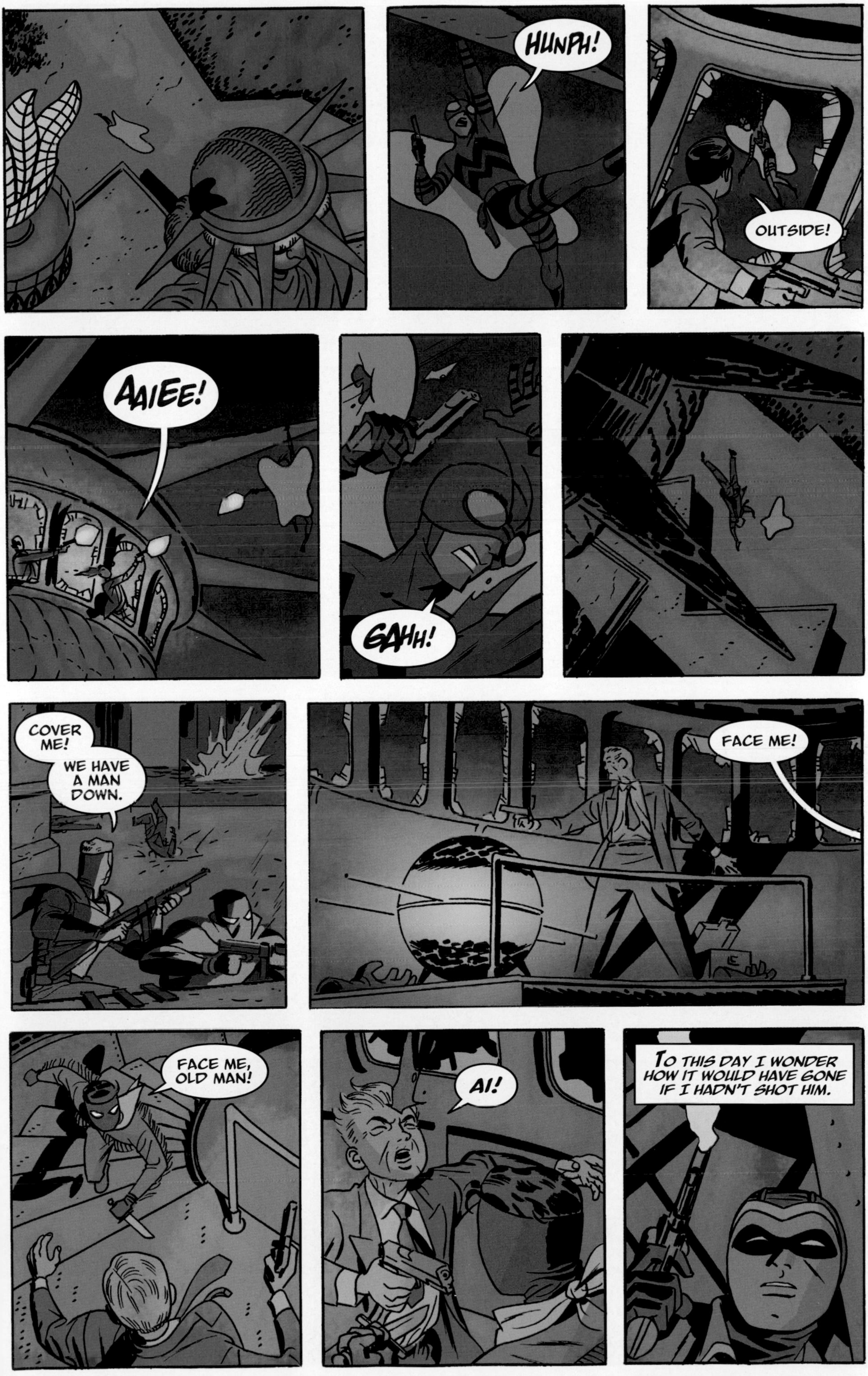
HUNPH!
OUTSIDE!
AAIEE!
GAHH!
COVER ME!
WE HAVE A MAN DOWN.
FACE ME!
FACE ME, OLD MAN!
AI!
TO THIS DAY I WONDER HOW IT WOULD HAVE GONE IF I HADN'T SHOT HIM.

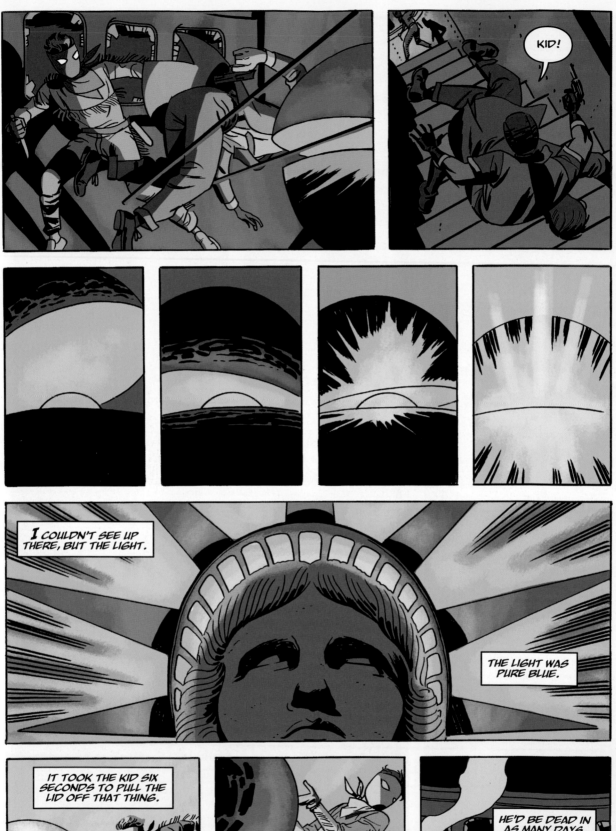

KID!

I COULDN'T SEE UP THERE, BUT THE LIGHT.

THE LIGHT WAS PURE BLUE.

IT TOOK THE KID SIX SECONDS TO PULL THE LID OFF THAT THING.

HE'D BE DEAD IN AS MANY DAYS.

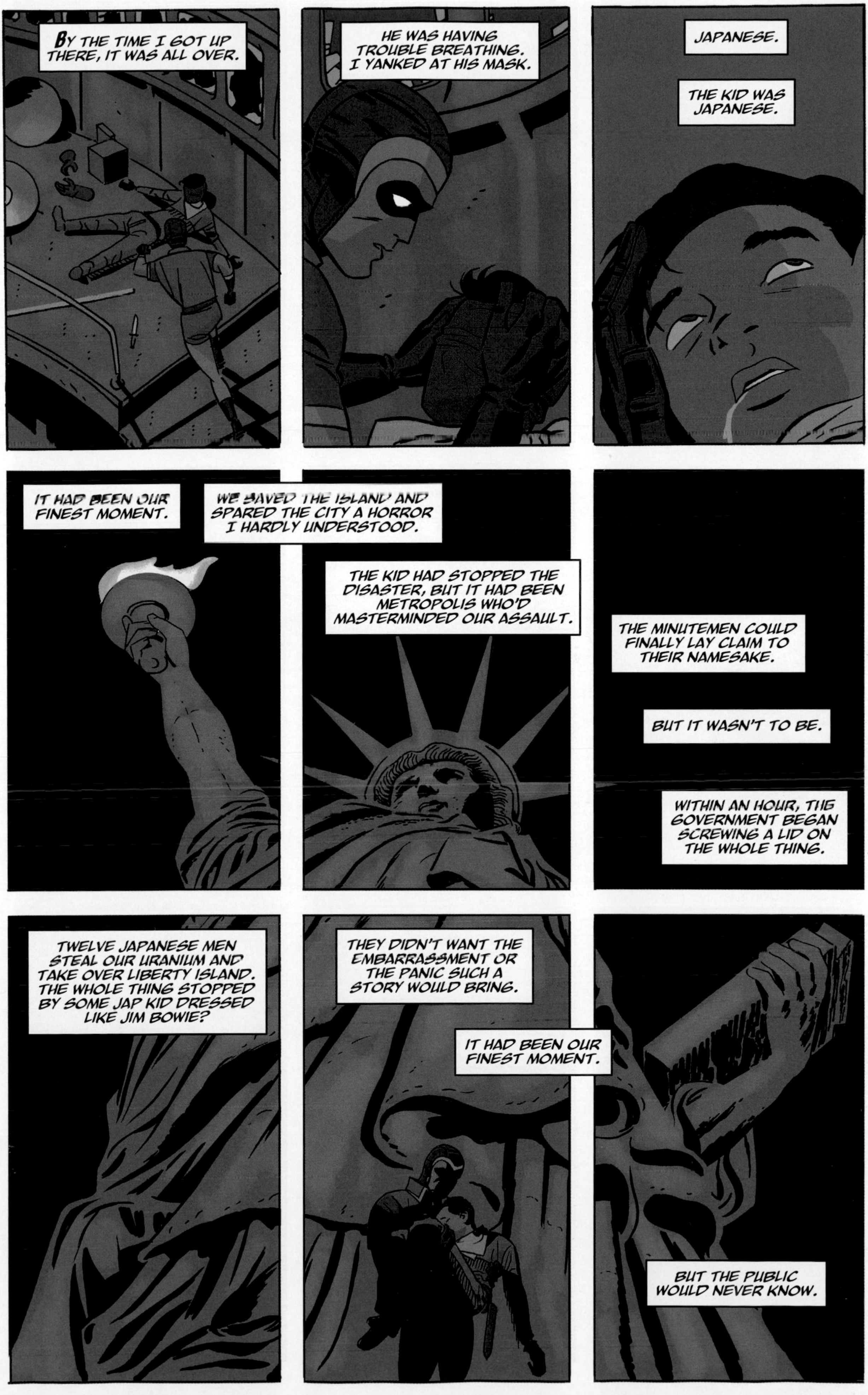
BY THE TIME I GOT UP THERE, IT WAS ALL OVER.
HE WAS HAVING TROUBLE BREATHING. I YANKED AT HIS MASK.
JAPANESE.
THE KID WAS JAPANESE.
IT HAD BEEN OUR FINEST MOMENT.
WE SAVED THE ISLAND AND SPARED THE CITY A HORROR I HARDLY UNDERSTOOD.
THE KID HAD STOPPED THE DISASTER, BUT IT HAD BEEN METROPOLIS WHO'D MASTERMINDED OUR ASSAULT.
THE MINUTEMEN COULD FINALLY LAY CLAIM TO THEIR NAMESAKE.
BUT IT WASN'T TO BE.
WITHIN AN HOUR, THE GOVERNMENT BEGAN SCREWING A LID ON THE WHOLE THING.
TWELVE JAPANESE MEN STEAL OUR URANIUM AND TAKE OVER LIBERTY ISLAND. THE WHOLE THING STOPPED BY SOME JAP KID DRESSED LIKE JIM BOWIE?
THEY DIDN'T WANT THE EMBARRASSMENT OR THE PANIC SUCH A STORY WOULD BRING.
IT HAD BEEN OUR FINEST MOMENT.
BUT THE PUBLIC WOULD NEVER KNOW.

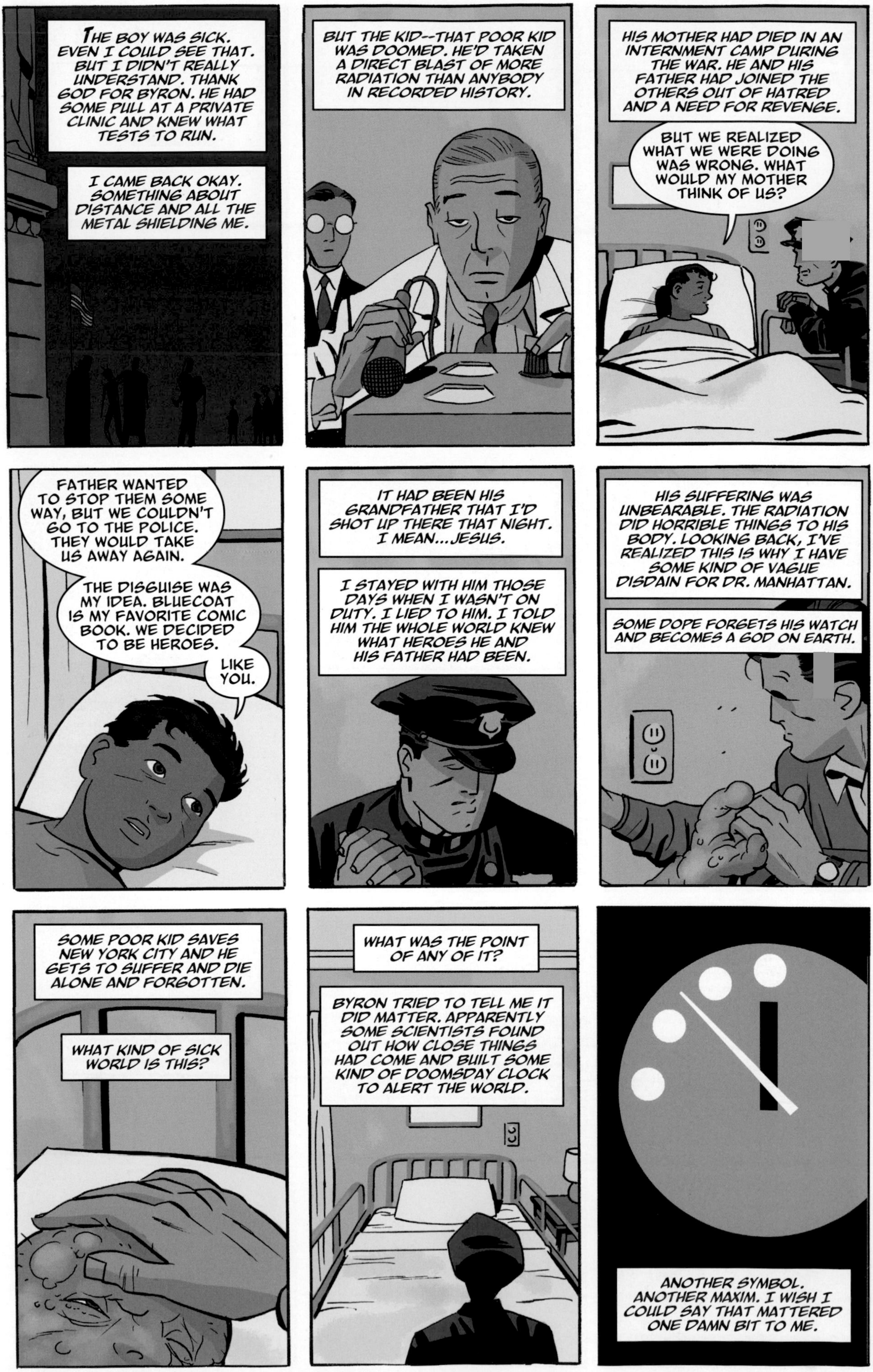
THE BOY WAS SICK. EVEN I COULD SEE THAT. BUT I DIDN'T REALLY UNDERSTAND. THANK GOD FOR BYRON. HE HAD SOME PULL AT A PRIVATE CLINIC AND KNEW WHAT TESTS TO RUN.
I CAME BACK OKAY. SOMETHING ABOUT DISTANCE AND ALL THE METAL SHIELDING ME.
BUT THE KID--THAT POOR KID WAS DOOMED. HE'D TAKEN A DIRECT BLAST OF MORE RADIATION THAN ANYBODY IN RECORDED HISTORY.
HIS MOTHER HAD DIED IN AN INTERNMENT CAMP DURING THE WAR. HE AND HIS FATHER HAD JOINED THE OTHERS OUT OF HATRED AND A NEED FOR REVENGE.
BUT WE REALIZED WHAT WE WERE DOING WAS WRONG. WHAT WOULD MY MOTHER THINK OF US?
FATHER WANTED TO STOP THEM SOME WAY, BUT WE COULDN'T GO TO THE POLICE. THEY WOULD TAKE US AWAY AGAIN.
THE DISGUISE WAS MY IDEA. BLUECOAT IS MY FAVORITE COMIC BOOK. WE DECIDED TO BE HEROES.
LIKE YOU.
IT HAD BEEN HIS GRANDFATHER THAT I'D SHOT UP THERE THAT NIGHT. I MEAN... JESUS.
I STAYED WITH HIM THOSE DAYS WHEN I WASN'T ON DUTY. I LIED TO HIM. I TOLD HIM THE WHOLE WORLD KNEW WHAT HEROES HE AND HIS FATHER HAD BEEN.
HIS SUFFERING WAS UNBEARABLE. THE RADIATION DID HORRIBLE THINGS TO HIS BODY. LOOKING BACK, I'VE REALIZED THIS IS WHY I HAVE SOME KIND OF VAGUE DISDAIN FOR DR. MANHATTAN.
SOME DOPE FORGETS HIS WATCH AND BECOMES A GOD ON EARTH.
SOME POOR KID SAVES NEW YORK CITY AND HE GETS TO SUFFER AND DIE ALONE AND FORGOTTEN.
WHAT KIND OF SICK WORLD IS THIS?
WHAT WAS THE POINT OF ANY OF IT?
BYRON TRIED TO TELL ME IT DID MATTER. APPARENTLY SOME SCIENTISTS FOUND OUT HOW CLOSE THINGS HAD COME AND BUILT SOME KIND OF DOOMSDAY CLOCK TO ALERT THE WORLD.
ANOTHER SYMBOL. ANOTHER MAXIM. I WISH I COULD SAY THAT MATTERED ONE DAMN BIT TO ME.

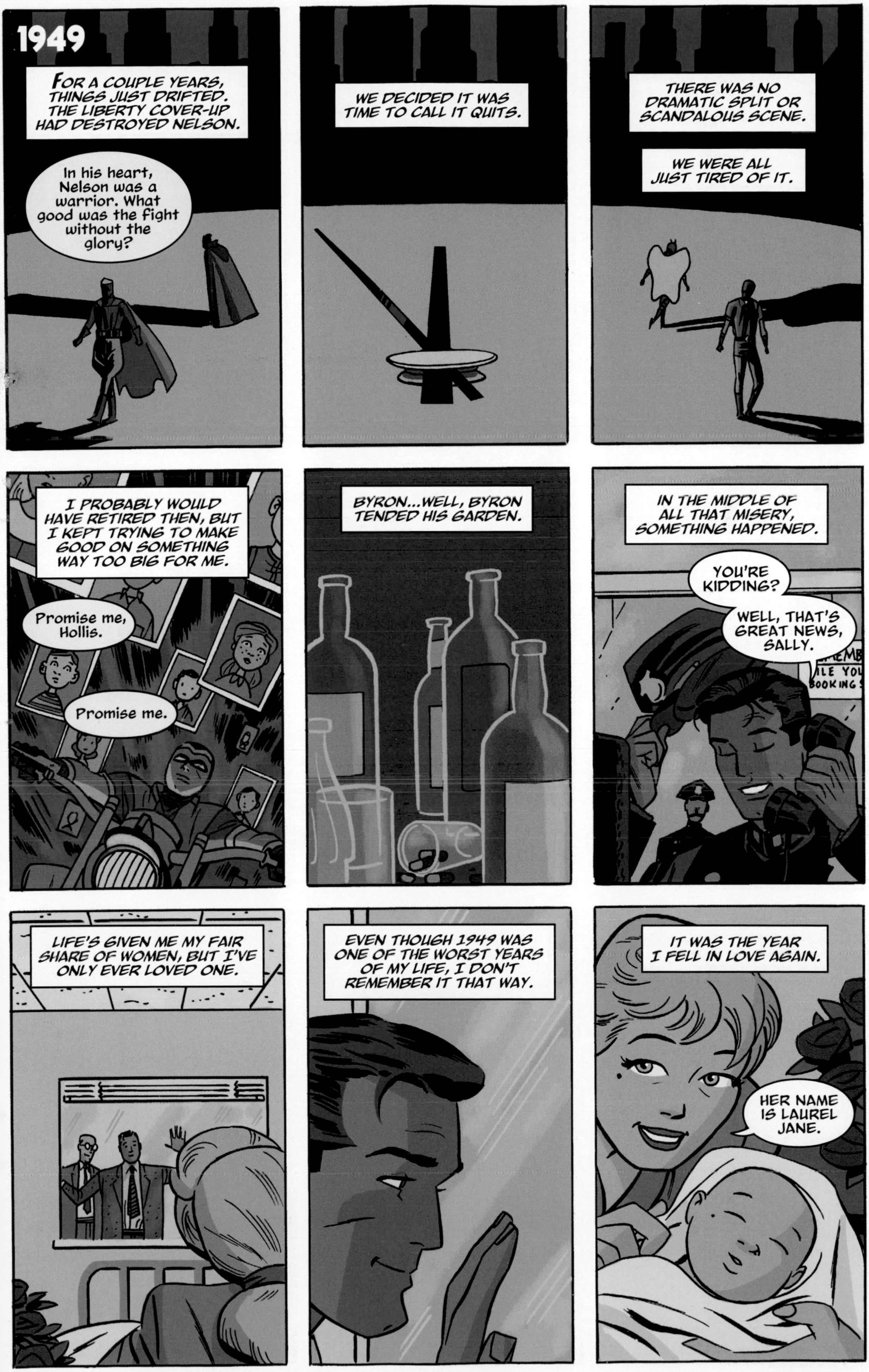
1949
FOR A COUPLE YEARS, THINGS JUST DRIFTED. THE LIBERTY COVER-UP HAD DESTROYED NELSON.
In his heart, Nelson was a warrior. What good was the fight without the glory?
WE DECIDED IT WAS TIME TO CALL IT QUITS.
THERE WAS NO DRAMATIC SPLIT OR SCANDALOUS SCENE.
WE WERE ALL JUST TIRED OF IT.
I PROBABLY WOULD HAVE RETIRED THEN, BUT I KEPT TRYING TO MAKE GOOD ON SOMETHING WAY TOO BIG FOR ME.
Promise me, Hollis.
Promise me.
BYRON...WELL, BYRON TENDED HIS GARDEN.
IN THE MIDDLE OF ALL THAT MISERY, SOMETHING HAPPENED.
YOU'RE KIDDING?
WELL, THAT'S GREAT NEWS, SALLY.
LIFE'S GIVEN ME MY FAIR SHARE OF WOMEN, BUT I'VE ONLY EVER LOVED ONE.
EVEN THOUGH 1949 WAS ONE OF THE WORST YEARS OF MY LIFE, I DON'T REMEMBER IT THAT WAY.
IT WAS THE YEAR I FELL IN LOVE AGAIN.
HER NAME IS LAUREL JANE.

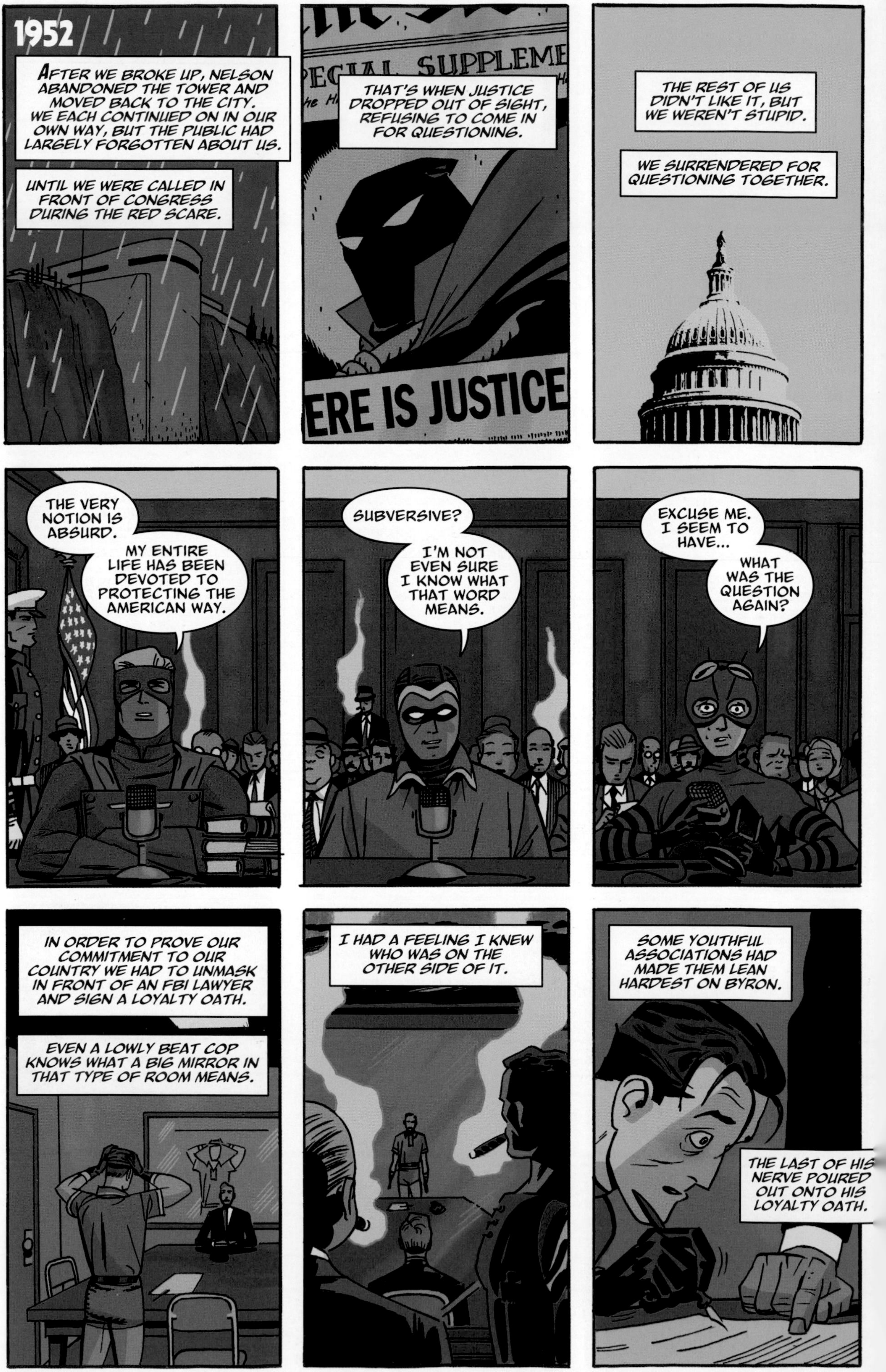
1952
AFTER WE BROKE UP, NELSON ABANDONED THE TOWER AND MOVED BACK TO THE CITY. WE EACH CONTINUED ON IN OUR OWN WAY, BUT THE PUBLIC HAD LARGELY FORGOTTEN ABOUT US.
UNTIL WE WERE CALLED IN FRONT OF CONGRESS DURING THE RED SCARE.
SPECIAL SUPPLEME
THAT'S WHEN JUSTICE DROPPED OUT OF SIGHT, REFUSING TO COME IN FOR QUESTIONING.
ERE IS JUSTICE
THE REST OF US DIDN'T LIKE IT, BUT WE WEREN'T STUPID.
WE SURRENDERED FOR QUESTIONING TOGETHER.
THE VERY NOTION IS ABSURD.
MY ENTIRE LIFE HAS BEEN DEVOTED TO PROTECTING THE AMERICAN WAY.
SUBVERSIVE?
I'M NOT EVEN SURE I KNOW WHAT THAT WORD MEANS.
EXCUSE ME. I SEEM TO HAVE...
WHAT WAS THE QUESTION AGAIN?
IN ORDER TO PROVE OUR COMMITMENT TO OUR COUNTRY WE HAD TO UNMASK IN FRONT OF AN FBI LAWYER AND SIGN A LOYALTY OATH.
EVEN A LOWLY BEAT COP KNOWS WHAT A BIG MIRROR IN THAT TYPE OF ROOM MEANS.
I HAD A FEELING I KNEW WHO WAS ON THE OTHER SIDE OF IT.
SOME YOUTHFUL ASSOCIATIONS HAD MADE THEM LEAN HARDEST ON BYRON.
THE LAST OF HIS NERVE POURED OUT ONTO HIS LOYALTY OATH.

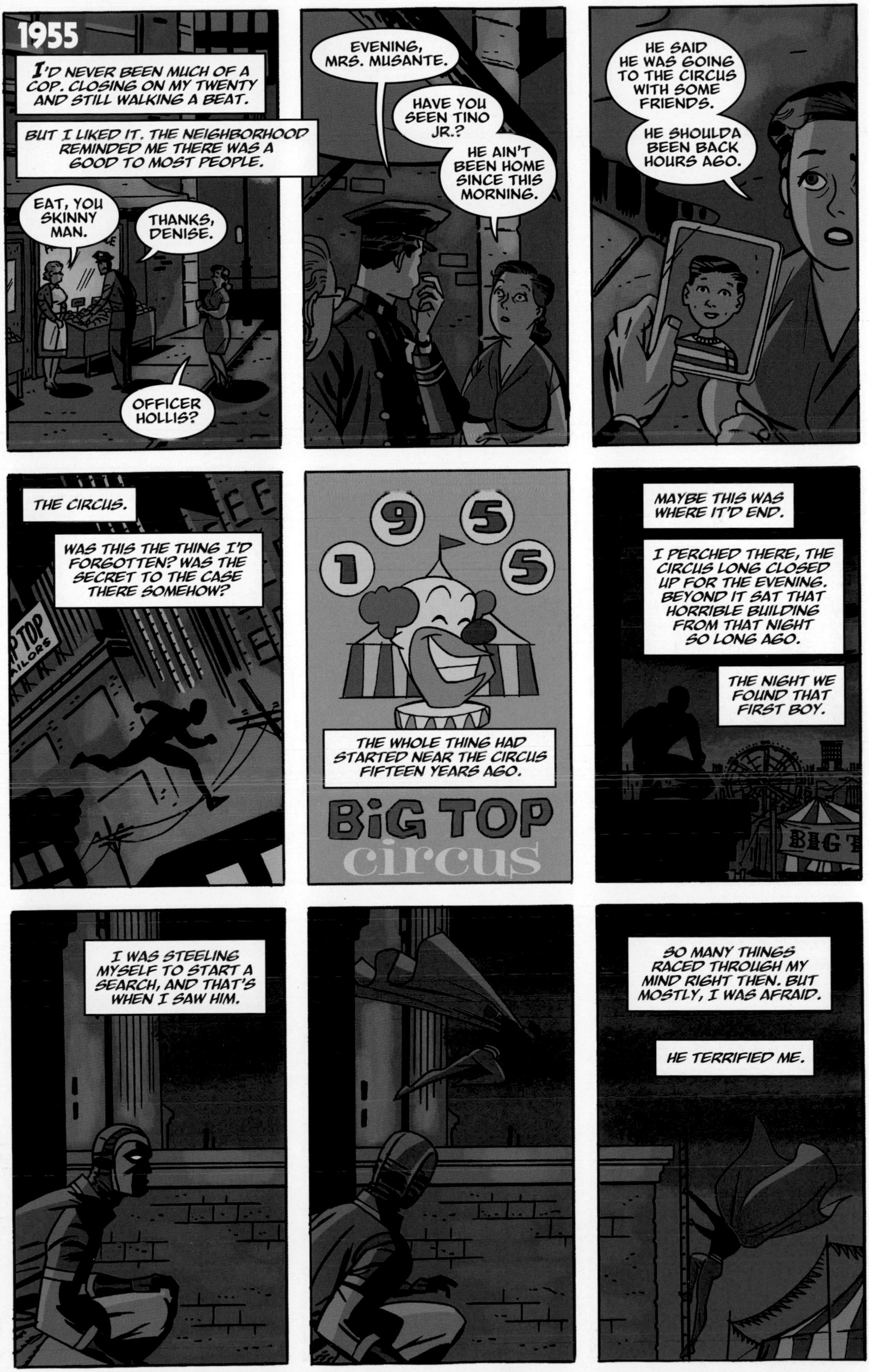
1955
I'D NEVER BEEN MUCH OF A COP. CLOSING ON MY TWENTY AND STILL WALKING A BEAT.
BUT I LIKED IT. THE NEIGHBORHOOD REMINDED ME THERE WAS A GOOD TO MOST PEOPLE.
EAT, YOU SKINNY MAN.
THANKS, DENISE.
OFFICER HOLLIS?
EVENING, MRS. MUSANTE.
HAVE YOU SEEN TINO JR.?
HE AIN'T BEEN HOME SINCE THIS MORNING.
HE SAID HE WAS GOING TO THE CIRCUS WITH SOME FRIENDS.
HE SHOULDA BEEN BACK HOURS AGO.
THE CIRCUS.
WAS THIS THE THING I'D FORGOTTEN? WAS THE SECRET TO THE CASE THERE SOMEHOW?
1955
THE WHOLE THING HAD STARTED NEAR THE CIRCUS FIFTEEN YEARS AGO.
BiG TOP circus
MAYBE THIS WAS WHERE IT'D END.
I PERCHED THERE, THE CIRCUS LONG CLOSED UP FOR THE EVENING. BEYOND IT SAT THAT HORRIBLE BUILDING FROM THAT NIGHT SO LONG AGO.
THE NIGHT WE FOUND THAT FIRST BOY.
I WAS STEELING MYSELF TO START A SEARCH, AND THAT'S WHEN I SAW HIM.
SO MANY THINGS RACED THROUGH MY MIND RIGHT THEN. BUT MOSTLY, I WAS AFRAID.
HE TERRIFIED ME.

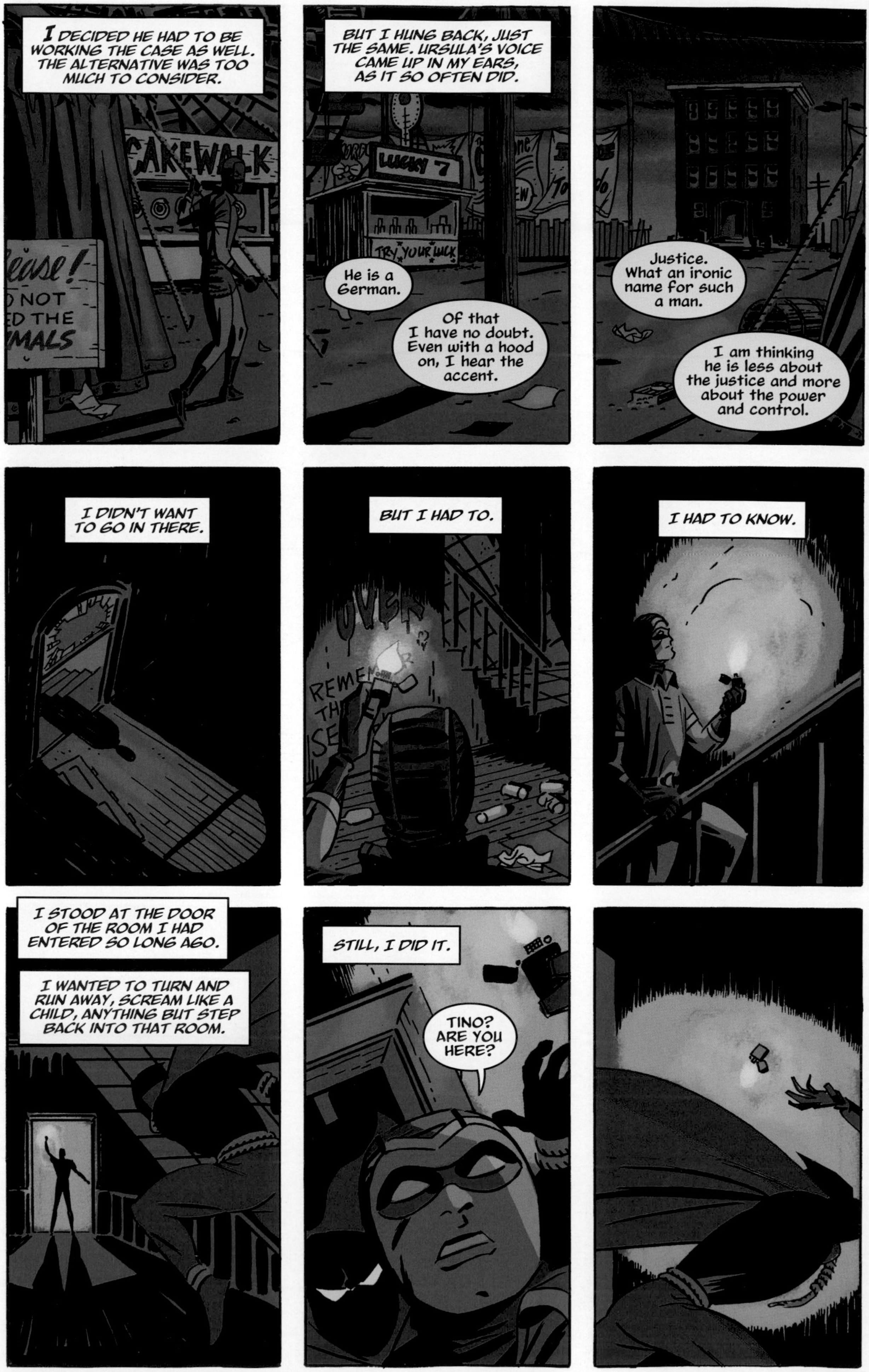
I DECIDED HE HAD TO BE WORKING THE CASE AS WELL. THE ALTERNATIVE WAS TOO MUCH TO CONSIDER.
CAKEWALK
Please! DO NOT FEED THE ANIMALS
BUT I HUNG BACK, JUST THE SAME. URSULA'S VOICE CAME UP IN MY EARS, AS IT SO OFTEN DID.
LUCKY 7
TRY YOUR LUCK
He is a German.
Of that I have no doubt. Even with a hood on, I hear the accent.
Justice. What an ironic name for such a man.
I am thinking he is less about the justice and more about the power and control.
I DIDN'T WANT TO GO IN THERE.
BUT I HAD TO.
I HAD TO KNOW.
I STOOD AT THE DOOR OF THE ROOM I HAD ENTERED SO LONG AGO.
I WANTED TO TURN AND RUN AWAY, SCREAM LIKE A CHILD, ANYTHING BUT STEP BACK INTO THAT ROOM.
STILL, I DID IT.
TINO? ARE YOU HERE?

I FLEW LIKE A RAG DOLL.

THERE WAS NO ESCAPING HIM.

I FELT RIBS GIVE WAY.

HE WAS TOO BIG.

TOO FAST.

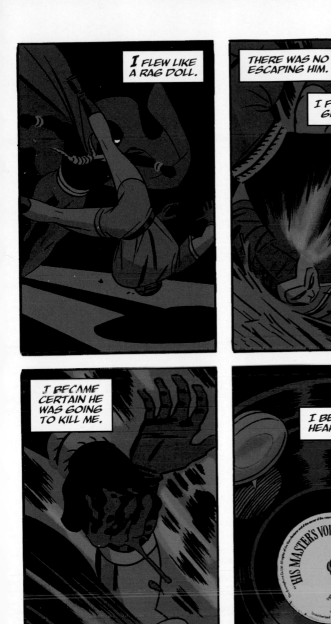

I BECAME CERTAIN HE WAS GOING TO KILL ME.

I BEGAN TO HEAR MUSIC.

THE SAD, SAD MUSIC.

HE STOPPED THEN, AND I HEARD HIM LEAVE. I LAY THERE LISTENING TO MY BREATHING.

IT SOUNDED LIKE IT WAS COMING FROM SOMEONE ELSE. IF I CLOSED MY EYES I WAS SURE I WOULD DIE.

I CLOSED THEM ANYWAY.

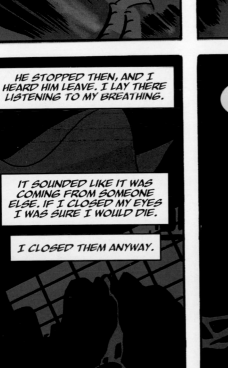

Wake up, Mister silly.

Wake up.

THE SUN WAS HIGH AND BRIGHT WHEN I CAME AROUND. MY FACE WAS THE SIZE OF A RIPE PUMPKIN AND MY LEGS WEREN'T WORKING.

I TRIED TO HAUL MYSELF UP.

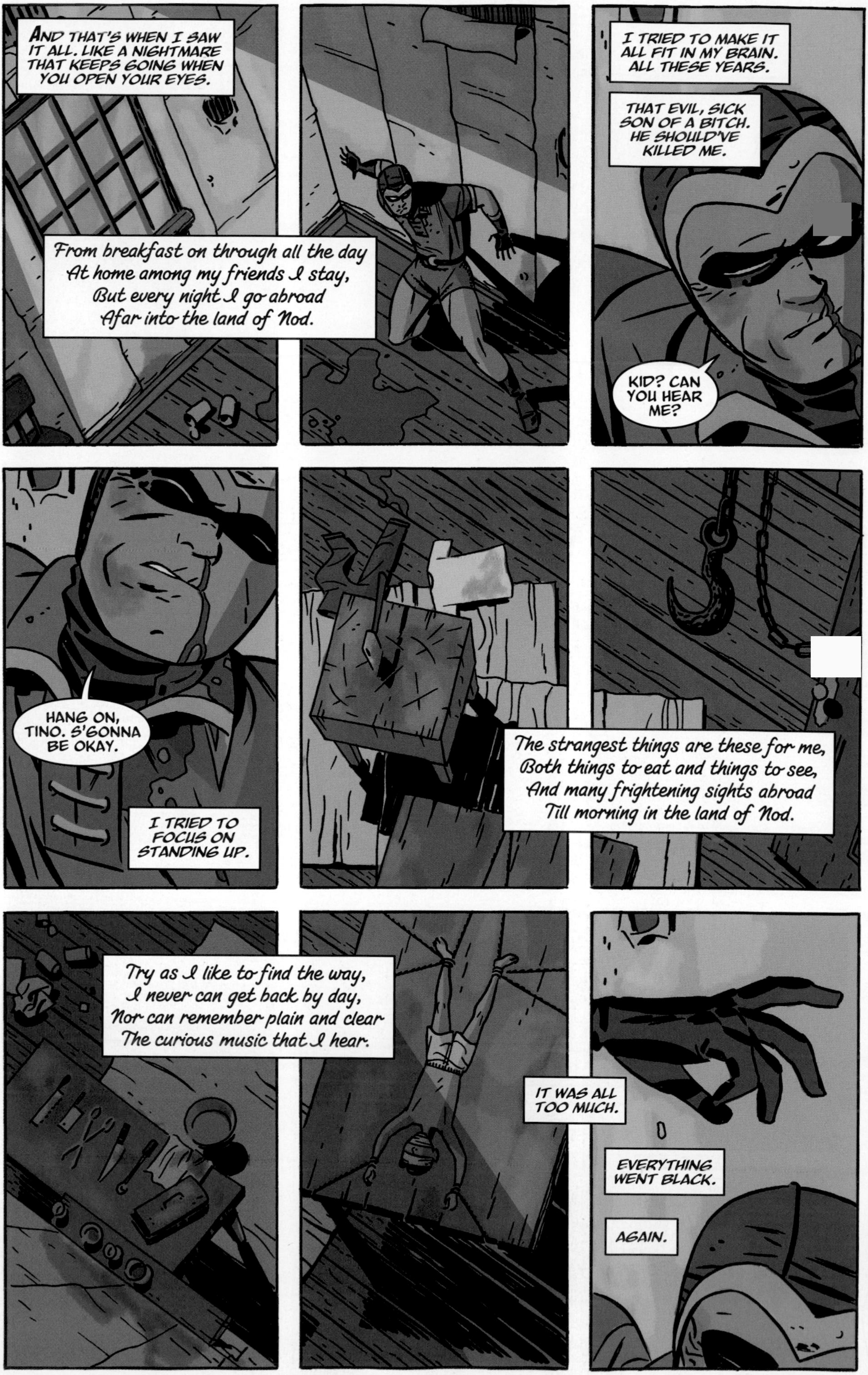
AND THAT'S WHEN I SAW IT ALL. LIKE A NIGHTMARE THAT KEEPS GOING WHEN YOU OPEN YOUR EYES.
From breakfast on through all the day
At home among my friends I stay,
But every night I go abroad
Afar into the land of Nod.
I TRIED TO MAKE IT ALL FIT IN MY BRAIN. ALL THESE YEARS.
THAT EVIL, SICK SON OF A BITCH. HE SHOULD'VE KILLED ME.
KID? CAN YOU HEAR ME?
HANG ON, TINO. S'GONNA BE OKAY.
I TRIED TO FOCUS ON STANDING UP.
The strangest things are these for me,
Both things to eat and things to see,
And many frightening sights abroad
Till morning in the land of Nod.
Try as I like to find the way,
I never can get back by day,
Nor can remember plain and clear
The curious music that I hear.
IT WAS ALL TOO MUCH.
EVERYTHING WENT BLACK.
AGAIN.

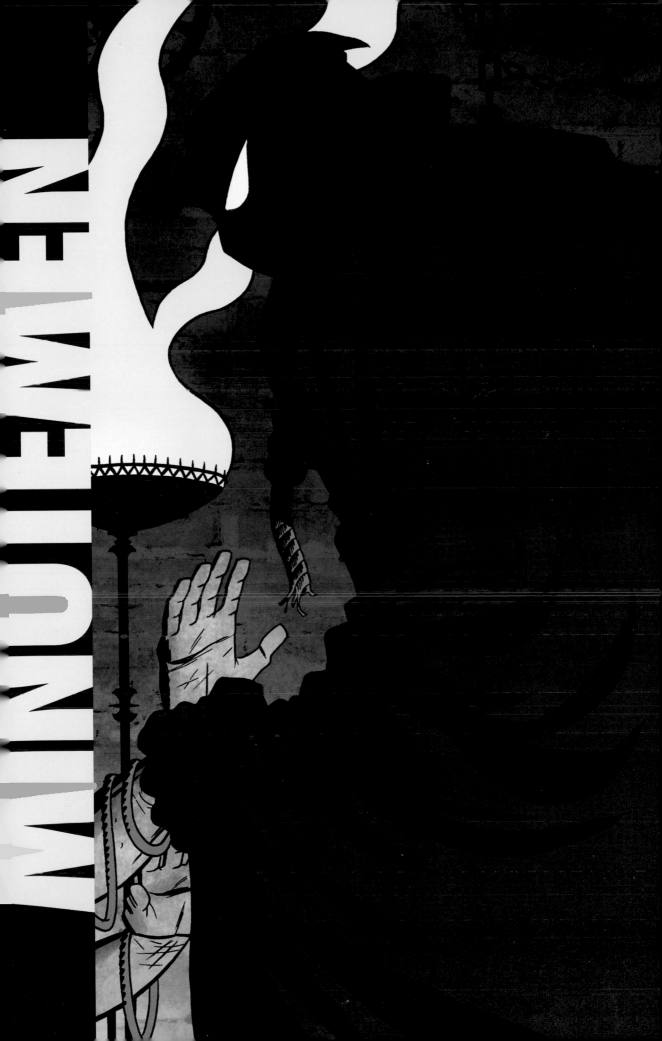

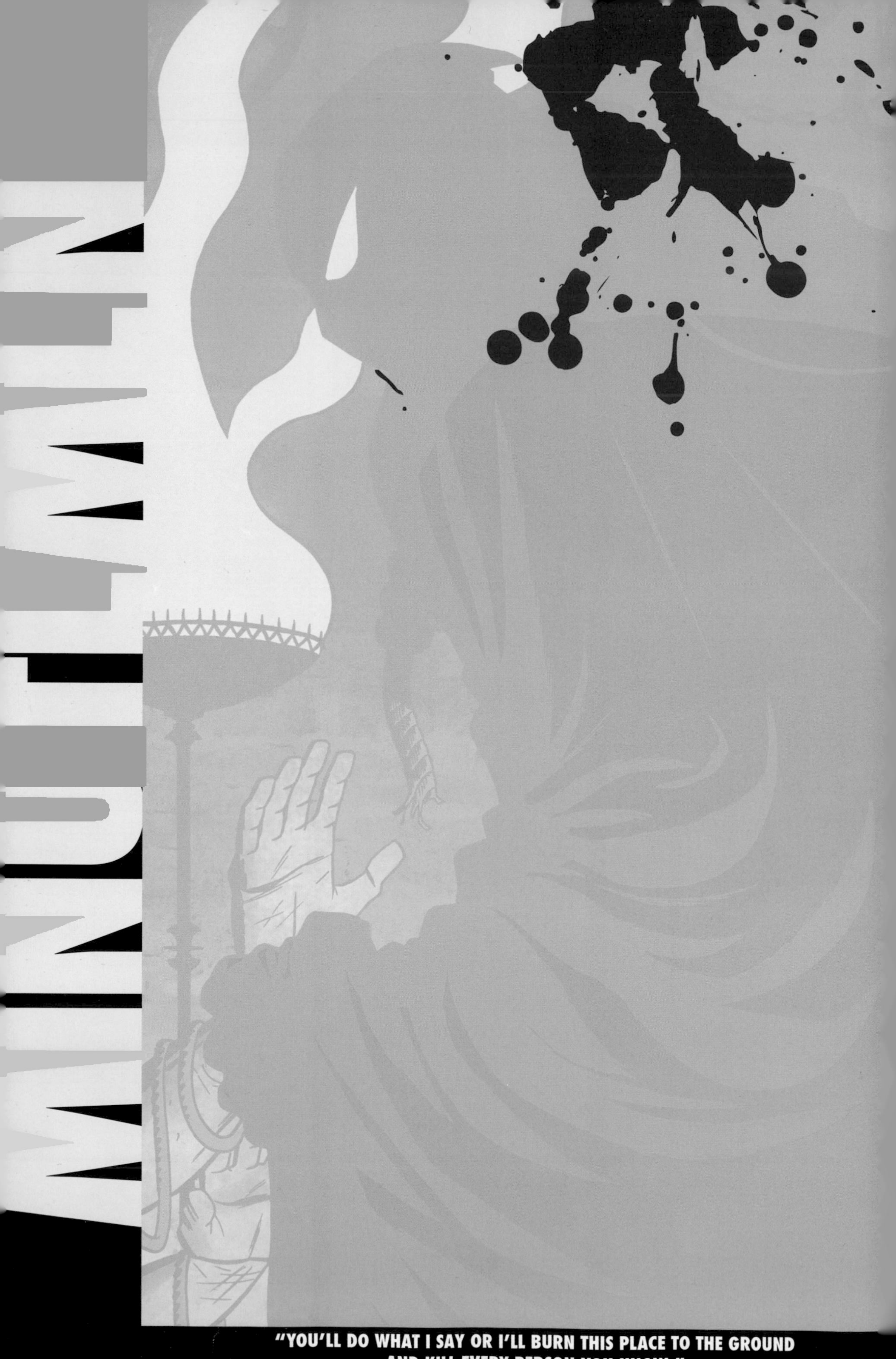

"YOU'LL DO WHAT I SAY OR I'LL BURN THIS PLACE TO THE GROUND AND KILL EVERY PERSON YOU KNOW."

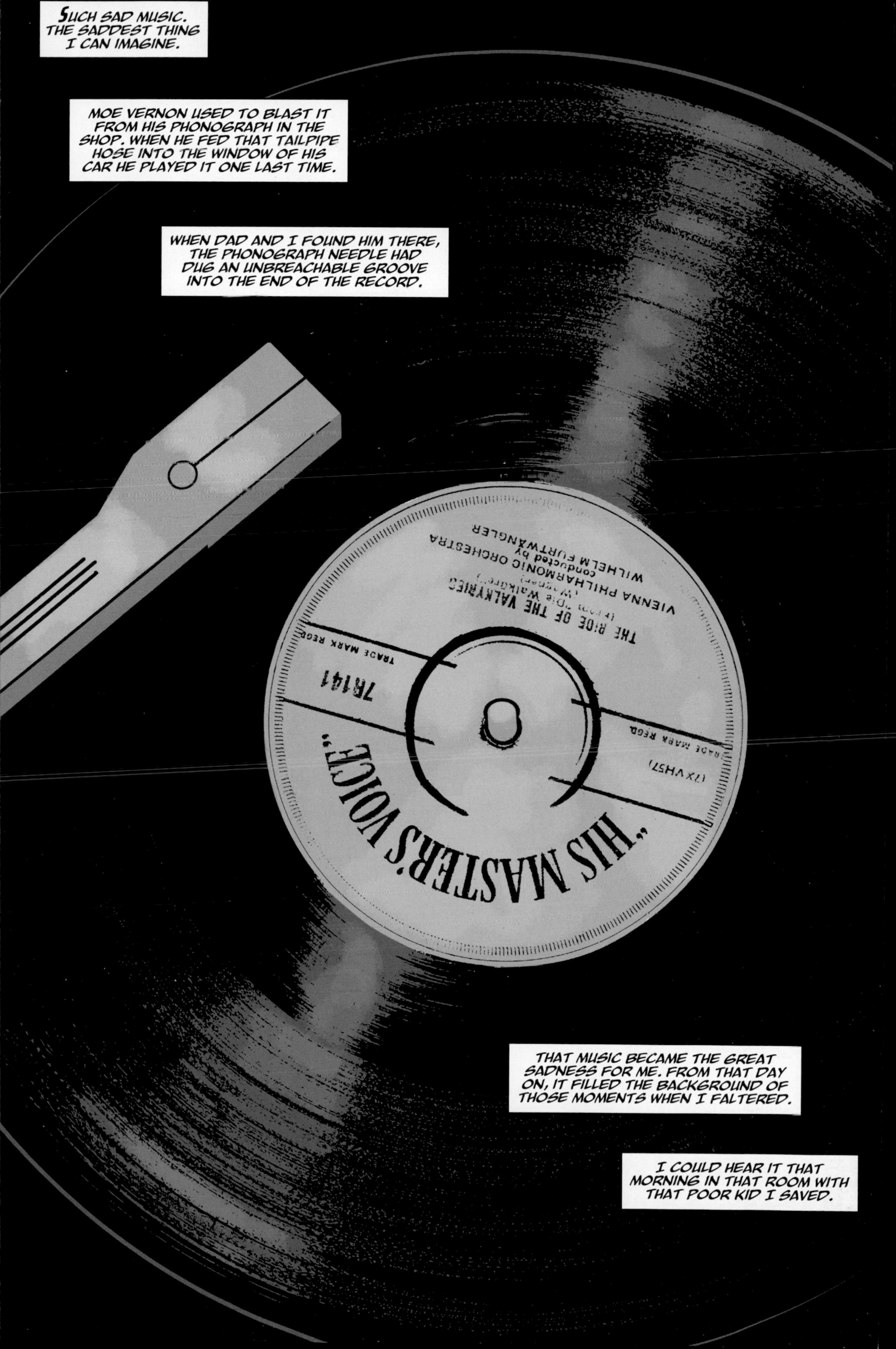
SUCH SAD MUSIC. THE SADDEST THING I CAN IMAGINE.
MOE VERNON USED TO BLAST IT FROM HIS PHONOGRAPH IN THE SHOP. WHEN HE FED THAT TAILPIPE HOSE INTO THE WINDOW OF HIS CAR HE PLAYED IT ONE LAST TIME.
WHEN DAD AND I FOUND HIM THERE, THE PHONOGRAPH NEEDLE HAD DUG AN UNBREACHABLE GROOVE INTO THE END OF THE RECORD.
"HIS MASTER'S VOICE."
TRADE MARK REGD.
7R141
THE RIDE OF THE VALKYRIES
VIENNA PHILHARMONIC ORCHESTRA
conducted by
WILHELM FURTWÄNGLER
TRADE MARK REGD.
(7XVH57)
THAT MUSIC BECAME THE GREAT SADNESS FOR ME. FROM THAT DAY ON, IT FILLED THE BACKGROUND OF THOSE MOMENTS WHEN I FALTERED.
I COULD HEAR IT THAT MORNING IN THAT ROOM WITH THAT POOR KID I SAVED.

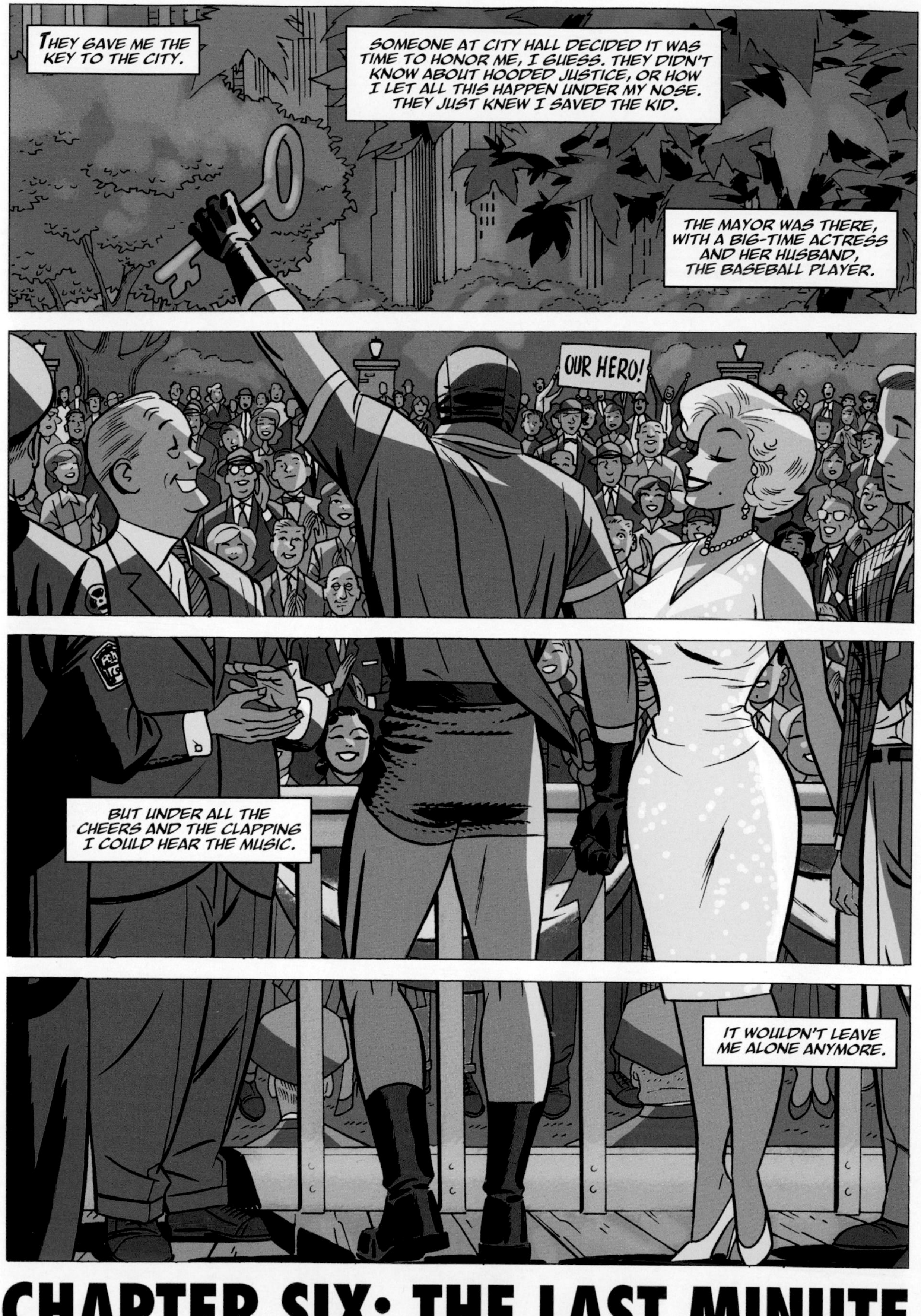
THEY GAVE ME THE KEY TO THE CITY.
SOMEONE AT CITY HALL DECIDED IT WAS TIME TO HONOR ME, I GUESS. THEY DIDN'T KNOW ABOUT HOODED JUSTICE, OR HOW I LET ALL THIS HAPPEN UNDER MY NOSE. THEY JUST KNEW I SAVED THE KID.
THE MAYOR WAS THERE, WITH A BIG-TIME ACTRESS AND HER HUSBAND, THE BASEBALL PLAYER.
OUR HERO!
BUT UNDER ALL THE CHEERS AND THE CLAPPING I COULD HEAR THE MUSIC.
IT WOULDN'T LEAVE ME ALONE ANYMORE.

CHAPTER SIX: THE LAST MINUTE

DARWYN COOKE WRITER & ARTIST

PHIL NOTO COLORIST **JARED K. FLETCHER** LETTERER **DARWYN COOKE** COVER ARTIST **BECKY CLOONAN** VARIANT COVER ARTIST

CAMILLA ZHANG ASSISTANT EDITOR **WIL MOSS** ASSOCIATE EDITOR **MARK CHIARELLO** EDITOR

WATCHMEN CREATED BY **ALAN MOORE** & **DAVE GIBBONS**

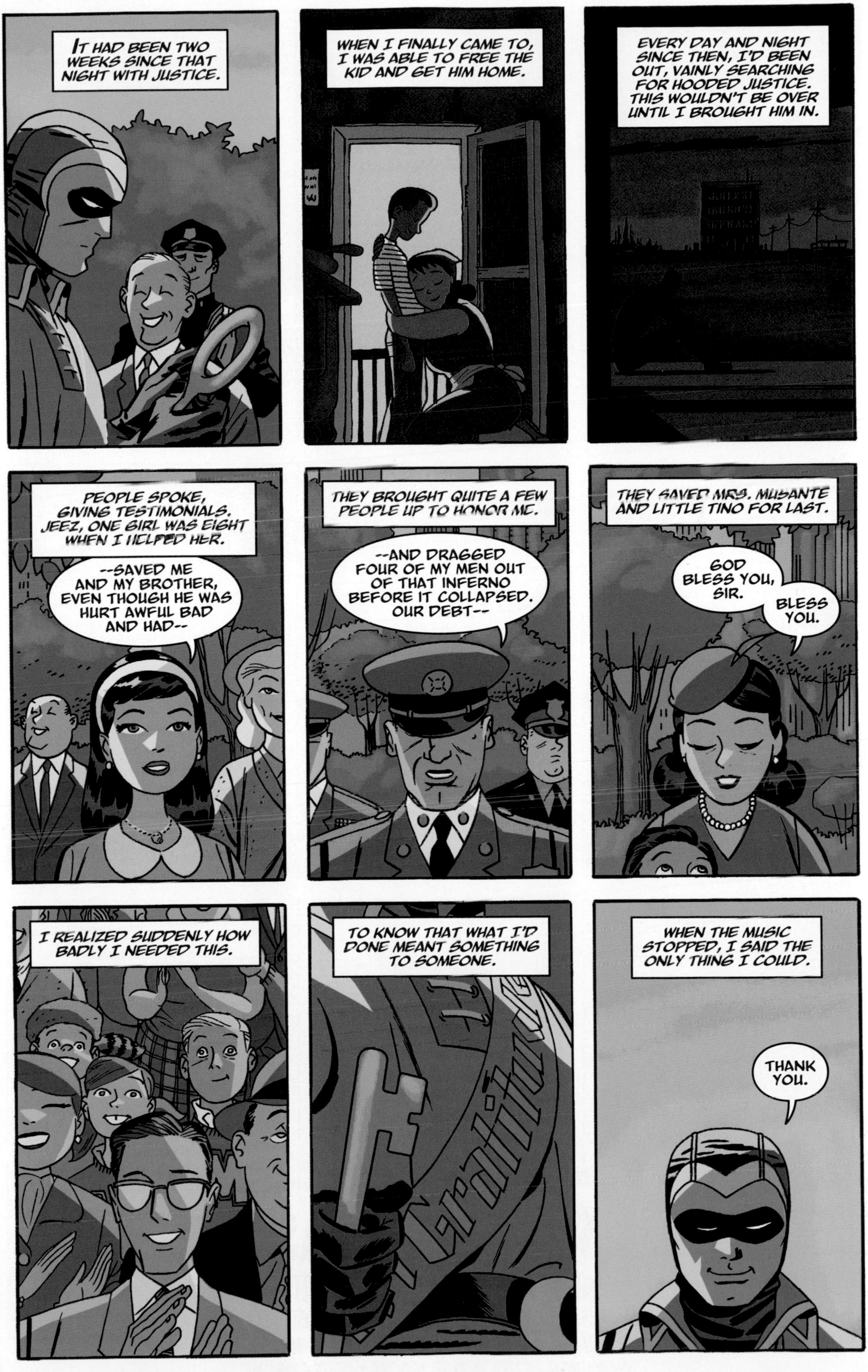
IT HAD BEEN TWO WEEKS SINCE THAT NIGHT WITH JUSTICE.
WHEN I FINALLY CAME TO, I WAS ABLE TO FREE THE KID AND GET HIM HOME.
EVERY DAY AND NIGHT SINCE THEN, I'D BEEN OUT, VAINLY SEARCHING FOR HOODED JUSTICE. THIS WOULDN'T BE OVER UNTIL I BROUGHT HIM IN.
PEOPLE SPOKE, GIVING TESTIMONIALS. JEEZ, ONE GIRL WAS EIGHT WHEN I HELPED HER.
--SAVED ME AND MY BROTHER, EVEN THOUGH HE WAS HURT AWFUL BAD AND HAD--
THEY BROUGHT QUITE A FEW PEOPLE UP TO HONOR ME.
--AND DRAGGED FOUR OF MY MEN OUT OF THAT INFERNO BEFORE IT COLLAPSED. OUR DEBT--
THEY SAVED MRS. MUSANTE AND LITTLE TINO FOR LAST.
GOD BLESS YOU, SIR.
BLESS YOU.
I REALIZED SUDDENLY HOW BADLY I NEEDED THIS.
TO KNOW THAT WHAT I'D DONE MEANT SOMETHING TO SOMEONE.
WHEN THE MUSIC STOPPED, I SAID THE ONLY THING I COULD.
THANK YOU.

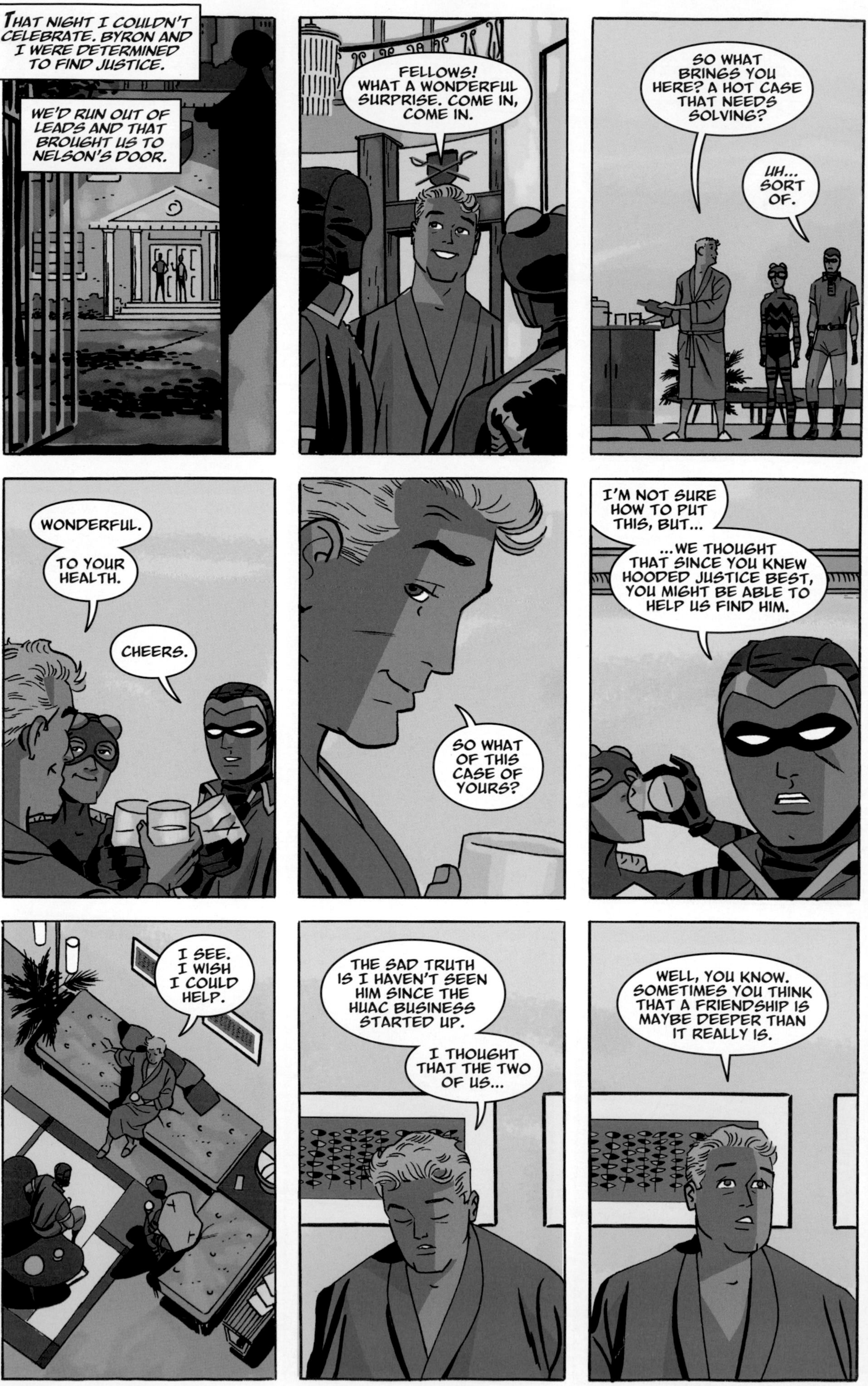
THAT NIGHT I COULDN'T CELEBRATE. BYRON AND I WERE DETERMINED TO FIND JUSTICE.
WE'D RUN OUT OF LEADS AND THAT BROUGHT US TO NELSON'S DOOR.
FELLOWS! WHAT A WONDERFUL SURPRISE. COME IN, COME IN.
SO WHAT BRINGS YOU HERE? A HOT CASE THAT NEEDS SOLVING?
UH... SORT OF.
WONDERFUL.
TO YOUR HEALTH.
CHEERS.
SO WHAT OF THIS CASE OF YOURS?
I'M NOT SURE HOW TO PUT THIS, BUT...
...WE THOUGHT THAT SINCE YOU KNEW HOODED JUSTICE BEST, YOU MIGHT BE ABLE TO HELP US FIND HIM.
I SEE. I WISH I COULD HELP.
THE SAD TRUTH IS I HAVEN'T SEEN HIM SINCE THE HUAC BUSINESS STARTED UP.
I THOUGHT THAT THE TWO OF US...
WELL, YOU KNOW. SOMETIMES YOU THINK THAT A FRIENDSHIP IS MAYBE DEEPER THAN IT REALLY IS.

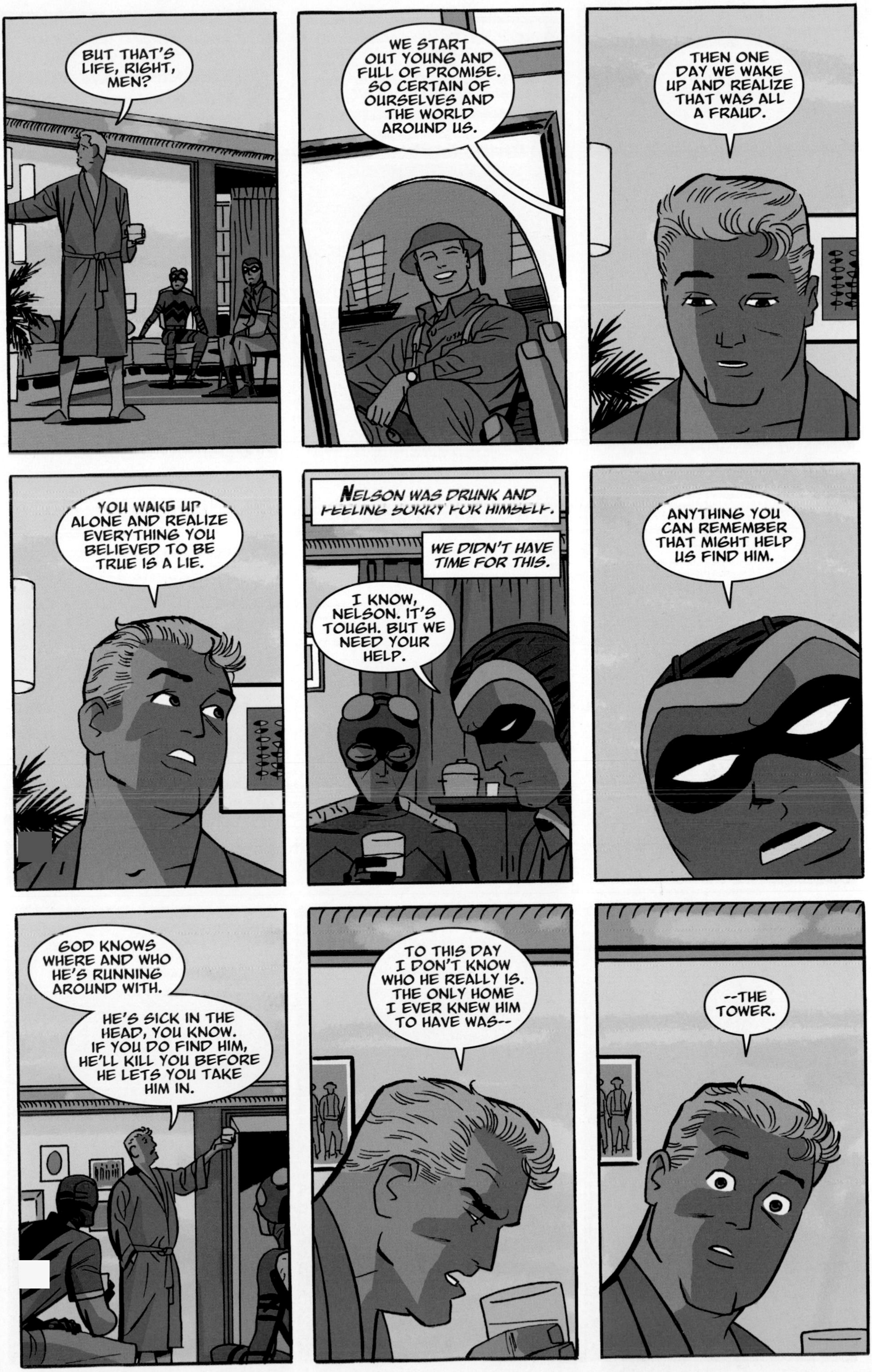
BUT THAT'S LIFE, RIGHT, MEN?
WE START OUT YOUNG AND FULL OF PROMISE. SO CERTAIN OF OURSELVES AND THE WORLD AROUND US.
THEN ONE DAY WE WAKE UP AND REALIZE THAT WAS ALL A FRAUD.
YOU WAKE UP ALONE AND REALIZE EVERYTHING YOU BELIEVED TO BE TRUE IS A LIE.
NELSON WAS DRUNK AND FEELING SORRY FOR HIMSELF.
WE DIDN'T HAVE TIME FOR THIS.
I KNOW, NELSON. IT'S TOUGH. BUT WE NEED YOUR HELP.
ANYTHING YOU CAN REMEMBER THAT MIGHT HELP US FIND HIM.
GOD KNOWS WHERE AND WHO HE'S RUNNING AROUND WITH.
HE'S SICK IN THE HEAD, YOU KNOW. IF YOU DO FIND HIM, HE'LL KILL YOU BEFORE HE LETS YOU TAKE HIM IN.
TO THIS DAY I DON'T KNOW WHO HE REALLY IS. THE ONLY HOME I EVER KNEW HIM TO HAVE WAS--
--THE TOWER.

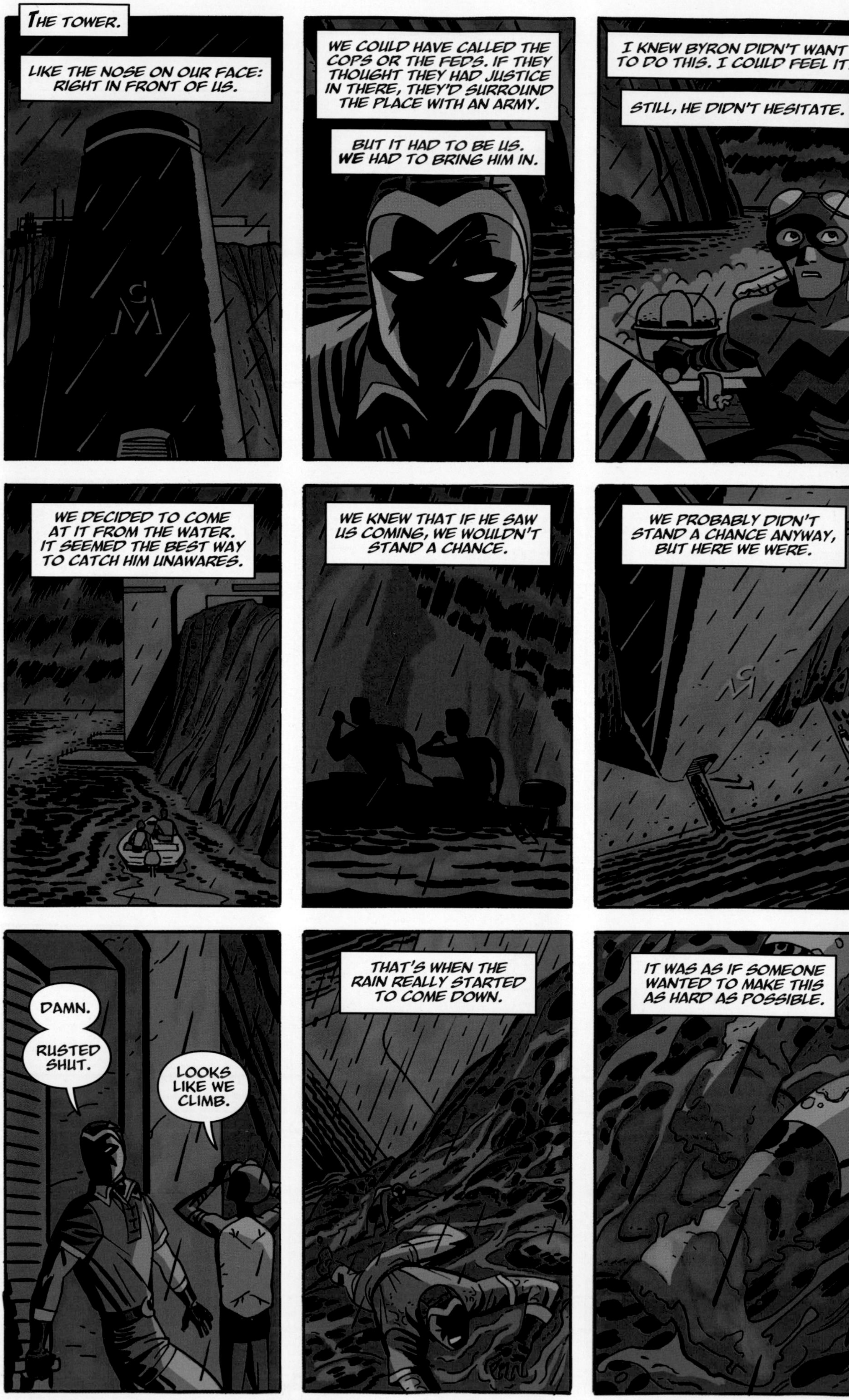
THE TOWER.
LIKE THE NOSE ON OUR FACE: RIGHT IN FRONT OF US.
WE COULD HAVE CALLED THE COPS OR THE FEDS. IF THEY THOUGHT THEY HAD JUSTICE IN THERE, THEY'D SURROUND THE PLACE WITH AN ARMY.
BUT IT HAD TO BE US. WE HAD TO BRING HIM IN.
I KNEW BYRON DIDN'T WANT TO DO THIS. I COULD FEEL IT.
STILL, HE DIDN'T HESITATE.
WE DECIDED TO COME AT IT FROM THE WATER. IT SEEMED THE BEST WAY TO CATCH HIM UNAWARES.
WE KNEW THAT IF HE SAW US COMING, WE WOULDN'T STAND A CHANCE.
WE PROBABLY DIDN'T STAND A CHANCE ANYWAY, BUT HERE WE WERE.
DAMN.
RUSTED SHUT.
LOOKS LIKE WE CLIMB.
THAT'S WHEN THE RAIN REALLY STARTED TO COME DOWN.
IT WAS AS IF SOMEONE WANTED TO MAKE THIS AS HARD AS POSSIBLE.

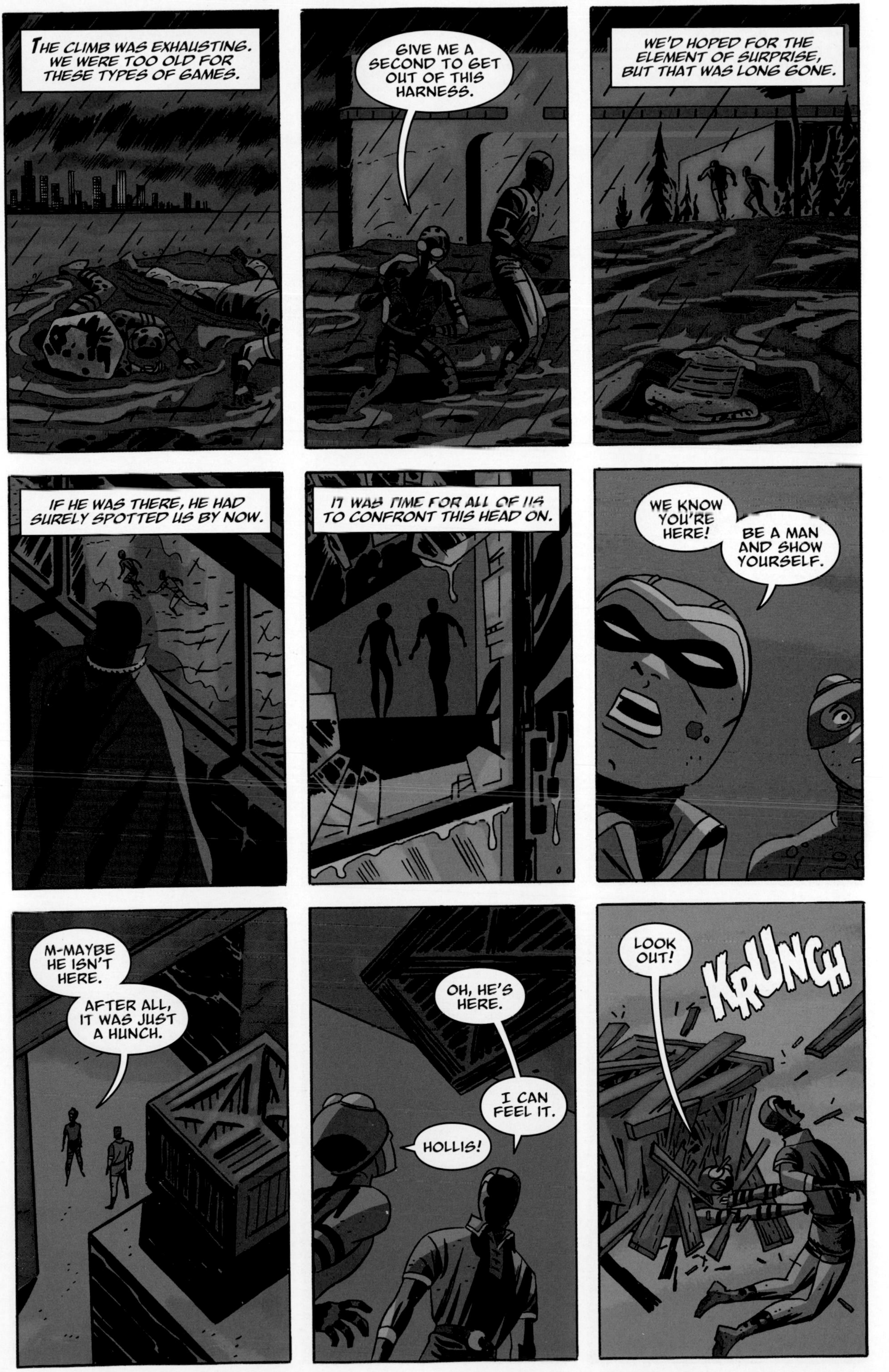
THE CLIMB WAS EXHAUSTING. WE WERE TOO OLD FOR THESE TYPES OF GAMES.
GIVE ME A SECOND TO GET OUT OF THIS HARNESS.
WE'D HOPED FOR THE ELEMENT OF SURPRISE, BUT THAT WAS LONG GONE.
IF HE WAS THERE, HE HAD SURELY SPOTTED US BY NOW.
IT WAS TIME FOR ALL OF US TO CONFRONT THIS HEAD ON.
WE KNOW YOU'RE HERE!
BE A MAN AND SHOW YOURSELF.
M-MAYBE HE ISN'T HERE.
AFTER ALL, IT WAS JUST A HUNCH.
OH, HE'S HERE.
I CAN FEEL IT.
HOLLIS!
LOOK OUT!
KRUNCH

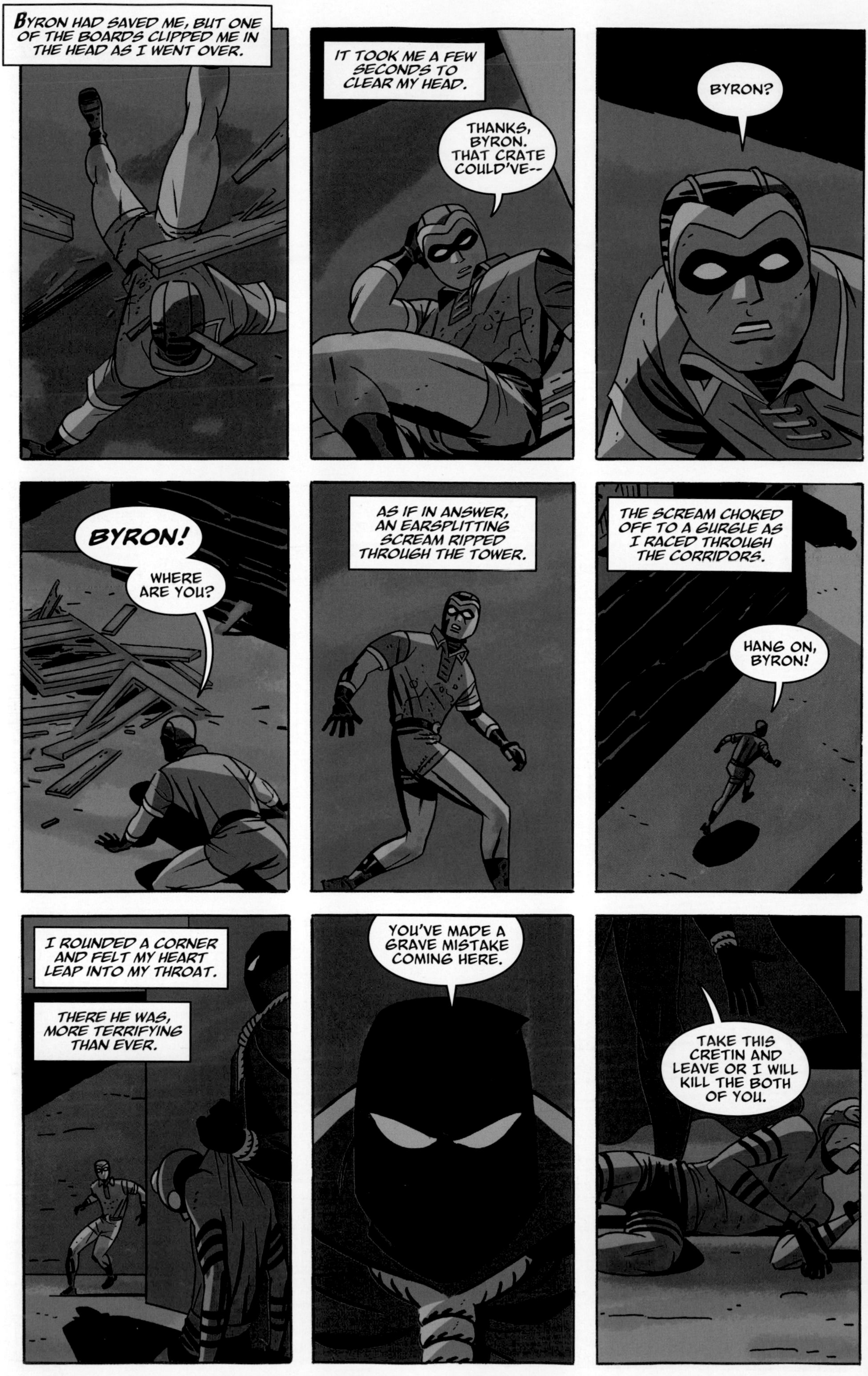
BYRON HAD SAVED ME, BUT ONE OF THE BOARDS CLIPPED ME IN THE HEAD AS I WENT OVER.
IT TOOK ME A FEW SECONDS TO CLEAR MY HEAD.
THANKS, BYRON. THAT CRATE COULD'VE--
BYRON?
BYRON!
WHERE ARE YOU?
AS IF IN ANSWER, AN EARSPLITTING SCREAM RIPPED THROUGH THE TOWER.
THE SCREAM CHOKED OFF TO A GURGLE AS I RACED THROUGH THE CORRIDORS.
HANG ON, BYRON!
I ROUNDED A CORNER AND FELT MY HEART LEAP INTO MY THROAT.
THERE HE WAS, MORE TERRIFYING THAN EVER.
YOU'VE MADE A GRAVE MISTAKE COMING HERE.
TAKE THIS CRETIN AND LEAVE OR I WILL KILL THE BOTH OF YOU.

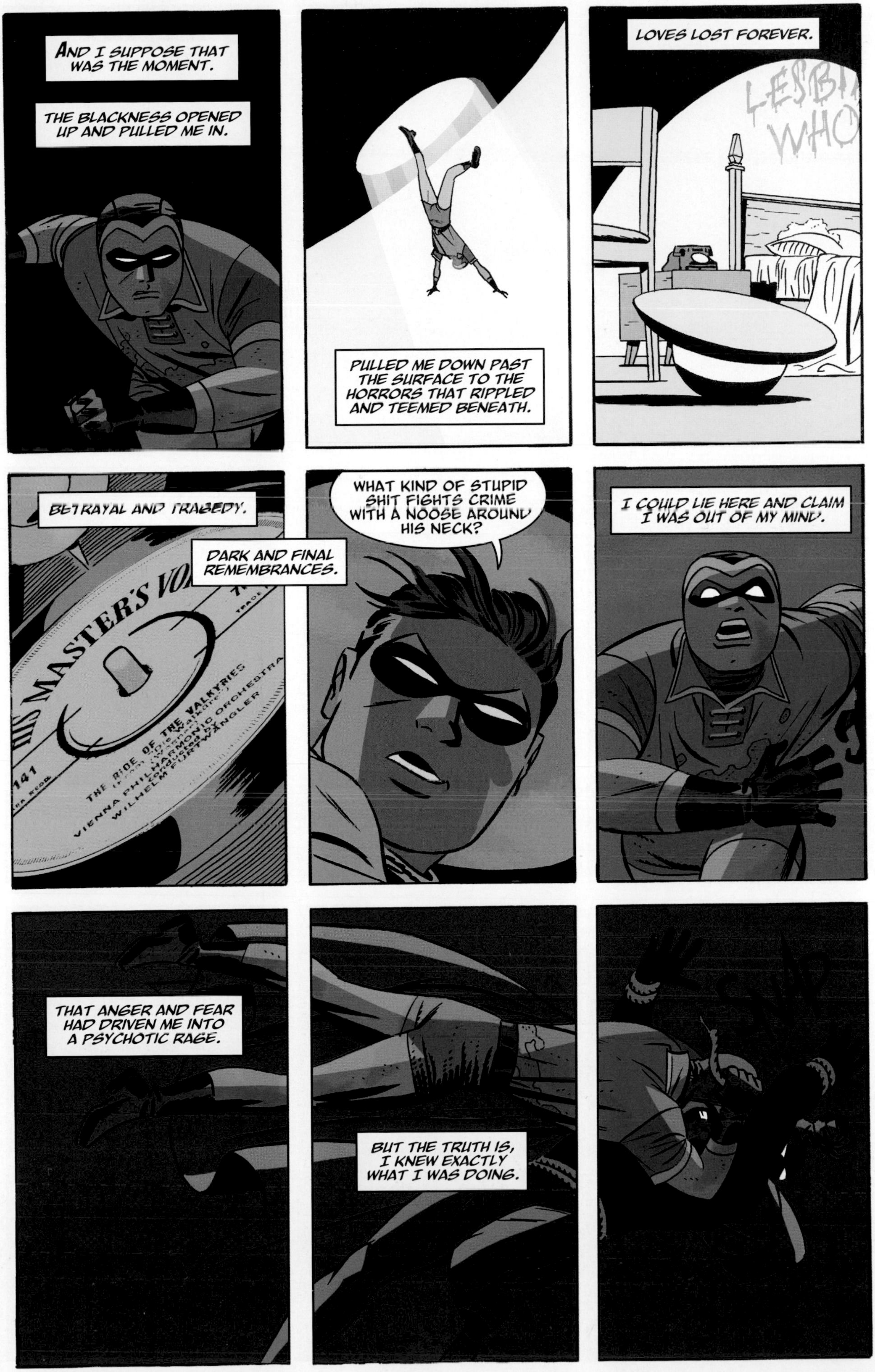
AND I SUPPOSE THAT WAS THE MOMENT.
THE BLACKNESS OPENED UP AND PULLED ME IN.
PULLED ME DOWN PAST THE SURFACE TO THE HORRORS THAT RIPPLED AND TEEMED BENEATH.
LOVES LOST FOREVER.
BETRAYAL AND TRAGEDY.
DARK AND FINAL REMEMBRANCES.
THE RIDE OF THE VALKYRIES
VIENNA PHILHARMONIC ORCHESTRA
WILHELM FURTWÄNGLER
WHAT KIND OF STUPID SHIT FIGHTS CRIME WITH A NOOSE AROUND HIS NECK?
I COULD LIE HERE AND CLAIM I WAS OUT OF MY MIND.
THAT ANGER AND FEAR HAD DRIVEN ME INTO A PSYCHOTIC RAGE.
BUT THE TRUTH IS, I KNEW EXACTLY WHAT I WAS DOING.

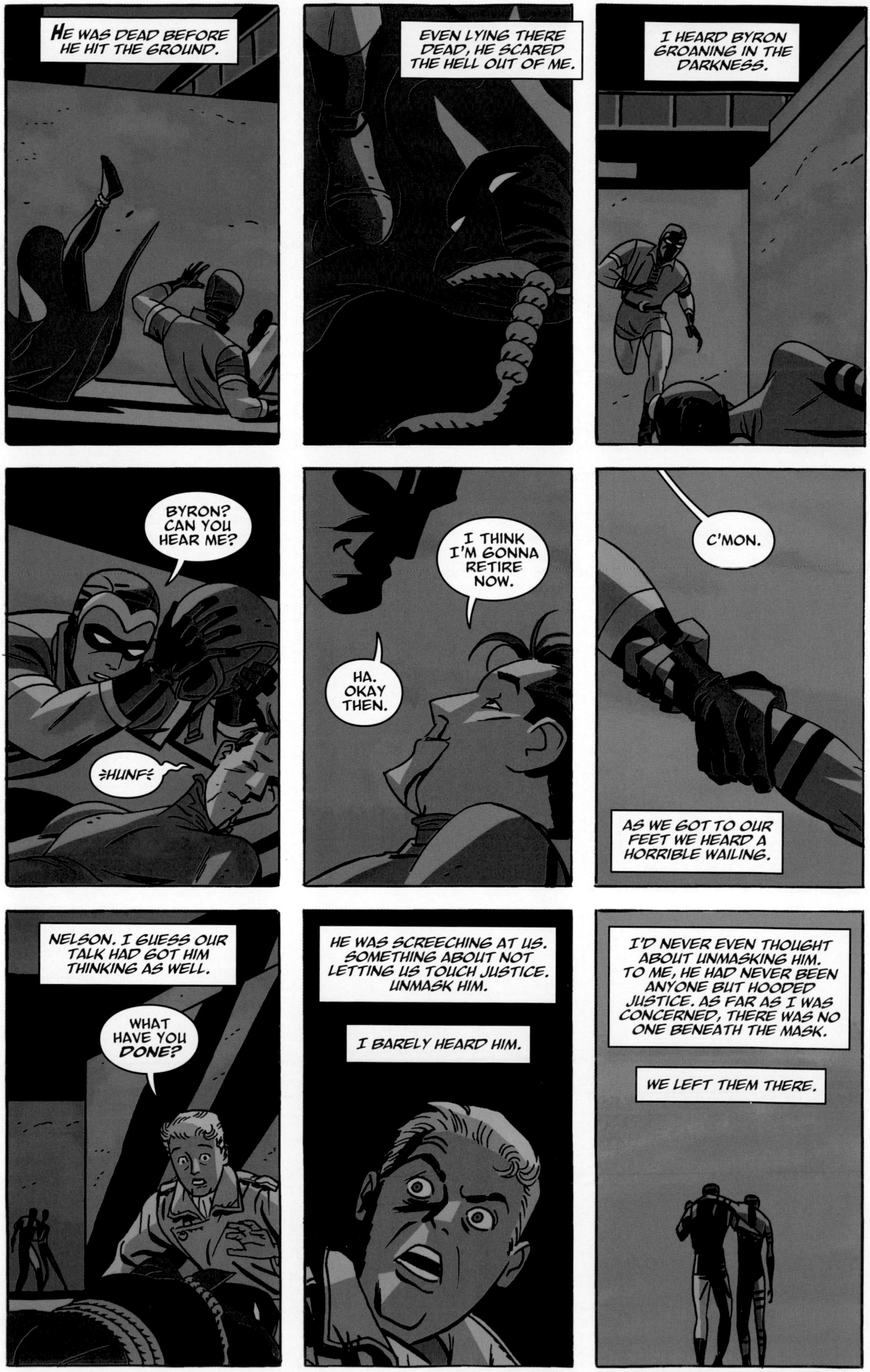
HE WAS DEAD BEFORE HE HIT THE GROUND.
EVEN LYING THERE DEAD, HE SCARED THE HELL OUT OF ME.
I HEARD BYRON GROANING IN THE DARKNESS.
BYRON? CAN YOU HEAR ME?
HUNF
I THINK I'M GONNA RETIRE NOW.
HA. OKAY THEN.
C'MON.
AS WE GOT TO OUR FEET WE HEARD A HORRIBLE WAILING.
NELSON. I GUESS OUR TALK HAD GOT HIM THINKING AS WELL.
WHAT HAVE YOU DONE?
HE WAS SCREECHING AT US. SOMETHING ABOUT NOT LETTING US TOUCH JUSTICE. UNMASK HIM.
I BARELY HEARD HIM.
I'D NEVER EVEN THOUGHT ABOUT UNMASKING HIM. TO ME, HE HAD NEVER BEEN ANYONE BUT HOODED JUSTICE. AS FAR AS I WAS CONCERNED, THERE WAS NO ONE BENEATH THE MASK.
WE LEFT THEM THERE.

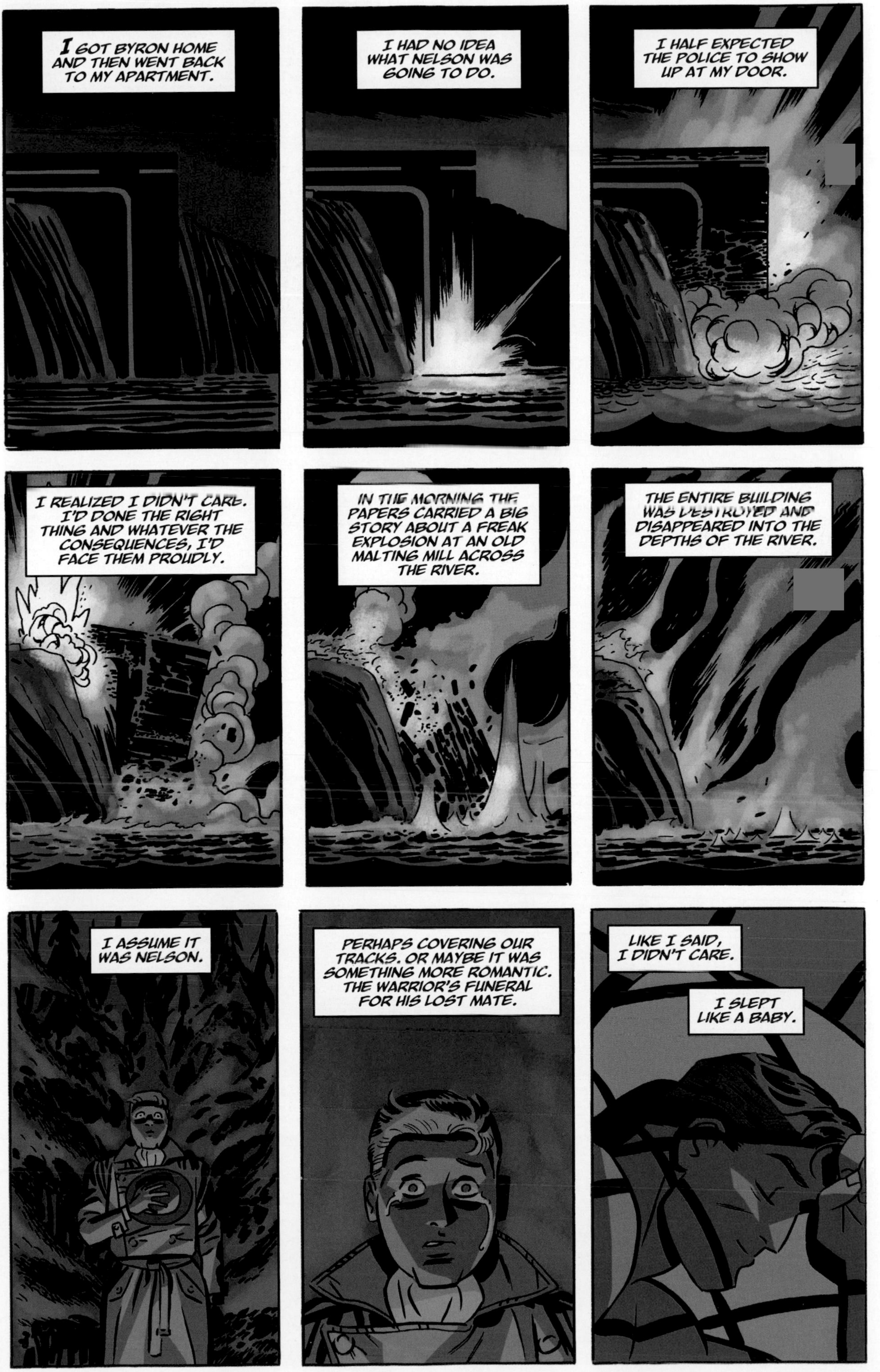
I GOT BYRON HOME AND THEN WENT BACK TO MY APARTMENT.
I HAD NO IDEA WHAT NELSON WAS GOING TO DO.
I HALF EXPECTED THE POLICE TO SHOW UP AT MY DOOR.
I REALIZED I DIDN'T CARE. I'D DONE THE RIGHT THING AND WHATEVER THE CONSEQUENCES, I'D FACE THEM PROUDLY.
IN THE MORNING THE PAPERS CARRIED A BIG STORY ABOUT A FREAK EXPLOSION AT AN OLD MALTING MILL ACROSS THE RIVER.
THE ENTIRE BUILDING WAS DESTROYED AND DISAPPEARED INTO THE DEPTHS OF THE RIVER.
I ASSUME IT WAS NELSON.
PERHAPS COVERING OUR TRACKS. OR MAYBE IT WAS SOMETHING MORE ROMANTIC. THE WARRIOR'S FUNERAL FOR HIS LOST MATE.
LIKE I SAID, I DIDN'T CARE.
I SLEPT LIKE A BABY.

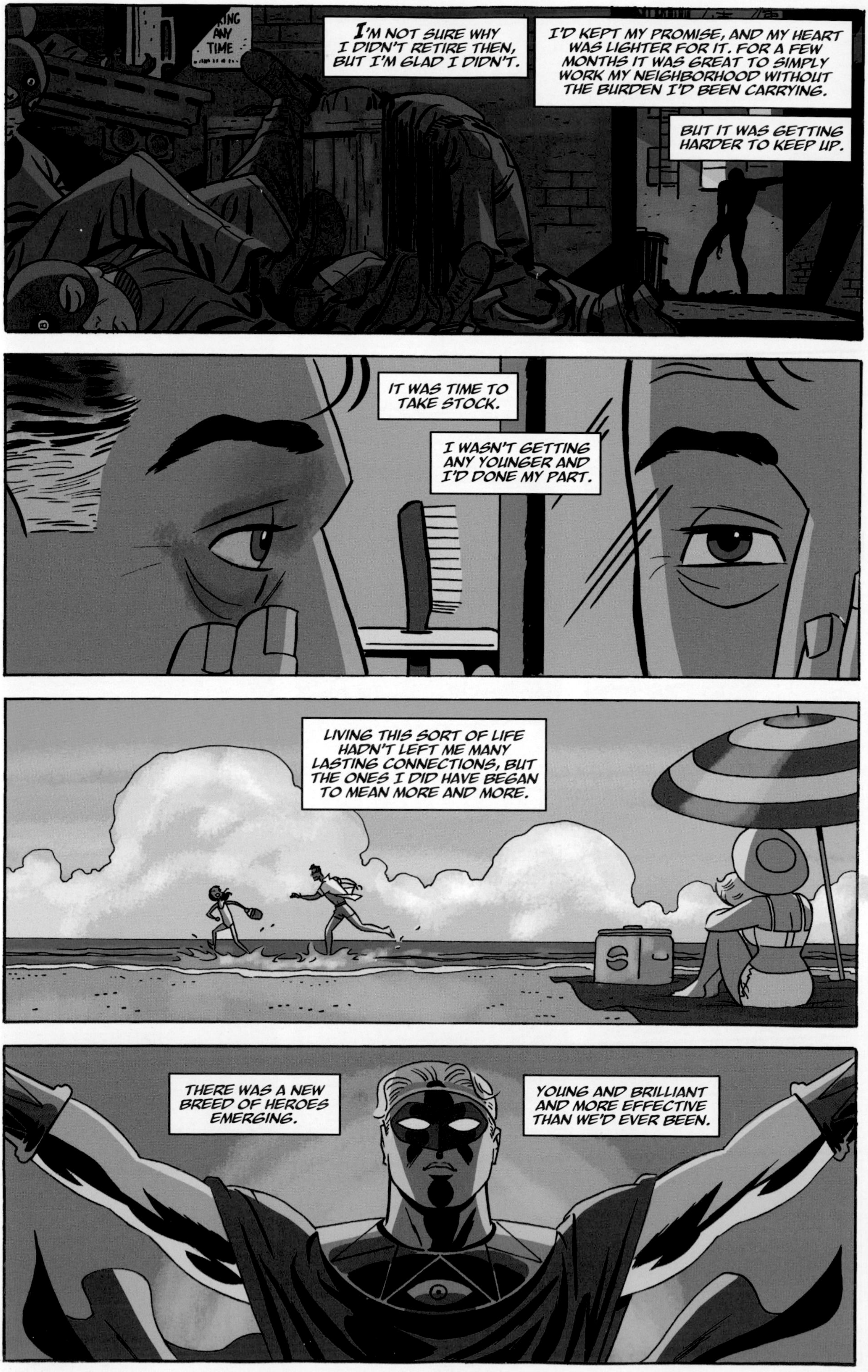
RING
ANY
TIME
I'M NOT SURE WHY I DIDN'T RETIRE THEN, BUT I'M GLAD I DIDN'T.
I'D KEPT MY PROMISE, AND MY HEART WAS LIGHTER FOR IT. FOR A FEW MONTHS IT WAS GREAT TO SIMPLY WORK MY NEIGHBORHOOD WITHOUT THE BURDEN I'D BEEN CARRYING.
BUT IT WAS GETTING HARDER TO KEEP UP.
IT WAS TIME TO TAKE STOCK.
I WASN'T GETTING ANY YOUNGER AND I'D DONE MY PART.
LIVING THIS SORT OF LIFE HADN'T LEFT ME MANY LASTING CONNECTIONS, BUT THE ONES I DID HAVE BEGAN TO MEAN MORE AND MORE.
THERE WAS A NEW BREED OF HEROES EMERGING.
YOUNG AND BRILLIANT AND MORE EFFECTIVE THAN WE'D EVER BEEN.

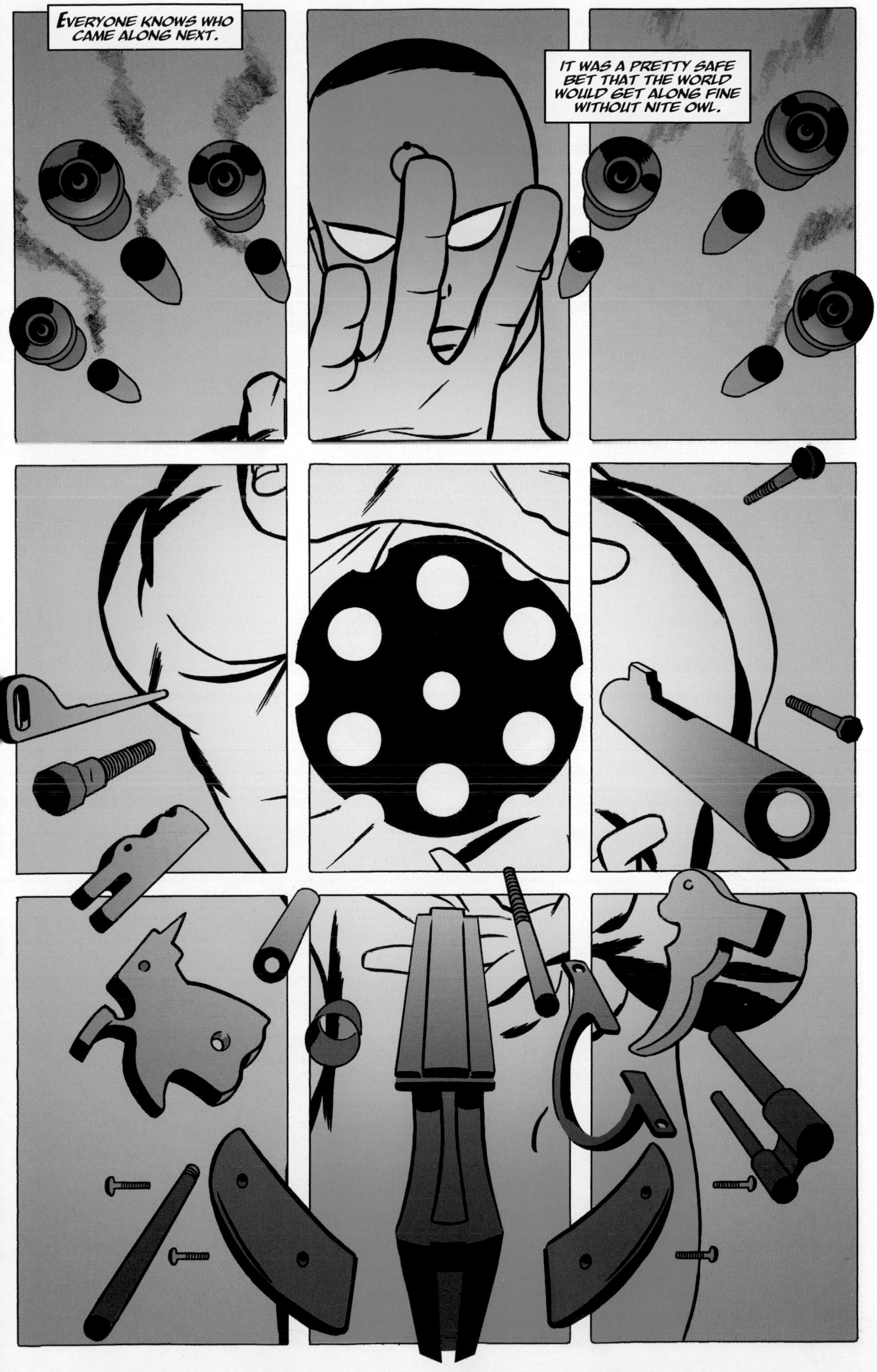
EVERYONE KNOWS WHO CAME ALONG NEXT.
IT WAS A PRETTY SAFE BET THAT THE WORLD WOULD GET ALONG FINE WITHOUT NITE OWL.

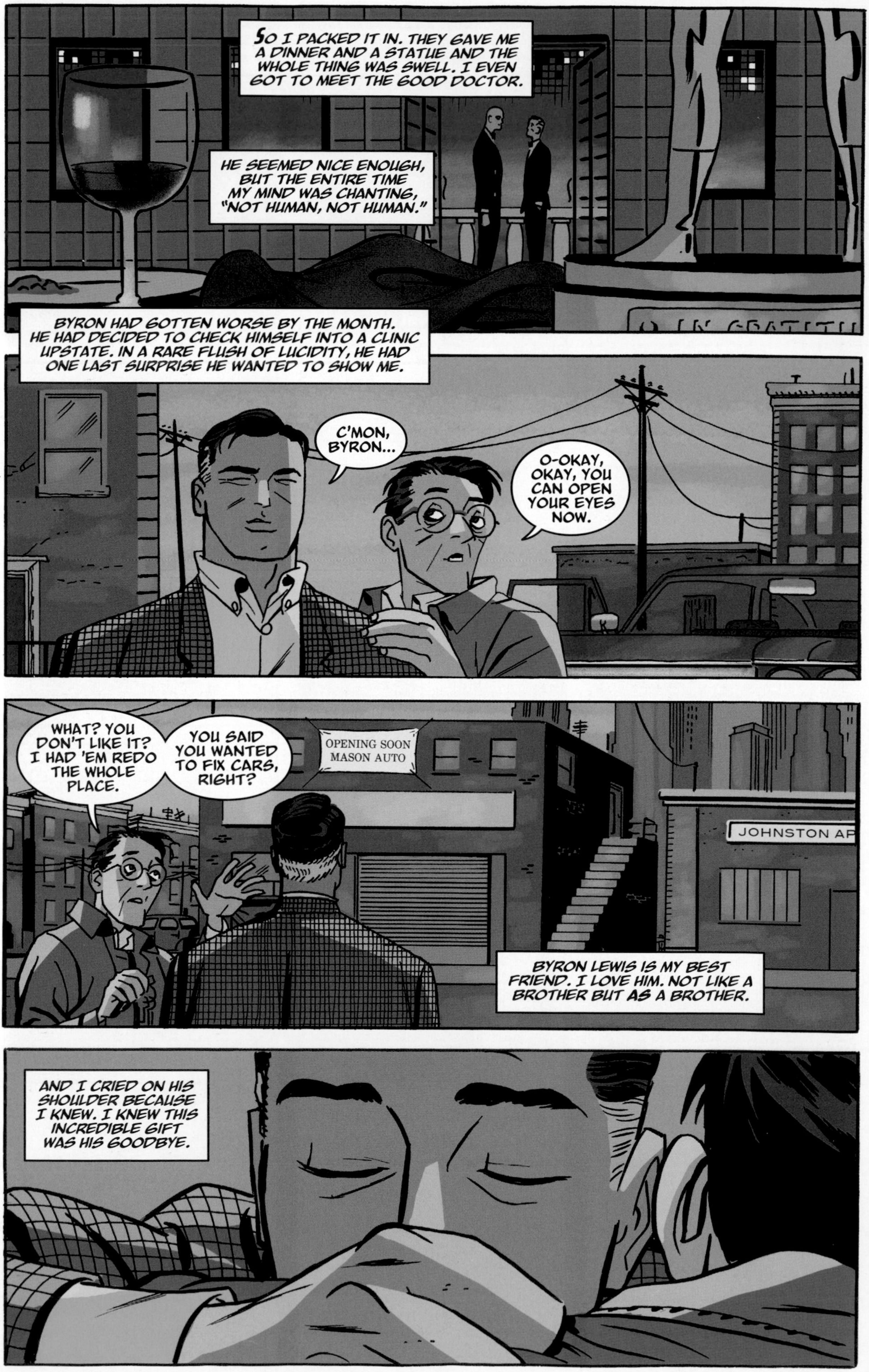
SO I PACKED IT IN. THEY GAVE ME A DINNER AND A STATUE AND THE WHOLE THING WAS SWELL. I EVEN GOT TO MEET THE GOOD DOCTOR.
HE SEEMED NICE ENOUGH, BUT THE ENTIRE TIME MY MIND WAS CHANTING, "NOT HUMAN, NOT HUMAN."
BYRON HAD GOTTEN WORSE BY THE MONTH. HE HAD DECIDED TO CHECK HIMSELF INTO A CLINIC UPSTATE. IN A RARE FLUSH OF LUCIDITY, HE HAD ONE LAST SURPRISE HE WANTED TO SHOW ME.
C'MON, BYRON...
O-OKAY, OKAY, YOU CAN OPEN YOUR EYES NOW.
WHAT? YOU DON'T LIKE IT? I HAD 'EM REDO THE WHOLE PLACE.
YOU SAID YOU WANTED TO FIX CARS, RIGHT?
OPENING SOON
MASON AUTO
JOHNSTON AP
BYRON LEWIS IS MY BEST FRIEND. I LOVE HIM. NOT LIKE A BROTHER BUT AS A BROTHER.
AND I CRIED ON HIS SHOULDER BECAUSE I KNEW. I KNEW THIS INCREDIBLE GIFT WAS HIS GOODBYE.

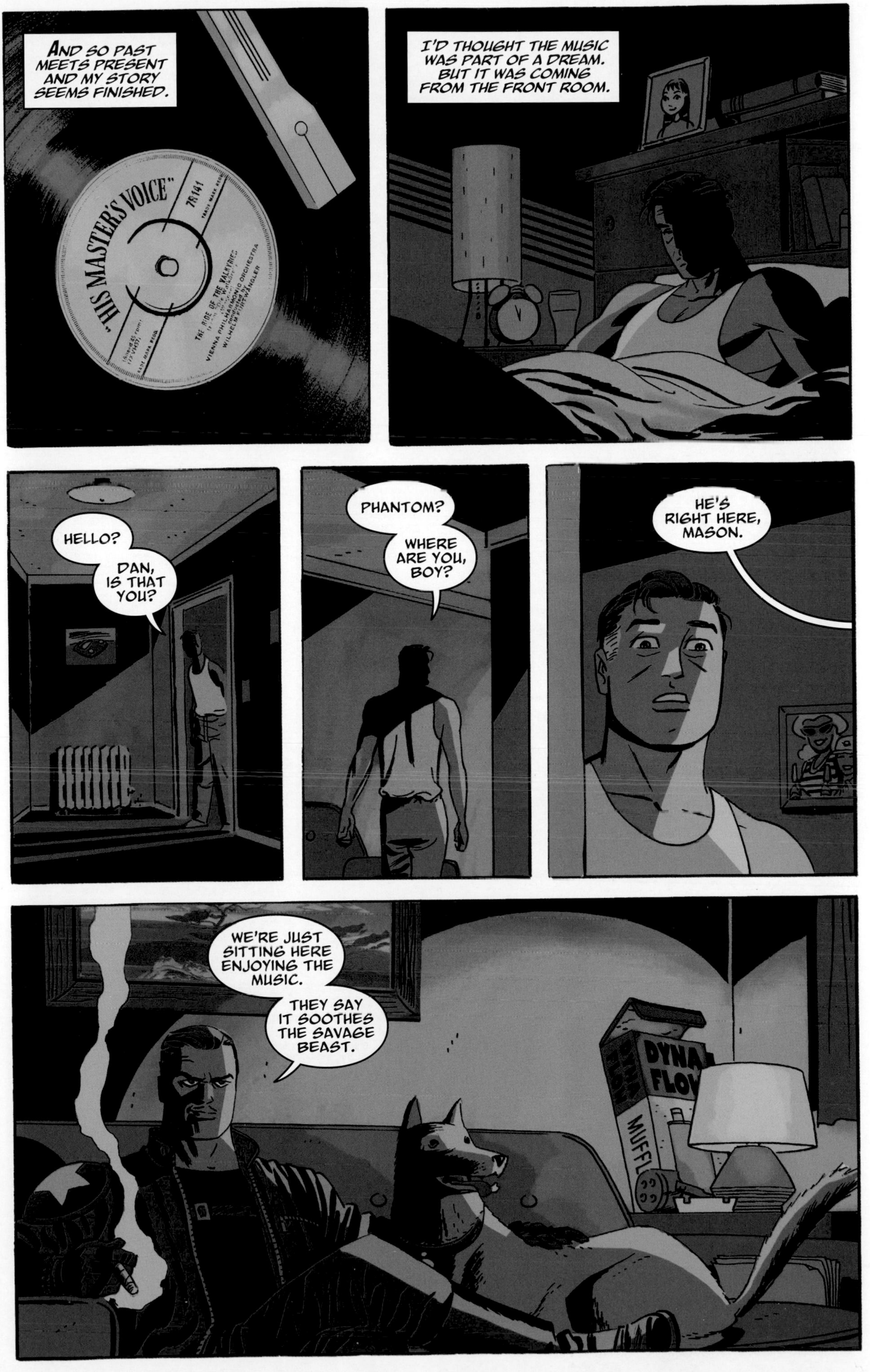
AND SO PAST MEETS PRESENT AND MY STORY SEEMS FINISHED.
"HIS MASTER'S VOICE"
I'D THOUGHT THE MUSIC WAS PART OF A DREAM. BUT IT WAS COMING FROM THE FRONT ROOM.
HELLO?
DAN, IS THAT YOU?
PHANTOM?
WHERE ARE YOU, BOY?
HE'S RIGHT HERE, MASON.
WE'RE JUST SITTING HERE ENJOYING THE MUSIC.
THEY SAY IT SOOTHES THE SAVAGE BEAST.

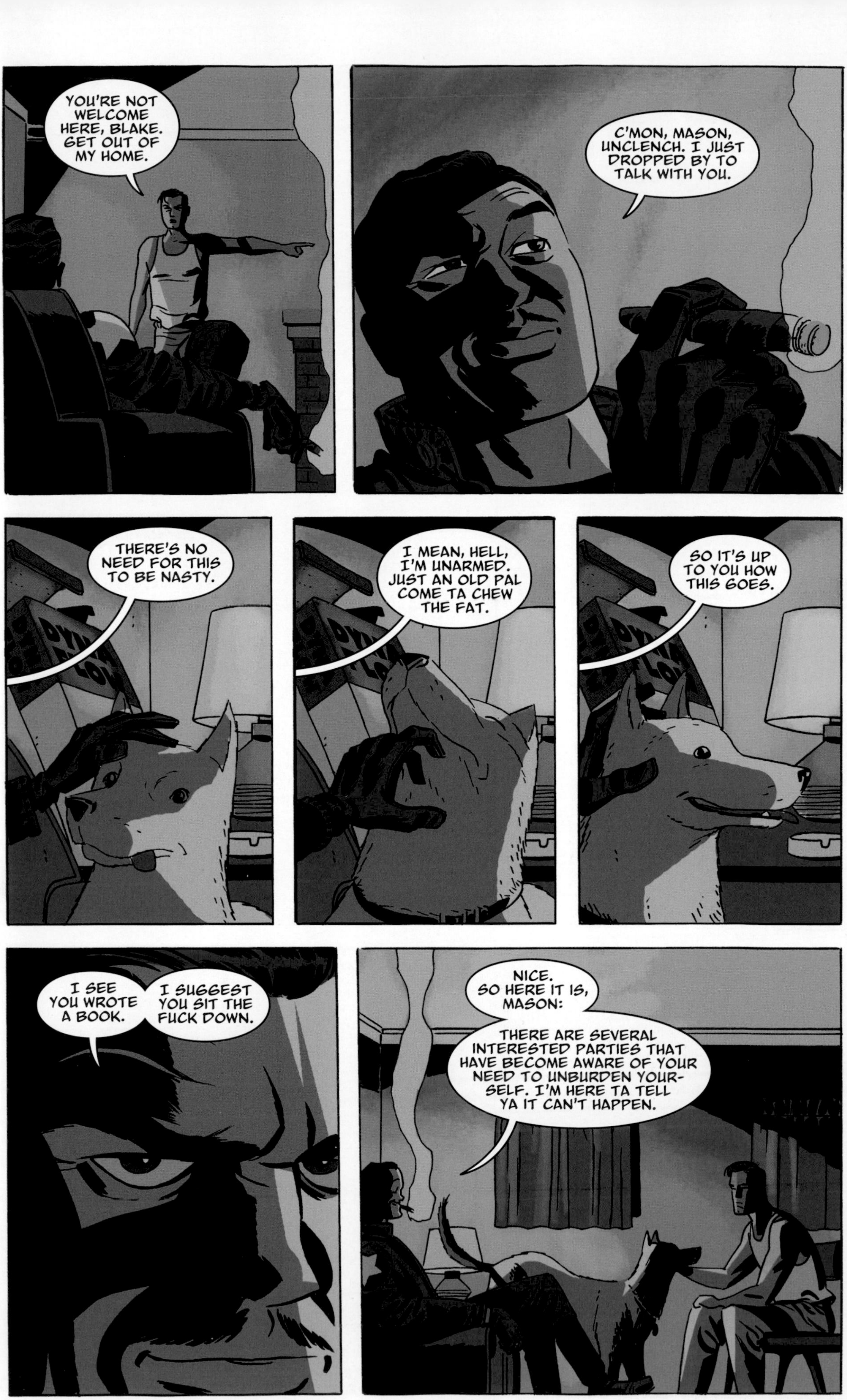
YOU'RE NOT WELCOME HERE, BLAKE. GET OUT OF MY HOME.
C'MON, MASON, UNCLENCH. I JUST DROPPED BY TO TALK WITH YOU.
THERE'S NO NEED FOR THIS TO BE NASTY.
I MEAN, HELL, I'M UNARMED. JUST AN OLD PAL COME TA CHEW THE FAT.
SO IT'S UP TO YOU HOW THIS GOES.
I SEE YOU WROTE A BOOK.
I SUGGEST YOU SIT THE FUCK DOWN.
NICE. SO HERE IT IS, MASON:
THERE ARE SEVERAL INTERESTED PARTIES THAT HAVE BECOME AWARE OF YOUR NEED TO UNBURDEN YOUR-SELF. I'M HERE TA TELL YA IT CAN'T HAPPEN.

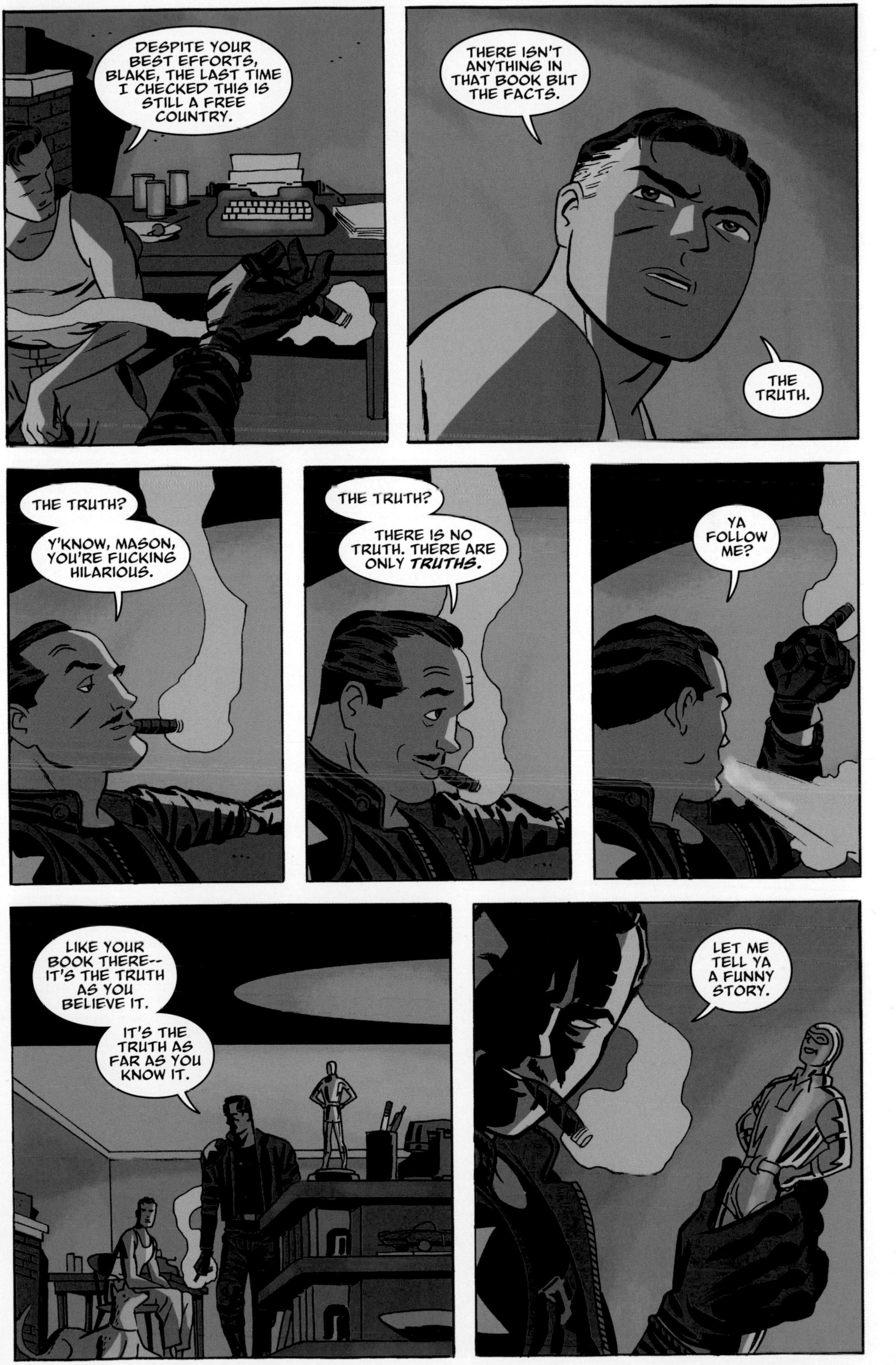
DESPITE YOUR BEST EFFORTS, BLAKE, THE LAST TIME I CHECKED THIS IS STILL A FREE COUNTRY.
THERE ISN'T ANYTHING IN THAT BOOK BUT THE FACTS.
THE TRUTH.
THE TRUTH?
Y'KNOW, MASON, YOU'RE FUCKING HILARIOUS.
THE TRUTH?
THERE IS NO TRUTH. THERE ARE ONLY *TRUTHS.*
YA FOLLOW ME?
LIKE YOUR BOOK THERE-- IT'S THE TRUTH AS YOU BELIEVE IT.
IT'S THE TRUTH AS FAR AS YOU KNOW IT.
LET ME TELL YA A FUNNY STORY.

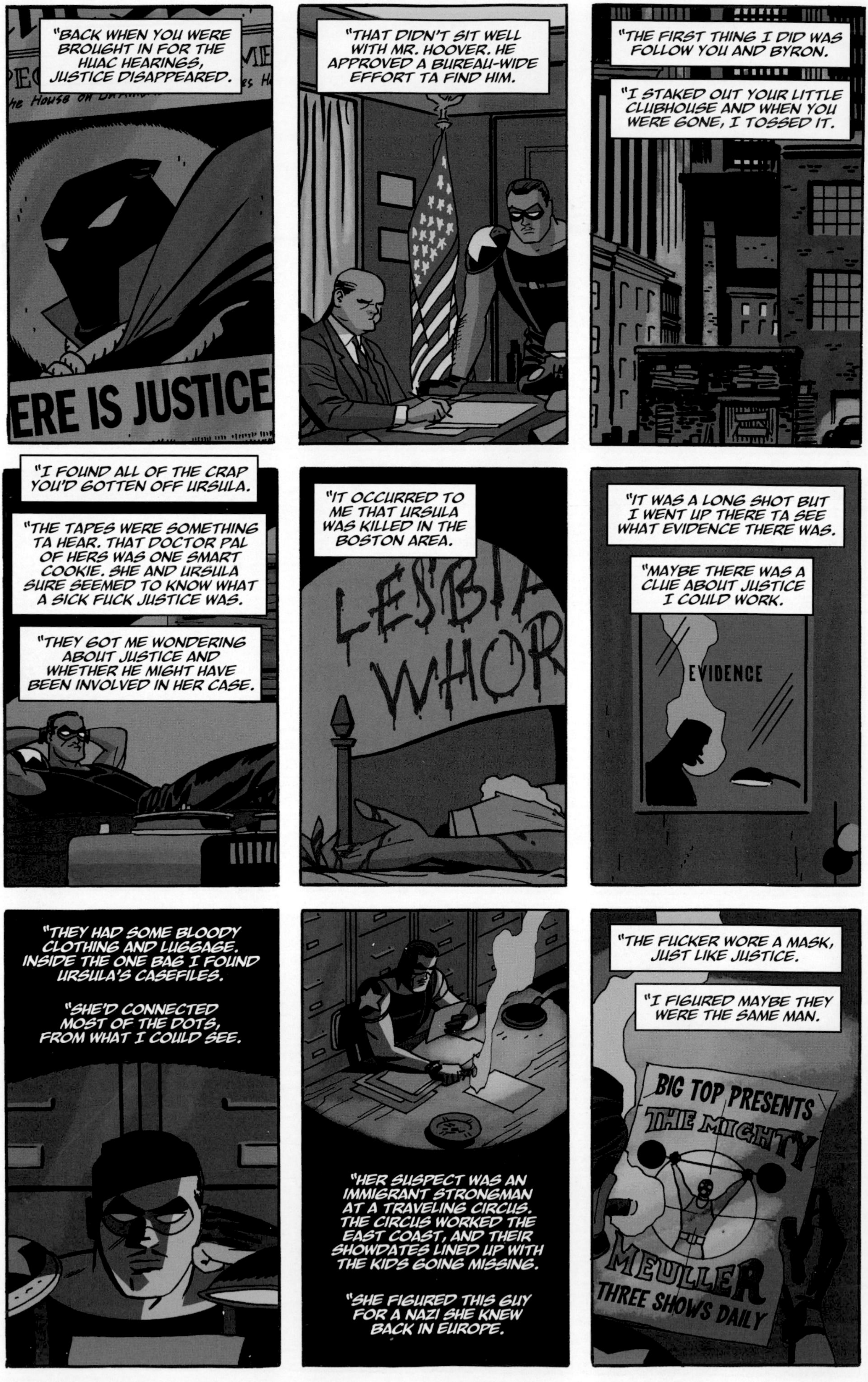
"BACK WHEN YOU WERE BROUGHT IN FOR THE HUAC HEARINGS, JUSTICE DISAPPEARED.
ERE IS JUSTICE
"THAT DIDN'T SIT WELL WITH MR. HOOVER. HE APPROVED A BUREAU-WIDE EFFORT TA FIND HIM.
"THE FIRST THING I DID WAS FOLLOW YOU AND BYRON.
"I STAKED OUT YOUR LITTLE CLUBHOUSE AND WHEN YOU WERE GONE, I TOSSED IT.
"I FOUND ALL OF THE CRAP YOU'D GOTTEN OFF URSULA.
"THE TAPES WERE SOMETHING TA HEAR. THAT DOCTOR PAL OF HERS WAS ONE SMART COOKIE. SHE AND URSULA SURE SEEMED TO KNOW WHAT A SICK FUCK JUSTICE WAS.
"THEY GOT ME WONDERING ABOUT JUSTICE AND WHETHER HE MIGHT HAVE BEEN INVOLVED IN HER CASE.
"IT OCCURRED TO ME THAT URSULA WAS KILLED IN THE BOSTON AREA.
LESBIA
WHOR
"IT WAS A LONG SHOT BUT I WENT UP THERE TA SEE WHAT EVIDENCE THERE WAS.
"MAYBE THERE WAS A CLUE ABOUT JUSTICE I COULD WORK.
EVIDENCE
"THEY HAD SOME BLOODY CLOTHING AND LUGGAGE. INSIDE THE ONE BAG I FOUND URSULA'S CASEFILES.
"SHE'D CONNECTED MOST OF THE DOTS, FROM WHAT I COULD SEE.
"HER SUSPECT WAS AN IMMIGRANT STRONGMAN AT A TRAVELING CIRCUS. THE CIRCUS WORKED THE EAST COAST, AND THEIR SHOWDATES LINED UP WITH THE KIDS GOING MISSING.
"SHE FIGURED THIS GUY FOR A NAZI SHE KNEW BACK IN EUROPE.
"THE FUCKER WORE A MASK, JUST LIKE JUSTICE.
"I FIGURED MAYBE THEY WERE THE SAME MAN.
BIG TOP PRESENTS
THE MIGHTY
MEULLER
THREE SHOWS DAILY

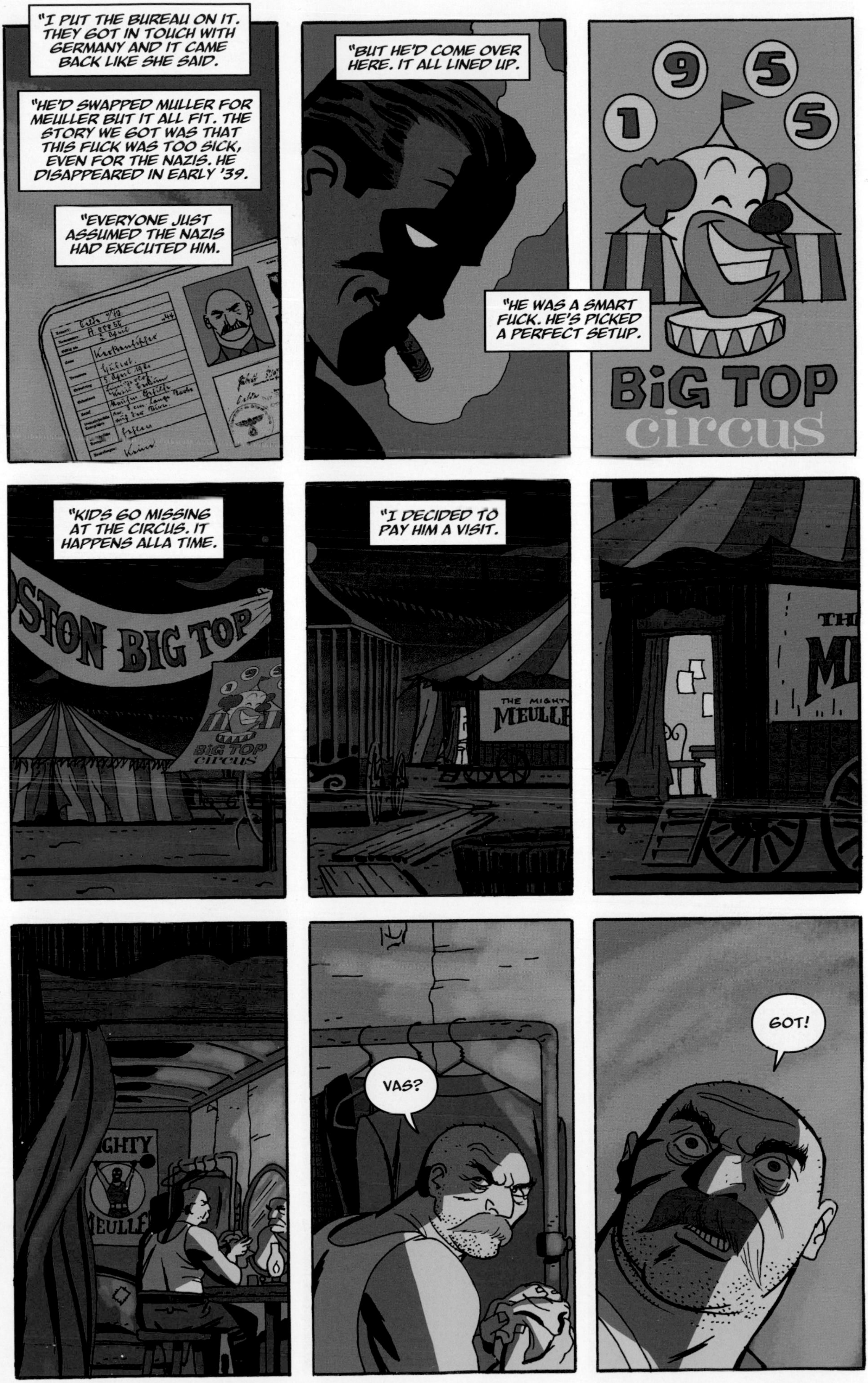
"I PUT THE BUREAU ON IT. THEY GOT IN TOUCH WITH GERMANY AND IT CAME BACK LIKE SHE SAID.
"HE'D SWAPPED MULLER FOR MEULLER BUT IT ALL FIT. THE STORY WE GOT WAS THAT THIS FUCK WAS TOO SICK, EVEN FOR THE NAZIS. HE DISAPPEARED IN EARLY '39.
"EVERYONE JUST ASSUMED THE NAZIS HAD EXECUTED HIM.
"BUT HE'D COME OVER HERE. IT ALL LINED UP.
"HE WAS A SMART FUCK. HE'S PICKED A PERFECT SETUP.
1955
BiG TOP
circus
"KIDS GO MISSING AT THE CIRCUS. IT HAPPENS ALLA TIME.
OSTON BIG TOP
BiG TOP
circus
"I DECIDED TO PAY HIM A VISIT.
THE MIGHTY
MEULLE
MIGHTY
MEULLE
VAS?
GOT!

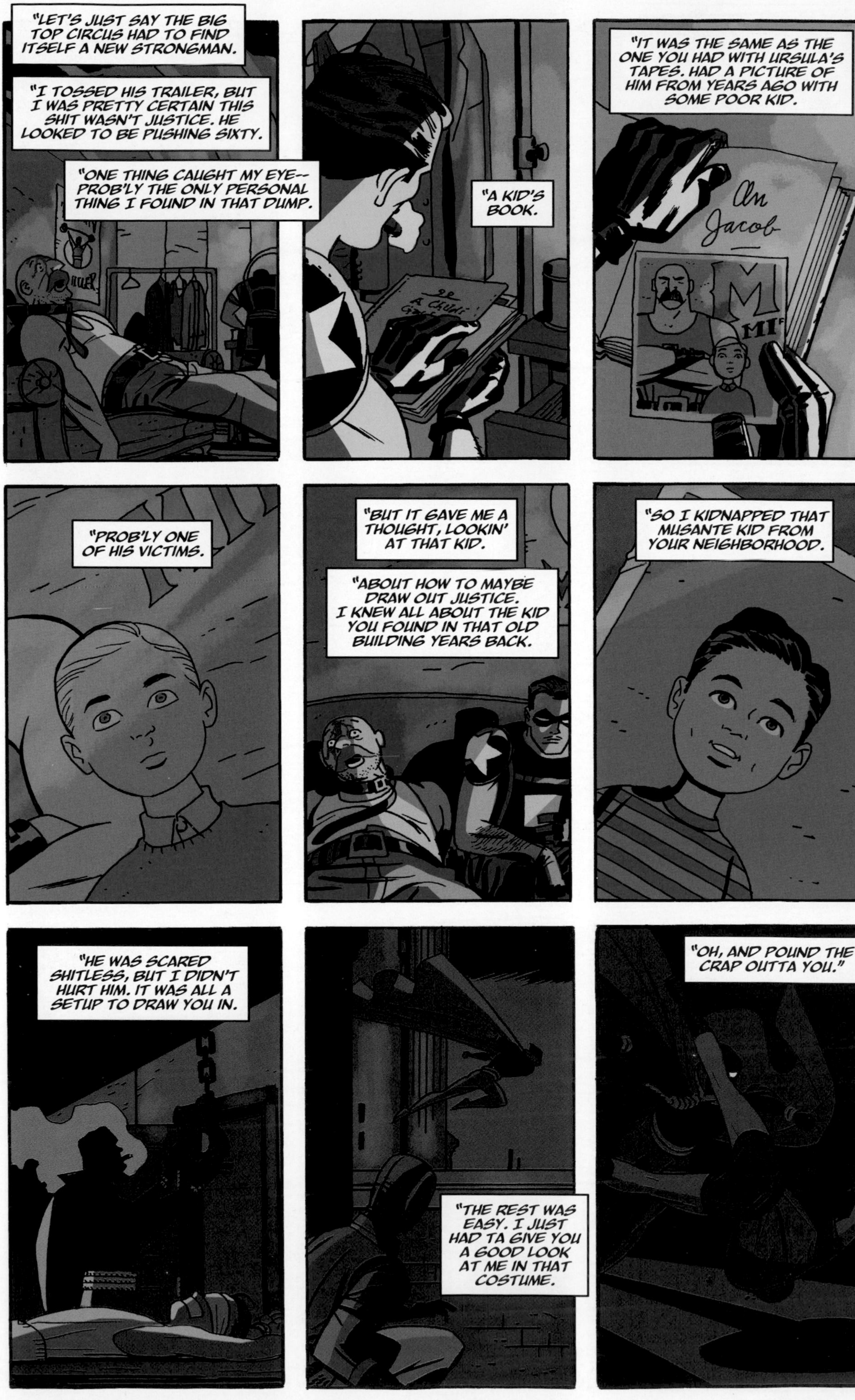
"LET'S JUST SAY THE BIG TOP CIRCUS HAD TO FIND ITSELF A NEW STRONGMAN.
"I TOSSED HIS TRAILER, BUT I WAS PRETTY CERTAIN THIS SHIT WASN'T JUSTICE. HE LOOKED TO BE PUSHING SIXTY.
"ONE THING CAUGHT MY EYE-- PROB'LY THE ONLY PERSONAL THING I FOUND IN THAT DUMP.
"A KID'S BOOK.
"IT WAS THE SAME AS THE ONE YOU HAD WITH URSULA'S TAPES. HAD A PICTURE OF HIM FROM YEARS AGO WITH SOME POOR KID.
Jacob
"PROB'LY ONE OF HIS VICTIMS.
"BUT IT GAVE ME A THOUGHT, LOOKIN' AT THAT KID.
"ABOUT HOW TO MAYBE DRAW OUT JUSTICE. I KNEW ALL ABOUT THE KID YOU FOUND IN THAT OLD BUILDING YEARS BACK.
"SO I KIDNAPPED THAT MUSANTE KID FROM YOUR NEIGHBORHOOD.
"HE WAS SCARED SHITLESS, BUT I DIDN'T HURT HIM. IT WAS ALL A SETUP TO DRAW YOU IN.
"THE REST WAS EASY. I JUST HAD TA GIVE YOU A GOOD LOOK AT ME IN THAT COSTUME.
"OH, AND POUND THE CRAP OUTTA YOU."

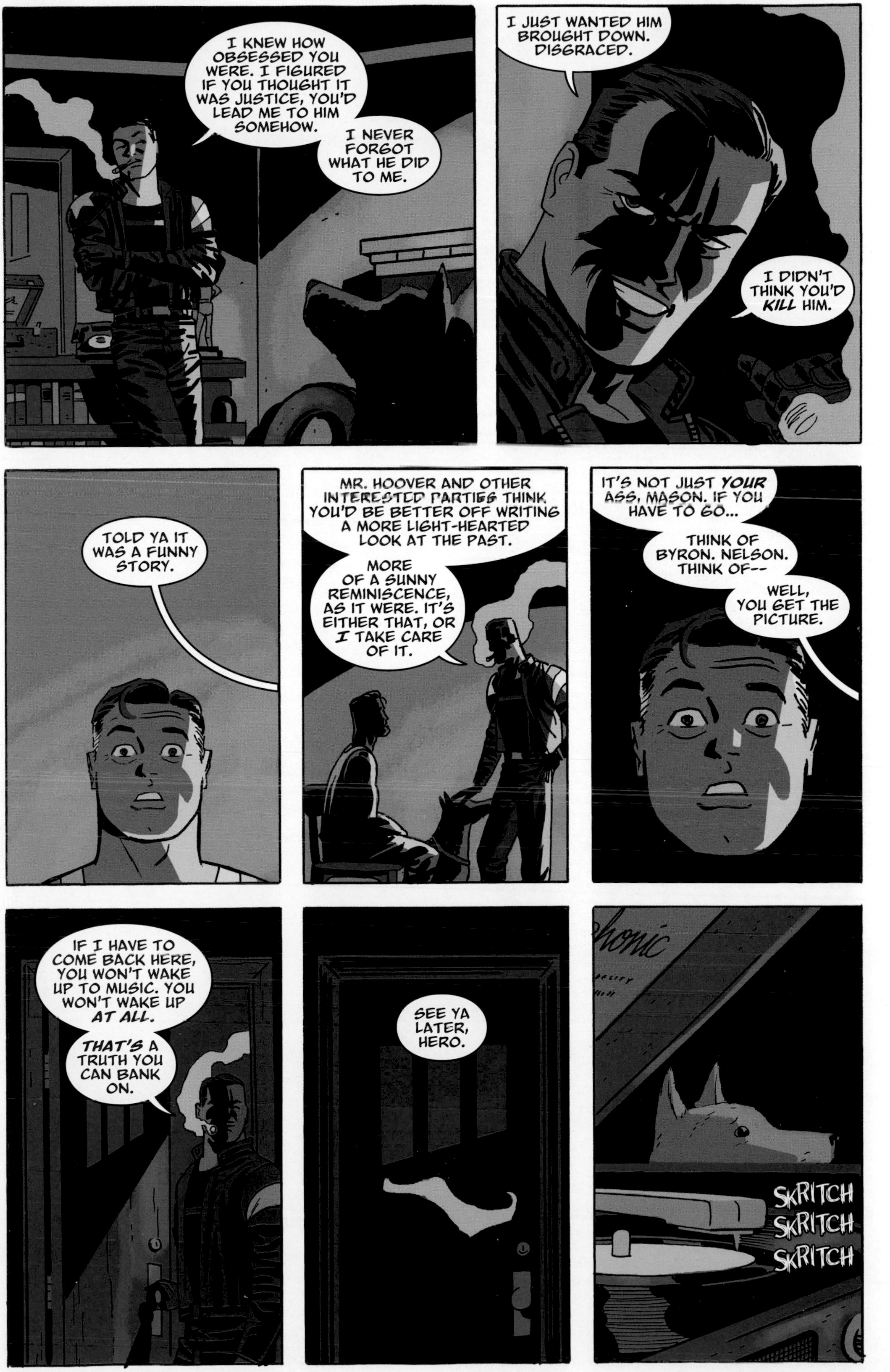
I KNEW HOW OBSESSED YOU WERE. I FIGURED IF YOU THOUGHT IT WAS JUSTICE, YOU'D LEAD ME TO HIM SOMEHOW.
I NEVER FORGOT WHAT HE DID TO ME.
I JUST WANTED HIM BROUGHT DOWN. DISGRACED.
I DIDN'T THINK YOU'D *KILL* HIM.
TOLD YA IT WAS A FUNNY STORY.
MR. HOOVER AND OTHER INTERESTED PARTIES THINK YOU'D BE BETTER OFF WRITING A MORE LIGHT-HEARTED LOOK AT THE PAST.
MORE OF A SUNNY REMINISCENCE, AS IT WERE. IT'S EITHER THAT, OR *I* TAKE CARE OF IT.
IT'S NOT JUST *YOUR* ASS, MASON. IF YOU HAVE TO GO...
THINK OF BYRON. NELSON. THINK OF--
WELL, YOU GET THE PICTURE.
IF I HAVE TO COME BACK HERE, YOU WON'T WAKE UP TO MUSIC. YOU WON'T WAKE UP *AT ALL*.
THAT'S A TRUTH YOU CAN BANK ON.
SEE YA LATER, HERO.
SKRITCH
SKRITCH
SKRITCH

HE LEFT ME THERE, STARING INTO A BLACKNESS OF MY OWN CREATION. I'D KILLED THE WRONG MAN.

THAT NIGHT IN THE TOWER, HE WOULD HAVE KILLED US. OF THAT I'M CERTAIN.

BUT IT WAS ALL MY FAULT. WE WOULDN'T HAVE EVEN BEEN THERE THAT NIGHT IF I HADN'T BEEN SO BLIND.

inference of the article was that Müller, whose family was East German, had gone on the run ... uncovered while the Communist witch hunts were at their most feverish. The ... d that Müller had probably been executed by his own Red superiors.

IRONICALLY, I'D SPENT THE LAST WEEK EDITING MY BOOK FOR THE SAKE OF MY OLD FRIENDS.

IT WAS LOOKING AT LITTLE LAURIE AND FINALLY REALIZING WHAT SALLY HAD BEEN TRYING TO GET THROUGH MY THICK HEAD.

CUT!

THERE WERE THINGS THAT WERE MORE IMPORTANT THAN THE TRUTH.

That was more than could be said for ... all had to testify before the House UnAmerican Activities Committee, and were all forced to reveal our true identities to one of ... Galling though this was, it didn't present any immediate problems for ... such an outstanding military record and with ...

IT DIDN'T TAKE MUCH WORK TO CUT OUT THE PARTS BLAKE WAS TALKING ABOUT.

THE ONE PART I DIDN'T CUT WAS BLAKE'S ATTACK ON SALLY.

FUCK HIM. HE CAN CARRY THAT, AND IF HE WANTS TO KILL ME, SO BE IT.

I BURNED EVERYTHING TO DO WITH IT.

I FIGURED I WOULD GO TO HELL NOW. THE WAY I WAS BROUGHT UP, THAT'S WHAT HAPPENS TO PEOPLE WHO DON'T CONFESS THEIR SINS.

BUT MY FRIENDS WON'T HAVE TO BEAR THE BURDEN OF MY GUILT.

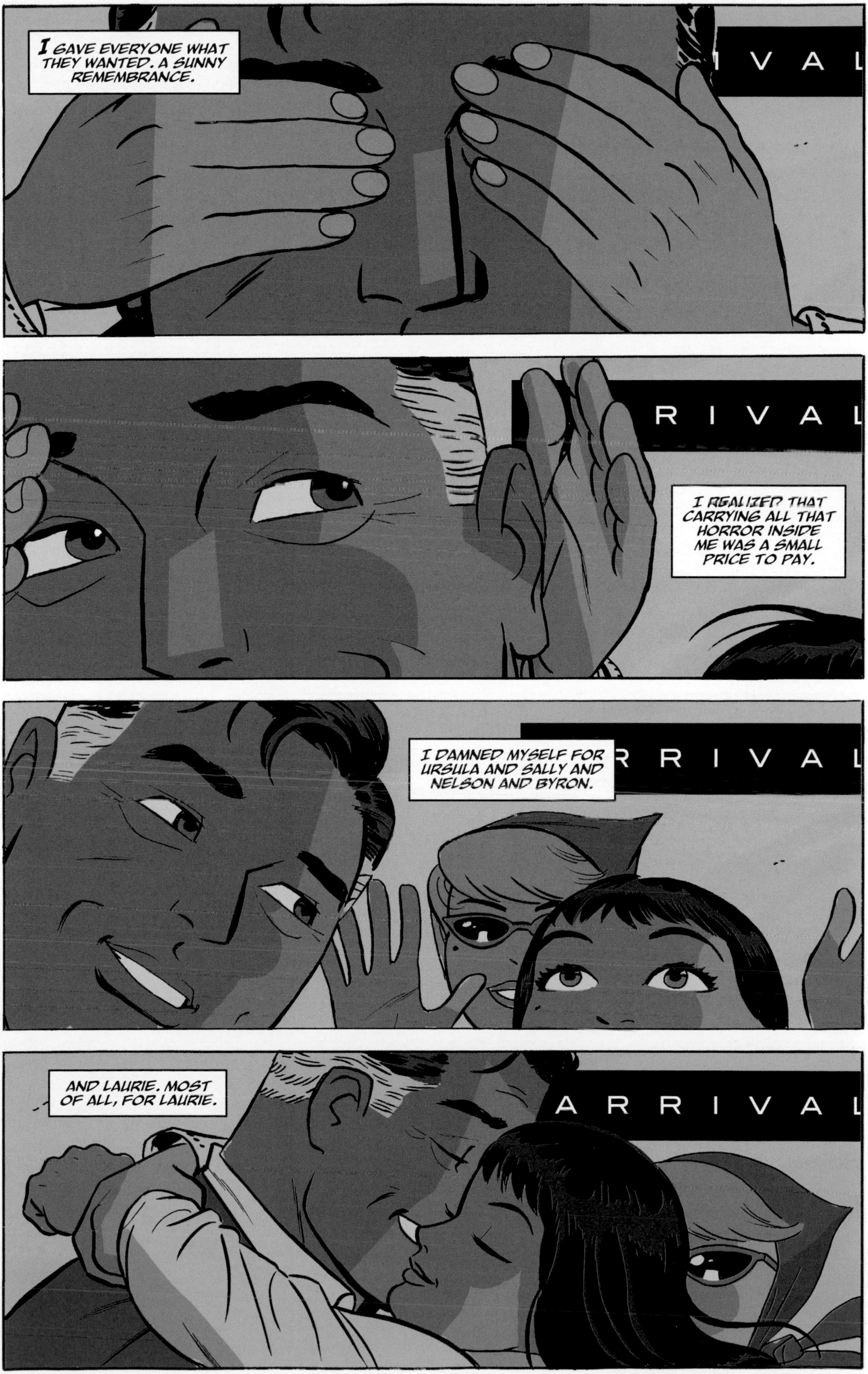
I GAVE EVERYONE WHAT THEY WANTED. A SUNNY REMEMBRANCE.
IVAL
RIVAL
I REALIZED THAT CARRYING ALL THAT HORROR INSIDE ME WAS A SMALL PRICE TO PAY.
I DAMNED MYSELF FOR URSULA AND SALLY AND NELSON AND BYRON.
RRIVAL
AND LAURIE. MOST OF ALL, FOR LAURIE.
ARRIVAL

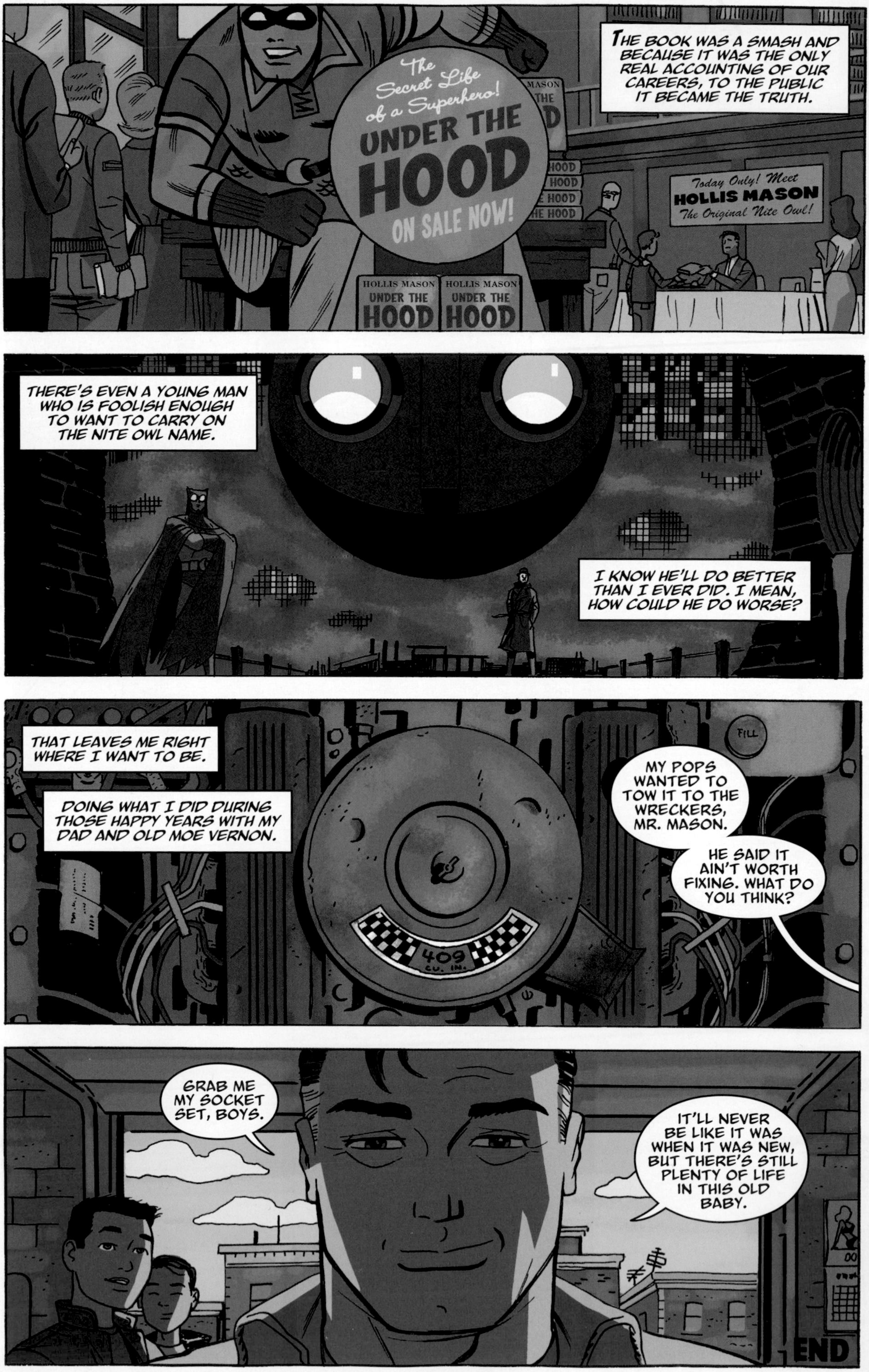
The Secret Life of a Superhero!
UNDER THE HOOD
ON SALE NOW!
THE BOOK WAS A SMASH AND BECAUSE IT WAS THE ONLY REAL ACCOUNTING OF OUR CAREERS, TO THE PUBLIC IT BECAME THE TRUTH.
Today Only! Meet HOLLIS MASON The Original Nite Owl!
HOLLIS MASON UNDER THE HOOD
HOLLIS MASON UNDER THE HOOD
THERE'S EVEN A YOUNG MAN WHO IS FOOLISH ENOUGH TO WANT TO CARRY ON THE NITE OWL NAME.
I KNOW HE'LL DO BETTER THAN I EVER DID. I MEAN, HOW COULD HE DO WORSE?
THAT LEAVES ME RIGHT WHERE I WANT TO BE.
DOING WHAT I DID DURING THOSE HAPPY YEARS WITH MY DAD AND OLD MOE VERNON.
FILL
409 CU. IN.
MY POPS WANTED TO TOW IT TO THE WRECKERS, MR. MASON.
HE SAID IT AIN'T WORTH FIXING. WHAT DO YOU THINK?
GRAB ME MY SOCKET SET, BOYS.
IT'LL NEVER BE LIKE IT WAS WHEN IT WAS NEW, BUT THERE'S STILL PLENTY OF LIFE IN THIS OLD BABY.
END

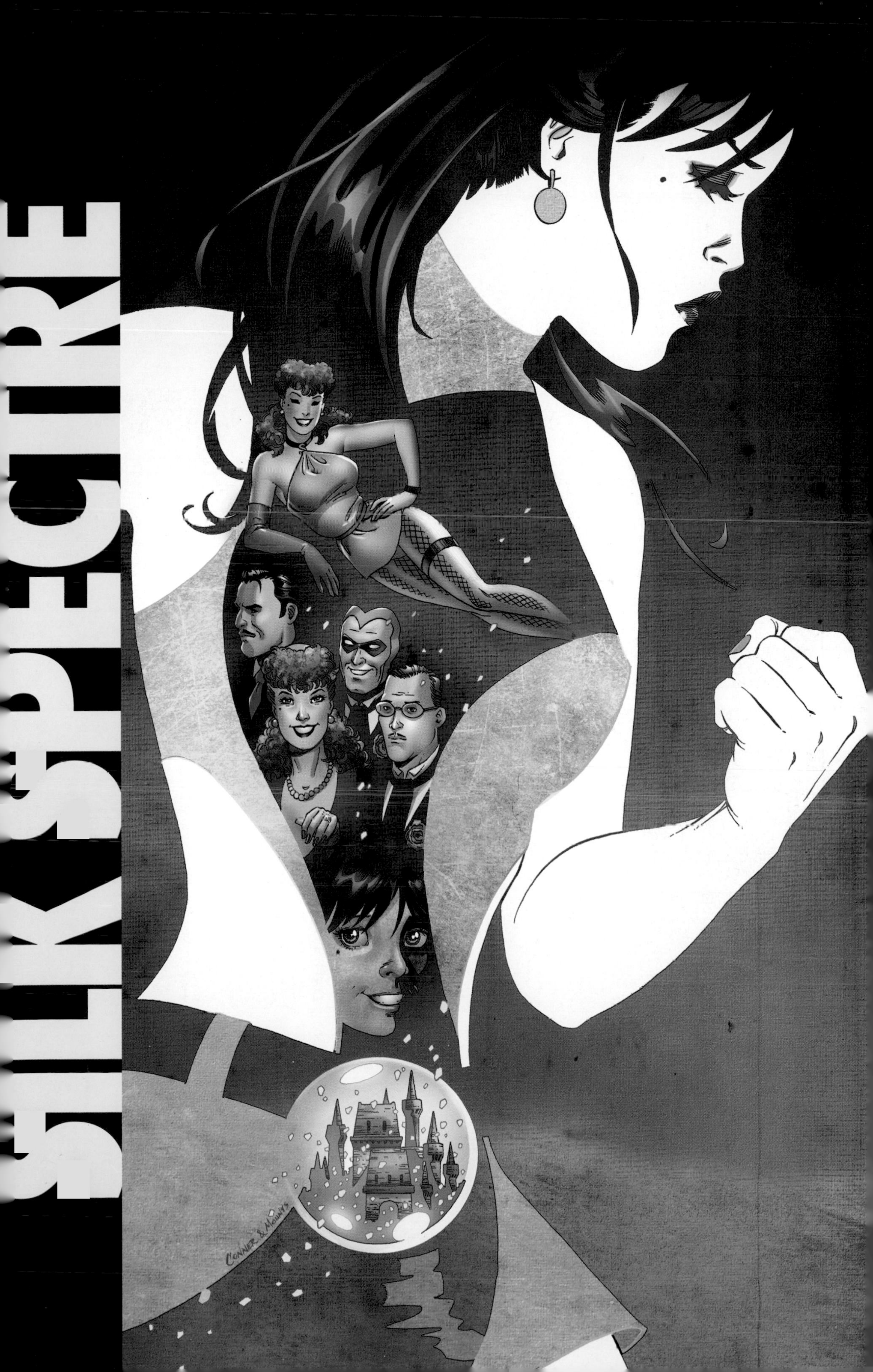
SILK SPECTRE
CONNER & MOUNTS

SILK SPECTRE

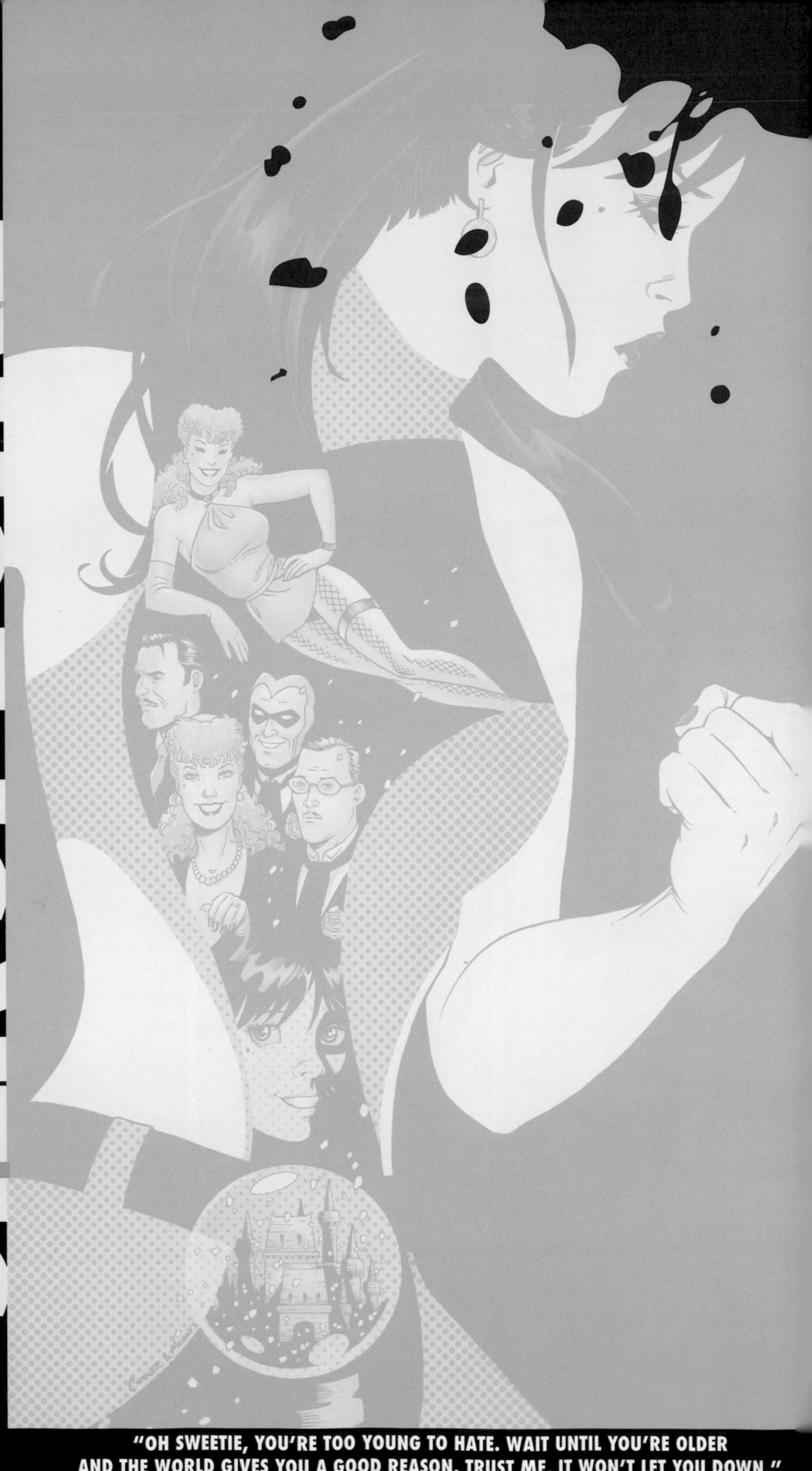
CONNER & MOUNTS

"OH SWEETIE, YOU'RE TOO YOUNG TO HATE. WAIT UNTIL YOU'RE OLDER AND THE WORLD GIVES YOU A GOOD REASON. TRUST ME, IT WON'T LET YOU DOWN."

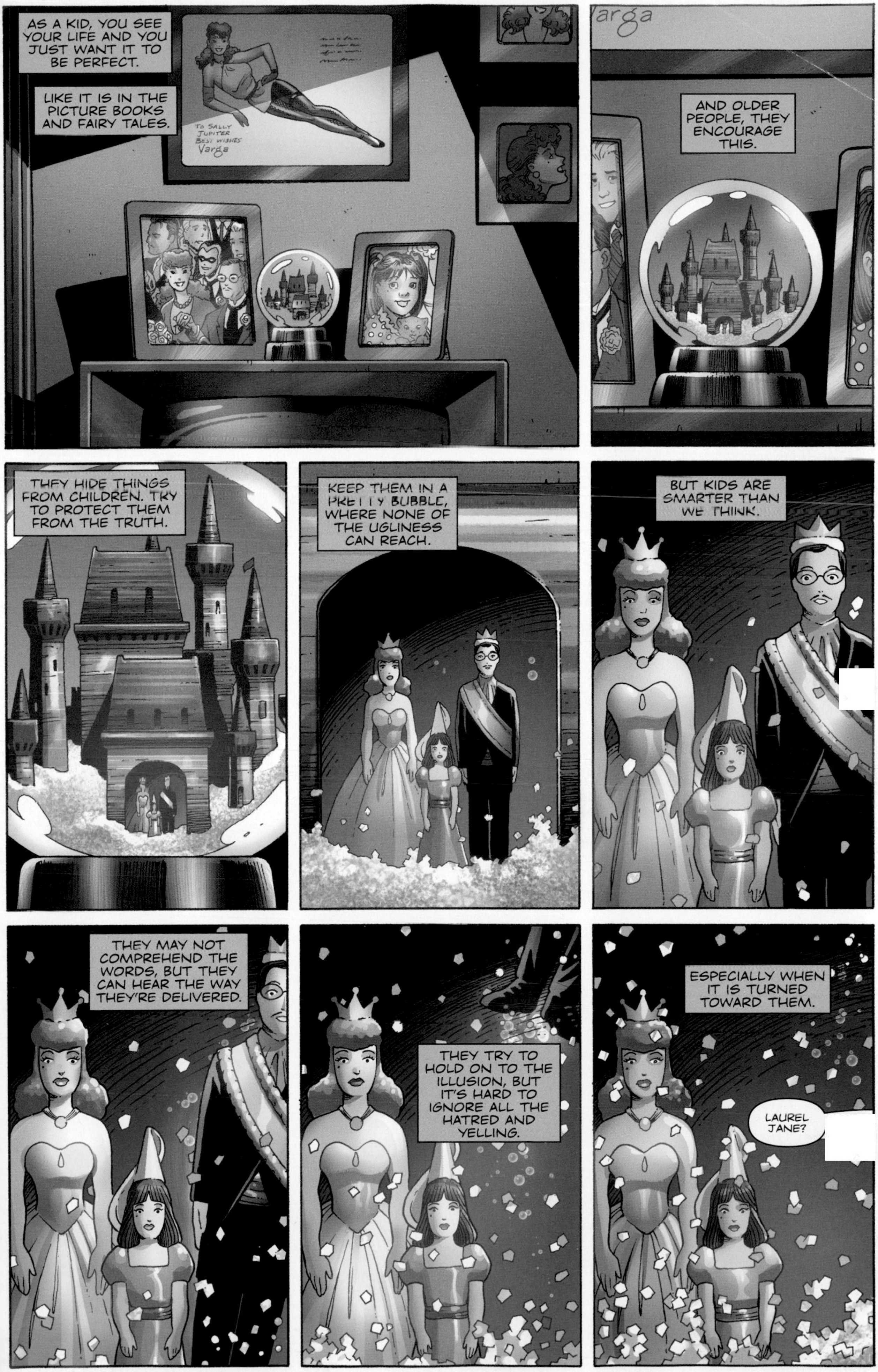
AS A KID, YOU SEE YOUR LIFE AND YOU JUST WANT IT TO BE PERFECT.
LIKE IT IS IN THE PICTURE BOOKS AND FAIRY TALES.
TO SALLY JUPITER BEST WISHES Varga
Varga
AND OLDER PEOPLE, THEY ENCOURAGE THIS.
THEY HIDE THINGS FROM CHILDREN. TRY TO PROTECT THEM FROM THE TRUTH.
KEEP THEM IN A PRETTY BUBBLE, WHERE NONE OF THE UGLINESS CAN REACH.
BUT KIDS ARE SMARTER THAN WE THINK.
THEY MAY NOT COMPREHEND THE WORDS, BUT THEY CAN HEAR THE WAY THEY'RE DELIVERED.
THEY TRY TO HOLD ON TO THE ILLUSION, BUT IT'S HARD TO IGNORE ALL THE HATRED AND YELLING.
ESPECIALLY WHEN IT IS TURNED TOWARD THEM.
LAUREL JANE?

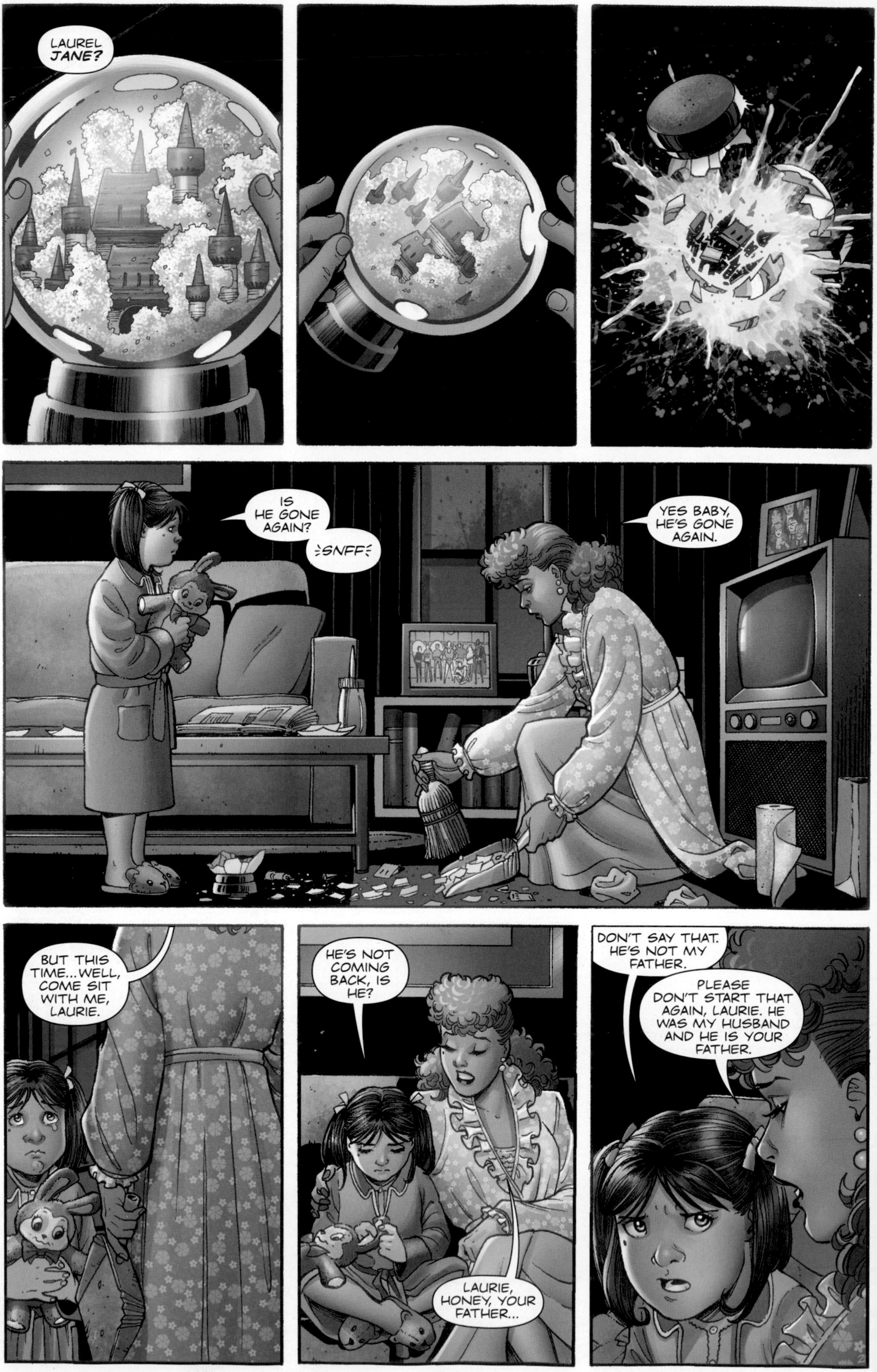
LAUREL JANE?
IS HE GONE AGAIN?
SNFF
YES BABY, HE'S GONE AGAIN.
BUT THIS TIME...WELL, COME SIT WITH ME, LAURIE.
HE'S NOT COMING BACK, IS HE?
LAURIE, HONEY, YOUR FATHER...
DON'T SAY THAT. HE'S NOT MY FATHER.
PLEASE DON'T START THAT AGAIN, LAURIE. HE WAS MY HUSBAND AND HE IS YOUR FATHER.

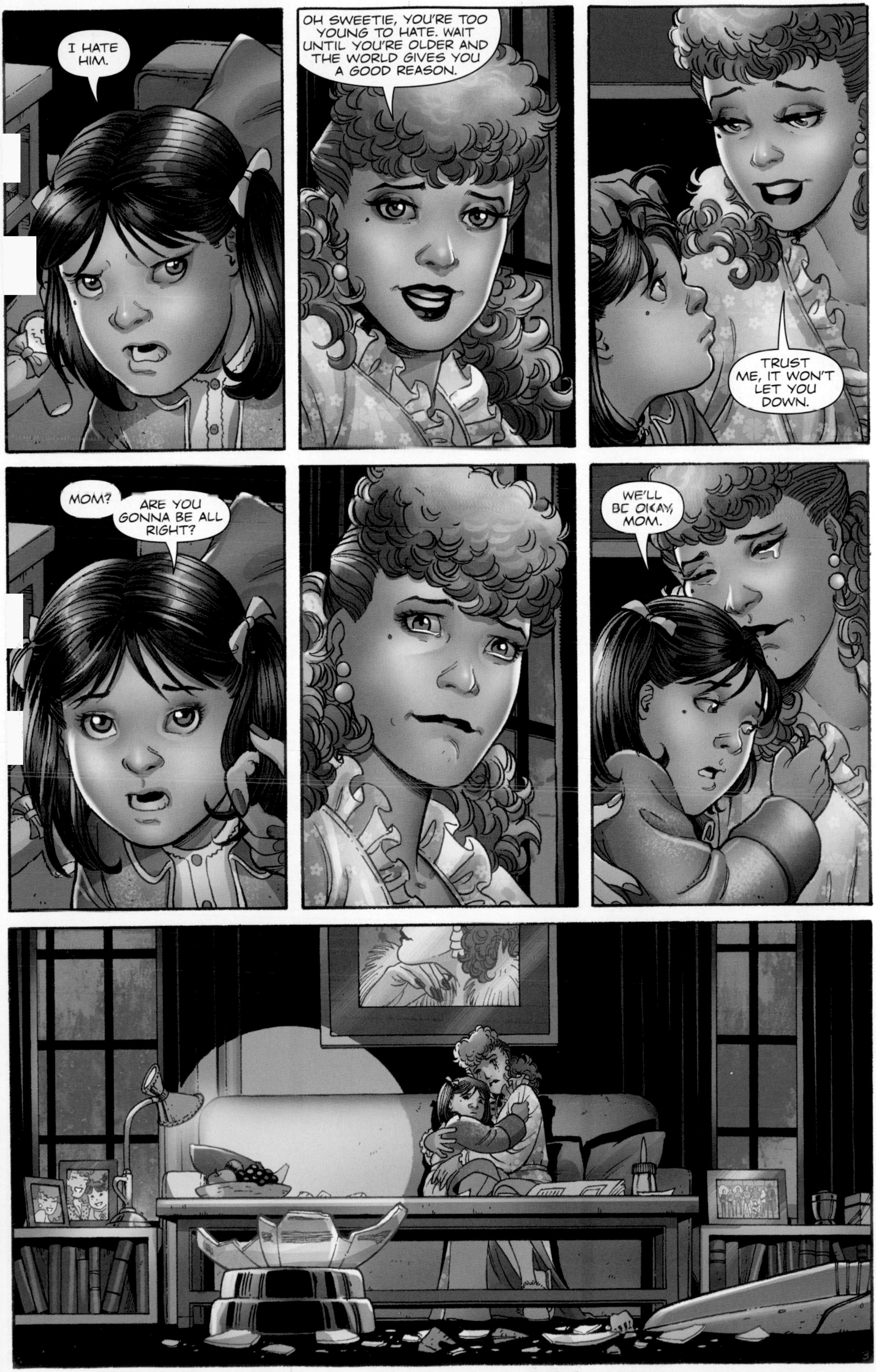
I HATE HIM.
OH SWEETIE, YOU'RE TOO YOUNG TO HATE. WAIT UNTIL YOU'RE OLDER AND THE WORLD GIVES YOU A GOOD REASON.
TRUST ME, IT WON'T LET YOU DOWN.
MOM?
ARE YOU GONNA BE ALL RIGHT?
WE'LL BE OKAY, MOM.

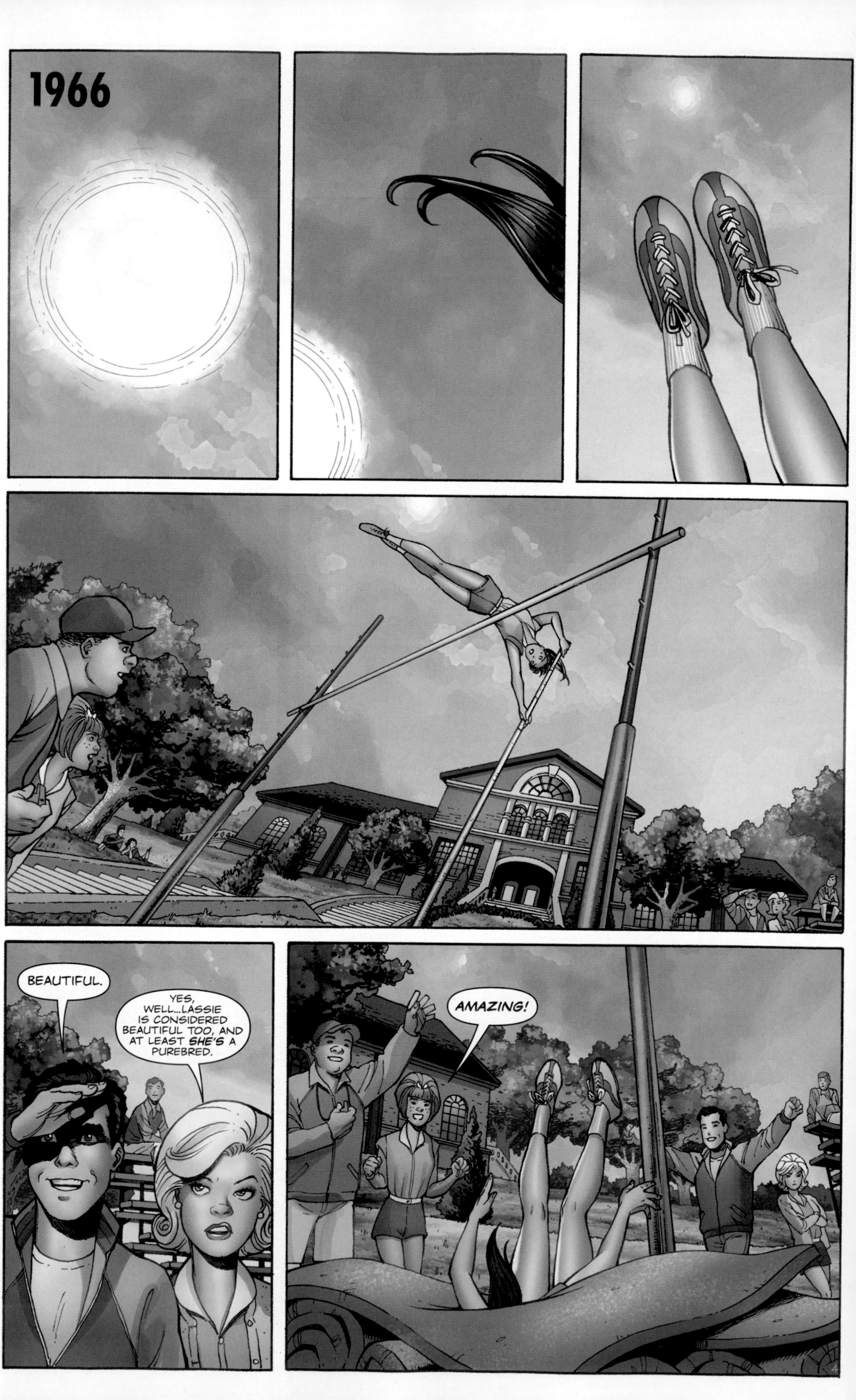
1966
BEAUTIFUL.
YES, WELL...LASSIE IS CONSIDERED BEAUTIFUL TOO, AND AT LEAST SHE'S A PUREBRED.
AMAZING!

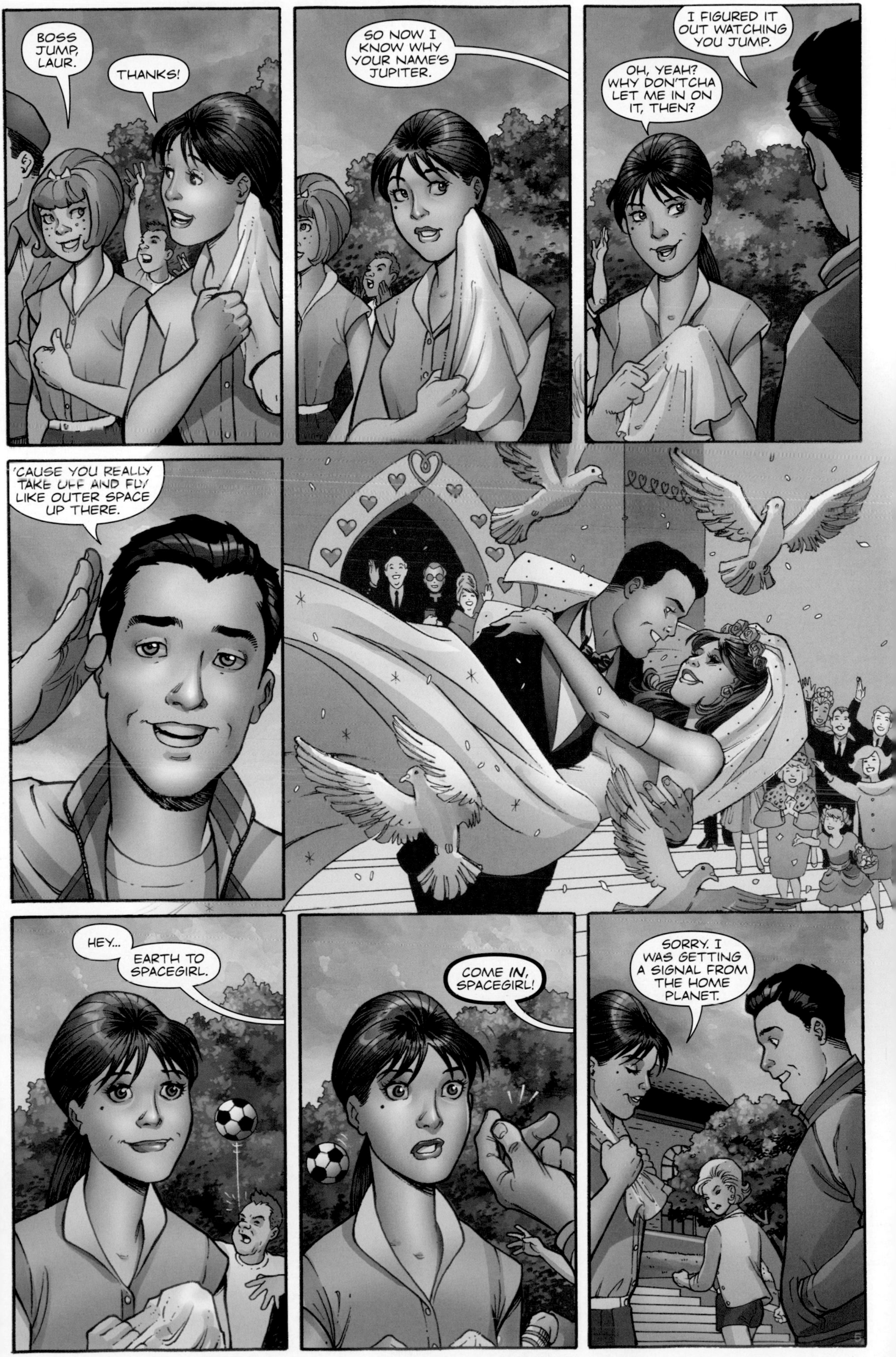
BOSS JUMP, LAUR.
THANKS!
SO NOW I KNOW WHY YOUR NAME'S JUPITER.
I FIGURED IT OUT WATCHING YOU JUMP.
OH, YEAH? WHY DON'TCHA LET ME IN ON IT, THEN?
'CAUSE YOU REALLY TAKE OFF AND FLY LIKE OUTER SPACE UP THERE.
HEY... EARTH TO SPACEGIRL.
COME IN, SPACEGIRL!
SORRY. I WAS GETTING A SIGNAL FROM THE HOME PLANET.

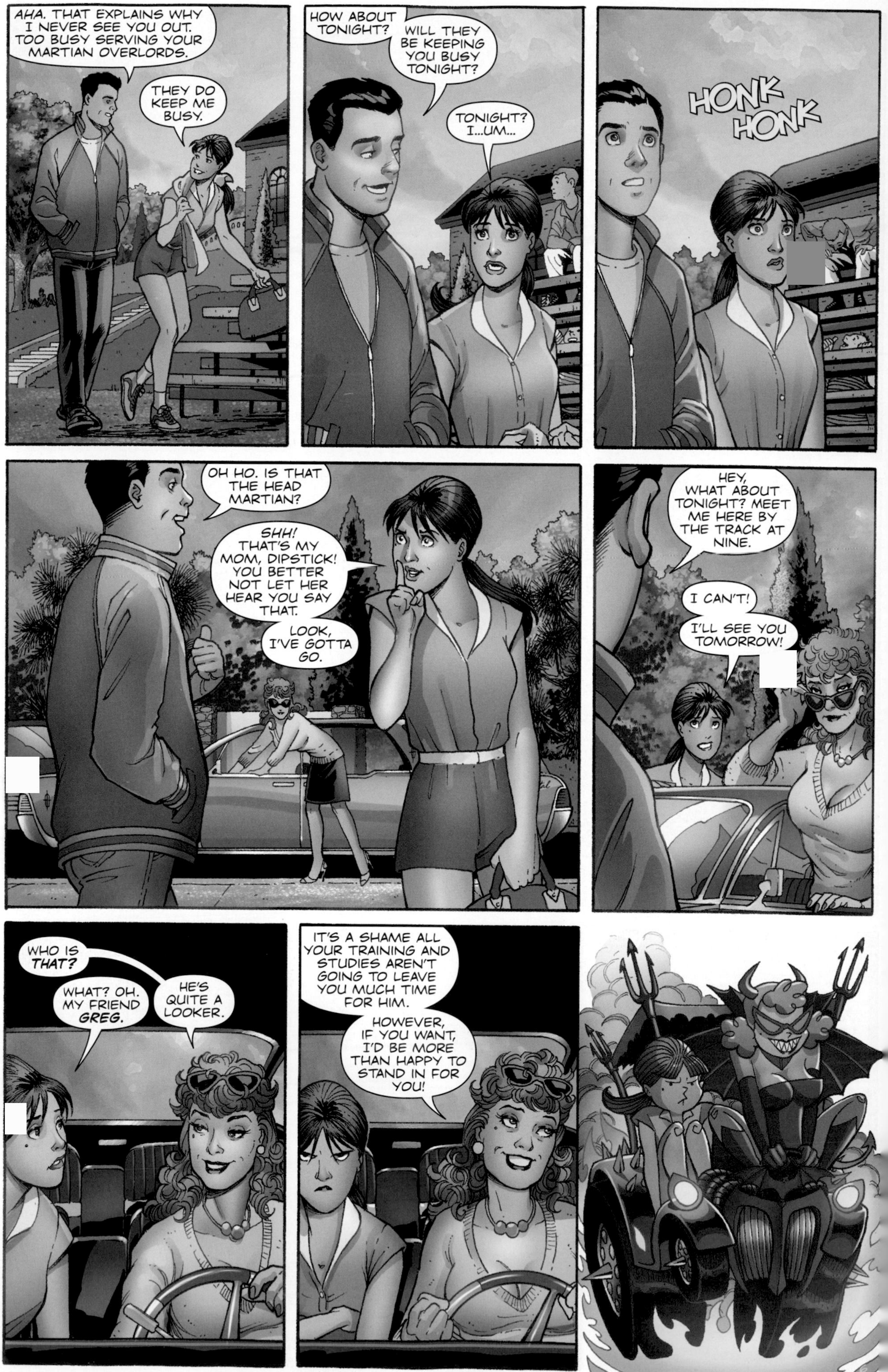
AHA. THAT EXPLAINS WHY I NEVER SEE YOU OUT. TOO BUSY SERVING YOUR MARTIAN OVERLORDS.
THEY DO KEEP ME BUSY.
HOW ABOUT TONIGHT?
WILL THEY BE KEEPING YOU BUSY TONIGHT?
TONIGHT? I...UM...
HONK HONK
OH HO. IS THAT THE HEAD MARTIAN?
SHH! THAT'S MY MOM, DIPSTICK! YOU BETTER NOT LET HER HEAR YOU SAY THAT.
LOOK, I'VE GOTTA GO.
HEY, WHAT ABOUT TONIGHT? MEET ME HERE BY THE TRACK AT NINE.
I CAN'T!
I'LL SEE YOU TOMORROW!
WHO IS THAT?
WHAT? OH. MY FRIEND GREG.
HE'S QUITE A LOOKER.
IT'S A SHAME ALL YOUR TRAINING AND STUDIES AREN'T GOING TO LEAVE YOU MUCH TIME FOR HIM.
HOWEVER, IF YOU WANT, I'D BE MORE THAN HAPPY TO STAND IN FOR YOU!

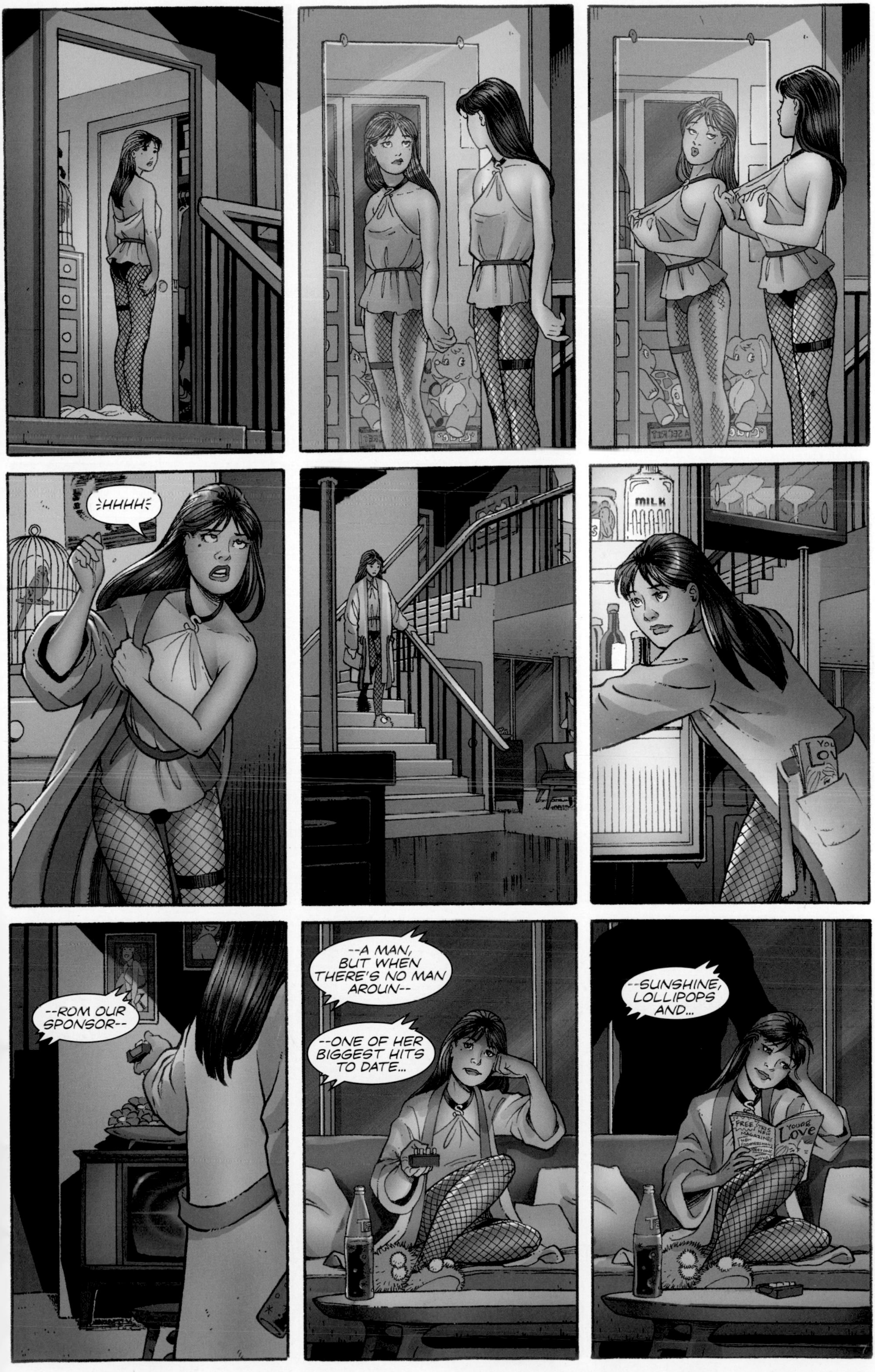
HHHH
MILK
--ROM OUR SPONSOR--
--A MAN, BUT WHEN THERE'S NO MAN AROUN--
--ONE OF HER BIGGEST HITS TO DATE...
--SUNSHINE, LOLLIPOPS AND...

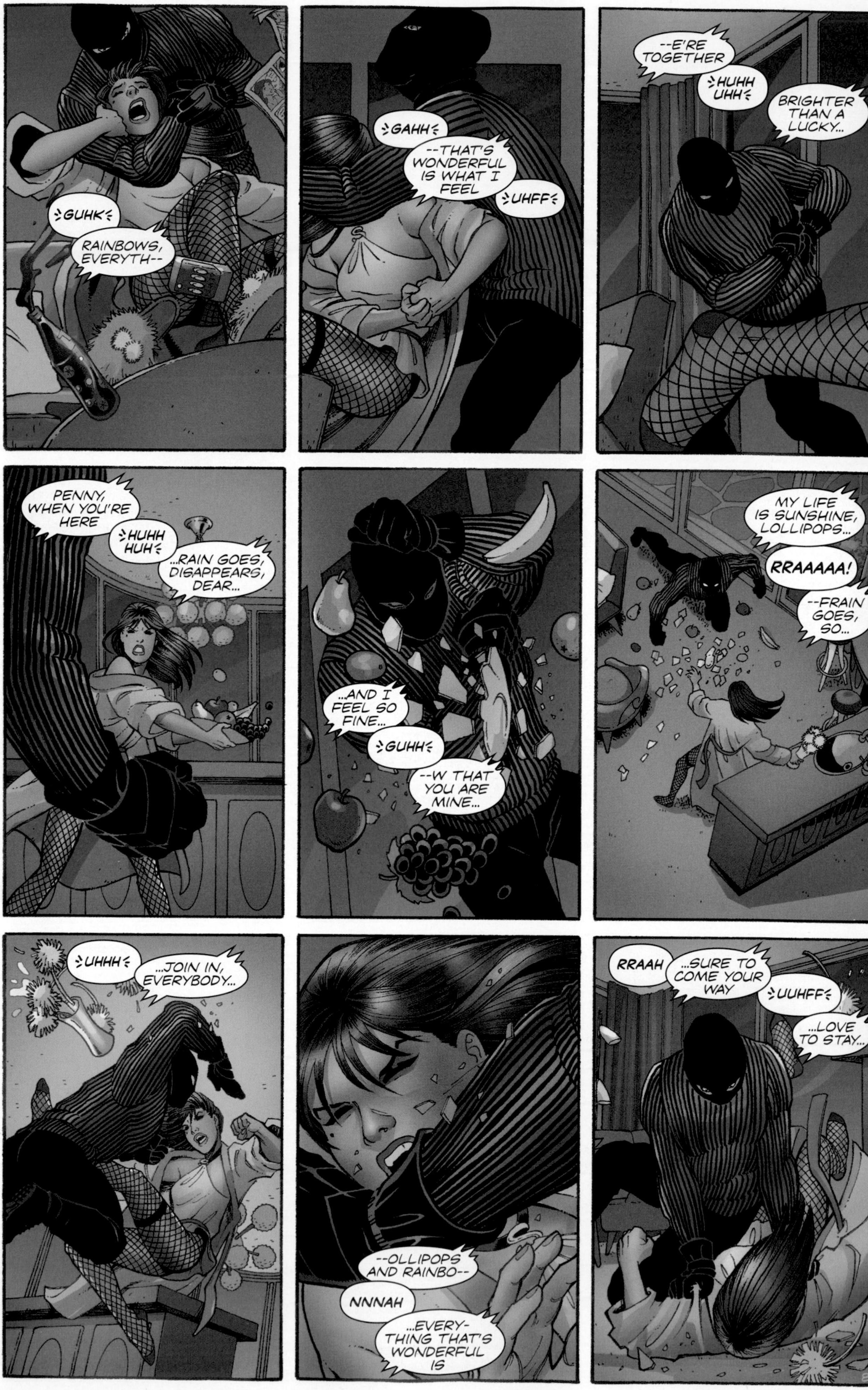
GUHK
RAINBOWS, EVERYTH--
GAHH
--THAT'S WONDERFUL IS WHAT I FEEL
UHFF
--E'RE TOGETHER
HUHH UHH
BRIGHTER THAN A LUCKY...
PENNY, WHEN YOU'RE HERE
HUHH HUH
...RAIN GOES, DISAPPEARS, DEAR...
...AND I FEEL SO FINE...
GUHH
--W THAT YOU ARE MINE...
MY LIFE IS SUNSHINE, LOLLIPOPS...
RRAAAAA!
--FRAIN GOES, SO...
UHHH
...JOIN IN, EVERYBODY...
--OLLIPOPS AND RAINBO--
NNNAH
...EVERY-THING THAT'S WONDERFUL IS
RRAAH
...SURE TO COME YOUR WAY
UUHFF
...LOVE TO STAY...

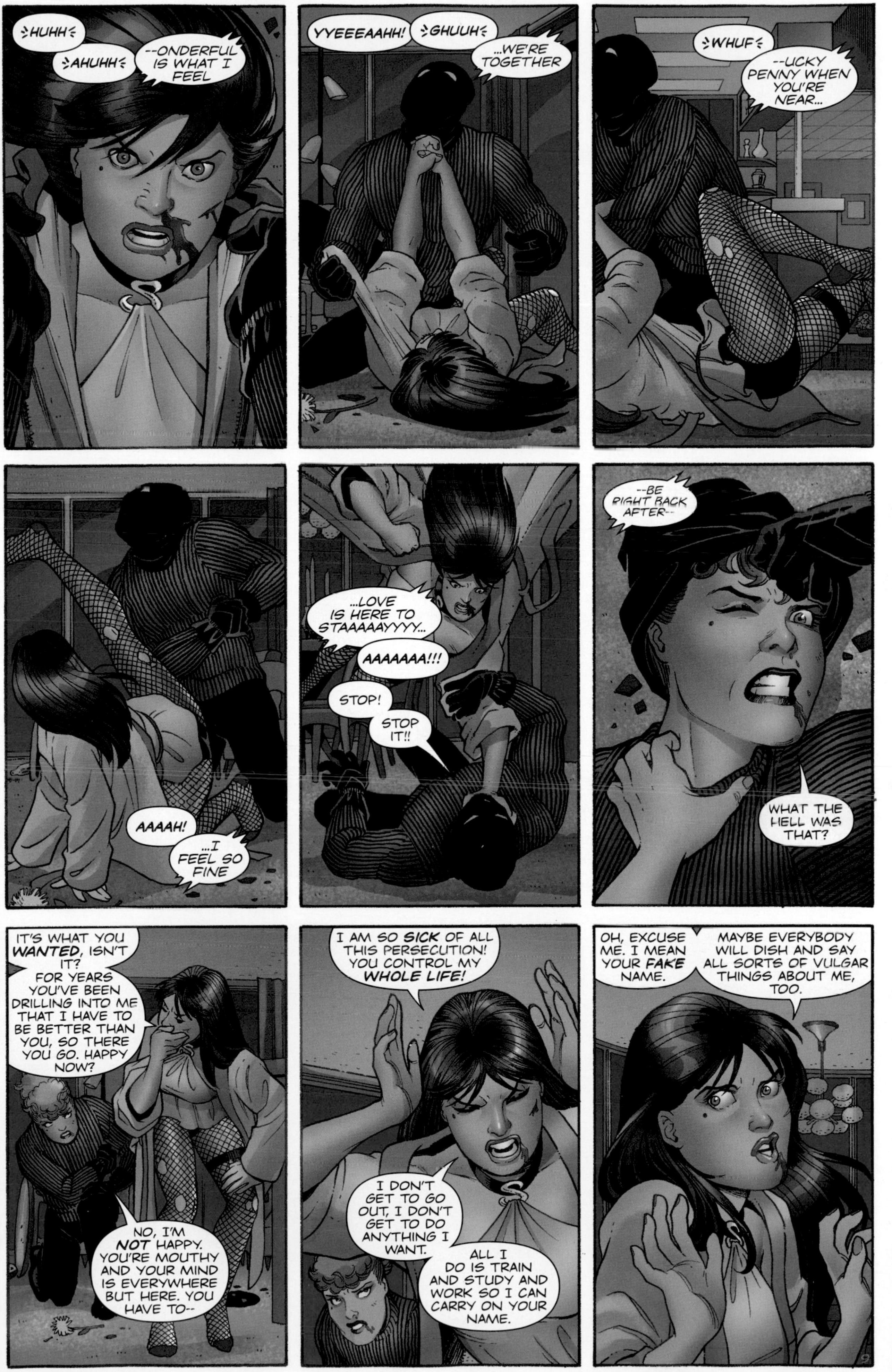
HUHH
AHUHH
--ONDERFUL IS WHAT I FEEL
YYEEEAAHH!
GHUUH
...WE'RE TOGETHER
WHUF
--UCKY PENNY WHEN YOU'RE NEAR...
AAAAH!
...I FEEL SO FINE
...LOVE IS HERE TO STAAAAAYYYY...
AAAAAAA!!!
STOP!
STOP IT!!
--BE RIGHT BACK AFTER--
WHAT THE HELL WAS THAT?
IT'S WHAT YOU WANTED, ISN'T IT? FOR YEARS YOU'VE BEEN DRILLING INTO ME THAT I HAVE TO BE BETTER THAN YOU, SO THERE YOU GO. HAPPY NOW?
NO, I'M NOT HAPPY. YOU'RE MOUTHY AND YOUR MIND IS EVERYWHERE BUT HERE. YOU HAVE TO--
I AM SO SICK OF ALL THIS PERSECUTION! YOU CONTROL MY WHOLE LIFE!
I DON'T GET TO GO OUT, I DON'T GET TO DO ANYTHING I WANT.
ALL I DO IS TRAIN AND STUDY AND WORK SO I CAN CARRY ON YOUR NAME.
OH, EXCUSE ME. I MEAN YOUR FAKE NAME.
MAYBE EVERYBODY WILL DISH AND SAY ALL SORTS OF VULGAR THINGS ABOUT ME, TOO.
9

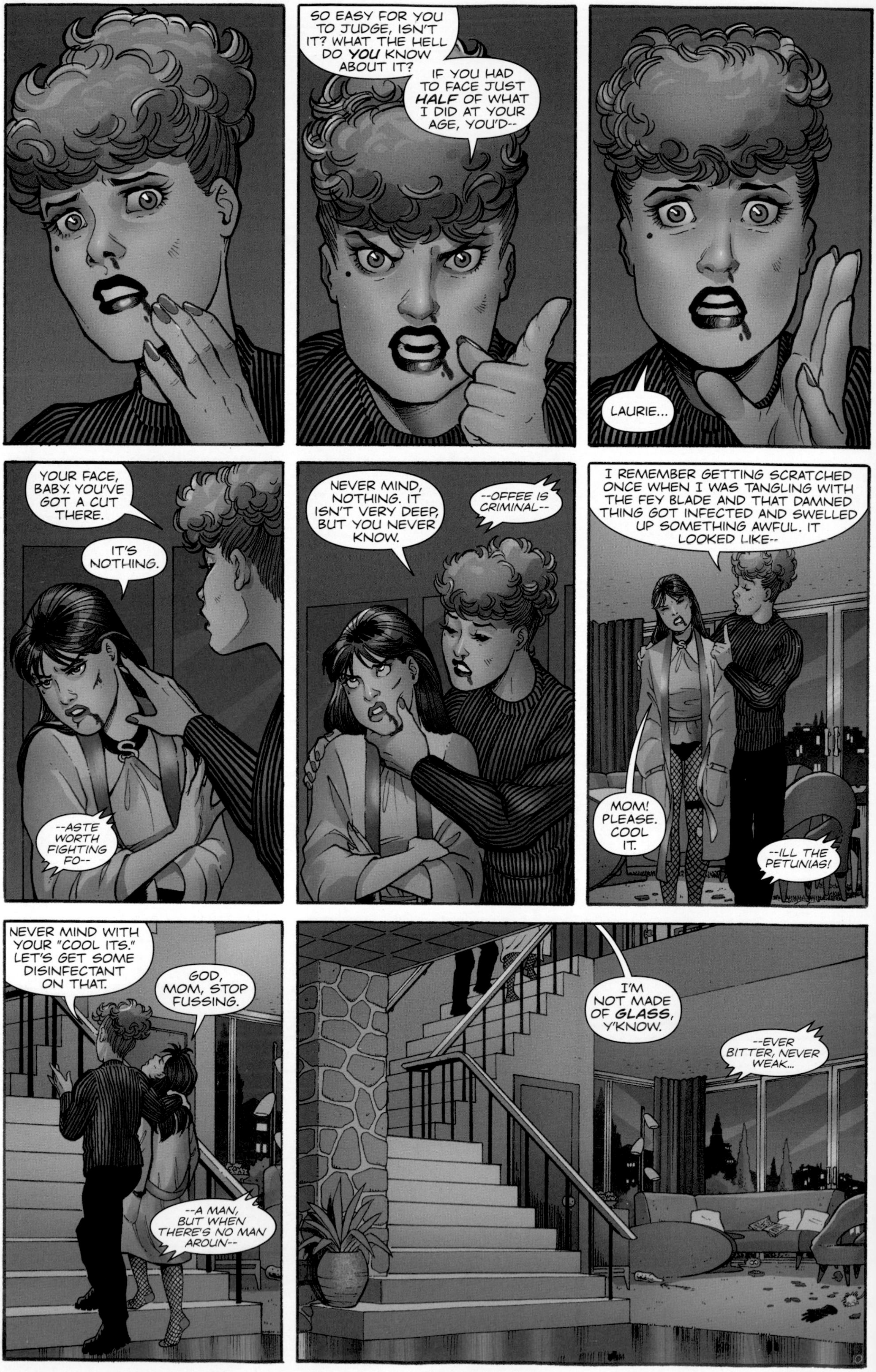
SO EASY FOR YOU TO JUDGE, ISN'T IT? WHAT THE HELL DO YOU KNOW ABOUT IT?
IF YOU HAD TO FACE JUST HALF OF WHAT I DID AT YOUR AGE, YOU'D--
LAURIE...
YOUR FACE, BABY. YOU'VE GOT A CUT THERE.
IT'S NOTHING.
--ASTE WORTH FIGHTING FO--
NEVER MIND, NOTHING. IT ISN'T VERY DEEP, BUT YOU NEVER KNOW.
--OFFEE IS CRIMINAL--
I REMEMBER GETTING SCRATCHED ONCE WHEN I WAS TANGLING WITH THE FEY BLADE AND THAT DAMNED THING GOT INFECTED AND SWELLED UP SOMETHING AWFUL. IT LOOKED LIKE--
MOM! PLEASE. COOL IT.
--ILL THE PETUNIAS!
NEVER MIND WITH YOUR "COOL ITS." LET'S GET SOME DISINFECTANT ON THAT.
GOD, MOM, STOP FUSSING.
--A MAN, BUT WHEN THERE'S NO MAN AROUN--
I'M NOT MADE OF GLASS, Y'KNOW.
--EVER BITTER, NEVER WEAK...

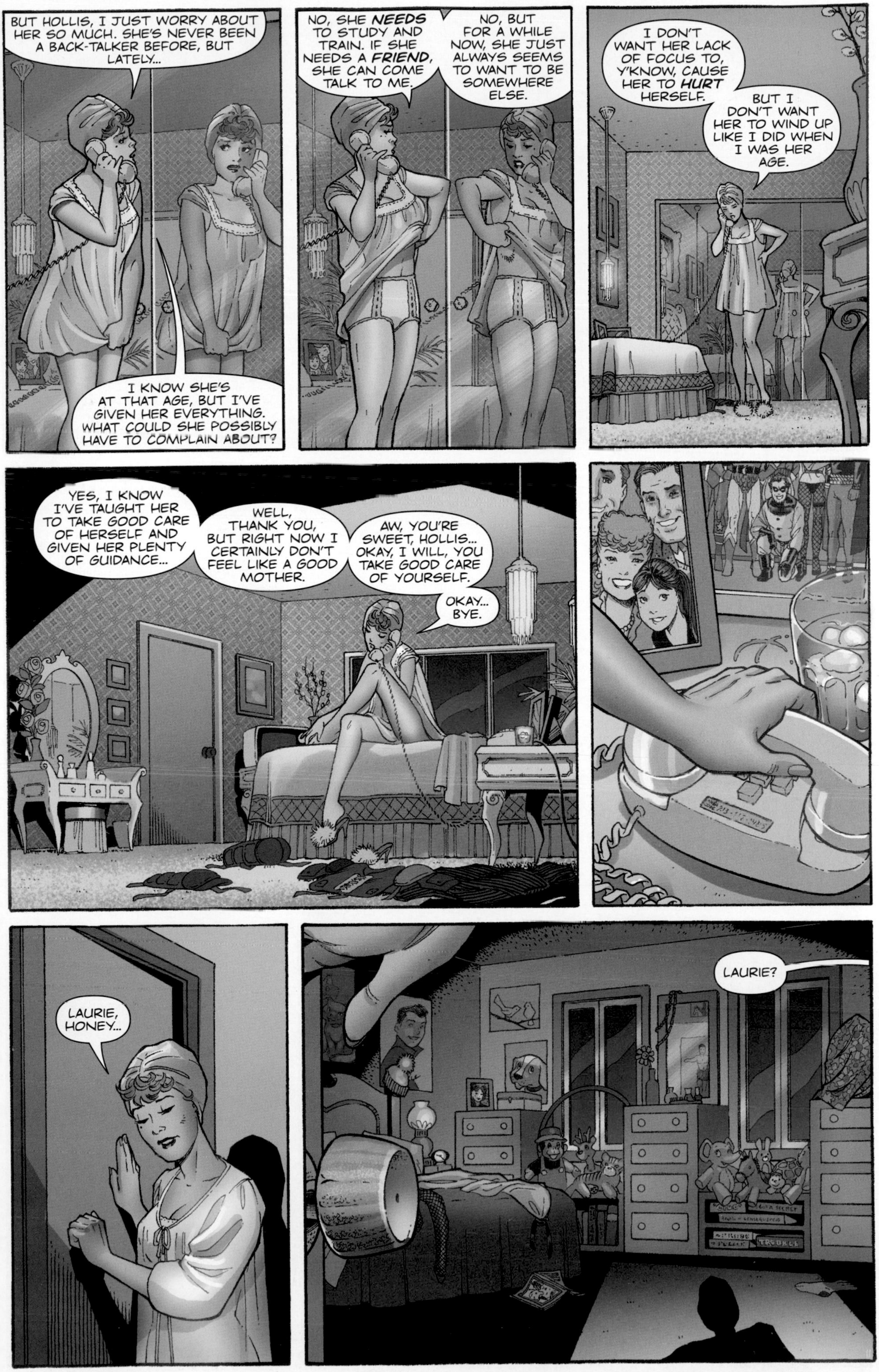

BUT HOLLIS, I JUST WORRY ABOUT HER SO MUCH. SHE'S NEVER BEEN A BACK-TALKER BEFORE, BUT LATELY...
I KNOW SHE'S AT THAT AGE, BUT I'VE GIVEN HER EVERYTHING. WHAT COULD SHE POSSIBLY HAVE TO COMPLAIN ABOUT?
NO, SHE NEEDS TO STUDY AND TRAIN. IF SHE NEEDS A FRIEND, SHE CAN COME TALK TO ME.
NO, BUT FOR A WHILE NOW, SHE JUST ALWAYS SEEMS TO WANT TO BE SOMEWHERE ELSE.
I DON'T WANT HER LACK OF FOCUS TO, Y'KNOW, CAUSE HER TO HURT HERSELF.
BUT I DON'T WANT HER TO WIND UP LIKE I DID WHEN I WAS HER AGE.
YES, I KNOW I'VE TAUGHT HER TO TAKE GOOD CARE OF HERSELF AND GIVEN HER PLENTY OF GUIDANCE...
WELL, THANK YOU, BUT RIGHT NOW I CERTAINLY DON'T FEEL LIKE A GOOD MOTHER.
AW, YOU'RE SWEET, HOLLIS... OKAY, I WILL, YOU TAKE GOOD CARE OF YOURSELF.
OKAY... BYE.
LAURIE, HONEY...
LAURIE?
TROUBLE

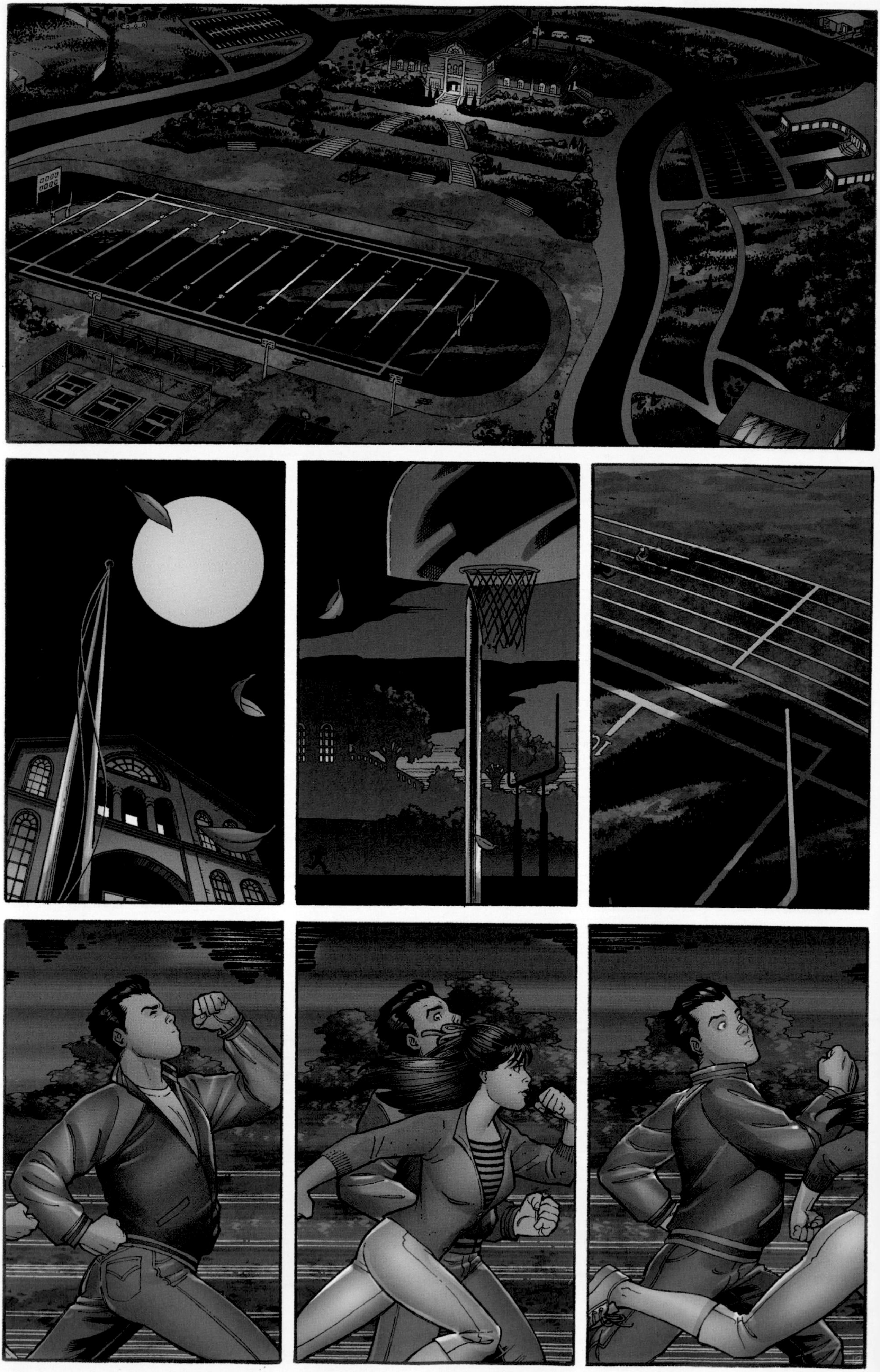

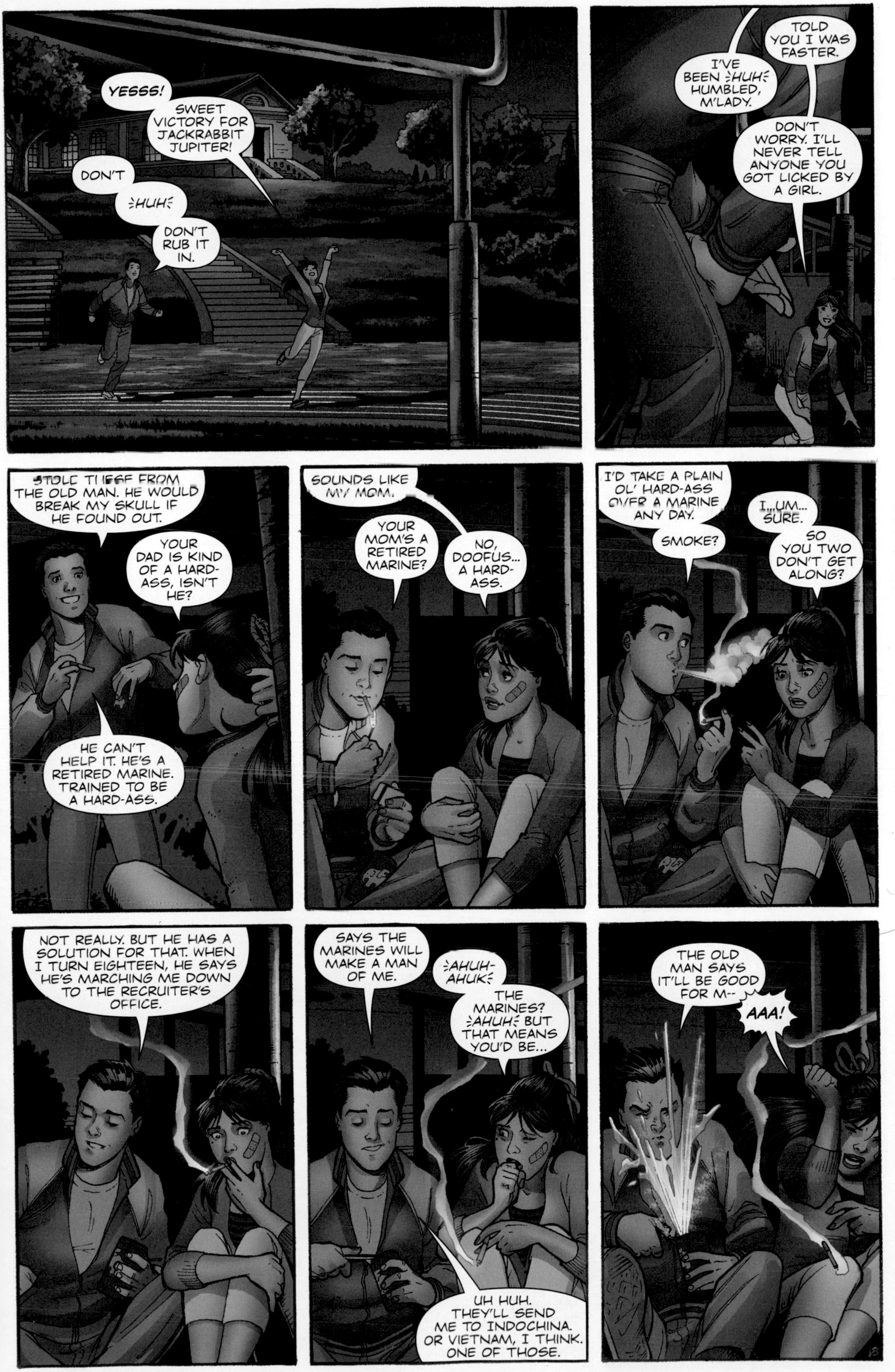
YESSS!
SWEET VICTORY FOR JACKRABBIT JUPITER!
DON'T
HUH
DON'T RUB IT IN.
I'VE BEEN HUH HUMBLED, M'LADY.
TOLD YOU I WAS FASTER.
DON'T WORRY. I'LL NEVER TELL ANYONE YOU GOT LICKED BY A GIRL.
STOLE THESE FROM THE OLD MAN. HE WOULD BREAK MY SKULL IF HE FOUND OUT.
YOUR DAD IS KIND OF A HARD-ASS, ISN'T HE?
HE CAN'T HELP IT. HE'S A RETIRED MARINE. TRAINED TO BE A HARD-ASS.
SOUNDS LIKE MY MOM.
YOUR MOM'S A RETIRED MARINE?
NO, DOOFUS... A HARD-ASS.
I'D TAKE A PLAIN OL' HARD-ASS OVER A MARINE ANY DAY.
SMOKE?
I...UM... SURE.
SO YOU TWO DON'T GET ALONG?
NOT REALLY. BUT HE HAS A SOLUTION FOR THAT. WHEN I TURN EIGHTEEN, HE SAYS HE'S MARCHING ME DOWN TO THE RECRUITER'S OFFICE.
SAYS THE MARINES WILL MAKE A MAN OF ME.
AHUH-AHUK
THE MARINES? AHUH BUT THAT MEANS YOU'D BE...
UH HUH. THEY'LL SEND ME TO INDOCHINA. OR VIETNAM, I THINK. ONE OF THOSE.
THE OLD MAN SAYS IT'LL BE GOOD FOR M--
AAA!

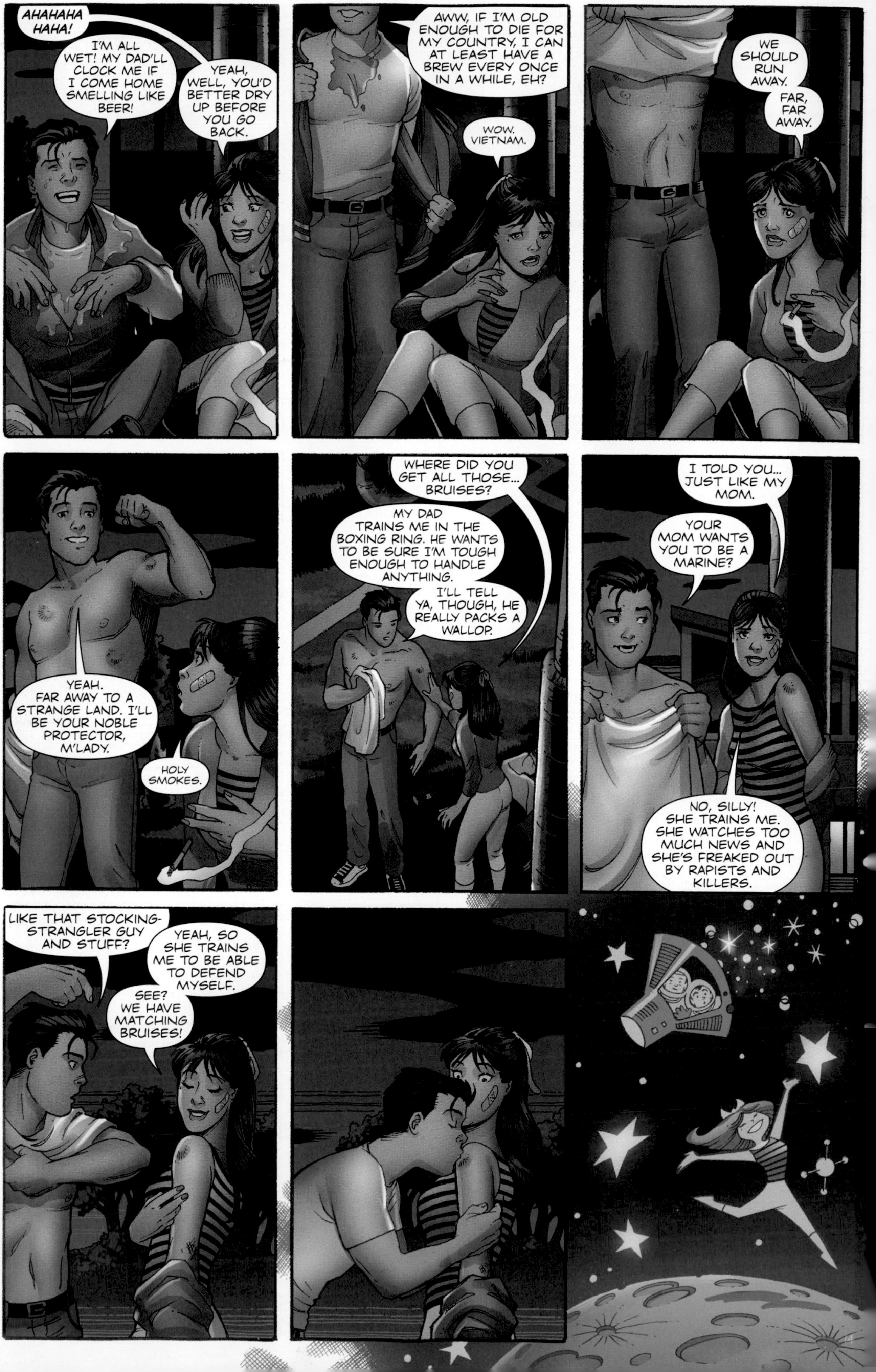
AHAHAHA HAHA!
I'M ALL WET! MY DAD'LL CLOCK ME IF I COME HOME SMELLING LIKE BEER!
YEAH, WELL, YOU'D BETTER DRY UP BEFORE YOU GO BACK.
AWW, IF I'M OLD ENOUGH TO DIE FOR MY COUNTRY, I CAN AT LEAST HAVE A BREW EVERY ONCE IN A WHILE, EH?
WOW. VIETNAM.
WE SHOULD RUN AWAY.
FAR, FAR AWAY.
YEAH. FAR AWAY TO A STRANGE LAND. I'LL BE YOUR NOBLE PROTECTOR, M'LADY.
HOLY SMOKES.
WHERE DID YOU GET ALL THOSE... BRUISES?
MY DAD TRAINS ME IN THE BOXING RING. HE WANTS TO BE SURE I'M TOUGH ENOUGH TO HANDLE ANYTHING.
I'LL TELL YA, THOUGH, HE REALLY PACKS A WALLOP.
I TOLD YOU... JUST LIKE MY MOM.
YOUR MOM WANTS YOU TO BE A MARINE?
NO, SILLY! SHE TRAINS ME. SHE WATCHES TOO MUCH NEWS AND SHE'S FREAKED OUT BY RAPISTS AND KILLERS.
LIKE THAT STOCKING-STRANGLER GUY AND STUFF?
YEAH, SO SHE TRAINS ME TO BE ABLE TO DEFEND MYSELF.
SEE? WE HAVE MATCHING BRUISES!

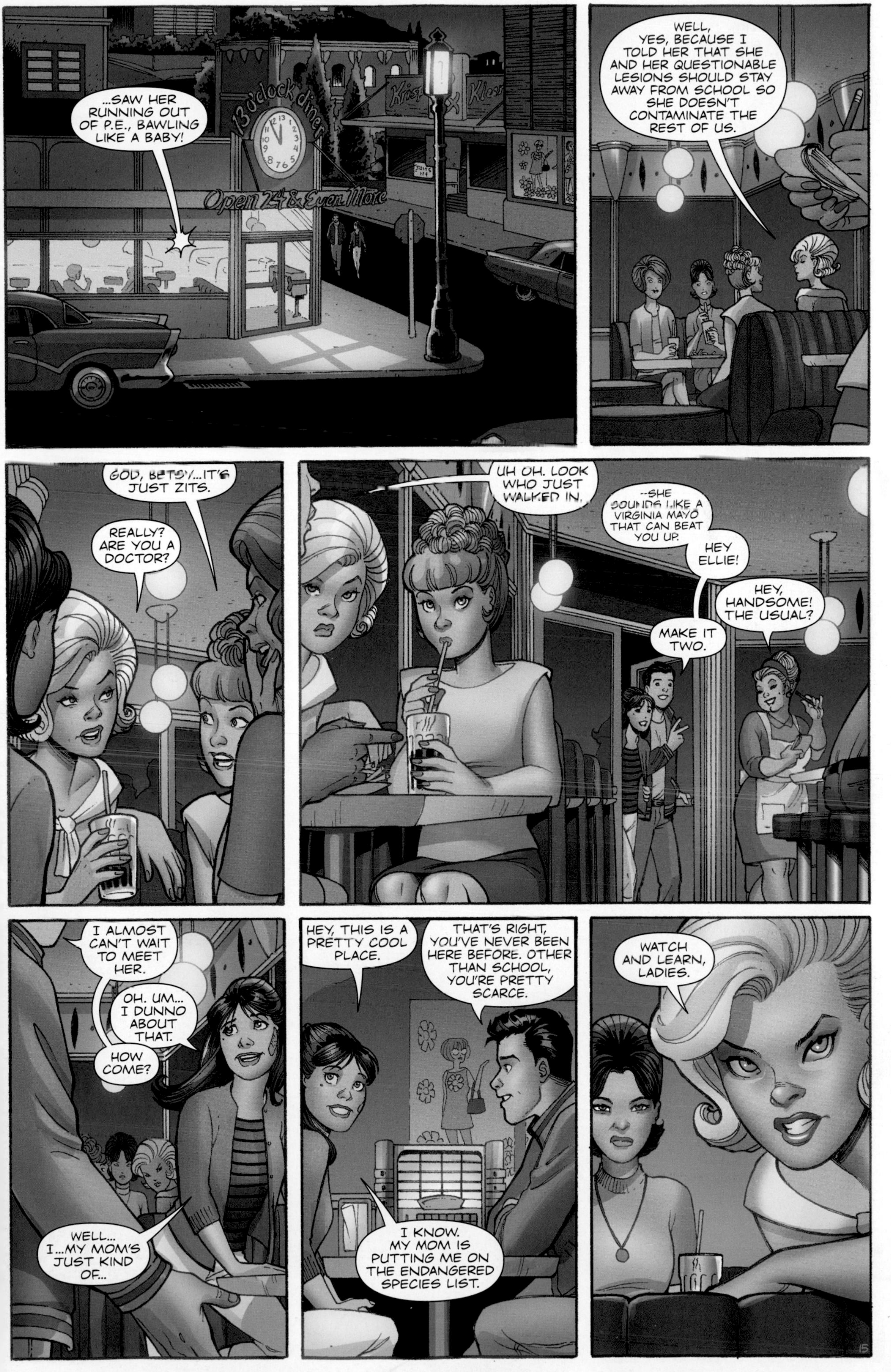
...SAW HER RUNNING OUT OF P.E., BAWLING LIKE A BABY!
13 o'clock diner
Open 24 & Even More
WELL, YES, BECAUSE I TOLD HER THAT SHE AND HER QUESTIONABLE LESIONS SHOULD STAY AWAY FROM SCHOOL SO SHE DOESN'T CONTAMINATE THE REST OF US.
GOD, BETSY...IT'S JUST ZITS.
REALLY? ARE YOU A DOCTOR?
UH OH. LOOK WHO JUST WALKED IN.
--SHE SOUNDS LIKE A VIRGINIA MAYO THAT CAN BEAT YOU UP.
HEY ELLIE!
HEY, HANDSOME! THE USUAL?
MAKE IT TWO.
I ALMOST CAN'T WAIT TO MEET HER.
OH. UM... I DUNNO ABOUT THAT.
HOW COME?
WELL... I...MY MOM'S JUST KIND OF...
HEY, THIS IS A PRETTY COOL PLACE.
THAT'S RIGHT, YOU'VE NEVER BEEN HERE BEFORE. OTHER THAN SCHOOL, YOU'RE PRETTY SCARCE.
I KNOW. MY MOM IS PUTTING ME ON THE ENDANGERED SPECIES LIST.
WATCH AND LEARN, LADIES.

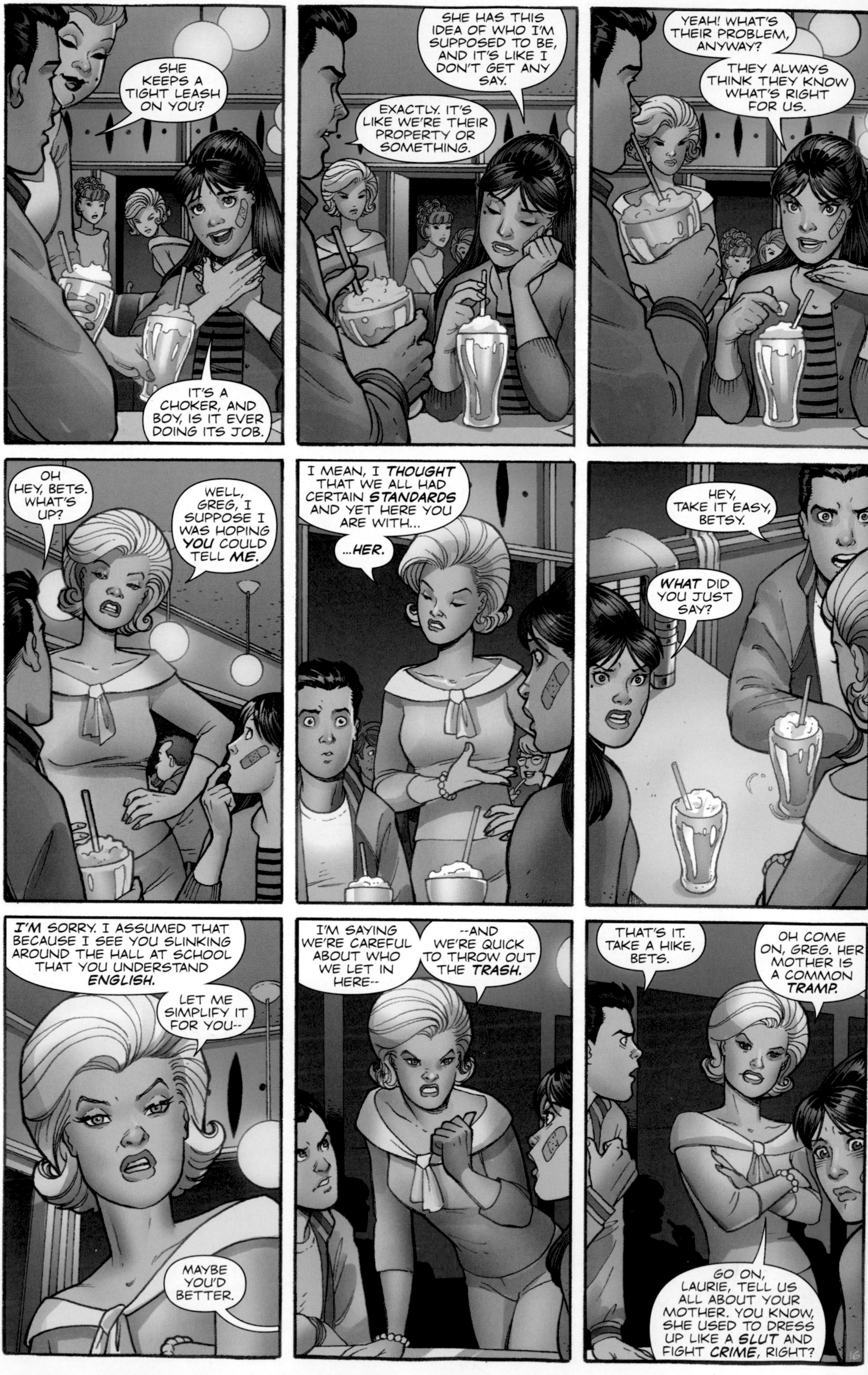
SHE KEEPS A TIGHT LEASH ON YOU?
IT'S A CHOKER, AND BOY, IS IT EVER DOING ITS JOB.
SHE HAS THIS IDEA OF WHO I'M SUPPOSED TO BE, AND IT'S LIKE I DON'T GET ANY SAY.
EXACTLY. IT'S LIKE WE'RE THEIR PROPERTY OR SOMETHING.
YEAH! WHAT'S THEIR PROBLEM, ANYWAY?
THEY ALWAYS THINK THEY KNOW WHAT'S RIGHT FOR US.
OH HEY, BETS. WHAT'S UP?
WELL, GREG, I SUPPOSE I WAS HOPING YOU COULD TELL ME.
I MEAN, I THOUGHT THAT WE ALL HAD CERTAIN STANDARDS AND YET HERE YOU ARE WITH...
...HER.
HEY, TAKE IT EASY, BETSY.
WHAT DID YOU JUST SAY?
I'M SORRY. I ASSUMED THAT BECAUSE I SEE YOU SLINKING AROUND THE HALL AT SCHOOL THAT YOU UNDERSTAND ENGLISH.
LET ME SIMPLIFY IT FOR YOU--
MAYBE YOU'D BETTER.
I'M SAYING WE'RE CAREFUL ABOUT WHO WE LET IN HERE--
--AND WE'RE QUICK TO THROW OUT THE TRASH.
THAT'S IT. TAKE A HIKE, BETS.
OH COME ON, GREG. HER MOTHER IS A COMMON TRAMP.
GO ON, LAURIE, TELL US ALL ABOUT YOUR MOTHER. YOU KNOW, SHE USED TO DRESS UP LIKE A SLUT AND FIGHT CRIME, RIGHT?
16

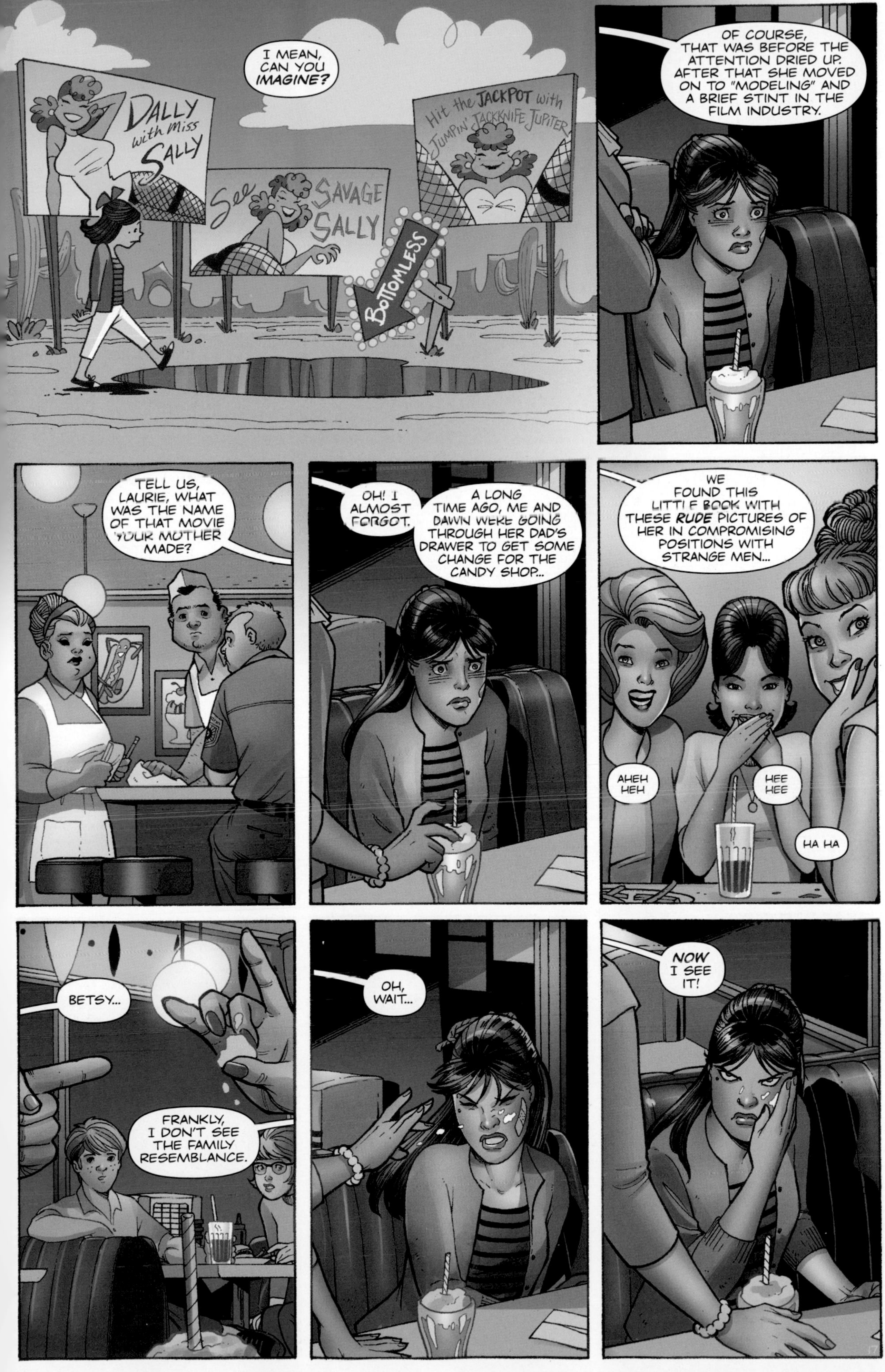
I MEAN, CAN YOU IMAGINE?
DALLY with Miss SALLY
See SAVAGE SALLY
Hit the JACKPOT with JUMPIN' JACKKNIFE JUPITER
BOTTOMLESS
OF COURSE, THAT WAS BEFORE THE ATTENTION DRIED UP. AFTER THAT SHE MOVED ON TO "MODELING" AND A BRIEF STINT IN THE FILM INDUSTRY.
TELL US, LAURIE, WHAT WAS THE NAME OF THAT MOVIE YOUR MOTHER MADE?
OH! I ALMOST FORGOT.
A LONG TIME AGO, ME AND DAWN WERE GOING THROUGH HER DAD'S DRAWER TO GET SOME CHANGE FOR THE CANDY SHOP...
WE FOUND THIS LITTLE BOOK WITH THESE RUDE PICTURES OF HER IN COMPROMISING POSITIONS WITH STRANGE MEN...
AHEH HEH
HEE HEE
HA HA
BETSY...
FRANKLY, I DON'T SEE THE FAMILY RESEMBLANCE.
OH, WAIT...
NOW I SEE IT!

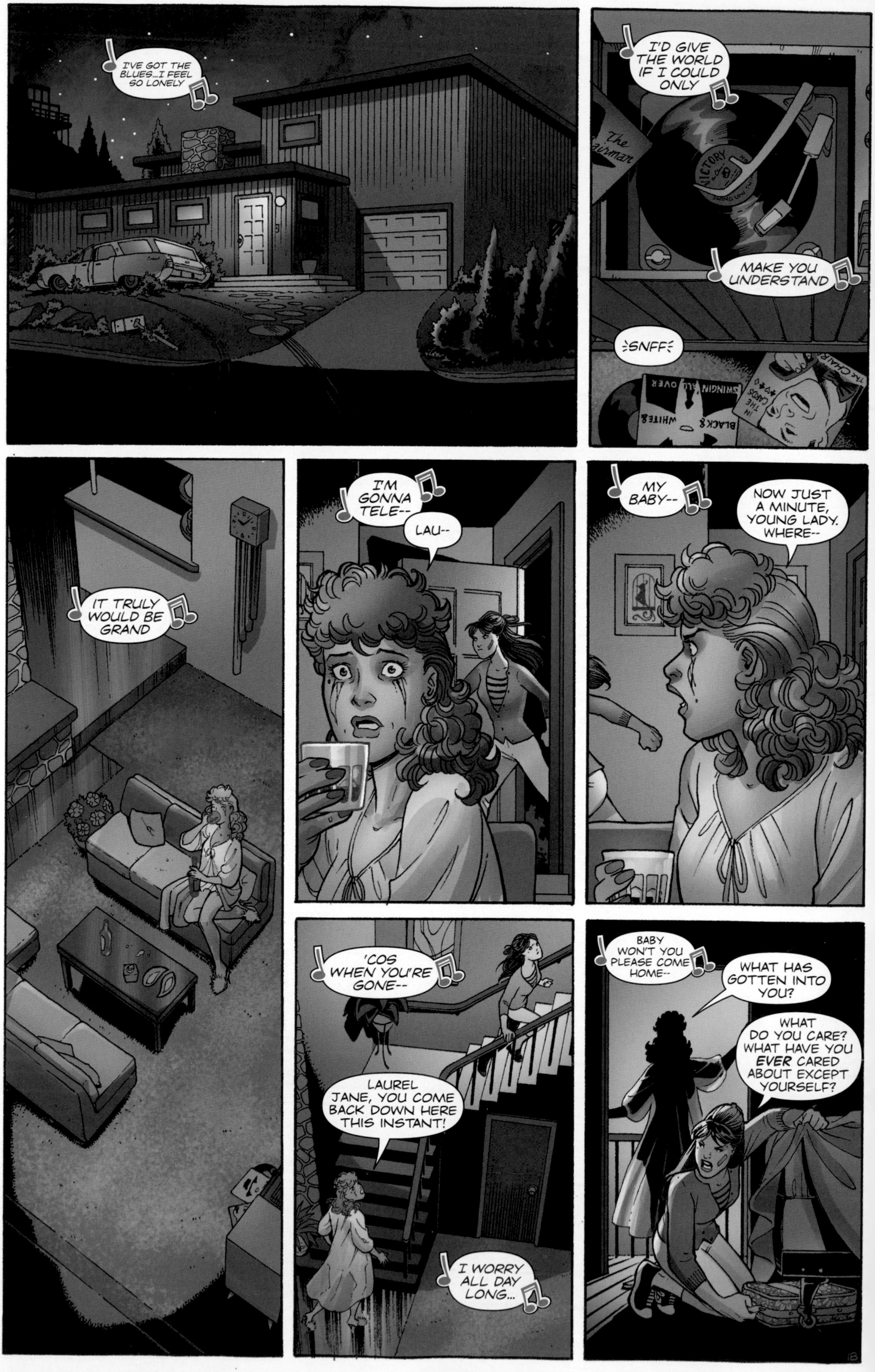
I'VE GOT THE BLUES...I FEEL SO LONELY
I'D GIVE THE WORLD IF I COULD ONLY
MAKE YOU UNDERSTAND
SNFF
IT TRULY WOULD BE GRAND
I'M GONNA TELE--
LAU--
MY BABY--
NOW JUST A MINUTE, YOUNG LADY. WHERE--
'COS WHEN YOU'RE GONE--
LAUREL JANE, YOU COME BACK DOWN HERE THIS INSTANT!
I WORRY ALL DAY LONG...
BABY WON'T YOU PLEASE COME HOME--
WHAT HAS GOTTEN INTO YOU?
WHAT DO YOU CARE? WHAT HAVE YOU EVER CARED ABOUT EXCEPT YOURSELF?

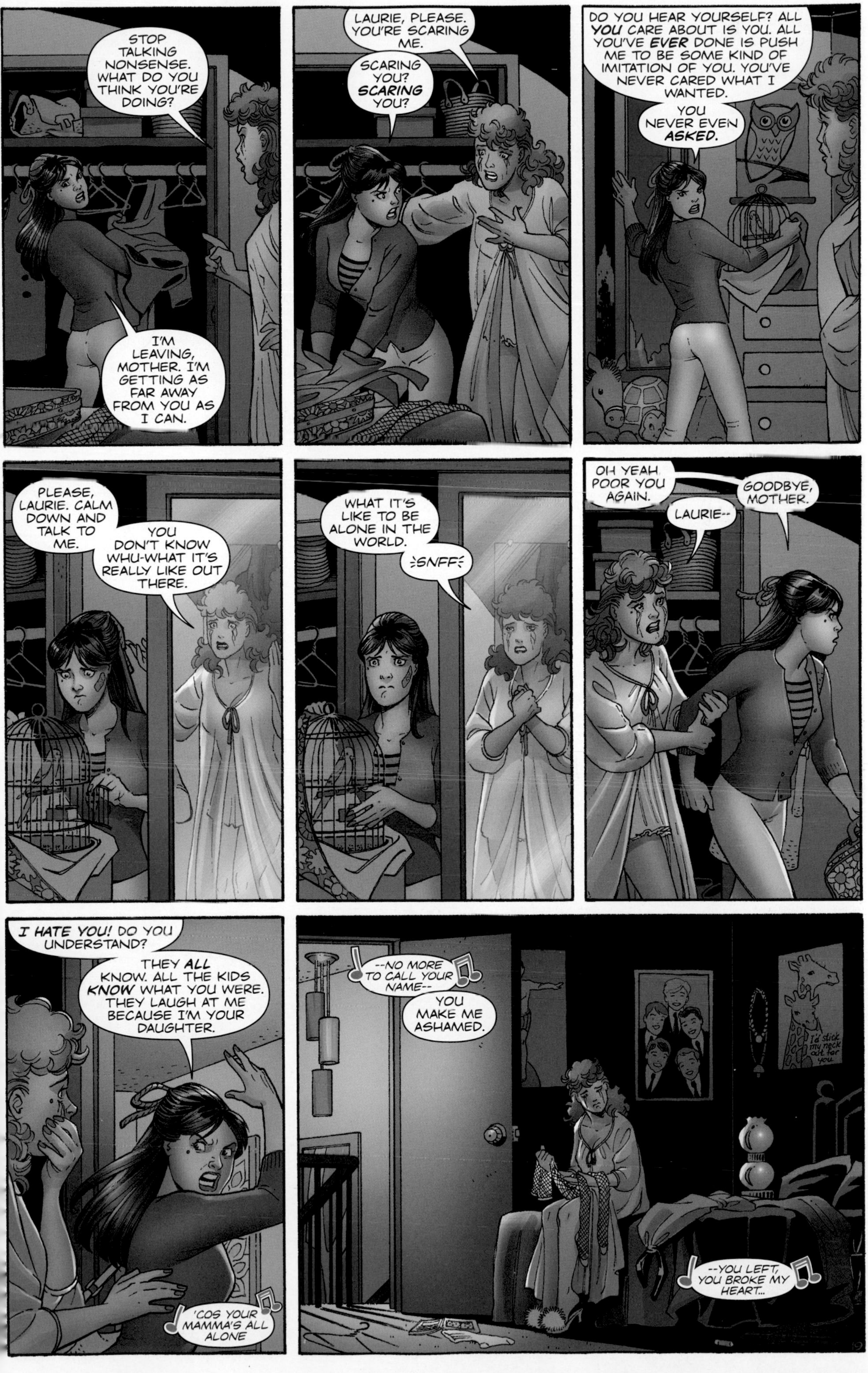
STOP TALKING NONSENSE. WHAT DO YOU THINK YOU'RE DOING?
I'M LEAVING, MOTHER. I'M GETTING AS FAR AWAY FROM YOU AS I CAN.
LAURIE, PLEASE. YOU'RE SCARING ME.
SCARING YOU? *SCARING* YOU?
DO YOU HEAR YOURSELF? ALL *YOU* CARE ABOUT IS YOU. ALL YOU'VE *EVER* DONE IS PUSH ME TO BE SOME KIND OF IMITATION OF YOU. YOU'VE NEVER CARED WHAT I WANTED.
YOU NEVER EVEN *ASKED.*
PLEASE, LAURIE. CALM DOWN AND TALK TO ME.
YOU DON'T KNOW WHU-WHAT IT'S REALLY LIKE OUT THERE.
WHAT IT'S LIKE TO BE ALONE IN THE WORLD.
SNFF
OH YEAH POOR YOU AGAIN.
LAURIE--
GOODBYE, MOTHER.
I HATE YOU! DO YOU UNDERSTAND?
THEY *ALL* KNOW. ALL THE KIDS *KNOW* WHAT YOU WERE. THEY LAUGH AT ME BECAUSE I'M YOUR DAUGHTER.
'COS YOUR MAMMA'S ALL ALONE
--NO MORE TO CALL YOUR NAME--
YOU MAKE ME ASHAMED.
I'd stick my neck out for you.
--YOU LEFT, YOU BROKE MY HEART...

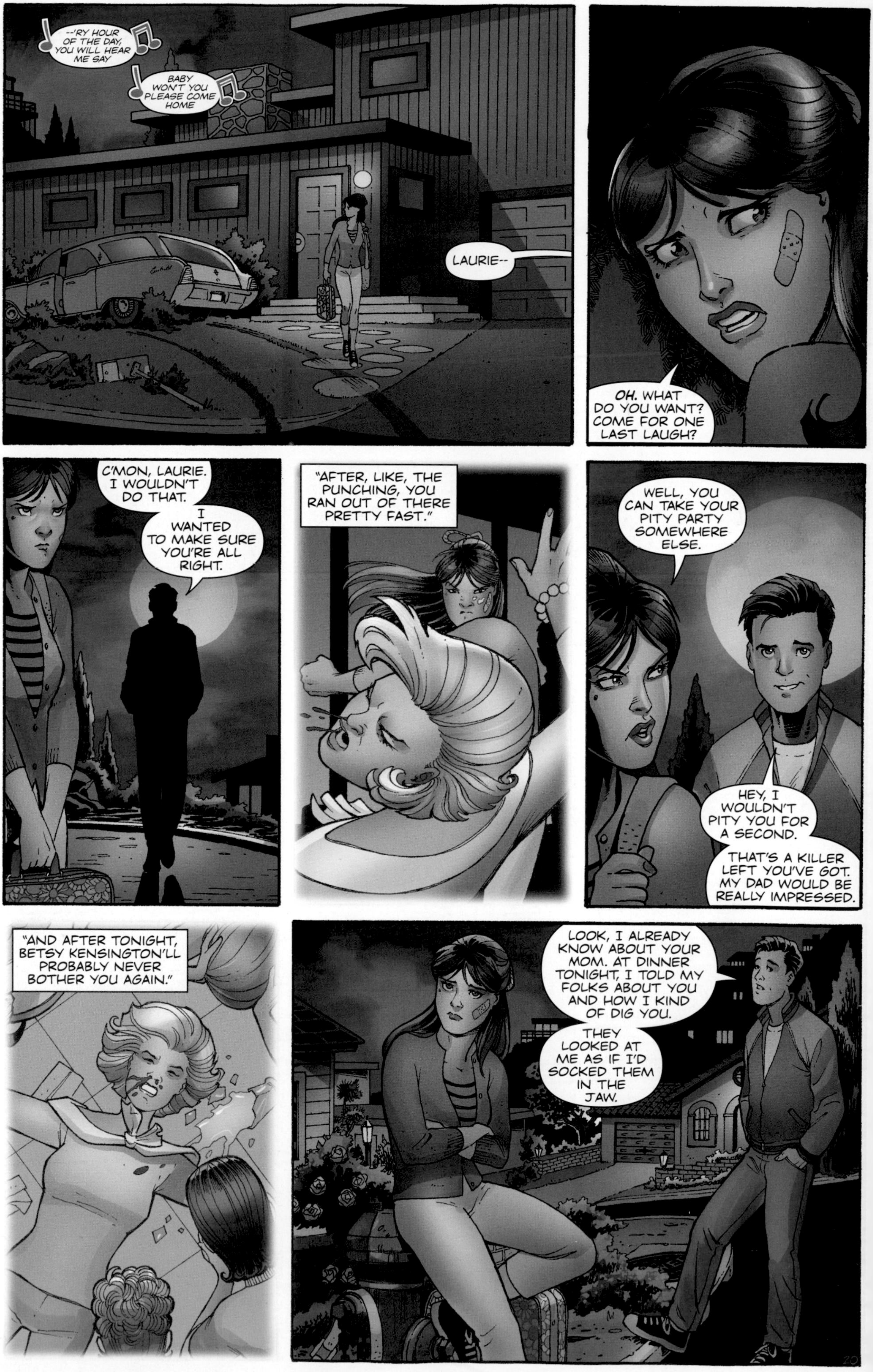
--'RY HOUR OF THE DAY, YOU WILL HEAR ME SAY
BABY WON'T YOU PLEASE COME HOME
LAURIE--
OH. WHAT DO YOU WANT? COME FOR ONE LAST LAUGH?
C'MON, LAURIE. I WOULDN'T DO THAT.
I WANTED TO MAKE SURE YOU'RE ALL RIGHT.
"AFTER, LIKE, THE PUNCHING, YOU RAN OUT OF THERE PRETTY FAST."
WELL, YOU CAN TAKE YOUR PITY PARTY SOMEWHERE ELSE.
HEY, I WOULDN'T PITY YOU FOR A SECOND.
THAT'S A KILLER LEFT YOU'VE GOT. MY DAD WOULD BE REALLY IMPRESSED.
"AND AFTER TONIGHT, BETSY KENSINGTON'LL PROBABLY NEVER BOTHER YOU AGAIN."
LOOK, I ALREADY KNOW ABOUT YOUR MOM. AT DINNER TONIGHT, I TOLD MY FOLKS ABOUT YOU AND HOW I KIND OF DIG YOU.
THEY LOOKED AT ME AS IF I'D SOCKED THEM IN THE JAW.
20

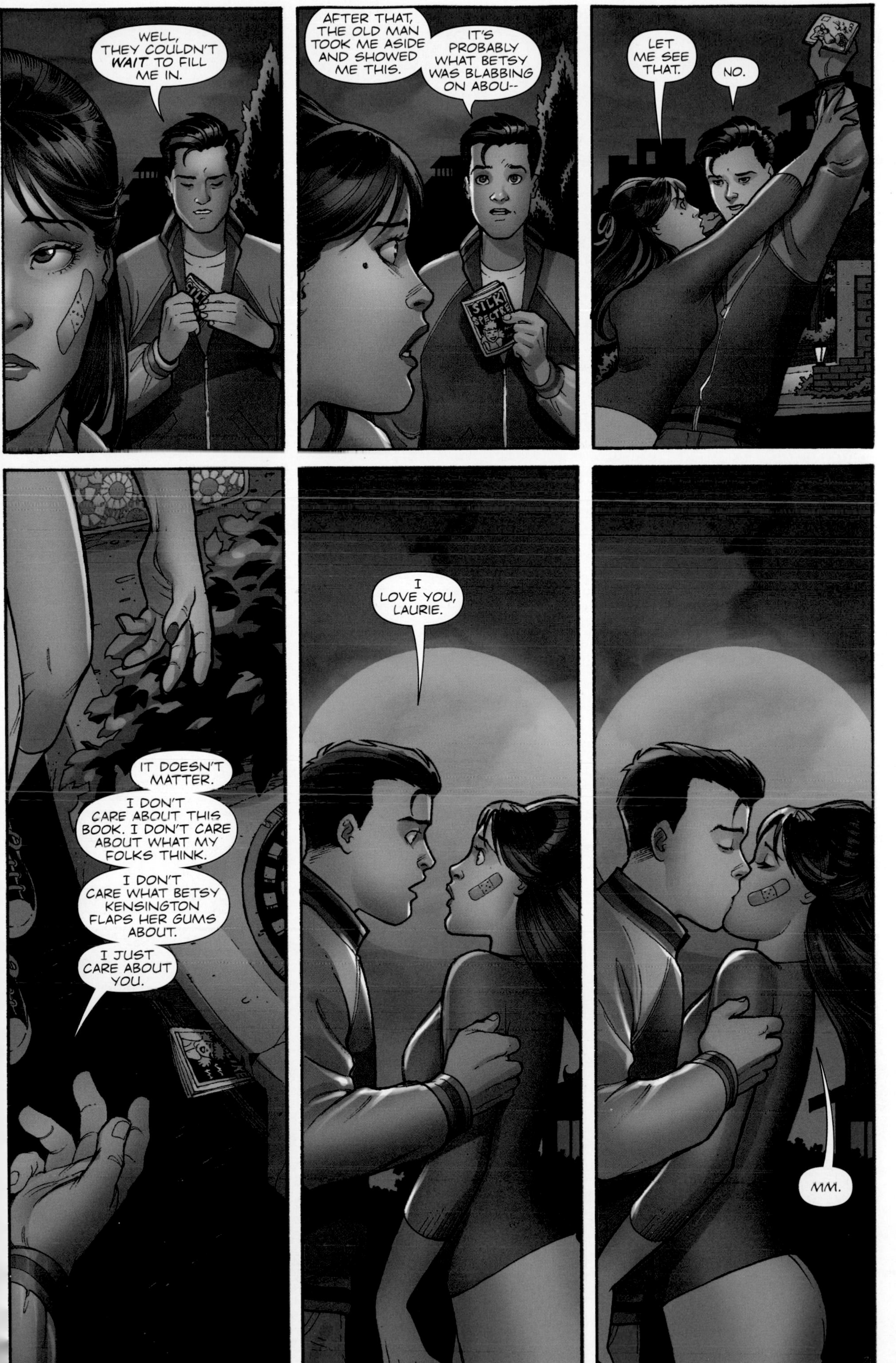
WELL, THEY COULDN'T *WAIT* TO FILL ME IN.
AFTER THAT, THE OLD MAN TOOK ME ASIDE AND SHOWED ME THIS.
IT'S PROBABLY WHAT BETSY WAS BLABBING ON ABOU--
SILK SPECTRE
LET ME SEE THAT.
NO.
IT DOESN'T MATTER.
I DON'T CARE ABOUT THIS BOOK. I DON'T CARE ABOUT WHAT MY FOLKS THINK.
I DON'T CARE WHAT BETSY KENSINGTON FLAPS HER GUMS ABOUT.
I JUST CARE ABOUT YOU.
I LOVE YOU, LAURIE.
MM.

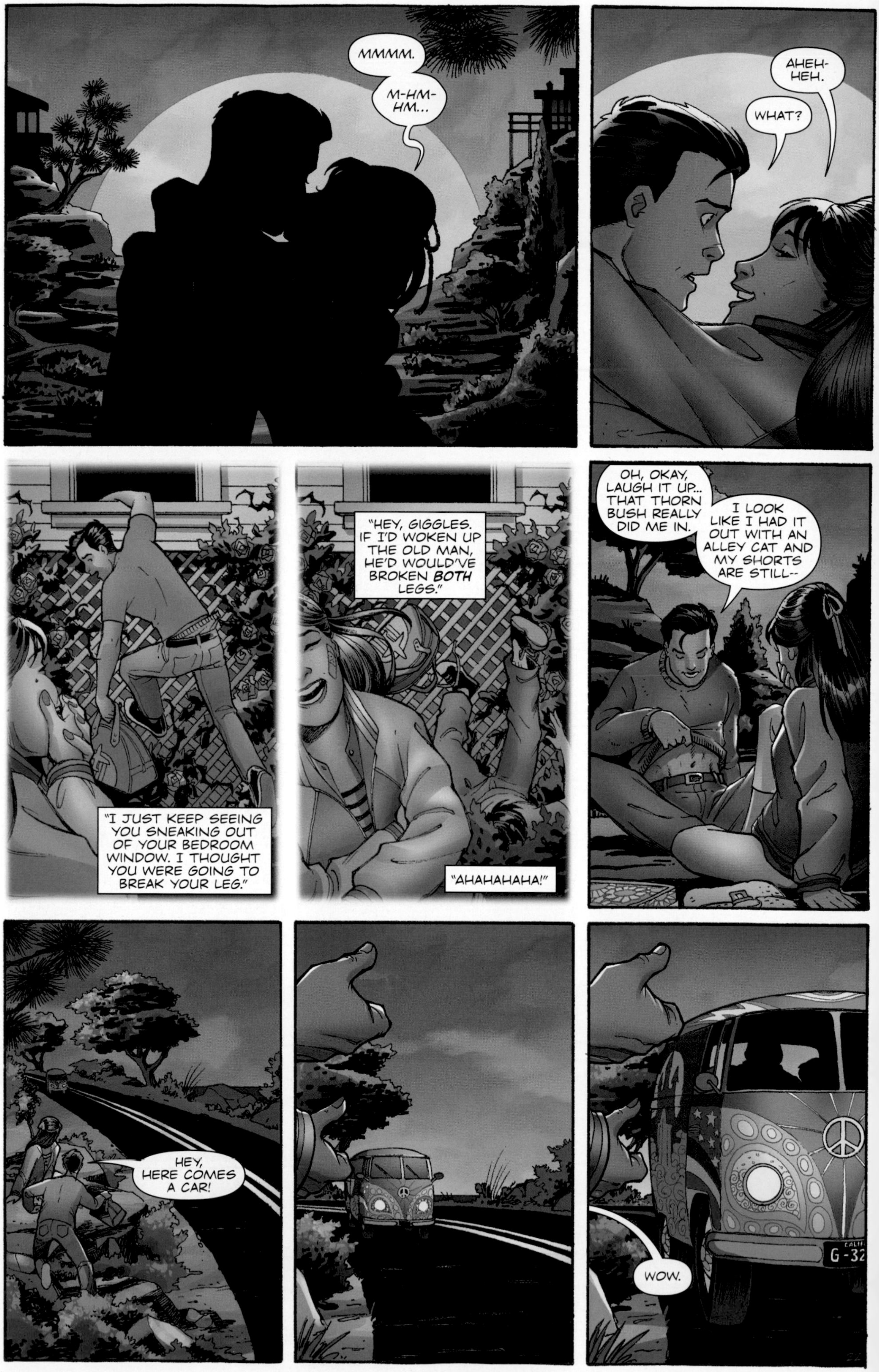
MMMM.
M-HM-HM...
AHEH-HEH.
WHAT?
"I JUST KEEP SEEING YOU SNEAKING OUT OF YOUR BEDROOM WINDOW. I THOUGHT YOU WERE GOING TO BREAK YOUR LEG."
"HEY, GIGGLES. IF I'D WOKEN UP THE OLD MAN, HE'D WOULD'VE BROKEN BOTH LEGS."
"AHAHAHAHA!"
OH, OKAY, LAUGH IT UP... THAT THORN BUSH REALLY DID ME IN.
I LOOK LIKE I HAD IT OUT WITH AN ALLEY CAT AND MY SHORTS ARE STILL--
HEY, HERE COMES A CAR!
WOW.

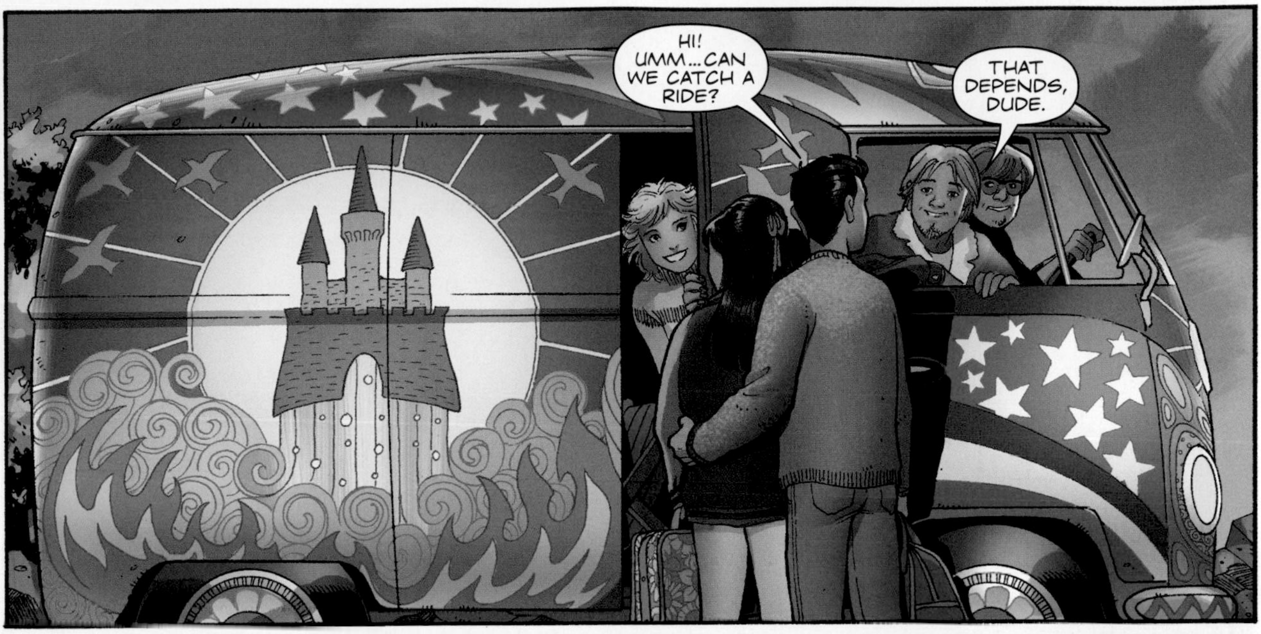
HI! UMM...CAN WE CATCH A RIDE?
THAT DEPENDS, DUDE.

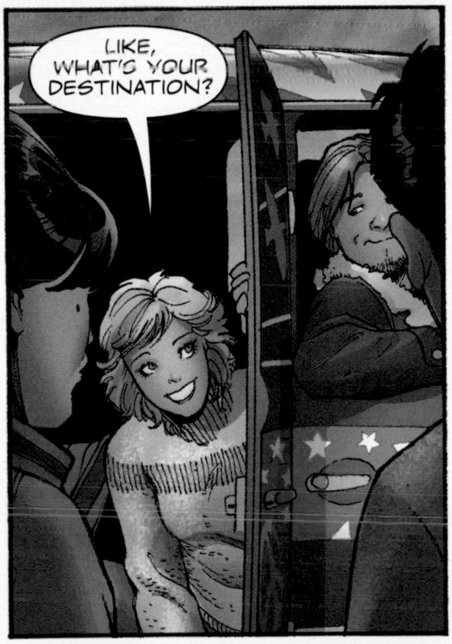
LIKE, WHAT'S YOUR DESTINATION?

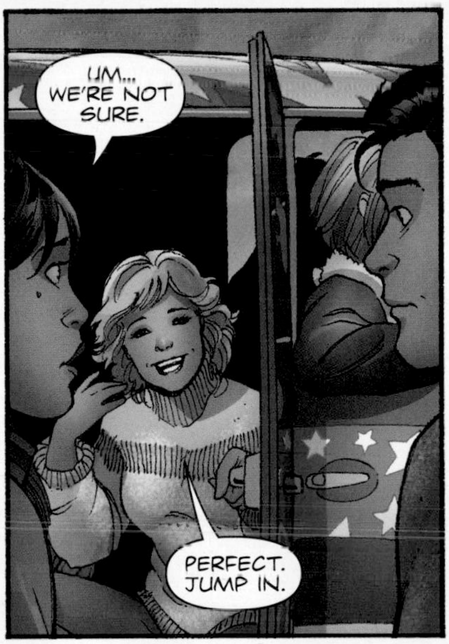
UM... WE'RE NOT SURE.
PERFECT. JUMP IN.

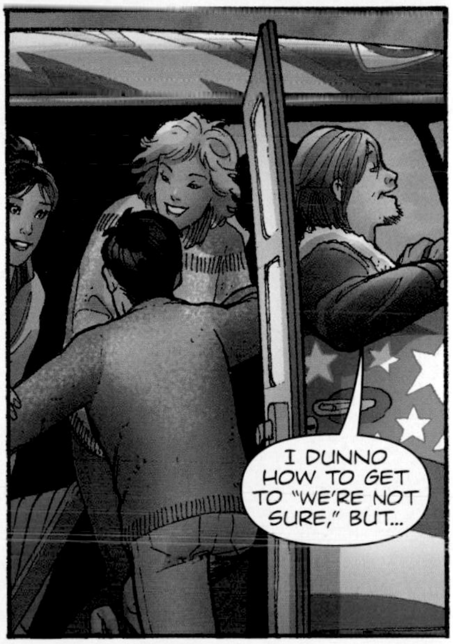
I DUNNO HOW TO GET TO "WE'RE NOT SURE," BUT...

MEAN GOODBYE

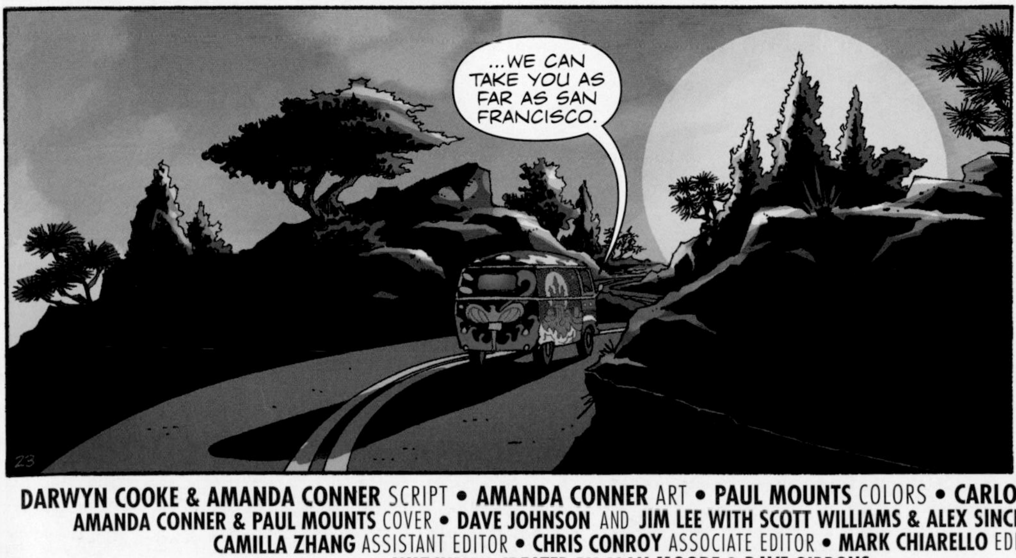
...WE CAN TAKE YOU AS FAR AS SAN FRANCISCO.

Please don't walk away,
pretty baby, with that
look in your eyes...
Don't say goodnight
and mean goodbye.
Charles Partee &
Joe DeAngelis

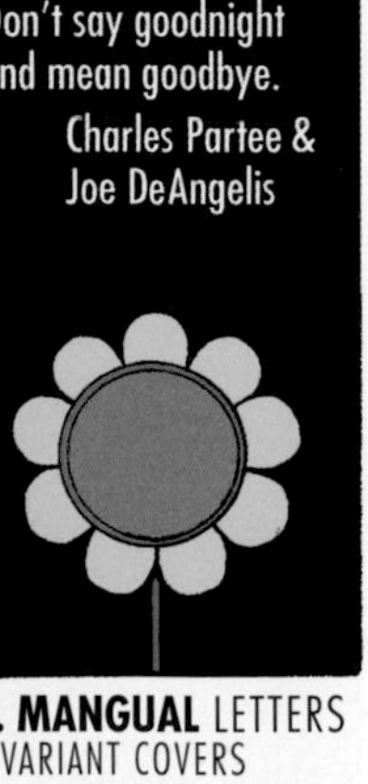

DARWYN COOKE & AMANDA CONNER SCRIPT • **AMANDA CONNER** ART • **PAUL MOUNTS** COLORS • **CARLOS M. MANGUAL** LETTERS
AMANDA CONNER & PAUL MOUNTS COVER • **DAVE JOHNSON** AND **JIM LEE WITH SCOTT WILLIAMS & ALEX SINCLAIR** VARIANT COVERS
CAMILLA ZHANG ASSISTANT EDITOR • **CHRIS CONROY** ASSOCIATE EDITOR • **MARK CHIARELLO** EDITOR
WATCHMEN CREATED BY ALAN MOORE & DAVE GIBBONS

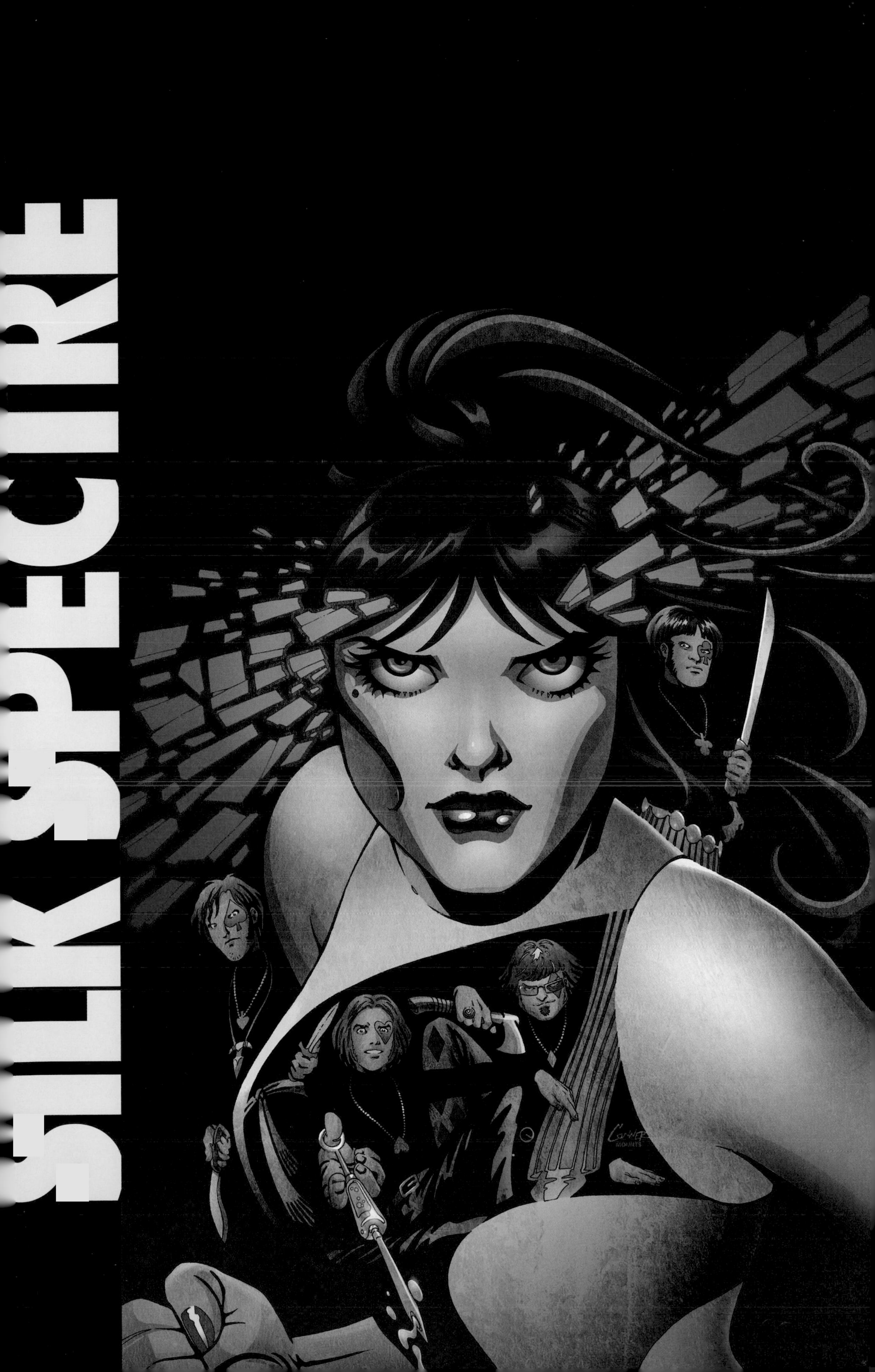
SILK SPECTRE

SILK SPECTRE

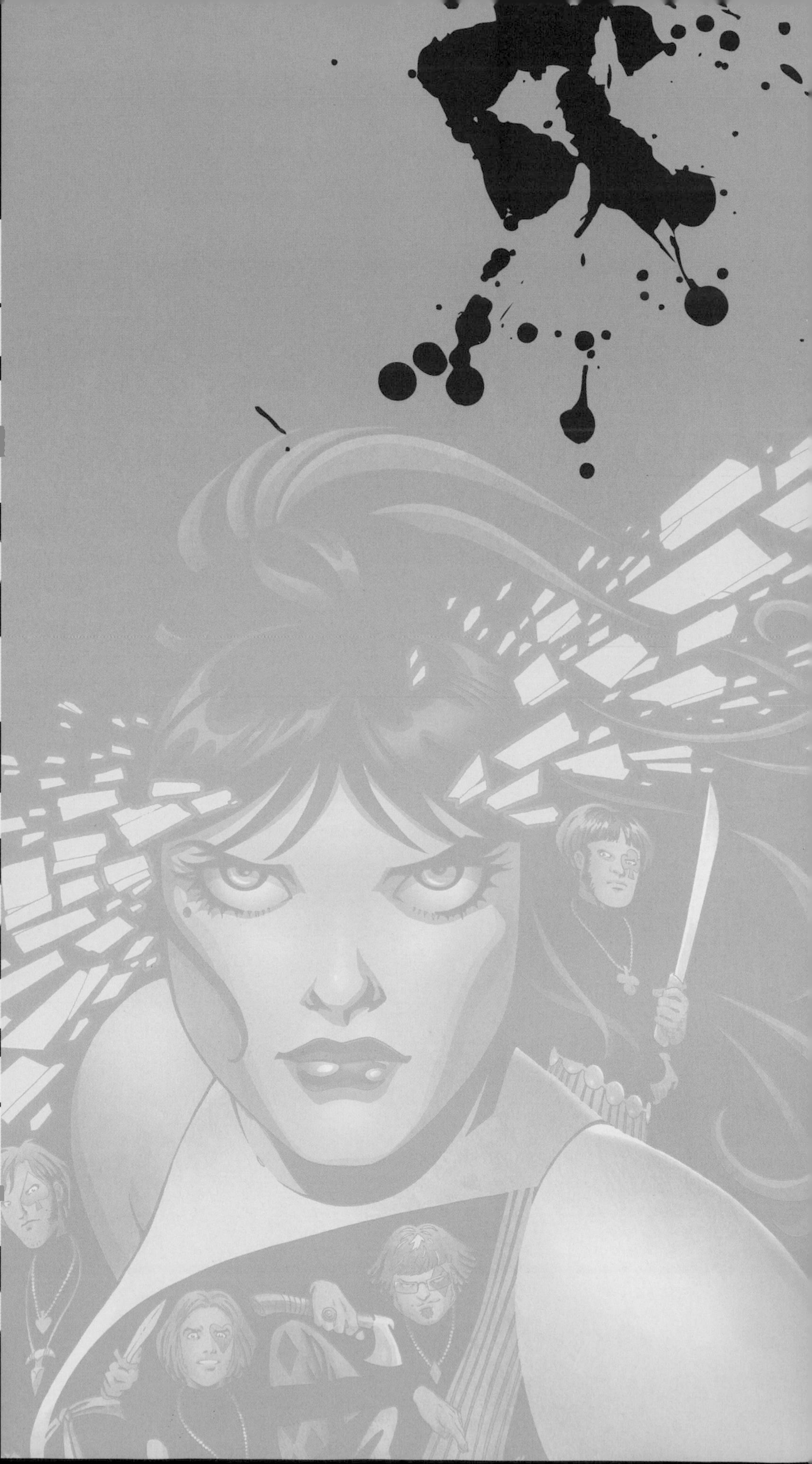

"I'VE JUST COME TO A HORRIBLE REALIZATION... MY MOM WOULD BE REALLY PROUD OF ME RIGHT NOW."

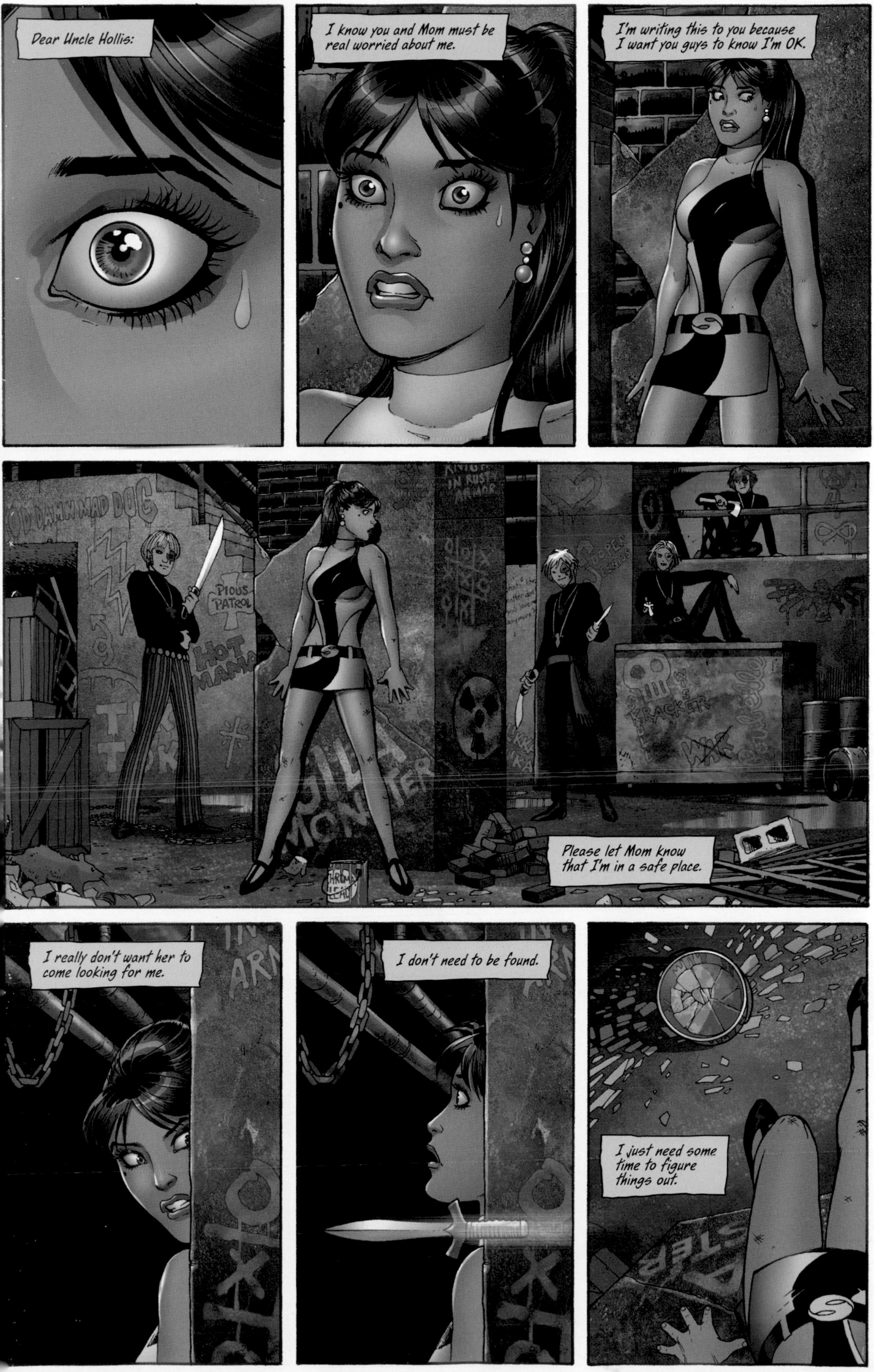
Dear Uncle Hollis:
I know you and Mom must be real worried about me.
I'm writing this to you because I want you guys to know I'm OK.
PIOUS PATROL
HOT MAMA
KRACKER
Please let Mom know that I'm in a safe place.
I really don't want her to come looking for me.
I don't need to be found.
I just need some time to figure things out.

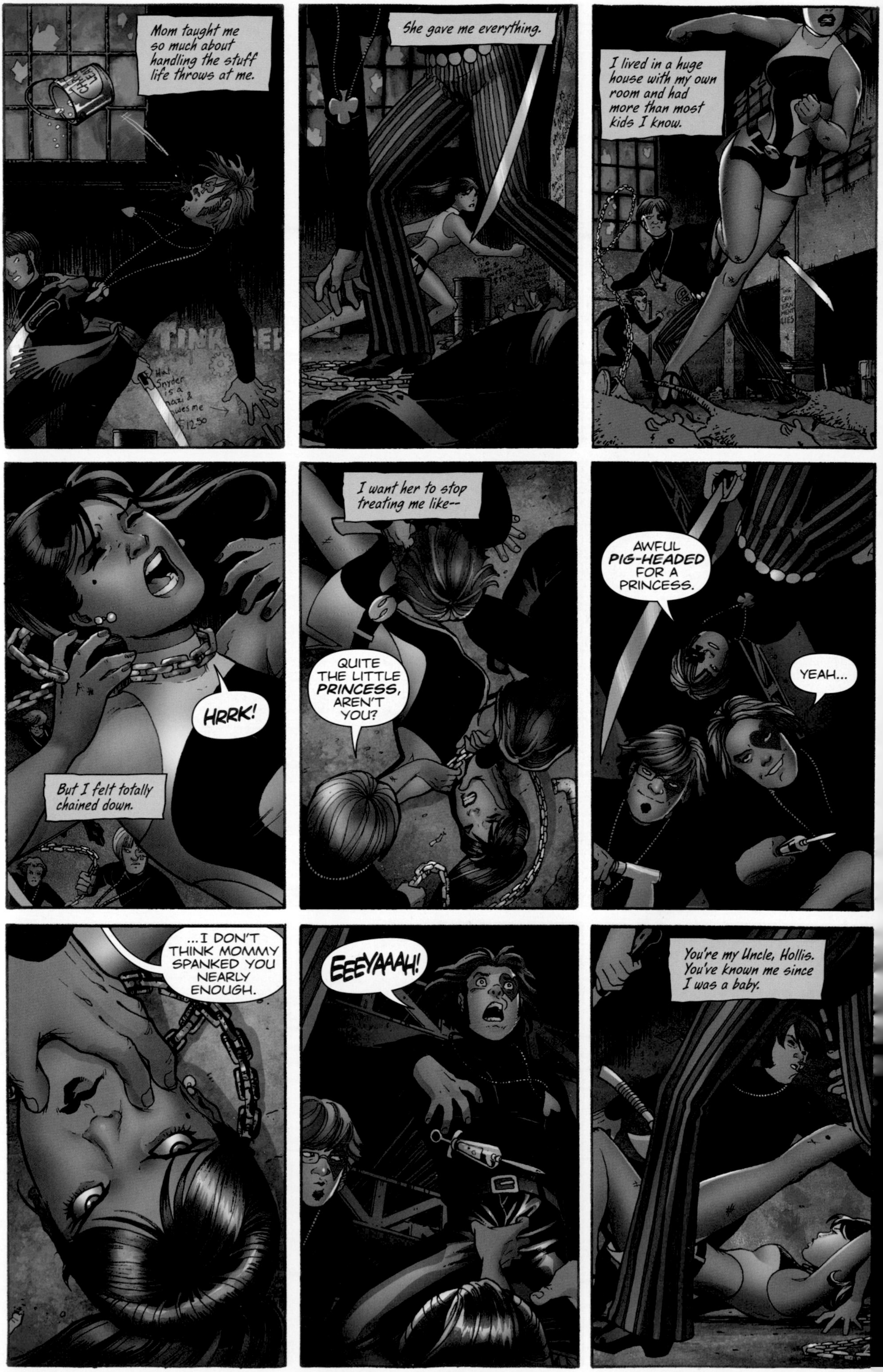

Mom taught me so much about handling the stuff life throws at me.
Hal Snyder is a nazi & owes me $12.50
She gave me everything.
I lived in a huge house with my own room and had more than most kids I know.
HRRK!
But I felt totally chained down.
I want her to stop treating me like--
QUITE THE LITTLE PRINCESS, AREN'T YOU?
AWFUL PIG-HEADED FOR A PRINCESS.
YEAH...
...I DON'T THINK MOMMY SPANKED YOU NEARLY ENOUGH.
EEEYAAAH!
You're my Uncle, Hollis. You've known me since I was a baby.

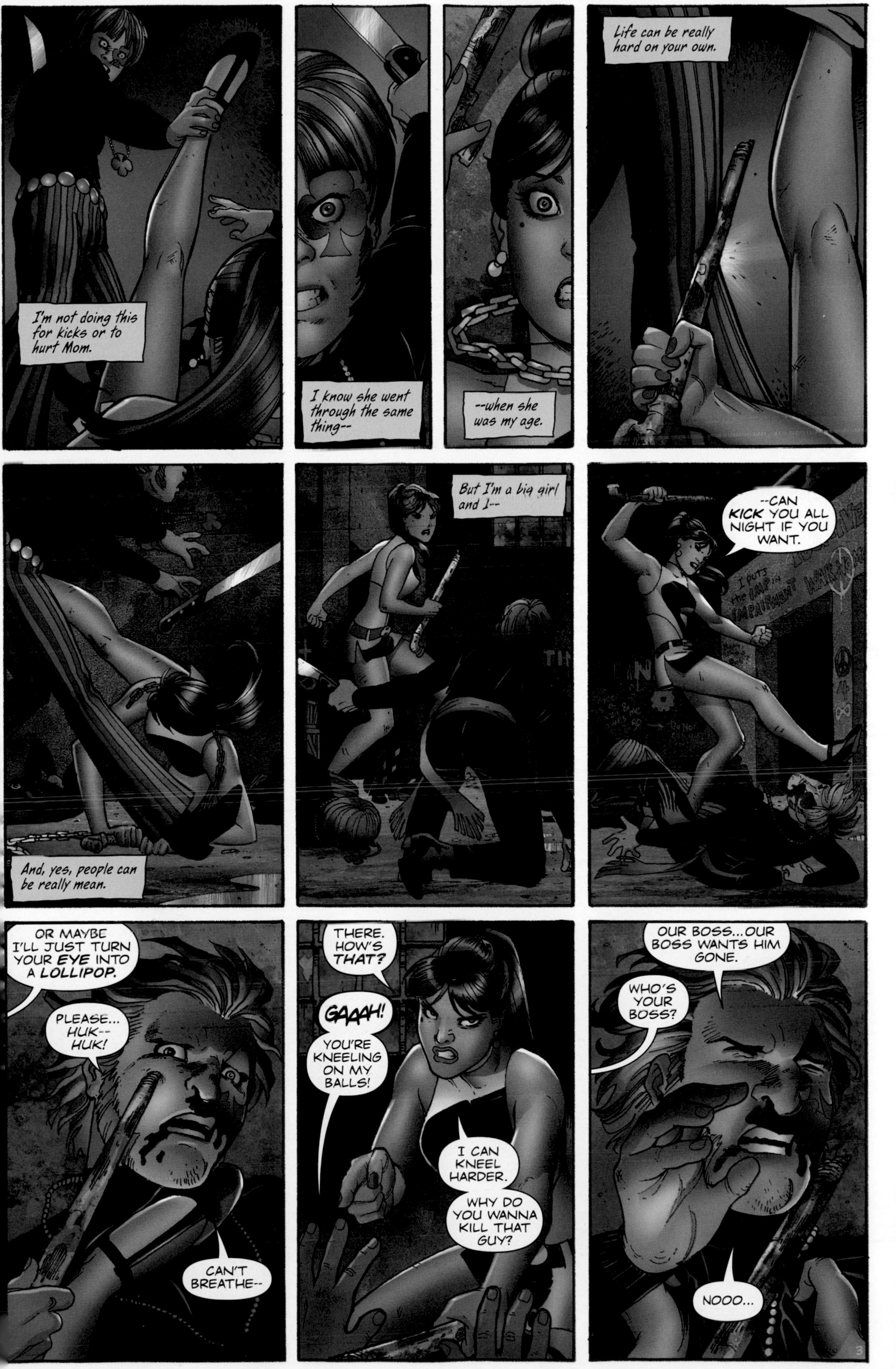

I'm not doing this for kicks or to hurt Mom.
I know she went through the same thing--
--when she was my age.
Life can be really hard on your own.
And, yes, people can be really mean.
But I'm a big girl and I--
--CAN KICK YOU ALL NIGHT IF YOU WANT.
I PUTS the IMP in IMPAIRMENT
OR MAYBE I'LL JUST TURN YOUR EYE INTO A LOLLIPOP.
PLEASE... HUK-- HUK!
CAN'T BREATHE--
THERE. HOW'S THAT?
GAAAH!
YOU'RE KNEELING ON MY BALLS!
I CAN KNEEL HARDER.
WHY DO YOU WANNA KILL THAT GUY?
OUR BOSS...OUR BOSS WANTS HIM GONE.
WHO'S YOUR BOSS?
NOOO...

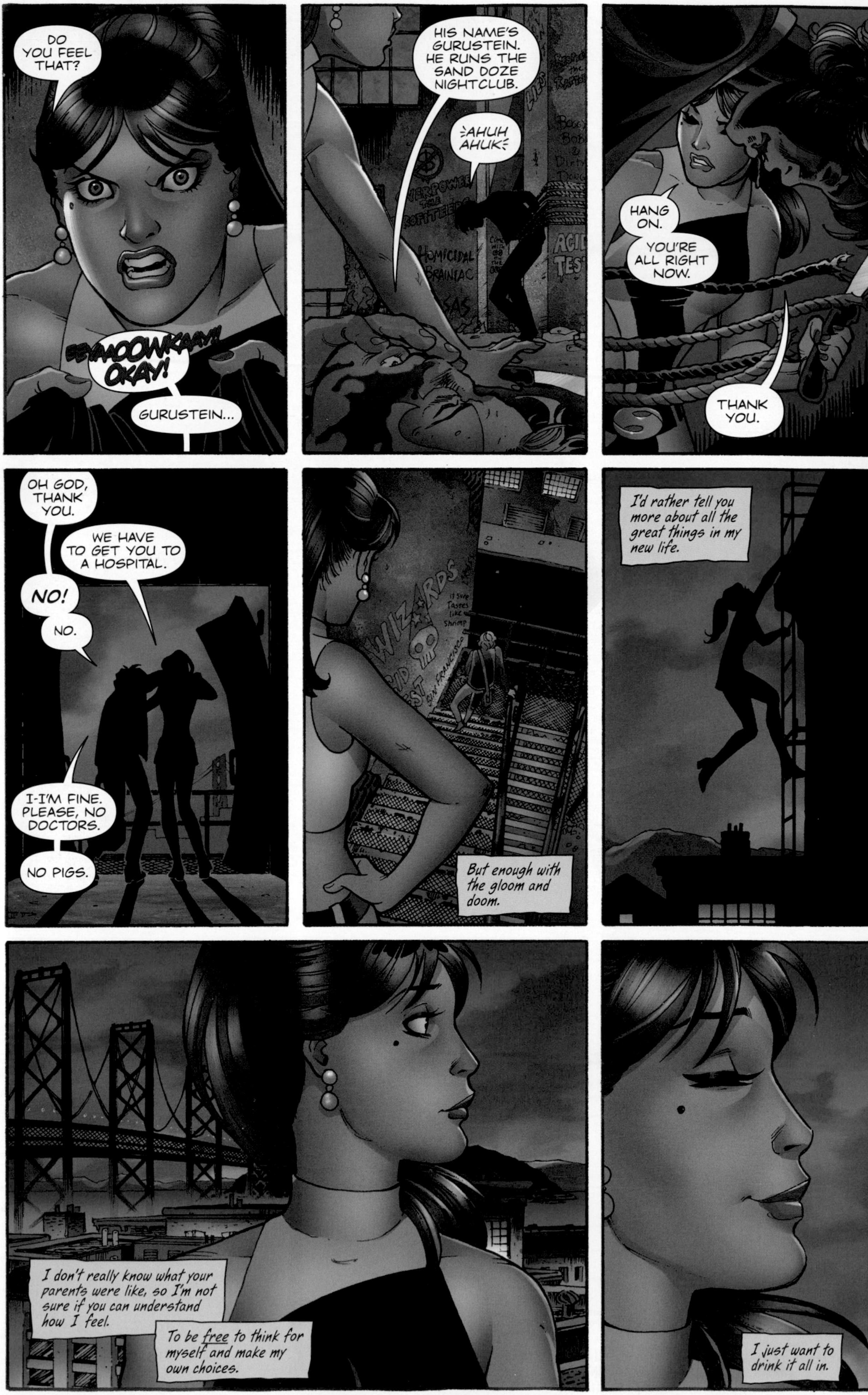
DO YOU FEEL THAT?
OKAY!
GURUSTEIN...
HIS NAME'S GURUSTEIN. HE RUNS THE SAND DOZE NIGHTCLUB.
AHUH AHUK
HANG ON.
YOU'RE ALL RIGHT NOW.
THANK YOU.
OH GOD, THANK YOU.
WE HAVE TO GET YOU TO A HOSPITAL.
NO!
NO.
I-I'M FINE. PLEASE, NO DOCTORS.
NO PIGS.
But enough with the gloom and doom.
I'd rather tell you more about all the great things in my new life.
I don't really know what your parents were like, so I'm not sure if you can understand how I feel.
To be free to think for myself and make my own choices.
I just want to drink it all in.

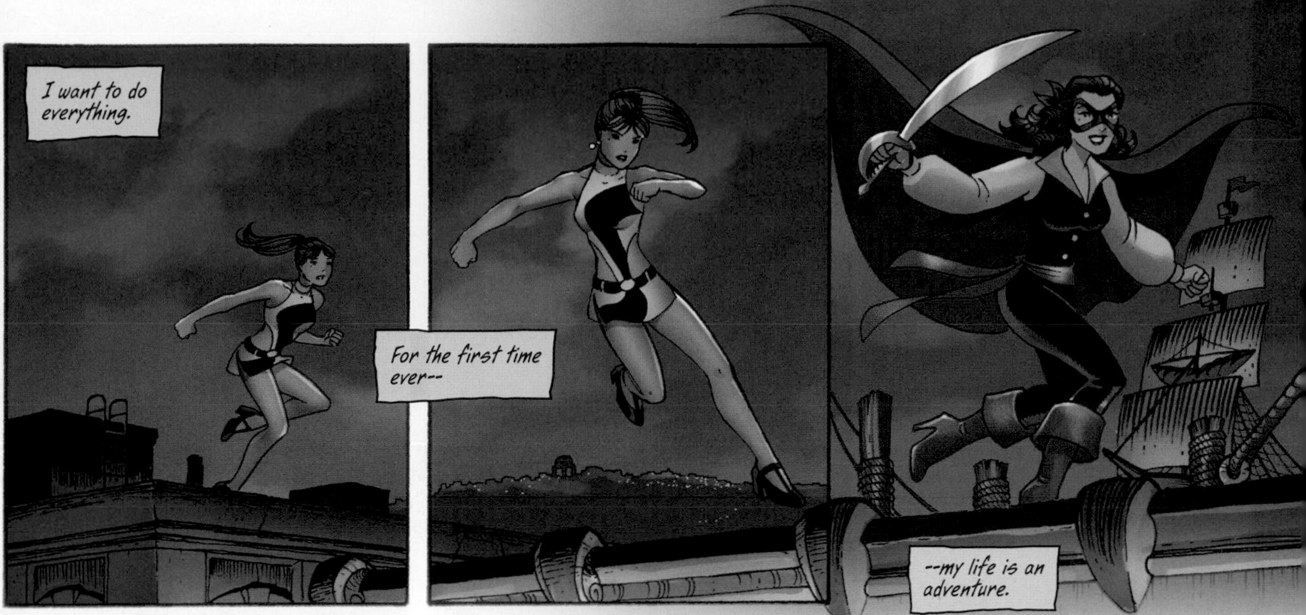
I want to do everything.
For the first time ever--
--my life is an adventure.

GETTING INTO THE WORLD

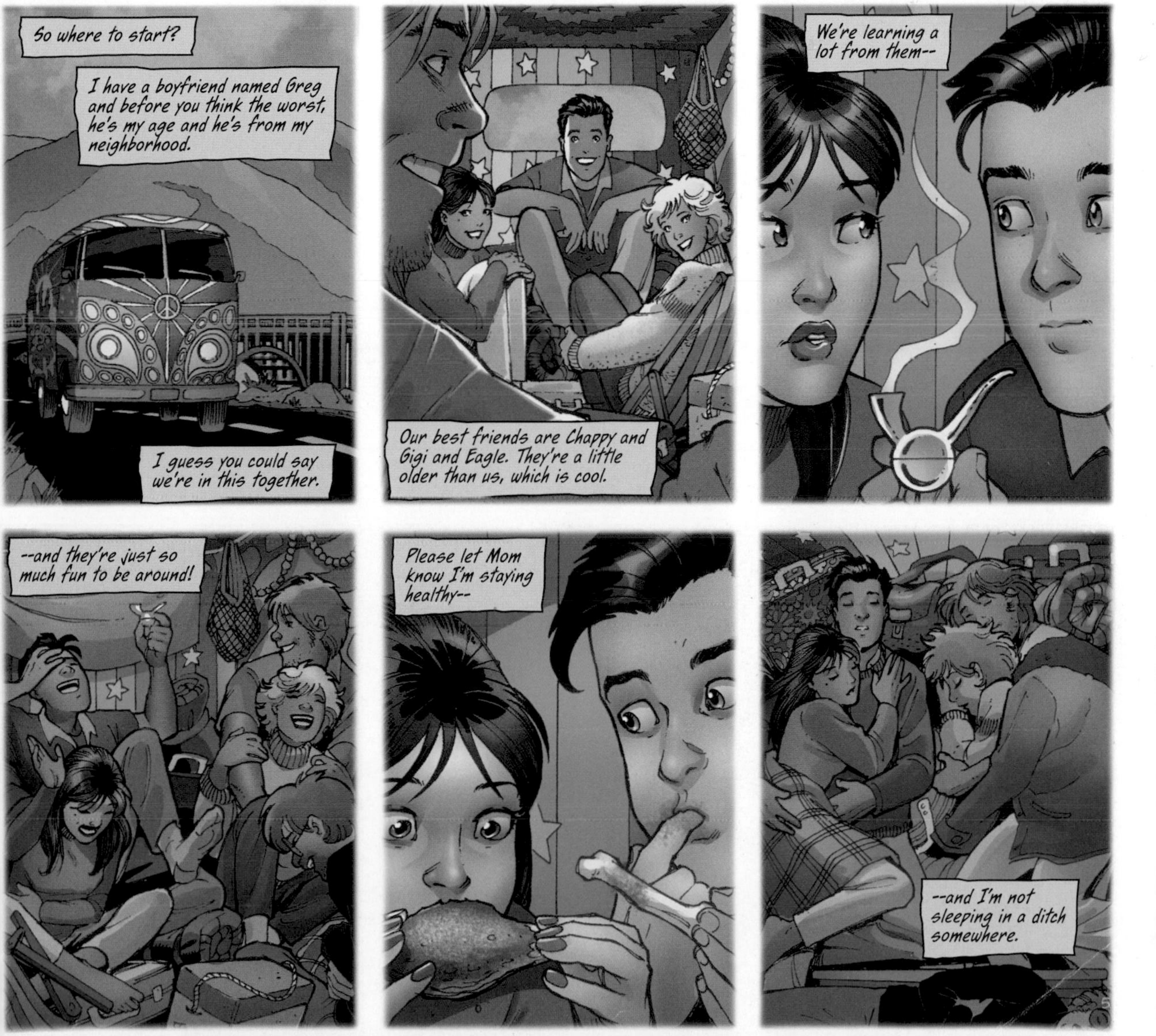
So where to start?
I have a boyfriend named Greg and before you think the worst, he's my age and he's from my neighborhood.
I guess you could say we're in this together.
Our best friends are Chappy and Gigi and Eagle. They're a little older than us, which is cool.
We're learning a lot from them--
--and they're just so much fun to be around!
Please let Mom know I'm staying healthy--
--and I'm not sleeping in a ditch somewhere.

DARWYN COOKE & AMANDA CONNER SCRIPT • **AMANDA CONNER** ART • **PAUL MOUNTS** COLORS • **CARLOS M. MANGUAL** LETTERS
AMANDA CONNER & PAUL MOUNTS COVER • **JOSH MIDDLETON** VARIANT COVER
CAMILLA ZHANG ASSISTANT EDITOR • **CHRIS CONROY** ASSOCIATE EDITOR • **MARK CHIARELLO** EDITOR
WATCHMEN CREATED BY ALAN MOORE & DAVE GIBBONS

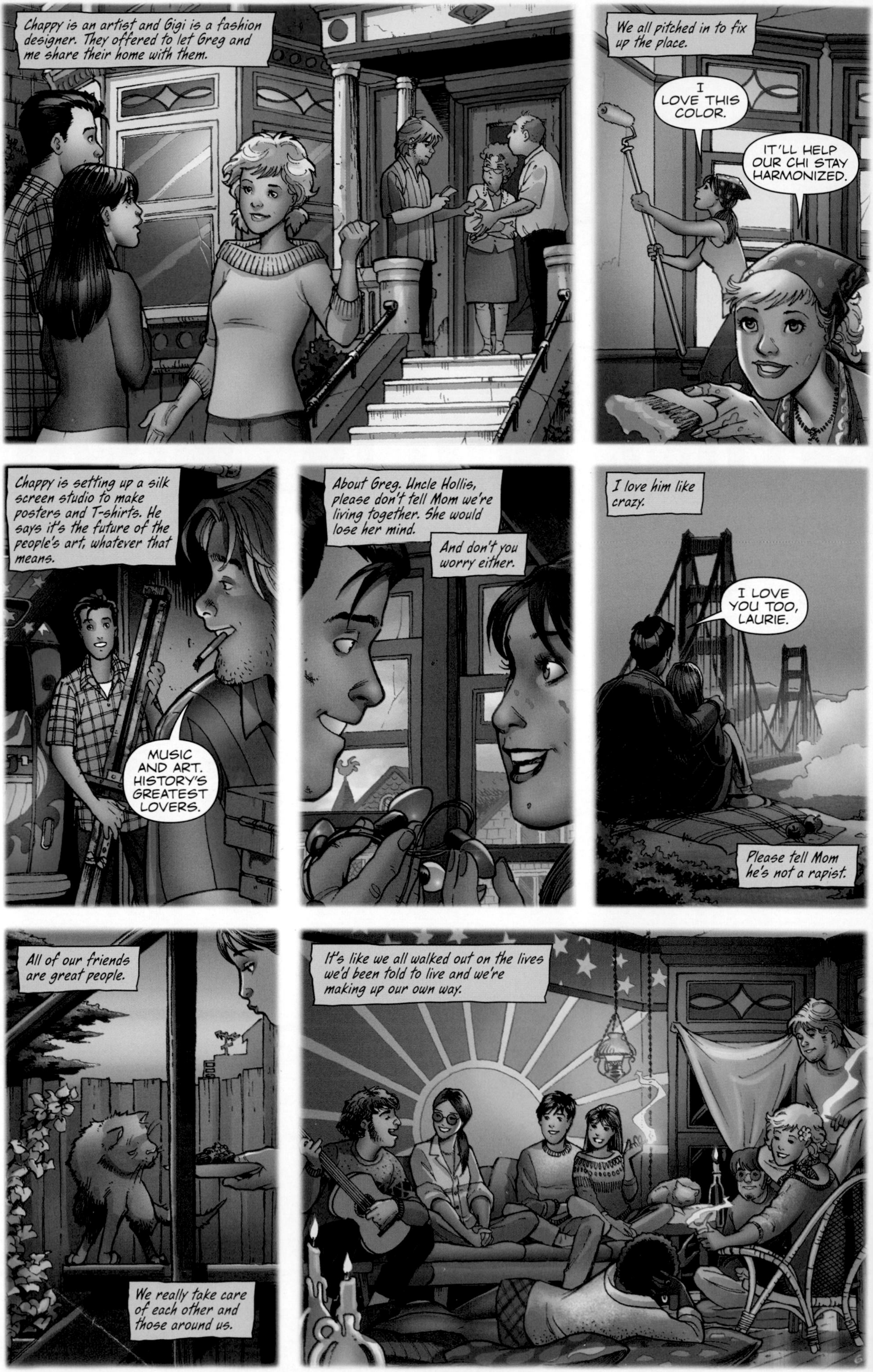
Chappy is an artist and Gigi is a fashion designer. They offered to let Greg and me share their home with them.
We all pitched in to fix up the place.
I LOVE THIS COLOR.
IT'LL HELP OUR CHI STAY HARMONIZED.
Chappy is setting up a silk screen studio to make posters and T-shirts. He says it's the future of the people's art, whatever that means.
MUSIC AND ART. HISTORY'S GREATEST LOVERS.
About Greg. Uncle Hollis, please don't tell Mom we're living together. She would lose her mind.
And don't you worry either.
I love him like crazy.
I LOVE YOU TOO, LAURIE.
Please tell Mom he's not a rapist.
All of our friends are great people.
We really take care of each other and those around us.
It's like we all walked out on the lives we'd been told to live and we're making up our own way.

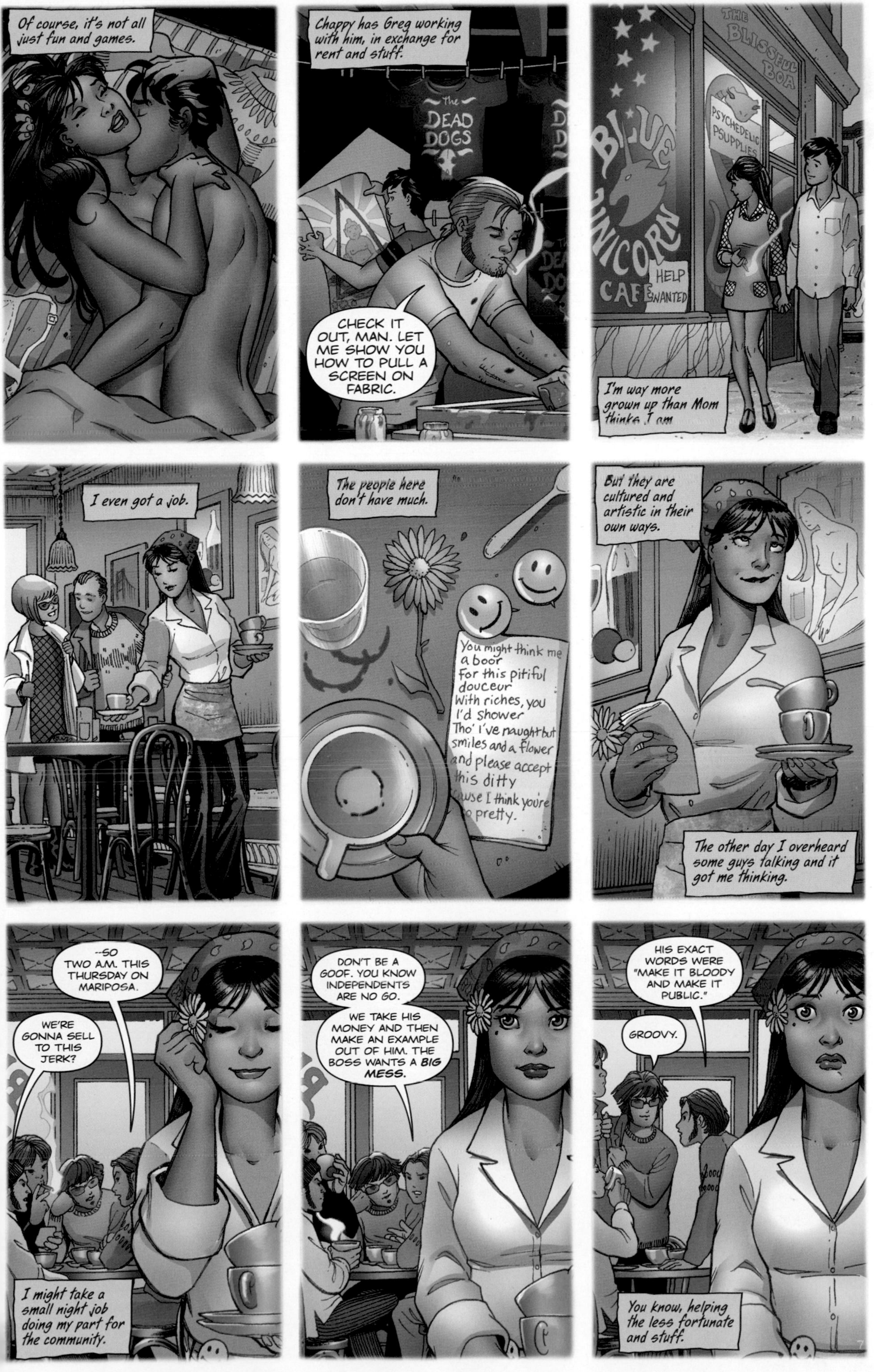
Of course, it's not all just fun and games.
Chappy has Greg working with him, in exchange for rent and stuff.
The DEAD DOGS
CHECK IT OUT, MAN. LET ME SHOW YOU HOW TO PULL A SCREEN ON FABRIC.
THE BLISSFUL BOA
PSYCHEDELIC PSUPPLIES
BLUE UNICORN CAFE
HELP WANTED
I'm way more grown up than Mom thinks I am
I even got a job.
The people here don't have much.
You might think me a boor
For this pitiful douceur
With riches, you I'd shower
Tho' I've naught but smiles and a flower
and please accept this ditty
'cause I think you're so pretty.
But they are cultured and artistic in their own ways.
The other day I overheard some guys talking and it got me thinking.
--SO TWO A.M. THIS THURSDAY ON MARIPOSA.
WE'RE GONNA SELL TO THIS JERK?
I might take a small night job doing my part for the community.
DON'T BE A GOOF. YOU KNOW INDEPENDENTS ARE NO GO.
WE TAKE HIS MONEY AND THEN MAKE AN EXAMPLE OUT OF HIM. THE BOSS WANTS A **BIG MESS**.
HIS EXACT WORDS WERE "MAKE IT BLOODY AND MAKE IT PUBLIC."
GROOVY.
You know, helping the less fortunate and stuff.

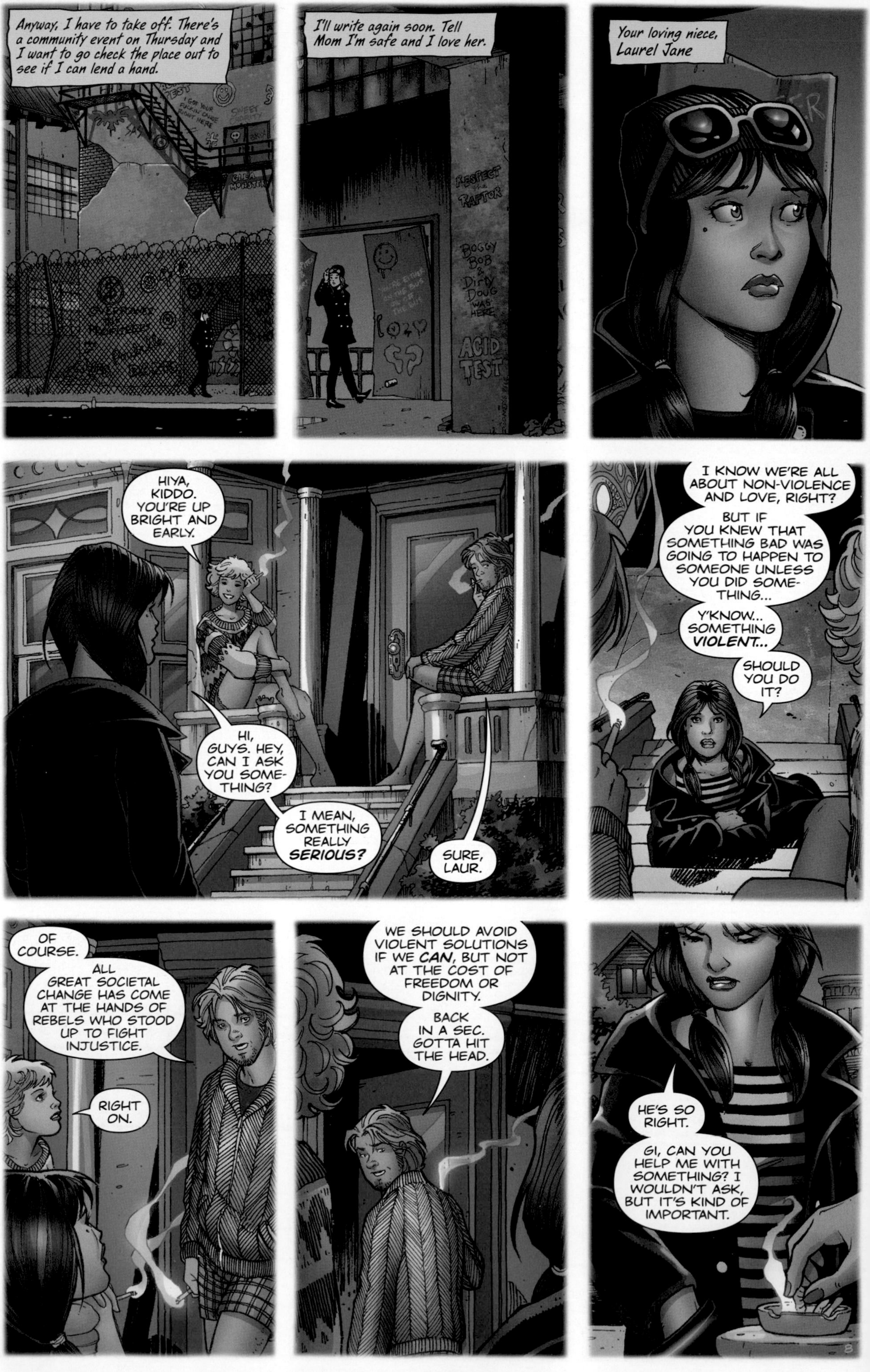
Anyway, I have to take off. There's a community event on Thursday and I want to go check the place out to see if I can lend a hand.
I'll write again soon. Tell Mom I'm safe and I love her.
RESPECT the RAPTOR
BOGGY BOB & DIRTY DOUG WAS HERE
ACID TEST
Your loving niece, Laurel Jane
HIYA, KIDDO. YOU'RE UP BRIGHT AND EARLY.
HI, GUYS. HEY, CAN I ASK YOU SOME-THING?
I MEAN, SOMETHING REALLY **SERIOUS?**
SURE, LAUR.
I KNOW WE'RE ALL ABOUT NON-VIOLENCE AND LOVE, RIGHT?
BUT IF YOU KNEW THAT SOMETHING BAD WAS GOING TO HAPPEN TO SOMEONE UNLESS YOU DID SOME-THING...
Y'KNOW... SOMETHING **VIOLENT...**
SHOULD YOU DO IT?
OF COURSE.
ALL GREAT SOCIETAL CHANGE HAS COME AT THE HANDS OF REBELS WHO STOOD UP TO FIGHT INJUSTICE.
RIGHT ON.
WE SHOULD AVOID VIOLENT SOLUTIONS IF WE **CAN**, BUT NOT AT THE COST OF FREEDOM OR DIGNITY.
BACK IN A SEC. GOTTA HIT THE HEAD.
HE'S SO RIGHT.
GI, CAN YOU HELP ME WITH SOMETHING? I WOULDN'T ASK, BUT IT'S KIND OF IMPORTANT.
8

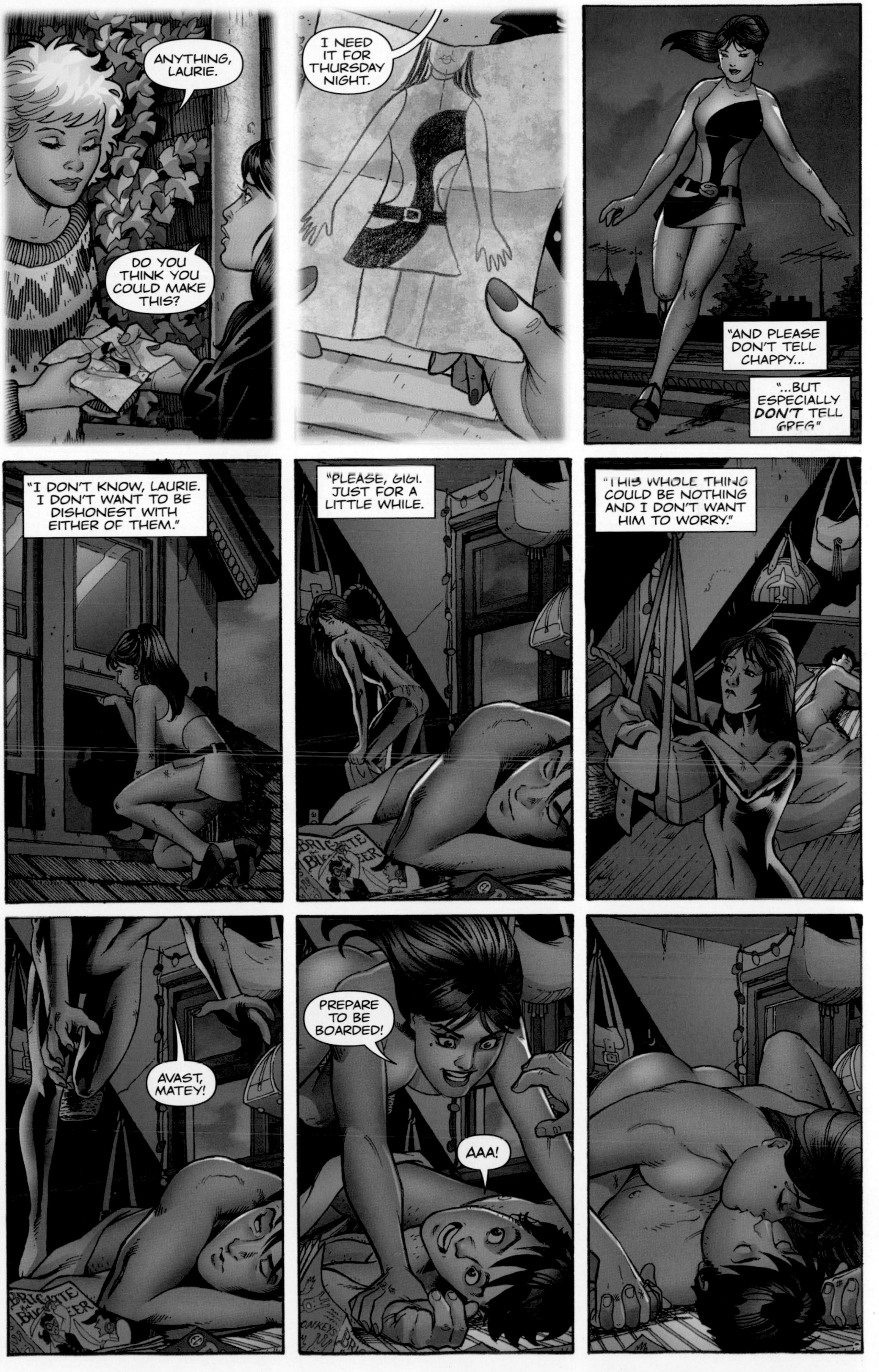
ANYTHING, LAURIE.
DO YOU THINK YOU COULD MAKE THIS?
I NEED IT FOR THURSDAY NIGHT.
"AND PLEASE DON'T TELL CHAPPY...
"...BUT ESPECIALLY DON'T TELL GREG"
"I DON'T KNOW, LAURIE. I DON'T WANT TO BE DISHONEST WITH EITHER OF THEM."
"PLEASE, GIGI. JUST FOR A LITTLE WHILE.
"THIS WHOLE THING COULD BE NOTHING AND I DON'T WANT HIM TO WORRY."
AVAST, MATEY!
PREPARE TO BE BOARDED!
AAA!

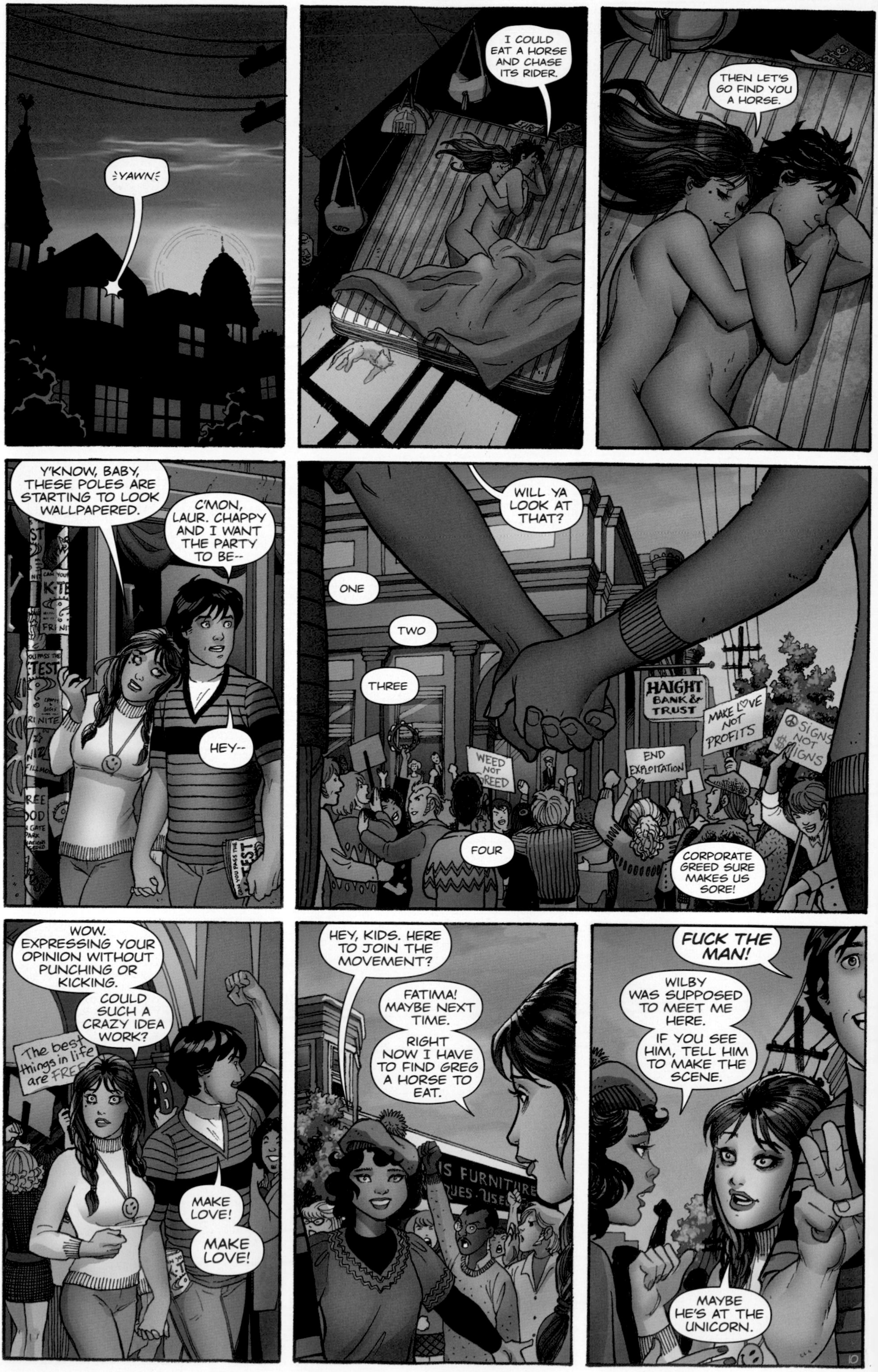
YAWN
I COULD EAT A HORSE AND CHASE ITS RIDER.
THEN LET'S GO FIND YOU A HORSE.
Y'KNOW, BABY, THESE POLES ARE STARTING TO LOOK WALLPAPERED.
C'MON, LAUR. CHAPPY AND I WANT THE PARTY TO BE--
HEY--
WILL YA LOOK AT THAT?
ONE
TWO
THREE
HAIGHT BANK & TRUST
MAKE LOVE NOT PROFITS
SIGNS NOT $IGNS
END EXPLOITATION
FOUR
CORPORATE GREED SURE MAKES US SORE!
WOW. EXPRESSING YOUR OPINION WITHOUT PUNCHING OR KICKING.
COULD SUCH A CRAZY IDEA WORK?
The best things in life are FREE
MAKE LOVE!
MAKE LOVE!
HEY, KIDS. HERE TO JOIN THE MOVEMENT?
FATIMA! MAYBE NEXT TIME.
RIGHT NOW I HAVE TO FIND GREG A HORSE TO EAT.
FUCK THE MAN!
WILBY WAS SUPPOSED TO MEET ME HERE.
IF YOU SEE HIM, TELL HIM TO MAKE THE SCENE.
MAYBE HE'S AT THE UNICORN.

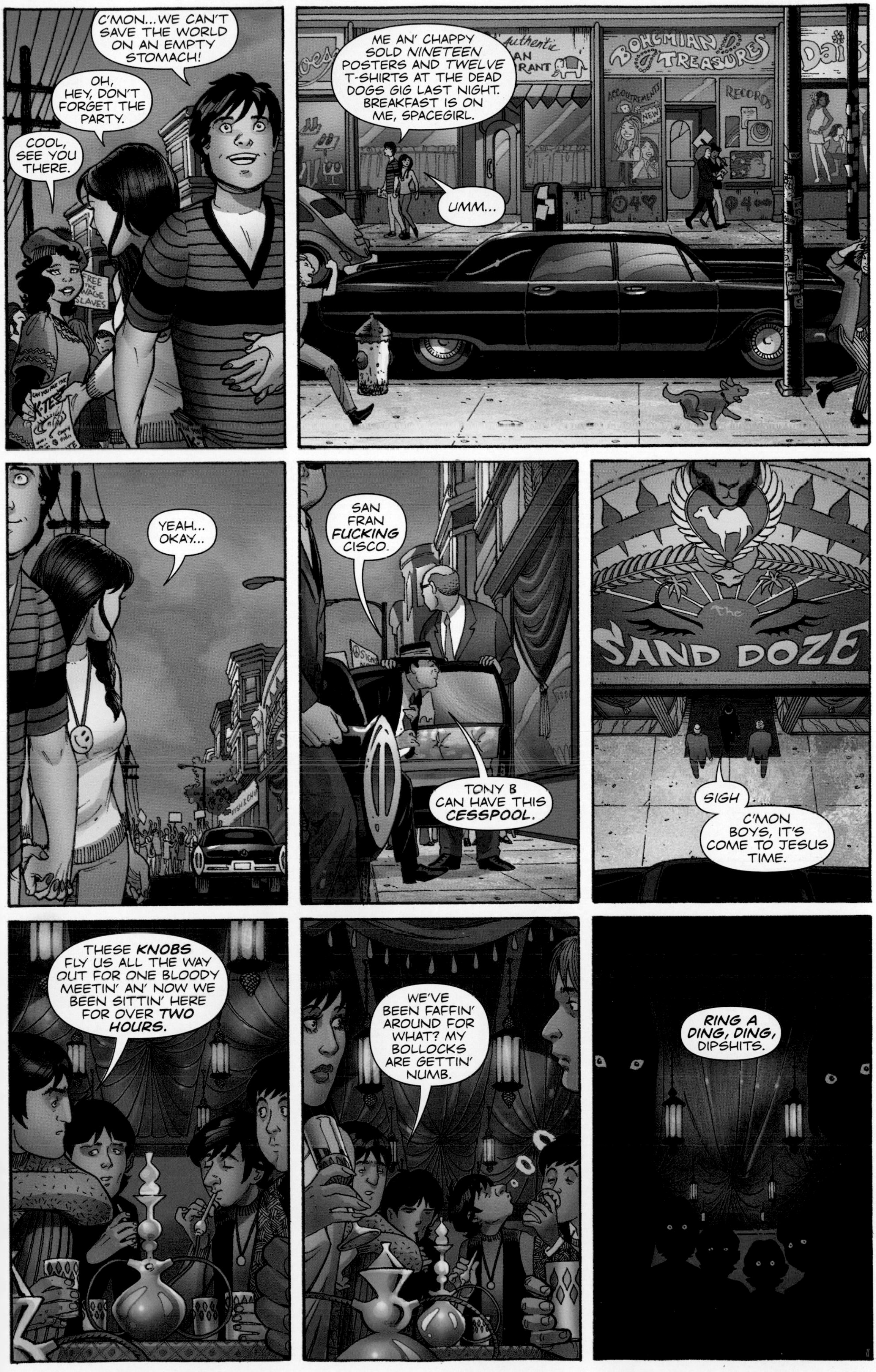
C'MON...WE CAN'T SAVE THE WORLD ON AN EMPTY STOMACH!
OH, HEY, DON'T FORGET THE PARTY.
COOL, SEE YOU THERE.
FREE THE WAGE SLAVES
ME AN' CHAPPY SOLD NINETEEN POSTERS AND TWELVE T-SHIRTS AT THE DEAD DOGS GIG LAST NIGHT. BREAKFAST IS ON ME, SPACEGIRL.
BOHEMIAN TREASURES
RECORDS
UMM...
YEAH... OKAY...
SAN FRAN FUCKING CISCO.
TONY B CAN HAVE THIS CESSPOOL.
The SAND DOZE
SIGH
C'MON BOYS, IT'S COME TO JESUS TIME.
THESE KNOBS FLY US ALL THE WAY OUT FOR ONE BLOODY MEETIN' AN' NOW WE BEEN SITTIN' HERE FOR OVER TWO HOURS.
WE'VE BEEN FAFFIN' AROUND FOR WHAT? MY BOLLOCKS ARE GETTIN' NUMB.
RING A DING, DING, DIPSHITS.

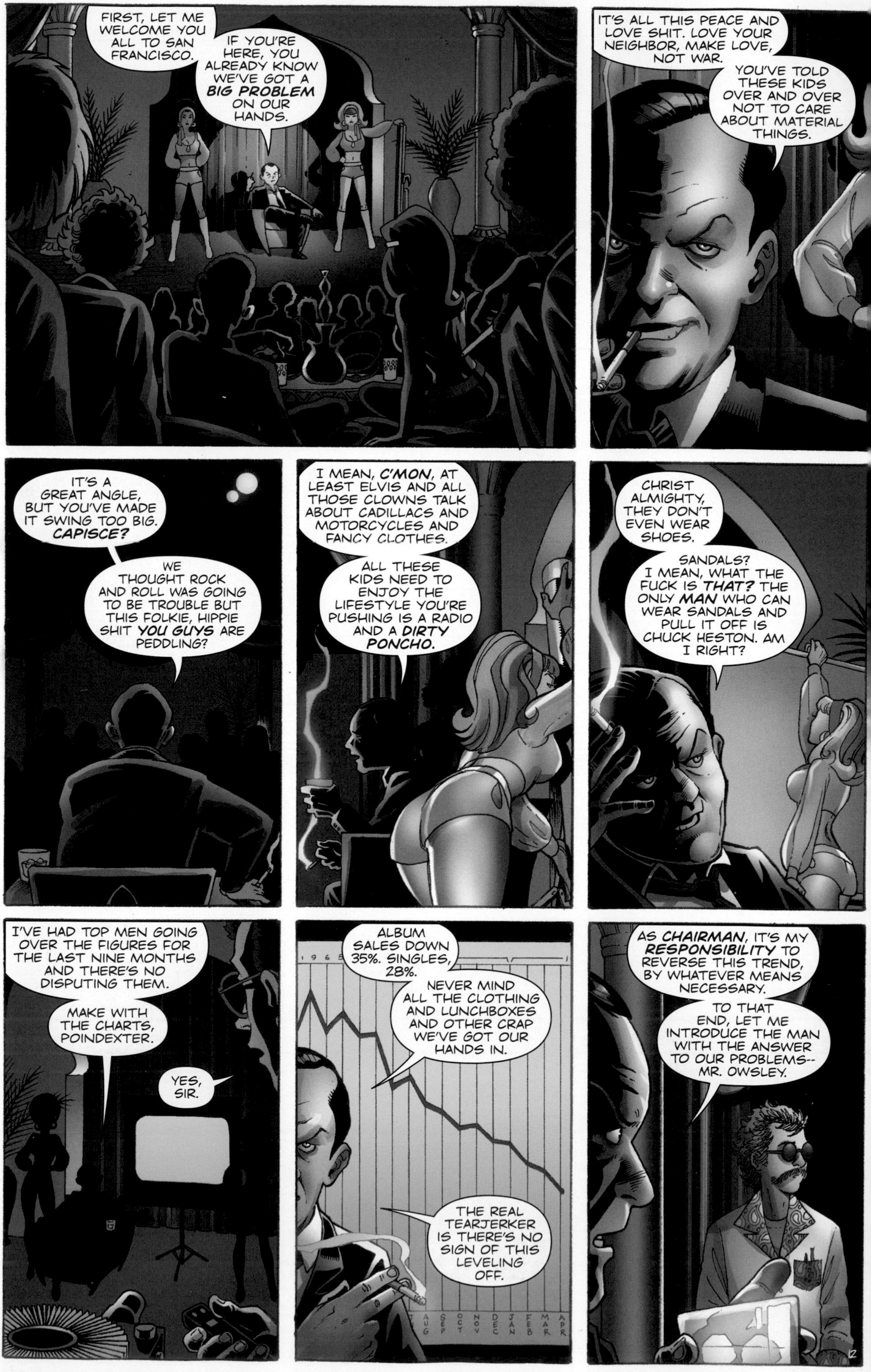
FIRST, LET ME WELCOME YOU ALL TO SAN FRANCISCO.
IF YOU'RE HERE, YOU ALREADY KNOW WE'VE GOT A ***BIG PROBLEM*** ON OUR HANDS.
IT'S ALL THIS PEACE AND LOVE SHIT. LOVE YOUR NEIGHBOR, MAKE LOVE, NOT WAR.
YOU'VE TOLD THESE KIDS OVER AND OVER NOT TO CARE ABOUT MATERIAL THINGS.
IT'S A GREAT ANGLE, BUT YOU'VE MADE IT SWING TOO BIG. ***CAPISCE?***
WE THOUGHT ROCK AND ROLL WAS GOING TO BE TROUBLE BUT THIS FOLKIE, HIPPIE SHIT ***YOU GUYS*** ARE PEDDLING?
I MEAN, ***C'MON***, AT LEAST ELVIS AND ALL THOSE CLOWNS TALK ABOUT CADILLACS AND MOTORCYCLES AND FANCY CLOTHES.
ALL THESE KIDS NEED TO ENJOY THE LIFESTYLE YOU'RE PUSHING IS A RADIO AND A ***DIRTY PONCHO.***
CHRIST ALMIGHTY, THEY DON'T EVEN WEAR SHOES.
SANDALS? I MEAN, WHAT THE FUCK IS ***THAT?*** THE ONLY ***MAN*** WHO CAN WEAR SANDALS AND PULL IT OFF IS CHUCK HESTON. AM I RIGHT?
I'VE HAD TOP MEN GOING OVER THE FIGURES FOR THE LAST NINE MONTHS AND THERE'S NO DISPUTING THEM.
MAKE WITH THE CHARTS, POINDEXTER.
YES, SIR.
1965
ALBUM SALES DOWN 35%. SINGLES, 28%.
NEVER MIND ALL THE CLOTHING AND LUNCHBOXES AND OTHER CRAP WE'VE GOT OUR HANDS IN.
THE REAL TEARJERKER IS THERE'S NO SIGN OF THIS LEVELING OFF.
AUG SEPT OCT NOV DEC JAN FEB MAR APR
AS ***CHAIRMAN***, IT'S MY ***RESPONSIBILITY*** TO REVERSE THIS TREND, BY WHATEVER MEANS NECESSARY.
TO THAT END, LET ME INTRODUCE THE MAN WITH THE ANSWER TO OUR PROBLEMS-- MR. OWSLEY.

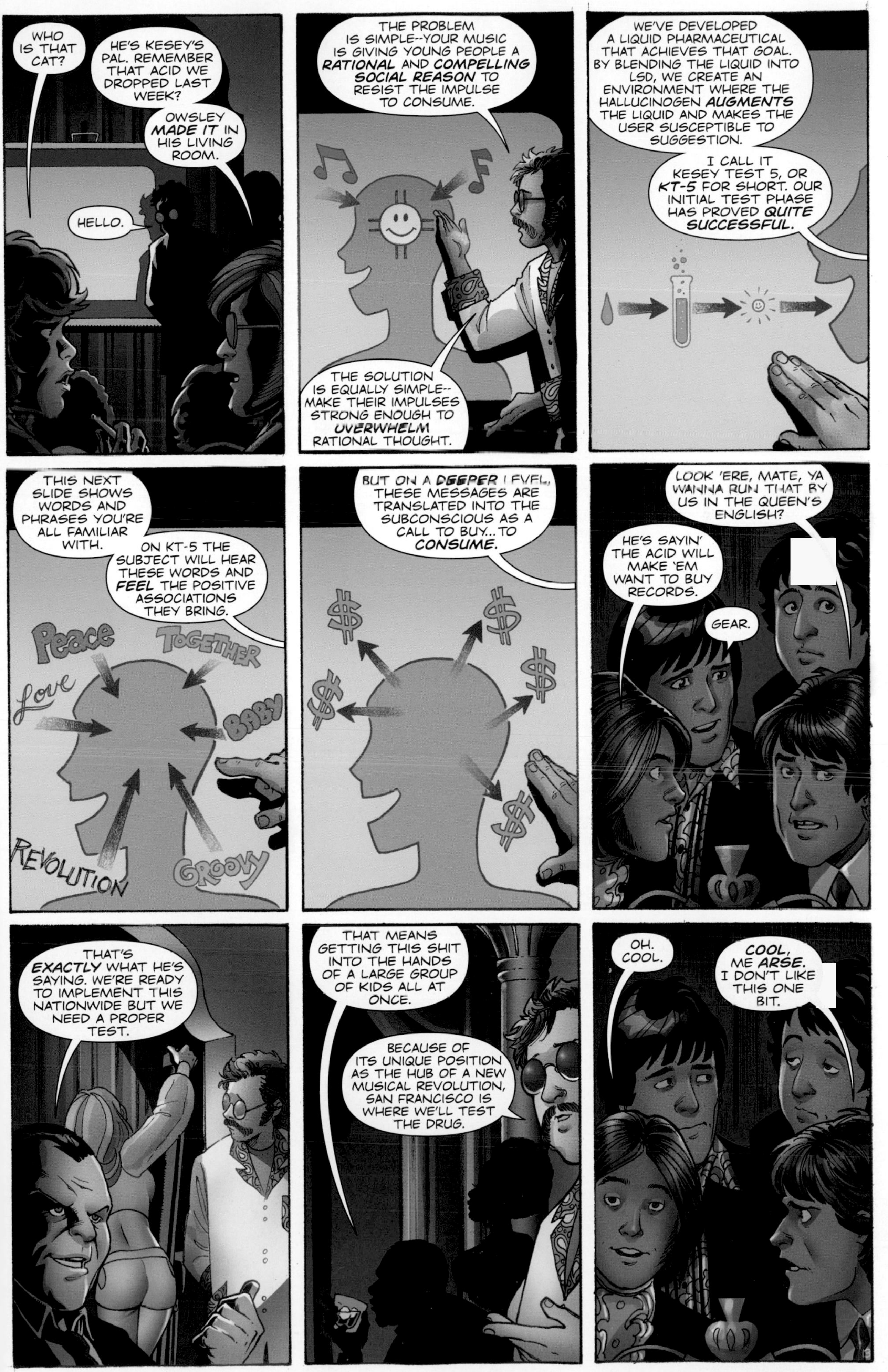
WHO IS THAT CAT?
HE'S KESEY'S PAL. REMEMBER THAT ACID WE DROPPED LAST WEEK?
OWSLEY MADE IT IN HIS LIVING ROOM.
HELLO.
THE PROBLEM IS SIMPLE--YOUR MUSIC IS GIVING YOUNG PEOPLE A RATIONAL AND COMPELLING SOCIAL REASON TO RESIST THE IMPULSE TO CONSUME.
THE SOLUTION IS EQUALLY SIMPLE--MAKE THEIR IMPULSES STRONG ENOUGH TO OVERWHELM RATIONAL THOUGHT.
WE'VE DEVELOPED A LIQUID PHARMACEUTICAL THAT ACHIEVES THAT GOAL. BY BLENDING THE LIQUID INTO LSD, WE CREATE AN ENVIRONMENT WHERE THE HALLUCINOGEN AUGMENTS THE LIQUID AND MAKES THE USER SUSCEPTIBLE TO SUGGESTION.
I CALL IT KESEY TEST 5, OR KT-5 FOR SHORT. OUR INITIAL TEST PHASE HAS PROVED QUITE SUCCESSFUL.
THIS NEXT SLIDE SHOWS WORDS AND PHRASES YOU'RE ALL FAMILIAR WITH.
ON KT-5 THE SUBJECT WILL HEAR THESE WORDS AND FEEL THE POSITIVE ASSOCIATIONS THEY BRING.
Peace
TOGETHER
Love
BABY
REVOLUTION
GROOVY
BUT ON A DEEPER LEVEL, THESE MESSAGES ARE TRANSLATED INTO THE SUBCONSCIOUS AS A CALL TO BUY...TO CONSUME.
LOOK 'ERE, MATE, YA WANNA RUN THAT BY US IN THE QUEEN'S ENGLISH?
HE'S SAYIN' THE ACID WILL MAKE 'EM WANT TO BUY RECORDS.
GEAR.
THAT'S EXACTLY WHAT HE'S SAYING. WE'RE READY TO IMPLEMENT THIS NATIONWIDE BUT WE NEED A PROPER TEST.
THAT MEANS GETTING THIS SHIT INTO THE HANDS OF A LARGE GROUP OF KIDS ALL AT ONCE.
BECAUSE OF ITS UNIQUE POSITION AS THE HUB OF A NEW MUSICAL REVOLUTION, SAN FRANCISCO IS WHERE WE'LL TEST THE DRUG.
OH. COOL.
COOL, ME ARSE. I DON'T LIKE THIS ONE BIT.

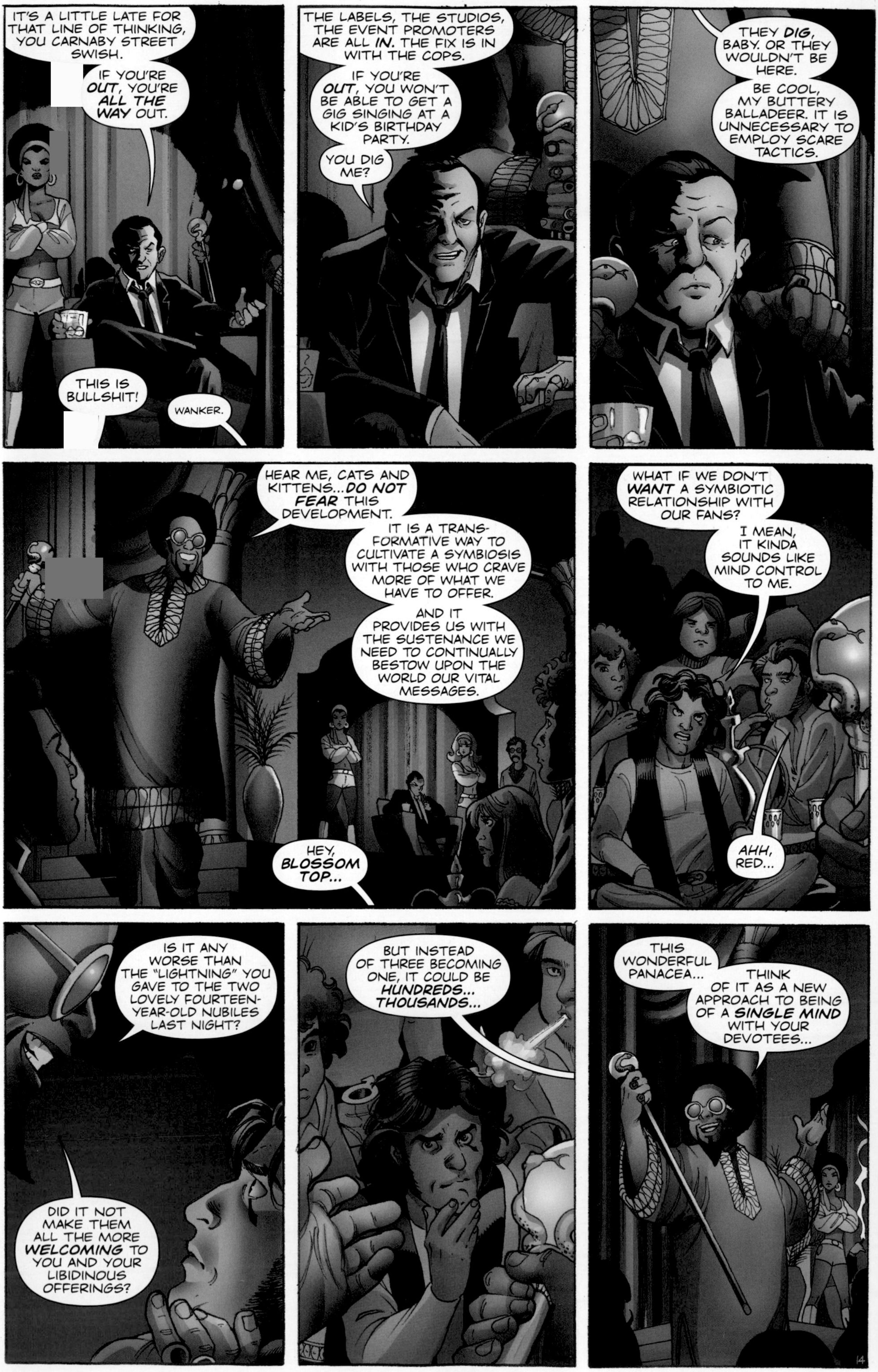
IT'S A LITTLE LATE FOR THAT LINE OF THINKING, YOU CARNABY STREET SWISH.
IF YOU'RE OUT, YOU'RE ALL THE WAY OUT.
THIS IS BULLSHIT!
WANKER.
THE LABELS, THE STUDIOS, THE EVENT PROMOTERS ARE ALL IN. THE FIX IS IN WITH THE COPS.
IF YOU'RE OUT, YOU WON'T BE ABLE TO GET A GIG SINGING AT A KID'S BIRTHDAY PARTY.
YOU DIG ME?
THEY DIG, BABY. OR THEY WOULDN'T BE HERE.
BE COOL, MY BUTTERY BALLADEER. IT IS UNNECESSARY TO EMPLOY SCARE TACTICS.
HEAR ME, CATS AND KITTENS...DO NOT FEAR THIS DEVELOPMENT.
IT IS A TRANS-FORMATIVE WAY TO CULTIVATE A SYMBIOSIS WITH THOSE WHO CRAVE MORE OF WHAT WE HAVE TO OFFER.
AND IT PROVIDES US WITH THE SUSTENANCE WE NEED TO CONTINUALLY BESTOW UPON THE WORLD OUR VITAL MESSAGES.
HEY, BLOSSOM TOP...
WHAT IF WE DON'T WANT A SYMBIOTIC RELATIONSHIP WITH OUR FANS?
I MEAN, IT KINDA SOUNDS LIKE MIND CONTROL TO ME.
AHH, RED...
IS IT ANY WORSE THAN THE "LIGHTNING" YOU GAVE TO THE TWO LOVELY FOURTEEN-YEAR-OLD NUBILES LAST NIGHT?
DID IT NOT MAKE THEM ALL THE MORE WELCOMING TO YOU AND YOUR LIBIDINOUS OFFERINGS?
BUT INSTEAD OF THREE BECOMING ONE, IT COULD BE HUNDREDS... THOUSANDS...
THIS WONDERFUL PANACEA...
THINK OF IT AS A NEW APPROACH TO BEING OF A SINGLE MIND WITH YOUR DEVOTEES...

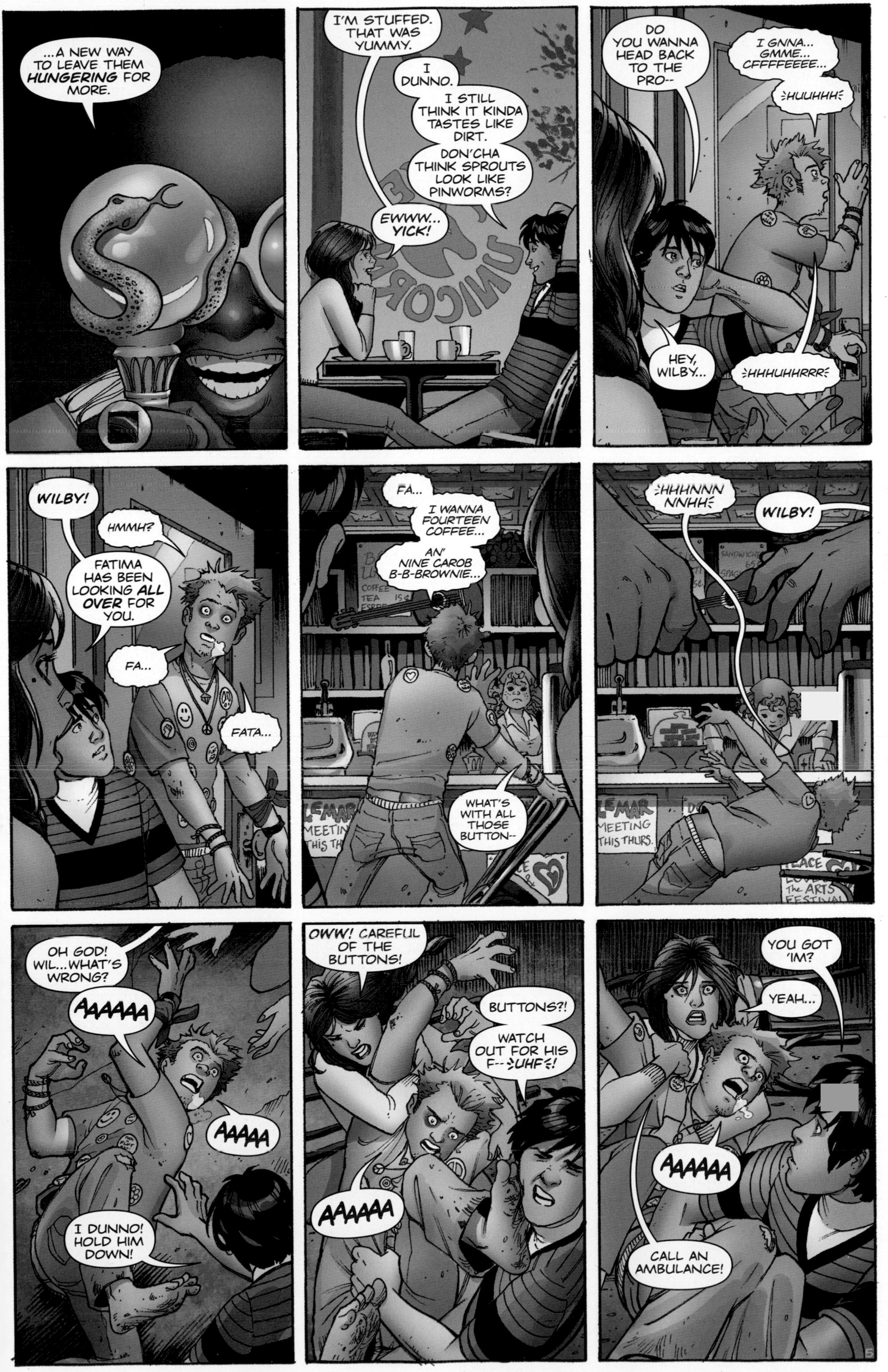
...A NEW WAY TO LEAVE THEM HUNGERING FOR MORE.
I'M STUFFED. THAT WAS YUMMY.
I DUNNO.
I STILL THINK IT KINDA TASTES LIKE DIRT.
DON'CHA THINK SPROUTS LOOK LIKE PINWORMS?
EWWW... YICK!
DO YOU WANNA HEAD BACK TO THE PRO--
I GNNA... GMME... CFFFFEEEE...
HUUHHH
HEY, WILBY...
HHHUHHRRR
WILBY!
HMMH?
FATIMA HAS BEEN LOOKING ALL OVER FOR YOU.
FA...
FATA...
FA...
I WANNA FOURTEEN COFFEE...
AN' NINE CAROB B-B-BROWNIE...
WHAT'S WITH ALL THOSE BUTTON--
HHHNNN NNHH
WILBY!
OH GOD! WIL...WHAT'S WRONG?
AAAAAA
AAAAA
I DUNNO! HOLD HIM DOWN!
OWW! CAREFUL OF THE BUTTONS!
BUTTONS?!
WATCH OUT FOR HIS F-- UHF!
AAAAAA
YOU GOT 'IM?
YEAH...
AAAAAA
CALL AN AMBULANCE!

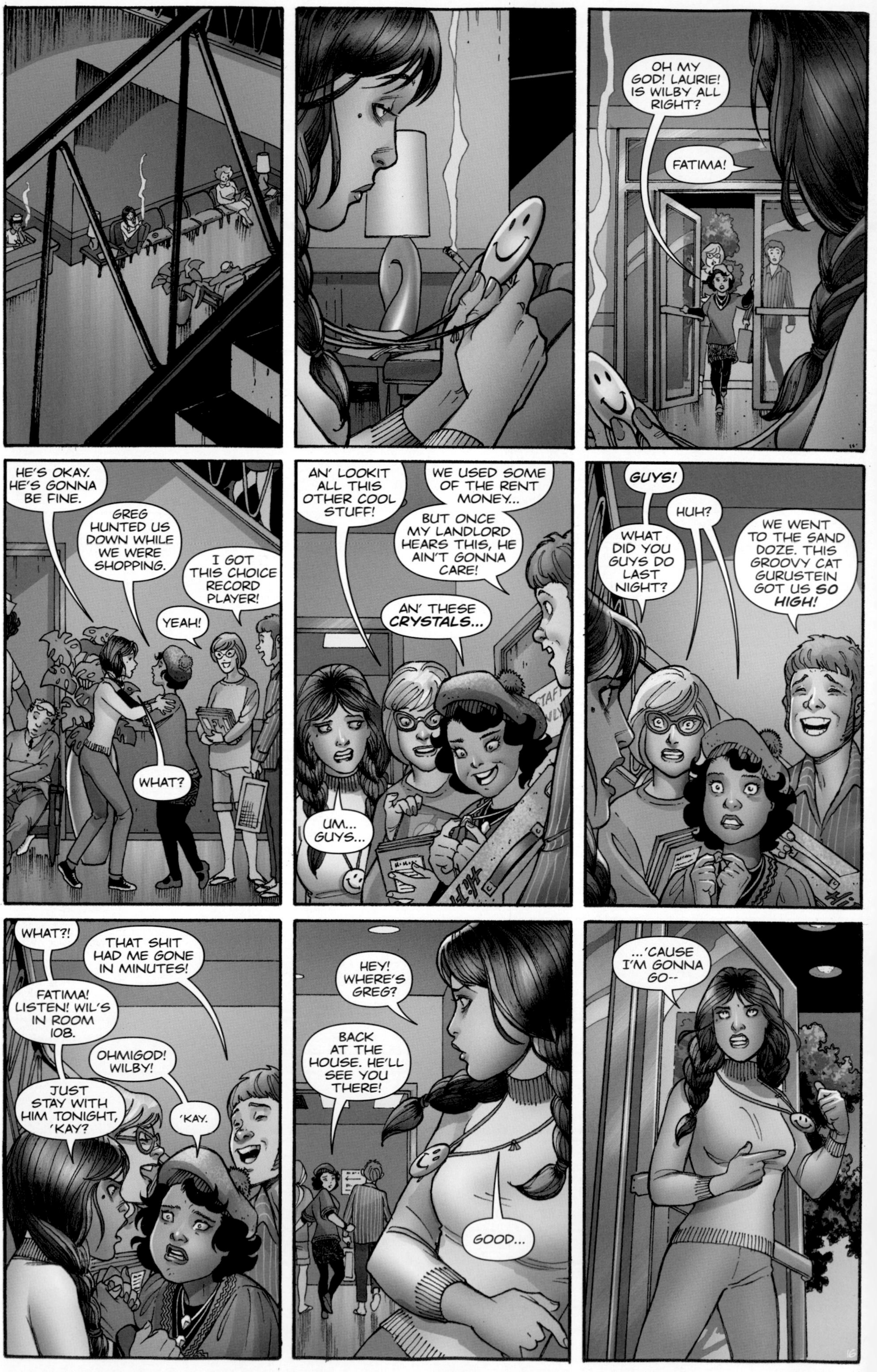
OH MY GOD! LAURIE! IS WILBY ALL RIGHT?
FATIMA!
HE'S OKAY. HE'S GONNA BE FINE.
GREG HUNTED US DOWN WHILE WE WERE SHOPPING.
I GOT THIS CHOICE RECORD PLAYER!
YEAH!
WHAT?
AN' LOOKIT ALL THIS OTHER COOL STUFF!
WE USED SOME OF THE RENT MONEY...
BUT ONCE MY LANDLORD HEARS THIS, HE AIN'T GONNA CARE!
AN' THESE CRYSTALS...
UM... GUYS...
GUYS!
WHAT DID YOU GUYS DO LAST NIGHT?
HUH?
WE WENT TO THE SAND DOZE. THIS GROOVY CAT GURUSTEIN GOT US SO HIGH!
WHAT?!
THAT SHIT HAD ME GONE IN MINUTES!
FATIMA! LISTEN! WIL'S IN ROOM 108.
OHMIGOD! WILBY!
JUST STAY WITH HIM TONIGHT, 'KAY?
'KAY.
HEY! WHERE'S GREG?
BACK AT THE HOUSE. HE'LL SEE YOU THERE!
GOOD...
...'CAUSE I'M GONNA GO--

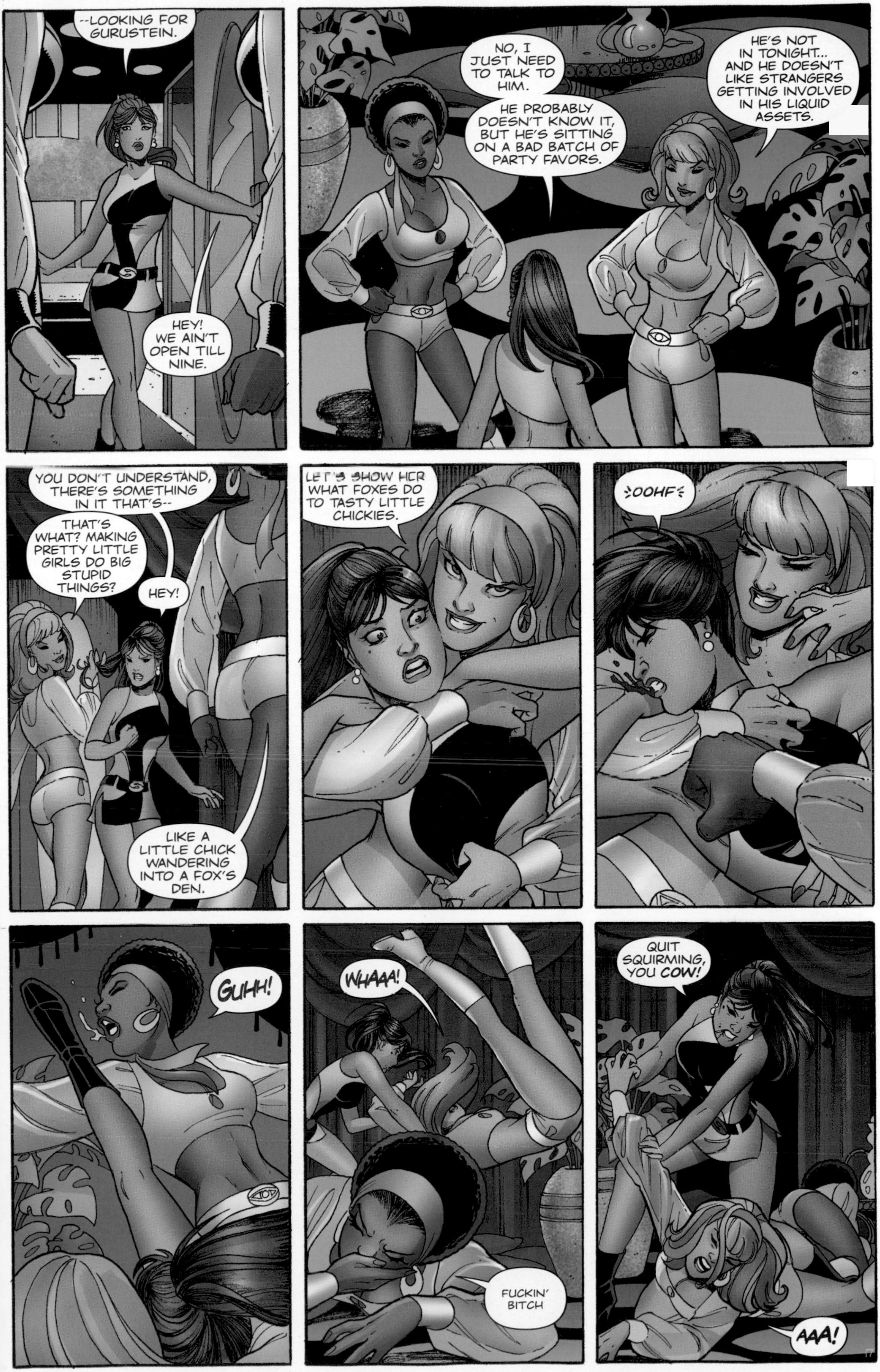
--LOOKING FOR GURUSTEIN.
HEY! WE AIN'T OPEN TILL NINE.
NO, I JUST NEED TO TALK TO HIM.
HE PROBABLY DOESN'T KNOW IT, BUT HE'S SITTING ON A BAD BATCH OF PARTY FAVORS.
HE'S NOT IN TONIGHT... AND HE DOESN'T LIKE STRANGERS GETTING INVOLVED IN HIS LIQUID ASSETS.
YOU DON'T UNDERSTAND, THERE'S SOMETHING IN IT THAT'S--
THAT'S WHAT? MAKING PRETTY LITTLE GIRLS DO BIG STUPID THINGS?
HEY!
LIKE A LITTLE CHICK WANDERING INTO A FOX'S DEN.
LET'S SHOW HER WHAT FOXES DO TO TASTY LITTLE CHICKIES.
OOHF
GUHH!
WHAAA!
FUCKIN' BITCH
QUIT SQUIRMING, YOU COW!
AAA!

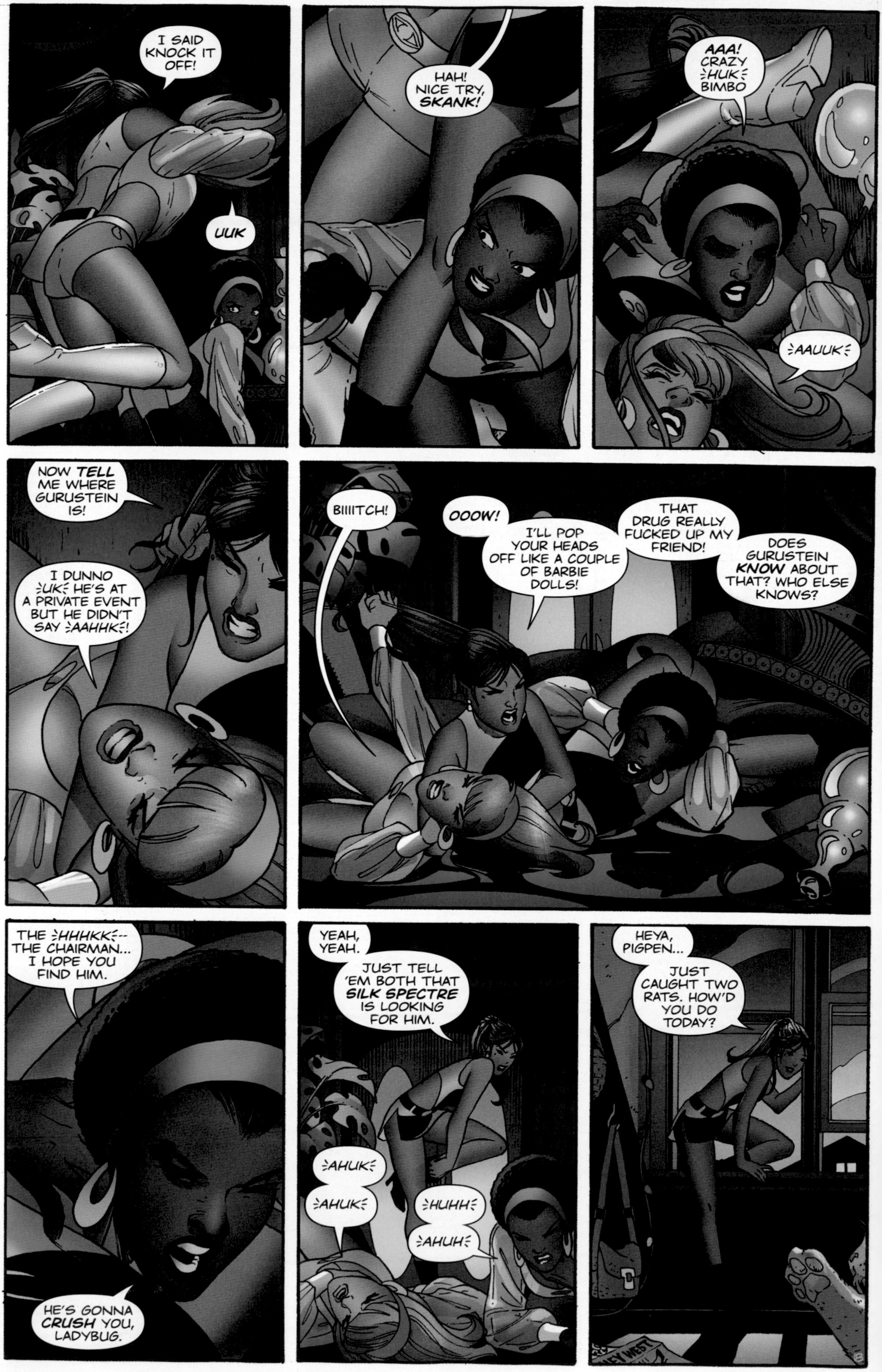

I SAID KNOCK IT OFF!
UUK
HAH! NICE TRY, SKANK!
AAA! CRAZY HUK BIMBO
AAUUK
NOW TELL ME WHERE GURUSTEIN IS!
I DUNNO UK HE'S AT A PRIVATE EVENT BUT HE DIDN'T SAY AAHHK!
BIIIITCH!
OOOW!
I'LL POP YOUR HEADS OFF LIKE A COUPLE OF BARBIE DOLLS!
THAT DRUG REALLY FUCKED UP MY FRIEND!
DOES GURUSTEIN KNOW ABOUT THAT? WHO ELSE KNOWS?
THE HHHKK-- THE CHAIRMAN... I HOPE YOU FIND HIM.
HE'S GONNA CRUSH YOU, LADYBUG.
YEAH, YEAH.
JUST TELL 'EM BOTH THAT SILK SPECTRE IS LOOKING FOR HIM.
AHUK
AHUK
HUHH
AHUH
HEYA, PIGPEN...
JUST CAUGHT TWO RATS. HOW'D YOU DO TODAY?

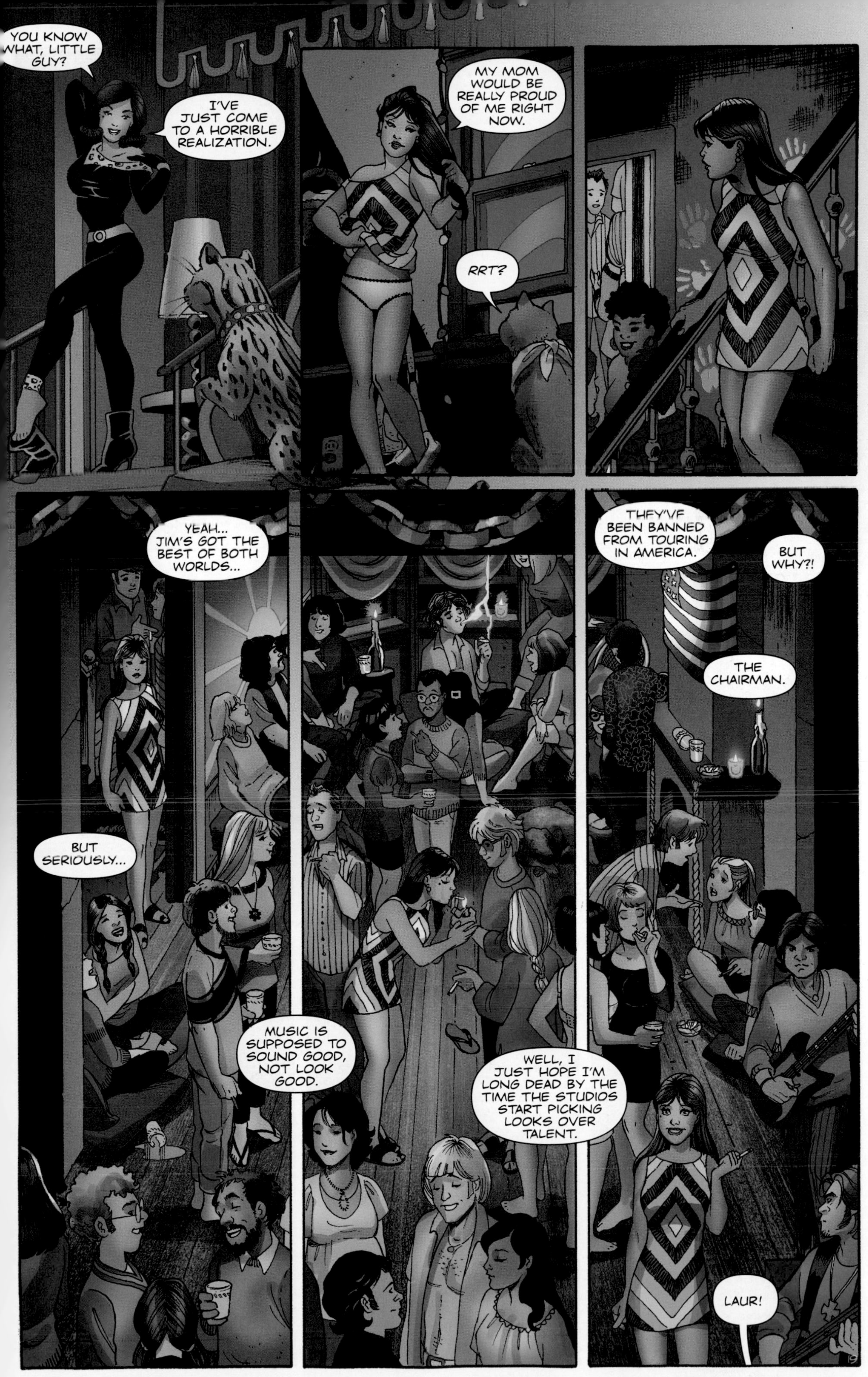
YOU KNOW WHAT, LITTLE GUY?
I'VE JUST COME TO A HORRIBLE REALIZATION.
MY MOM WOULD BE REALLY PROUD OF ME RIGHT NOW.
RRT?
YEAH... JIM'S GOT THE BEST OF BOTH WORLDS...
BUT SERIOUSLY...
MUSIC IS SUPPOSED TO SOUND GOOD, NOT LOOK GOOD.
WELL, I JUST HOPE I'M LONG DEAD BY THE TIME THE STUDIOS START PICKING LOOKS OVER TALENT.
THFY'VF BEEN BANNED FROM TOURING IN AMERICA.
BUT WHY?!
THE CHAIRMAN.
LAUR!

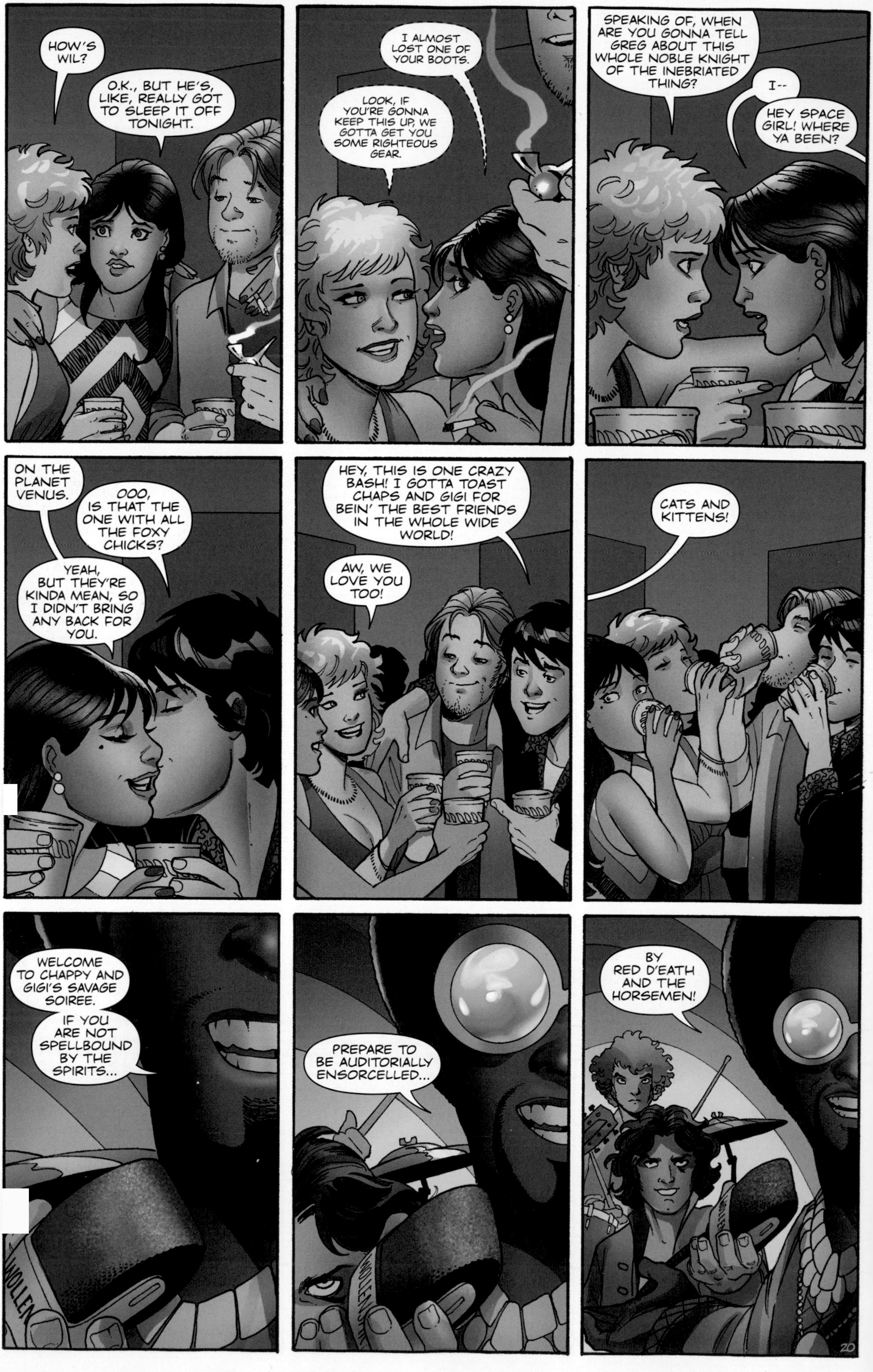
HOW'S WIL?
O.K., BUT HE'S, LIKE, REALLY GOT TO SLEEP IT OFF TONIGHT.
I ALMOST LOST ONE OF YOUR BOOTS.
LOOK, IF YOU'RE GONNA KEEP THIS UP, WE GOTTA GET YOU SOME RIGHTEOUS GEAR.
SPEAKING OF, WHEN ARE YOU GONNA TELL GREG ABOUT THIS WHOLE NOBLE KNIGHT OF THE INEBRIATED THING?
I--
HEY SPACE GIRL! WHERE YA BEEN?
ON THE PLANET VENUS.
OOO, IS THAT THE ONE WITH ALL THE FOXY CHICKS?
YEAH, BUT THEY'RE KINDA MEAN, SO I DIDN'T BRING ANY BACK FOR YOU.
HEY, THIS IS ONE CRAZY BASH! I GOTTA TOAST CHAPS AND GIGI FOR BEIN' THE BEST FRIENDS IN THE WHOLE WIDE WORLD!
AW, WE LOVE YOU TOO!
CATS AND KITTENS!
WELCOME TO CHAPPY AND GIGI'S SAVAGE SOIREE.
IF YOU ARE NOT SPELLBOUND BY THE SPIRITS...
WOLLEN
PREPARE TO BE AUDITORIALLY ENSORCELLED...
WOLLEN
BY RED D'EATH AND THE HORSEMEN!

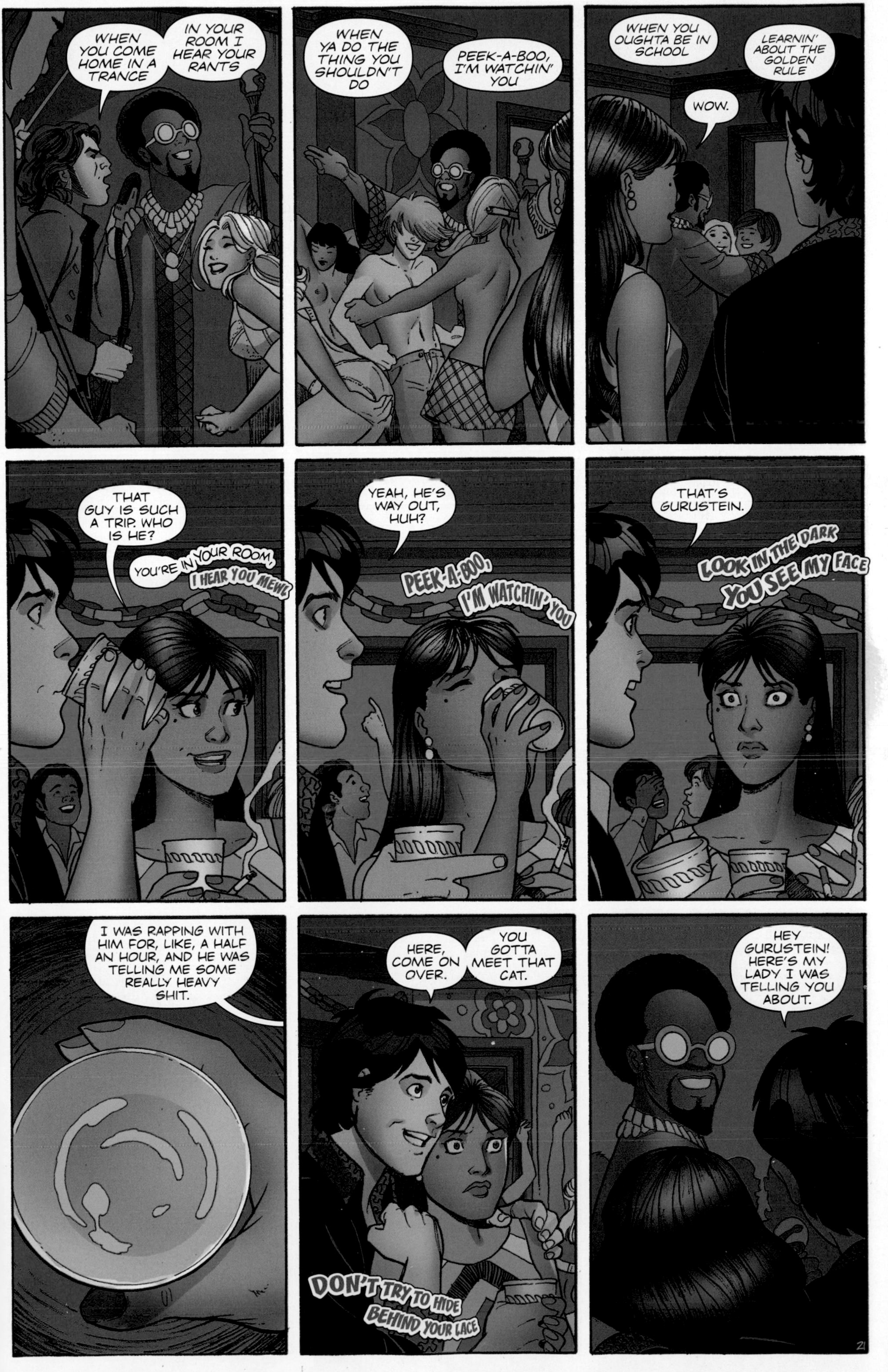
WHEN YOU COME HOME IN A TRANCE
IN YOUR ROOM I HEAR YOUR RANTS
WHEN YA DO THE THING YOU SHOULDN'T DO
PEEK-A-BOO, I'M WATCHIN' YOU
WHEN YOU OUGHTA BE IN SCHOOL
LEARNIN' ABOUT THE GOLDEN RULE
WOW.
THAT GUY IS SUCH A TRIP. WHO IS HE?
YOU'RE IN YOUR ROOM, I HEAR YOU MEWL
YEAH, HE'S WAY OUT, HUH?
PEEK-A-BOO, I'M WATCHIN' YOU
THAT'S GURUSTEIN.
LOOK IN THE DARK YOU SEE MY FACE
I WAS RAPPING WITH HIM FOR, LIKE, A HALF AN HOUR, AND HE WAS TELLING ME SOME REALLY HEAVY SHIT.
HERE, COME ON OVER.
YOU GOTTA MEET THAT CAT.
DON'T TRY TO HIDE BEHIND YOUR LACE
HEY GURUSTEIN! HERE'S MY LADY I WAS TELLING YOU ABOUT.

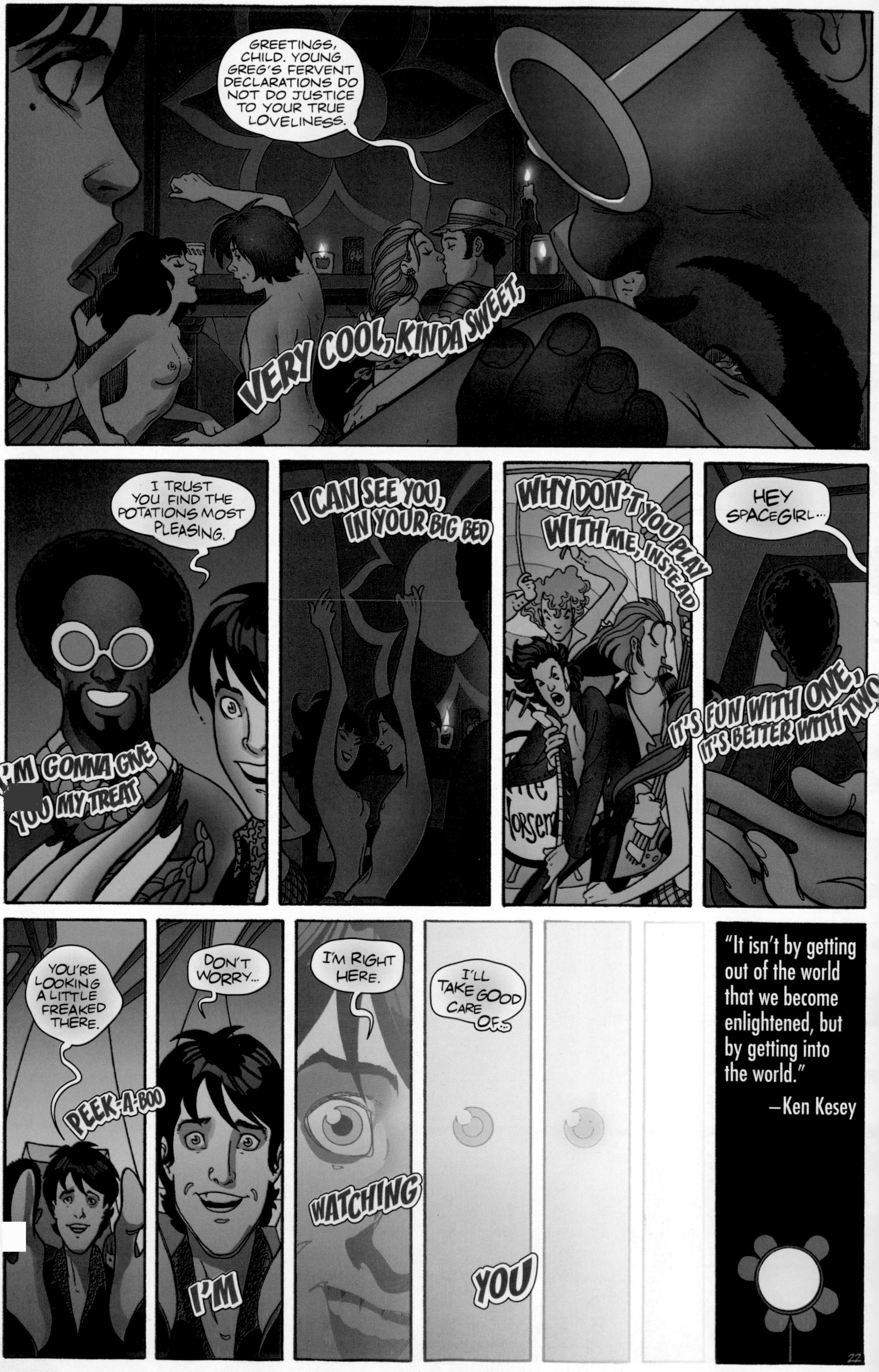
GREETINGS, CHILD. YOUNG GREG'S FERVENT DECLARATIONS DO NOT DO JUSTICE TO YOUR TRUE LOVELINESS.
VERY COOL, KINDA SWEET,
I TRUST YOU FIND THE POTATIONS MOST PLEASING.
I'M GONNA GIVE YOU MY TREAT
I CAN SEE YOU, IN YOUR BIG BED
WHY DON'T YOU PLAY WITH ME, INSTEAD
HEY SPACEGIRL...
IT'S FUN WITH ONE, IT'S BETTER WITH TWO
YOU'RE LOOKING A LITTLE FREAKED THERE.
PEEK-A-BOO
DON'T WORRY...
I'M
I'M RIGHT HERE.
WATCHING
I'LL TAKE GOOD CARE OF...
YOU
"It isn't by getting out of the world that we become enlightened, but by getting into the world."
—Ken Kesey

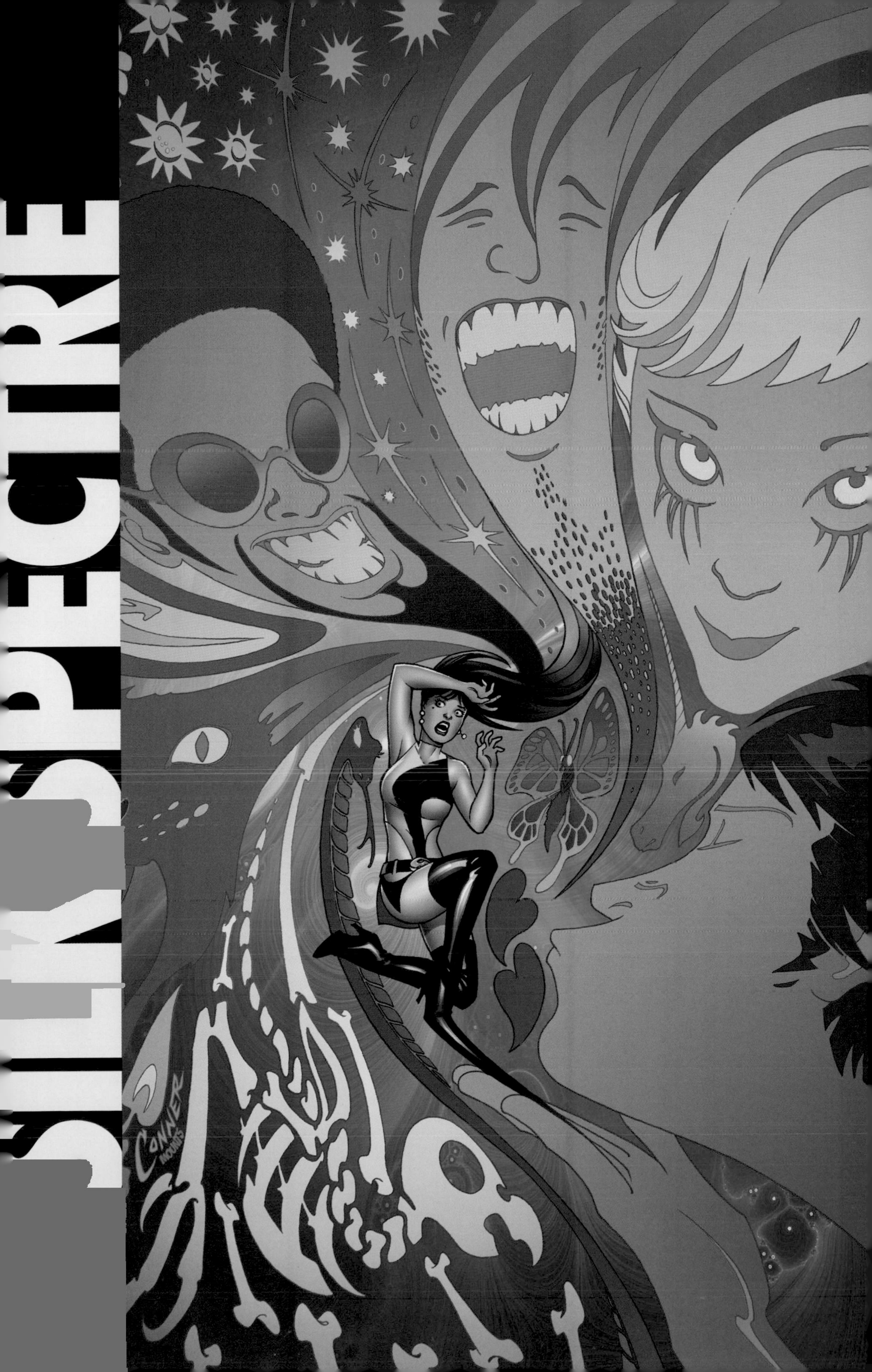
SILK SPECTRE

SILK SPECTRE

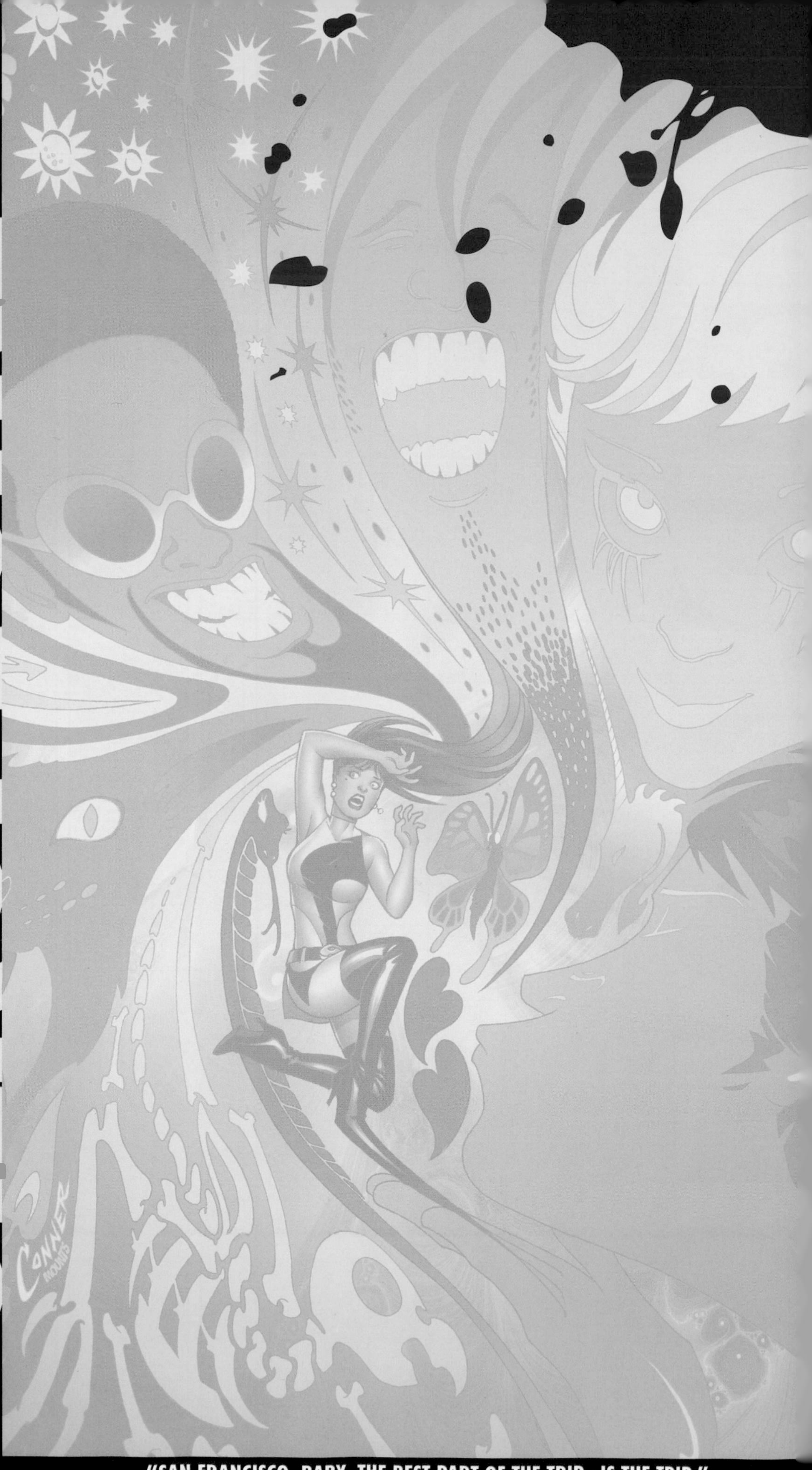

"SAN FRANCISCO, BABY. THE BEST PART OF THE TRIP...IS THE TRIP."

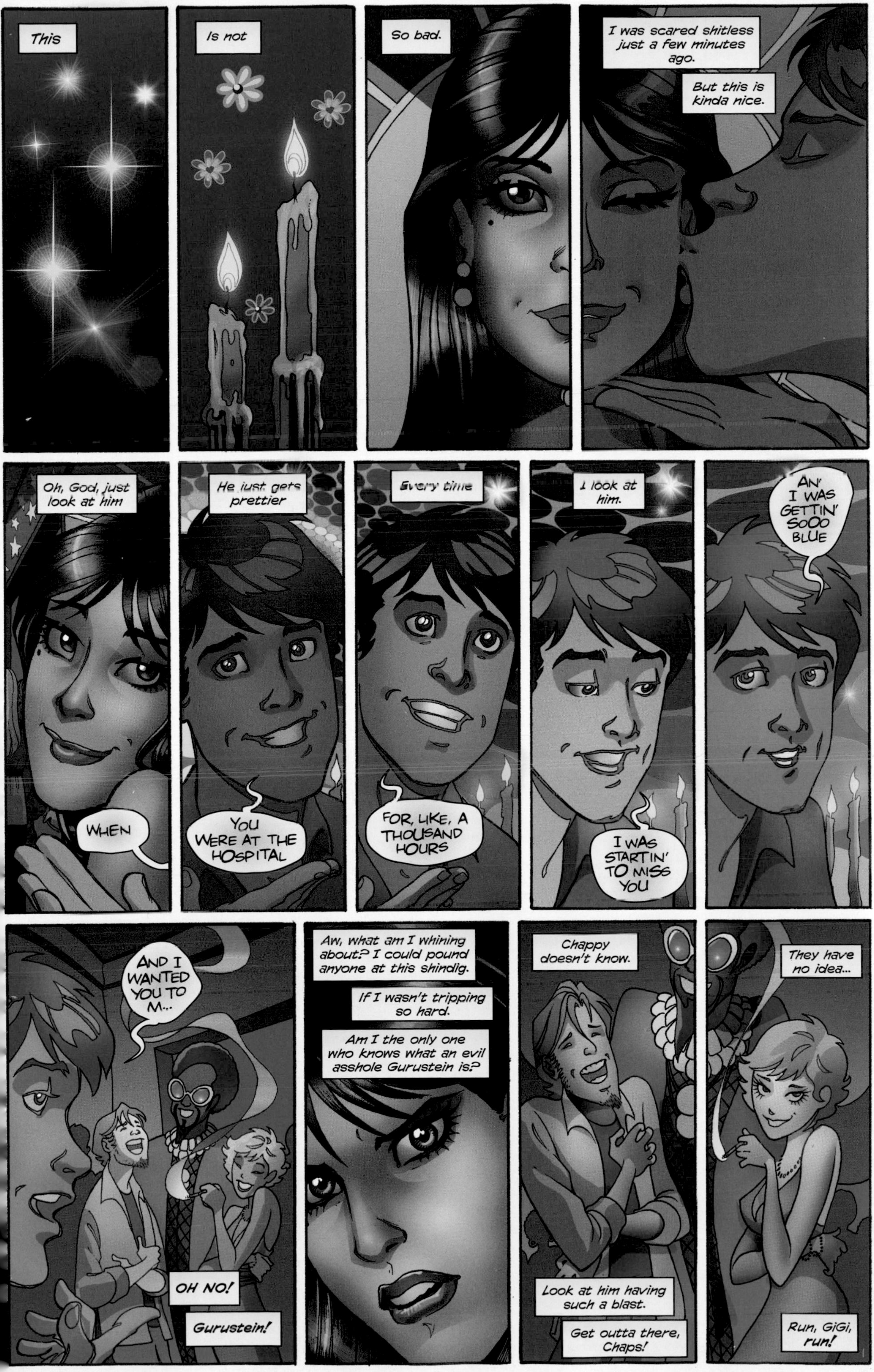
This
Is not
So bad.
I was scared shitless just a few minutes ago.
But this is kinda nice.
Oh, God, just look at him
WHEN
He just gets prettier
YOU WERE AT THE HOSPITAL
Every time
FOR, LIKE, A THOUSAND HOURS
I look at him.
I WAS STARTIN' TO MISS YOU
AN' I WAS GETTIN' SoOO BLUE
AND I WANTED YOU TO M...
OH NO!
Gurustein!
Aw, what am I whining about? I could pound anyone at this shindig.
If I wasn't tripping so hard.
Am I the only one who knows what an evil asshole Gurustein is?
Chappy doesn't know.
Look at him having such a blast.
Get outta there, Chaps!
They have no idea...
Run, GiGi, run!

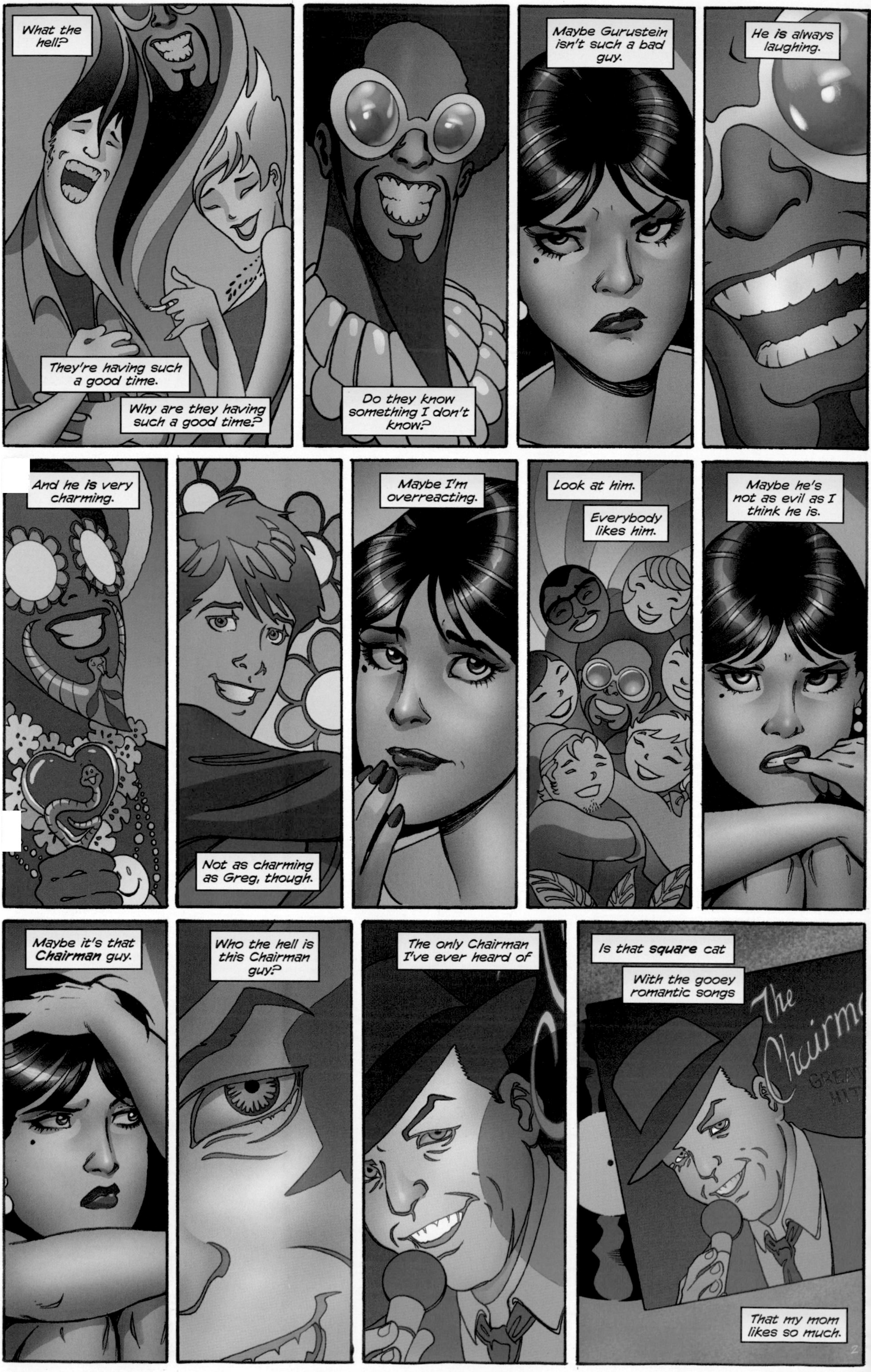
What the hell?
They're having such a good time.
Why are they having such a good time?
Do they know something I don't know?
Maybe Gurustein isn't such a bad guy.
He is always laughing.
And he is very charming.
Not as charming as Greg, though.
Maybe I'm overreacting.
Look at him.
Everybody likes him.
Maybe he's not as evil as I think he is.
Maybe it's that Chairman guy.
Who the hell is this Chairman guy?
The only Chairman I've ever heard of
Is that square cat
With the gooey romantic songs
The Chairm
GREAT HIT
That my mom likes so much.

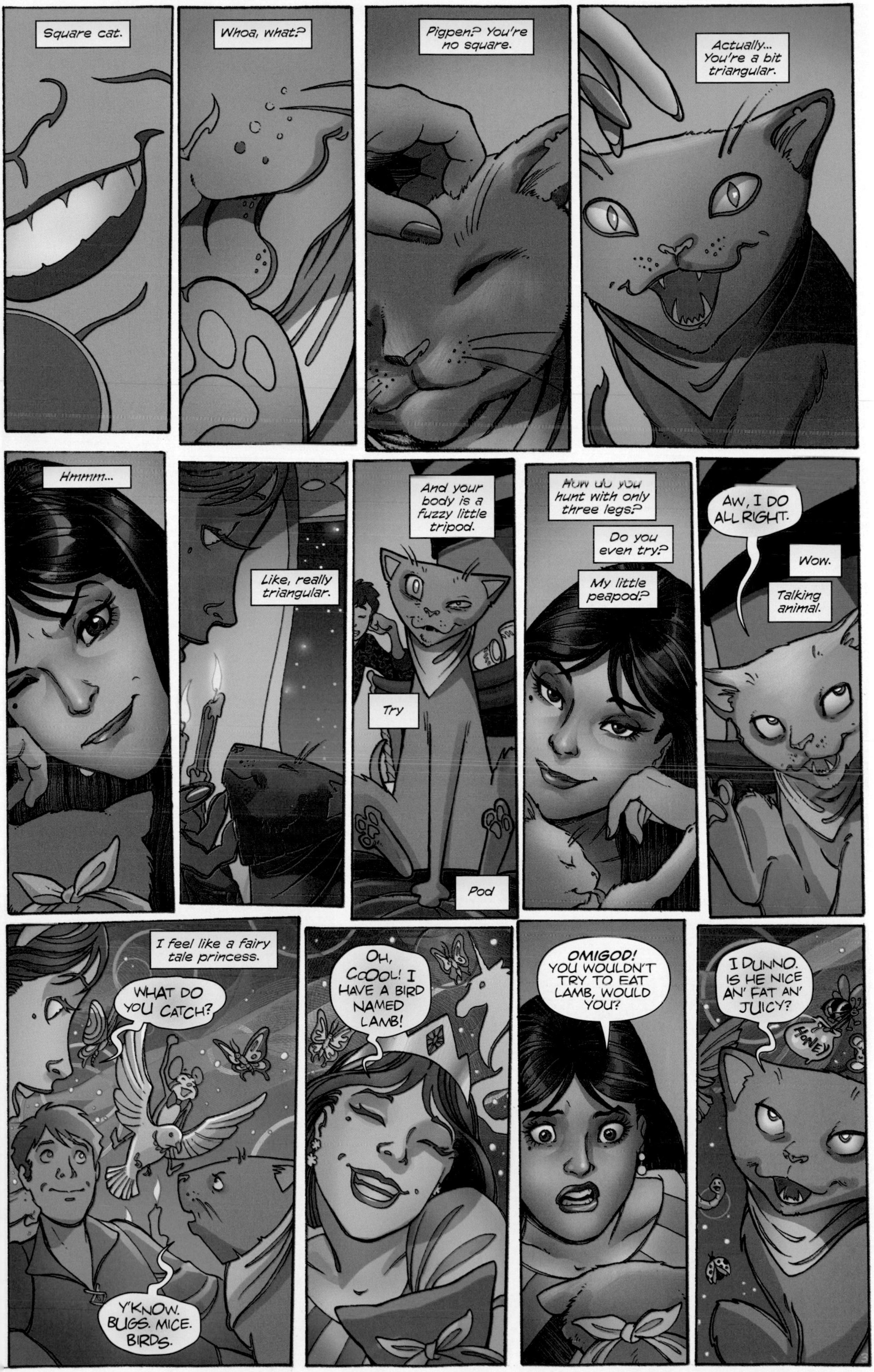
Square cat.
Whoa, what?
Pigpen? You're no square.
Actually... You're a bit triangular.
Hmmm...
Like, really triangular.
And your body is a fuzzy little tripod.
Try
Pod
How do you hunt with only three legs?
Do you even try?
My little peapod?
AW, I DO ALL RIGHT.
Wow.
Talking animal.
I feel like a fairy tale princess.
WHAT DO YOU CATCH?
Y'KNOW. BUGS. MICE. BIRDS.
OH, COOOL! I HAVE A BIRD NAMED LAMB!
OMIGOD! YOU WOULDN'T TRY TO EAT LAMB, WOULD YOU?
I DUNNO. IS HE NICE AN' FAT AN' JUICY?
HONEY

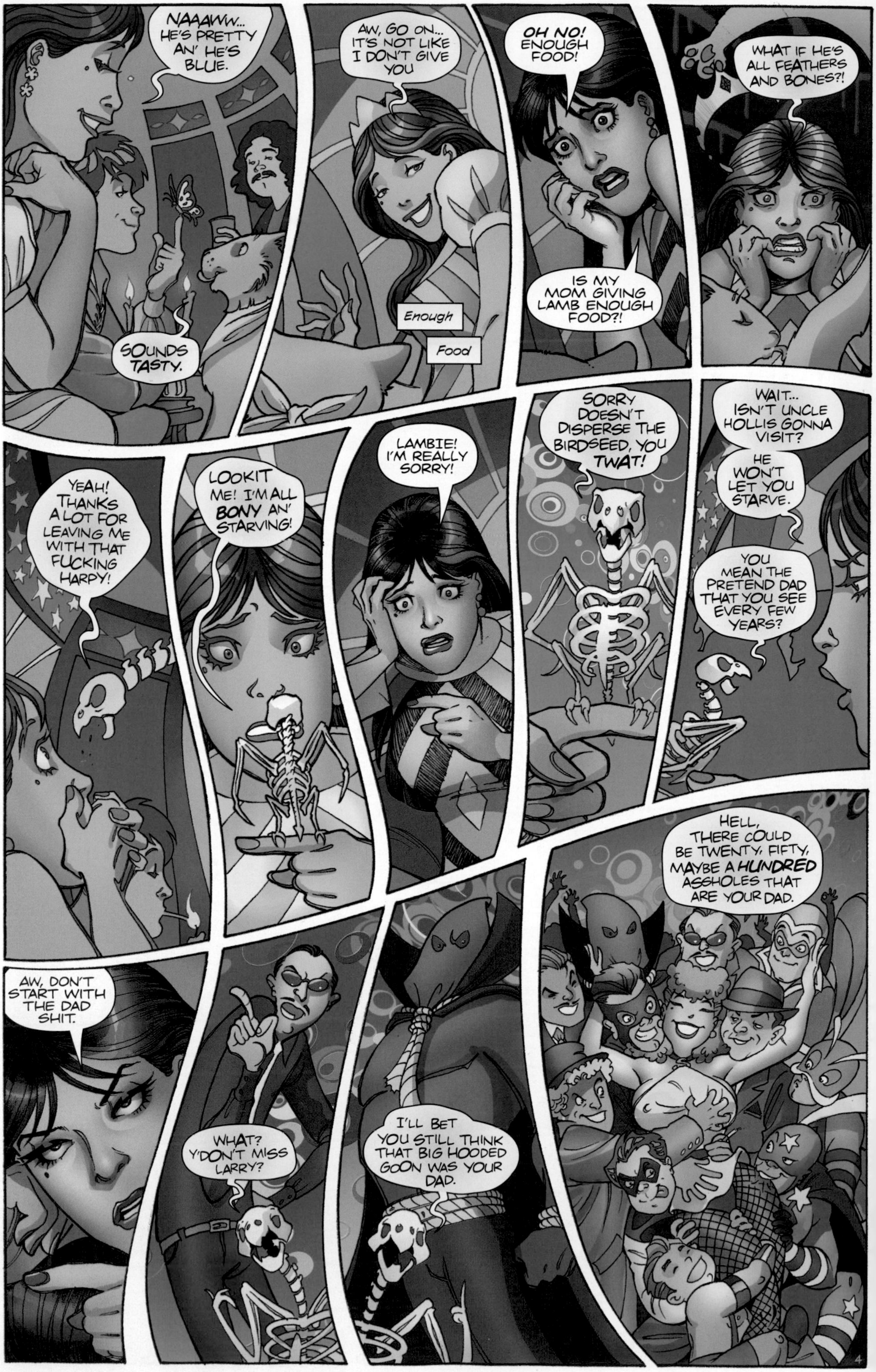
NAAAWW... HE'S PRETTY AN' HE'S BLUE.
SOUNDS TASTY.
AW, GO ON... IT'S NOT LIKE I DON'T GIVE YOU
Enough
Food
OH NO! ENOUGH FOOD!
IS MY MOM GIVING LAMB ENOUGH FOOD?!
WHAT IF HE'S ALL FEATHERS AND BONES?!
YEAH! THANKS A LOT FOR LEAVING ME WITH THAT FUCKING HARPY!
LOOKIT ME! I'M ALL BONY AN' STARVING!
LAMBIE! I'M REALLY SORRY!
SORRY DOESN'T DISPERSE THE BIRDSEED, YOU TWAT!
WAIT... ISN'T UNCLE HOLLIS GONNA VISIT?
HE WON'T LET YOU STARVE.
YOU MEAN THE PRETEND DAD THAT YOU SEE EVERY FEW YEARS?
AW, DON'T START WITH THE DAD SHIT.
WHAT? Y'DON'T MISS LARRY?
I'LL BET YOU STILL THINK THAT BIG HOODED GOON WAS YOUR DAD.
HELL, THERE COULD BE TWENTY, FIFTY, MAYBE A HUNDRED ASSHOLES THAT ARE YOUR DAD.

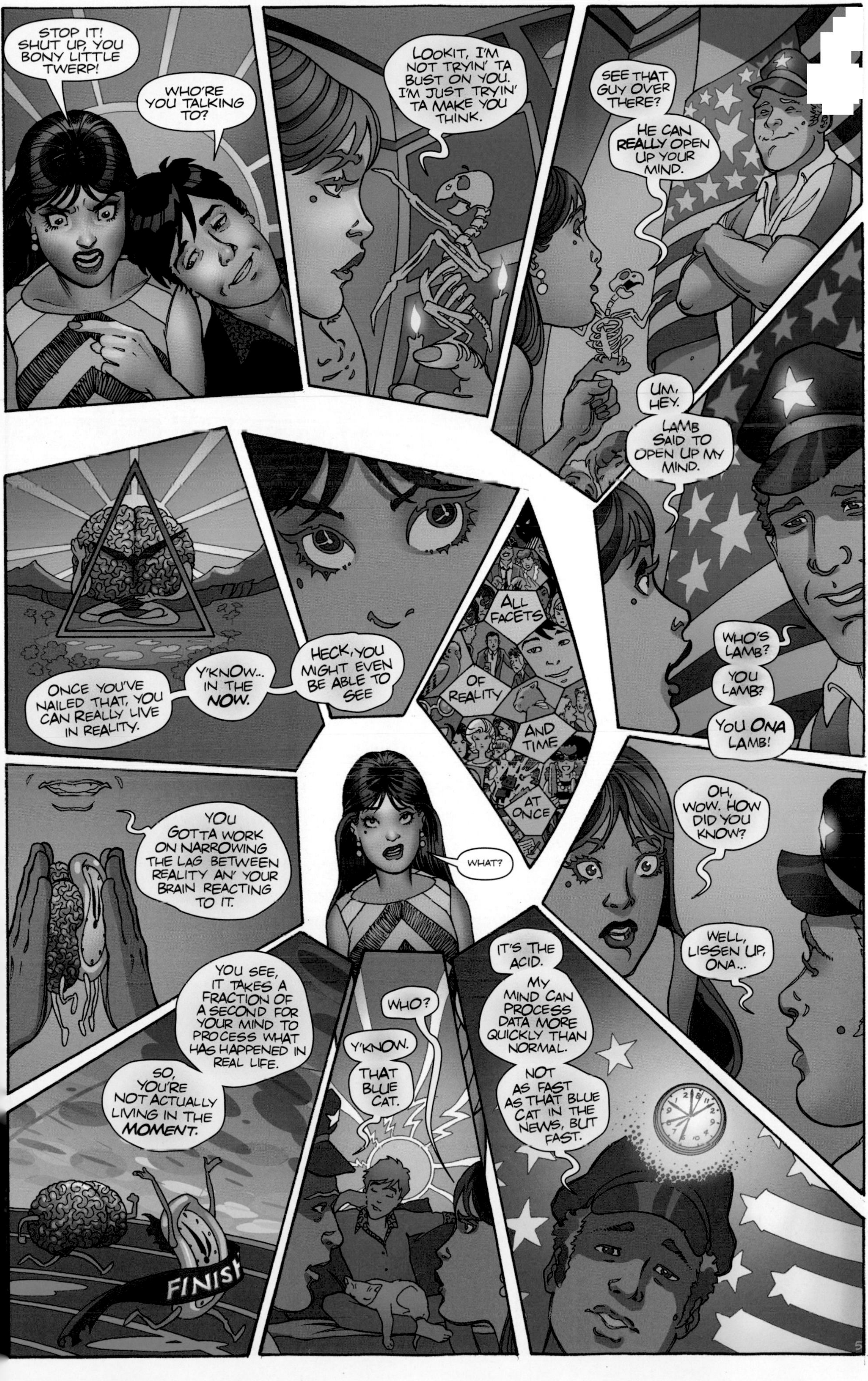
STOP IT! SHUT UP, YOU BONY LITTLE TWERP!
WHO'RE YOU TALKING TO?
LOOKIT, I'M NOT TRYIN' TA BUST ON YOU. I'M JUST TRYIN' TA MAKE YOU THINK.
SEE THAT GUY OVER THERE?
HE CAN REALLY OPEN UP YOUR MIND.
UM, HEY.
LAMB SAID TO OPEN UP MY MIND.
WHO'S LAMB?
YOU LAMB?
YOU ONA LAMB!
ONCE YOU'VE NAILED THAT, YOU CAN REALLY LIVE IN REALITY.
Y'KNOW... IN THE NOW.
HECK, YOU MIGHT EVEN BE ABLE TO SEE
ALL FACETS
OF REALITY
AND TIME
AT ONCE
OH, WOW. HOW DID YOU KNOW?
YOU GOTTA WORK ON NARROWING THE LAG BETWEEN REALITY AN' YOUR BRAIN REACTING TO IT.
WHAT?
WELL, LISSEN UP, ONA...
YOU SEE, IT TAKES A FRACTION OF A SECOND FOR YOUR MIND TO PROCESS WHAT HAS HAPPENED IN REAL LIFE.
SO, YOU'RE NOT ACTUALLY LIVING IN THE MOMENT.
FINISH
WHO?
Y'KNOW.
THAT BLUE CAT.
IT'S THE ACID.
MY MIND CAN PROCESS DATA MORE QUICKLY THAN NORMAL.
NOT AS FAST AS THAT BLUE CAT IN THE NEWS, BUT FAST.

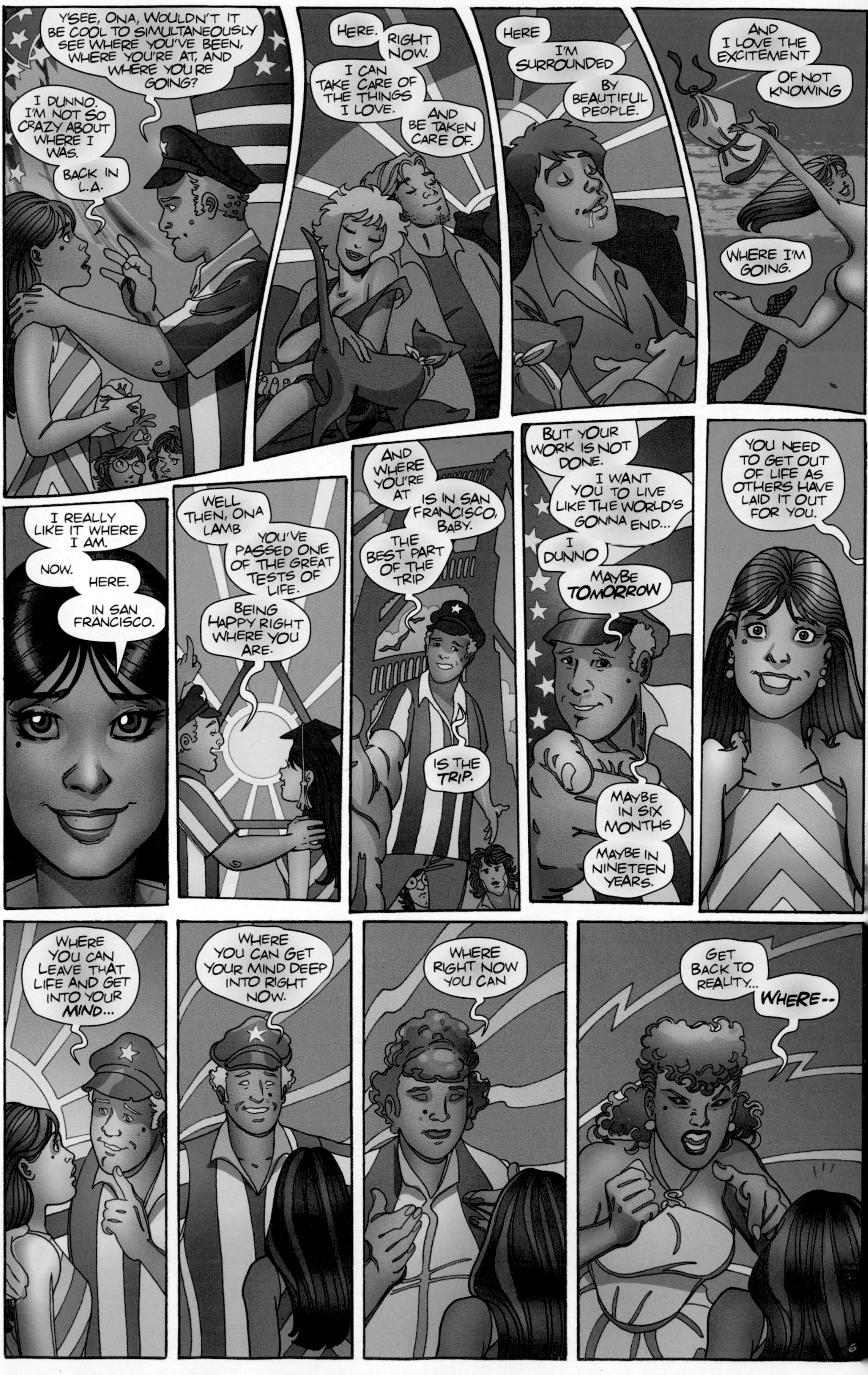
Y'SEE, ONA, WOULDN'T IT BE COOL TO SIMULTANEOUSLY SEE WHERE YOU'VE BEEN, WHERE YOU'RE AT, AND WHERE YOU'RE GOING?
I DUNNO. I'M NOT SO CRAZY ABOUT WHERE I WAS.
BACK IN L.A.
HERE.
RIGHT NOW.
I CAN TAKE CARE OF THE THINGS I LOVE.
AND BE TAKEN CARE OF.
HERE
I'M SURROUNDED
BY BEAUTIFUL PEOPLE.
AND I LOVE THE EXCITEMENT
OF NOT KNOWING
WHERE I'M GOING.
I REALLY LIKE IT WHERE I AM.
NOW.
HERE.
IN SAN FRANCISCO.
WELL THEN, ONA LAMB
YOU'VE PASSED ONE OF THE GREAT TESTS OF LIFE.
BEING HAPPY RIGHT WHERE YOU ARE.
AND WHERE YOU'RE AT
IS IN SAN FRANCISCO, BABY.
THE BEST PART OF THE TRIP
IS THE TRIP.
BUT YOUR WORK IS NOT DONE.
I WANT YOU TO LIVE LIKE THE WORLD'S GONNA END...
I DUNNO
MAYBE TOMORROW
MAYBE IN SIX MONTHS
MAYBE IN NINETEEN YEARS.
YOU NEED TO GET OUT OF LIFE AS OTHERS HAVE LAID IT OUT FOR YOU.
WHERE YOU CAN LEAVE THAT LIFE AND GET INTO YOUR MIND...
WHERE YOU CAN GET YOUR MIND DEEP INTO RIGHT NOW.
WHERE RIGHT NOW YOU CAN
GET BACK TO REALITY... WHERE--

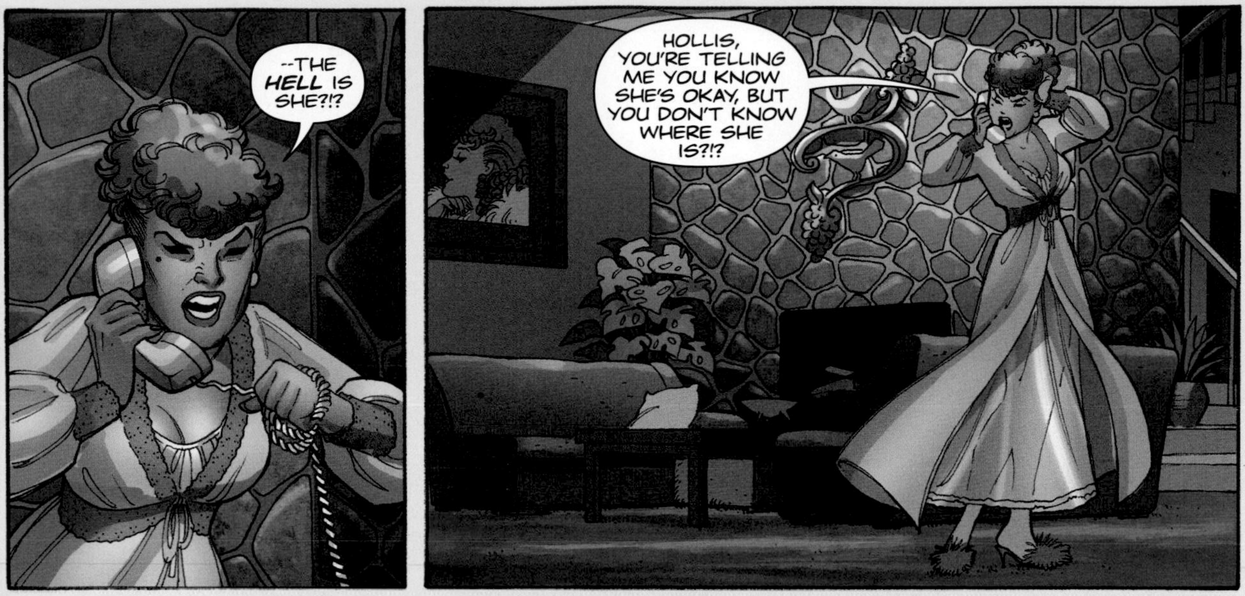
--THE HELL IS SHE?!?
HOLLIS, YOU'RE TELLING ME YOU KNOW SHE'S OKAY, BUT YOU DON'T KNOW WHERE SHE IS?!?

NO ILLUSION

DARWYN COOKE & AMANDA CONNER SCRIPT
AMANDA CONNER ART
PAUL MOUNTS COLORS
CARLOS M. MANGUAL LETTERS

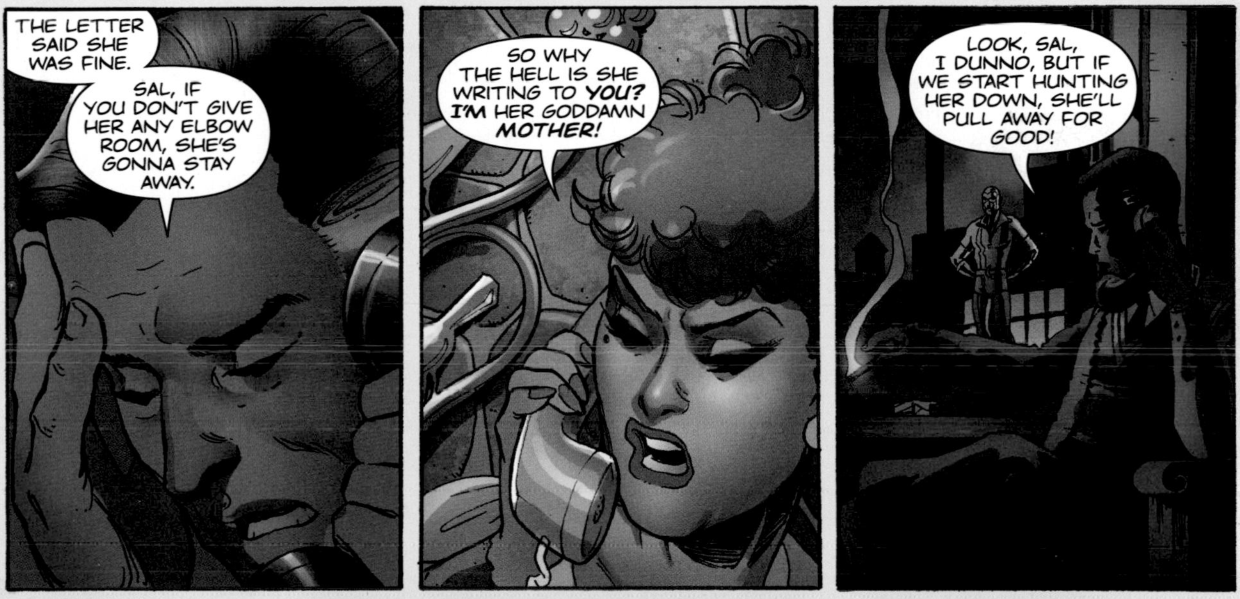
THE LETTER SAID SHE WAS FINE.
SAL, IF YOU DON'T GIVE HER ANY ELBOW ROOM, SHE'S GONNA STAY AWAY.
SO WHY THE HELL IS SHE WRITING TO YOU? I'M HER GODDAMN MOTHER!
LOOK, SAL, I DUNNO, BUT IF WE START HUNTING HER DOWN, SHE'LL PULL AWAY FOR GOOD!

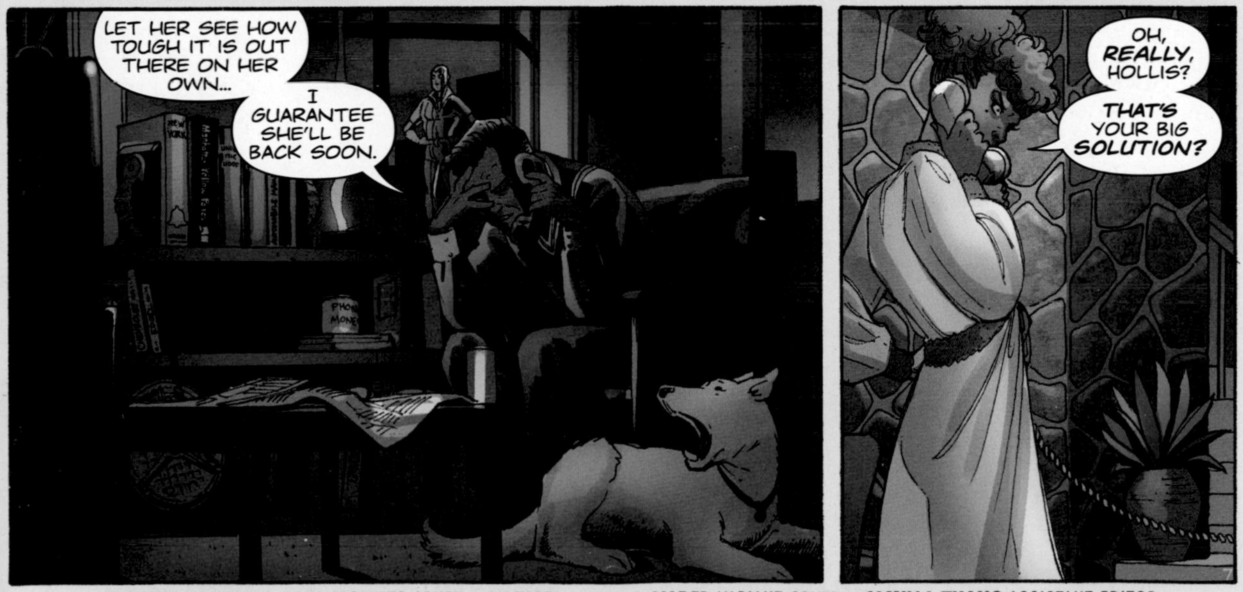
LET HER SEE HOW TOUGH IT IS OUT THERE ON HER OWN...
I GUARANTEE SHE'LL BE BACK SOON.
OH, REALLY, HOLLIS?
THAT'S YOUR BIG SOLUTION?

AMANDA CONNER & PAUL MOUNTS COVER • **MICHAEL & LAURA ALLRED** VARIANT COVER • **CAMILLA ZHANG** ASSISTANT EDITOR
CHRIS CONROY ASSOCIATE EDITOR • **MARK CHIARELLO** EDITOR • **WATCHMEN CREATED BY ALAN MOORE & DAVE GIBBONS**

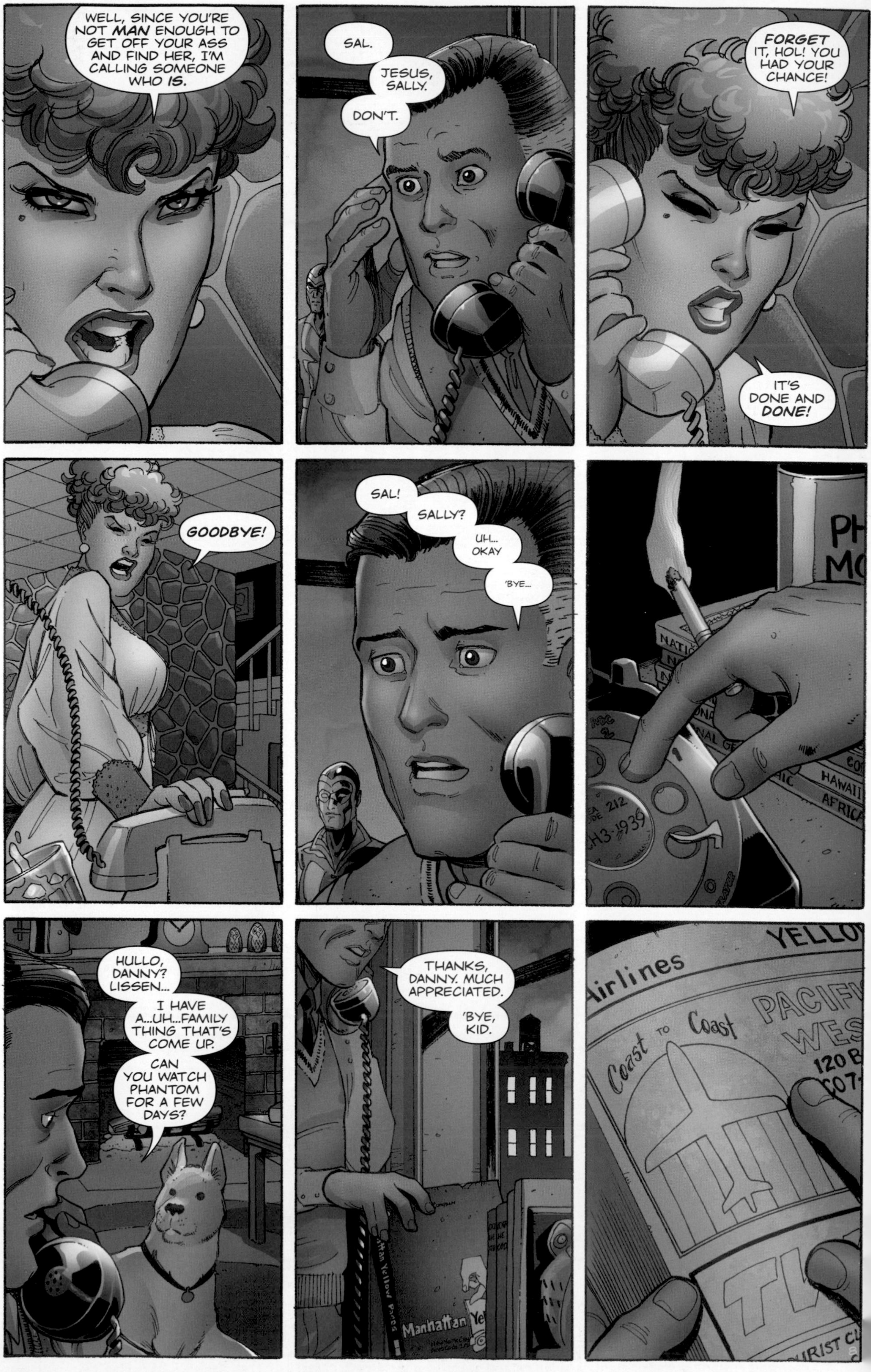

WELL, SINCE YOU'RE NOT **MAN** ENOUGH TO GET OFF YOUR ASS AND FIND HER, I'M CALLING SOMEONE WHO **IS.**
SAL.
JESUS, SALLY.
DON'T.
FORGET IT, HOL! YOU HAD YOUR CHANCE!
IT'S DONE AND **DONE!**
GOODBYE!
SAL!
SALLY?
UH... OKAY
'BYE...
HULLO, DANNY? LISSEN...
I HAVE A...UH...FAMILY THING THAT'S COME UP.
CAN YOU WATCH PHANTOM FOR A FEW DAYS?
THANKS, DANNY. MUCH APPRECIATED.
'BYE, KID.
Airlines
Coast to Coast
Manhattan Yellow Pages

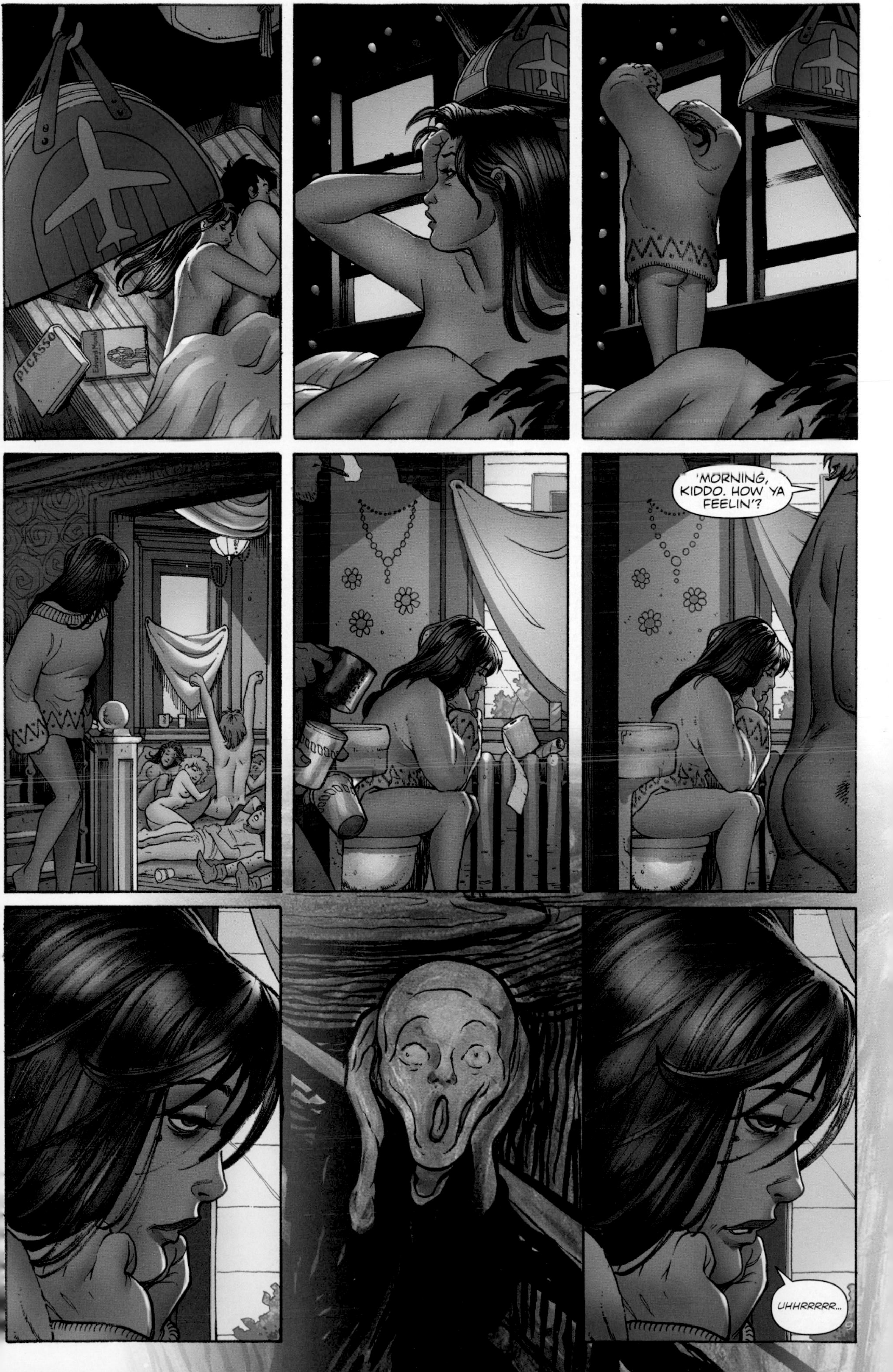
PICASSO
'MORNING, KIDDO. HOW YA FEELIN'?
UHHRRRRR...

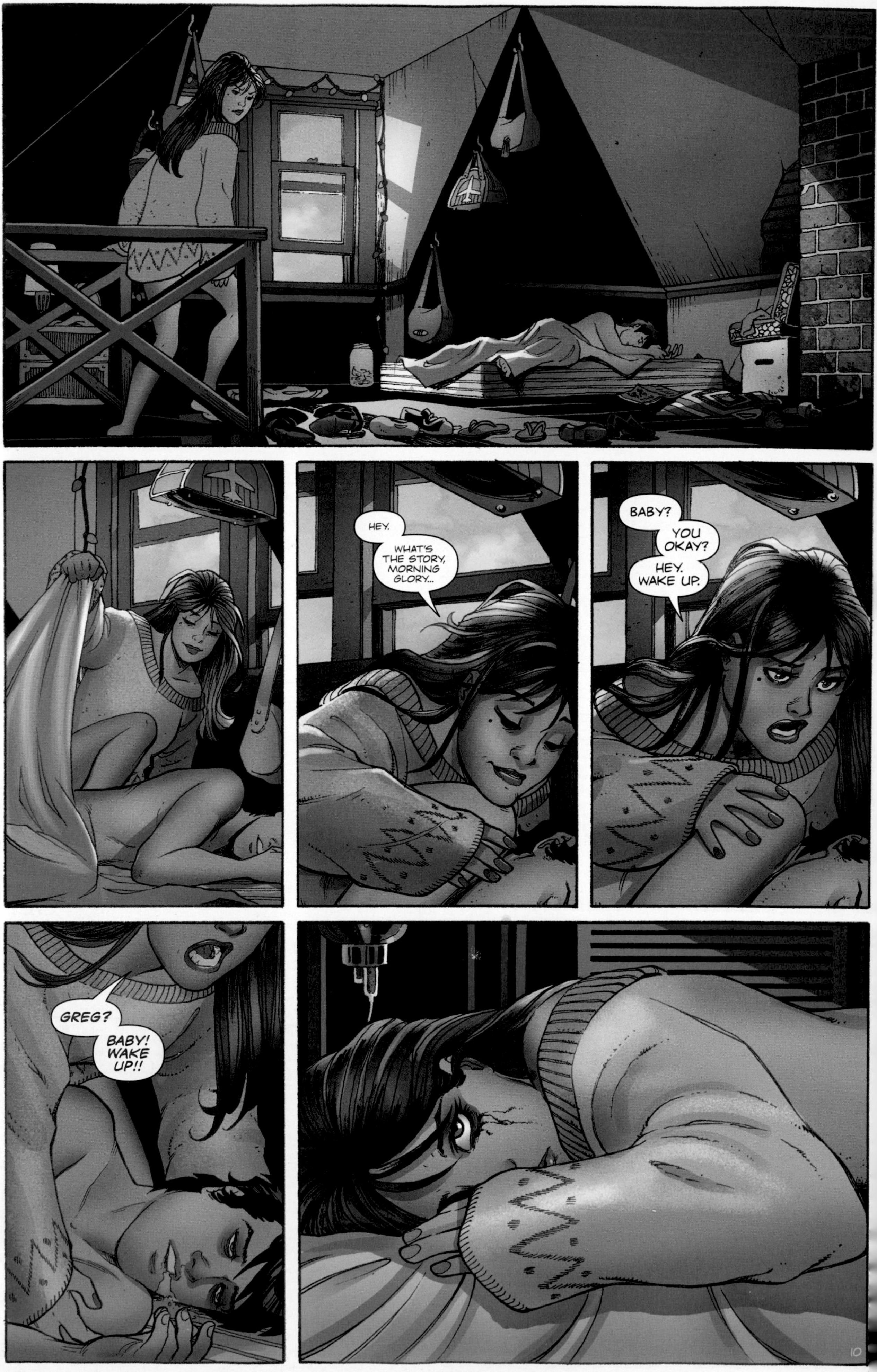
HEY.
WHAT'S THE STORY, MORNING GLORY...
BABY?
YOU OKAY?
HEY. WAKE UP.
GREG?
BABY! WAKE UP!!

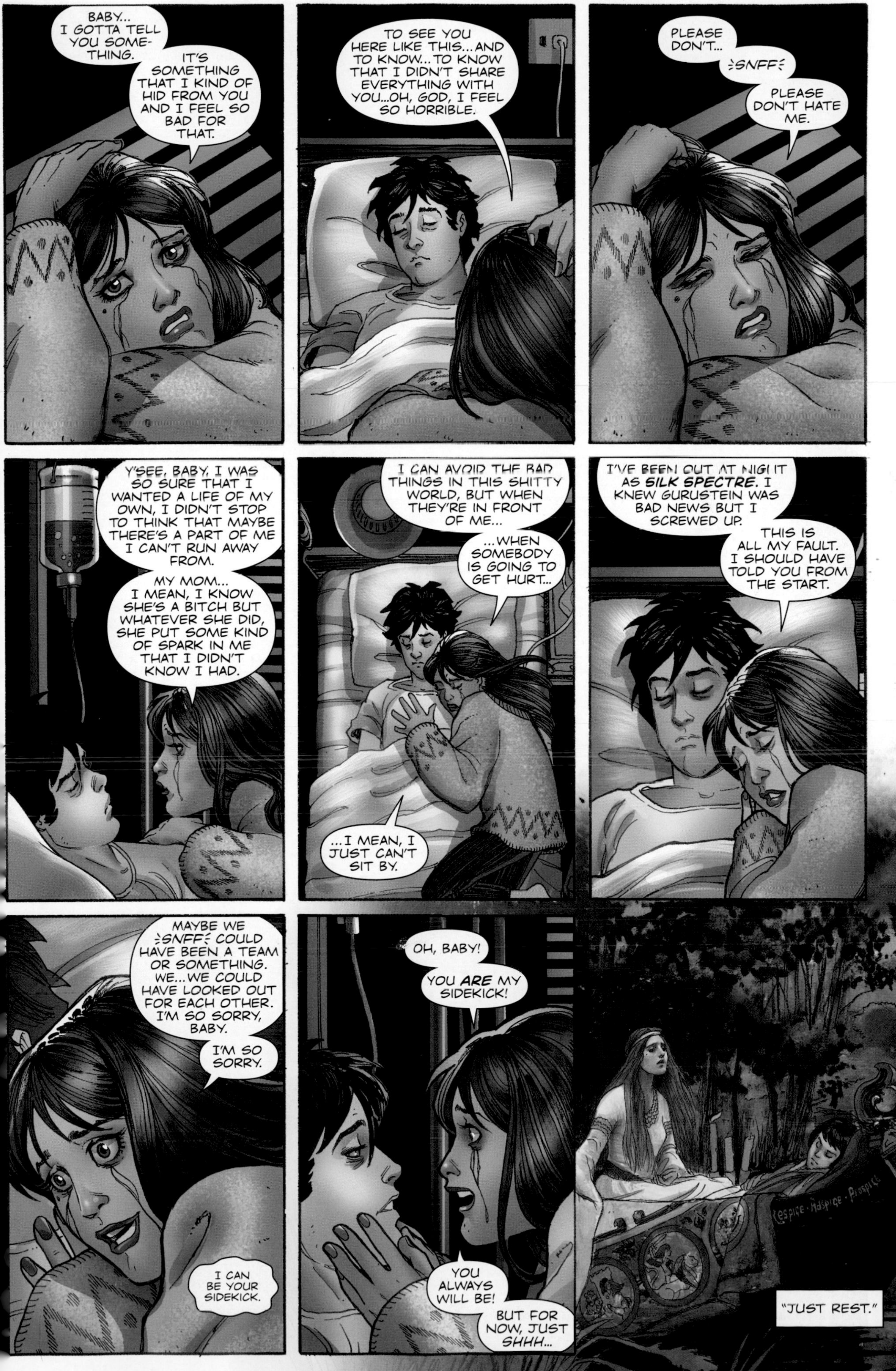
BABY... I GOTTA TELL YOU SOME-THING.
IT'S SOMETHING THAT I KIND OF HID FROM YOU AND I FEEL SO BAD FOR THAT.
TO SEE YOU HERE LIKE THIS... AND TO KNOW... TO KNOW THAT I DIDN'T SHARE EVERYTHING WITH YOU...OH, GOD, I FEEL SO HORRIBLE.
PLEASE DON'T...
SNFF
PLEASE DON'T HATE ME.
Y'SEE, BABY, I WAS SO SURE THAT I WANTED A LIFE OF MY OWN, I DIDN'T STOP TO THINK THAT MAYBE THERE'S A PART OF ME I CAN'T RUN AWAY FROM.
MY MOM... I MEAN, I KNOW SHE'S A BITCH BUT WHATEVER SHE DID, SHE PUT SOME KIND OF SPARK IN ME THAT I DIDN'T KNOW I HAD.
I CAN AVOID THE BAD THINGS IN THIS SHITTY WORLD, BUT WHEN THEY'RE IN FRONT OF ME...
...WHEN SOMEBODY IS GOING TO GET HURT...
...I MEAN, I JUST CAN'T SIT BY.
I'VE BEEN OUT AT NIGHT AS SILK SPECTRE. I KNEW GURUSTEIN WAS BAD NEWS BUT I SCREWED UP.
THIS IS ALL MY FAULT. I SHOULD HAVE TOLD YOU FROM THE START.
MAYBE WE SNFF COULD HAVE BEEN A TEAM OR SOMETHING. WE...WE COULD HAVE LOOKED OUT FOR EACH OTHER. I'M SO SORRY, BABY.
I'M SO SORRY.
I CAN BE YOUR SIDEKICK.
OH, BABY!
YOU ARE MY SIDEKICK!
YOU ALWAYS WILL BE!
BUT FOR NOW, JUST SHHH...
Respice · Adspice · Prospice
"JUST REST."

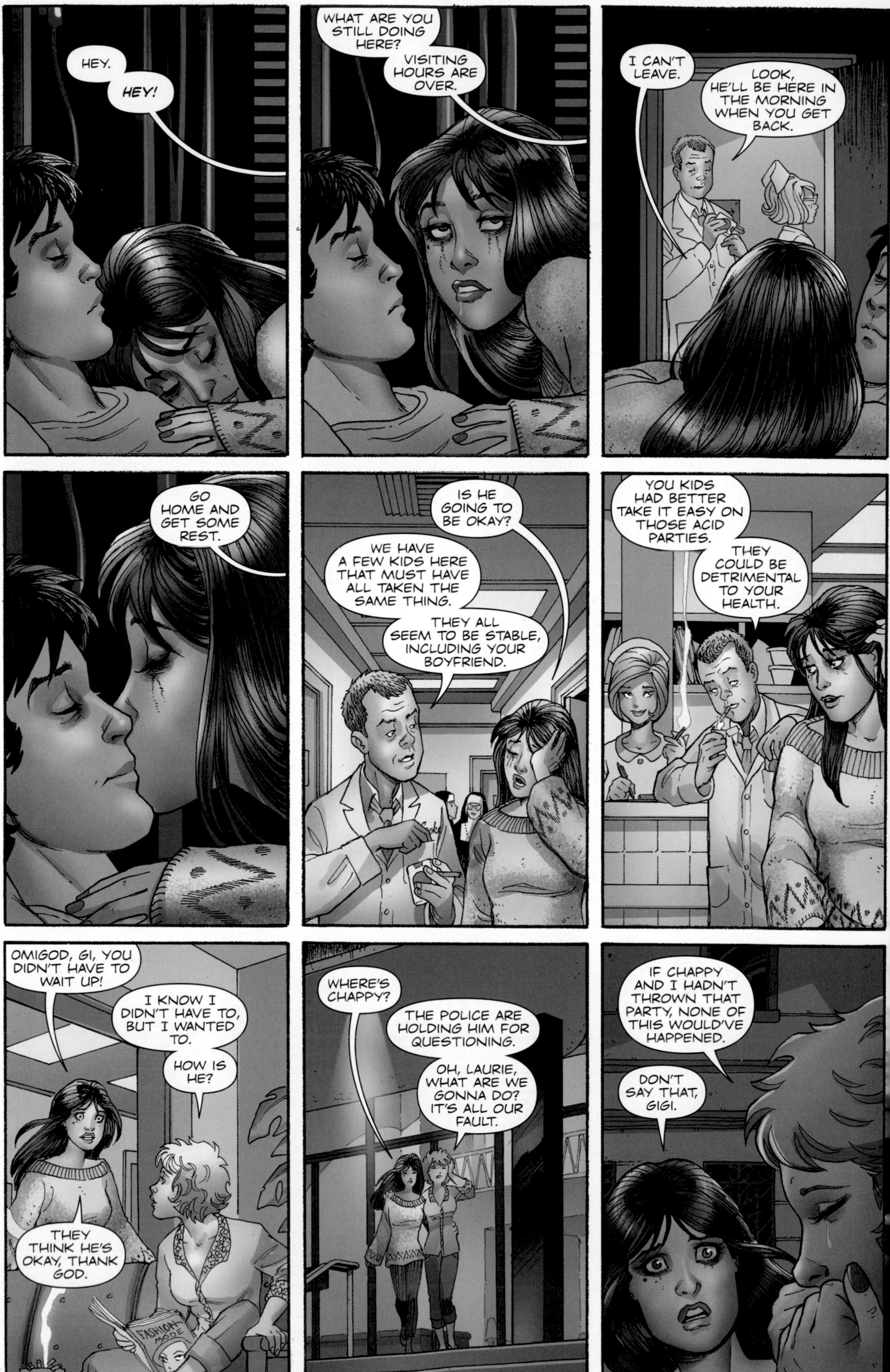
HEY.
HEY!
WHAT ARE YOU STILL DOING HERE?
VISITING HOURS ARE OVER.
I CAN'T LEAVE.
LOOK, HE'LL BE HERE IN THE MORNING WHEN YOU GET BACK.
GO HOME AND GET SOME REST.
IS HE GOING TO BE OKAY?
WE HAVE A FEW KIDS HERE THAT MUST HAVE ALL TAKEN THE SAME THING.
THEY ALL SEEM TO BE STABLE, INCLUDING YOUR BOYFRIEND.
YOU KIDS HAD BETTER TAKE IT EASY ON THOSE ACID PARTIES.
THEY COULD BE DETRIMENTAL TO YOUR HEALTH.
OMIGOD, GI, YOU DIDN'T HAVE TO WAIT UP!
I KNOW I DIDN'T HAVE TO, BUT I WANTED TO.
HOW IS HE?
THEY THINK HE'S OKAY, THANK GOD.
FASHION MODE
WHERE'S CHAPPY?
THE POLICE ARE HOLDING HIM FOR QUESTIONING.
OH, LAURIE, WHAT ARE WE GONNA DO? IT'S ALL OUR FAULT.
IF CHAPPY AND I HADN'T THROWN THAT PARTY, NONE OF THIS WOULD'VE HAPPENED.
DON'T SAY THAT, GIGI.

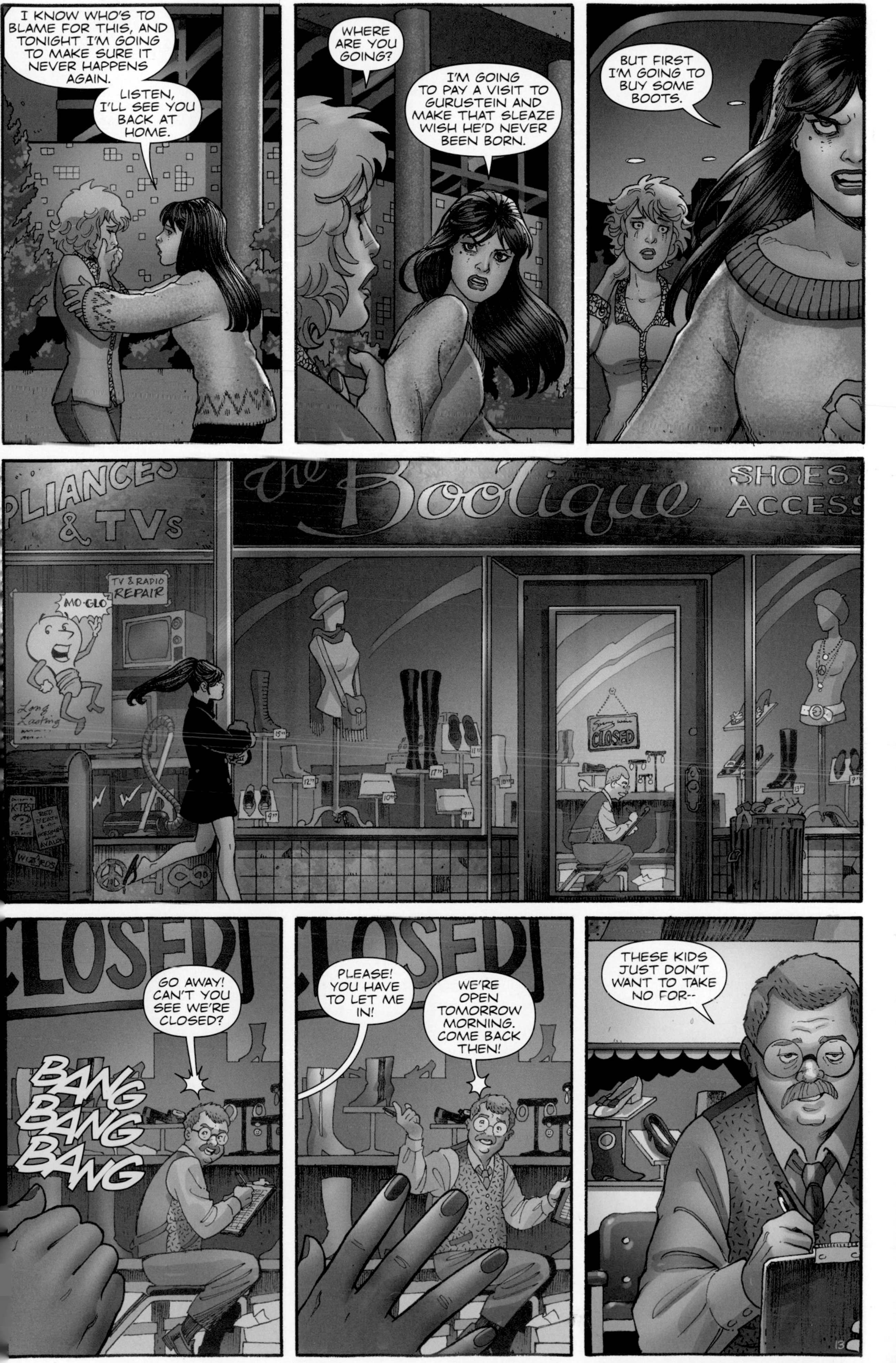
I KNOW WHO'S TO BLAME FOR THIS, AND TONIGHT I'M GOING TO MAKE SURE IT NEVER HAPPENS AGAIN.
LISTEN, I'LL SEE YOU BACK AT HOME.
WHERE ARE YOU GOING?
I'M GOING TO PAY A VISIT TO GURUSTEIN AND MAKE THAT SLEAZE WISH HE'D NEVER BEEN BORN.
BUT FIRST I'M GOING TO BUY SOME BOOTS.
PLIANCES & TVs
The Bootique
SHOES & ACCESS
TV & RADIO REPAIR
MO-GLO
CLOSED
CLOSED
GO AWAY! CAN'T YOU SEE WE'RE CLOSED?
BANG BANG BANG
PLEASE! YOU HAVE TO LET ME IN!
WE'RE OPEN TOMORROW MORNING. COME BACK THEN!
THESE KIDS JUST DON'T WANT TO TAKE NO FOR--
13

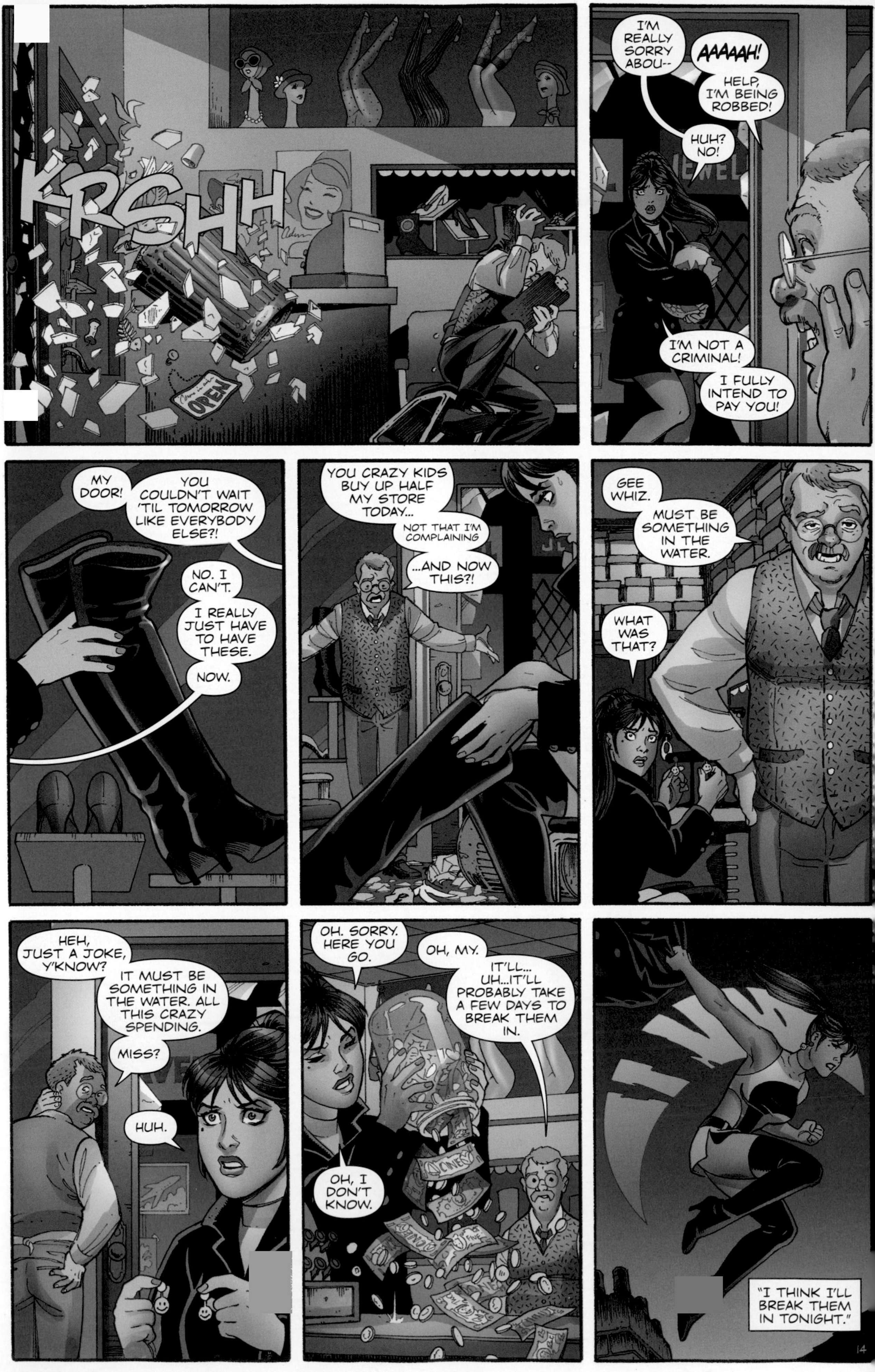
KRSHH
OPEN
I'M REALLY SORRY ABOU--
AAAAAH!
HELP, I'M BEING ROBBED!
HUH? NO!
I'M NOT A CRIMINAL!
I FULLY INTEND TO PAY YOU!
MY DOOR!
YOU COULDN'T WAIT 'TIL TOMORROW LIKE EVERYBODY ELSE?!
NO. I CAN'T.
I REALLY JUST HAVE TO HAVE THESE.
NOW.
YOU CRAZY KIDS BUY UP HALF MY STORE TODAY...
NOT THAT I'M COMPLAINING
...AND NOW THIS?!
GEE WHIZ.
MUST BE SOMETHING IN THE WATER.
WHAT WAS THAT?
HEH, JUST A JOKE, Y'KNOW?
IT MUST BE SOMETHING IN THE WATER. ALL THIS CRAZY SPENDING.
MISS?
HUH.
OH. SORRY. HERE YOU GO.
OH, MY.
IT'LL... UH...IT'LL PROBABLY TAKE A FEW DAYS TO BREAK THEM IN.
OH, I DON'T KNOW.
"I THINK I'LL BREAK THEM IN TONIGHT."

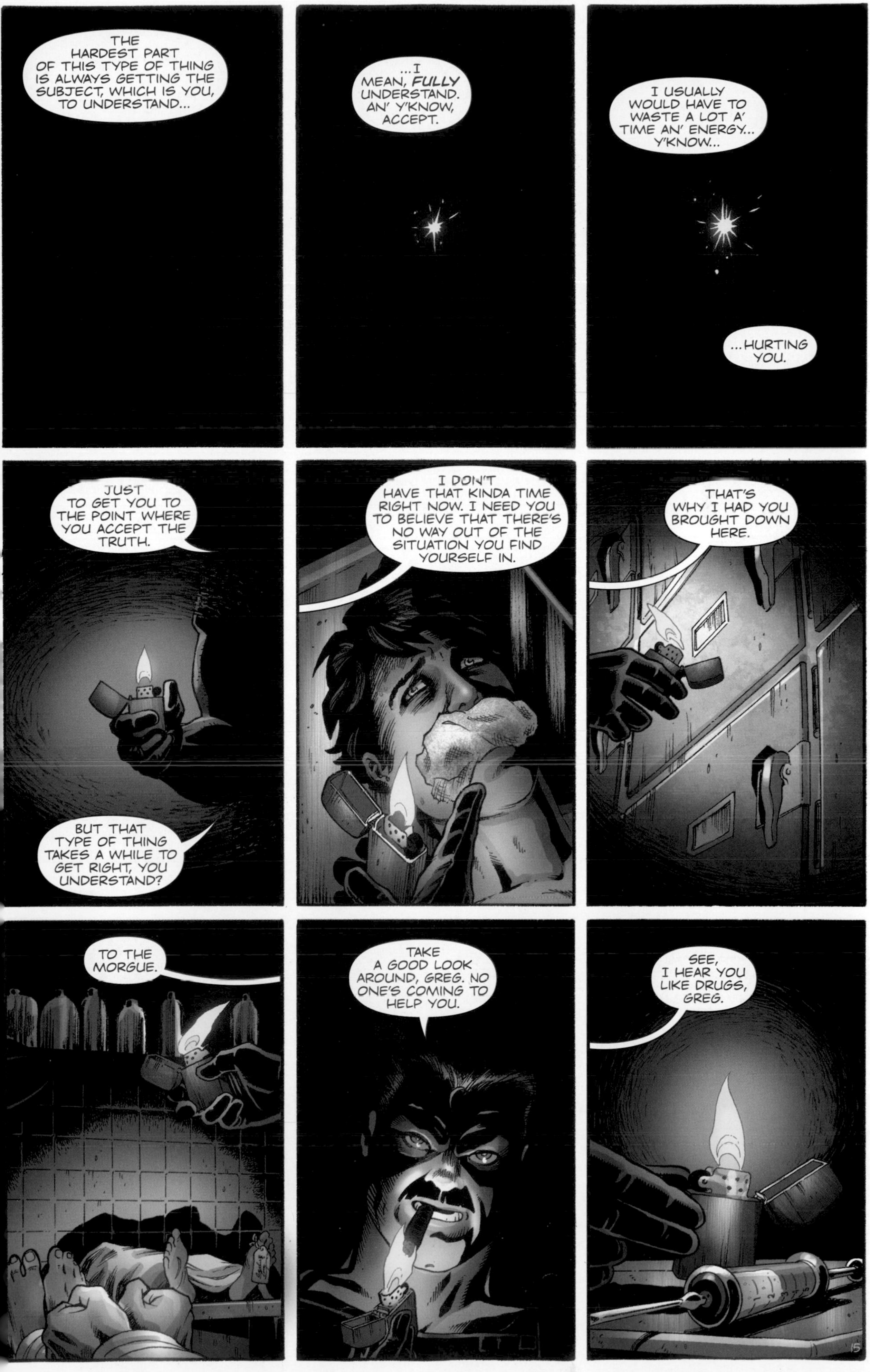

THE HARDEST PART OF THIS TYPE OF THING IS ALWAYS GETTING THE SUBJECT, WHICH IS YOU, TO UNDERSTAND...
...I MEAN, FULLY UNDERSTAND. AN' Y'KNOW, ACCEPT.
I USUALLY WOULD HAVE TO WASTE A LOT A' TIME AN' ENERGY... Y'KNOW...
...HURTING YOU.
JUST TO GET YOU TO THE POINT WHERE YOU ACCEPT THE TRUTH.
BUT THAT TYPE OF THING TAKES A WHILE TO GET RIGHT, YOU UNDERSTAND?
I DON'T HAVE THAT KINDA TIME RIGHT NOW. I NEED YOU TO BELIEVE THAT THERE'S NO WAY OUT OF THE SITUATION YOU FIND YOURSELF IN.
THAT'S WHY I HAD YOU BROUGHT DOWN HERE.
TO THE MORGUE.
TAKE A GOOD LOOK AROUND, GREG. NO ONE'S COMING TO HELP YOU.
SEE, I HEAR YOU LIKE DRUGS, GREG.

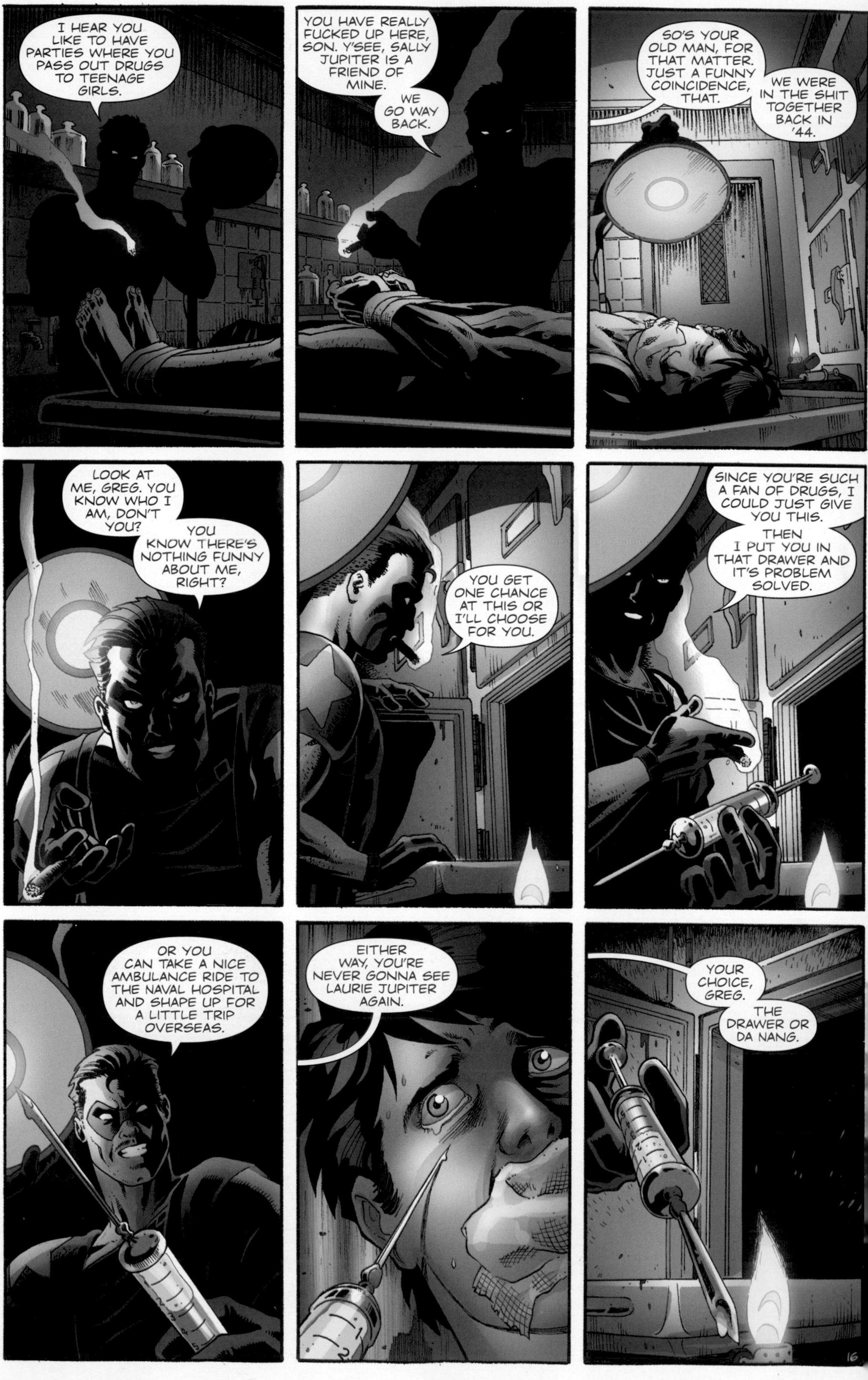
I HEAR YOU LIKE TO HAVE PARTIES WHERE YOU PASS OUT DRUGS TO TEENAGE GIRLS.
YOU HAVE REALLY FUCKED UP HERE, SON. Y'SEE, SALLY JUPITER IS A FRIEND OF MINE.
WE GO WAY BACK.
SO'S YOUR OLD MAN, FOR THAT MATTER. JUST A FUNNY COINCIDENCE, THAT.
WE WERE IN THE SHIT TOGETHER BACK IN '44.
LOOK AT ME, GREG. YOU KNOW WHO I AM, DON'T YOU?
YOU KNOW THERE'S NOTHING FUNNY ABOUT ME, RIGHT?
YOU GET ONE CHANCE AT THIS OR I'LL CHOOSE FOR YOU.
SINCE YOU'RE SUCH A FAN OF DRUGS, I COULD JUST GIVE YOU THIS.
THEN I PUT YOU IN THAT DRAWER AND IT'S PROBLEM SOLVED.
OR YOU CAN TAKE A NICE AMBULANCE RIDE TO THE NAVAL HOSPITAL AND SHAPE UP FOR A LITTLE TRIP OVERSEAS.
EITHER WAY, YOU'RE NEVER GONNA SEE LAURIE JUPITER AGAIN.
YOUR CHOICE, GREG.
THE DRAWER OR DA NANG.

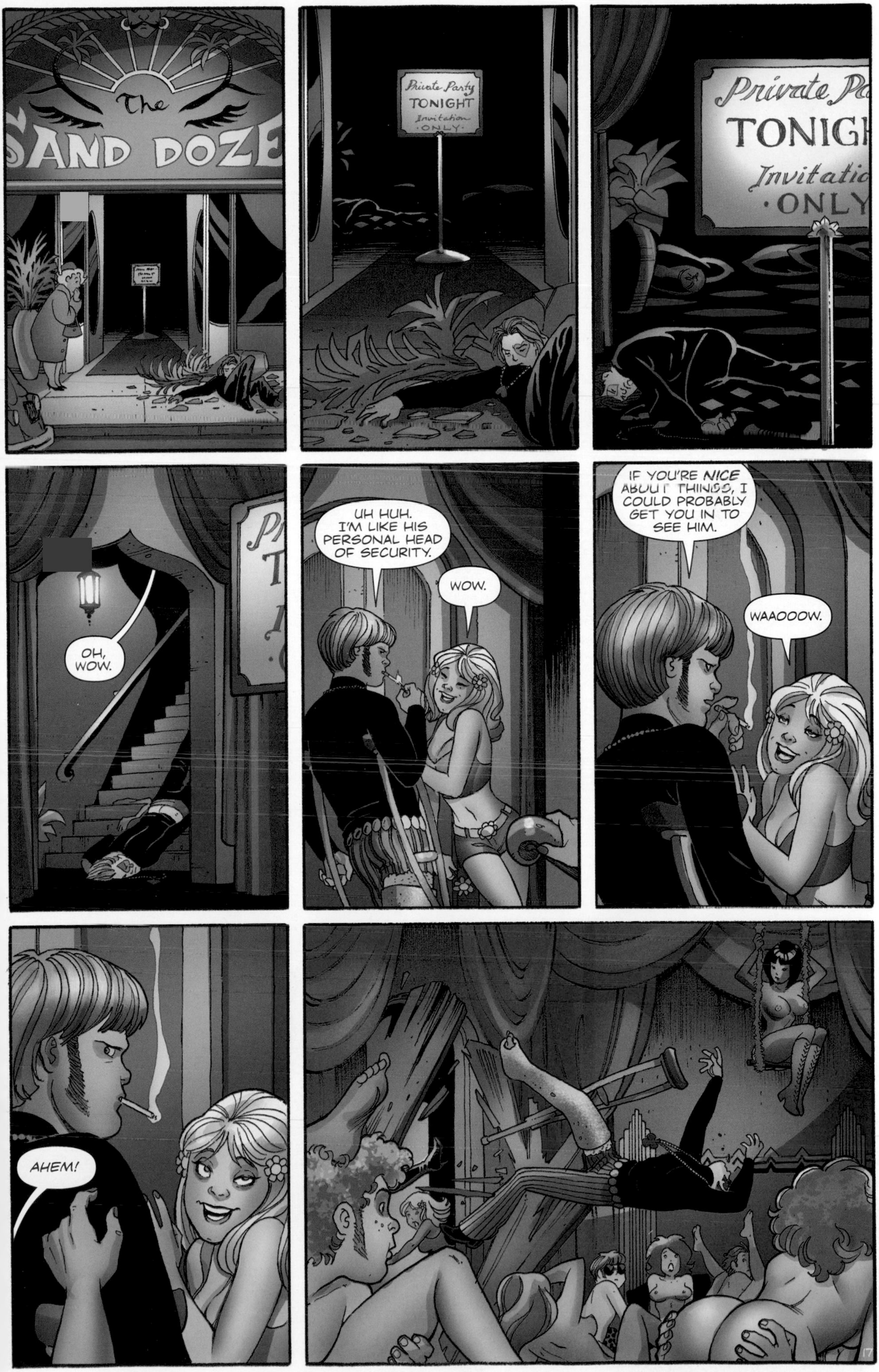
The
SAND DOZE
Private Party
TONIGHT
Invitation
ONLY
Private Pa
TONIGH
Invitatio
ONLY
OH, WOW.
UH HUH. I'M LIKE HIS PERSONAL HEAD OF SECURITY.
WOW.
IF YOU'RE NICE ABOUT THINGS, I COULD PROBABLY GET YOU IN TO SEE HIM.
WAAOOOW.
AHEM!

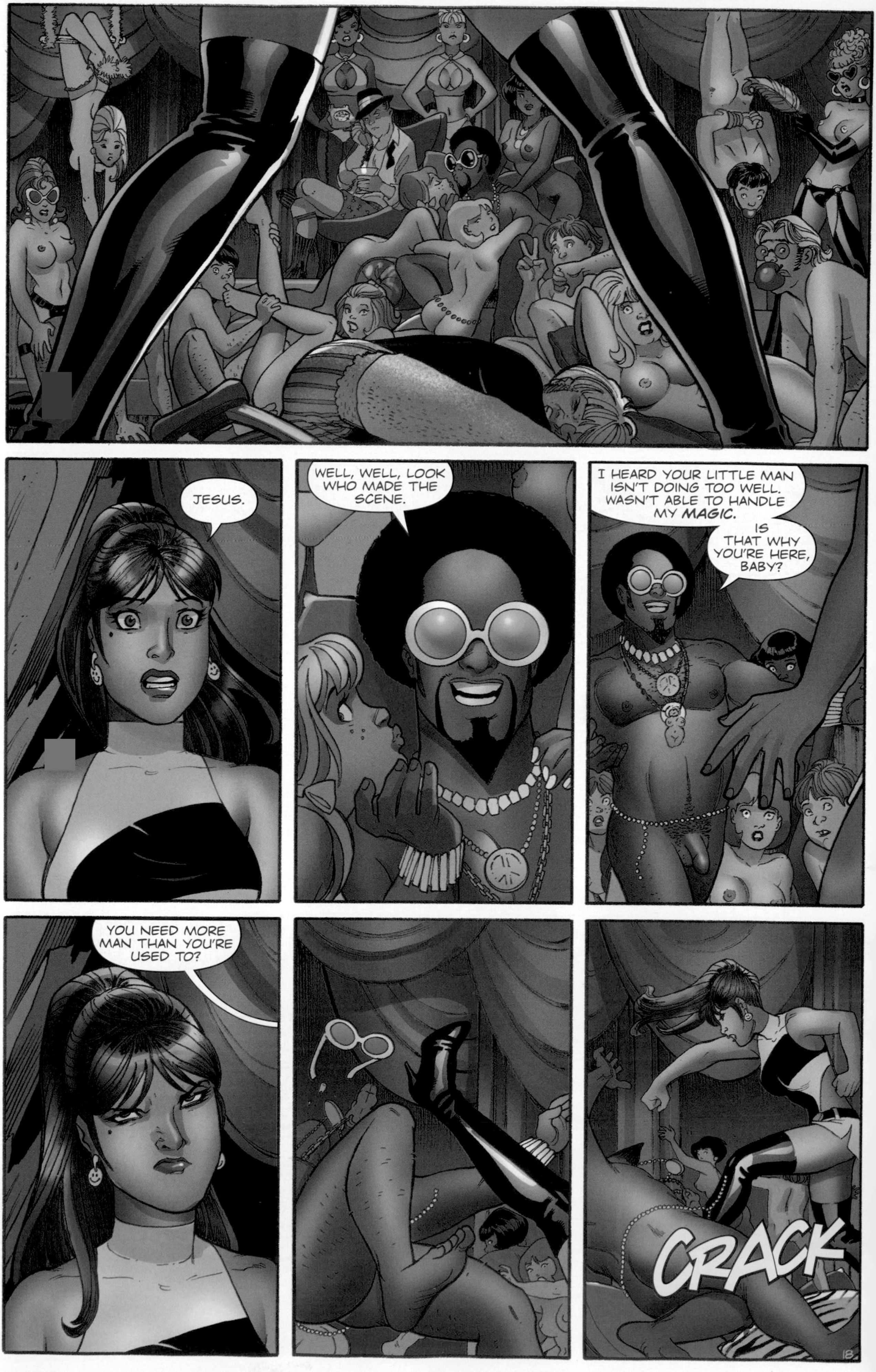
JESUS.
WELL, WELL, LOOK WHO MADE THE SCENE.
I HEARD YOUR LITTLE MAN ISN'T DOING TOO WELL. WASN'T ABLE TO HANDLE MY MAGIC.
IS THAT WHY YOU'RE HERE, BABY?
YOU NEED MORE MAN THAN YOU'RE USED TO?
CRACK

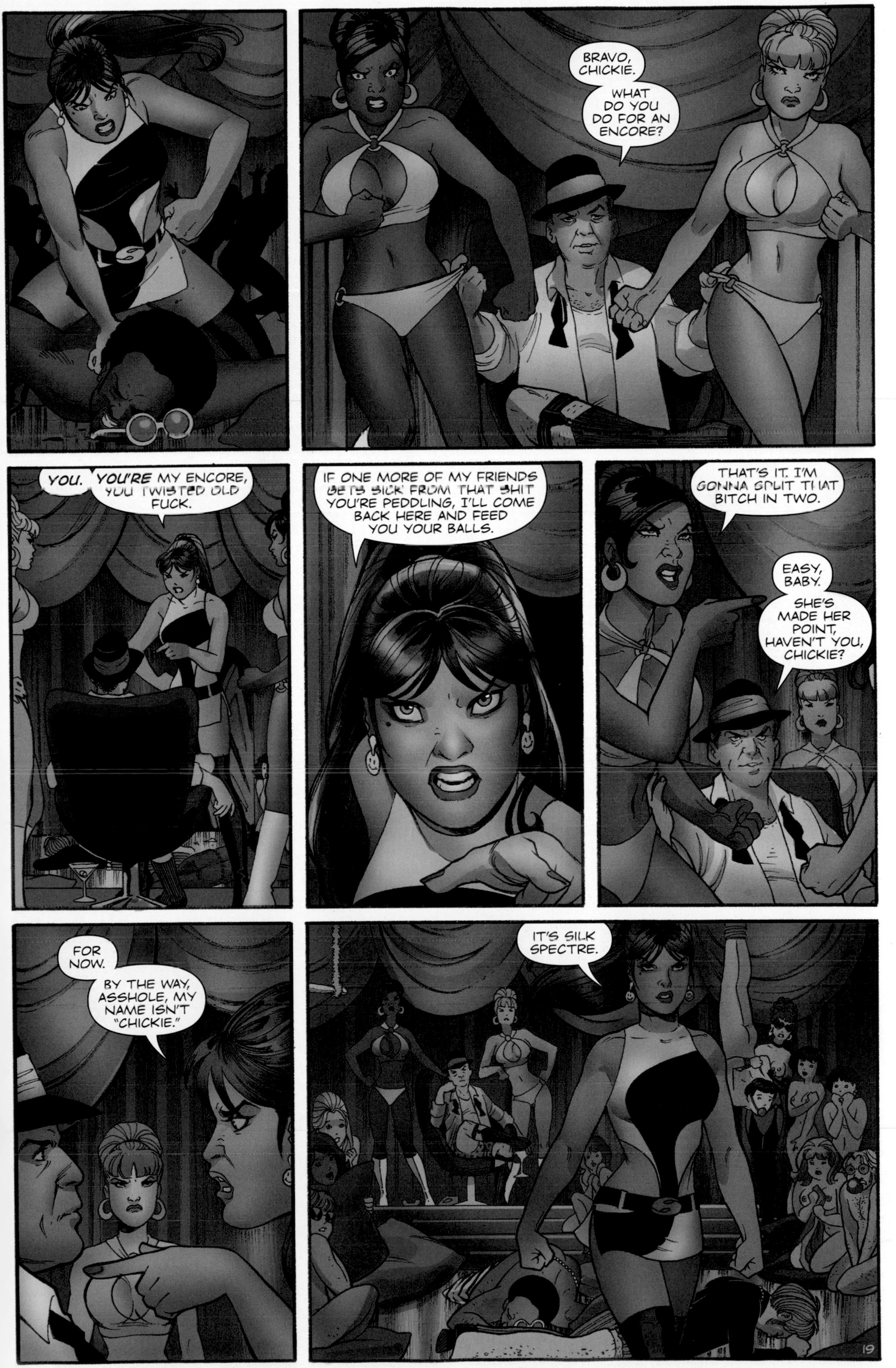
BRAVO, CHICKIE.
WHAT DO YOU DO FOR AN ENCORE?
YOU.
YOU'RE MY ENCORE, YOU TWISTED OLD FUCK.
IF ONE MORE OF MY FRIENDS GETS SICK FROM THAT SHIT YOU'RE PEDDLING, I'LL COME BACK HERE AND FEED YOU YOUR BALLS.
THAT'S IT. I'M GONNA SPLIT THAT BITCH IN TWO.
EASY, BABY.
SHE'S MADE HER POINT, HAVEN'T YOU, CHICKIE?
FOR NOW.
BY THE WAY, ASSHOLE, MY NAME ISN'T "CHICKIE."
IT'S SILK SPECTRE.
19

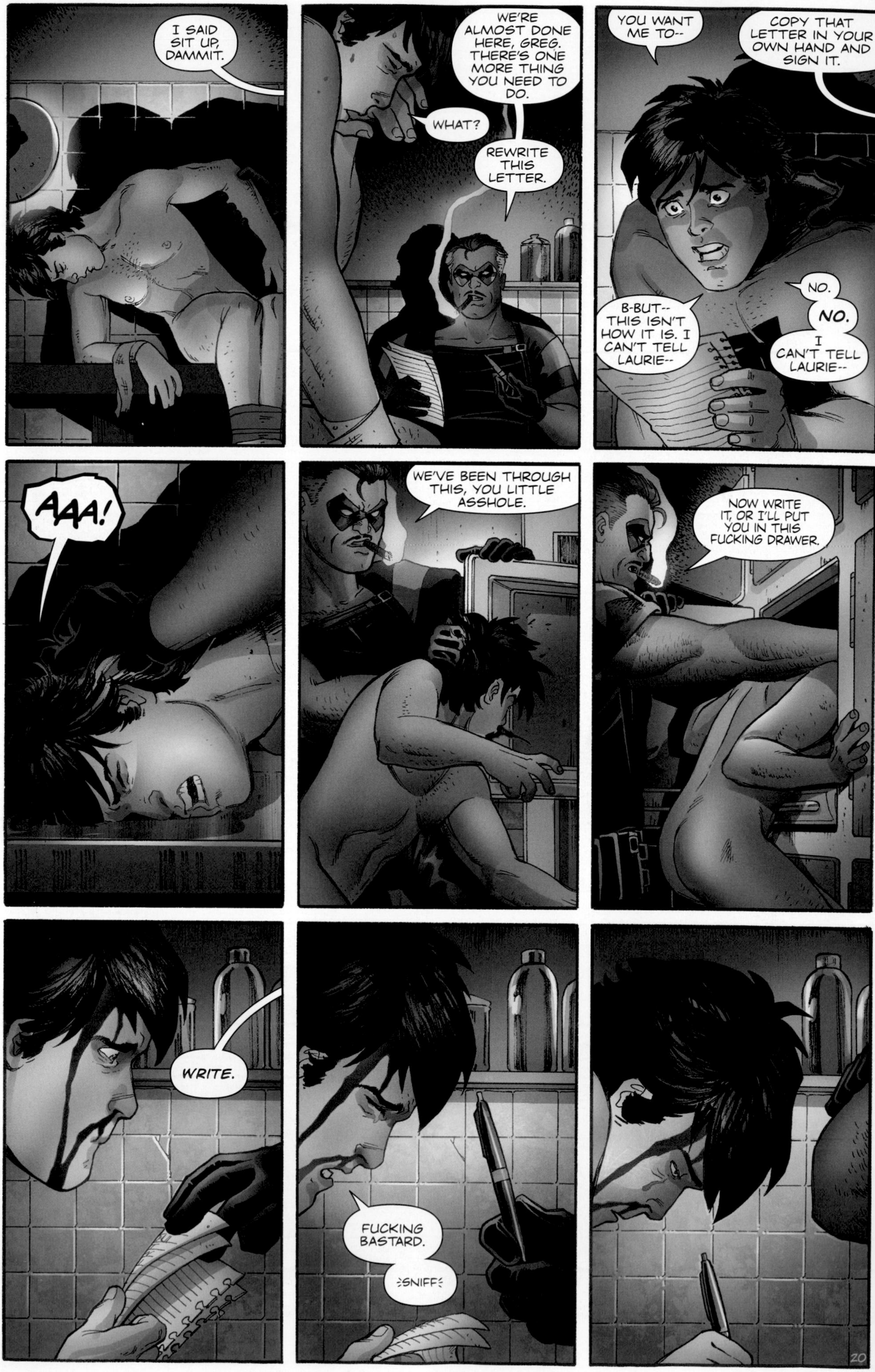
I SAID SIT UP, DAMMIT.
WE'RE ALMOST DONE HERE, GREG. THERE'S ONE MORE THING YOU NEED TO DO.
WHAT?
REWRITE THIS LETTER.
YOU WANT ME TO--
COPY THAT LETTER IN YOUR OWN HAND AND SIGN IT.
B-BUT-- THIS ISN'T HOW IT IS. I CAN'T TELL LAURIE--
NO.
NO.
I CAN'T TELL LAURIE--
AAA!
WE'VE BEEN THROUGH THIS, YOU LITTLE ASSHOLE.
NOW WRITE IT, OR I'LL PUT YOU IN THIS FUCKING DRAWER.
WRITE.
FUCKING BASTARD.
SNIFF

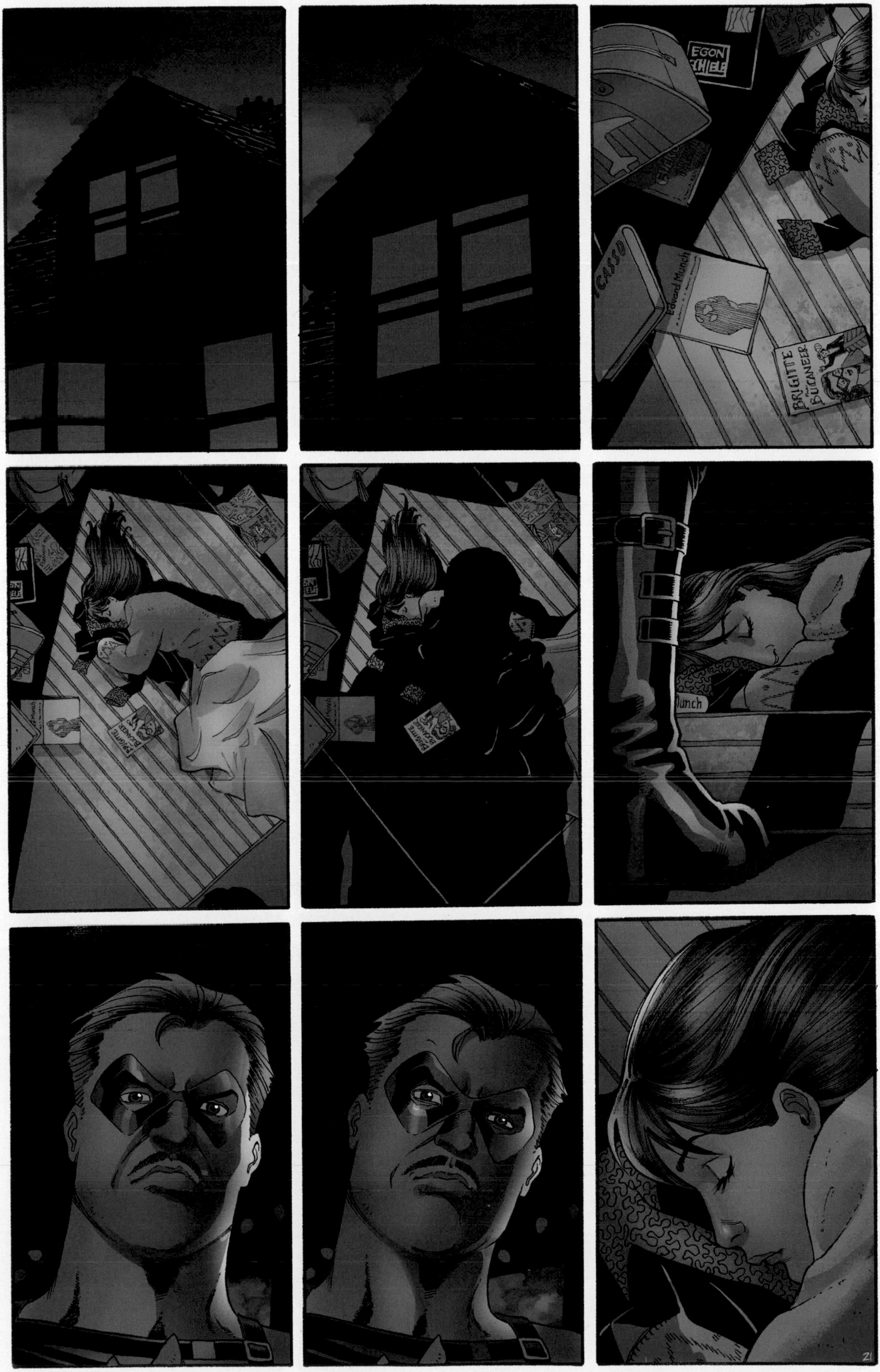
EGON
Edvard Munch
BRIGITTE
Munch

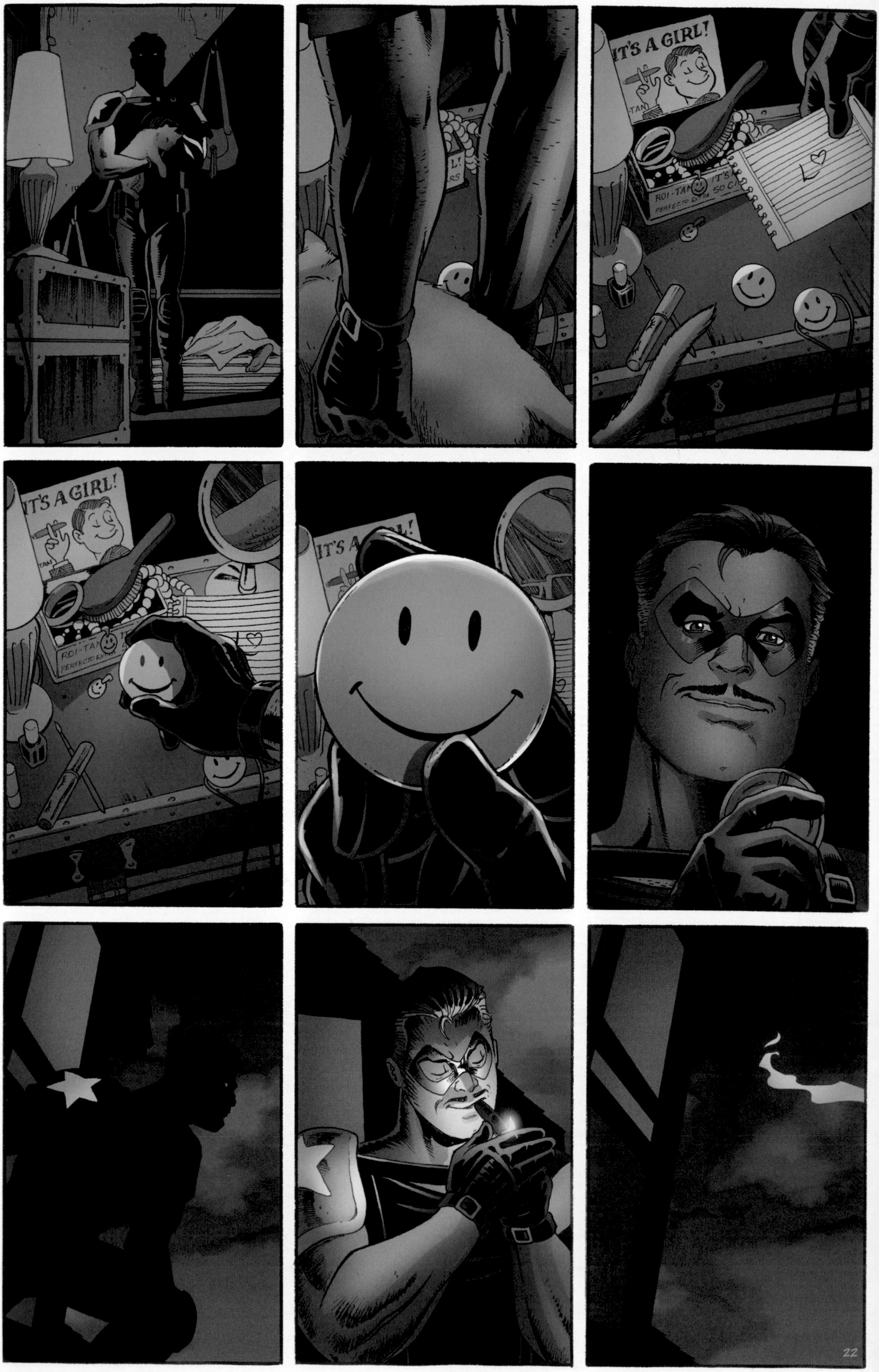
IT'S A GIRL!
ROI-TAN
PERFECTO EXTRA

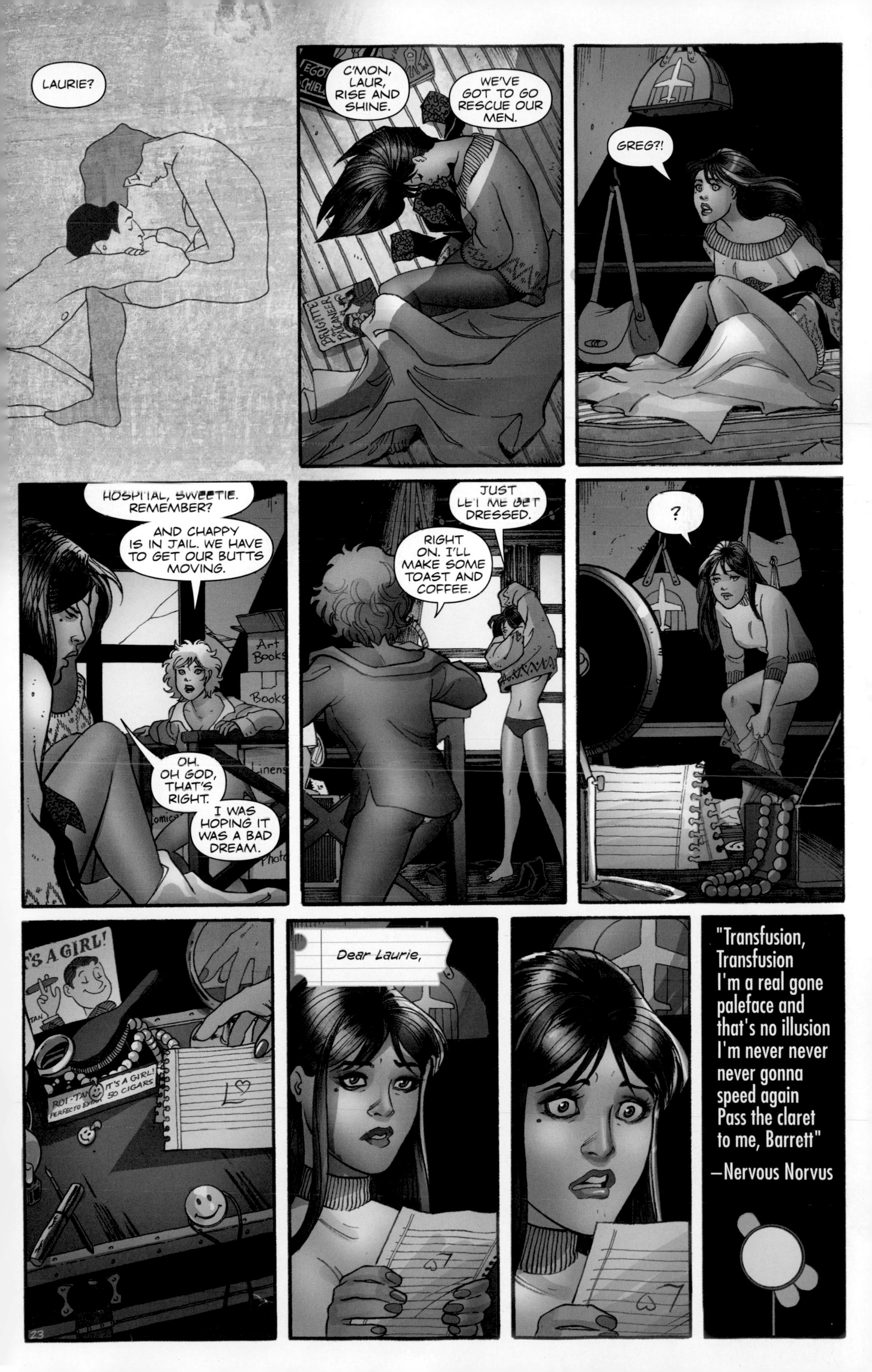
LAURIE?
C'MON, LAUR, RISE AND SHINE.
WE'VE GOT TO GO RESCUE OUR MEN.
GREG?!
HOSPITAL, SWEETIE. REMEMBER?
AND CHAPPY IS IN JAIL. WE HAVE TO GET OUR BUTTS MOVING.
OH. OH GOD, THAT'S RIGHT.
I WAS HOPING IT WAS A BAD DREAM.
Art Books
Books
Linens
Photo
JUST LET ME GET DRESSED.
RIGHT ON. I'LL MAKE SOME TOAST AND COFFEE.
?
IT'S A GIRL!
IT'S A GIRL! 50 CIGARS
Dear Laurie,
"Transfusion, Transfusion I'm a real gone paleface and that's no illusion I'm never never never gonna speed again Pass the claret to me, Barrett"
—Nervous Norvus

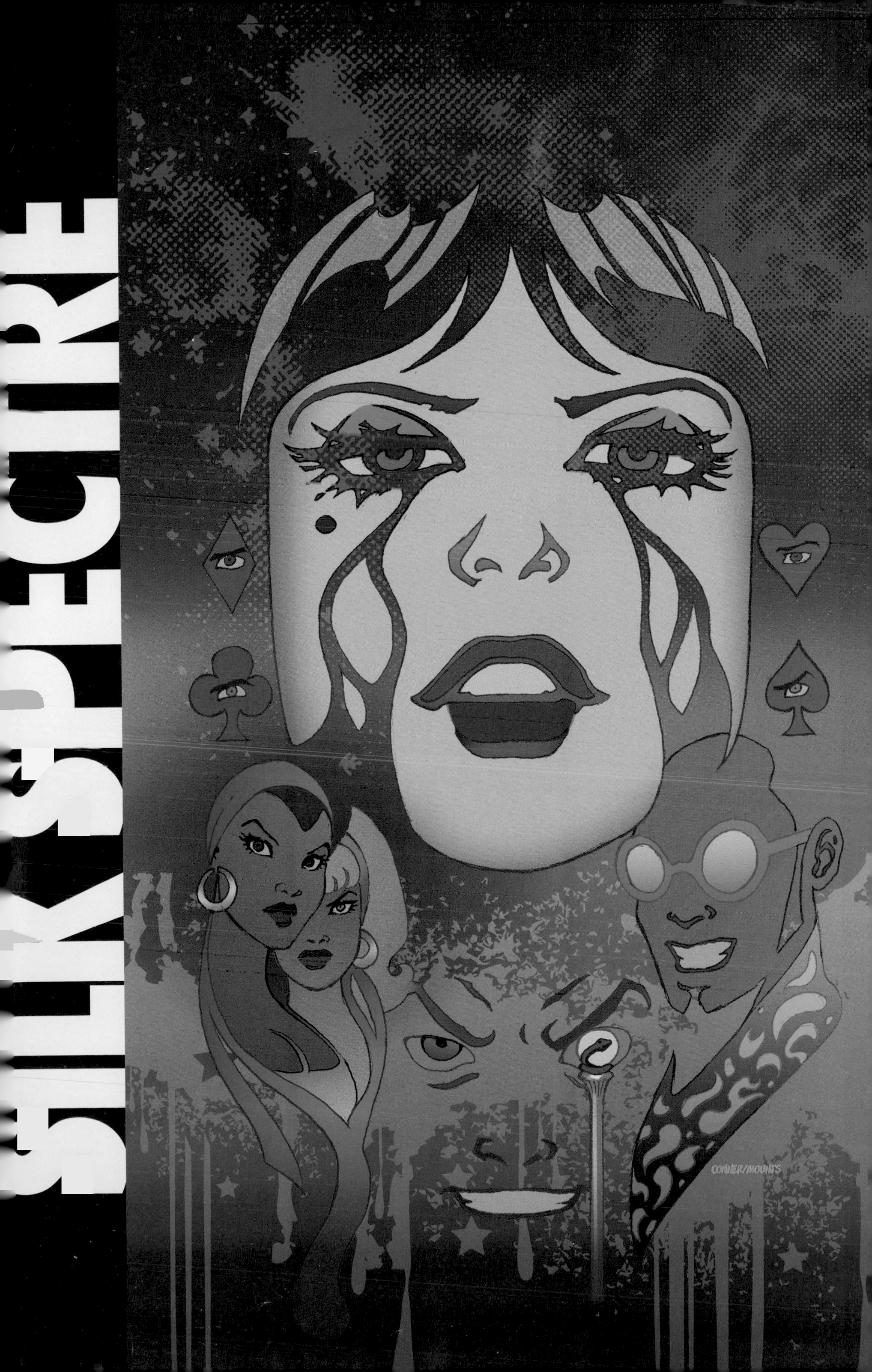
SILK SPECTRE
CONNER/MOUNTS

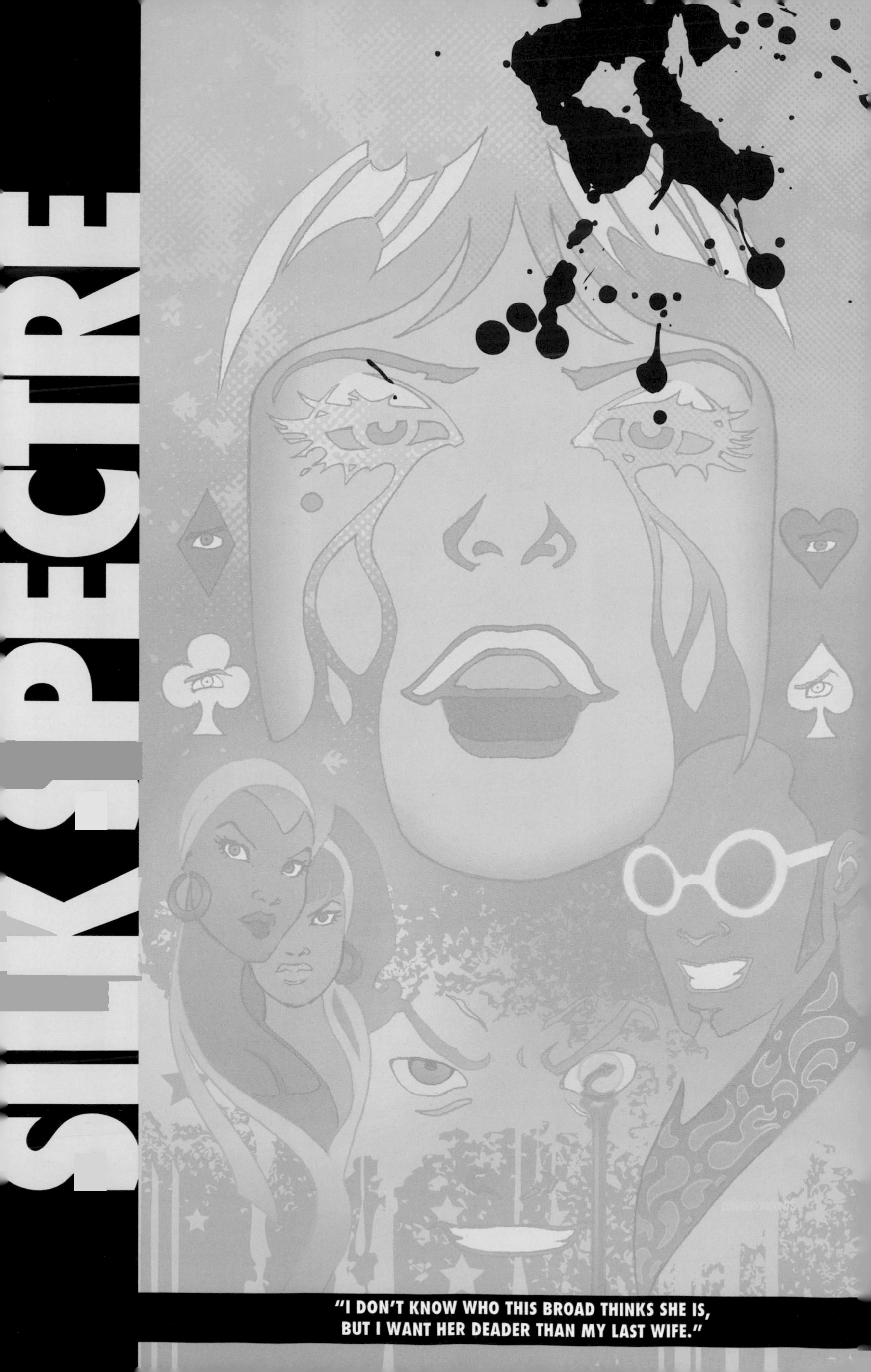
SILK SPECTRE
"I DON'T KNOW WHO THIS BROAD THINKS SHE IS,
BUT I WANT HER DEADER THAN MY LAST WIFE."

1960

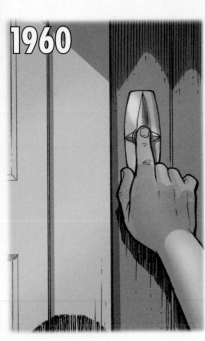

HELLO, MISSUS JUPITER. CAN LAURIE COME OUT TO PLAY?

NOW WHO, PRAY TELL, MIGHT YOU BE?

I'M SIMON. I GO TO SCHOOL WITH LAURIE.

I SEE.

AND YOU WANT TO PLAY WITH MY LAURIE?

YES MA'AM.

MA'AM?

MA'AM.

WELL LET ME TELL 'YOU A THING OR TWO, SCHOOLBOY SIMON.

SOMETHING ALL THE BOYS ON THIS STREET ALREADY KNOW.

LAURIE IS TRYING TO PLAY A TRICK ON YOU. SHE ONLY PRETENDS TO LIKE BOYS.

SHE'LL PRETEND SHE'S YOUR FRIEND, BUT WHEN YOU GET TO THE PARK...

WELL...

YOU KNOW WHAT SHE'LL DO?

UH UH.

FIRST, SHE'LL—

AND THEN SHE'LL PULL DOWN YOUR SHORTS SO EVERYONE CAN SEE YOUR UNDERWEAR.

I'VE SEEN HER DO IT.

SAYONARA, SIMON.

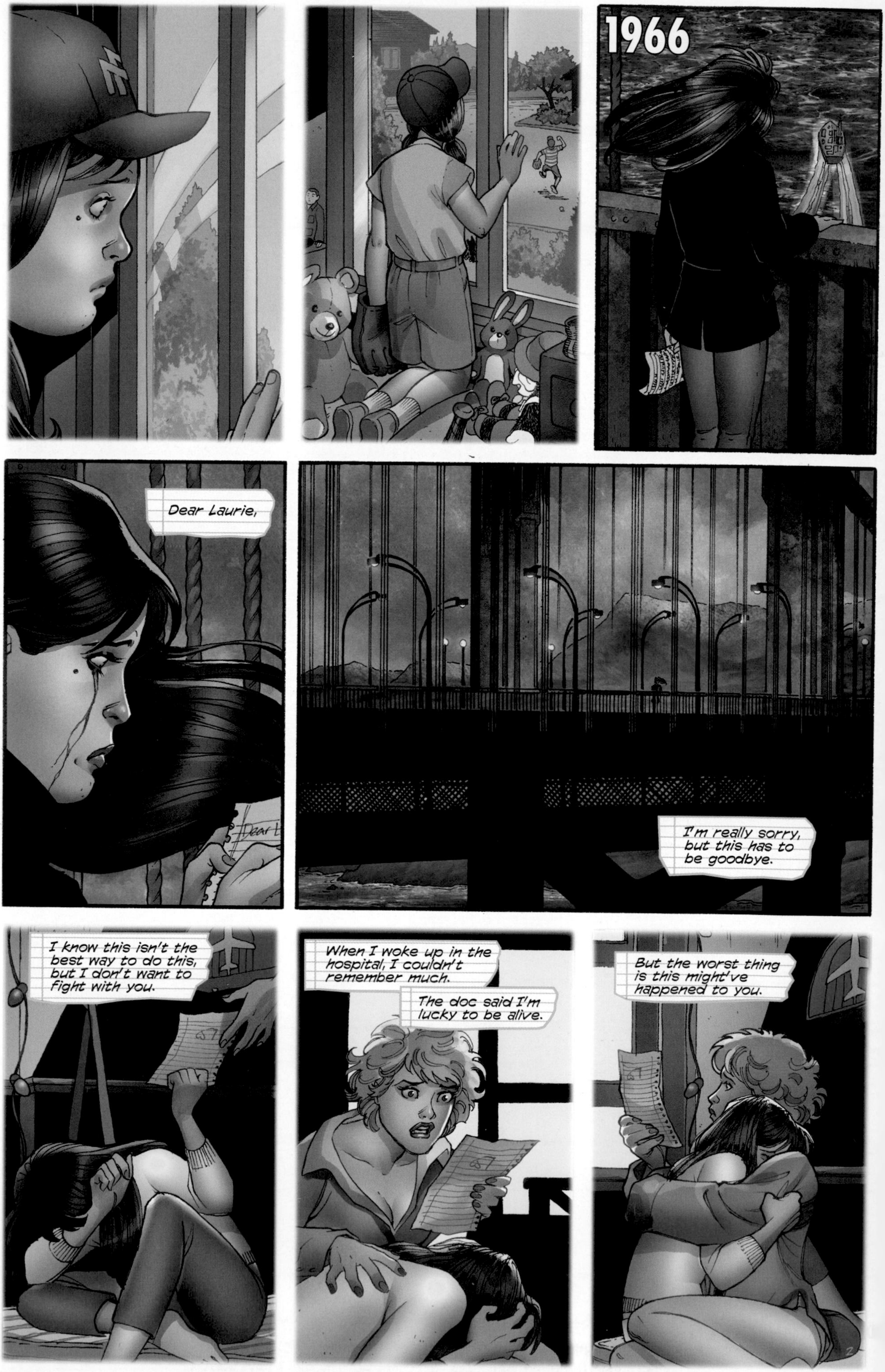

1966
Dear Laurie,
I'm really sorry, but this has to be goodbye.
I know this isn't the best way to do this, but I don't want to fight with you.
When I woke up in the hospital, I couldn't remember much.
The doc said I'm lucky to be alive.
But the worst thing is this might've happened to you.

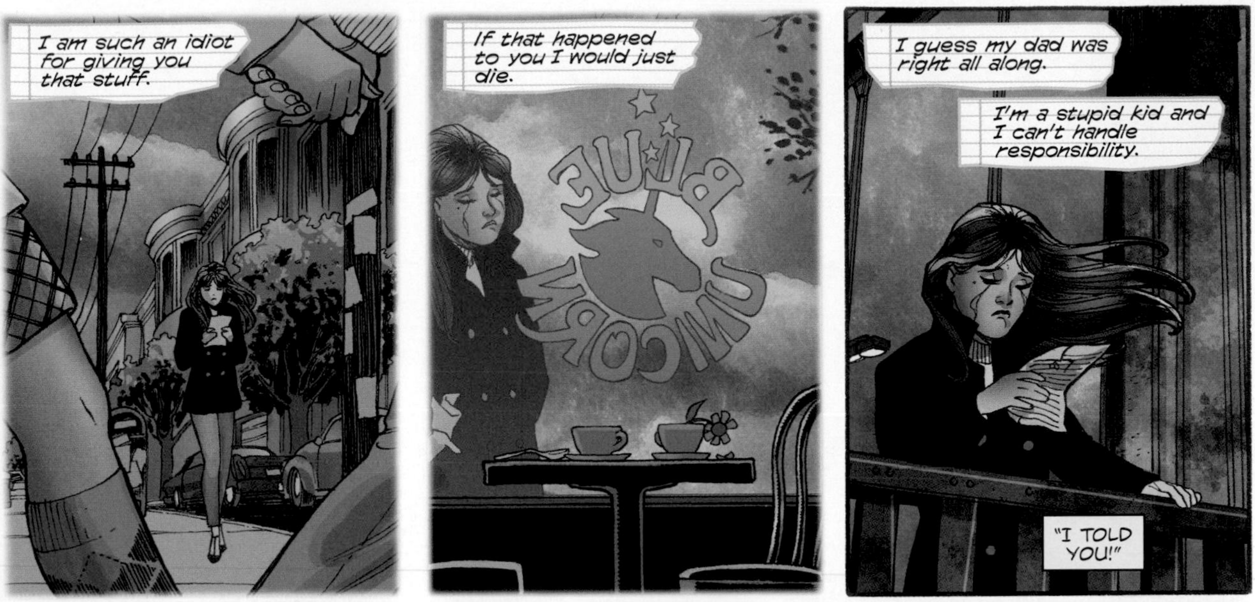
I am such an idiot for giving you that stuff.
If that happened to you I would just die.
BLUE UNICORN
I guess my dad was right all along.
I'm a stupid kid and I can't handle responsibility.
"I TOLD YOU!"

THE END OF THE RAINBOW

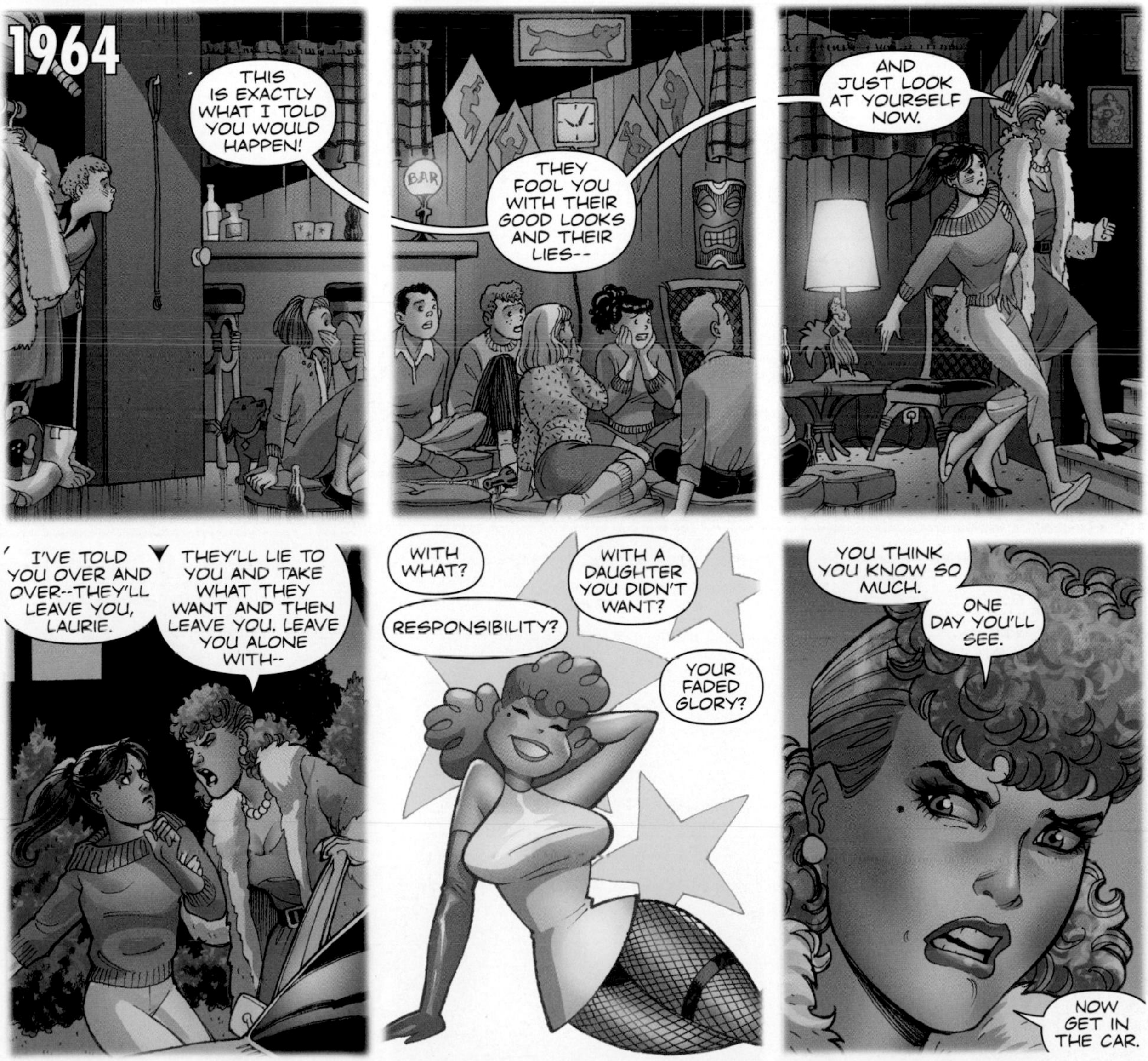
1964
THIS IS EXACTLY WHAT I TOLD YOU WOULD HAPPEN!
BAR
THEY FOOL YOU WITH THEIR GOOD LOOKS AND THEIR LIES--
AND JUST LOOK AT YOURSELF NOW.
I'VE TOLD YOU OVER AND OVER--THEY'LL LEAVE YOU, LAURIE.
THEY'LL LIE TO YOU AND TAKE WHAT THEY WANT AND THEN LEAVE YOU. LEAVE YOU ALONE WITH--
WITH WHAT?
RESPONSIBILITY?
WITH A DAUGHTER YOU DIDN'T WANT?
YOUR FADED GLORY?
YOU THINK YOU KNOW SO MUCH.
ONE DAY YOU'LL SEE.
NOW GET IN THE CAR.

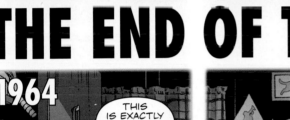

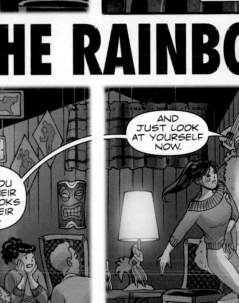

DARWYN COOKE & AMANDA CONNER SCRIPT • **AMANDA CONNER** ART • **PAUL MOUNTS** COLORS • **CARLOS M. MANGUAL** LETTERS
AMANDA CONNER & PAUL MOUNTS COVER • **BRUCE TIMM** VARIANT COVER • **CAMILLA ZHANG** ASSISTANT EDITOR • **CHRIS CONROY** ASSOCIATE EDITOR
MARK CHIARELLO EDITOR • **WATCHMEN CREATED BY ALAN MOORE & DAVE GIBBONS**

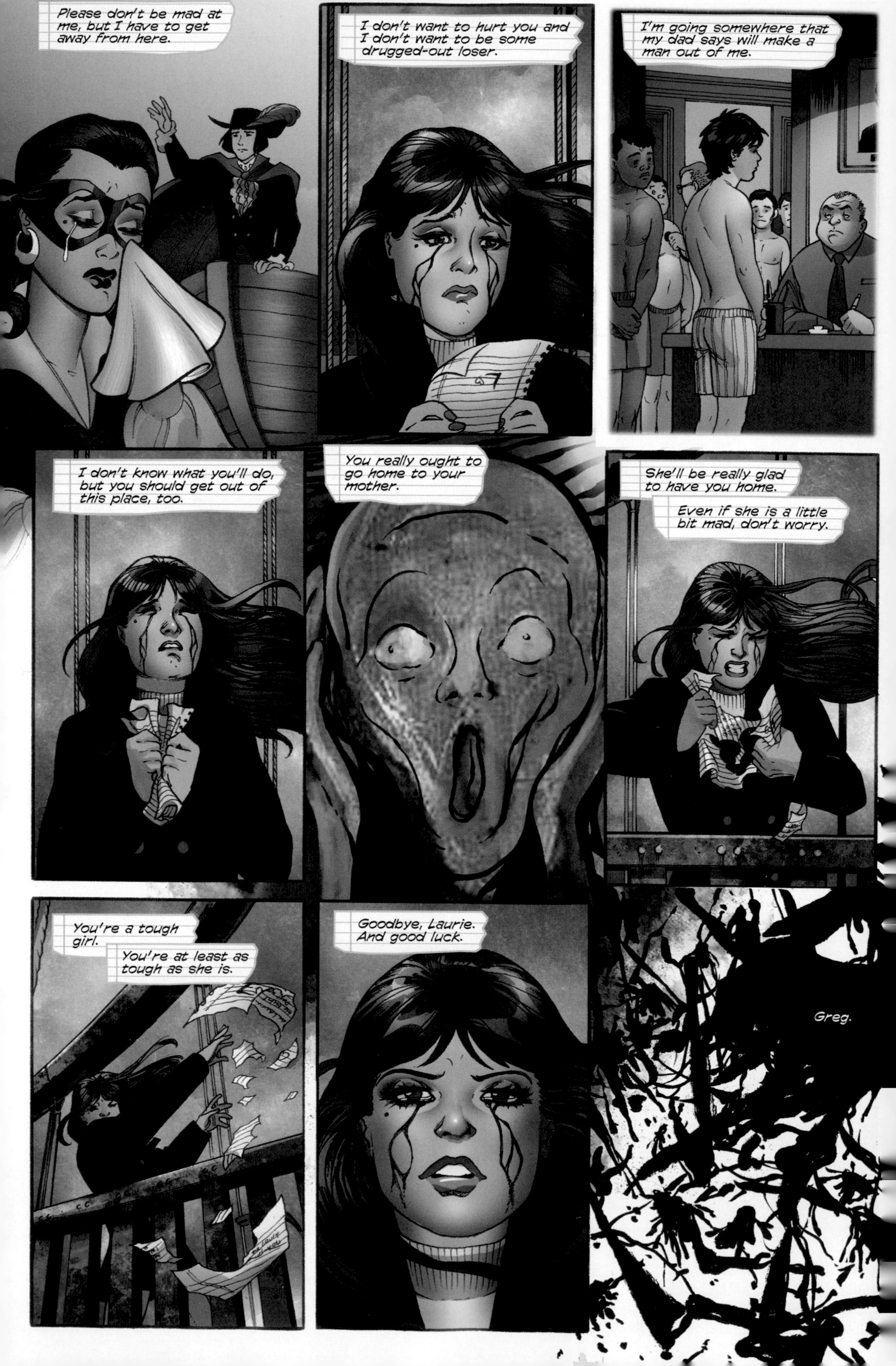
Please don't be mad at me, but I have to get away from here.
I don't want to hurt you and I don't want to be some drugged-out loser.
I'm going somewhere that my dad says will make a man out of me.
I don't know what you'll do, but you should get out of this place, too.
You really ought to go home to your mother.
She'll be really glad to have you home.
Even if she is a little bit mad, don't worry.
You're a tough girl.
You're at least as tough as she is.
Goodbye, Laurie. And good luck.
Greg.

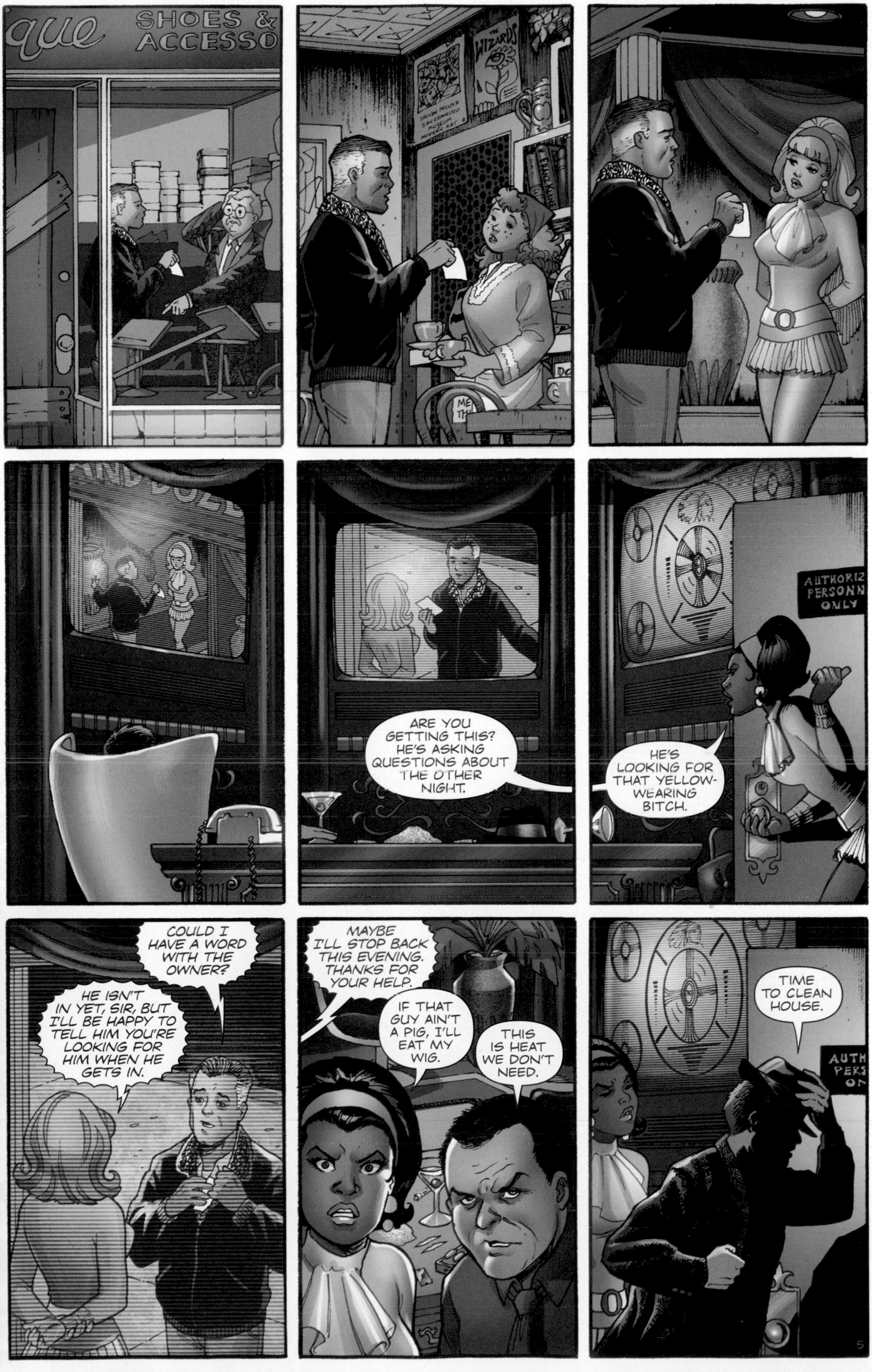
que
SHOES & ACCESSO
THE WIZARDS
AUTHORIZ PERSONN ONLY
ARE YOU GETTING THIS? HE'S ASKING QUESTIONS ABOUT THE OTHER NIGHT.
HE'S LOOKING FOR THAT YELLOW-WEARING BITCH.
COULD I HAVE A WORD WITH THE OWNER?
HE ISN'T IN YET, SIR, BUT I'LL BE HAPPY TO TELL HIM YOU'RE LOOKING FOR HIM WHEN HE GETS IN.
MAYBE I'LL STOP BACK THIS EVENING. THANKS FOR YOUR HELP.
IF THAT GUY AIN'T A PIG, I'LL EAT MY WIG.
THIS IS HEAT WE DON'T NEED.
TIME TO CLEAN HOUSE.

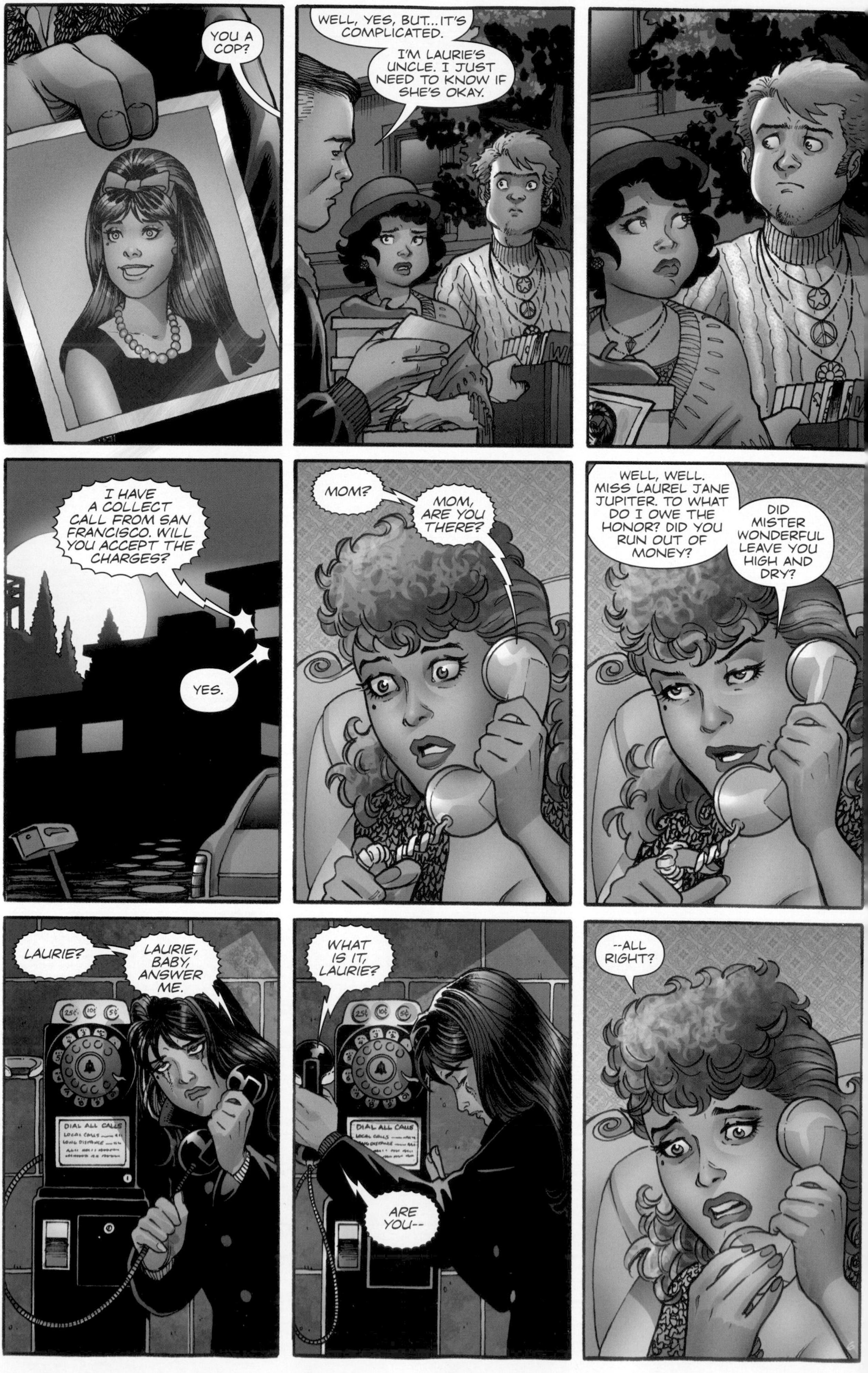
YOU A COP?
WELL, YES, BUT...IT'S COMPLICATED.
I'M LAURIE'S UNCLE. I JUST NEED TO KNOW IF SHE'S OKAY.
I HAVE A COLLECT CALL FROM SAN FRANCISCO. WILL YOU ACCEPT THE CHARGES?
YES.
MOM?
MOM, ARE YOU THERE?
WELL, WELL. MISS LAUREL JANE JUPITER. TO WHAT DO I OWE THE HONOR? DID YOU RUN OUT OF MONEY?
DID MISTER WONDERFUL LEAVE YOU HIGH AND DRY?
LAURIE?
LAURIE, BABY, ANSWER ME.
DIAL ALL CALLS
WHAT IS IT, LAURIE?
ARE YOU--
DIAL ALL CALLS
--ALL RIGHT?

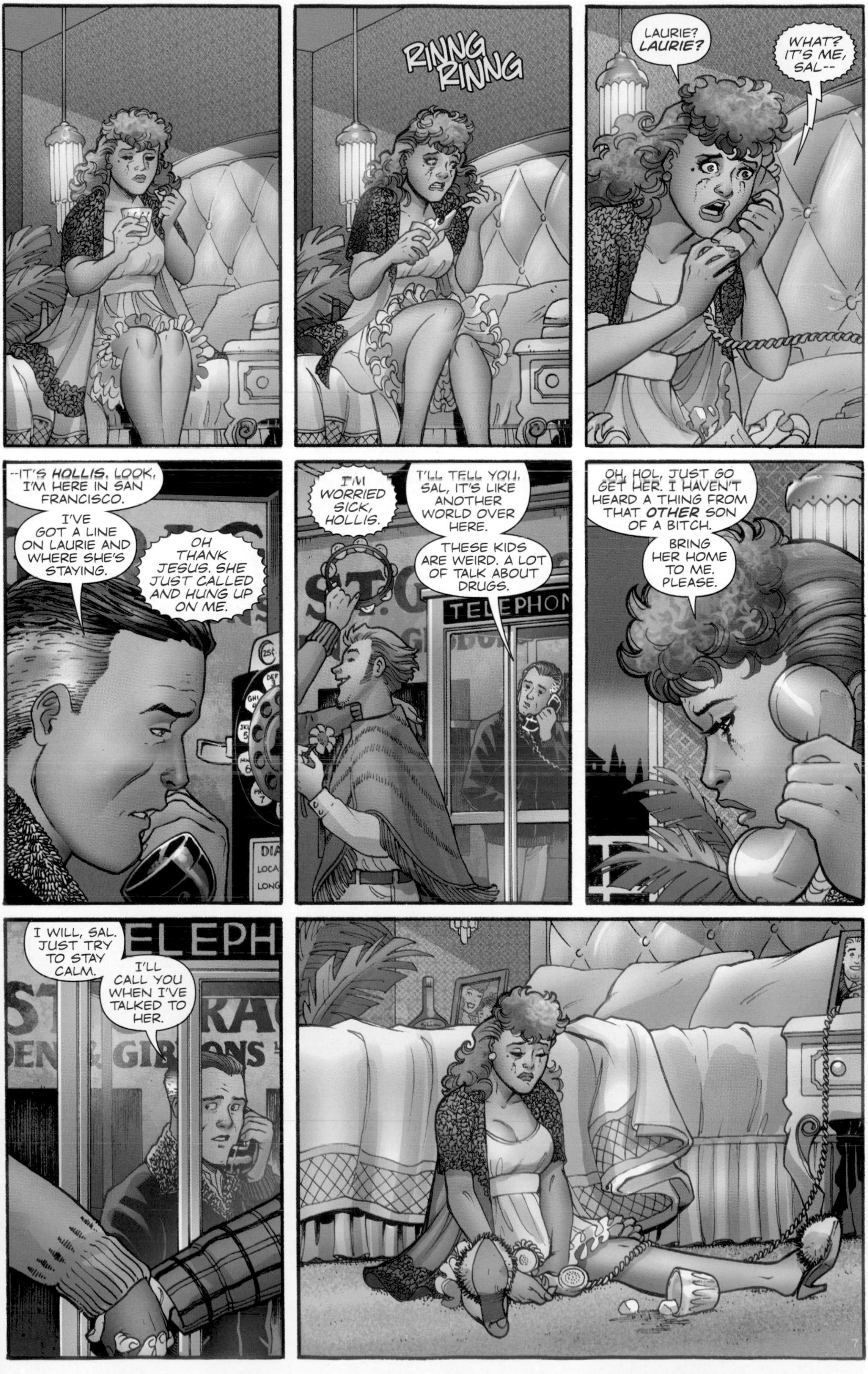
RINNG RINNG
LAURIE? LAURIE?
WHAT? IT'S ME, SAL--
--IT'S HOLLIS. LOOK, I'M HERE IN SAN FRANCISCO.
I'VE GOT A LINE ON LAURIE AND WHERE SHE'S STAYING.
OH THANK JESUS. SHE JUST CALLED AND HUNG UP ON ME.
I'M WORRIED SICK, HOLLIS.
I'LL TELL YOU, SAL, IT'S LIKE ANOTHER WORLD OVER HERE.
THESE KIDS ARE WEIRD. A LOT OF TALK ABOUT DRUGS.
TELEPHON
OH, HOL, JUST GO GET HER. I HAVEN'T HEARD A THING FROM THAT OTHER SON OF A BITCH.
BRING HER HOME TO ME. PLEASE.
TELEPH
I WILL, SAL. JUST TRY TO STAY CALM.
I'LL CALL YOU WHEN I'VE TALKED TO HER.

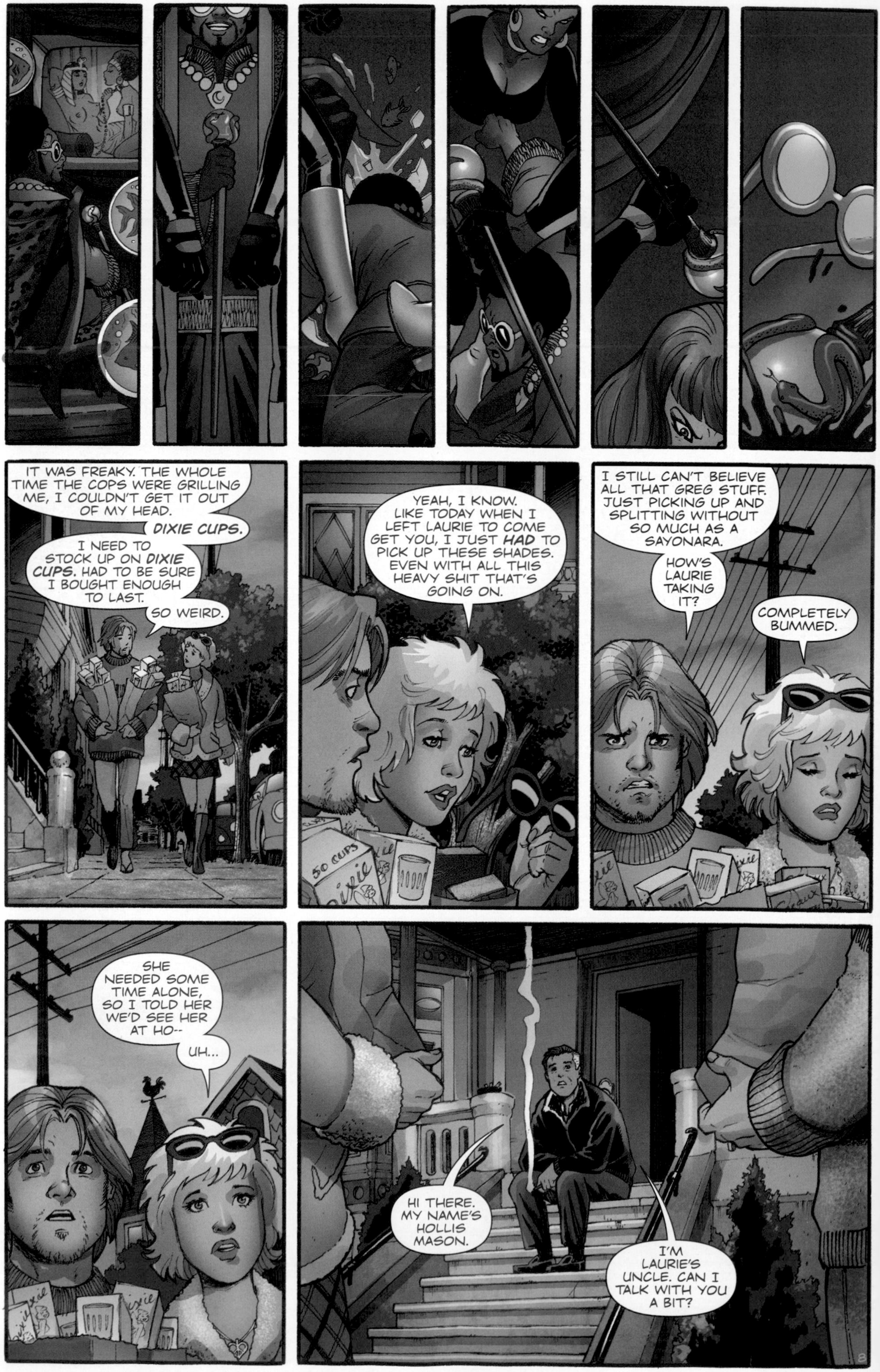
IT WAS FREAKY. THE WHOLE TIME THE COPS WERE GRILLING ME, I COULDN'T GET IT OUT OF MY HEAD.
DIXIE CUPS.
I NEED TO STOCK UP ON DIXIE CUPS. HAD TO BE SURE I BOUGHT ENOUGH TO LAST.
SO WEIRD.
YEAH, I KNOW. LIKE TODAY WHEN I LEFT LAURIE TO COME GET YOU, I JUST HAD TO PICK UP THESE SHADES. EVEN WITH ALL THIS HEAVY SHIT THAT'S GOING ON.
50 CUPS
I STILL CAN'T BELIEVE ALL THAT GREG STUFF. JUST PICKING UP AND SPLITTING WITHOUT SO MUCH AS A SAYONARA.
HOW'S LAURIE TAKING IT?
COMPLETELY BUMMED.
SHE NEEDED SOME TIME ALONE, SO I TOLD HER WE'D SEE HER AT HO--
UH...
HI THERE. MY NAME'S HOLLIS MASON.
I'M LAURIE'S UNCLE. CAN I TALK WITH YOU A BIT?

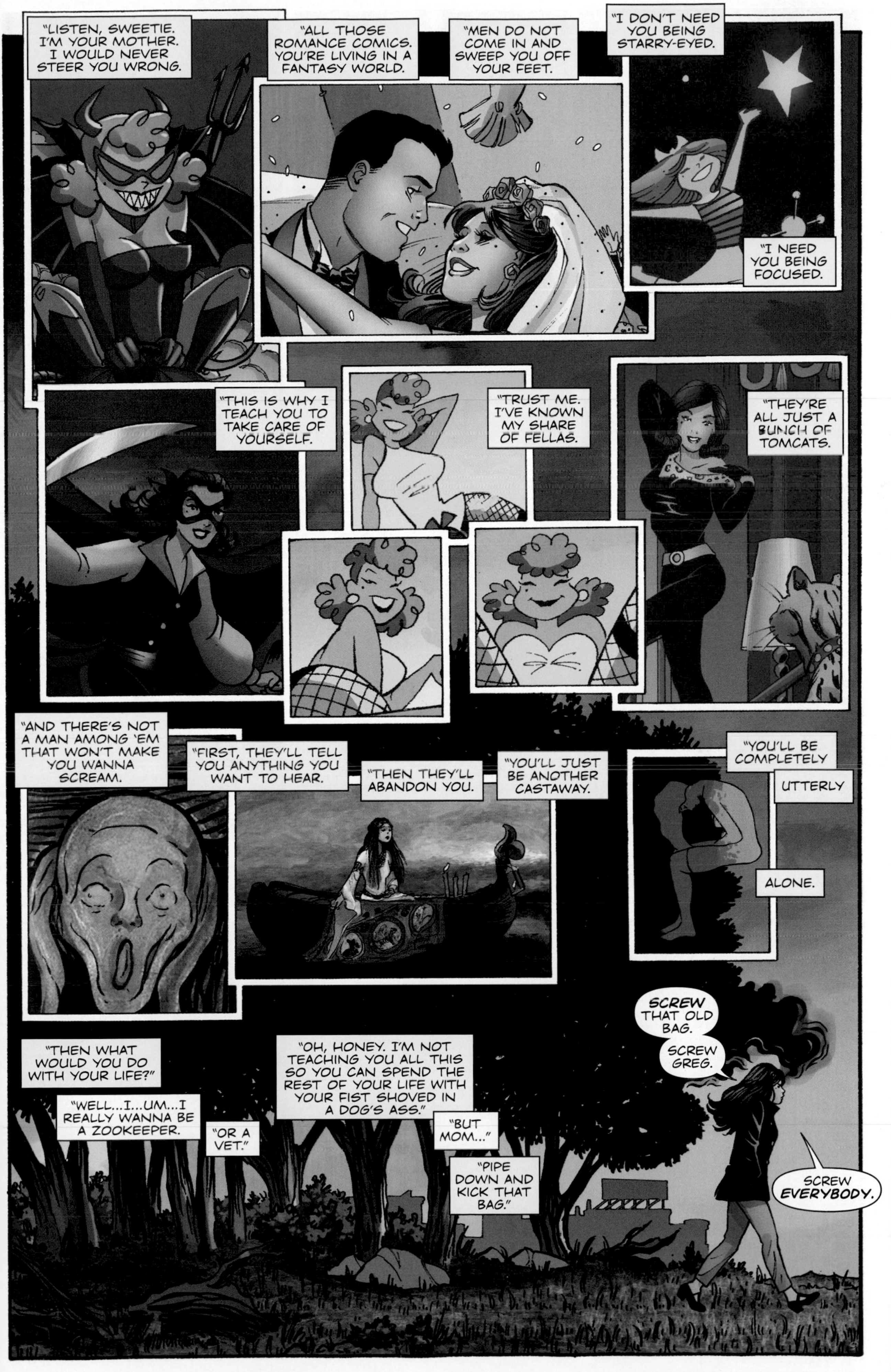
"LISTEN, SWEETIE. I'M YOUR MOTHER. I WOULD NEVER STEER YOU WRONG.
"ALL THOSE ROMANCE COMICS. YOU'RE LIVING IN A FANTASY WORLD.
"MEN DO NOT COME IN AND SWEEP YOU OFF YOUR FEET.
"I DON'T NEED YOU BEING STARRY-EYED.
"I NEED YOU BEING FOCUSED.
"THIS IS WHY I TEACH YOU TO TAKE CARE OF YOURSELF.
"TRUST ME. I'VE KNOWN MY SHARE OF FELLAS.
"THEY'RE ALL JUST A BUNCH OF TOMCATS.
"AND THERE'S NOT A MAN AMONG 'EM THAT WON'T MAKE YOU WANNA SCREAM.
"FIRST, THEY'LL TELL YOU ANYTHING YOU WANT TO HEAR.
"THEN THEY'LL ABANDON YOU.
"YOU'LL JUST BE ANOTHER CASTAWAY.
"YOU'LL BE COMPLETELY
UTTERLY
ALONE.
"THEN WHAT WOULD YOU DO WITH YOUR LIFE?"
"WELL...I...UM...I REALLY WANNA BE A ZOOKEEPER.
"OR A VET."
"OH, HONEY. I'M NOT TEACHING YOU ALL THIS SO YOU CAN SPEND THE REST OF YOUR LIFE WITH YOUR FIST SHOVED IN A DOG'S ASS."
"BUT MOM..."
"PIPE DOWN AND KICK THAT BAG."
SCREW THAT OLD BAG.
SCREW GREG.
SCREW EVERYBODY.

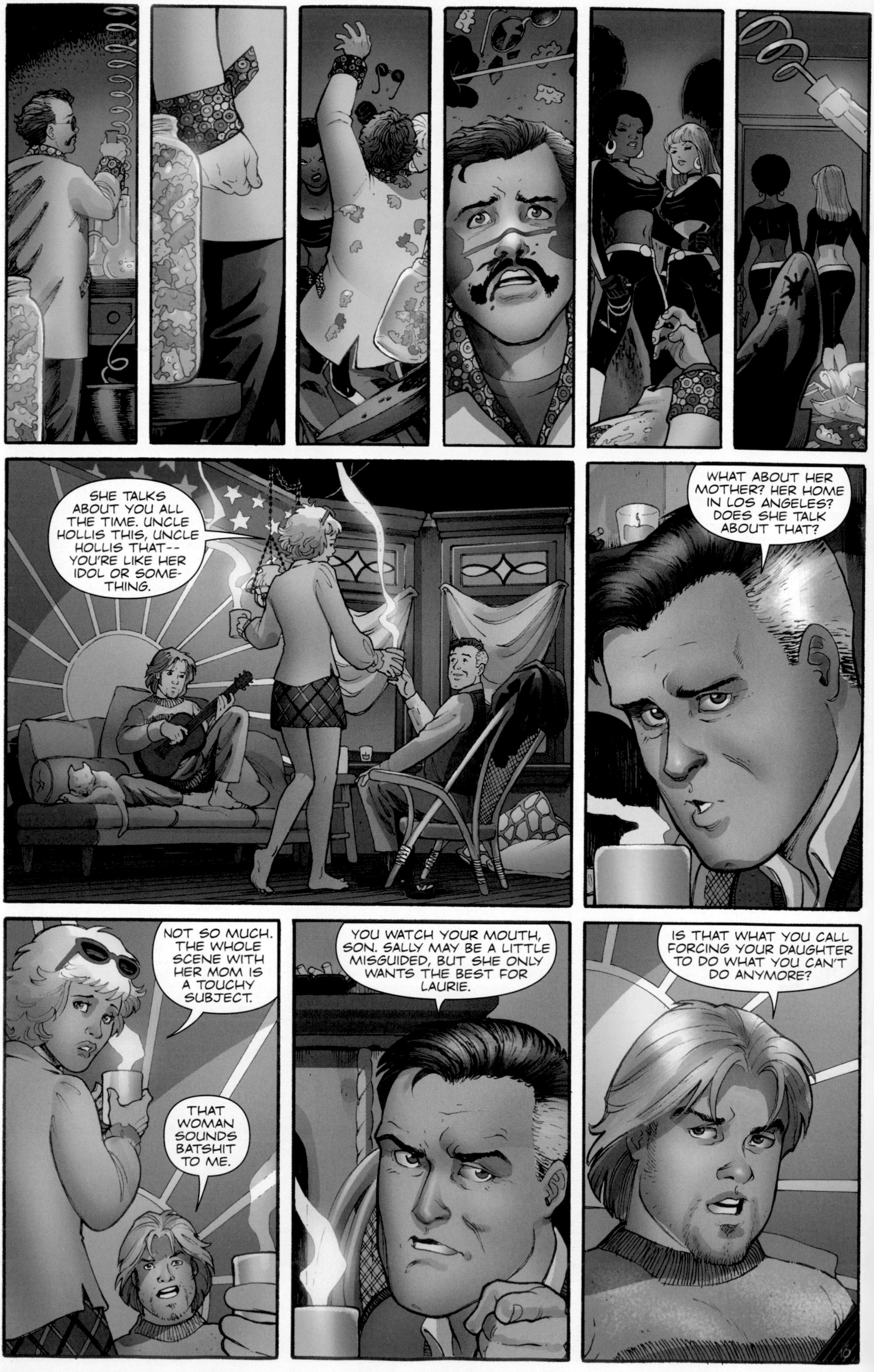
SHE TALKS ABOUT YOU ALL THE TIME. UNCLE HOLLIS THIS, UNCLE HOLLIS THAT-- YOU'RE LIKE HER IDOL OR SOME-THING.
WHAT ABOUT HER MOTHER? HER HOME IN LOS ANGELES? DOES SHE TALK ABOUT THAT?
NOT SO MUCH. THE WHOLE SCENE WITH HER MOM IS A TOUCHY SUBJECT.
THAT WOMAN SOUNDS BATSHIT TO ME.
YOU WATCH YOUR MOUTH, SON. SALLY MAY BE A LITTLE MISGUIDED, BUT SHE ONLY WANTS THE BEST FOR LAURIE.
IS THAT WHAT YOU CALL FORCING YOUR DAUGHTER TO DO WHAT YOU CAN'T DO ANYMORE?
10

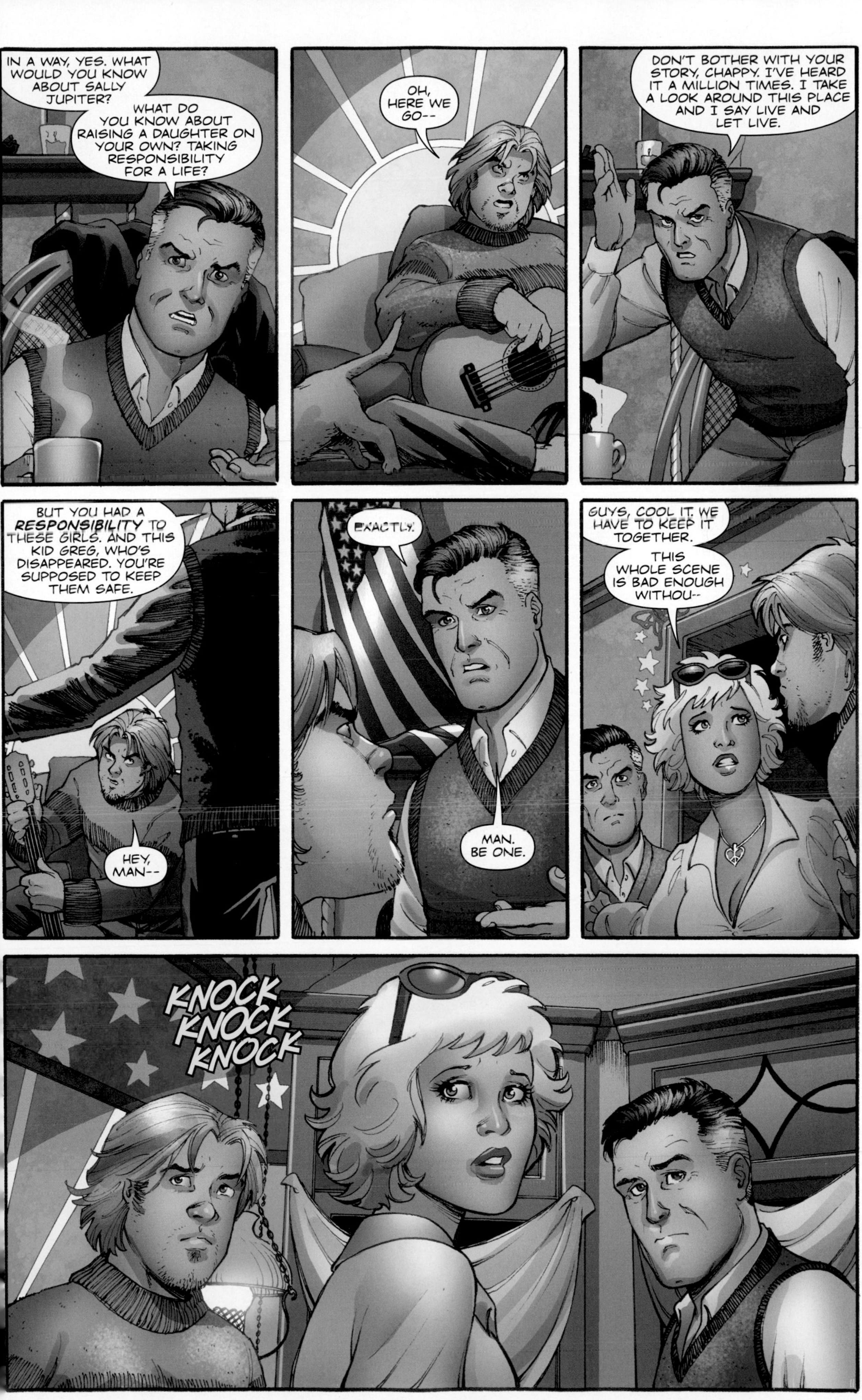
IN A WAY, YES. WHAT WOULD YOU KNOW ABOUT SALLY JUPITER?
WHAT DO YOU KNOW ABOUT RAISING A DAUGHTER ON YOUR OWN? TAKING RESPONSIBILITY FOR A LIFE?
OH, HERE WE GO--
DON'T BOTHER WITH YOUR STORY, CHAPPY. I'VE HEARD IT A MILLION TIMES. I TAKE A LOOK AROUND THIS PLACE AND I SAY LIVE AND LET LIVE.
BUT YOU HAD A RESPONSIBILITY TO THESE GIRLS. AND THIS KID GREG, WHO'S DISAPPEARED. YOU'RE SUPPOSED TO KEEP THEM SAFE.
HEY, MAN--
EXACTLY.
MAN. BE ONE.
GUYS, COOL IT. WE HAVE TO KEEP IT TOGETHER.
THIS WHOLE SCENE IS BAD ENOUGH WITHOU--
KNOCK KNOCK KNOCK

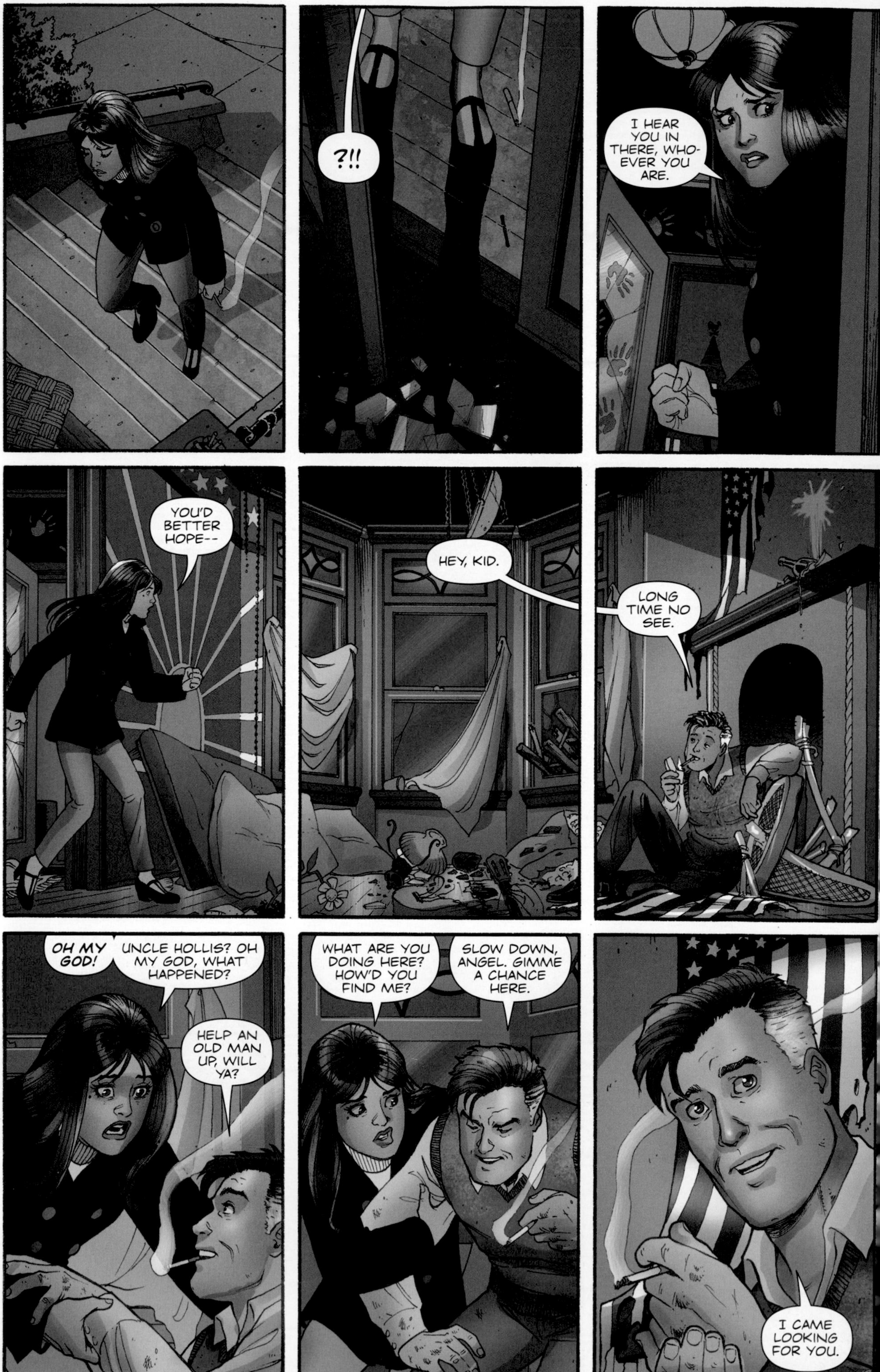
?!!
I HEAR YOU IN THERE, WHO-EVER YOU ARE.
YOU'D BETTER HOPE--
HEY, KID.
LONG TIME NO SEE.
OH MY GOD!
UNCLE HOLLIS? OH MY GOD, WHAT HAPPENED?
HELP AN OLD MAN UP, WILL YA?
WHAT ARE YOU DOING HERE? HOW'D YOU FIND ME?
SLOW DOWN, ANGEL. GIMME A CHANCE HERE.
I CAME LOOKING FOR YOU.

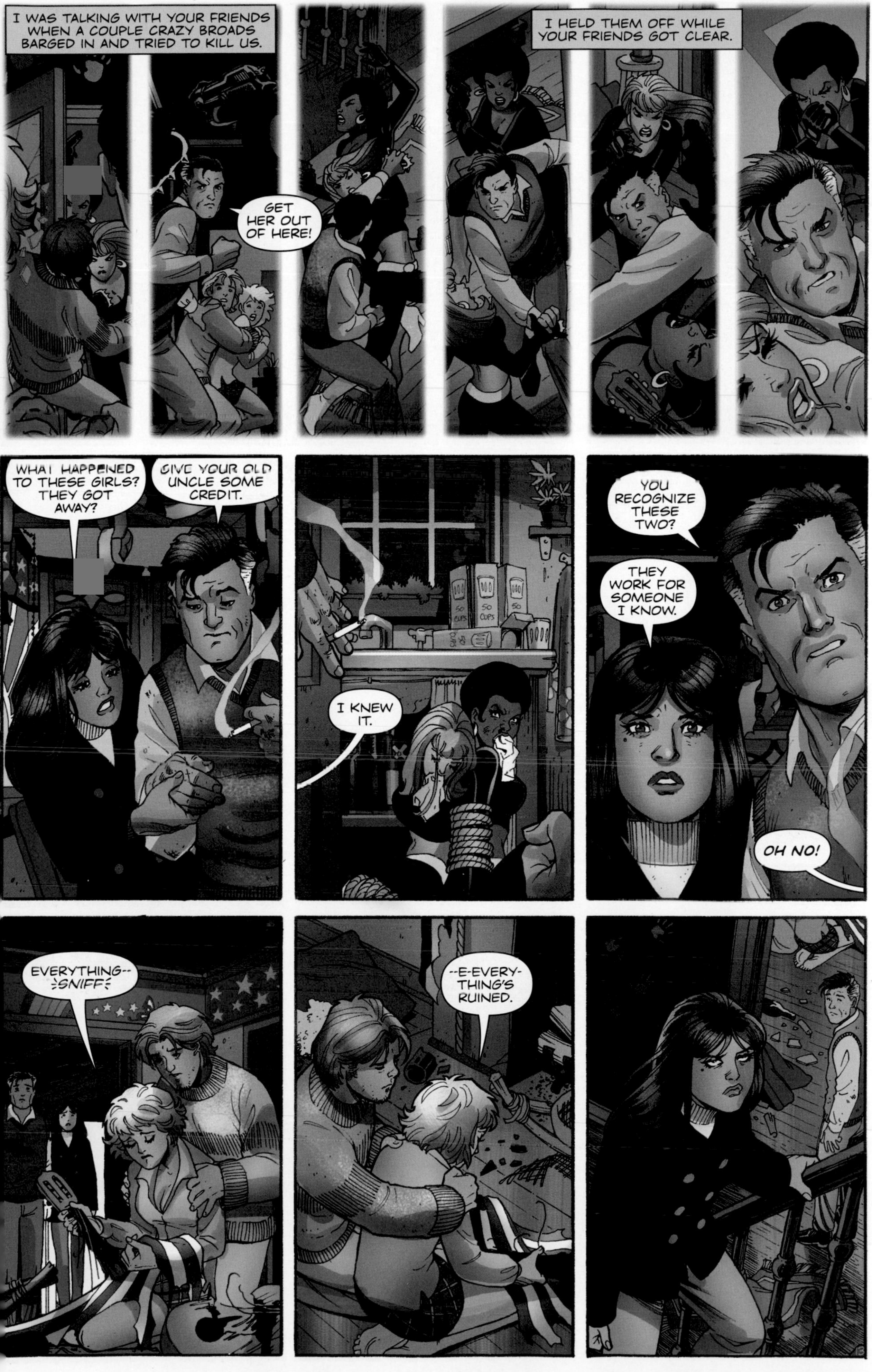
I WAS TALKING WITH YOUR FRIENDS WHEN A COUPLE CRAZY BROADS BARGED IN AND TRIED TO KILL US.
GET HER OUT OF HERE!
I HELD THEM OFF WHILE YOUR FRIENDS GOT CLEAR.
WHAT HAPPENED TO THESE GIRLS? THEY GOT AWAY?
GIVE YOUR OLD UNCLE SOME CREDIT.
50 CUPS
50 CUPS
I KNEW IT.
YOU RECOGNIZE THESE TWO?
THEY WORK FOR SOMEONE I KNOW.
OH NO!
EVERYTHING--
SNIFF
--E-EVERY-THING'S RUINED.

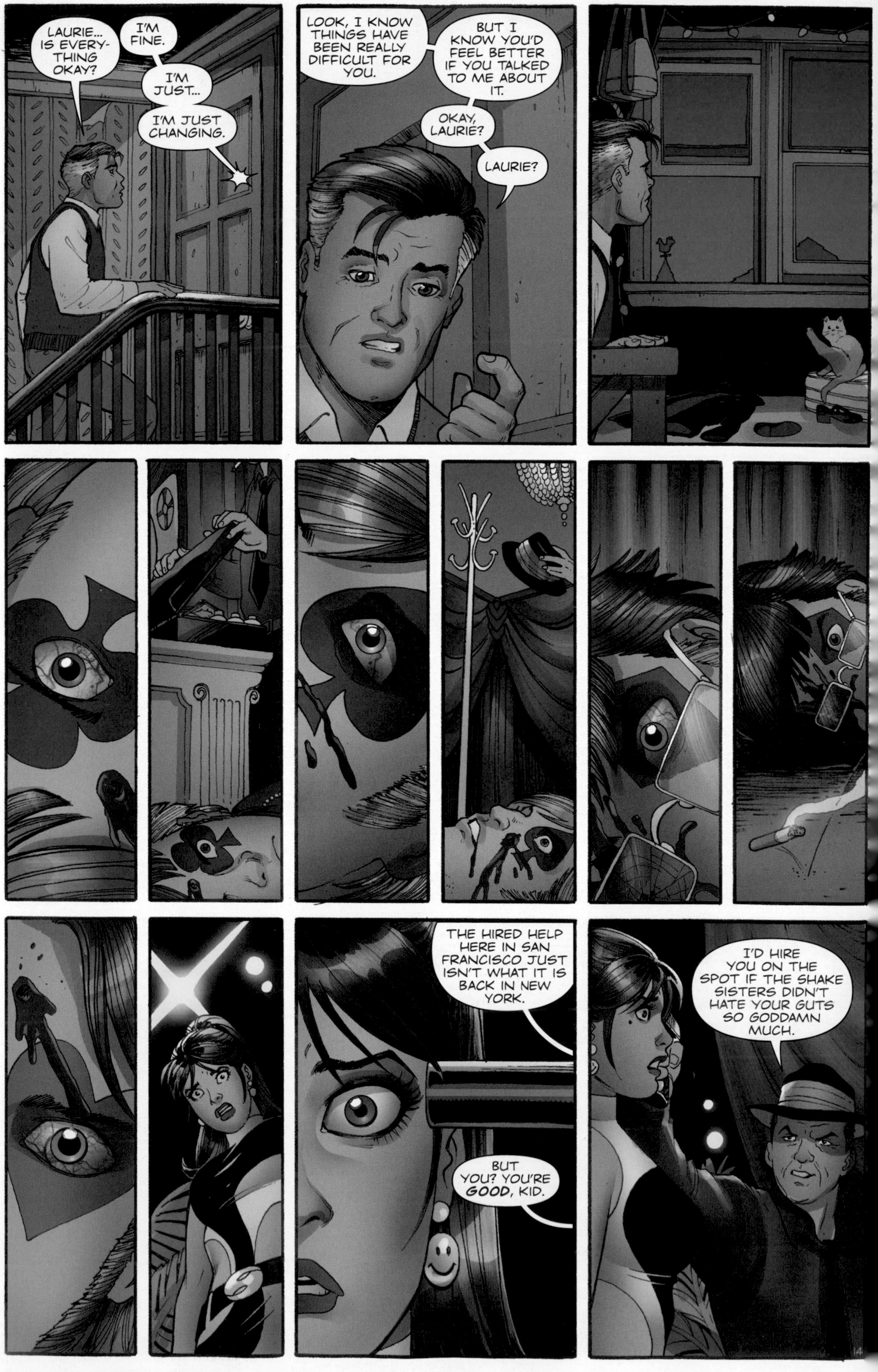

LAURIE... IS EVERY-THING OKAY?
I'M FINE.
I'M JUST...
I'M JUST CHANGING.
LOOK, I KNOW THINGS HAVE BEEN REALLY DIFFICULT FOR YOU.
BUT I KNOW YOU'D FEEL BETTER IF YOU TALKED TO ME ABOUT IT.
OKAY, LAURIE?
LAURIE?
THE HIRED HELP HERE IN SAN FRANCISCO JUST ISN'T WHAT IT IS BACK IN NEW YORK.
BUT YOU? YOU'RE GOOD, KID.
I'D HIRE YOU ON THE SPOT IF THE SHAKE SISTERS DIDN'T HATE YOUR GUTS SO GODDAMN MUCH.

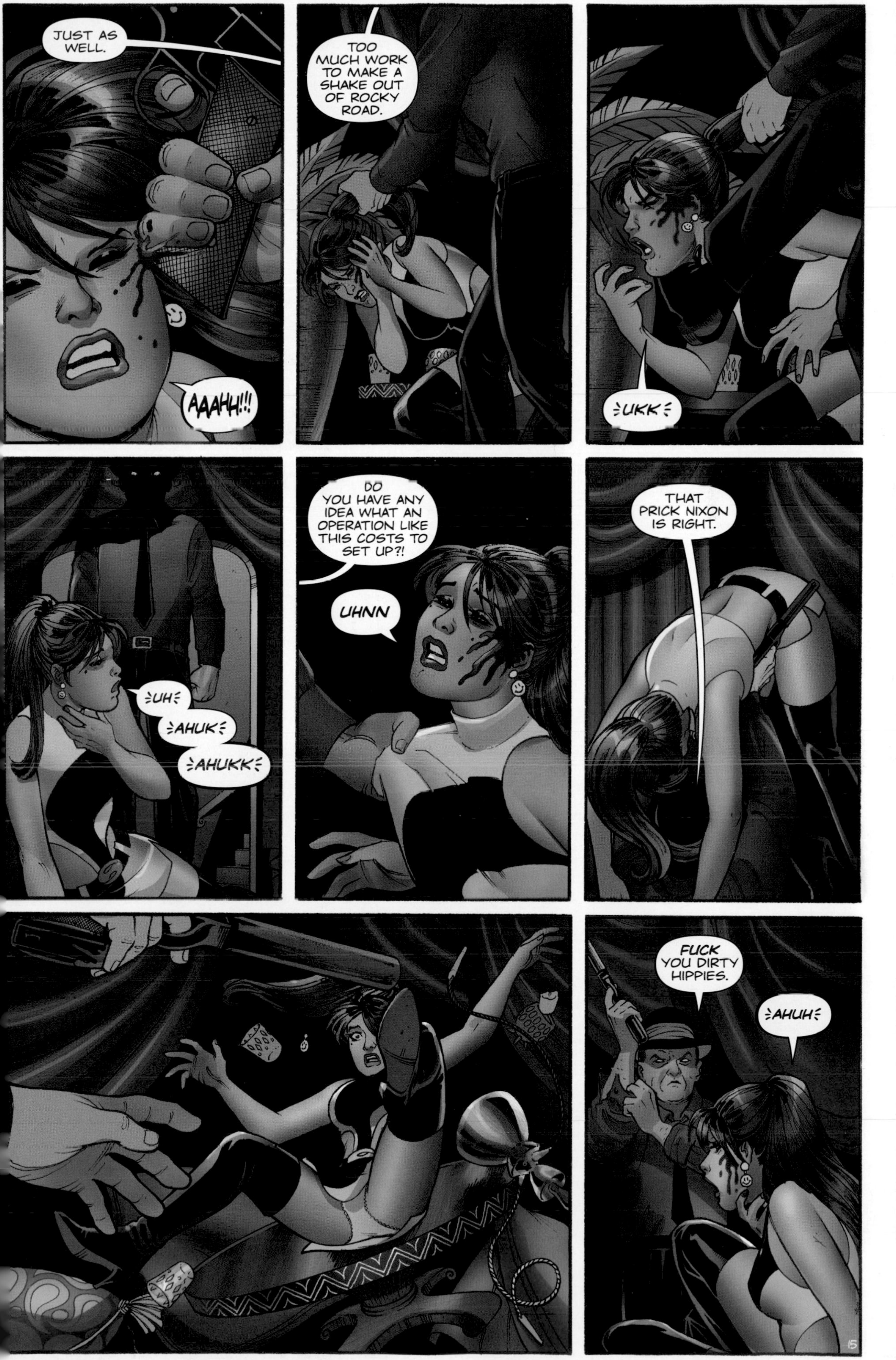
JUST AS WELL.
AAAHH!!!
TOO MUCH WORK TO MAKE A SHAKE OUT OF ROCKY ROAD.
UKK
UH
AHUK
AHUKK
DO YOU HAVE ANY IDEA WHAT AN OPERATION LIKE THIS COSTS TO SET UP?!
UHNN
THAT PRICK NIXON IS RIGHT.
FUCK YOU DIRTY HIPPIES.
AHUH

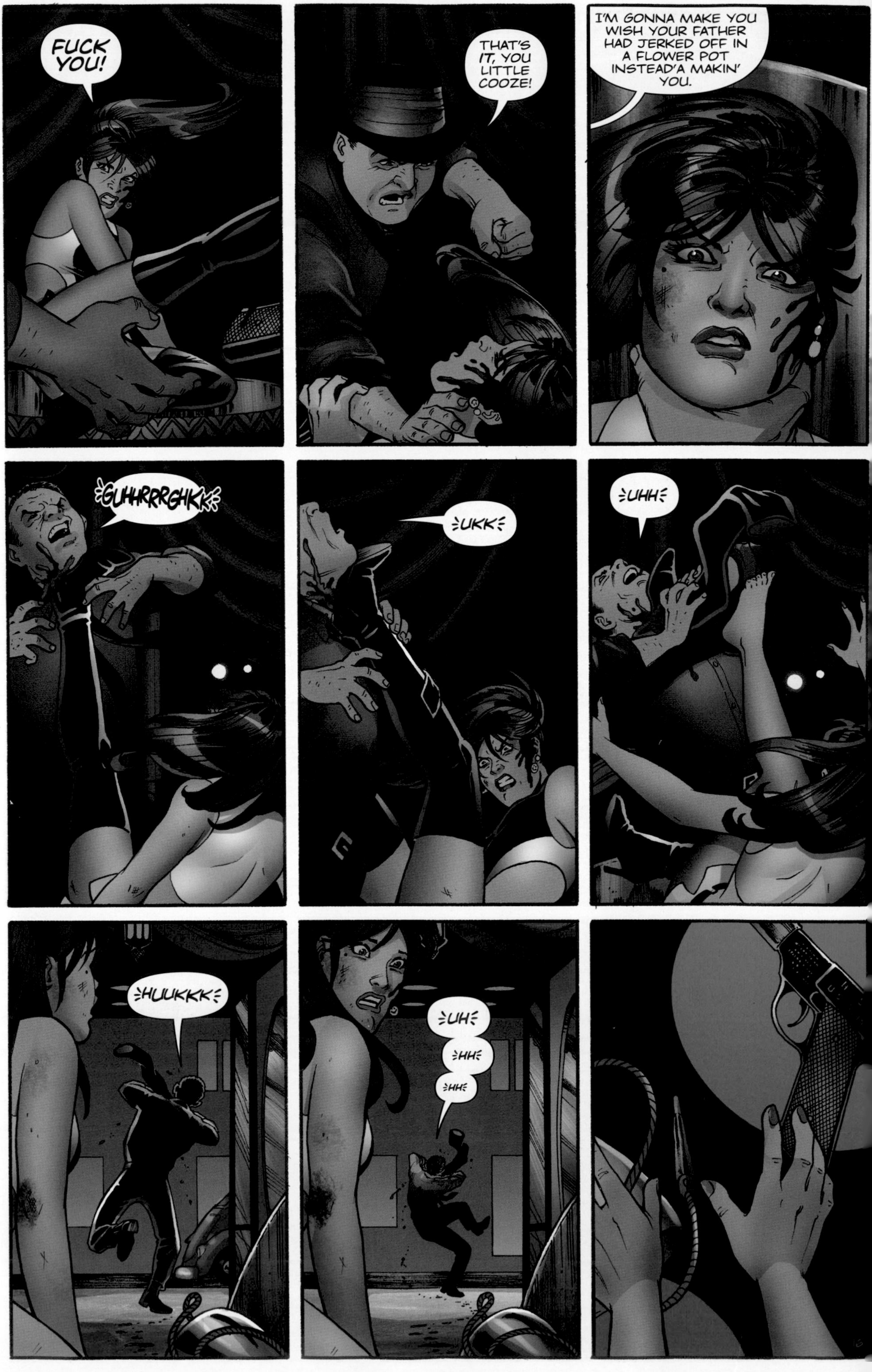
FUCK YOU!
THAT'S IT, YOU LITTLE COOZE!
I'M GONNA MAKE YOU WISH YOUR FATHER HAD JERKED OFF IN A FLOWER POT INSTEAD'A MAKIN' YOU.
GUHHRRRGHKK
UKK
UHH
HUUKKK
UH
HH
HH

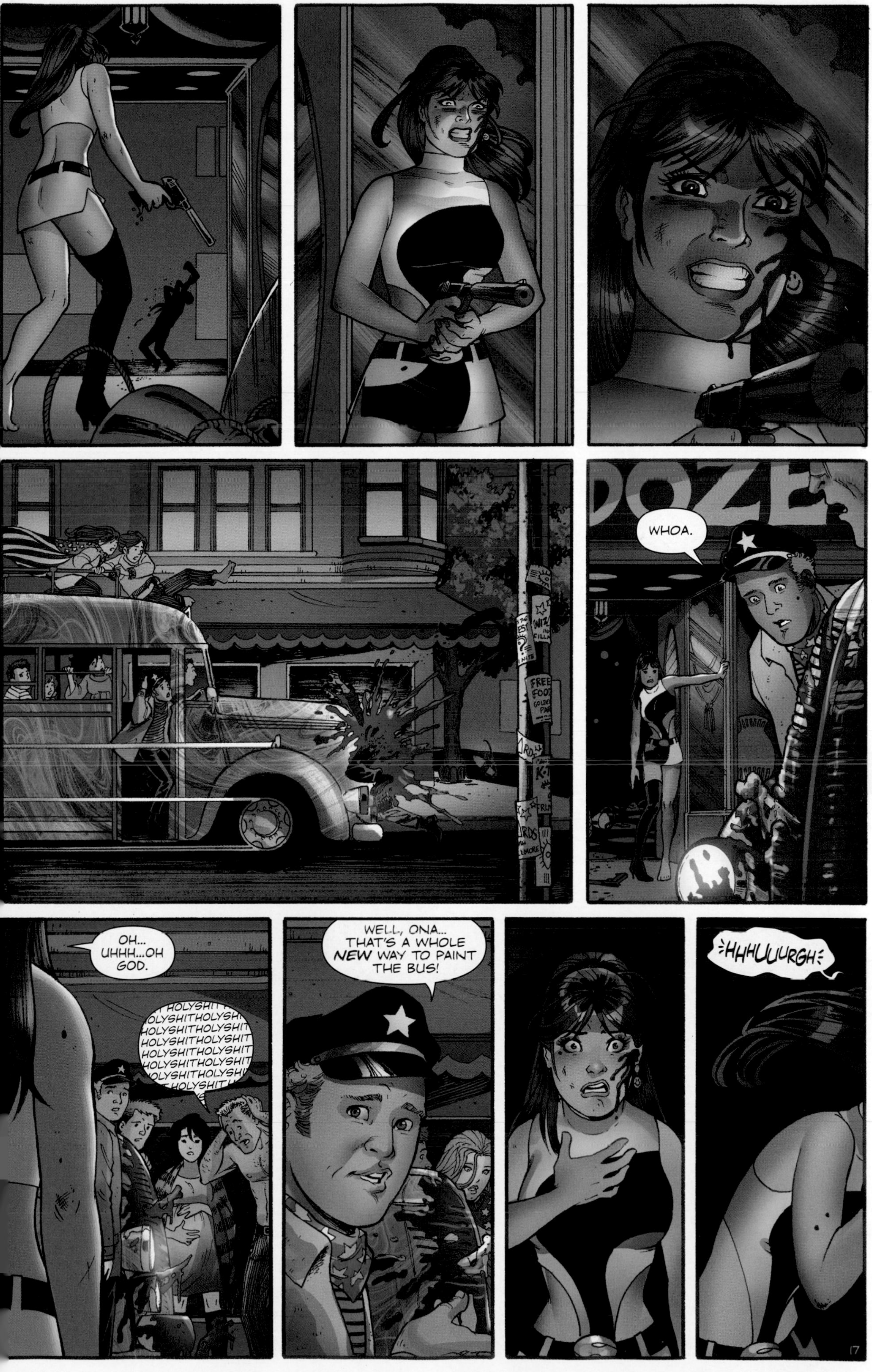
DOZE
WHOA.
OH... UHHH...OH GOD.
HOLYSHITHOLYSHIT HOLYSHITHOLYSHIT HOLYSHITHOLYSHIT HOLYSHITHOLYSHIT HOLYSHITHOLYSHIT HOLYSHITHOLYSHI HOLYSHIT
WELL, ONA... THAT'S A WHOLE NEW WAY TO PAINT THE BUS!
HHHUUURGH
FREE FOOD

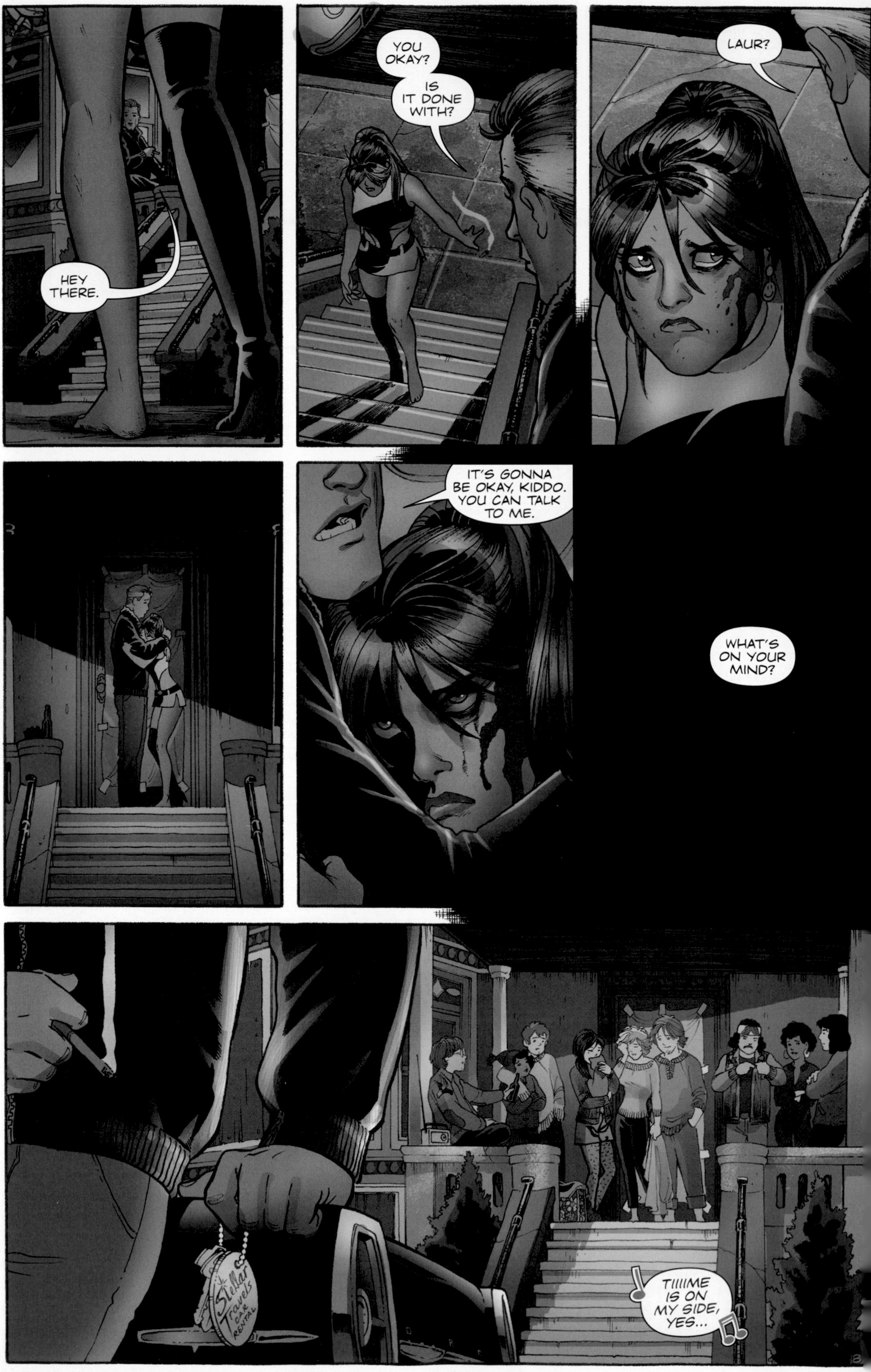
HEY THERE.
YOU OKAY?
IS IT DONE WITH?
LAUR?
IT'S GONNA BE OKAY, KIDDO. YOU CAN TALK TO ME.
WHAT'S ON YOUR MIND?
Stellar Travels CAR RENTAL
TIIIIME IS ON MY SIDE, YES...

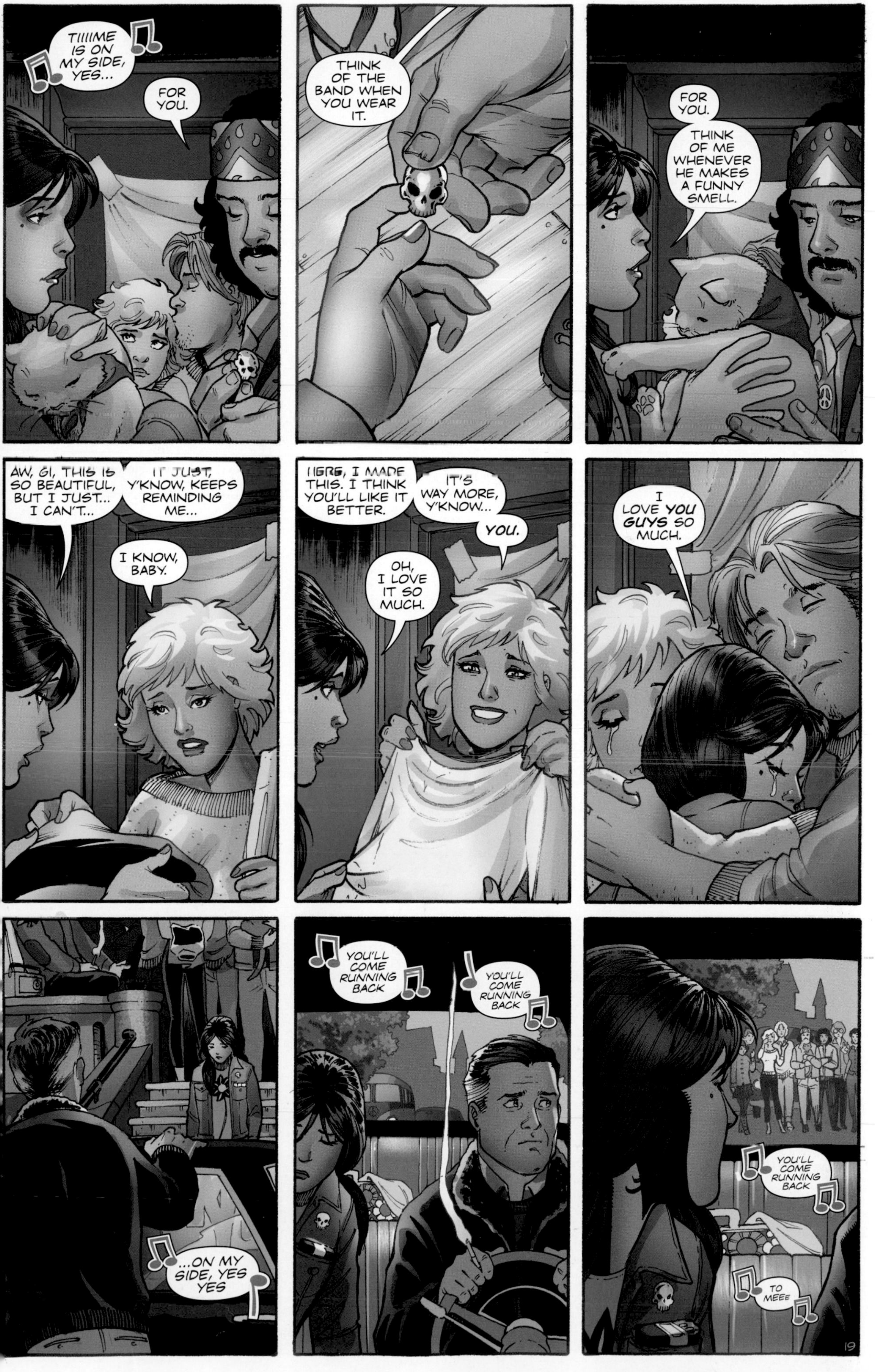
TIIIIME IS ON MY SIDE, YES...
FOR YOU.
THINK OF THE BAND WHEN YOU WEAR IT.
FOR YOU.
THINK OF ME WHENEVER HE MAKES A FUNNY SMELL.
AW, GI, THIS IS SO BEAUTIFUL, BUT I JUST... I CAN'T...
IT JUST, Y'KNOW, KEEPS REMINDING ME...
I KNOW, BABY.
HERE, I MADE THIS. I THINK YOU'LL LIKE IT BETTER.
IT'S WAY MORE, Y'KNOW...
YOU.
OH, I LOVE IT SO MUCH.
I LOVE YOU GUYS SO MUCH.
...ON MY SIDE, YES YES
YOU'LL COME RUNNING BACK
YOU'LL COME RUNNING BACK
YOU'LL COME RUNNING BACK
TO MEEE

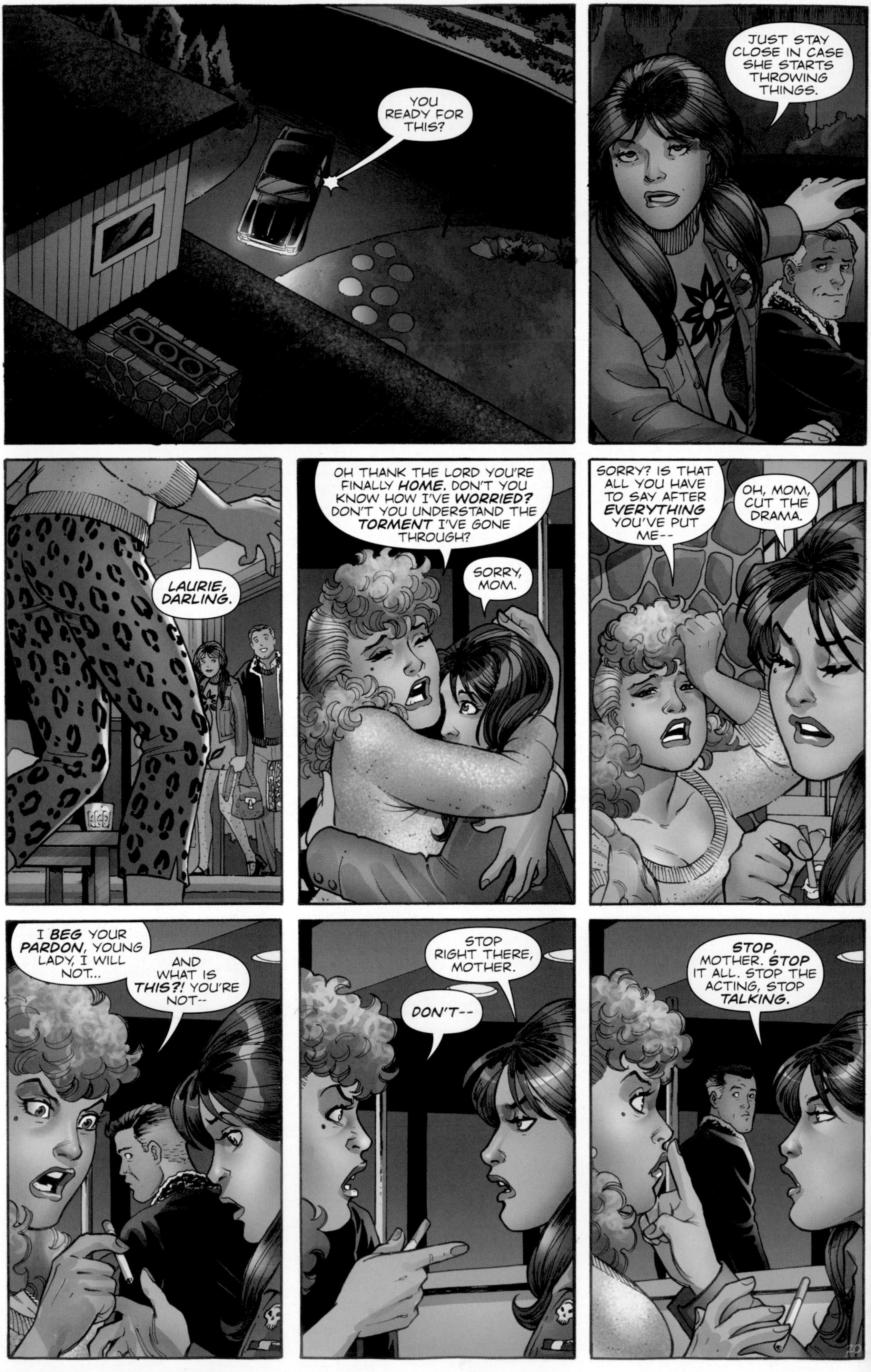
YOU READY FOR THIS?
JUST STAY CLOSE IN CASE SHE STARTS THROWING THINGS.
LAURIE, DARLING.
OH THANK THE LORD YOU'RE FINALLY HOME. DON'T YOU KNOW HOW I'VE WORRIED? DON'T YOU UNDERSTAND THE TORMENT I'VE GONE THROUGH?
SORRY, MOM.
SORRY? IS THAT ALL YOU HAVE TO SAY AFTER EVERYTHING YOU'VE PUT ME--
OH, MOM, CUT THE DRAMA.
I BEG YOUR PARDON, YOUNG LADY, I WILL NOT...
AND WHAT IS THIS?! YOU'RE NOT--
STOP RIGHT THERE, MOTHER.
DON'T--
STOP, MOTHER. STOP IT ALL. STOP THE ACTING, STOP TALKING.

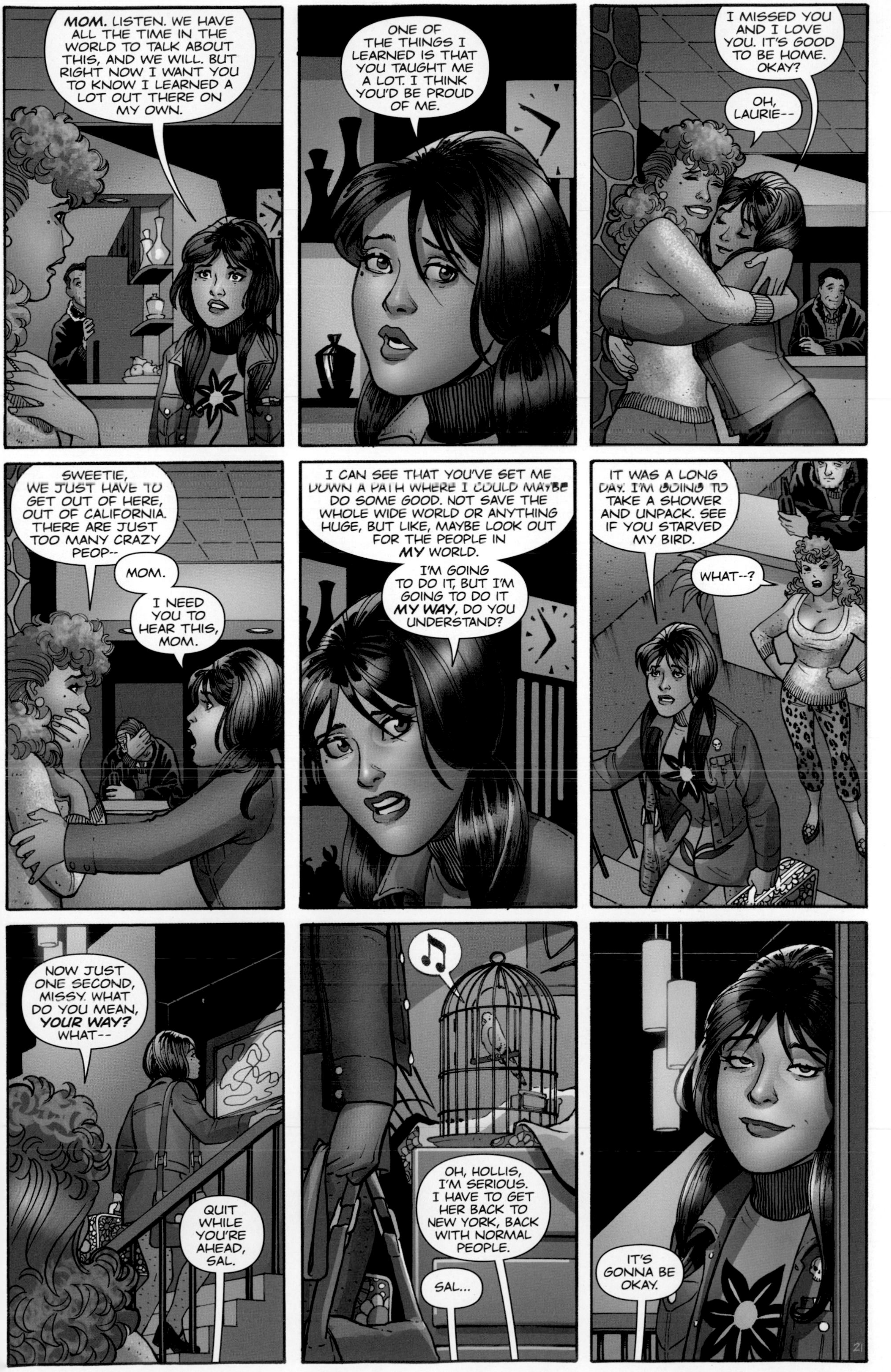
MOM. LISTEN. WE HAVE ALL THE TIME IN THE WORLD TO TALK ABOUT THIS, AND WE WILL. BUT RIGHT NOW I WANT YOU TO KNOW I LEARNED A LOT OUT THERE ON MY OWN.
ONE OF THE THINGS I LEARNED IS THAT YOU TAUGHT ME A LOT. I THINK YOU'D BE PROUD OF ME.
I MISSED YOU AND I LOVE YOU. IT'S GOOD TO BE HOME. OKAY?
OH, LAURIE--
SWEETIE, WE JUST HAVE TO GET OUT OF HERE, OUT OF CALIFORNIA. THERE ARE JUST TOO MANY CRAZY PEOP--
MOM.
I NEED YOU TO HEAR THIS, MOM.
I CAN SEE THAT YOU'VE SET ME DOWN A PATH WHERE I COULD MAYBE DO SOME GOOD. NOT SAVE THE WHOLE WIDE WORLD OR ANYTHING HUGE, BUT LIKE, MAYBE LOOK OUT FOR THE PEOPLE IN MY WORLD.
I'M GOING TO DO IT, BUT I'M GOING TO DO IT MY WAY, DO YOU UNDERSTAND?
IT WAS A LONG DAY. I'M GOING TO TAKE A SHOWER AND UNPACK. SEE IF YOU STARVED MY BIRD.
WHAT--?
NOW JUST ONE SECOND, MISSY. WHAT DO YOU MEAN, YOUR WAY? WHAT--
QUIT WHILE YOU'RE AHEAD, SAL.
♪
OH, HOLLIS, I'M SERIOUS. I HAVE TO GET HER BACK TO NEW YORK, BACK WITH NORMAL PEOPLE.
SAL...
IT'S GONNA BE OKAY.
21

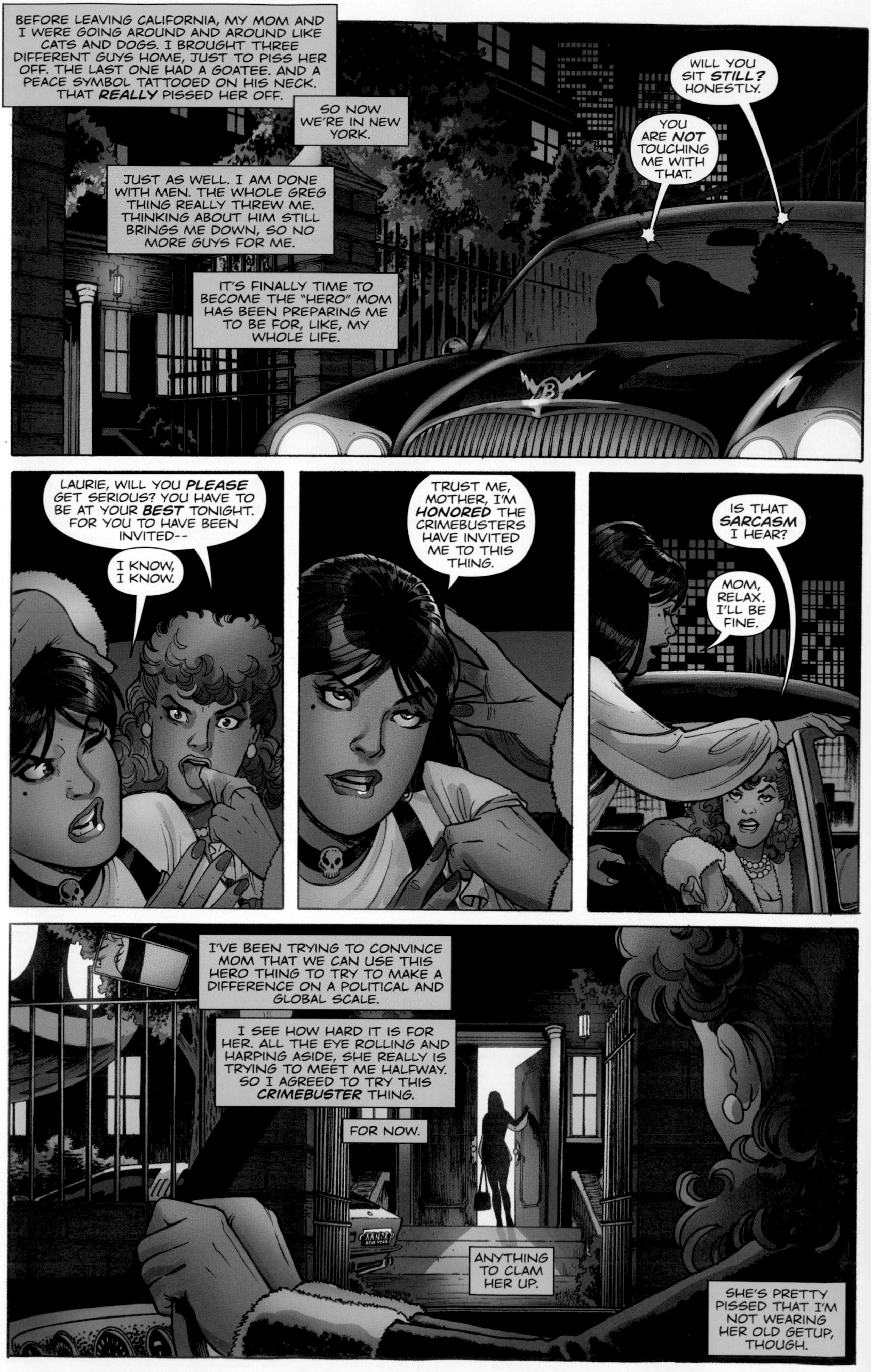
BEFORE LEAVING CALIFORNIA, MY MOM AND I WERE GOING AROUND AND AROUND LIKE CATS AND DOGS. I BROUGHT THREE DIFFERENT GUYS HOME, JUST TO PISS HER OFF. THE LAST ONE HAD A GOATEE. AND A PEACE SYMBOL TATTOOED ON HIS NECK. THAT **REALLY** PISSED HER OFF.
SO NOW WE'RE IN NEW YORK.
JUST AS WELL. I AM DONE WITH MEN. THE WHOLE GREG THING REALLY THREW ME. THINKING ABOUT HIM STILL BRINGS ME DOWN, SO NO MORE GUYS FOR ME.
IT'S FINALLY TIME TO BECOME THE "HERO" MOM HAS BEEN PREPARING ME TO BE FOR, LIKE, MY WHOLE LIFE.
WILL YOU SIT **STILL?** HONESTLY.
YOU ARE **NOT** TOUCHING ME WITH THAT.
LAURIE, WILL YOU **PLEASE** GET SERIOUS? YOU HAVE TO BE AT YOUR **BEST** TONIGHT. FOR YOU TO HAVE BEEN INVITED--
I KNOW, I KNOW.
TRUST ME, MOTHER, I'M **HONORED** THE CRIMEBUSTERS HAVE INVITED ME TO THIS THING.
IS THAT **SARCASM** I HEAR?
MOM, RELAX. I'LL BE FINE.
I'VE BEEN TRYING TO CONVINCE MOM THAT WE CAN USE THIS HERO THING TO TRY TO MAKE A DIFFERENCE ON A POLITICAL AND GLOBAL SCALE.
I SEE HOW HARD IT IS FOR HER. ALL THE EYE ROLLING AND HARPING ASIDE, SHE REALLY IS TRYING TO MEET ME HALFWAY. SO I AGREED TO TRY THIS **CRIMEBUSTER** THING.
FOR NOW.
ANYTHING TO CLAM HER UP.
SHE'S PRETTY PISSED THAT I'M NOT WEARING HER OLD GETUP, THOUGH.

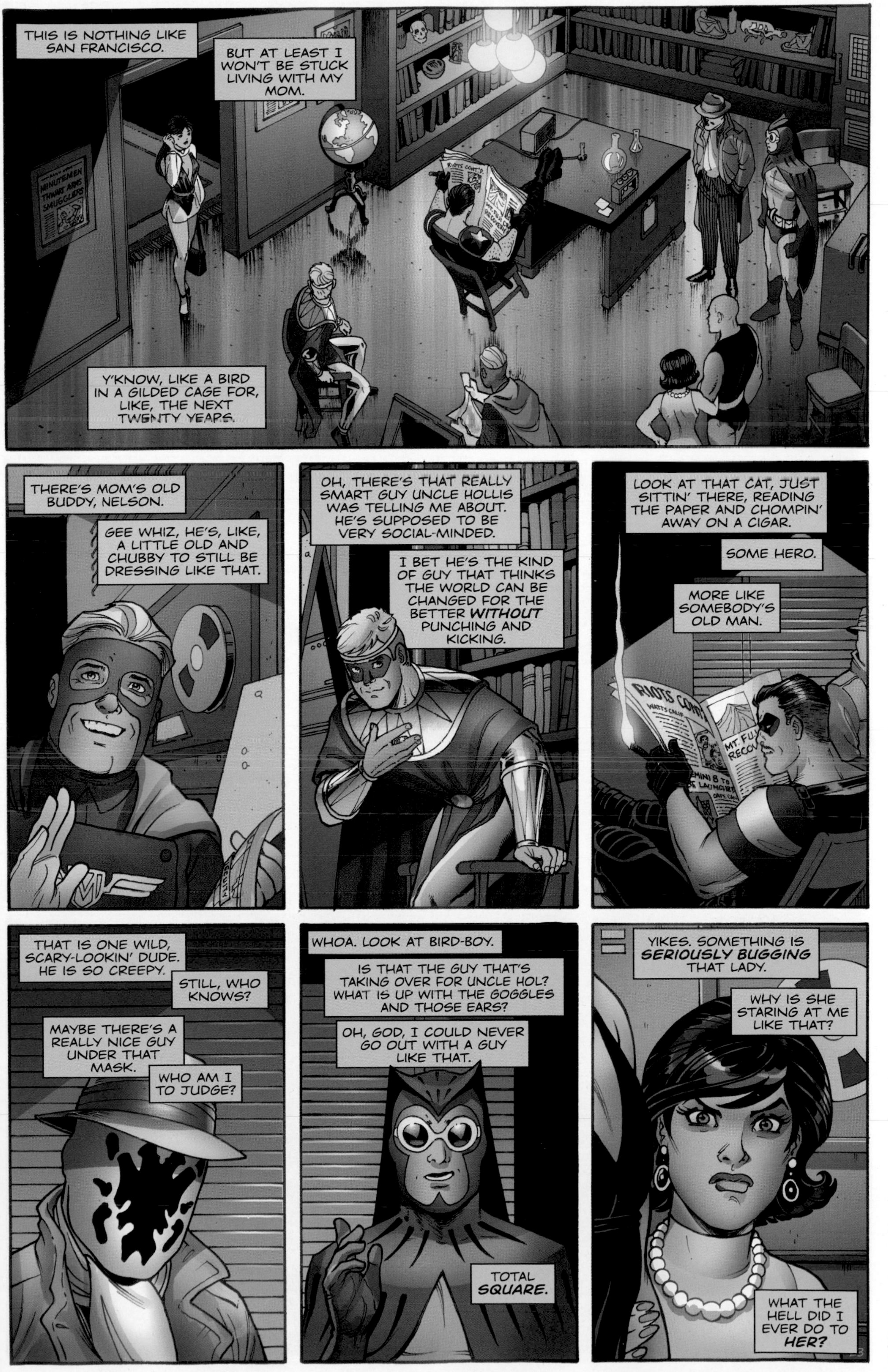
THIS IS NOTHING LIKE SAN FRANCISCO.
BUT AT LEAST I WON'T BE STUCK LIVING WITH MY MOM.
MINUTEMEN THWART ARMS SMUGGLERS
Y'KNOW, LIKE A BIRD IN A GILDED CAGE FOR, LIKE, THE NEXT TWENTY YEARS.
THERE'S MOM'S OLD BUDDY, NELSON.
GEE WHIZ, HE'S, LIKE, A LITTLE OLD AND CHUBBY TO STILL BE DRESSING LIKE THAT.
OH, THERE'S THAT REALLY SMART GUY UNCLE HOLLIS WAS TELLING ME ABOUT. HE'S SUPPOSED TO BE VERY SOCIAL-MINDED.
I BET HE'S THE KIND OF GUY THAT THINKS THE WORLD CAN BE CHANGED FOR THE BETTER ***WITHOUT*** PUNCHING AND KICKING.
LOOK AT THAT CAT, JUST SITTIN' THERE, READING THE PAPER AND CHOMPIN' AWAY ON A CIGAR.
SOME HERO.
MORE LIKE SOMEBODY'S OLD MAN.
THAT IS ONE WILD, SCARY-LOOKIN' DUDE. HE IS SO CREEPY.
STILL, WHO KNOWS?
MAYBE THERE'S A REALLY NICE GUY UNDER THAT MASK.
WHO AM I TO JUDGE?
WHOA. LOOK AT BIRD-BOY.
IS THAT THE GUY THAT'S TAKING OVER FOR UNCLE HOL? WHAT IS UP WITH THE GOGGLES AND THOSE EARS?
OH, GOD, I COULD NEVER GO OUT WITH A GUY LIKE THAT.
TOTAL ***SQUARE.***
YIKES. SOMETHING IS ***SERIOUSLY BUGGING*** THAT LADY.
WHY IS SHE STARING AT ME LIKE THAT?
WHAT THE HELL DID I EVER DO TO ***HER?***

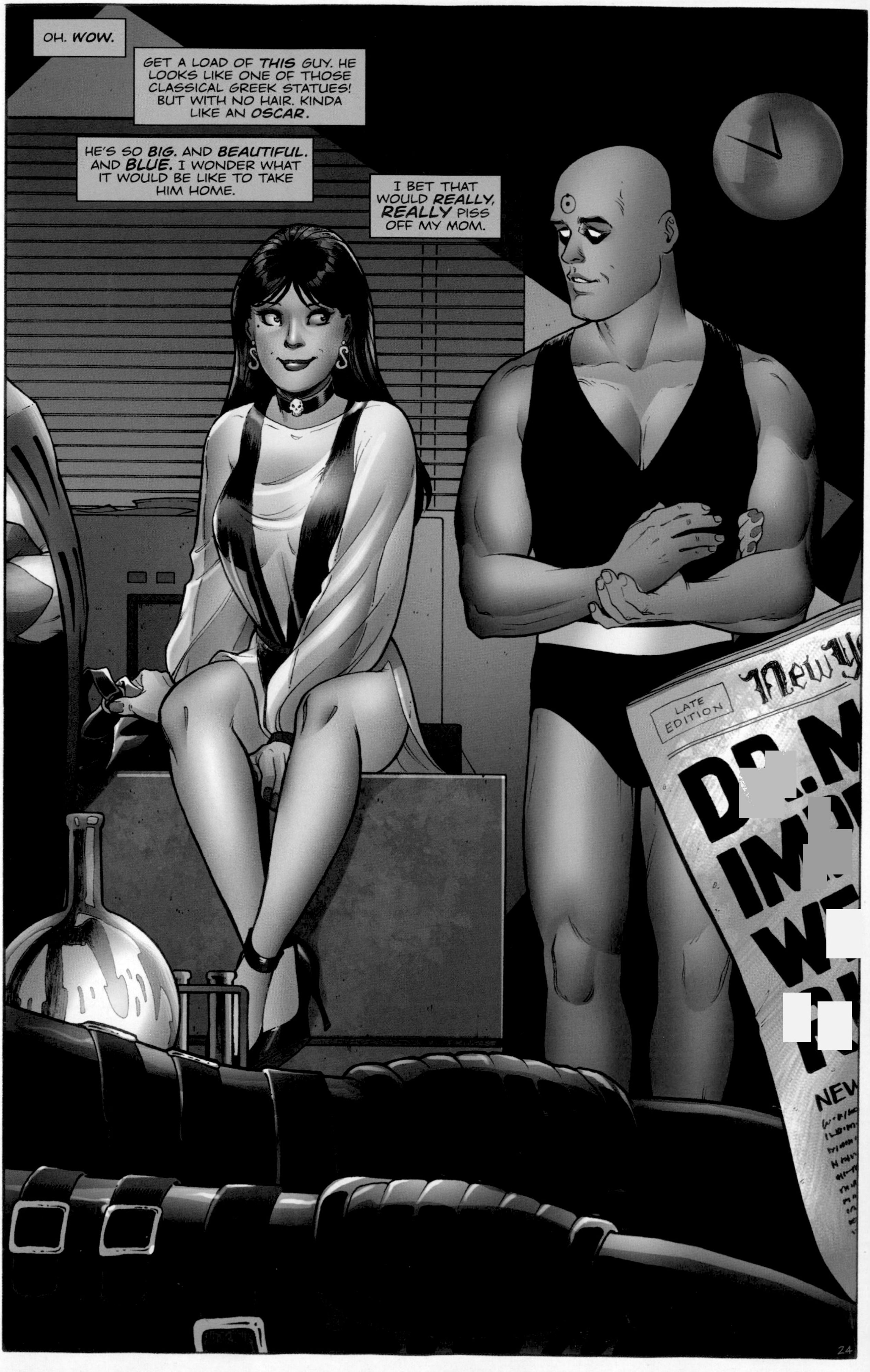
OH. WOW.
GET A LOAD OF THIS GUY. HE LOOKS LIKE ONE OF THOSE CLASSICAL GREEK STATUES! BUT WITH NO HAIR. KINDA LIKE AN OSCAR.
HE'S SO BIG. AND BEAUTIFUL. AND BLUE. I WONDER WHAT IT WOULD BE LIKE TO TAKE HIM HOME.
I BET THAT WOULD REALLY, REALLY PISS OFF MY MOM.
LATE EDITION
NEW

"You're the end of the
rainbow, my pot of gold,
You're daddy's little girl
to have and hold.
A precious gem is what
you are,
You're mommy's bright
and shining star."

- Edward Madden

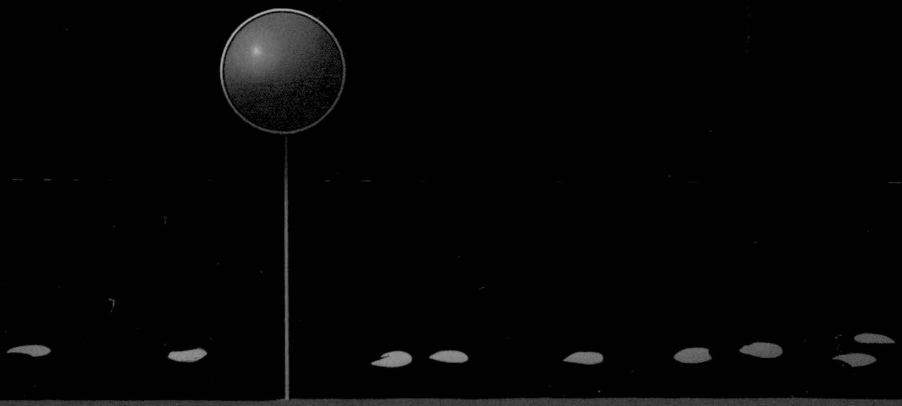

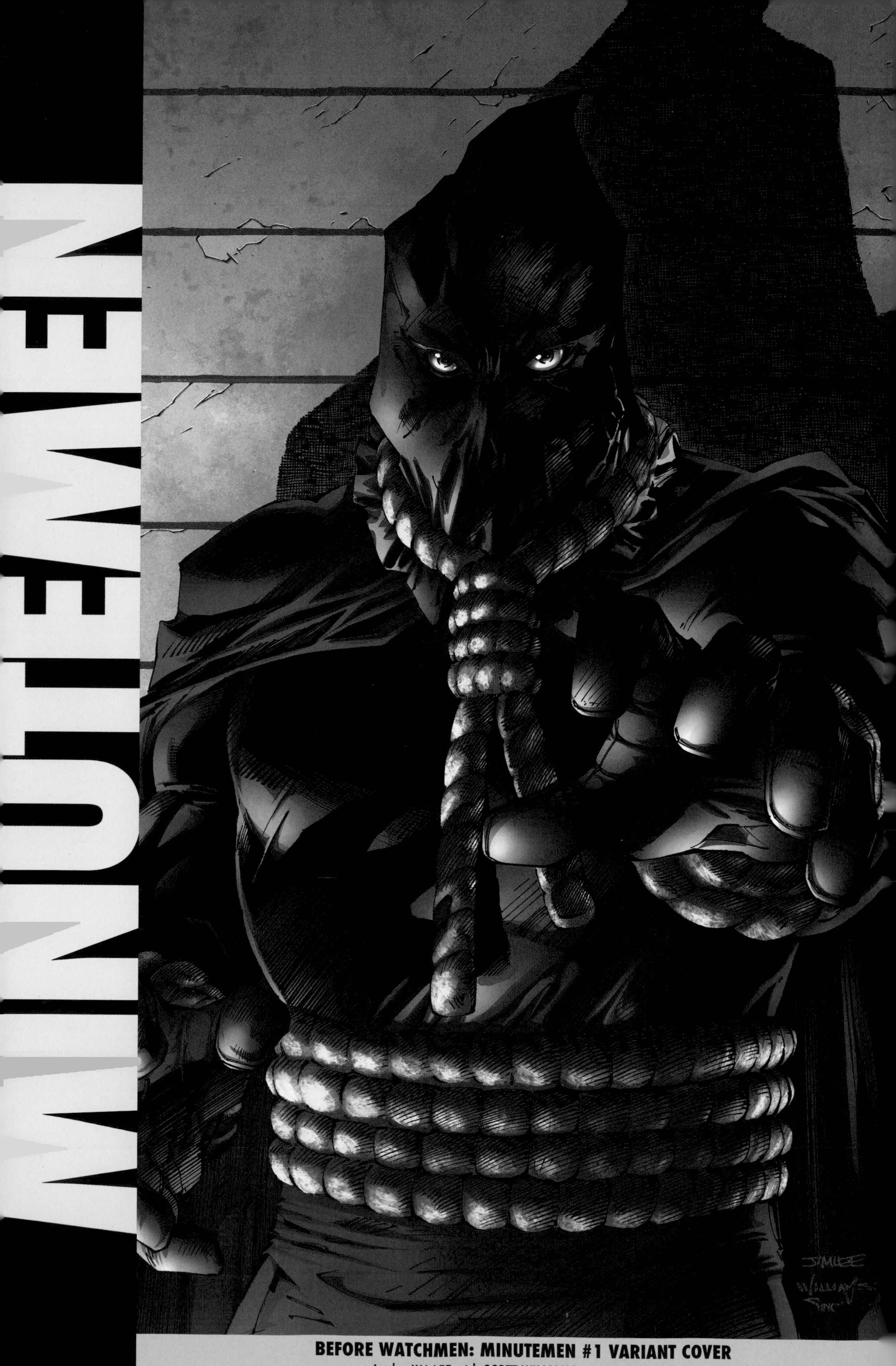
MINUTEMEN

BEFORE WATCHMEN: MINUTEMEN #1 VARIANT COVER
Art by JIM LEE with SCOTT WILLIAMS & ALEX SINCLAIR

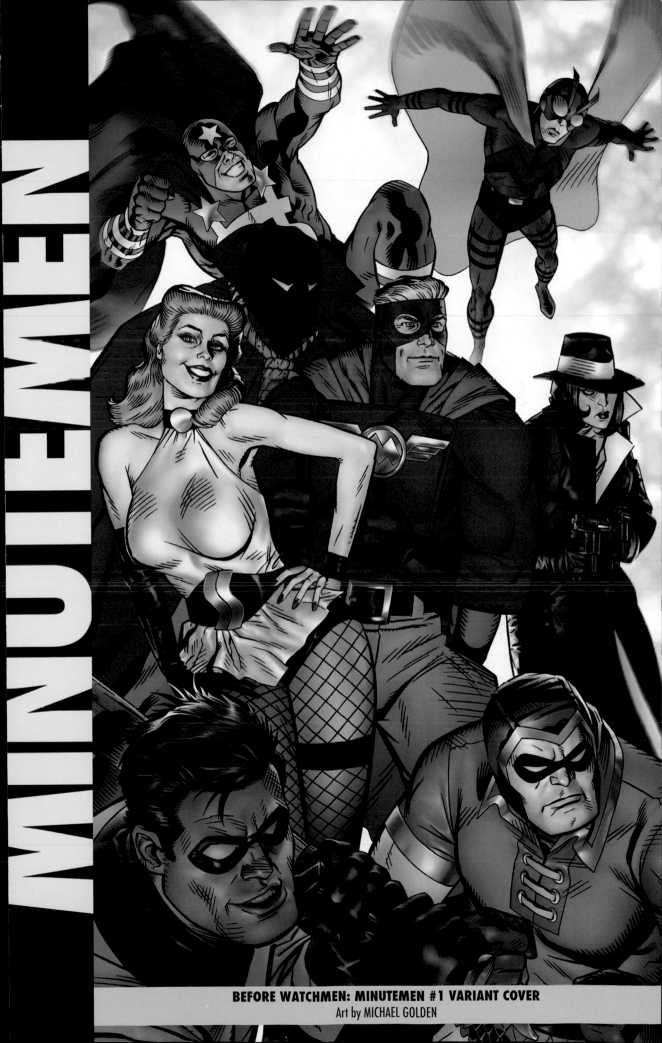

BEFORE WATCHMEN: MINUTEMEN #1 VARIANT COVER
Art by MICHAEL GOLDEN

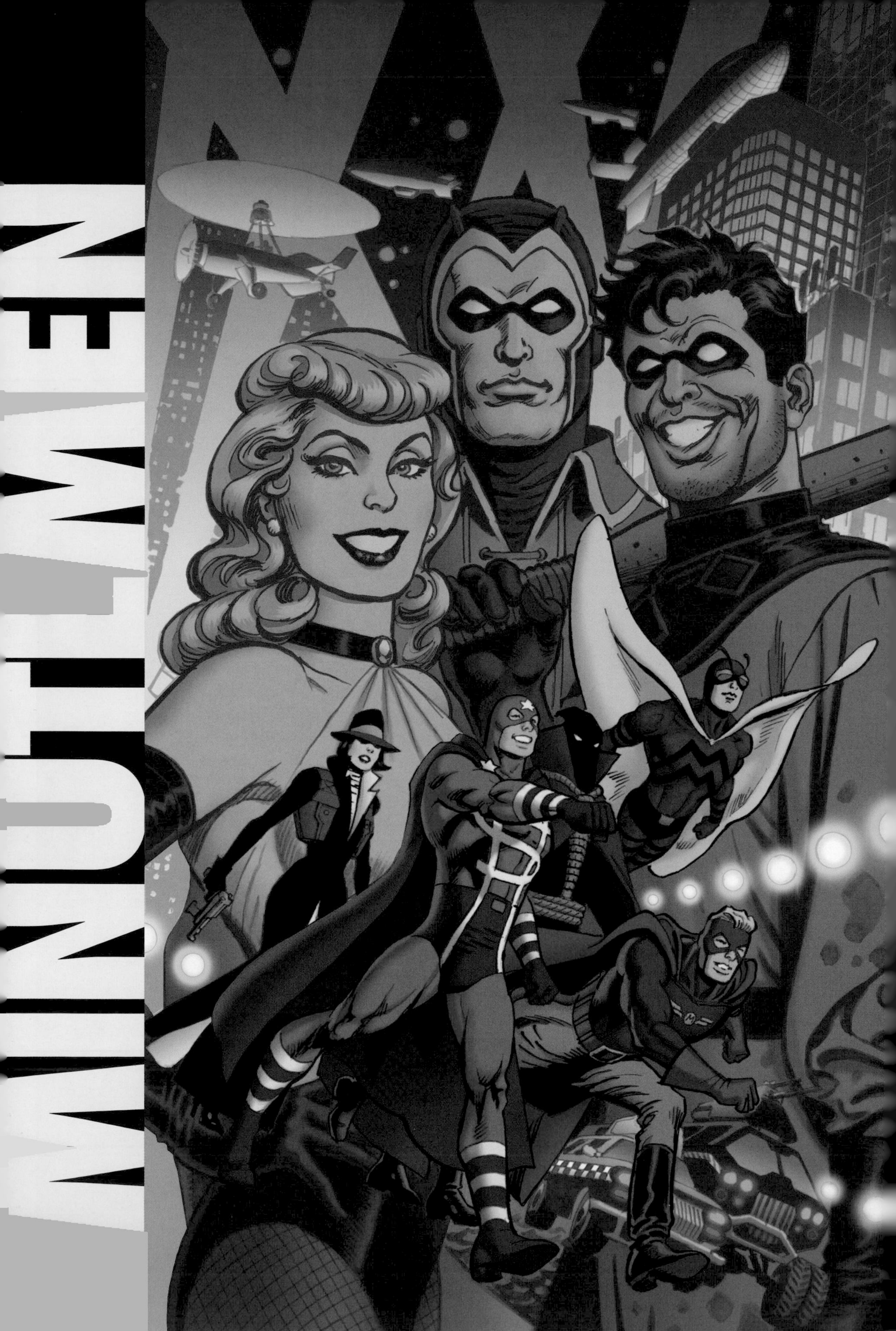
MINUTEMEN

BEFORE WATCHMEN: MINUTEMEN #2 VARIANT COVER
Art by JOSÉ LUIS GARCÍA-LÓPEZ & TRISH MULVIHILL

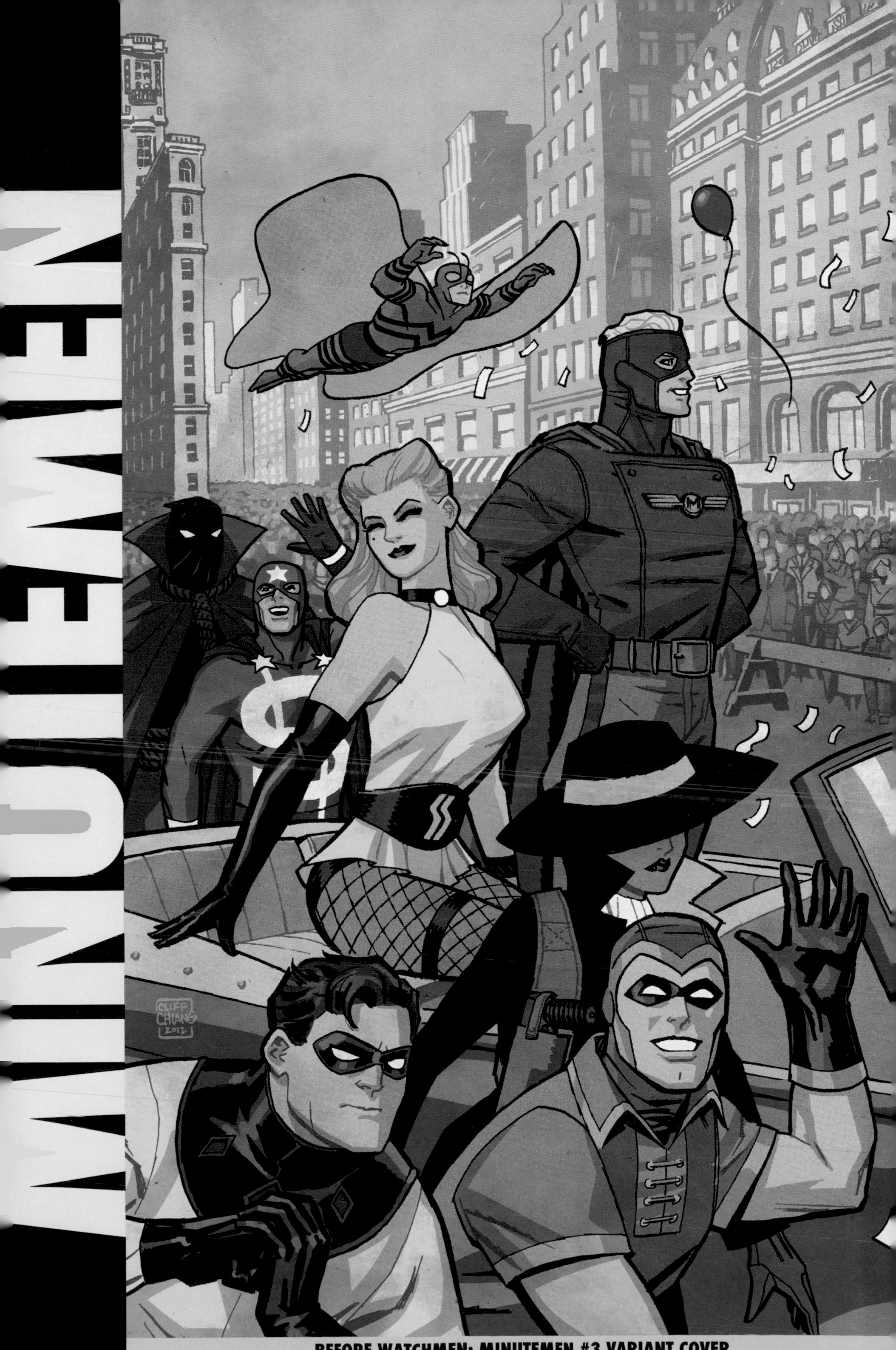
MINUTEMEN
CLIFF CHIANG 2012

BEFORE WATCHMEN: MINUTEMEN #3 VARIANT COVER

Art by CLIFF CHIANG

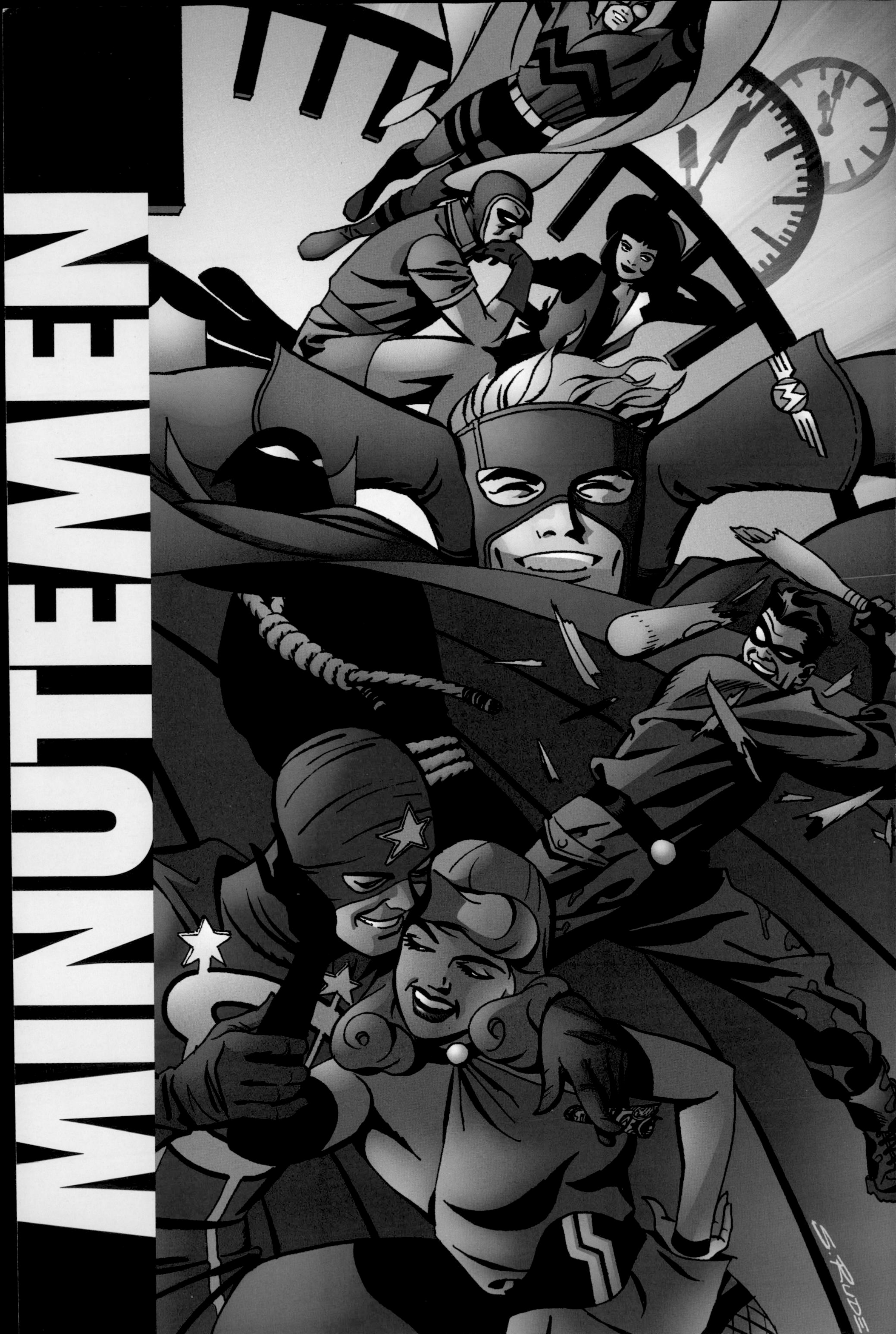
MINUTEMEN
S. RUDE

BEFORE WATCHMEN: MINUTEMEN #4 VARIANT COVER
Art by STEVE RUDE & GLEN WHITMORE

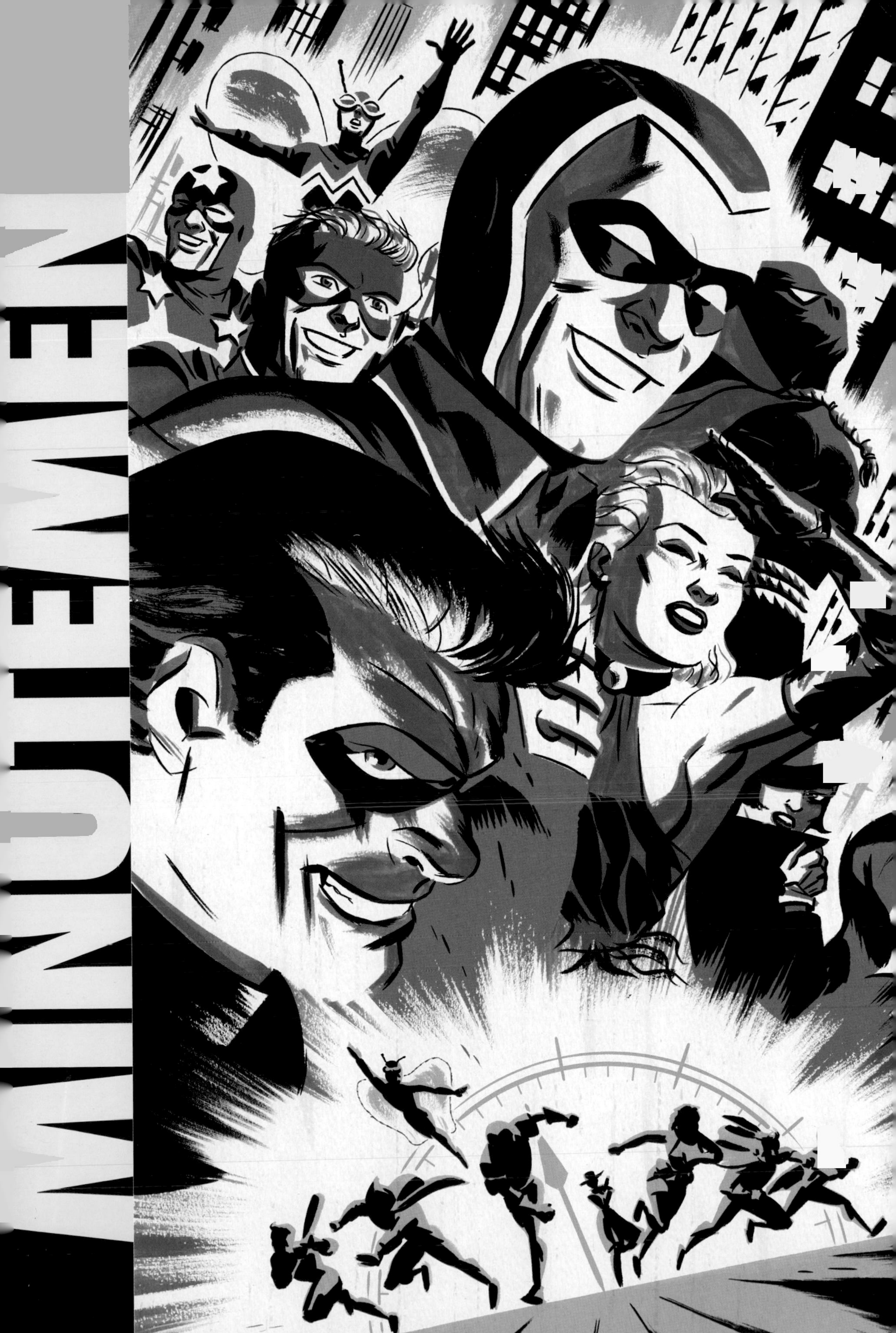
MINUTEMEN

BEFORE WATCHMEN: MINUTEMEN #5 VARIANT COVER
Art by MICHAEL CHO

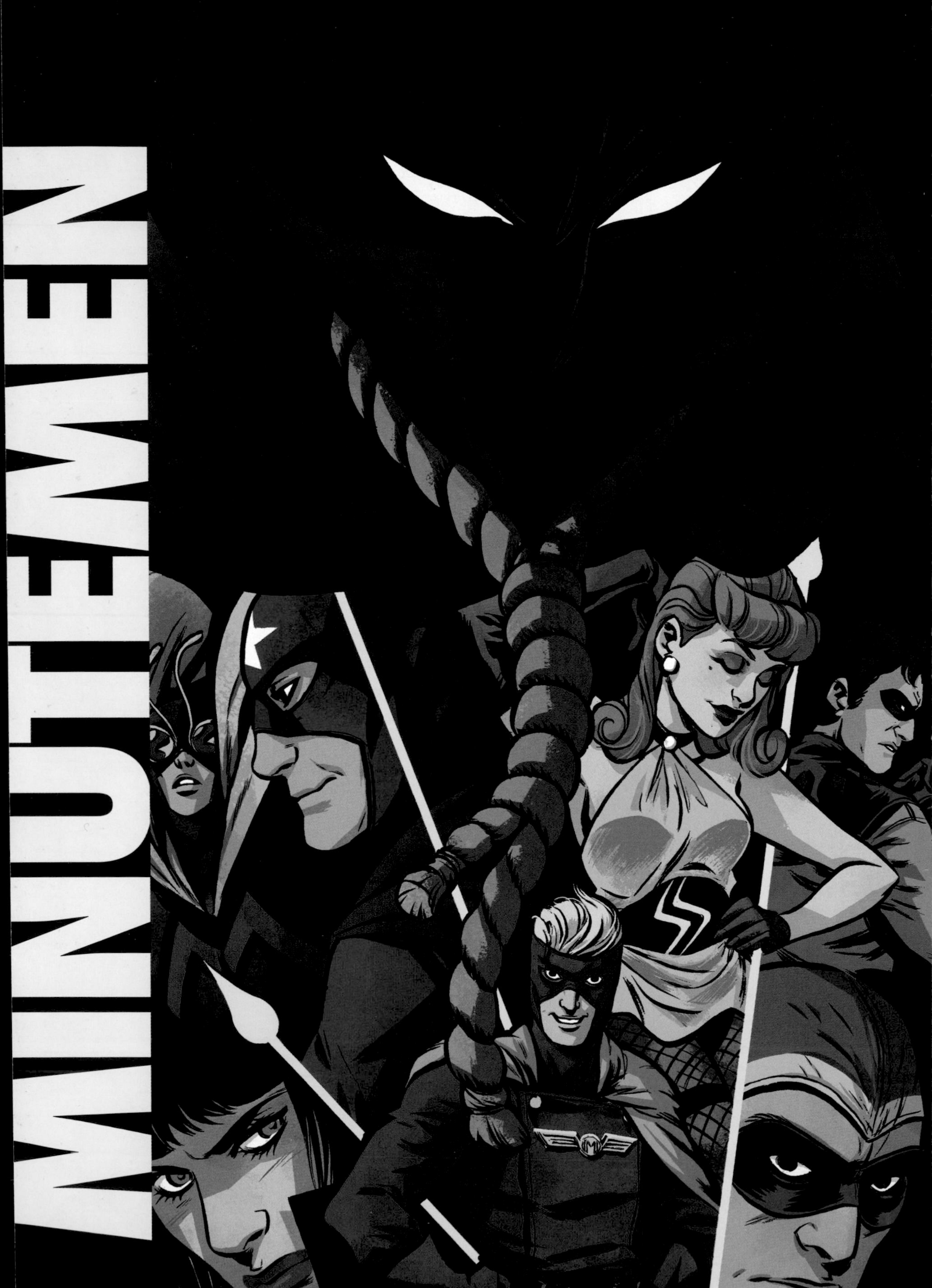
MINUTEMEN

BEFORE WATCHMEN: MINUTEMEN #6 VARIANT COVER
Art by BECKY CLOONAN

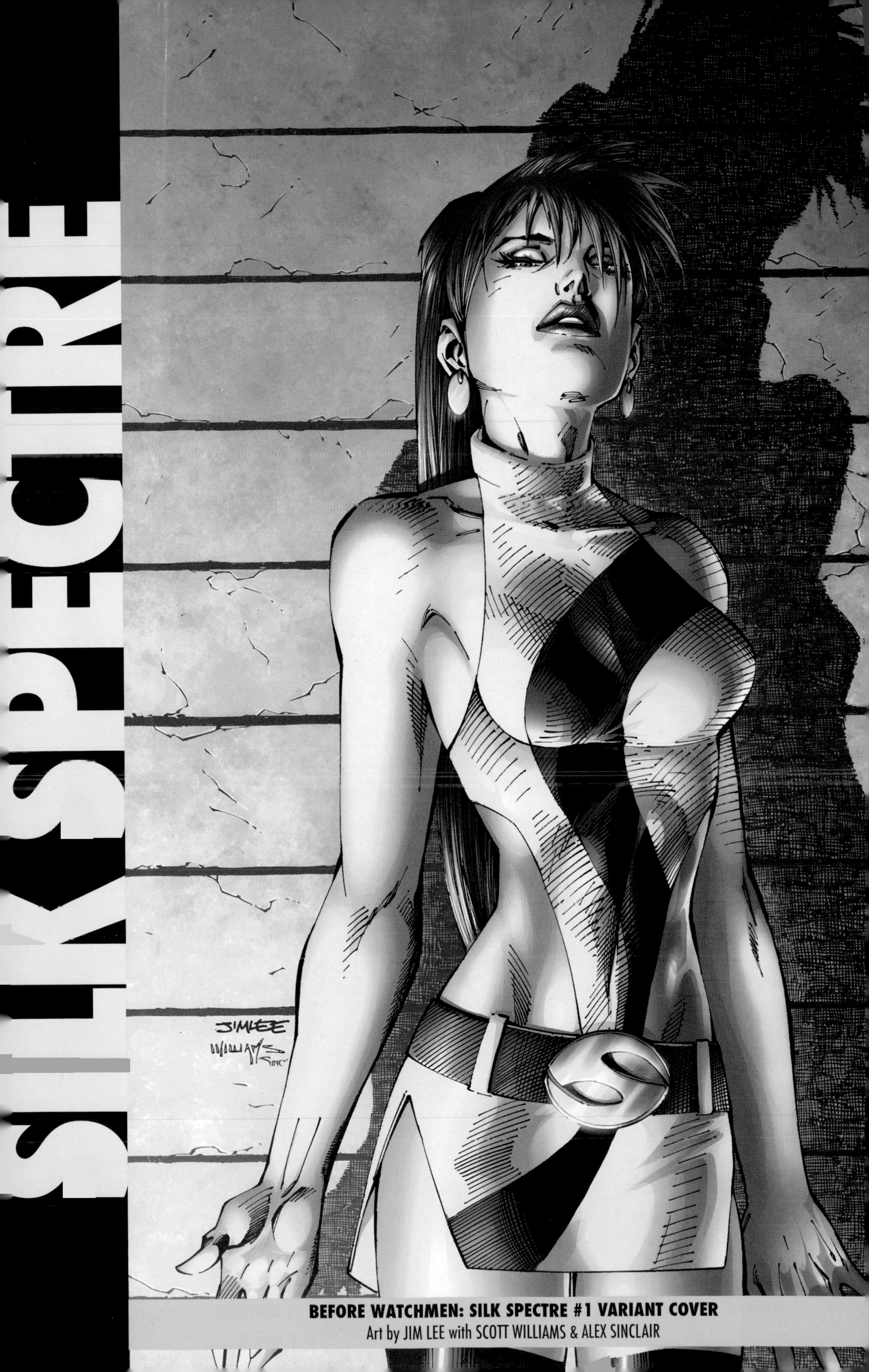
SILK SPECTRE

BEFORE WATCHMEN: SILK SPECTRE #1 VARIANT COVER
Art by JIM LEE with SCOTT WILLIAMS & ALEX SINCLAIR

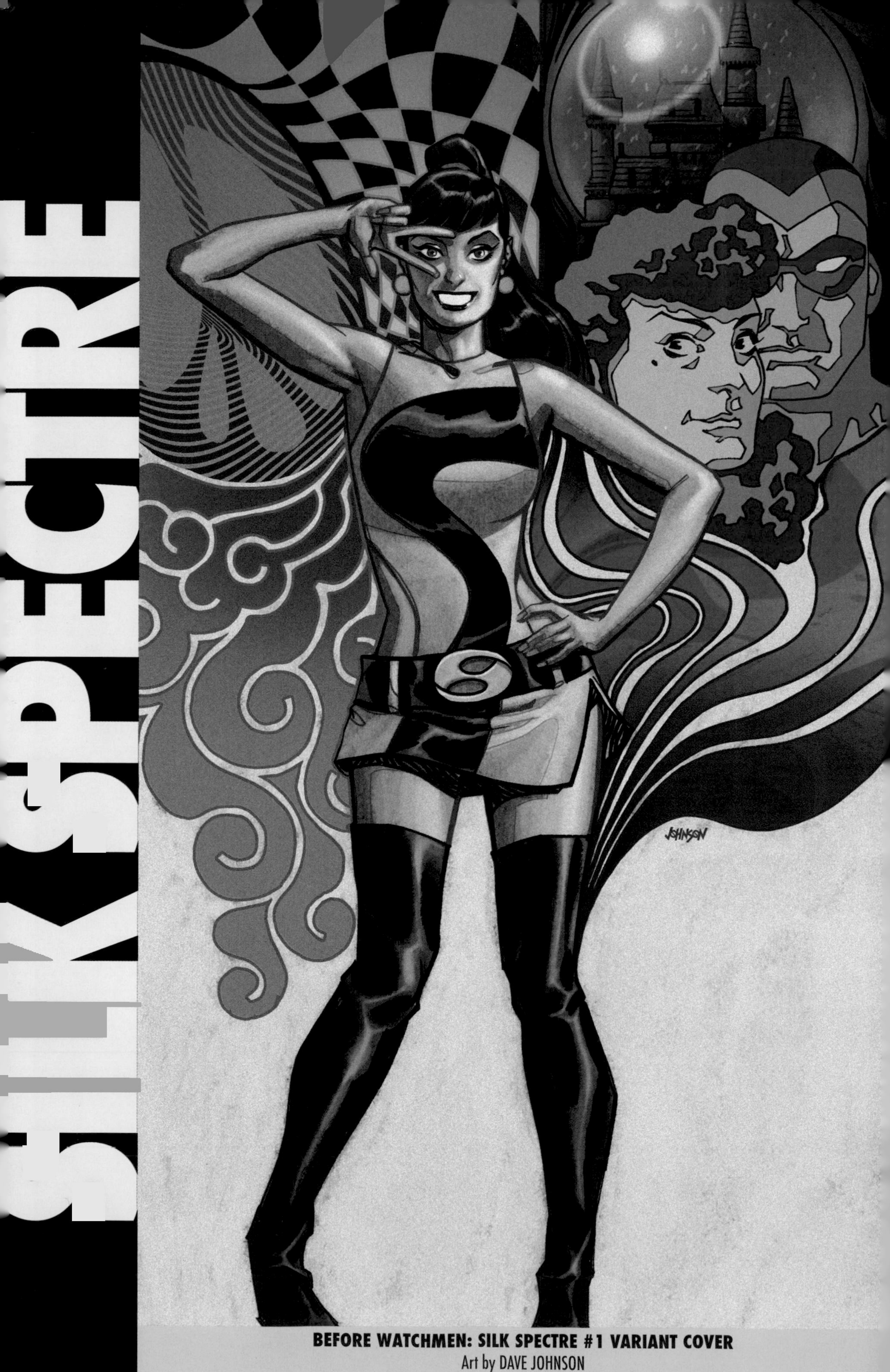
SILK SPECTRE
JOHNSON

BEFORE WATCHMEN: SILK SPECTRE #1 VARIANT COVER
Art by DAVE JOHNSON

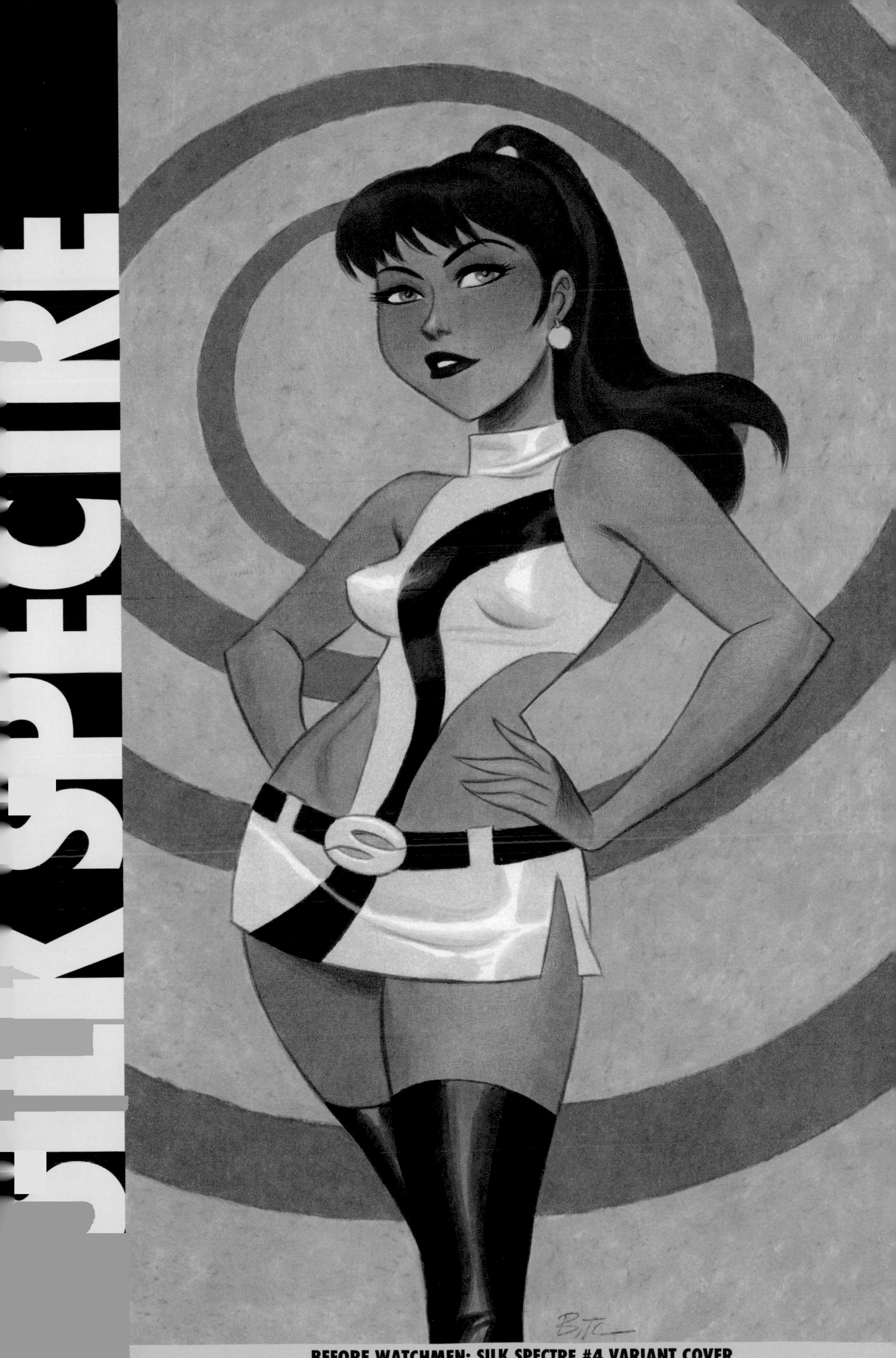

SILK SPECTRE

BEFORE WATCHMEN: SILK SPECTRE #4 VARIANT COVER
Art by BRUCE TIMM

COMEDIAN

DOLLAR BILL

GRAND OPENIN

Solo character studies by DARWYN COOKE

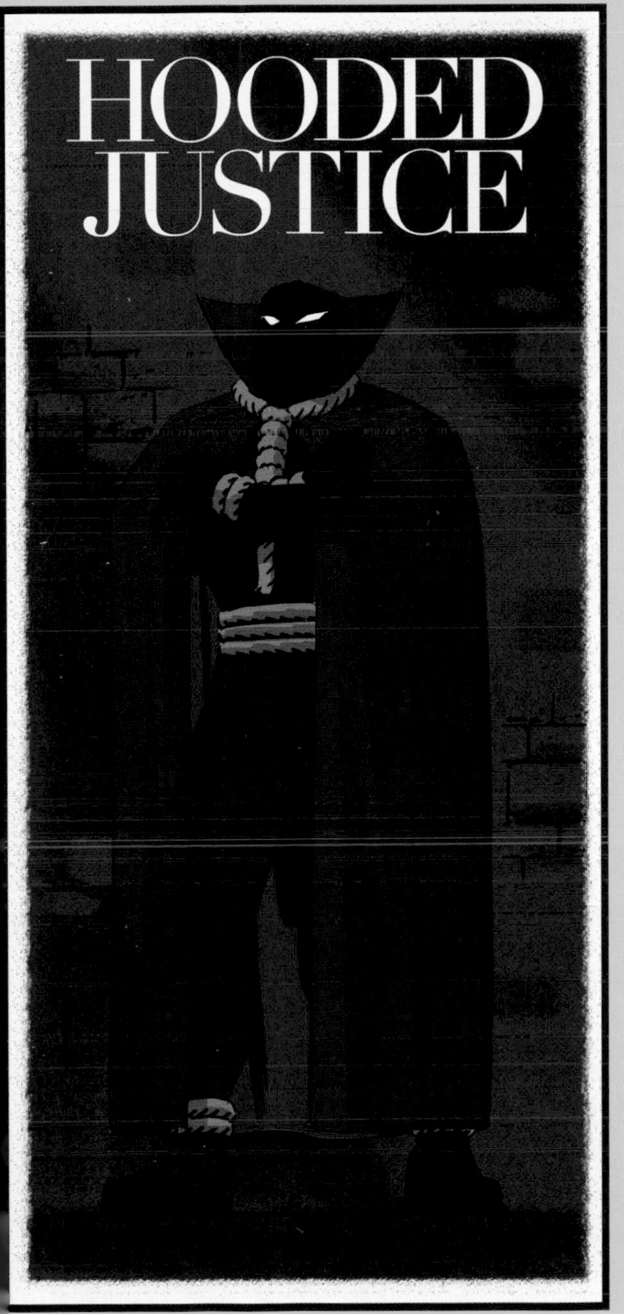
HOODED
JUSTICE

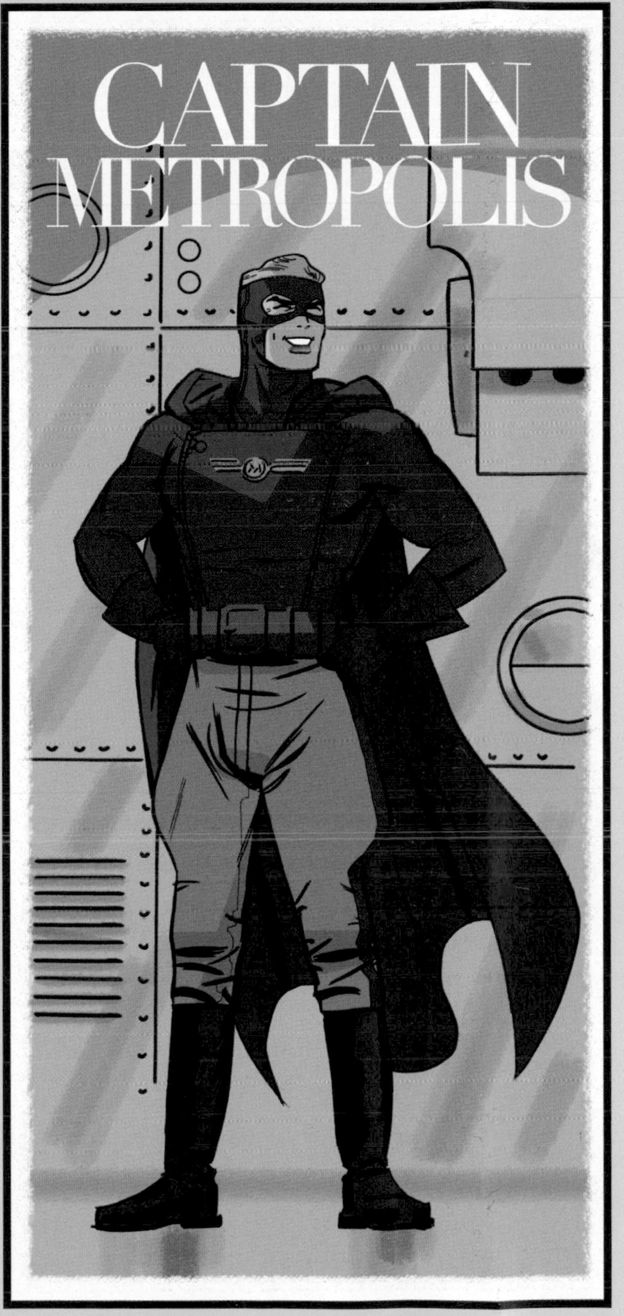
CAPTAIN
METROPOLIS

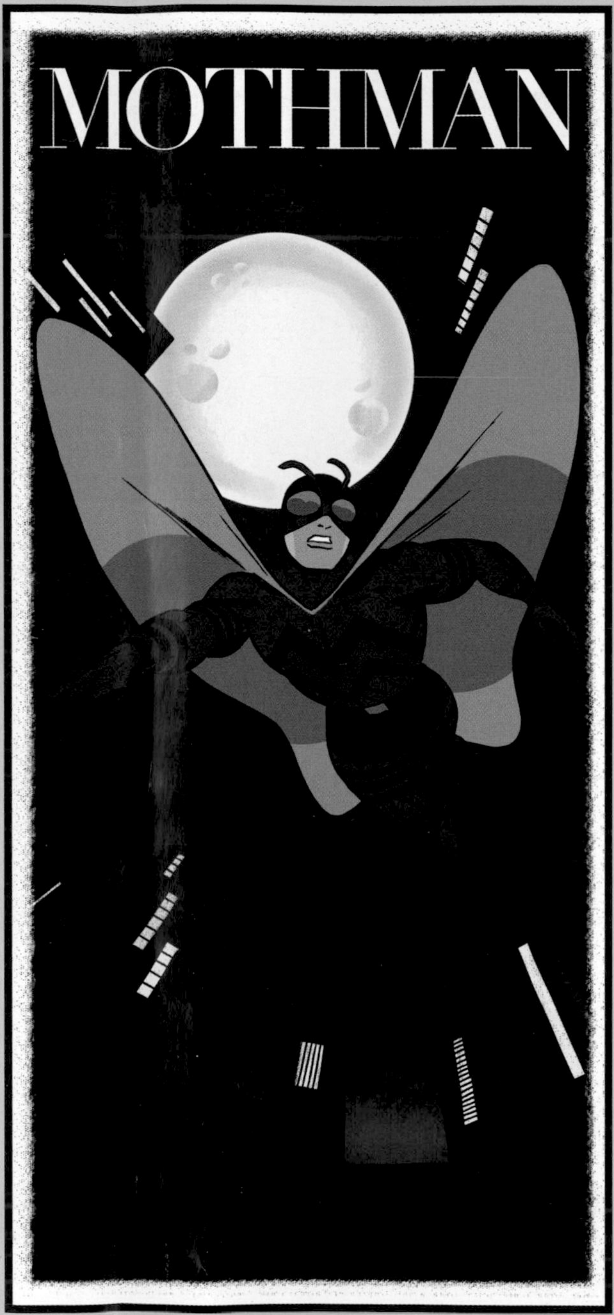
MOTHMAN

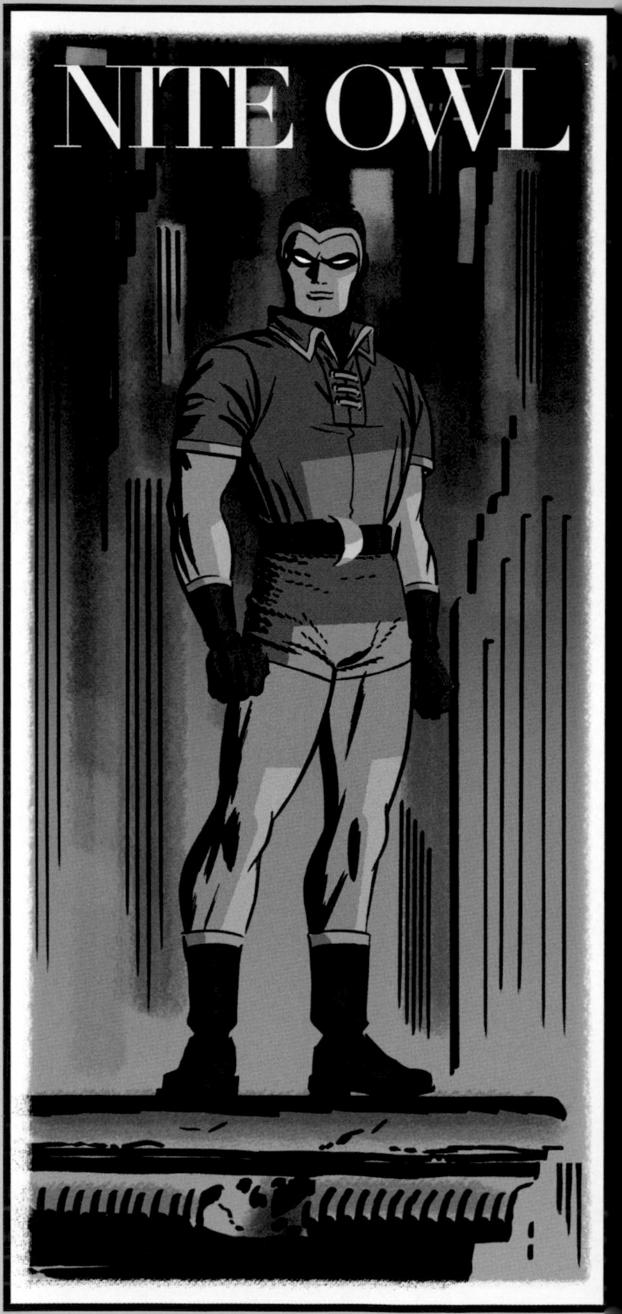
NITE OWL

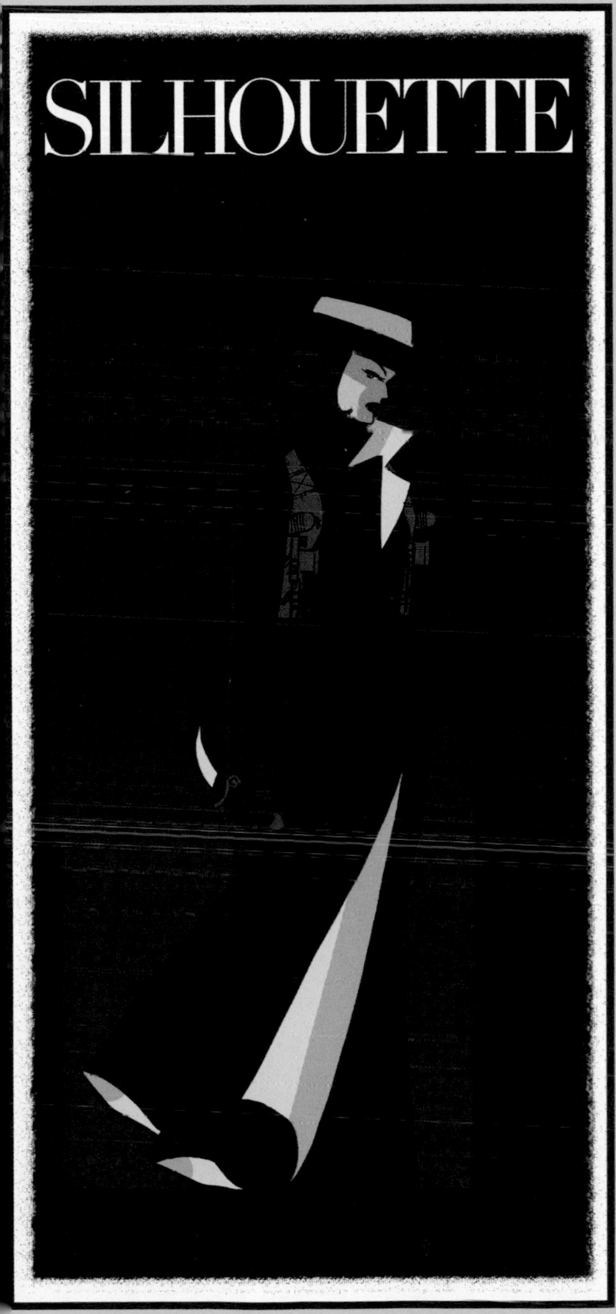
SILHOUETTE

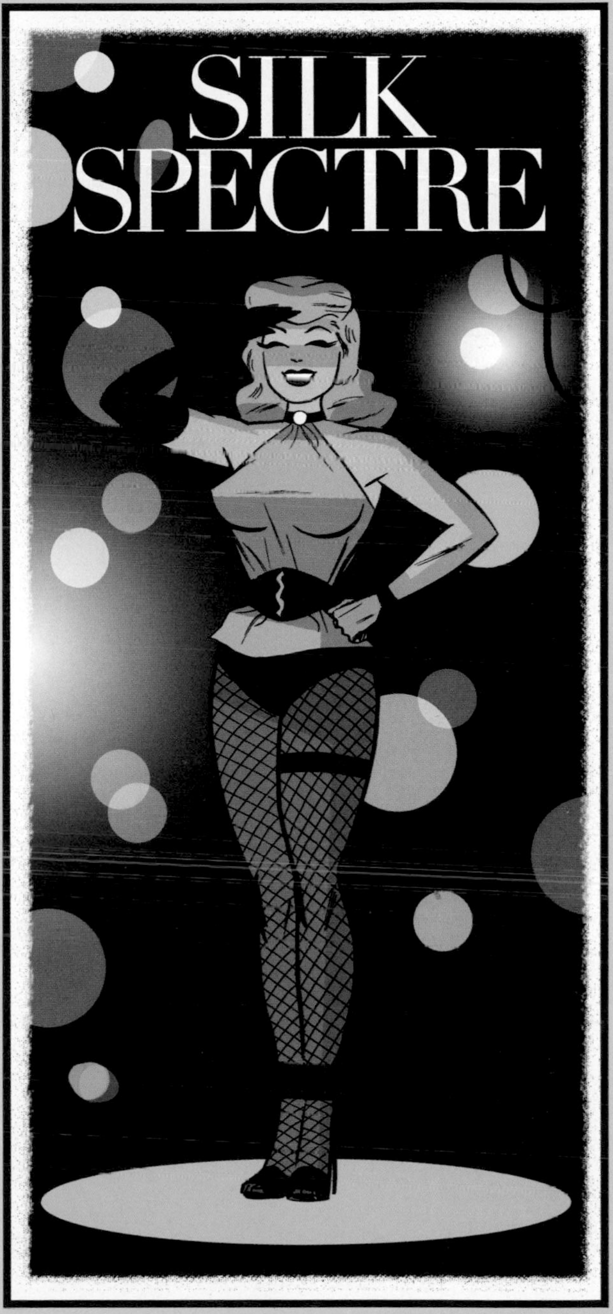
SILK SPECTRE

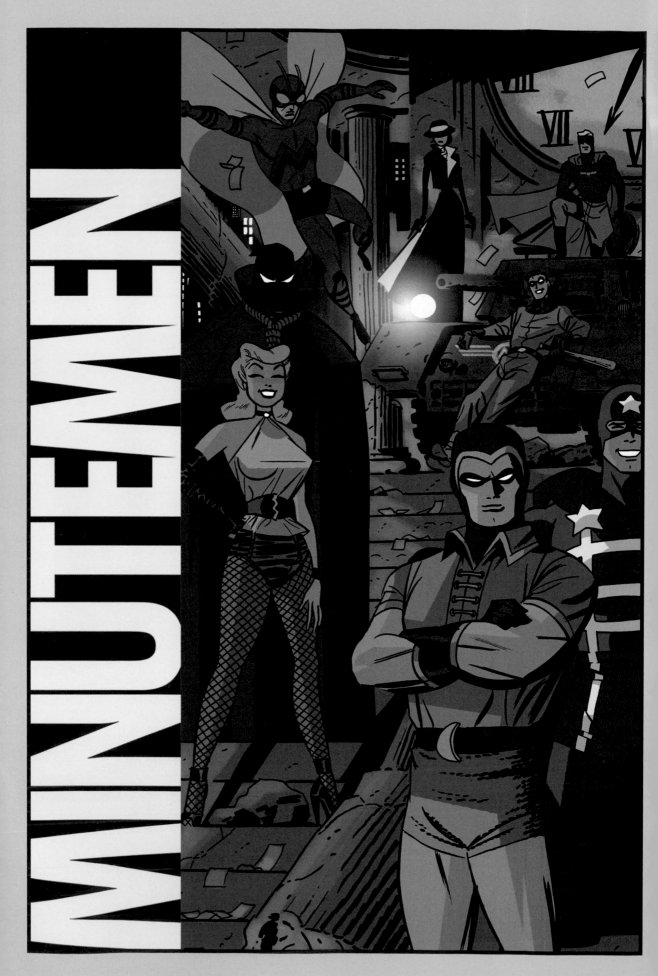

MINUTEMEN

Initial group shot by **DARWYN COOKE**

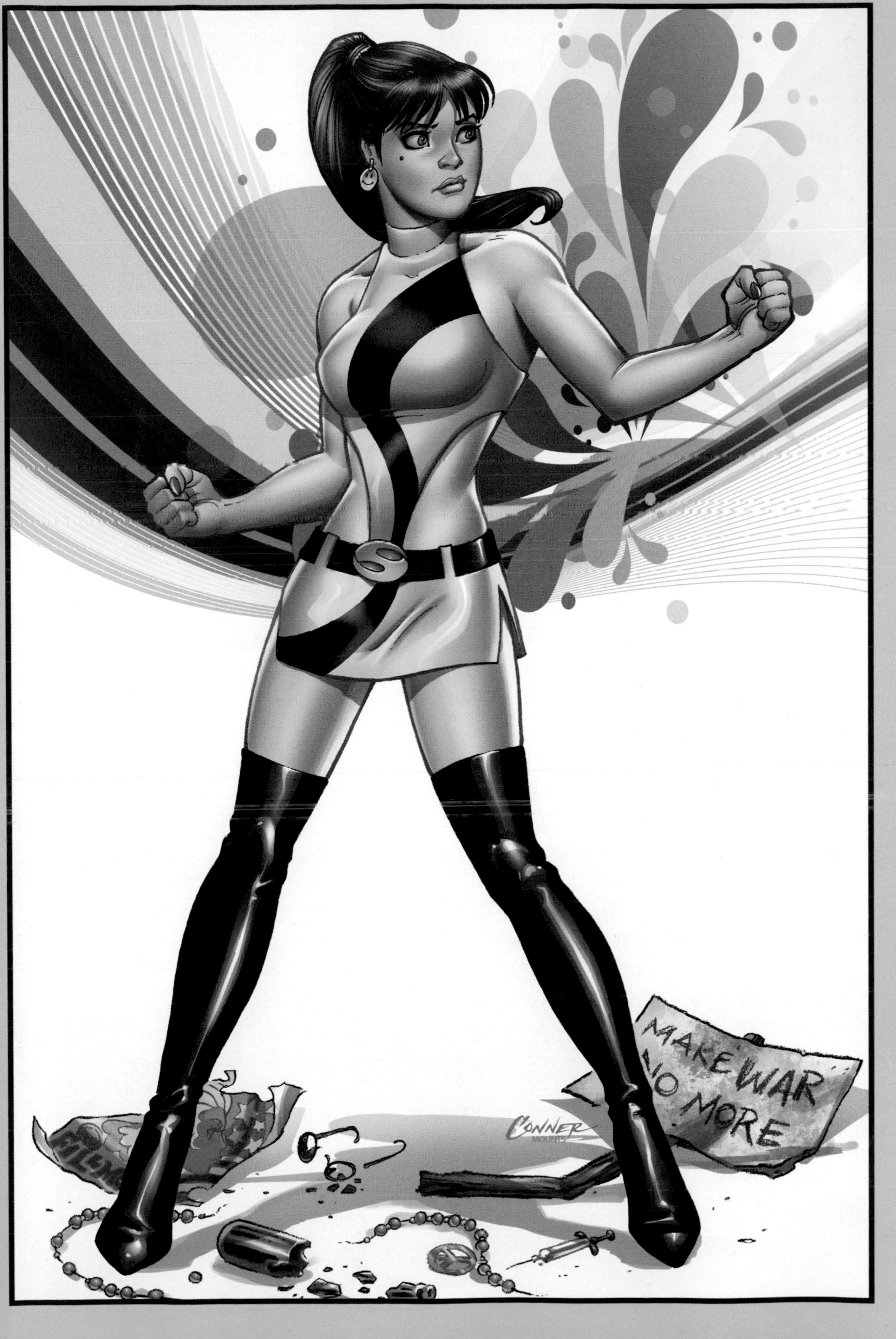
MAKE WAR
NO MORE
CONNER
MOUNTS

Before Watchmen: Silk Spectre Statue design by AMANDA CONNER with PAUL MOUNTS

SO working on this book turned me into a complete asshole for around eight or nine months. Aside from those who would insist that I still am, for tackling this project in the first place, here are a few of the reasons that I was an asshole at that particular time:

I turned a completely happy mate (Jimmy Palmiotti) into a discontented roommate who got stuck going to see movies and having lunches all by himself, because I was too busy obsessing over this book and not giving myself any play time. More often than not, I would wind up going to bed at five in the morning, and it would feel like I only got to see Jimmy for an hour and a half each day.

I became even worse than I already am at answering e-mail, and I am certain that there are people out there who are wondering "What the hell...?!?". I still need to go through a bunch of old e-mail and apologize profusely to those people I didn't respond to.

I didn't take very good care of myself at all. I got no exercise whatsoever, and I think my organs and my lower back were making me pay for it.

I drove my editor, Mark Chiarello, and his intrepid assistant editor Camilla completely batshit. I'm actually very relieved that all those windows at the DC offices don't open.

And I plotted with Darwyn Cooke to take a sweet, sheltered sixteen-year-old girl and turn her life completely upside-down, sideways, and inside-out.

Hopefully I'm on my way to becoming more of an incomplete asshole. I'm still working on it, and I'd like to apologize to all those that I've pissed off. I hope this book was worth all of the sweat and aggravation, because I'm sure as hell not ever working like that again.

That said, the book was fun to work on, and I'm really happy with how it turned out...

I'd like to dedicate this book to Dave Gibbons, who told me, "Relax, it's just a comic book!"

Hope you like it!

Amanda Conner

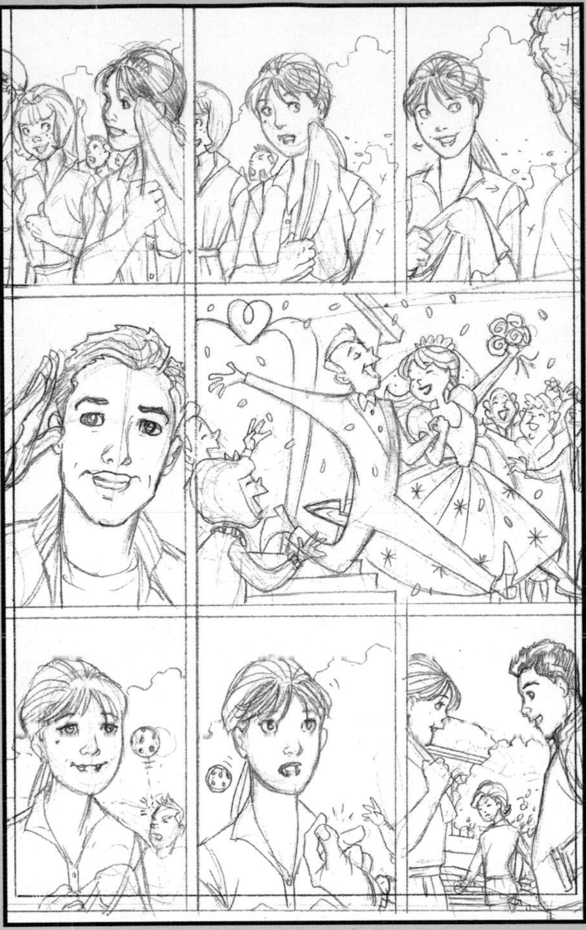

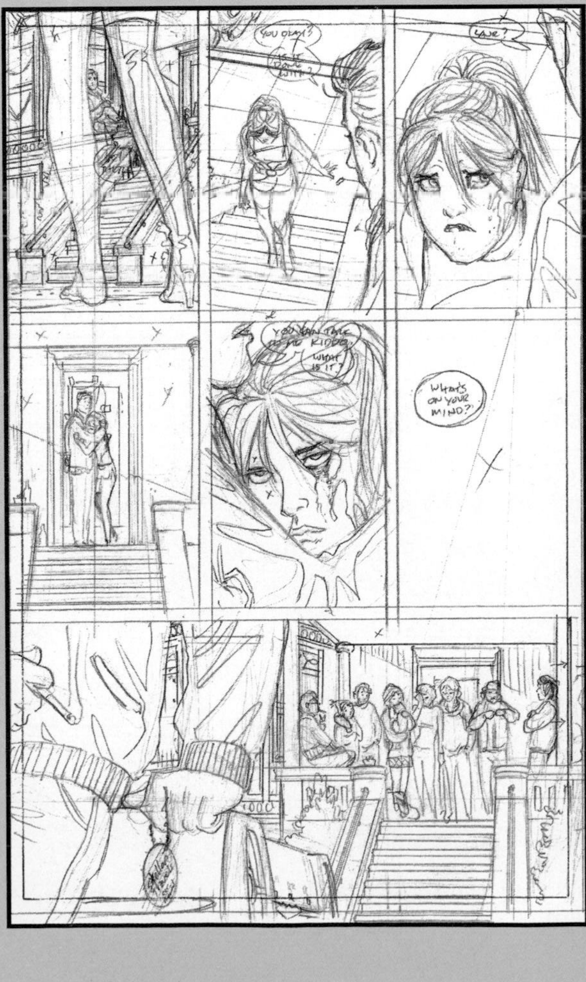
YOU OKAY?
WHAT IS IT?
WHAT'S ON YOUR MIND?

BIOGRAPHIES

DARWYN COOKE is an Eisner Award-winning cartoonist and animator. After spending several years as a magazine art director and graphic designer, Cooke switched careers and began working in animation, where he contributed to such shows as *Batman: The Animated Series*, *Superman: The Animated Series* and *Men In Black: The Series*. From there, DC Comics approached Cooke to write and illustrate a project that the artist had submitted to the company years earlier: BATMAN: EGO. The critical success of the title led to more freelance work, including the relaunch of the CATWOMAN series with writer Ed Brubaker (which inspired Cooke to write and draw the graphic novel CATWOMAN: SELINA'S BIG SCORE) and assignments on *X-Force* and *Spider-Man's Tangled Web* for Marvel.

Cooke then spent several years writing and drawing the ambitious epic THE NEW FRONTIER, a six-issue miniseries bridging the gap between the end of the Golden Age of comics and the beginnings of the Silver Age. He also recently illustrated and wrote (with friends) a highly acclaimed issue of DC's artist-centric series SOLO. He is currently working on a new incarnation of THE SPIRIT for DC while living in Nova Scotia, Canada, with his lovely wife Marsha.

AMANDA CONNER began her professional art career as an illustrator for New York City ad agencies. Her love of comic books and cartooning soon led her to the comics world where she initially found work at companies including Archie, Marvel and Claypool Comics. Since then she has worked on a number of high-profile projects spanning a variety of genres. Her work includes *Vampirella,* and *Painkiller Jane,* as well as such creator-owned projects as *Gatecrasher* (with co-creators Jimmy Palmiotti and Mark Waid) and *The Pro* (with co-creators Jimmy Palmiotti and Garth Ennis). Her work for DC Comics includes CODENAME KNOCKOUT, BIRDS OF PREY, TERRA, a well-regarded run on POWER GIRL and BEFORE WATCHMEN: SILK SPECTRE.

Along with her artist/writer/fiancé Jimmy Palmiotti, Amanda and writer Justin Gray currently work together via PaperFilms, a multimedia entertainment studio engaged in screenwriting, art production and development.

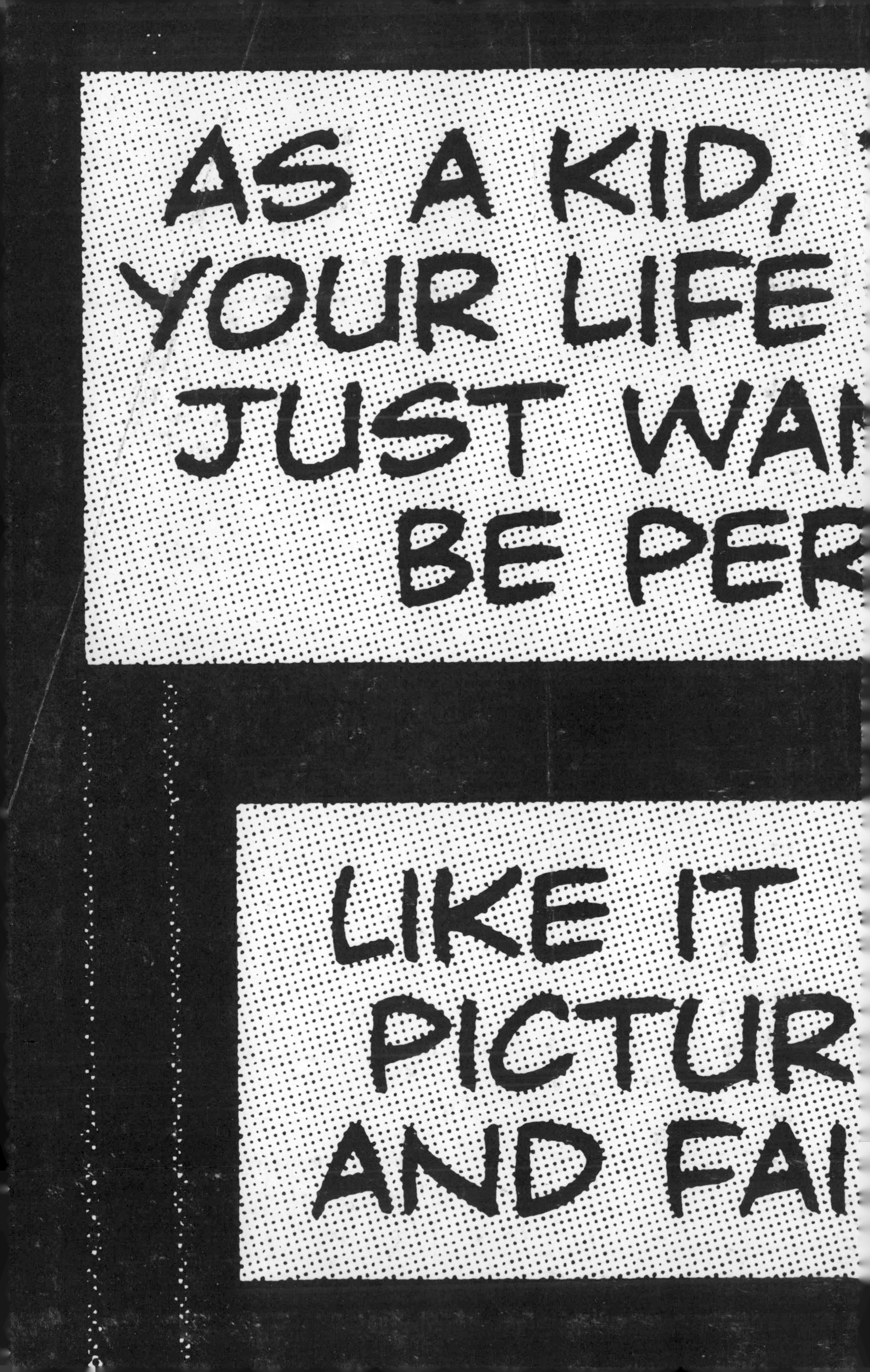
AS A KID, YOUR LIFE JUST WAN BE PER
LIKE IT PICTUR AND FAI